SOCIETY IN QUESTION

Sociological Readings for the 21st Century

Robert J. Brym
University of Toronto

HARCOURT
BRACE
CANADA

Harcourt Brace & Company, Canada

Toronto Montreal Fort Worth New York Orlando
Philadelphia San Diego London Sydney Tokyo

Canadian Cataloguing in Publication Data

Main entry under title:

Society in question : sociological readings for
    the 21st century

Includes bibliographical references and index.
ISBN 0-7747-3516-3

1. Sociology.   I. Brym, Robert J., 1951–   .

HM51.S63 1996   301   C95-931516-0

Publisher: Heather McWhinney
Senior Acquisitions Editor: Daniel J. Brooks
Projects Manager: Liz Radojkovic
Developmental Editor: Megan Mueller
Director of Publishing Services: Jean Davies
Editorial Manager: Marcel Chiera
Supervising Editor: Semareh Al-Hillal
Production Manager: Sue-Ann Becker
Production Co-ordinator: Sheila Barry
Copy Editor: Jim Lyons
Cover and Interior Design: Steve Eby Production and Design
Typesetting and Assembly: IBEX Graphic Communications Inc.
Printing and Binding: Webcom Limited

Cover Art: Trigo Piula, *Ta Tele* (1988), oil on canvas, 100 x 100 cm. Slide provided by The Museum for African Art, New York, N.Y. Reproduced with permission of the artist. *Artist's Statement: "The dreams and escapist fantasies that TV satisfies are depicted in the images that appear on the rear screens, while each [audience member's] personal dream appears inside his or her own head.... The word 'ta' in the title corresponds to the Kikongo word for father. The word 'tele' means television in French, the national language of Zaire. In Kikongo 'tele' means said. Thus, in French, the title means 'your television,' and in Kikongo it means 'Father said.'"*

This book was printed in Canada.

3 4 5   00 99 98 97

For Rhonda, Shira, Talia, and Ariella.

—— RJB

PREFACE

SOCIETY IN QUESTION is designed to supplement the main textbook in an introductory sociology course. I have therefore aimed for balanced coverage of major topics, approaches, and methods in current sociology. However, as the title and subtitle suggest, this book also tries to convey more than just a sense of what sociologists do for a living. The chapters, and my introductions to them, are intended to speak plainly and vividly to contemporary Canadians about how sociology can help them make sense of their lives in a rapidly changing and often confusing world. The book's title is thus an intentional pun: as the nature of social life is called into question by vast and sometimes frightening forces over which we appear to have little control, sociological questioning offers the prospect of helping us understand those forces and make informed choices about how we can best deal with them.

Let me substantiate my claim to balance. The placement of a chapter in one part or another is to a degree arbitrary since most items cover two or more subject areas. In order to supplement the information about coverage contained in the Table of Contents, please see Table p.1. There I list 27 sociological key words and six methodologies, showing which chapters devote significant attention to each topic. (Instructors may wish to use Table p.1 as a guide to how chapters can be reordered to reflect their own teaching priorities.)

The fact that so many entries are required to give an adequate sense of the book's content is itself an indication of breadth. Equally telling are the key words with the most frequent counts. Leading the inventory, with nine citations, is "public policy." This reflects students' increasing desire — which I have witnessed over two decades of teaching introductory courses — for sociological material that has practical applications. Next are "economy" and "gender," each with seven citations. Here we see the imprint of what are undoubtedly the two most important developments in Canadian sociology over the past 25 years: the emergence and popularization of political economy and feminist approaches. Key words with between four and six citations reflect traditional and current sociological preoccupations with class, crime, culture, development, ethnicity, families, globalization, interaction, politics, race, and religion.

The methodological breakdown shows similar diversity. All the major sociological methods are illustrated in this collection, and in proportions that, I think, roughly mirror the distribution of methods used in the discipline.

This is a non-parochial collection of chapters. I have not felt obliged to select only the works of authors who are Canadian citizens and hold Ph.D.s in sociology (although 70 percent of the authors are and do). The sociological imagination has influenced anthropology, political science, economics, history, and law, among other disciplines. I have chosen some works by scholars in these fields because they are particularly striking examples of how cognate disciplines have repaid the favour by enriching sociological thought. Moreover, I strongly believe that, especially in this era of globalization, Canadian sociologists have as much to learn from non-Canadians as from non-sociologists. That is why several non-Canadians are among the authors represented here.

I consider some of the pieces reprinted here to be modern classics, but I have tried wherever possible to select items that speak to key issues of social life today. Specifically, over 60 percent of the chapters in this book were written in the 1990s and over 25 percent in the 1980s.

Finally, although I selected a few chapters just because they cover important topics concisely and clearly, more rigorous criteria guided most of my choices. As I

Table p.1 Key Words by Chapter

Topic	Chapter	Count
Class	2, 11, 12, 13	4
Cities	9	1
Community	8, 9	2
Crime	26, 27, 28, 29	4
Culture	5, 6, 7, 13, 17, 29	6
Development	24, 30, 32, 31, 33	5
Economy	21, 24, 25, 30, 32, 31, 33	7
Environment	30, 31	2
Ethnicity	14, 15, 16, 20	4
Families	12, 17, 18, 19	4
Gender	3, 11, 12, 17, 18, 19, 31	7
Globalization	20, 21, 30, 32, 33	5
Interaction	3, 4, 5, 13, 19	5
Law	18, 23	2
Organizations	25	1
Politics	20, 21, 22, 23	4
Population	31	1
Postindustrialism	12, 30	2
Public policy	17, 18, 20, 23, 23, 30, 31, 32, 33	9
Race	14, 15, 16, 23, 28, 29	6
Religion	5, 6, 7, 19, 20	5
Socialization	3, 4	2
Social movements	10, 19	2
Social structure	8, 9, 10	3
Sociology	1	1
Theory	1, 2	2
Work	25	1
METHOD		
Historical	10, 13, 14, 20, 21, 22, 23, 24, 32	9
In-depth interviews	5, 13, 15, 26	4
Official statistics	10, 11, 15, 16, 21, 27, 28, 29, 31, 33	10
Participant-observation	3, 4, 5, 7, 8, 11, 30	7
Survey	3, 6, 9, 12, 15, 17, 18, 19, 25, 27, 29	11
Theoretical	1, 2	2

reviewed material for this collection, I tried to place myself in the shoes of a contemporary Canadian undergraduate who, entirely sensibly, takes the time to read only material that says something significant and non-obvious. Most of the chapters in this book surprised me when I first read them and they continue to affect the way I see the world. Accordingly, the best indicator of the usefulness of this book will be the number of students who complete it and say that it helped ensure that they can no longer pick up a newspaper without thinking about the broader sociological significance of what they've read. That is just about the highest praise an introductory sociology instructor can receive.

ACKNOWLEDGEMENTS

My research assistant, Ivanka Knezevic, helped me to locate, gather, and sift through scores of articles that were potential candidates for inclusion in this book and she brought several gems to my attention. I am very grateful for her energetic, punctual, and thoughtful work. I am also indebted to the Harcourt Brace Canada team of

Dan Brooks (Senior Acquisitions Editor), Megan Mueller (Developmental Editor), Semareh Al-Hillal (Supervising Editor), and Jim Lyons (Copy Editor) for their assistance in shaping this collection. I am happy to say that it was not only a pleasure working with them. It was a pleasure as usual.

Robert J. Brym
University of Toronto

Readers wishing further information on data provided by Statistics Canada may obtain copies of related publications by mail from Publications Sales, Statistics Canada, Ottawa, Ontario, K1A 0T6, by phone at (613) 951-7277 or toll-free 1-800-267-6677. You may also fax your order to (613) 951-1584.

A Note from the Publisher

Thank you for selecting *Society in Question: Sociological Readings for the 21st Century*, by Robert J. Brym. The author and publisher have devoted considerable time to the careful development of this book. We appreciate your recognition of this effort and accomplishment.

We want to hear what you think about *Society in Question*. Please take a few minutes to fill in the stamped reader reply card at the back of the book. Your comments and suggestions will be valuable to us as we prepare new editions and other books.

CONTENTS

PART 1

THE FIELD OF SOCIOLOGY

I HAVE BEEN WRITING my autobiography for twenty years. As autobiographies go, it is pretty unconventional. It records no personal events or dates, nor does it sketch interesting characters. My friends, enemies, colleagues, parents, wife, and children are not mentioned in it. It is not written as a personal narrative. Yet, indirectly, it is the story of my life.

My life story is embedded in my sociological writings. The pressing issues that trouble me have somehow been transformed into a research agenda. I can plainly see the connection between my life and my writings; nobody else can — nor would they particularly care to. To the degree that my writings have any value to others, it lies in their contribution, however slight, to conversations and debates that people who call themselves sociologists have engaged in for more than a century. Those sociologists couldn't care less about whether I have found my research and writing useful in answering the political, ethnic, and economic issues that have weighed on me over the years.

Nor should they. Sociology is a science — a science that is not as precise as physics, which doesn't have to contend with human caprice, but a science nonetheless. That is, sociologists try to observe their chosen corner of reality in a systematic and controlled manner and to evaluate the validity of their ideas on the basis of whether their observations confirm or disconfirm them. The origins of those ideas are irrelevant, scientifically speaking. That is, I think, what the American writer Kurt Vonnegut meant when he wrote that the most beautiful marigold he ever saw was growing in a bucket of cat manure.

Here we have the great irony of much scholarship, sociology included. Scholars try to be dispassionate and objective, yet a great deal of scholarly activity is animated by real-life experiences and individual passions. For example, Albert Einstein believed on philosophical grounds that the universe is a deterministic system operating according to iron laws and that it is the physicist's job to discover those laws. When he was confronted by evidence that certain subatomic processes can be described only in terms of probable rather than certain outcomes, he objected: "God does not play dice with the universe." In this case, Einstein was not swayed by the evidence; his personal bent of mind, even his religious outlook, affected his evaluation of the evidence.

1

In their laudable efforts to be objective, some scholars lose sight of the fact that personal experiences and individual passions help them define certain problems as urgent and certain solutions to those problems as preferable. But few thoughtful and honest scholars can fool themselves for long with pious statements about being purely objective in their research. The plain fact is that objectivity and subjectivity each have an important role to play in science, including sociology. Objectivity is a "reality check"; subjectivity leads us to define which aspect of reality is worth checking on in the first place.

In contrast to the misguided scientist, who believes that objectivity is everything, most non-scientists are under the equally misguided impression that subjectivity tells all, that their own experience is the sole reliable guide to action, that their personal troubles are theirs and theirs alone. In his 1959 classic work *The Sociological Imagination*, a portion of which is reprinted here as Chapter 1, the late C. Wright Mills shows how wrong this common-sense view is.

When one person in a community is unemployed, says Mills, that is a personal trouble and perhaps a personal failing. When 30 percent of a country's work force is unemployed, as was the case in North America during the Great Depression of 1929–39, that is a massive social issue. The best sociologists try to show how personal troubles are tied to social issues and how social issues, in turn, have developed historically. From Mills's point of view, good sociology is liberating. It promises to broaden your sense of what you can do with your life by showing how your subjective feelings and actions are a product of broad social and historical forces, and how you can act to alter those social and historical forces and thus improve the quality of your life. Although in some respects dated — Mills's tone was influenced by the fact that he wrote at the height of the Cold War; his language is sexist — his main argument is as true and as inspiring today as it was 37 years ago.

It is generally agreed that the three most important figures in the early history of sociology were Karl Marx, Max Weber, and Émile Durkheim. They lived in Germany, France, and England in the period 1820–1920, and they therefore witnessed the consequences of one of the greatest social transformations the world has ever seen: the Industrial Revolution. They were disturbed and excited by what they witnessed: peasants moving to the cities, becoming workers in giant factories, doing routine, backbreaking labour for long hours in horrid conditions, facing anonymous bureaucracies, losing faith in their religions, protesting the conditions of their existence, engaging in criminal behaviour. Marx detected in these changes the seeds of a worldwide revolution. Capitalism, he believed, would create social conditions that would propel workers to overthrow their unjust rulers, take power themselves, and create a more just society. Durkheim, of a decidedly more conservative frame of mind, hoped that new forms of social solidarity would replace the social disorganization he witnessed and make society whole and stable again. Weber, more cynical, believed he was witnessing the rationalization and routinization of social life, the forcing of the human spirit into an iron cage.

In Chapter 2, I set out some of the important issues raised in the writings of Marx, Weber, and Durkheim. Their ideas, I argue, are not just a matter of historical curiosity. They constitute the core problems of sociology and are therefore worth studying in depth.

Chapter 1

THE SOCIOLOGICAL IMAGINATION

C. WRIGHT MILLS

Nowadays men often feel that their private lives are a series of traps. They sense that within their everyday worlds, they cannot overcome their troubles, and in this feeling, they are often quite correct: What ordinary men are directly aware of and what they try to do are bounded by the private orbits in which they live; their visions and their powers are limited to the close-up scenes of job, family, neighborhood; in other milieux, they move vicariously and remain spectators. And the more aware they become, however vaguely, of ambitions and of threats which transcend their immediate locales, the more trapped they seem to feel.

Underlying this sense of being trapped are seemingly impersonal changes in the very structure of continent-wide societies. The facts of contemporary history are also facts about the success and the failure of individual men and women. When a society is industrialized, a peasant becomes a worker; a feudal lord is liquidated or becomes a businessman. When classes rise or fall, a man is employed or unemployed; when the rate of investment goes up or down, a man takes new heart or goes broke. When wars happen, an insurance salesman becomes a rocket launcher; a store clerk, a radar man; a wife lives alone; a child grows up without a father. Neither the life of an individual nor the history of a society can be understood without understanding both.

Yet men do not usually define the troubles they endure in terms of historical change and institutional contradiction. The well-being they enjoy, they do not usually impute to the big ups and downs of the societies in which they live. Seldom aware of the intricate connection between the patterns of their own lives and the course of world history, ordinary men do not usually know what this connection means for the kinds of men they are becoming and for the kinds of history-making in which they might take part. They do not possess the quality of mind essential to grasp the interplay of man and society, of biography and history, of self and world. They cannot cope with their personal troubles in such ways as to control the structural transformations that usually lie behind them.

Surely it is no wonder. In what period have so many men been so totally exposed at so fast a pace to such earthquakes of change? That Americans have not known such catastrophic changes as have the men and women of other societies is due to historical facts that are now quickly becoming "merely history." The history that now affects every man is world history. Within this scene and this period, in the course of a single generation, one sixth of mankind is transformed from all that is feudal and backward into all that is modern, advanced, and fearful. Political colonies are freed; new and less visible forms of imperialism installed. Revolutions occur; men feel the intimate grip of new kinds of authority. Totalitarian societies rise, and are smashed to bits — or succeed fabulously. After two centuries of ascendancy, capitalism is shown up as only one way to make society into an industrial apparatus. After two centuries of hope, even formal democracy is restricted to a quite small portion of mankind.

Source: The Sociological Imagination (New York: Oxford University Press, 1959), pp. 3–13. Copyright © 1959 by Oxford University Press, Inc. Renewed 1987 by Yaraslava Mills. Reprinted by permission of the publisher.

Everywhere in the underdeveloped world, ancient ways of life are broken up and vague expectations become urgent demands. Everywhere in the overdeveloped world, the means of authority and of violence become total in scope and bureaucratic in form. Humanity itself now lies before us, the super-nation at either pole concentrating its most co-ordinated and massive efforts upon the preparation of World War Three.

The very shaping of history now outpaces the ability of men to orient themselves in accordance with cherished values. And which values? Even when they do not panic, men often sense that older ways of feeling and thinking have collapsed and that newer beginnings are ambiguous to the point of moral stasis. Is it any wonder that ordinary men feel they cannot cope with the larger worlds with which they are so suddenly confronted? That they cannot understand the meaning of their epoch for their own lives? That — in defense of selfhood — they become morally insensible, trying to remain altogether private men? Is it any wonder that they come to be possessed by a sense of the trap?

It is not only information that they need — in this Age of Fact, information often dominates their attention and overwhelms their capacities to assimilate it. It is not only the skills of reason that they need — although their struggles to acquire these often exhaust their limited moral energy.

What they need, and what they feel they need, is a quality of mind that will help them to use information and to develop reason in order to achieve lucid summations of what is going on in the world and of what may be happening within themselves. It is this quality, I am going to contend, that journalists and scholars, artists and publics, scientists and editors are coming to expect of what may be called the sociological imagination.

1

The sociological imagination enables its possessor to understand the larger historical scene in terms of its meaning for the inner life and the external career of a variety of individuals. It enables him to take into account how individuals, in the welter of their daily experience, often become falsely conscious of their social positions. Within that welter, the framework of modern society is sought, and within that framework the psychologies of a variety of men and women are formulated. By such means the personal uneasiness of individuals is focused upon explicit troubles and the indifference of publics is transformed into involvement with public issues.

The first fruit of this imagination — and the first lesson of the social science that embodies it — is the idea that the individual can understand his own experience and gauge his own fate only by locating himself within his period, that he can know his own chances in life only by becoming aware of those of all individuals in his circumstances. In many ways it is a tenable lesson; in many ways a magnificent one. We do not know the limits of man's capacities for supreme effort or willing degradation, for agony or glee, for pleasurable brutality or the sweetness of reason. But in our time we have come to know that the limits of "human nature" are frighteningly broad. We have come to know that every individual lives, from one generation to the next, in some society; that he lives out a biography, and that he lives it out within some historical sequence. By the fact of his living he contributes, however minutely, to the shaping of this society and to the course of its history, even as he is made by society and by its historical push and shove.

The sociological imagination enables us to grasp history and biography and the relations between the two within society. That is its task and its promise. To recognize this task and this promise is the mark of the classic social analyst. It is characteristic of Herbert Spencer — turgid, polysyllabic, comprehensive; of E.A. Ross — graceful, muckraking, upright; of Auguste Comte and Emile Durkheim; of the intricate and subtle Karl Mannheim. It is the quality of all that is intellectually excellent in Karl Marx; it is the clue to Thorstein Veblen's brilliant and ironic insight, to Joseph Schumpeter's many-sided constructions of reality; it is the basis of the psychological sweep of W.E.H. Lecky no less than of the profundity and clarity of Max Weber. And it is the signal of what is best in contemporary studies of man and society.

No social study that does not come back to the problems of biography, of history and of their intersections within a society has completed its intellectual journey. Whatever the specific problems of the classic social analysts, however limited or however broad the features of social reality they have examined, those who have been imaginatively aware of the promise of their work have consistently asked three sorts of questions:

1. What is the structure of this particular society as a whole? What are its essential components, and how are they related to one another? How does it differ from other varieties of social order? Within it, what is the meaning of any particular feature for its continuance and for its change?

2. Where does this society stand in human history? What are the mechanics by which it is changing?

What is its place within and its meaning for the development of humanity as a whole? How does any particular feature we are examining affect, and how is it affected by, the historical period in which it moves? And this period — what are its essential features? How does it differ from other periods? What are its characteristic ways of history-making?

3. What varieties of men and women now prevail in this society and in this period? And what varieties are coming to prevail? In what ways are they selected and formed, liberated and repressed, made sensitive and blunted? What kinds of "human nature" are revealed in the conduct and character we observe in this society in this period? And what is the meaning for "human nature" of each and every feature of the society we are examining?

Whether the point of interest is a great power state or a minor literary mood, a family, a prison, a creed — these are the kinds of questions the best social analysts have asked. They are the intellectual pivots of classic studies of man in society — and they are the questions inevitably raised by any mind possessing the sociological imagination. For that imagination is the capacity to shift from one perspective to another — from the political to the psychological; from examination of a single family to comparative assessment of the national budgets of the world; from the theological school to the military establishment; from considerations of an oil industry to studies of contemporary poetry. It is the capacity to range from the most impersonal and remote transformations to the most intimate features of the human self — and to see the relations between the two. Back of its use there is always the urge to know the social and historical meaning of the individual in the society and in the period in which he has his quality and his being.

That, in brief, is why it is by means of the sociological imagination that men now hope to grasp what is going on in the world, and to understand what is happening in themselves as minute points of the intersections of biography and history within society. In large part, contemporary man's self-conscious view of himself as at least an outsider, if not a permanent stranger, rests upon an absorbed realization of social relativity and of the transformative power of history. The sociological imagination is the most fruitful form of this self-consciousness. By its use men whose mentalities have swept only a series of limited orbits often come to feel as if suddenly awakened in a house with which they had only supposed themselves to be familiar. Correctly or incorrectly, they often come to feel that they can now provide themselves with adequate summations, cohesive assessments, comprehensive orientations. Older decisions that once appeared sound now seem to them products of a mind unaccountably dense. Their capacity for astonishment is made lively again. They acquire a new way of thinking, they experience a transvaluation of values: in a word, by their reflection and by their sensibility, they realize the cultural meaning of the social sciences.

2

Perhaps the most fruitful distinction with which the sociological imagination works is between "the personal troubles of milieu" and "the public issues of social structure." This distinction is an essential tool of the sociological imagination and a feature of all classic work in social science.

Troubles occur within the character of the individual and within the range of his immediate relations with others; they have to do with his self and with those limited areas of social life of which he is directly and personally aware. Accordingly, the statement and the resolution of troubles properly lie within the individual as a biographical entity and within the scope of his immediate milieu — the social setting that is directly open to his personal experience and to some extent his willful activity. A trouble is a private matter: values cherished by an individual are felt by him to be threatened.

Issues have to do with matters that transcend these local environments of the individual and the range of his inner life. They have to do with the organization of many such milieux into the institutions of an historical society as a whole, with the ways in which various milieux overlap and interpenetrate to form the larger structure of social and historical life. An issue is a public matter: some value cherished by publics is felt to be threatened. Often there is a debate about what that value really is and about what it is that really threatens it. This debate is often without focus if only because it is the very nature of an issue, unlike even widespread trouble, that it cannot very well be defined in terms of the immediate and everyday environments of ordinary men. An issue, in fact, often involves a crisis in institutional arrangements, and often too it involves what Marxists call "contradictions" or "antagonisms."

In these terms, consider unemployment. When, in a city of 100,000, only one man is unemployed, that is his personal trouble, and for its relief we properly look to the character of the man, his skills, and his immediate opportunities. But when in a nation of 50 million employees, 15 million men are unemployed, that is an issue, and we may not hope to find its solution within the range of opportunities open to any one individual. The very structure of opportunities has collapsed. Both the correct statement of the problem and the range of possible solutions require us to consider the economic and political institutions of the society, and not merely the personal situation and character of a scatter of individuals.

Consider war. The personal problem of war, when it occurs, may be how to survive it or how to die in it with honor; how to make money out of it; how to climb into the higher safety of the military apparatus; or how to contribute to the war's termination. In short, according to one's values, to find a set of milieux and within it to survive the war or make one's death in it meaningful. But the structural issues of war have to do with its causes; with what types of men it throws up into command; with its effects upon economic and political, family and religious institutions; with the unorganized irresponsibility of a world of nation-states.

Consider marriage. Inside a marriage a man and a woman may experience personal troubles, but when the divorce rate during the first four years of marriage is 250 out of every 1,000 attempts, this is an indication of a structural issue having to do with the institutions of marriage and the family and other institutions that bear upon them.

Or consider the metropolis — the horrible, beautiful, ugly, magnificent sprawl of the great city. For many upper-class people, the personal solution to "the problem of the city" is to have an apartment with private garage under it in the heart of the city, and forty miles out, a house by Henry Hill, garden by Garrett Eckbo, on a hundred acres of private land. In these two controlled environments — with a small staff at each end and a private helicopter connection — most people could solve many of the problems of personal milieux caused by the facts of the city. But all this, however splendid, does not solve the public issues that the structural fact of the city poses. What should be done with this wonderful monstrosity? Break it all up into scattered units, combining residence and work? Refurbish it as it stands? Or, after evacuation, dynamite it and build new cities according to new plans in new places? What should those plans be? And who is to decide and to accomplish whatever choice is made? These are structural issues; to confront them and to solve them requires us to consider political and economic issues that affect innumerable milieux.

In so far as an economy is so arranged that slumps occur, the problem of unemployment becomes inca-

pable of personal solution. In so far as war is inherent in the nation-state system and in the uneven industrialization of the world, the ordinary individual in his restricted milieu will be powerless — with or without psychiatric aid — to solve the troubles this system or lack of system imposes upon him. In so far as the family as an institution turns women into darling little slaves and men into their chief providers and unweaned dependents, the problem of a satisfactory marriage remains incapable of purely private solution. In so far as the overdeveloped megalopolis and the overdeveloped automobile are built-in features of the overdeveloped society, the issues of urban living will not be solved by personal ingenuity and private wealth.

What we experience in various and specific milieux, I have noted, is often caused by structural changes. Accordingly, to understand the changes of many personal milieux we are required to look beyond them. And the number and variety of such structural changes increase as the institutions within which we live become more embracing and more intricately connected with one another. To be aware of the idea of social structure and to use it with sensibility is to be capable of tracing such linkages among a great variety of milieux. To be able to do that is to possess the sociological imagination.

3

What are the major issues for publics and the key troubles of private individuals in our time? To formulate issues and troubles, we must ask what values are cherished yet threatened, and what values are cherished and supported, by the characterizing trends of our period. In the case both of threat and of support we must ask what salient contradictions of structure may be involved.

When people cherish some set of values and do not feel any threat to them, they experience *well-being*. When they cherish values but *do* feel them to be threatened, they experience a crisis — either as a personal trouble or as a public issue. And if all their values seem involved, they feel the total threat of panic.

But suppose people are neither aware of any cherished values nor experience any threat? That is the experience of *indifference*, which, if it seems to involve all their values, becomes apathy. Suppose, finally, they are unaware of any cherished values, but still are very much aware of a threat? That is the experience of *uneasiness*, of anxiety, which, if it is total enough, becomes a deadly unspecified malaise.

Ours is a time of uneasiness and indifference — not yet formulated in such ways as to permit the work of reason and the play of sensibility. Instead of troubles — defined in terms of values and threats — there is often the misery of vague uneasiness; instead of explicit issues there is often merely the beat feeling that all is somehow not right. Neither the values threatened nor whatever threatens them has been stated; in short, they have not been carved to the point of decision. Much less have they been formulated as problems of social science.

In the 'thirties there was little doubt — except among certain deluded business circles — that there was an economic issue which was also a pack of personal troubles. In these arguments about "the crisis of capitalism," the formulations of Marx and the many unacknowledged re-formulations of his work probably set the leading terms of the issue, and some men came to understand their personal troubles in these terms. The values threatened were plain to see and cherished by all; the structural contradictions that threatened them also seemed plain. Both were widely and deeply experienced. It was a political age.

But the values threatened in the era after World War Two are often neither widely acknowledged as values nor widely felt to be threatened. Much private uneasiness goes unformulated; much public malaise and many decisions of enormous structural relevance never become public issues. For those who accept such inherited values as reason and freedom, it is the uneasiness itself that is the trouble; it is the indifference itself that is the issue. And it is this condition, of uneasiness and indifference, that is the signal feature of our period.

All this is so striking that it is often interpreted by observers as a shift in the very kinds of problems that need now to be formulated. We are frequently told that the problems of our decade, or even the crises of our period, have shifted from the external realm of economics and now have to do with the quality of individual life — in fact with the question of whether there is soon going to be anything that can properly be called individual life. Not child labor but comic books, not poverty but mass leisure, are at the center of concern. Many great public issues as well as many private troubles are described in terms of "the psychiatric" — often, it seems, in a pathetic attempt to avoid the large issues and problems of modern society. Often this statement seems to rest upon a provincial narrowing of interest to the Western societies, or even to the United States — thus ignoring two-thirds of mankind; often, too, it arbitrarily divorces the individual life from the larger institutions within which that life is enacted, and which on occasion bear upon it more grievously than do the intimate environments of childhood.

Problems of leisure, for example, cannot even be stated without considering problems of work. Family troubles over comic books cannot be formulated as problems without considering the plight of the contemporary family in its new relations with the newer institutions of the social structure. Neither leisure nor its debilitating uses can be understood as problems without recognition of the extent to which malaise and indifference now form the social and personal climate of contemporary American society. In this climate, no problems of "the private life" can be stated and solved without recognition of the crisis of ambition that is part of the very career of men at work in the incorporated economy.

It is true, as psychoanalysts continually point out, that people do often have "the increasing sense of being moved by obscure forces within themselves which they are unable to define." But it is *not* true, as Ernest Jones asserted, that "man's chief enemy and danger is his own unruly nature and the dark forces pent up within him." On the contrary: "Man's chief danger" today lies in the unruly forces of contemporary society itself, with its alienating methods of production, its enveloping techniques of political domination, its international anarchy — in a word, its pervasive transformations of the very "nature" of man and the conditions and aims of his life.

It is now the social scientist's foremost political and intellectual task — for here the two coincide — to make clear the elements of contemporary uneasiness and indifference. It is the central demand made upon him by other cultural workmen — by physical scientists and artists, by the intellectual community in general. It is because of this task and these demands, I believe, that the social sciences are becoming the common denominator of our cultural period, and the sociological imagination our most needed quality of mind.

Chapter 2

FOUNDATIONS OF SOCIOLOGICAL THEORY

ROBERT J. BRYM

INTRODUCTION

Sociology will inevitably appear a confusing enterprise to students just beginning to study it. Sociologists occupy themselves with problems that also concern political scientists, economists, psychologists, social workers, urban planners, psychiatrists and lawyers. In what sense, then, is sociology distinct from these other disciplines?

The answer has more to do with the unique *approach* of sociologists to their subject matter than with the nature of the subject matter itself. While many kinds of scholars are interested in, say, crime, economic development, elections and mental disorders, sociologists ask relatively distinct questions about these and other social issues.

I will examine three of the main questions that have animated sociology since its origins in the nineteenth century: (1) What is the relationship between the individual and society? (2) Are the most important determinants of social behaviour cultural or economic? (3) What are the bases of social inequality?

The debates surrounding these questions are recurrent. It is the tenacity and longevity of these disputes that allows me to characterize them as key issues in sociology. But the enduring character of these disputes may also be a source of frustration to the introductory student. It may appear that nothing ever gets resolved in sociology. However, careful study of the discipline demonstrates that sociological knowledge is, to a degree, cumulative. In other words, although soci-

ologists ask much the same questions today as they did a century ago, their answers are now much more precise, complex and enlightening than they were then; the classic questions of sociology continue to engage lively minds in a debate that gets more and more sophisticated over time.

Let us begin by examining Emile Durkheim's *Suicide*, which, a century ago, set out a highly controversial idea about the individual's relationship to society.

INDIVIDUAL AND SOCIETY

Durkheim on "Social Facts" and Suicide

Usually we assume that any act — a suicide, a marriage, a revolution, extraordinary economic success — is the outcome of an individual's (or many individuals') motives. Features of society are, in turn, usually viewed as the result of many individual passions and decisions. Durkheim, however, turned this conventional wisdom on its head. He argued that individual passions and decisions are the result of certain features of society, that the social whole is greater than the sum of its individual parts. And, according to Durkheim, the study of how social forces influence individual behaviour is what sociology is all about (Durkheim 1966 [1895]).

Consider, for example, the act of suicide. For two reasons, no act appears to be more personal than the taking of one's own life. First, common sense suggests that suicide is the outcome of some profound problem

Source: "Foundations of Sociological Theory," in Lorne Tepperman and James Curtis, eds., *Everyday Life: A Reader* (Toronto: McGraw-Hill Ryerson, 1992), pp. 14–23. Reprinted by permission of the author.

in the mind of the *individual*. Second, suicide seems the most *anti-social* act imaginable: it negates — indeed, destroys — society, at least for one person.

Yet in 1897 Durkheim proposed the controversial idea that the causes of suicide are not just personal. If suicide rates are high in one group of people and low in another, that is due, said Durkheim, to the operation of *social facts*: impersonal social forces that lie outside an individual's mind and compel him or her to act in certain ways.

In order to make his case Durkheim first disposed of psychological and other common explanations of suicide.[1] For example, Durkheim examined the association between rates of suicide (the number of suicides among 100,000 people) and rates of psychological disorder (the number of cases of psychological disorder among 100,000 people) in various groups. The notion that psychological disorder causes suicide is supported, Durkheim reasoned, only if suicide rates tend to be high where rates of psychological disorder are high, and if suicide rates tend to be low where rates of psychological disorder are low.

Durkheim's analysis of European government statistics, hospital records, and other sources revealed nothing of the kind. For example, he discovered that: (1) There were slightly more women than men in European insane asylums. But there were four male suicides for every female suicide. (2) Jews had the highest rate of psychological disorder among the major religious groups in France. But they had the lowest suicide rate. (3) Psychological disorders occurred most frequently when a person reached maturity. But suicide rates increased steadily with age.

Clearly, suicide rates and rates of psychological disorder did not vary directly; in fact, they often appeared to vary inversely. Why, then, did men commit suicide more frequently than women, the aged more than the young, Jews less than Catholics, and Catholics less than Protestants? Durkheim saw these regularities as results of variations in the degree of *social solidarity* in different categories of the population. Accordingly, he expected groups whose members interact more frequently and intensely to exhibit lower suicide rates. For instance, Durkheim found that married adults were half as likely as unmarried adults to commit suicide. He explained this difference as a result of the fact that marriage creates social ties that bind the individual to society. Likewise, large families provide their members with more social ties than do small families; that is why, wrote Durkheim, the suicide rate is lower in large families. In general, he wrote, "suicide varies with the degree of integration of the social groups of which the

individual forms a part.... The more weakened the groups to which he[2] belongs, the less he depends on them, the more he consequently depends only on himself and recognizes no other rules of conduct than what are founded on his private interests," the greater the chance that an individual will take his or her own life (Durkheim 1951 [1897]: 209). Of course, this generalization tells us nothing about why any particular individual may take his or her life. It does, however, say something uniquely sociological about why the suicide rate varies from group to group.

The Phenomenological Response

Many contemporary sociologists continue to argue that the proper focus of the discipline is the study of social pressures that constrain or influence individuals. Today, researchers can use statistical techniques to measure the independent and combined effects of many social variables on many types of behaviour. The choice of a marriage partner may, for example, seem to be a question exclusively of love. But even love is constrained by social facts: research reveals that a very large proportion of marriages join partners from the same ethnic groups and classes.

However, not all marriages take place within ethnic groups and class groupings. This, opponents of the Durkheimian position argue, points to an important flaw in his theory. They argue that Durkheim paints an altogether too mechanical and deterministic view of the individual in society, making it seem as if people behave like billiard balls, knocked about on predetermined trajectories, unable to choose to alter their destinations. But, Durkheim's critics continue, we know from our everyday experience that this is not the case. People *do* make choices — often difficult ones — about what career to follow, what country to live in, whether and in what form they will adopt an established religion, whether to engage in heterosexual or homosexual relationships (or both), and so forth. Two people with similar social characteristics may react quite differently to similar social circumstances because, according to Durkheim's detractors, they may *interpret* these circumstances differently. In the opinion of such *phenomenological* sociologists, an adequate explanation of social phenomena requires that we understand the *subjective meanings* that people attach to social facts and the ways in which they actively *create* these social facts.

In order better to understand the phenomenological school of thought, let us return to the problem of suicide. If a police officer discovers a dead person at the wheel of a car that has run into a tree, it may be very difficult to establish with any certainty whether the death was accidental or suicidal. Interviewing friends and relatives in order to find out the dead person's state of mind immediately before the crash may help to rule out the possibility of suicide. But, as this example illustrates, understanding the intention or motive of the actor is critical to explaining or labelling a social action. Suicide, then, is not just an objective social fact, but an inferred, and therefore subjective, social fact. A state of mind must be interpreted — usually by a coroner — before the dead body becomes a suicide statistic (Douglas 1967).

Because social stigma is attached to suicide, coroners are inclined to classify deaths as accidental whenever such an interpretation is at all plausible. Experts believe that, for this reason, official suicide rates are about one-third lower than actual suicide rates. The phenomenological study of social life reveals many such inconsistencies between objective and subjective reality. For instance, if increased crime rates among aboriginal Canadians are reported in the newspapers, this may reflect more crimes being committed by aboriginal Canadians. But the phenomenological sociologist is unlikely to accept such reports at face value. The higher crime rate may result from a politically motivated change in the official definition of what constitutes a crime, or increased police surveillance in areas where aboriginal Canadians reside. Here, inquiry into the subjective underside of the official picture may deepen our understanding of how society works.

Some phenomenological sociologists tend to ignore the impact of objective, outside social forces on the lives of men and women, reducing the study of society to an analysis of subjective interactions in small settings: how person A perceives person B's actions, how person A responds to these actions, and so forth (Goffman 1959). Just as one-sidedly, strict Durkheimians ignore the subjective side of social life, and draw attention only to objective, outside forces. But many modern sociologists endorse neither extreme. They think it makes more sense to combine the Durkheimian and phenomenological approaches and analyze how men and women interpret, create, and change their social existence — but within the limits imposed on them by powerful social constraints. This synthetic approach is found in the work of Karl Marx and, to an even greater degree, Max Weber, who, along with Durkheim, established the groundwork of modern sociology. Let us now turn to a brief examination of their work.

STRUCTURE VERSUS CULTURE

Marx's Legacy

Both Marx and Weber stressed the importance of analyzing subjective social actions *and* objective social constraints (Marx 1972 [1932]: 118; Weber 1947 [1922]: 103; Gerth and Mills 1946: 57–58). They also had compatible (though different) ideas about the *nature* of these constraints.

Marx, like Weber, recognized that the external determinants of behaviour consist of economic, political, and cultural forces. Marx tended to assign overwhelming causal priority to the economic realm. Weber did not deny the primacy of economic arrangements, but he rounded out Marx's analysis by showing how the political and cultural facts of life can act as important, independent causes of many social phenomena.

In the middle of the nineteenth century Marx proposed a sweeping theory of the development of human societies. In this theory the locus of change is economic organization — more precisely, society's class structure and its technological base. In 1859 Marx succinctly put his argument as follows:

> At a certain stage of their development, the material forces of production in society come into conflict with the existing relations of production, or — what is but a legal expression of the same thing — with the property relations within which they had been at work before. From forms of development of the forces of production these relations turn into fetters. Then occurs a period of social revolution. With the change of the economic foundation the entire immense superstructure is more or less rapidly transformed. (Marx 1904 [1859]: 11–12)

How does Marx's theory apply to the rise of capitalism? In European feudal society peasants tilled small plots of land that were owned not by the peasants themselves but by landlords. Peasants were legally bound to the land, obliged to give landlords a set proportion of their harvest and to continue working for them under any circumstances. In turn, landlords were expected to protect peasants against poor economic conditions and marauders.

By the late fifteenth century, certain processes had been set in motion that eventually transformed feudal society into a modern capitalist system. Most important was the growth of exploration and trade, which increased the demand for many goods and services in commerce, navigation, and industry. By the seventeenth and eighteenth centuries some urban dwellers — successful artisans and merchants — had accumulated sufficient capital to expand their production significantly. In order to maximize their profits, these capitalists required an abundant supply of workers who could be hired in periods of high demand and fired without obligation during slack times. It was therefore necessary to induce and coerce indentured peasants to leave the soil and transform them into legally free workers who would work for wages (Marx and Engels 1972 [1848]: 336 ff.).

In Marx's view, the relations between wage labourers and capitalists at first facilitated rapid technological innovation and economic growth. Capitalists were keen to adopt new tools, machines, and production techniques. These changes allowed capitalists to produce more efficiently, earn higher profits, and drive their competitors out of business. Efficiency also required that workers be concentrated in larger and larger industrial establishments, that wages be kept as low as possible, and that as little as possible be invested in improving working conditions. Thus, according to Marx, workers and capitalists would stand face-to-face in factory and mine: a large and growing class of relatively impoverished workers opposing a small and shrinking class of increasingly wealthy owners.

Marx argued that in due course all workers would become aware of belonging to the same exploited class. This sense of *class consciousness* would, he felt, encourage the growth of working-class organizations, such as trade unions and political parties. These organizations would be bent on overthrowing the capitalist system and establishing a classless society. According to Marx, this revolutionary change was bound to occur during one of the recurrent and worsening *crises of overproduction* characteristic of the capitalist era. The productive capacity of the system would, Marx said, come to far outstrip the ability of the relatively impoverished workers to purchase goods and services. Thus, in order to sell goods and services, capitalists would be forced to lower their prices. Profits would then fall, the less efficient capitalists would go bankrupt, and massive unemployment of workers would result — thus deepening the economic crisis still further. The capitalist class system had originally encouraged economic growth. Eventually the crises of overproduction it generated would hinder such growth. At that time the capitalist class system would be destroyed and replaced by socialism, Marx argued.

As this thumbnail sketch shows, beliefs, symbols, and values — in short, culture — play a quite minor independent causal role in Marx's theory. Marx analyzed how, under most circumstances, ruling-class ideology forms a legitimizing cement in society and how, under rare circumstances, subordinate class consciousness can become an important force for change. But in his work it is always the material circumstances of existence that ultimately determine the role ideas play.

Weber on Capitalism and the World Religions

Weber, like Marx, was interested in explaining the rise of modern capitalism. And, like Marx, he was prepared to recognize the "fundamental importance of the economic factor" in his explanation (Weber 1958 [1904–5]: 26). But Weber was also bent on demonstrating the one-sidedness of any *exclusively* economic interpretation. After all, the economic conditions that Marx said were necessary for capitalist development existed in Catholic France during the reign of Louis XIV; yet the wealth generated in France by international trade and commerce tended to be consumed by war and the luxurious lifestyle of the aristocracy rather than invested in the growth of capitalist enterprise. For Weber, what prompted vigorous capitalist development in non-Catholic Europe and North America was a combination of (1) favourable economic conditions such as those discussed by Marx and (2) the spread of certain moral values by the Protestant reformers of the sixteenth century and their followers in the seventeenth century.

For specifically *religious* reasons, followers of the Protestant theologian John Calvin stressed the need to engage in intense worldly activity, to demonstrate industry, punctuality, and frugality in one's everyday life. In the view of men like John Wesley and Benjamin Franklin, religious doubts could be reduced, and a state of grace assured, if one worked diligently and lived ascetically. This idea was taken up by Puritanism, Methodism, and other Protestant denominations; Weber called it the *Protestant work ethic* (Weber 1958 [1904–5]: 183).

According to Weber, this ethic had wholly unexpected economic consequences: where it took root, and where economic conditions were favourable, early capitalist enterprise grew robustly. In other words, two independent developments — the Protestant work ethic (which derived from purely religious considerations) and the material conditions favouring capitalist growth (which derived from specifically economic circumstances) — interacted to invigorate capitalism. Weber made his case even more persuasive by comparing Protestant Western Europe and North America with India and China. He concluded that the latter cases differed from the former in one decisive (but certainly not exclusive) respect: Indian and Chinese religions inhibited capitalist economic action. In contrast to ancient Judaism and Christianity, Asiatic religions had strong other-worldly, magical, and antirational components that hindered worldly success in competition and accumulation. As a result, capitalism developed very slowly in India and China (Zeitlin 1987 [1968]: 135–50).

Subsequent research has demonstrated that the association between the Protestant ethic and the strength of capitalist development is weaker than Weber thought (Brym 1986: 24–27; Samuelsson 1961 [1957]). In some places, Catholicism has co-existed with vigorous capitalist growth and Protestantism with relative stagnation. Nonetheless, even if Weber was wrong about this particular case, his *general* view — that religious developments cannot be reduced to economic developments, and that religious ideas have economic consequences — is still widely regarded as a brilliant and valid insight.

Just as some Marxist sociologists have adopted a strict economic determinism, some Weberians have misinterpreted Weber's ideas in a way that supports a sort of cultural determinism. But the plain fact is that Weber assigned nearly the same relative weight to economic and cultural forces as did Marx; and there is nothing in Marx's work that is incompatible with Weber's insights into the relative autonomy of religious developments. Disputes between orthodox Marxists and orthodox Weberians over the relative weight of economic versus cultural causes of change may thus be as specious as the disagreement between rigid Durkheimians and equally rigid phenomenologists.

THE BASES OF SOCIAL INEQUALITY

Marx versus Weber

Thus far I have singled out areas of similarity or compatibility in the thought of Marx and Weber. In Weber's "long and intense debate with the ghost of Karl Marx" (Albert Salomon, quoted in Zeitlin 1987 [1968]): xi), there also emerged some ideas that are incompatible with those of Marx. This is especially obvious in Weber's work on social inequality.

Marx regarded ownership or non-ownership of property as the fundamental basis of inequality in capitalist society. In his view, there are two main classes under capitalism. Members of the capitalist class, or

bourgeoisie, own means of production (tools, factories, etc.) but they do not work them. Members of the working class, or *proletariat,* work but do not own means of production. In addition, Marx discussed some minor classes that are vestiges of pre-capitalist times. Most important, members of the *petite bourgeoisie* (e.g., farmers, owners of small family businesses) own and work means of production. Marx also analyzed various divisions within the major classes. These class segments were distinguished from one another by their sources of income (e.g., financial versus industrial capitalists) or skill level (e.g., skilled versus unskilled manual workers).

In defining classes in this way, Marx was not trying to account for gradations of rank in society. Instead, he sought to explain the massive historical change that results from the materially grounded opposition of interests between classes. In his view, the major classes were potentially self-conscious groups engaged in conflict that would eventually result in societal transformation.

Weber agreed that "'property' and 'lack of property' are... the basic categories of all class situations" (Weber 1946 [1922]: 182). But his analysis of inequality differed from Marx's in three main ways. First, he was profoundly sceptical about Marx's interpretation of historical development. As a result he stressed that members of classes do not necessarily become class-conscious and act in concert. Second, Weber argued that property relations are just one aspect of a more general "market situation" that determines class position. For example, expertise acquired through formal education is a scarce commodity on the labour market. Such expertise increases one's advantages or "life-chances" and is therefore an important factor structuring the class system. On this basis, and in addition to the capitalist and manual working classes, Weber distinguished large and growing classes of technical/managerial personnel and white-collar workers who perform routine tasks.

Third, Weber was less concerned than Marx with the sources of conflict between discrete classes and more concerned with the structure of complex social hierarchies. For this reason he showed that the bases of social inequality are not exclusively economic. One non-economic source of inequality is the way honour (or esteem or prestige) is distributed in society. Weber referred to groups distinguished from one another in terms of prestige as *status groups.* For example, line of descent (including ethnic origin) may account for the level of esteem in which a status group is held, and esteem affects the life-chances of status-group members. A second non-economic source of inequality is the political party. A party, in Weber's definition, is an association that seeks to gain control over an organization — ranging all the way from, say, a sports club to a state — for purposes of implementing specific policies. Parties may recruit members from specific classes or status groups, or both. As such, and to the degree that they achieve organizational control, parties bestow more advantages on their supporters than on non-supporters.

If parties and status groups are independent bases of social inequality, then, according to Weber, they are not wholly independent, especially in capitalist societies. There is an association between status-group and party membership, on the one hand, and class position on the other. The structure of class inequality helps to shape status-group and party membership; in fact, "today the class situation is by far the predominant factor" (Weber 1946 [1922]: 190).[3]

Much of modern sociology has been devoted to exploring the ramifications of Weber's refinement of Marx's stratification model. What are the economic determinants of class that do not derive from ownership versus non-ownership of property? How does the concentration of ethnic and other status groups in particular class locations reinforce status-group cohesion? How do ethnic and other forms of status-group identification serve to reinforce patterns of inequality? To what degree do classes serve as recruitment bases for political parties? To what degree do different types of political parties enact policies that redistribute income? These are among the most popular questions asked by modern sociologists, and they are all indebted to Weber's elaboration of the Marxian schema.

Gender Inequality

Recent years have also witnessed an important addition to the stratification model sketched above. It is now generally acknowledged that gender is a basis of social inequality quite on a par with status groups, parties, and classes (see Figure 2.1). Thus, in Canada and elsewhere, gender is as important a determinant of annual income as class (Ornstein 1983b) because women in the paid labour force tend to be segregated in low-pay, low-prestige jobs (Fox and Fox 1986; 1987). One study conducted in the early 1980s found that even if one matches a group of Canadian men and a group of Canadian women in terms of education, occupation, amount of time worked each year, and years of job experience, one discovers that the women

Figure 2.1 The Main Sources of Social Inequality

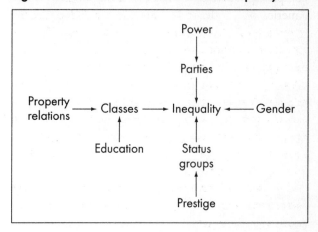

earn only 63 per cent of what the men earn (Goyder 1981: 328). Meanwhile, the great bulk of household labour continues to be performed by women, even if both spouses work; one study conducted in Vancouver found that when their wives entered the paid labour force, husbands did on average only one hour more of housework per week (Meissner et al. 1975).

Classical theories teach us little about the causes of such gender inequality. That is, while Marx and Weber offered important insights into the reasons for the expansion and contraction of particular locations in the stratification system, they "give no clues about why *women* are subordinate to *men* inside and outside the family and why it is not the other way around" (Hartmann 1984 [1978]: 174).

Over the past 25 years, biological, cultural, and social-structural theories of gender inequality have been proposed. Accumulated research suggests that while biological factors — especially women's childbearing function — may have encouraged some division of labour between the sexes in primitive societies, there is no biological reason why male and female jobs should have been rewarded differently, let alone why they continue to be rewarded differently today. Cultural theories, which locate the causes of gender inequality in the way people learn established practices, cannot account either for the origins of gender inequality or for the sources of variation in such inequality. Explanations that root gender inequality in social structure appear more promising. While the subordination of women is evident in virtually every known society, it takes on different forms and degrees in different times and places. Unravelling the relationship between social structure, on the one hand, and the form and degree of gender inequality, on the other, is a complex task that lies at the cutting edge of contemporary research on social inequality.

CONCLUSION

In this brief essay I have set out three questions that lie at the foundation of classical sociology. I have emphasized that the significance of these questions derives from their proven ability to continue provoking the sociological imagination. The remainder of this book demonstrates the soundness of my assertion. As you will see, the value of most of the readings in this volume derives in part from their indebtedness to the first practitioners of the discipline.

NOTES

I would like to thank Jim Curtis, Jim Richardson and Lorne Tepperman for helpful comments on a draft of this article.

1. Durkheim actually analyzed several types of suicide and disposed of several types of explanations. However, strict space limitations preclude a full discussion of these.
2. For the most part, classical sociology (as well as history, political science, economics, and so forth) virtually ignored the existence of women in society. This was reflected not only in the use of sexist language, but in major oversights and imbalances in sociological theorizing, as will be illustrated later in this essay.
3. Unfortunately, many modern sociologists, particularly in the United States, have trivialized Weber — and rendered him much more "anti-Marxist" than he in fact was — by exaggerating the independence of the various bases of inequality, unnecessarily multiplying the number of bases, regarding inequality as a continuous ranking of statistical categories, and highlighting the subjective evaluation of prestige as the major basis of inequality. For a critique of these tendencies, see (Parkin, 1972 [1971]: esp. pp. 13–47).

REFERENCES

Brym, Robert J. "Anglo-Canadian Sociology," *Current Sociology*, Vol. 34, No. 1 (pp. 1–152), 1986.

Douglas, John D. *The Social Meaning of Suicide.* Princeton: Princeton University Press, 1967.

Durkheim, Émile. *The Rules of the Sociological Method,* 8th ed., C. Catlin, ed., S. Solovay and J. Mueller, trans. New York: The Free Press, 1966 (1895).

Fox, Bonnie J. and John Fox. "Women in the labour market, 1931–81: exclusion and competition," *Canadian Review of Sociology and Anthropology*, Vol. 23 (pp. 1–21), 1986.

Gerth, H.H. and C. Wright Mills. "The man and his work," in *From Max Weber: Essays in Sociology*, H. Gerth and C. Mills, eds. and trans., pp. 1–74. New York: Oxford University Press, 1946.

Goffman, Erving. *The Presentation of Self in Everyday Life.* Garden City, N.Y.: Anchor, 1959.

Goyder, John C. "Income differences between the sexes: findings from a national Canadian survey," *Canadian Review of Sociology and Anthropology*, Vol. 18 (pp. 321–42), 1981.

Hartmann, Heidi I. "The unhappy marriage of Marxism and feminism: towards a more progressive union," in *Feminist Frameworks: Alternative Theoretical Accounts of the Relations between Women and Men*, 2nd ed., A. Jaggar and P. Rothenberg, eds., pp. 172–89. New York: McGraw-Hill, 1984 (1978).

Marx, Karl. *A Contribution to the Critique of Political Economy*, N. Stone, trans. Chicago: Charles H. Kerr, 1904 (1859).

———. "The German ideology: Part I," in *The Marx–Engels Reader*, R. Tucker, ed., pp. 110–64. New York: Praeger, 1972 (1932).

Marx, Karl and Friedrich Engels. "Manifesto of the Communist Party," in *The Marx–Engels Reader*, R. Tucker, ed., pp. 331–62. New York: Praeger, 1972 (1848).

Meissner, Martin et al. "No exit for wives: sexual division of labour and the culmination of household demands," *Canadian Review of Sociology and Anthropology*, Vol. 12 (pp. 424–39), 1975.

Ornstein, Michael D. "Class, gender and job income in Canada," *Research in Social Stratification and Mobility*, Vol. 2 (pp. 41–75), 1983.

Parkin, Frank. *Class Inequality and Political Order: Social Stratification in Capitalist and Communist Societies.* London: Paladin, 1972 (1971).

Samuelsson, Kurt. *Religion and Economic Action*, E. French, trans. Stockholm: Scandinavian University Books, 1961 (1957).

Weber, Max. "Class, status, party," in *From Max Weber: Essays in Sociology*, H. Gerth and C. Mills, eds. and trans., pp. 180–95. New York: Oxford University Press, 1946 (1922).

———. *The Protestant Ethic and the Spirit of Capitalism*, T. Parsons, trans. New York: Charles Scribner's Sons, 1958 (1904–5).

———. *The Theory of Social and Economic Organization*, T. Parsons, ed. New York: The Free Press, 1947 (1922).

Zeitlin, Irving. *Ideology and the Development of Sociological Theory*, 2nd ed. Englewood Cliffs, N.J.: Prentice-Hall, 1987.

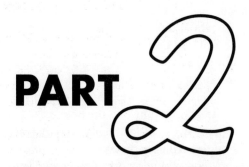

PART 2

FOUNDATIONS OF SOCIETY

*I*MAGINE STANDING AT THE END of a road 30 kilometres long. Allow each metre of the road to represent 100 000 years. The entire road will then signify the amount of time that has passed since life first appeared on the planet: about 3 billion years. From this long view, human beings are very recent arrivals, first assuming their present form only about 100 000 years ago, or just a metre down the road.

Recorded human history spans a much shorter distance. The development of agriculture, undoubtedly the single most important event in human history, took place about 10 000 years ago (only 10 centimetres down the road). The beginning of modern industry, arguably the second most important event in human history, dates from just over 200 years ago (a mere 2 millimetres down the road).

The evolution of agriculture and modern industry hint at what makes humans different from other animals: our ability to create symbols (**abstraction**), to make and use tools that improve our ability to take what we want from nature (**production**), and to develop a complex social life (**co-operation**). These are the characteristics that enabled humans to survive and multiply despite a harsh natural environment and poor physical endowments. Let us consider each of the three distinctive human features in turn.

Abstraction is the capacity to create symbols, including languages, mathematical notations, and signs, in order to classify experience and generalize from it. For example, we recognize that there are many objects on which we can sit but that only some of them are equipped with legs and backs. We distinguish the latter from other objects by giving them a name: "chairs." By the time a baby reaches the end of her first year she has heard that word repeatedly and understands well that it refers to a certain class of objects. No animal apart from humans can create such symbols.

The ability to abstract enables humans to learn in a way that no other animal can. For instance, all animals take from nature in order to subsist. But because humans can learn by conceptualizing, we are able to modify nature substantially in order to try (albeit not always successfully) to improve our survival chances and enhance the quality of our lives. An ape may occasionally use a rock to break another object. But only humans are sufficiently intelligent and dexterous to construct tools and use them to produce everything from food to computers. Understood in this sense, *production* is a uniquely human activity.

The capacity to create complex communities, to develop advanced forms of *co-operation*, is the third human characteristic that enhances our survival chances. Co-operation is needed to reproduce the human race and raise children. Moreover, communities enable people to pool resources and acquire specialized skills, thus accomplishing things that no person could possibly do on his or her own. An enormous variety of social arrangements and institutions ranging from health-care systems to forms of religious worship to political parties demonstrates the advanced human capacity to co-operate. Of course, there is also plenty of war, crime, and revolution in the world, but even when people engage in conflict, they must co-operate or fail to achieve their survival aims. The bank robber who is left stranded by his getaway man will be caught; the navy captain whose sailors mutiny will lose the battle.

The chapters in this part of the book focus on the building blocks of social life, the basic social mechanisms and processes involved in human abstraction, production, and co-operation. You will explore how face-to-face symbolic communication, or **social interaction**, enables people to engage in social learning, or **socialization**. By means of socialization people acquire the languages, laws, science, values, customs, and beliefs — in short, the **culture** — of the groups to which they belong. When social interaction assumes a regular or patterned form, the *relations* among people form a **social structure**. Social structures may be, for example, hierarchical or egalitarian, tightly integrated or loosely organized; and different social-structural forms influence human thoughts and actions in different ways. The patterned behaviour of people embedded in a social structure is called a **role**. For instance, in some types of hierarchy, some people perform the role of slave, others the role of master. You will see that social structures and cultures are paradoxical features of social life. On the one hand, they are constructed anew, and often modified, at least a little, by each person in society. On the other hand, because social structures and cultures exist before any particular individual does, they help define and limit what the individual can think and what he or she can do. Hence the sociologist's answer to the philosopher's debate about whether people are free or determined: They are both.

GLOSSARY

Abstraction is the human ability to create symbols in order to classify experience and generalize from it.

Co-operation is the human ability to give and receive aid from other humans; social structures are typically created in order to facilitate co-operation.

Culture is the stock of human learning, the sum of human creations, as expressed symbolically in custom, language, art, law, science, etc.

Production is a distinctively human mode of interacting with nature; it involves inventing tools and using them to make and improve the means of survival.

Roles are the behaviour patterns of people embedded in a social structure.

Social interaction is meaningful communication between people.

Socialization is the social process by which culture is learned.

Social structures are the patterns of social relations in which people are embedded and that provide opportunities for, and constrain, action.

PART 2A

SOCIALIZATION AND SOCIAL INTERACTION

What could be more natural than sex? Don't men tend to be masculine and women feminine because they are born that way? Sociology disputes this common-sense view. As Marlene Mackie of the University of Calgary shows in Chapter 3, anatomical and hormonal differences between women and men are slight compared with the enormous **gender** differences that are socially constructed on top of them. (While sex refers to biological differences between women and men, gender refers to socially constructed definitions of femininity and masculinity.) Babies who are identified as girls or boys are systematically *taught* to assume feminine or masculine roles by parents, schools, and the mass media. And early gender socialization shapes one's fate as few other social forces do. Learn to "act like a man" and you can reasonably expect a position of authority as an adult; learn to "be a good little girl" and you can reasonably expect a job nurturing others.

Socialization does not, of course, end in early childhood. It is a lifelong process. In Chapter 4, Jack Haas and William Shaffir of McMaster University provide an extended example of **secondary socialization** in their analysis of how medical students learn to perform the role of doctor. They demonstrate that medical students become adept at **impression management** in order not to be judged incompetent by their teachers and patients. That is, they learn to consciously and often cynically manipulate the way they present themselves to others in order to be seen in the best possible light. They adopt a new vocabulary and way of dress to set themselves off from patients. They try to model their behaviour after that of doctors who have authority over them. By engaging in these symbolic interaction practices, they reduce the distance between their selves and the role of doctor. They eventually learn the role so well that, by the time they complete medical school, they fail to see any difference between their selves and their role. They come to take for granted a fact they once had to socially construct, painstakingly and imaginatively: the fact that they are doctors.

The example of medical student socialization shows that roles are not handed to people like so many ready-to-wear suits of clothing. Individuals assist in tailoring roles to match their individual needs and capabilities. As Haas and Shaffir emphasize, learning a role is a creative endeavour, often requiring keen interpersonal skills. Roles are not passively learned but actively negotiated.

GLOSSARY

Gender refers to socially constructed definitions of femininity and masculinity and is thus different from sex, which refers to biological differences between men and women.

Impression management is the conscious manipulation of how one presents one's self to others for the purpose of achieving a desired result.

Secondary socialization is social learning that takes place after early childhood in public school, during professional training, etc.

Chapter 3

BIOLOGICAL AND SOCIALIZATION EXPLANATIONS OF GENDER

MARLENE MACKIE

BIOLOGICAL EXPLANATIONS OF GENDER

To what extent are men masculine and women feminine because they were born that way? In particular, is women's social subordination a reflection of their biological inferiority? These questions have concerned practitioners of many academic disciplines.

Animal Research

Studies have been made of our evolutionary cousins the monkeys and apes in an attempt to determine whether human sex/gender differences are innate or learned (Tavris and Wade 1984). The logic here rests on the assumption that primates are like human beings but do not undergo the intensive social learning that humans do. Primate sex differences that parallel human sex differences therefore constitute evidence for biological causation of human sex differences.

This type of argument-by-analogy (Tavris and Wade 1984) presents at least three problems. First, the conclusion reached depends greatly on the particular species chosen (Rosenberg 1976). The male baboon is much more aggressive than the female baboon; both male and female gibbons are highly aggressive (Lancaster 1976). As far as human differences are concerned, do baboons support biological causation and gibbons social learning? Second, extrapolation from lower-animal behaviour to human behaviour is risky "for the simple reason that humans are not non-humans" (Weisstein 1971). As the evolutionary ladder is ascended, the effects of physiology on behaviour become less dramatic and the role of learning more important (Frieze et al. 1978). Third, even when the same label is used for human and animal behaviour, the behaviours may not be at all comparable. Consider, for example, sex differences in aggression. The animal findings refer to such measures as threat displays, the latency of initial attack, and the outcome of fights, whereas the human studies refer to quite different measures, such as verbal aggression, teachers' ratings of assertiveness, questionnaire responses, and so on (Archer 1976).

Do criticisms like these mean that animal studies are worthless to students of human sex/gender differences? Not at all. But research into animal differences is best viewed as a source of hypotheses, rather than definitive answers concerning differences in *Homo sapiens* (Sperling 1991).

The Anthropological Approach

Anthropologists have provided yet another perspective on the question "To what extent do gender questions stem from essential human nature?" Put another way, are the division of labour and male superiority that characterize contemporary Western societies biologically based? See Rosaldo and Lamphere (1974); Friedl (1975); Martin and Voorhies (1975); Ortner and Whitehead (1981); Sanday (1981); Leacock (1982); Liebowitz (1983); and di Leonardo (1991).

Source: "Gender Relations," in Robert Hagedorn, ed., *Sociology*, 5th ed. (Toronto: Harcourt Brace, 1994), pp. 128–44. Reprinted by permission of the publisher.

The presence or absence of *cultural universals* in the anthropological record is taken to be evidence for or against a biological explanation. If a certain type of behaviour is found in many cultures, despite other variations in cultural patterns, that behaviour is assumed to be biologically determined, or at least linked in some way to physiology. According to this conservative position, existing gender arrangements being "essentially natural, they *should* stay about what they are: major change would be unsuccessful, or would exact too high a price in emotional strain" (Friedl 1975). If, however, cultural comparisons show inconsistency, if social arrangements are sometimes this way and sometimes that, this cross-cultural inconsistency is interpreted as evidence that gender differences are socially caused.

Debate has centred on two interrelated and apparently universal aspects of the anthropological record: male dominance and the division of labour between the sexes. The first cultural universal refers to the fact that although women sometimes have a good deal of informal influence, "societies in which women are consistently dominant do not exist and have never existed" (Friedl 1978).

The second cultural universal summarizes anthropological evidence that all societies distinguish between tasks usually performed by men and tasks usually performed by women. These arrangements appear to have had their original source in women's reproductive capacities, the long helplessness of the human infant, and the generally greater size and strength of men. Since women were tied down with pregnancy and breastfeeding, their activities were restricted to a home base. They were responsible for feeding and nurturing family members of all ages, and for gathering food available near home. Men, by necessity, filled the more public roles of hunter, political leader, soldier, and religious official (Rosaldo 1974).

Most feminist anthropologists acknowledge the near-universality of male dominance and sexually based divisions of labour. However, they challenge the biological inevitability of these gender arrangements. According to them, the cultural meanings given these "natural" facts merit special attention. They point out that considerable cross-cultural variability exists in determining which sex performs which tasks. Feminist anthropologists argue that women's status and the way work is organized have a lot to do with a society's level of technology (Friedl 1975). In hunting and gathering societies, which prevailed for 98 percent of human history, the sexes are generally full economic partners. In horticultural societies, in which food is cultivated by

hoe, relations between the sexes tend to be relatively egalitarian (Basow 1992). However, women's status varies with the existence of other customs, such as polygamy. Men's monopoly over large game and warfare gave them advantages over women.

With the rise of agrarian societies some 5000 to 6000 years ago, women's status declined. Sociologist Rae Blumberg (1978) warns: If you believe in reincarnation, hope that you will never come back as a woman in a traditional agrarian society! Because plough cultivation requires few workers at sites farther from the home base, men dominate the economy. As land became property to be owned, defended, and inherited, concern for paternity increased men's desire to control women's sexuality. When class societies developed and goods were produced for exchange rather than for sharing, women's child-care responsibilities rendered them economically dependent on men (Sayers 1982).

Every one of today's industrialized societies emerged from an agrarian base (Basow 1992). Women's status worsened with the Industrial Revolution, which began in England and northwest Europe in the 1800s. Tasks formerly performed in the home were transferred to the factory and taken over by men. Women from the poorer classes also worked in the factories. However, their presence in the workplace was defined as merely temporary diversion from females' primary responsibility to children and home. These women entered the labour force either when factories were especially short of workers or when extra wages were badly needed at home. The dead-end, poorly paid, low-level jobs they filled did little to improve women's status. At the same time, women in the higher social classes were discouraged from working outside the home.

As Basow (1992) points out, the above pattern of viewing women as cheap temporary labour when a society begins industrializing is strikingly evident in many developing countries today, such as Mexico. Manufacturing industries, especially electronics and textiles, have transferred production to export-processing zones in the Third World. "These industries have shown an overwhelming preference for female workers, who are viewed as a cheap, abundant, and politically docile labour force."

As a result of these developments, men increasingly assumed dominance in the public sphere. Men's public activities gave them privileged access to resources and symbols that enhanced their power and provided disproportionate rewards. As dominant groups usually do, males propagated definitions of the situation that aggrandized themselves and their work. There is considerable pressure on subordinate groups, such as women, to accept the dominant groups' definitions.

The real issue then is cultural meanings, not reproductive capabilities. As human products, ideas are subject to revision (Richardson 1981). The notion of male superiority is therefore open to question; moreover, "technology permits humans to transcend biology — people can fly although no one was born with wings" (Huber 1976). Technology has made it possible for the average woman in industrialized nations to be pregnant only a few months of her life. Inventions such as bottle feeding and day-care centres have made the child-bearing function separable from the child-rearing function. The allocation of domestic tasks to women and public tasks to men can no longer be justified on biological grounds. In short, male dominance is universal but not inevitable (Richardson 1981).

Psychosexual Deviations

Gender identity (a person's conviction of being male or female) and genitals usually match. Children born with penises believe themselves to be males and display masculine personalities and behaviour. Similarly, children born with vaginas develop female gender identities and feminine characteristics. Occasionally, ambiguous genitals occur through birth defects or accidents. People with psychosexual abnormalities function, to a certain extent, as natural experiments that provide some insight into the question of the relative weight of biological and social causation in the development of gender. Evidence on both sides has been reported. However, the case described below suggests that *gender assignment* is socially caused.

In the 1960s, the parents of perfectly normal seven-month-old twin boys took their children to a hospital to be circumcised:

> *The physician elected to use an electric cauterizing needle instead of a scalpel to remove the foreskin of the one who chanced to be brought to the operating room first. When this baby's foreskin didn't give on the first try, or on the second, the doctor stepped up the current. On the third try, the surge of heat from the electricity literally cooked the baby's penis. Unable to heal, the penis dried up, and in a few days sloughed off completely, like the stub of an umbilical cord.* (Money and Tucker 1975)

Doctors recommended that the boy's sex be reassigned and that female external genitals be surgically constructed. The child's name, clothes, and hairstyle

were feminized as the parents made every effort to rear twins, one male and one female. As the following anecdotes concerning the twins at age four-and-a-half show, both parents and children successfully developed gender-appropriate attitudes and behaviour. The mother, talking about the boy, reported, "In the summer time, one time I caught him — he went out and took a leak in the flower garden in the front yard, you know. He was quite happy with himself. And I just didn't say anything. I just couldn't. I started laughing and I told daddy about it." The corresponding comments about the girl went this way: "I've never had a problem with her. She did once when she was little, she took off her panties and threw them over the fence. And she didn't have no panties on. But I just gave her a little swat on the rear, and I told her that nice little girls didn't do that, and she should keep her pants on" (Money and Ehrhardt 1972). For Christmas, the girl wanted dolls, a doll house, and a doll carriage. The boy wanted a toy garage with cars, gas pumps, and tools. We are told that the feminized twin grew up to be a healthy young "woman" (Schulz 1984).

This case and others suggest that sex by assignment outweighs biological factors in determining gender identity. For example, of 44 cases of individuals with female XX chromosomes, ovaries, excessive male hormones, and ambiguous external genitals, 39 were assigned as female at birth. Thirty-seven of them developed a female identity. In contrast, all five assigned and reared as males developed male gender identity (Green 1974). However, gender reassignment is usually unsuccessful after the age of 18 months (Money and Ehrhardt 1972). By then, the child has the ability to understand verbal labels for gender and to view the world from a "female" or "male" perspective. Finally, we must point out that the conclusions of psychosexual abnormality research have been criticized because gender reassignment has been supplemented by appropriate surgery and hormone treatment. That is, the individual's biology has been modified to correspond to the assigned gender (Hyde 1979).

Hormonal Explanations of Sex/Gender Differences

Humans' growth, reproduction, aging, reaction to attack, as well as the experience of moods that range from elation to depression are all governed by some 45 hormones. These chemical substances also influence sexuality. When hormones flood into the bloodstream at puberty, boys get erections, girls get menstrual periods, and everyone gets acne (Clark et al. 1987).

Moreover, the prenatal development of female and male forms of internal reproductive structures and external genitalia is controlled by the secretion of male hormones. Without these hormones, the fetus will differentiate as female, regardless of genetic sex (Williams 1987). Given the significance of hormones and their connection with sexuality, it is understandable why some scientists have posited hormones as the key to gender.

The spectacular growth of endocrinology (the study of hormones) stimulated these and other questions: Do very aggressive men have extraordinarily high levels of testosterone coursing through their bloodstream? Do hormones equip women for lives of baby-tending and sweeping the hearth, and make men natural leaders? Does the volatility of moods associated with premenstrual syndrome disqualify women of child-bearing age from responsible positions (Parlee 1973, 1982)? Taking the argument one step further, they ask: Do biochemical variations among people of the same sex account for variations in sex-typed behaviour? Are macho men loaded with testosterone and dainty women with estrogen? Did homosexuals get that way because of hormone imbalances?

Although testosterone administered to animals enhances levels of aggression and produces masculinized behaviour in females, authorities disagree about the connection in humans between testosterone and behaviour (Doyle 1989). Although many studies have found little or no relationship between testosterone levels and various measures of aggression (Lowe 1983), other researchers continue to pursue a link. The dramatic psychological changes, including hostility or "raid rage," in athletes who have used anabolic steroids (Taylor 1985) encourages this line of research.

Are women incapacitated by emotional instability during the premenstrual period? Despite the embarrassment in our culture that surrounds menstruation, premenstrual syndrome (PMS) has recently become a topic for magazine advice columns and TV talk shows. Courts in France now recognize PMS as a legal insanity defense (Tavris 1992). Nevertheless, "half a century's work on the premenstrual syndrome has been flawed by faulty methodology and unfounded interpretations" (Tavris and Wade 1984). Available studies, most clinical and lacking control groups, do not establish that mood changes are strongly correlated with phases of menstrual cycle (Tavris and Wade 1984). Although this does not mean that all menstrual distress is in women's heads, "it would be a mistake to assume that menstruating women are more anxious, tense, or antisocial than the average man" (Tavris and Wade

1984). Women have much lower rates of crime and accidents than do men, whether or not these rates are associated with menstrual periods (Epstein 1988).

So what if premenstrual women are moody and men get more aggressive as their testosterone level rises? Although reliable research fails to underwrite these conclusions, "the question relevant to the genders in society is the *meaning* of differences in hormonal levels" (Epstein 1988). While raging female hormones are widely believed to be detrimental to women's participation in public affairs, no similar hormonal barriers disqualify testosterone-maddened males from sensitive decision-making posts. Having the "right" hormones does not explain masculine advantage; having the "wrong" hormones cannot account for women's lower status. Neither sex can use its hormones as an excuse for antisocial behaviour. Since society "expects people to manage their moods and assume responsibility for harming others," feminists worry about criminal court decisions that let "women get away with murder — literally — because it's their 'time of the month'" (Tavris and Wade 1984).

All human fetuses begin by being female; inputs of male hormones are required to differentiate male characteristics in those fetuses having an XY genetic structure. Various sorts of sex/gender nonconformity (cross-dressing, homosexuality, transsexualism) appear to be more common in males than females. These two factors, taken together, make provocative the hypothesis that prenatal hormone imbalances are linked with postnatal departures from masculinity (Green 1974). Because research techniques of the future might reveal hormonal influences, we should remain open-minded about this possibility (Bell, Weinberg, and Hammersmith 1981; Ross 1986). Nevertheless, at the present time, there is very little evidence for hormonal (or genetic) abnormality in homosexuals or transvestites (Baker 1980; Geer et al. 1984; Huston 1983) or transsexuals (Bolin 1987; Ross 1986).

Conclusions

Every approach to the problem of the biological foundation of female/male differences raises more questions than it answers. Biology may be directly involved in social-psychological traits such as aggressiveness, and indirectly involved in the gender division of labour. The secondary sex characteristics of male size and strength may also contribute indirectly to gender differences. In American and Canadian cultures, which value "sheer bigness," the generally greater male body size may translate into status (Garn 1966). The gender-role implications of strength are more obvious. Superior male strength is an ingredient in the traditional gender division of labour. More important, however, is the implicit or actual physical threat that males present to females. As Goffman (1977) points out, "Selective mating ensures that with almost no exceptions husbands are bigger than wives and boyfriends are bigger than girlfriends."

The biological differences between females and males are really very slight in comparison with the immense gender differences erected on this substructure. However, to search for either biological or environmental causation of gender patterns, to pose the issue as nature versus nurture, is a misleading and simplistic formulation of a complex question. In gender patterns, as in social behaviour in general, both biology and environment are implicated. Biochemical and genetic factors set the stage, but culture and history provide the script for social life (Kunkel 1977). The fact that socialization often emphasizes "natural" sex differences further complicates the situation. For example, our society provides more athletic facilities and opportunities for the physically stronger males. However, because most of the psychosocial differences between the sexes involve learning in one way or another, let us look at socialization as an explanation of gender.

SOCIALIZATION EXPLANATIONS OF GENDER

Socialization is defined as the lifelong learning process through which individuals develop selfhood and acquire the knowledge, skills, and motivations required for participation in social life. *Gender socialization* involves the particular processes through which people learn to be masculine and feminine according to the expectations current in their society. There are a number of theoretical approaches to socialization: the learning, Freudian, cognitive developmental, and symbolic-interaction perspectives. Symbolic interaction will be emphasized here.

Each society has its scripts for femininity and masculinity. The emotions, thoughts, and behaviour of children are shaped in approximate conformity with these gender scripts. However, the content of gender socialization is not uniform for all citizens of a country. Gender scripts are differently interpreted in different social classes, racial/ethnic groups, and regions of a country. In addition, these scripts are age-graded: the gender norms that pertain to given individuals change as they move through the life cycle. Gender stereotypes

and gender-role attitudes tell us something about society's scripts for gender socialization.

Gender Stereotypes

Imagine yourself talking with a friend who describes two people whom you have never met. One person is said to be independent, adventurous, and dominant, while the other is described as sentimental, submissive, emotional, and affectionate. Would it be easier to picture one of these persons as male and the other as female? If you visualize the first person as male and the second as female, you have demonstrated your knowledge of gender stereotypes. What is more, you could be Canadian, American, Nigerian, Pakistani, or Japanese. Cross-cultural research shows that citizens of 30 nations share similar general beliefs about the sexes (Williams and Best 1982).

A *stereotype* refers to those folk beliefs about the attributes characterizing a social category on which there is substantial agreement (Mackie 1973). The term refers to consensual beliefs about the traits people choose to describe categories of people, such as ethnic groups, old people, or university students. In themselves, stereotypes are not good or bad; they simply are. Some stereotype traits are false — for example, that women are illogical. Other traits may be generally fitting but, like all generalizations, fail to take into account individual differences within the sexes or the degree of overlap between the sexes (Williams and Best 1982). For example, the male stereotype contains the trait aggressiveness. Our previous discussion noted both the accuracy of this sex difference and the female/male overlap. In short, "stereotypes both represent and distort reality" (Eagly and Steffen 1984).

Gender stereotypes capture folk beliefs about the nature of females and males generally. Many studies show that, despite the activities of the women's movement, gender stereotypes are "widely held, persistent, and highly traditional in content" (Ward and Balswick 1978). When researchers (Broverman et al. 1972) ask respondents to describe the average man and the average woman, the gender traits fall into a feminine *warmth–expressiveness* cluster and a masculine *competency* cluster. The latter cluster includes such characteristics as being independent, active, competitive, and ambitious. A relative absence of these traits supposedly characterizes women. In other words, relative to men, women are seen to be dependent, passive, noncompetitive, and not ambitious. The warmth–expressiveness cluster, on the other hand, consists of such attributes as being gentle, quiet, and sensitive to the feelings of others. Relative to women, men are perceived as lacking these traits. Gender-stereotype studies (Broverman et al. 1972) also report that many more of the characteristics valued in Western societies are seen as masculine rather than feminine traits.

Gender stereotypes embody the edicts of societal scripts regarding appropriate major time and energy investments for women and men. According to this "ideal" division of labour, men are expected to work outside the home, marry, and support their families, while women are expected to marry, carry the major responsibility for child-rearing, and rely on men for financial support and social status. Increasingly, it is expected that Canadian and American women will also work outside the home. Nevertheless, attracting a suitable mate and looking after his interests (and eventually those of their children) still take priority over serious occupational commitment. The two clusters of traits reflect this division of labour.

It appears that beliefs about gender develop, at least in part, from people's observations of women and men playing these traditional social roles. For example, children are more likely to encounter women taking care of babies and men wielding authority in the workplace than the other way around, and they come to believe that the characteristics thought to be necessary for child care (nurturance, warmth) and for success in the labour force (dominance, objectivity) are typical of women and men, respectively. It is likely that fundamental changes in the "pictures in people's heads" (Lippmann 1922) about men and women reflect social change. In other words, "Gender stereotypes ... will not disappear until people divide social roles equally — that is, until child care and household responsibilities are shared equally by women and men and the responsibility to be employed outside the home is borne equally" (Eagly and Steffen 1984).

The gender stereotypes themselves, since they function as self-fulfilling prophecies, constitute an important impediment to social change. If women are assumed to be less competent, their performance may be judged less successful than it actually is. In addition, if women are assumed to be less competent, they may be given fewer opportunities to assert themselves.

Gender-Role Attitudes

A second component of societal scripts that are learned through socialization are gender-role attitudes. While gender stereotypes refer to shared beliefs about feminine and masculine psychological makeup, *gender-role attitudes* point to people's beliefs about the status of the sexes and the appropriate gender division of labour in the home and workplace. They range from traditional to egalitarian, "from the view that women belong in the home and are responsible for child-rearing, to the view that women and men should have equal access to identical positions and rewards" (Boyd 1984).

Table 3.1 lists six questions that were asked of Canadian national probability samples by researchers Gibbins, Ponting, and Symons (1978) and Ponting (1986). Since four of the six questions from the earlier survey were asked again in 1986, we can draw some conclusions about changes over time. First of all, Canadians' attitudes concerning gender arrangements in the domestic sphere are more traditional than their public-sphere attitudes. In 1986, 64 percent felt that a mother with young children belongs in the home. Moreover, 40 percent believed that a wife should give her husband's career higher priority than her own.

When questions focus exclusively on the woman in the workplace — that is, the implications of her work for her family are left unmentioned — Canadians' attitudes become more egalitarian. Seventy-seven percent said more women should be promoted into senior management positions. Three-quarters of the sample expressed verbal support for the women's movement (questions #5 and #6). Finally, two-thirds said women should have the right to decide whether or not to have an abortion (question #4).

Another important conclusion that can be derived from Table 3.1 is that Canadians' gender-role attitudes have become more egalitarian. The sensitive domestic issues show especially large shifts over time (questions #1 and #2). Ponting's findings agree with several American studies (Cherlin and Walters 1981; Thornton, Alwin, and Camburn 1983). This historical change may be attributed to such factors as the growing labour-force participation of women, public debate and media attention to gender, higher education, and the declining birth rate.

Some categories of Canadians are more liberal than others. Francophones were significantly more liberal than anglophones on questions #3 to #6; no language group differences emerged for the family-related questions (#1 and #2). There is a slight tendency for women to be more liberal than men (questions #3, #5, and #6). However, significantly more men gave the egalitarian response to question #2; sex differences in replies to questions #1 and #4 were not statistically significant. Finally, according to data not shown on Table 3.1, people with more formal education tend to hold more egalitarian attitudes.

Table 3.1 Canadian Gender-Role Attitudes

Attitudinal Item		% Agree	% Disagree	% Undecided/ Neutral**
1. When children are young, a mother's place is in the home.	TOTAL (1986)	64	20	16
	TOTAL (1976)	81	10	9
	Male*	62	19	18
	Female*	65	20	13
	Anglophone*	63	20	16
	Francophone*	62	22	16
2. Although a wife's career may be important, she should give priority to helping her husband advance in his career.	TOTAL (1986)	40	47	13
	TOTAL (1976)	74	21	5
	Male	35	51	13
	Female	44	42	12
	Anglophone	40	47	14
	Francophone	41	47	11
3. In the business world more women should be promoted into senior management positions.	TOTAL (1986)	77	8	14
	TOTAL (1976)	72	14	13
	Male	72	10	18
	Female	82	6	11
	Anglophone	73	9	17
	Francophone	87	4	8
4. A woman should have the sole right to decide whether or not to have an abortion.	TOTAL (1986)	66	26	7
	TOTAL (1976)	56	34	9
	Male	67	24	8
	Female	65	27	6
	Anglophone	65	27	6
	Francophone	70	22	8
5. Overall, the women's movement has had more of a positive effect than a negative effect on Canadian society.	TOTAL (1986)***	73	11	12
	Male	71	12	14
	Female	75	11	10
	Anglophone	73	13	10
	Francophone	71	8	15
6. There should be more laws to get rid of differences in the way women are treated, compared with men.	TOTAL (1986)***	74	13	11
	Male	68	18	13
	Female	80	9	9
	Anglophone	72	15	12
	Francophone	80	9	9

*All sex and language group results refer to 1986 data.
**Because of rounding and "don't know" answers or refusals, some totals do not equal 100%.
***Questions 5 and 6 were not asked in 1976.

Sources: Roger Gibbins, J. Rick Ponting, Gladys L. Symons, "Attitudes and ideology: Correlates of liberal attitudes towards the role of women," *Journal of Comparative Family Studies* 9(1978):19–40; and J. Rick Ponting (unpublished 1986 data).

The impact of the women's movement on Canadians' (and Americans') thinking about the sexes has been significant. However, after analyzing 30 years of Gallup poll data, Boyd (1984) concluded that while enormous changes have occurred with respect to gender issues, Canadians' gender-role attitudes "also reveal a residue of earlier norms and practices."

The Role of the Mass Media in Gender Socialization

The mass media are impersonal communication sources that reach large audiences. As such, they function as symbolic socialization agents. Because the media keep people in touch with what is happening in the world and co-ordinate other societal institutions, they have been described as the "cement of modern social life" (Tuchman 1978).

Since the advent of the women's movement, concern has been voiced over the impact of the media on the development of gender attitudes and behaviour. Although exceptions certainly exist within and among media, mass-communication sources convey traditional, often sexist, messages about gender relations. As a quick survey of magazine ads or newspaper comic strips will illustrate, the media exaggerate the dividing lines between females and males. Their caricatured portraits often rely on gender stereotypes. Women (and to some extent, men) are objectified as sexual beings.

Two main factors explain why the media often depict gender stereotypes and devalue females' status. First, despite some improvement over the past two decades, relatively few women hold positions of authority in media industries. Indeed, feminist critics have accused both Canadian and American media of "widespread discrimination against women in broadcast industry employment practices (Cantor 1988). Moreover, it is hard for those few women who are employed in the media to resist ideas and attitudes that disparage women. Consider the press. Only 6 percent of publishers in Canada are women; 9 percent of editors-in-chief and 6 percent of managing editors are women (Smith 1990: D8). Yet more than half the students in North American journalism classes are now women. "However, change has come hard in a traditionally male-dominated workplace. Women have had to do all the pushing so far and the pace of change has been glacial" (Smith 1990: D8). A professor at an American school of journalism agrees: "Women are creeping ever so slowly toward the year 2055 when projections indicate they will attain levels in newspaper editorships on a par with their level in the population [53 percent]" (Beasley 1989).

Second, the media are sexist because they mirror cultural notions about gender — they take and accentuate societal images of gender and sexuality — and, in turn, they shape and strengthen these views. To be acceptable, media content must contain dominant social beliefs and images. Mass media represent conservative interests. Large audiences are needed to make profits. These mass audiences respond to contemporary, but familiar images. Therefore "content cannot 'move ahead of' public opinion" (Wilson 1981). There is cause for feminist critics to remain troubled about the impressions of masculinity and femininity conveyed by these powerful, ubiquitous symbolic socialization agencies.

Music provides a good example of the gender imagery conveyed by popular culture. Music is an important source of enjoyment for 89 percent of Canadian teenagers (Bibby and Posterski 1992). "Golden oldies" often idealize women ("Earth An-gel, Earth An-gel, will you be mine?"); country ballads sing about strong cowboys and their unrequited love for bad women. Rock music has been criticized for its misogyny (Harding and Nett 1984). For example, a member of Kiss ("Burn Bitch Burn") boasts about having "bedded down" 3000 women during his rock-band travels (*Herald Sunday Magazine*, September 4, 1988). The message of the rap group 2 Live Crew album "As Nasty As They Wanna Be" also glorifies male studs and submissive women. Bibby and Posterski (1992) quote a study by the Quebec Status of Women Council of 338 rock videos: "More than half the rock videos broadcast on television are blatantly sexist, and the most flagrant offenders tend to get the most air time."

Considerable variation exists in the content of the media. For example, movies vary from *Slumber Party Massacre*, which featured female victims of slashing, to *The Accused*, which tried to convince audiences that no woman, regardless of provocative dress, suggestive behaviour, or unsavoury reputation, deserves to be raped. Nevertheless, traditional gender imagery predominates. It is important to note psychologists' conclusion that "there is solid evidence that the way sex roles are portrayed in the mass media can affect children's and adolescents' attitudes and perceptions of what is and is not appropriate for the two sexes" (Roberts and Maccoby 1985).

The Symbolic-Interaction Perspective on Gender Socialization

Symbolic interactionists, such as Cooley and Mead, view "reality" as a matter of social definition. Socialization involves the acquisition of a self, which is also socially defined. The "looking-glass self" notion holds that children learn who they are by adopting other people's attitudes toward themselves. The roles played by language and significant others in the socialization process are emphasized in this perspective. In this section, we want to apply some of these themes to gender socialization. Because gender consists of social constructions built on female/male physiological differences, symbolic interaction seems a particularly appropriate theoretical approach to the questions we have been asking (Mackie 1987).

Development of Gender Identity

As a first step to self-awareness, the child differentiates herself or himself from other objects in the environment. Mead hypothesizes that the capacity to use language allows the child to learn the meaning of many things, including himself or herself. Names form a basis, then, for the development of the self. A given name individualizes the infant and usually classifies it by gender. That is, baptizing a child "Barbara" simultaneously separates this infant from other infants and signifies its femaleness. Often, parents dress youngsters to advertise their gender. They may be colour-coded in traditional masculine blue and feminine pink, or dressed in miniature versions of adult genderized clothing (baseball caps for infant boys and bows taped to female infants' hairless heads) (Cahill 1989).

Gender classification influences caregivers to treat the infant as a boy or as a girl. For example, for the first six months or so, male infants are touched more, while female infants are talked to more (Lewis 1972). Later, the male toddler is tossed into the air ("How's my big boy?"), while the female child is tickled under the chin ("How's my sweet little girl?") (Richmond-Abbott 1983). In other words, when we attach gender-designating labels, we invite gender-specific interactional experiences based on stereotypes (Cahill 1989). The child with a bow taped on her head is regarded as delicate; when she cries, she is seen to be frightened rather than angry. In contrast, adults are likely to view the baby wearing a baseball cap as hardy, and to interpret his crying as anger rather than fear (Cahill 1989).

Although the adults who socialize a child place it in a gender class at birth, some time must pass before the child responds to its own self in terms of gender. As noted above, gender reassignment becomes less successful after eighteen months. One reason may be that by that age the child is labelling itself "male" or "female." By the age of three, a child can accurately and consistently answer the question "Are you a girl or a boy?" At the same age, children show preferences for either "girl" or "boy" toys and activities (Kessler and McKenna 1978). This self-categorization as male or female becomes a major axis of identity. However, young children do not necessarily interpret gender in the same way that adults do. For instance, they use facial hair and clothing, not genitals, as gender cues (Cahill 1989). Lindesmith, Strauss, and Denzin (1977) tell the story of the five-year-old acquaintance of theirs who attended a party at which children of both sexes bathed in the nude. When asked how many boys and how many girls were at the party, she

answered, "I couldn't tell because they all had their clothes off." This misconception is understandable in a society such as ours, where the naked body is usually covered.

Socialization agents such as the family, peers, mass media, and schools teach children what sorts of traits and behaviours go along with the female/male distinction. Parents admonish that "Boys don't cry" and "Girls don't sit with their legs apart." In the past, children's storybooks were sex-typed. Pyke's (1975) survey of Canadian children's books found few women in jobs outside the home. Women's trademark was the "perennial apron," worn "even by female squirrels." Storybook characters who had interesting adventures were most often male. A recent survey of American children's books discovered that girls are increasingly the active central characters who are having fun. However, the women in these stories are still portrayed as homebound mothers without extrafamilial roles (Grauerholz and Pescosolido 1989). Let us turn now to some examples of how language reinforces the ranking of the sexes.

Language and the Ranking of the Sexes

In many ways, female inferiority is conveyed through language forms and usage. For instance, women's speech is viewed as frivolous and unimportant:

> In the English language, we talk and we chat, we jabber and we chatter while men speak, proclaim and express concerns. In the French language, "elle parlote, babille, bavarde, jase, cause" while men "parlent, discourent, discutent." (Martel and Peterat 1984: 43)

Moreover, words label. Speaking of women as "the opposite sex" exaggerates male–female differences. In addition to naming, these labels often imply hidden messages about their referents (a father nicknames his small son "Tiger" and his daughter "Dolly"). Emotionally charged verbal labels also serve to control behaviour. Male children are effectively chastised by being called "fags" or "girls." (A basketball coach yells at a boy who isn't playing well, "Where's your purse, Mrs. — ?"). Similarly, the expletive "bitch" carries the connotation that the woman has failed to observe traditional gender standards.

Terms of address also convey gender messages. For one thing, people feel free to be more familiar semantically with women. In the 1990 Liberal Party leadership contest, the frontrunners were "Chrétien," "Martin," and "Sheila." Observations of males and females in parallel positions in various companies and public places showed that women were more often addressed by first names or nicknames, while men were generally dealt with more formally, by title or last name (Eakins and Eakins 1978). Usually men are at the top of work hierarchies and women are at the bottom. Men call the women by their first names, and the women more often address the men by last name plus title (Thorne and Henley 1975).

Despite innovations such as hyphenated surnames, most women continue to lose their surname upon marriage. Men, however, not only keep their last name for life, but pass it on intact to sons. In general, women are labelled in terms of the men with whom they are associated — "Mrs. Jones," "Harvey Hart's daughter." The significance of the now widely accepted neologism "Ms." has been described as follows: "The new privacy regarding marital status symbolically elevated women to personhood from their previous commodity status in the marriage market where "Miss" meant "for sale," and "Mrs." meant "sold" (Davy 1978).

Clearly, language evaluates the sexes. For example, masculine connotations tend to be strong and positive, while feminine connotations tend to be negative, weak, or trivial. All references to God are masculine: Father, Lord, King. The negative connotations attached to the word "woman" become obvious when we compare taking defeat "like a man" and taking defeat "like a woman." The order of word usage also communicates differential evaluation: "men and women," "boys and girls," "husbands and wives." As Spender (1985) points out, it is appropriate "to call a mixed sex group 'guys' or 'men' but it is a mistake — and an insult — to refer to a group which contains even one male as 'gals' or 'women.'"

While individual examples of sexism in language may seem trivial, their combined impact is profound when we remember that people's perceptions of the world are linked closely to their language. As children learn a language, they also learn gender lessons about women's and men's places in society.

Parents as Significant Others

The provocative ideas of David Lynn (1959, 1969) emphasize the significance of parents in gender socialization. Lynn postulates that, because of the greater availability of the mother and the relative absence of the father during early childhood, little girls easily develop their gender identity through imitation and positive reinforcement. However, little boys must shift from their initial identification with the mother to identification with the father. Because male models are scarce, they have greater difficulty than females in achieving gender identity. According to Lynn, males must learn through abstractly piecing together the intellectual problem of what it means to be male. Some of this learning comes from peers and from media presentations of gender stereotypes. Some results from punishment for displays of feminine behaviour. Masculine behaviour is rarely defined positively as something the boy *should* do. One reason is that the male gender role is "so strongly defined in terms of work and sexuality, both of which are usually hidden from the eyes of children" (Colwill 1982). Instead, undesirable feminine behaviour is indicated negatively as something he should not do. Consequently, males remain anxious about gender. Females freely imitate males (in fashion, for example), but not vice versa. As adults, men are more hostile than women toward both the opposite sex and homosexuals. Nevertheless, the boy learns to prefer the masculine role to the feminine because being male implies countless privileges.

During childhood, the male role is the more inflexible. More pressure is placed on boys to act like boys than on girls to act like girls. Girls' problems start with adolescence:

> Since girls are less likely to masturbate, run away from home, or bite and draw blood, their lives are relatively free from crisis until puberty. Before that, girls do not have to conform to threatening new criteria of acceptability to anywhere near the extent that boys do. (Bardwick and Douvan 1971)

As children of both sexes reach the teenage years, they are exposed to more complex and more precisely defined norms of gender-appropriate behaviour. According to Gilligan (1982), girls' socialization makes connectedness to others all-important to females throughout the life cycle; ruptured relationships, power, and aggression all deeply threaten them. Males, on the other hand, see the world in terms of autonomy, hierarchy, and conflict; it is intimacy that threatens them.

Peers as Significant Others

Children's experience with age-mates is also important in learning masculine or feminine behaviour. Boys and girls have different friendship patterns and different forms of play. Consequently, they acquire different sorts of social skills that may well have implications for their later adult behaviour. Peer activities also reinforce the notion that males are more important than females.

Engaging in what sociologist Fine (1986) has labelled "dirty play" seems important in the gender socialization of little boys. Pre-adolescent pranks such as "mooning" cars (pulling down one's trousers while facing away from the traffic), "egging" cars, and ringing doorbells and running away are thoroughly disapproved of by adults. However, these activities serve as anticipatory socialization for manhood. Males are supposed to be tough, cool, and aggressive. "There is risk involved in throwing eggs at houses or at moving cars; one could get caught, beaten, grounded, or even arrested" (Fine 1986). Boys gain status within their peer group for behaviour adults regard as troublesome. Boys' identity as males is enhanced by engaging in "dirty play," partly because it is "dirty" play (that is, it defies adult, especially female, authority), and partly because it is not *girls'* play.

After formal schooling begins, children's play becomes increasingly sex-segregated. The rare cross-sex play that does occur tends to be courtship activity at an unsophisticated level. According to one study (Richer 1984), the most common type is a chasing game in which girls chase boys and kiss them when they are caught. When boys do bother to chase girls, they pull their hair or push them. Both courtship games (where the desirable males are chased) and the general tendency of both sexes to evaluate boys' activities and boys more positively than girls' activities and girls tend to perpetuate traditional gender arrangements (Richer 1984).

A gender difference exists in the size of children's sex-segregated play groups (Eder and Hallinan 1978). Girls tend to play in small groups, especially dyads (two-person groups). Boys prefer to congregate in larger groups. Thus girls tend to learn the type of interpersonal skills required by small, intimate groups, such as sensitivity to others' feelings, the ability to disclose information about themselves, and the ability to show affection. Boys learn other sorts of skills; in general they learn something about group leadership and decision-making. In addition, girls protect their exclusive groups against the advances of newcomers, while boys tend to welcome new members. Little girls probably blame themselves for the greater trouble they have in making friends.

The type of play preferred by boys versus that enjoyed by girls partly explains the size difference of their friendship groups (Lever 1978). Although such differences seem to be diminishing somewhat, boys tend to play competitive games requiring teams of interdependent players with definite roles. Such games are played according to specific rules (hockey is a good example). In comparison, girls prefer to converse or to engage in physically undemanding activities in an indoor setting that require few participants. Playing dolls or board games does not demand the co-ordination of effort that hockey or baseball does. One result is the learning of different types of skills — and, again, these very likely carry over into adulthood.

Boys acquire the ability to co-ordinate their actions, to cope with impersonal rules, to work for collective as well as individual goals, to deal with competition and criticism. Girls learn to be imaginative, to converse, and to be empathetic. All these social experiences would be valuable for both sexes. While sex differences in play are lessening (many girls now play hockey, soccer, and baseball), the data suggest that the female differentiation and impression of male superiority conveyed by peer socialization are still very strong (Best 1983; Richer 1984).

Conclusions

Symbolic interactionists view gender as a matter of social definition and social behaviour learned through interaction during the socialization process. Other theoretical viewpoints on gender socialization are also useful. For example, Lynn's (1959, 1969) ideas incorporate psychoanalytic ideas that are developed more fully in Chodorow's (1978) analysis of mothering. Learning by imitation is very important in gender socialization. Children growing up in a home organized according to traditional gender patterns regard this organization as perfectly normal and readily accept gender stereotypes (Lambert 1971).

Many social scientists are convinced that the traditional gender stereotypes are arbitrary and even damaging gender scripts for socialization. During the 1970s, some became intrigued with the possibility of making androgyny rather than sex-typing the goal of socialization. The term *androgyny* combines the Greek words for male (*andros*) and female (*gyne*), and refers to the presence of both feminine and masculine elements within individuals of both sexes. Allowing people to have both instrumental and expressive capabilities within their repertoires may help to free the human personality from the restricting prison of stereotyping (Bem 1976). An androgynous person might characterize himself or herself as understanding and compassionate, and assertive, self-reliant, and ambitious. A sex-typed person, on the other hand, might use either the first two or the last three traits in self-description. In recent years, the ideal of androgyny has been criticized on the grounds that it does not eliminate gender stereotypes; it just combines them in new ways (Lott 1981).

The current ideal of *gender transcendence* looks to a state where femininity and masculinity are superseded as ways of labelling and experiencing psychological traits (Garnets and Pleck 1979). In a utopian society where gender has been transcended, each child would be taught that the distinctions of girl/boy and female/male are exclusively biological. The multitude of sociocultural elaborations on sex would disappear. Personality traits, interests, hobbies, toys, clothing, occupations, domestic division of labour — none would any longer be a function of sex (Bem 1983).

REFERENCES

Archer, John. 1976. "Biological explanations of psychological sex differences." *Exploring Sex Differences*. Barbara Lloyd and John Archer, eds. New York: Academic.

Baker, S.W. 1980. "Biological influences on human sex and gender." *Signs* 6: 80–96.

Bardwick, Judith M., and Elizabeth Douvan. 1971. "Ambivalence: The socialization of women." In *Women in Sexist Society*. Vivian Gornick and Barbara K. Moran, eds. New York: Signet.

Basow, Susan A. 1992. *Gender stereotypes and roles.* 3rd ed. Pacific Grove, CA: Brooks/Cole.

Beasley, Maurine. 1989. "Newspapers: Is there a new majority defining the news?" In *Women in Mass Communication: Challenging Gender Values.* Pamela J. Creedon, ed. Newbury Park, CA: Sage Publications.

Bell, Alan P., Martin S. Weinberg, and Sue K. Hammersmith. 1981. *Homosexualities: A Study of Diversity among Men and Women.* New York: Simon and Schuster.

Bem, Sandra L. 1976. "Probing the promise of androgyny." In *Beyond Sex-Role Stereotypes: Readings toward a Psychology of Androgyny.* Alexander G. Kaplan and Joan P. Bean, eds. Boston: Little, Brown.

———. 1983. "Gender schema theory and its implications for child development: Raising gender-aschematic children in a gender-schematic society." *Signs* 8: 598–616.

Best, Raphaela. 1983. *We've All Got Scars: What Boys and Girls Learn in Elementary School.* Bloomington, IN: Indiana University Press.

Bibby, Reginald W., and Donald C. Posterski. 1992. *Teen Trends: A Nation in Motion.* Toronto: Stoddart.

Blumberg, Rae L. 1978. *Stratification: Socioeconomic and Sexual Inequality.* Dubuque, IA: Wm. C. Brown

Bolin, Anne. 1987. "Transsexualism and the limits of traditional analysis." *American Behavioral Scientist* 31: 41–65.

Boyd, Monica. 1984. *Canadian Attitudes Toward Women: Thirty Years of Change.* Ottawa: Women's Bureau, Labour Canada.

Broverman, I.K., et al. 1972. "Sex-role stereotypes: A current appraisal." *Journal of Social Issues* 28: 59–78.

Cahill, Spencer E. 1989. "Fashioning males and females: Appearance management and the social reproduction of gender." *Symbolic Interaction* 12: 281–98.

Cantor, Muriel G. 1988. "Feminism and the media." *Society* 25: 76–81.

Cherlin, Andrew, and Pamela Barnhouse Walters. 1981. "Trends in United States men's and women's sex-role attitudes: 1972–1978." *American Sociological Review* 46: 453–60.

Chodorow, Nancy. 1978. *The Reproduction of Mothering: Psychoanalysis and the Sociology of Gender.* Berkeley, CA: University of California Press.

Clark, Matt, and David Gelman, with Mariana Gosnell, Mary Hager, and Barbara Schuler. 1987. "A user's guide to hormones." *Newsweek* (January 12): 50–59.

Colwill, Nina L. 1982. *The New Partnership: Women and Men in Organizations.* Palo Alto, CA: Mayfield Publishing.

Davy, Shirley. 1978. "Miss to Mrs.: Going, going, gone!" *Canadian Women's Studies* 1: 47–48.

di Leonardo, Micaela, ed. 1991. *Gender at the Crossroads of Knowledge: Feminist Anthropology in the Post-modern Era.* Berkeley, CA: University of California Press.

Doyle, James A. 1989. *The Male Experience.* 2nd ed. Dubuque, IA: Wm. C. Brown.

Eagly, Alice H., and Valerie J. Steffen. 1984. "Gender stereotypes stem from the distribution of women and men into social roles." *Journal of Personality and Social Psychology* 46: 735–54.

Eakins, Barbara Westbrook, and R. Gene Eakins. 1978. *Sex Differences in Human Communication.* Boston: Houghton Mifflin.

Eder, Donna, and Maureen T. Hallinan. 1978. "Sex differences in children's friendships." *American Sociological Review* 43: 237–50.

Epstein, Cynthia Fuchs. 1988. *Deceptive Distinctions: Sex, Gender, and the Social Order.* New York: Russell Sage Foundation and Yale University Press.

Fine, Gary Alan. 1986. "The dirty play of little boys." *Society* 24 (November/December): 63–67.

Friedl, Ernestine. 1975. *Women and Men: An Anthropologist's View.* New York: Holt, Rinehart and Winston.

———. 1978. "Society and sex roles." *Human Nature* (April): 70.

Frieze, Irene H., et al. 1978. *Women and Sex Roles: A Social Psychological Perspective.* New York: W.W. Norton.

Garn, Stanley M. 1966. "Body size and its implications." In *Review of Child Development Research* 2. Lois W. Hoffman and Martin L. Hoffman, eds. New York: Sage.

Garnets, Linda, and Joseph H. Pleck. 1979. "Sex role identity, androgyny, and sex role transcendence: A sex role strain analysis." *Psychology of Women Quarterly* 3: 270–83.

Geer, James, Julia Heiman, and Harold Leitenberg. 1984. *Human Sexuality*. Englewood Cliffs, NJ: Prentice-Hall.

Gibbins, Roger, J. Rick Ponting, and Gladys L. Symons. 1978. "Attitudes and Ideology: Correlates of liberal attitudes towards the role of women." *Journal of Comparative Family Studies* 9: 19–40.

Gilligan, Carol. 1982. *In a Different Voice*. Cambridge, MA: Harvard University Press.

Goffman, Erving. 1977. "The arrangement between the sexes." *Theory and Society* 4: 301–31.

Grauerholz, Elizabeth, and Bernice A. Pescosolido. 1989. "Gender representation in children's literature: 1900–1984." *Gender and Society* 3: 113–25.

Green, Richard. 1974. *Sexual Identity Conflict in Children and Adults*. Baltimore: Penguin.

Harding, Deborah, and Emily Nett. 1984. "Women and rock music." *Atlantis* 10: 60–76.

Huber, Joan. 1976. "Toward a socio-technological theory of the women's movement." *Social Problems* 23: 371–88.

Huston, Aletha C. 1983. "Sex typing." In *Handbook of Child Psychology* 4. Paul H. Mussen, ed.; E. Mavis Hetherington, vol. ed. New York: John Wiley.

Hyde, Janet. 1979. *Understanding Human Sexuality*. New York: McGraw-Hill.

Kessler, Suzanne J., and Wendy McKenna. 1978. *Gender: An Ethnomethodological Approach*. New York: John Wiley.

Kunkel, John H. 1977. "Sociobiology vs biosociology." *American Sociologist* 12: 69–73.

Lambert, Ronald D. 1971. *Sex Role Imagery in Children: Social Origins of Mind*. Study 6. Royal Commission on the Status of Women in Canada. Ottawa: Information Canada.

Lancaster, Jane Beckman. 1976. "Sex roles in primate societies." In *Sex Differences: Social and Biological Perspectives*. Michael S. Teitelbaum, ed. Garden City, NY: Doubleday Anchor.

Leacock, Eleanor B. 1982. *Myths of Male Dominance*. New York: Monthly Review.

Lever, Janet. 1978. "Sex differences in the complexity of children's play." *American Sociological Review* 43: 471–83.

Lewis, Michael. 1972. "Culture and gender roles: There's no unisex in the nursery." *Psychology Today* 5 (May): 54–57.

Liebowitz, Lila. 1983. "Origins of the sexual division of labor." In *Woman's Nature: Rationalizations of Inequality*. Marian Lowe and Ruth Hubbard, eds. New York: Pergamon.

Lindesmith, Alfred R., Anselm L. Strauss, and Norman K. Denzin. 1977. *Social Psychology*. 5th ed. New York: Holt, Rinehart and Winston.

Lippmann, Walter. 1922. *Public Opinion*. New York: Harcourt and Brace.

Lott, Bernice. 1981. "A feminist critique of androgyny: Toward the elimination of gender attributions for learned behavior." In *Gender and Nonverbal Behavior*. Clara Mayo and Nancy M. Henley, eds. New York: Springer-Verlag.

Lowe, Marian. 1983. "The dialectic of biology and culture." In *Woman's Nature: Rationalizations of Inequality*. Marian Lowe and Ruth Hubbard, eds. New York: Pergamon.

Lynn, David B. 1959. "A note on sex differences in the development of masculine and feminine identification." *Psychological Review* 66: 126–35.

———. 1969. *Parental and Sex-Role Identification: A Theoretical Formulation*. Berkeley, CA: McCutchan.

Mackie, Marlene. 1973. "Arriving at 'truth' by definition: The case of stereotype inaccuracy." *Social Problems* 20: 431–47.

———. 1987. *Constructing Women and Men: Gender Socialization*. Toronto: Holt, Rinehart and Winston.

Martel, Angeline, and Lina Peterat. 1984. "Naming the world: Consciousness in a patriarchal iceberg." In *Taking Sex into Account: The Policy Consequences of Sexist Research*. Jill McCalla Vickers, ed. Ottawa: Carleton University Press.

Martin, M. Kay, and Barbara Voorhies. 1975. *Female of the Species*. Toronto: Methuen.

Money, John, and A.A. Ehrhardt. 1972. *Man and Woman, Boy and Girl: The Differentiation and Dimorphism of Gender Identity from Conception to Maturity*. Baltimore: Johns Hopkins University Press.

Money, John, and Patricia Tucker. 1975. *Sexual Signatures: On Being a Man or a Woman*. Boston: Little, Brown.

Ortner, Sherry B., and Harriet Whitehead. 1981. *Sexual Meanings: The Cultural Construction of Gender and Sexuality*. Cambridge, UK: Cambridge University Press.

Parlee, Mary Brown. 1973. "The premenstrual syndrome." *Psychological Bulletin* 80: 454–65.

Ponting, J. Rick. 1986. "Canadian gender-role attitudes." Unpublished manuscript. University of Calgary.

Pyke, S.W. 1975. "Children's literature: Conceptions of sex roles." In *Socialization and Values in Canadian Society* (Vol. 2). Robert M. Pike and Elia Zureik, eds. Toronto: McClelland and Stewart.

Richardson, Laurel Walum. 1981. *The Dynamics of Sex and Gender*. 2nd edition. Boston: Houghton Mifflin.

Richer, Stephen. 1984. "Sexual inequality and children's play." *Canadian Review of Sociology and Anthropology* 21: 166–80.

Richmond-Abbott, Marie. 1983. *Masculine and Feminine: Sex Roles over the Life Cycle*. Reading, MA: Addison-Wesley.

Roberts, Donald F., and Nathan Maccoby. 1985. "Effects of mass communication." In *The Handbook of Social Psychology* (Vol. 2). Garner Lindzey and Elliot Aronson, eds. 3rd ed. New York: Random House.

Rosaldo, Michelle Zimbalist. 1974. "Woman, culture, and society: A theoretical overview." In *Woman, Culture and Society*. Michelle Zimbalist Rosaldo and Louise Lamphere, eds. Stanford, CA: Stanford University Press.

Rosaldo, Michelle Zimbalist, and Louise Lamphere, eds. 1974. *Woman, Culture and Society*. Stanford, CA: Stanford University Press.

Rosenberg, Miriam. 1976. "The biological basis for sex role stereotypes." In *Beyond Sex-Role Stereotypes: Readings toward a Psychology of Androgyny*. Alexandra G. Kaplan and Joan P. Bean, eds. Boston: Little, Brown.

Ross, Michael W. 1986. "Causes of gender dysphoria: How does transsexualism develop and why?" In *Transsexualism and Sex Reassignment*. William A.W. Waters and Michael W. Ross, eds. New York: Oxford University Press.

Sanday, P.R. 1981. *Female Power and Male Dominance: On the Origins of Sexual Inequality*. Cambridge, UK: Cambridge University Press.

Sayers, Janet. 1982. *Biological Politics: Feminist and Antifeminist Perspectives*. London: Tavistock.

Schulz, David A. 1984. *Human Sexuality*. 2nd ed. Englewood Cliffs, NJ: Prentice Hall.

Smith, Vivian. 1990. "Women of the press." *The Globe and Mail* (March 24): D1, D8.

Spender, Dale. 1985. *Man Made Language*. 2nd ed. London: Routledge and Kegan Paul.

Sperling, Susan. 1991. "Baboons with briefcases: Feminism, functionalism, and sociobiology in the evolution of primate gender." *Signs* 17: 1–27.

Tavris, Carol. 1992. *The Mismeasure of Women*. New York: Simon & Schuster.

Tavris, Carol, and Carole Wade. 1984. *The Longest War*. 2nd ed. San Diego, CA: Harcourt Brace Jovanovich.

Taylor, W. 1985 *Hormonal Manipulation: A New Era of Monstrous Athletes*. Jefferson, NC: McFarland.

Thorne, Barrie, and Nancy Henley. 1975. "Difference and dominance: An overview of language, gender, and society." In *Language and Sex: Difference and Dominance*. Barrie Thorne and Nancy Henley, eds. Rowley, MA: Newbury House.

Thornton, Arland, Duane F. Alwin, and Donald Camburn. 1983. "Causes and consequences of sex-role attitudes and change." *American Sociological Review* 48 211–27.

Tuchman, Gaye. 1978. "Introduction: The symbolic annihilation of women by the mass media." In *Hearth and Home: Images of Women in the Mass Media*. Gaye Tuchman, Arlene Kaplan Daniels, and James Benet, eds. New York: Oxford University Press.

Ward, Dawn, and Jack Balswick. 1978. "Strong men and virtuous women: A content analysis of sex role stereotypes." *Pacific Sociological Review* 21: 45–53.

Weisstein, Naomi. 1971. "Psychology constructs the female, or the fantasy life of the male psychologist." In *Roles Women Play: Readings toward Women's Liberation*. Michele Hoffnung Garskof, ed. Belmont, CA: Brooks/Cole.

Williams, John E., and Deborah L. Best. 1982. *Measuring Sex Stereotypes: A Thirty-Nation Study*. Beverly Hills, CA: Sage.

Williams, Juanita H. 1987. *Psychology of Women: Behavior in a Biosocial Context*. 3rd ed. New York: W.W. Norton.

Wilson, Susannah J. 1981. "The image of women in Canadian magazines." In *Mass Media and Social Change*. Elihu Katz and Tamas Szeckso, eds. Beverly Hills, CA: Sage.

Chapter 4

IMPRESSION MANAGEMENT: BECOMING A DOCTOR AT McMASTER

JACK HAAS AND WILLIAM SHAFFIR

In his seminal work on social interaction, Goffman (1959) draws attention to the significance of impression management in everyday life. In order to explore this dimension of social life, sociologists have focused mainly on people involved in deviant and low status occupations (Ball, 1967; Edgerton, 1967; Goffman, 1961; Henslin, 1968; Maurer, 1962; Prus and Sharper, 1979; Scott, 1968). Yet as Hughes (1951a) suggests, a comparative study of occupations often reveals similar adaptive mechanisms. In occupations that demand a measure of trust from clients, participants must convince legitimating audiences of their credibility. The importance of playing an adequate role in order to exact the right kind of response from clients is true of both shady and respectable occupations.

Although impression management and role playing are essential parts of this kind of sociological interaction, effective performance becomes even more crucial when participants perceive an audience that is potentially critical and condemning. This is especially true when an audience has high expectations of competence in others. If those in whom competence is expected also have a concomitant responsibility of making decisions that affect the well-being of others, the situation is even more crucial. Audiences then look for cues and indications of personal and/or collective (institutional) competence and in response practitioners organize a carefully managed presentation of self intended to create an aura of competence.

Concern about the competence of those granted rights and responsibilities affecting others is very much

a part of the relationship existing between patients and medical professionals. Patients look for competent advice and assistance and medical professionals, particularly doctors, want to convince those they treat that they are indeed competent and trustworthy. It is only when a patient believes a doctor possesses these attributes that diagnostic intervention and prescribed treatment can affect the course of the illness in any positive way.

Studies of professional socialization (Becker et al., 1961; Bloom, 1973; Broadhead, 1983; Light, 1980; Merton et al., 1957; Olesen and Whittaker, 1968; Ross, 1961) show how trainees adopt a professional image as they proceed through the socialization process. Sociological studies of noncollege, school and other training situations (Geer, 1972) indicate that the socialization experience involves learning specific skills and techniques as well as taking on an occupational culture which includes a new or altered identity. Such studies describe a process whereby students or trainees adapt in order to develop a new view of the self.

As students are professionalized, they are initiated into a new culture wherein they gradually adopt those symbols which represent the profession and its generally accepted authority. These symbols (language, tools, clothing, and demeanor) establish, identify and separate the bearer from the outsider, particularly from the client and the paraprofessional audience. Professionalization, as we observed it, involves the adoption and manipulation of symbols and symbolic behavior which creates an imagery of competence. The net

Source: Becoming Doctors: The Adoption of a Cloak of Competence (Greenwich, CT: JAI Press, 1987), pp. 53–83. Reprinted by permission of the publisher.

result of this process separates the profession from those they are intended to serve.

Faced with inordinately high audience expectations, medical students begin the process of professionalization by distancing themselves from those they interact with. They manipulate the symbols of their new status in order to distinguish their activity as one grounded in mystery and sciences unfathomable to others. Their performance is intended to convince both themselves and others that they are competent and confident to face the immense responsibilities imposed by their privileged role.

This chapter will demonstrate the ways in which the medical students we studied attempted to communicate trustworthiness by impression-management. The focus is mainly on the clinical, or clerkship experience, this being the critical phase of the ritual ordeal where the professionalization process is most intense. We begin by outlining the general expectations that delineate the physician's role and the perceived expectations of the student in clinical training. Then we describe the importance of the manipulation and control of people, symbols, and ideas that is necessary for meeting both generalized and situational expectations. We especially note the specific problems involved in the process by students in the innovative program.

As students become successful at controlling and manipulating others' impressions in order to be perceived as competent and trustworthy, they increasingly identify with the role and with the ways that qualified practitioners handle their problems. Successful control of professionalizing situations, it would seem, has a self-fulfilling quality which allows authoritative performances to contribute to the neophytes' changing perceptions of the self. If initiation is rigorous, students learn to adopt a symbolic-ideological cloak of competence that they perceive initiated members of the medical fraternity to wear. It is thus that the image of authority and trustworthiness is created. By way of a conclusion we will point out that the nature of legitimating audience expectations are perceived by newcomers as requiring conformity to a role that is exaggerated and thus demands an exaggerated performance.

GENERALIZED EXPECTATIONS OF COMPETENCE

The medical profession is a unique one in that so much of its authority depends on the effective communication of trust. Freidson (1970: 10–11) outlines the characteristics of this occupation that serve to set it apart from others. These are:

- A general public belief in the consulting occupation's competence, in the value of its professed knowledge and skill.
- The occupational group ... must be the prime source of the criteria that qualify a person to work in an acceptable fashion.
- The occupation has gained command of the exclusive competence to determine the proper content and effective method of performing some tasks.

Medicine's position, Freidson (1970: 5) notes, is equivalent to that of a state religion: "... it has an officially approved monopoly of the right to define health and illness and to treat illness."

Doctors possess a special authority because of their accepted expertise about human health. Their work is believed to constitute a social and individual good. Their authority is further enhanced by the historical linking of medicine and religion: the physician mediates the mysteries of scientific research through a ritual system where the doctor assumes a priest-like role (Siegler and Osmond, 1973: 42)[1]

To create a physician's authority requires the manipulation of an effective symbol system which is accepted and shared by participants. The moral authority of the physician is most apparent as being complete and unassailable when the doctor is involved with decisions affecting life and death. The fact that death strikes fear in human beings gives impressive, Aesculapian authority to those who are believed able to ward it off or postpone it (Siegler and Osmond, 1973).[2]

Because of the authority invested in them, medical practitioners, students and physician alike, must deal with the inordinate and exaggerated demands of those they treat. The problem is somewhat less in magnitude for the medical student, who is generally protected from situations which would prematurely or inappropriately demand his exercise of inappropriate responsibility. Students, however, realize that the outcome of their socialization will, in the future, require them to deal with life and death situations. It is thus their hope that the socialization process will prepare them to meet the responsibilities imposed by their profession with both confidence and competence. According to one student:

I think you're faced with a problem, that in a large way the public has unrealistic expectations about the medical profession. It puts the doctor in a very difficult position because you know yourself you don't know it all, but the public thinks you know it all and puts you in a position where you have to be a good actor (Interview: Winter, second year).

The Problems of Perceived Expectations in Clerkship

During the rotating clerkship assignments, the students are exposed to many different audiences which all have different expectations about the proper performance of the role. In fact, in the hospital setting, the role itself is ambiguous and raises the question, is the individual primarily student, clerk or physician? As a result, the "clinical jerk" is constantly faced with new situations that do not relate in a clear way to his or her new status. In consequence he or she finds it difficult to assume an appropriate role and to project a "correct" identity.

Another confusing aspect of the clinical clerk's situation concerns the responsibility he or she is expected to assume. In earlier phases of the program the student examined patients as part of a learning experience; clerkship demands that the students do more than learn. They must assume a degree of responsibility for patient well-being. A student summarizes this difference when he says.

> Well, from my perception, even in Phase II and Phase III, we played around with real patients in a Phase I sort of thing.... It was sort of a game. You were trying to find out what was the interesting clinical sign. Whereas now (clerkship) when you see a patient you are doing a history and physical on a patient and it sort of focuses on you.... The intern may or may not go over the bloody patient because he's really trusting you to pick up what you should pick up ... so you're always trying to think, "Well, if I don't pick these up, and the resident doesn't get them, I'm the one who has done the history and physical. If I miss something then somebody is going to be after my ass for it" (Interview: Winter, third year).

As students in clerkship become more integral members of a health care team, they are delegated some tasks which require the exercise of personal responsibility, and thus they become accountable in ways almost always new to them. The taking on of increased responsibility and the concomitant exercise of medical judgment makes them accountable to a variety of professionals. The prevalent response of the clinical clerk is to develop an increasingly sympathetic attitude towards their future profession. The following examples gleaned from clinical clerks illustrate this point:

> (The conversation centers around clerkship and whether this phase of the program alters one's view of the medical profession.) I think it does from the point of view that you can more or less see other peoples' situations much more because you're in their boat.... Having been in it (medicine), I can see why some patients are dealt with quickly perhaps (Interview: Spring, second year).

> I remember when we were way back in Phase II and Phase I, we would go see a patient with a clinical skills preceptor, and he might have said something to the patient that seemed rude, and I'd get all very indignant about it and say: "My God, you're not being sensitive." While that may have been justified, now that I'm on the ward I can see that in a way it's a bit silly to take that one episode, because what you are seeing is one episode in a long history of the relationship between that patient and his doctor. You're taking this totally out of context and it's really not relevant to criticize unless you really know the relationship. Now I'm much less free with those sorts of criticisms (Interview: Spring, second year).

Students are confronted with a dilemma. On the one hand they try to prove themselves as competent to others, while on the other, they remain concerned about the limits of their competence which might cause them to act inappropriately, perhaps with dire consequences. Two students summarize this ambiguous response to the taking on of responsibility this way:

> Jim complains to Claudette that on one of his rotations he was given too much responsibility. He says, "I don't mind it if I'm ready for it, but I just didn't feel I was ready for it. The resident thought I was ready for it. He thought I knew more than I did. Maybe I did, maybe I didn't. If I did, I suppose I was ready for it, but I didn't feel I was ready for it. I didn't feel I knew enough but he tells me I knew enough. I felt uncomfortable and asked that I not be given the responsibility" (Field notes: Spring, third year).

While students are generally protected from meeting all the expectations of patients, they do face the unpredictable nature of faculty expectations; in fact, faculty become the major reference group or audience that students feel most demand and evaluate competence. The teaching staff is responsible for evaluating and determining the progress of the students. The students, in turn, attempt to estimate teachers' demands, although at times they are ill-defined and sometimes contradictory. Defining and attempting to meet faculty expectations is often difficult. The students' problem is dealing with staff who have widely divergent approaches to the practice of medicine. Faced with a threatening ambiguity, students try to find out the particular biases and special areas of interest of those with whom they must interact (Becker et al., 1961). This is because they soon realize that their teachers are convinced of the correctness and validity of their expertise and approach. In this sort of situation the students find their competence and learning assessed in situations in which they are vulnerable and therefore easily reminded of their incompetence.

For professional students the short-term goal of a "good" evaluation is vital because this kind of assessment demonstrates their developing competence to those who control their careers. To a lesser extent this is also true of students in traditional medical school settings. Although these students initially impress the faculty by their skill at passing examinations, they must eventually demonstrate competence. This is similar to students in the innovative program, through the exercise of selective interactional skills. Both types of students, those in traditional and innovative learning environments, then exhibit a common reaction to evaluation in the face of uncertain expectations. When individuals are uncertain about what they should know or how they should apply it, they "cover" themselves by deflecting others from probing their ignorance (Edgerton, 1967; Goffman, 1963; Haas, 1972, 1977; Haas and Shaffir, 1977; Olesen and Whittaker, 1968). This "cloaking" behavior is often accompanied by initiative-taking behavior intended to impress others with their competence. This phenomenon is well-documented. For example, Becker et al. state:

Perhaps the most noticeable form of attempting to make a good impression is the use of trickery of various kinds to give the appearance of knowing what one thinks the faculty wants one to know or having done what the faculty wants done, even though these appearances are false (1961: 284).

Bucher and Stelling also report that students, themselves, are aware that impression management is crucial to their progress.

The residents have learned that they could contribute considerably to the nature and outcome of the supervisory process.... The most common tactic was that the resident psyched out what the superior wanted to hear and presented his material accordingly (1977: 107, 109).

THE SYMBOLS OF PROFESSIONALISM

The professionalization of medical students is facilitated and intensified by symbols the neophytes manipulate. The manipulation serves to announce to insiders and outsiders alike how they are to be identified. During the first weeks of their studies students begin wearing white lab jackets with plastic name tags which identify them as medical students. In addition, since from the beginning clinical skills sessions are included in the curriculum, students participate in a variety of settings with the tools of the doctor's trade carried on their person. This attire clearly identifies students to participants and visitors of the hospital/school setting. Then, equipped with their identity kit, students begin to learn and express themselves in the medical vernacular, often referred to as "McBabble" or "medspeak." Distinctive dress, badges, tools and language provide the student with symbols which announce their role and activity.

The significance of these symbols to the professionalization process is critical. The symbols serve, on the one hand, to identify and unite the bearers as members of a community of shared interests, purpose and identification (Roth, 1957), and on the other these symbols distinguish and separate their possessors from lay people, making their role seem more mysterious, shrouded, and priest-like (Bramson, 1973). The early manipulation of these symbols serves to heighten identification and commitment to the profession, while at the same time facilitates students' separation from the lay world. As one student candidly remarks:

Wearing the jacket seems to give you carte blanche to just about go anywhere you want in the hospital. People assume that you belong and that you know what you're doing (Field notes: Spring, second year).

The importance of the white coat as a symbol is reinforced by the faculty and staff who, with the exception of the psychiatry department, mandate that it be worn. As the following incident illustrates, this expectation is rigorously adhered to, and is justified in terms of patients' expectations:

The rheumatology session tutorial group assembled and walked to the room where Dr. Gordon would be met. Dr. Gordon said, "Well you know in order to see any of the patients you have to wear a white jacket and a tie." The group was very surprised by his remark and, in fact, John and Ken looked at each other in disbelief. John said, "No, I didn't know that."

Dr. Gordon says, "Well you do know that in order to see any of the patients you have to wear a white coat. They expect that. You will agree that they expect that. Wouldn't you agree with that?"

John says, "No, I wouldn't. I mean that hasn't been my experience."

Dr. Gordon says, "Well, have you ever visited any of the patients in the hospital?"

John says, "Yes, for about a year and a half now."

Dr. Gordon says, "Those people who have the white jackets on will be able to visit the patients. Those who don't, won't be able to." (Field notes: Winter, second year).

One of the first difficult tasks that faces students is to begin to learn and communicate within the symbolic system that serves to define medical work and workers. Learning to use the "correct" language is part of this. From the beginning, in tutorials, readings, demonstrations, and rounds, students are exposed to a language in which they are expected to become facile. A student explains the importance of replacing his lay vocabulary:

When I was just beginning, I would use my own words to describe how a lesion looked or how a patient felt ... because they were more immediate to me and more accessible to me. And on many occasions I was corrected. The way you describe that is such and such because that is the vocabulary of the profession and that is the only way you can be understood (Interview: Winter, third year).

Another incident that took place in a tutorial captures the students' difficulties in knowing when use of the symbol system may be inappropriate:

At one point Dr. Smith asked, "What is it, what is the name for this kind of phenomenon that gives this kind of pain?" E.C. volunteered a term and she ended it with a question mark. She was tentatively offering a term. Dr. Smith said, "Just use the plain language, what is the plain everyday word for that?" There was a pause and he said, "Heartburn, that's what everybody calls it and that's good enough" (Field notes: Spring, first year).

The separation between "we" and "they" becomes clearer to the students as they learn the professional symbol system and are absorbed into the medical culture. As they move through the culture, they learn how symbols are used to communicate and enforce certain definitions of the situations they are exposed to. Students must learn how practicing physicians manipulate these symbols to this end.

The ability to use the linguistic symbols of medicine defines members of the profession and creates a boundary that is not often crossed. Two students reflect on the significance of technical terminology:

... so you could talk about things in front of a patient that would totally baffle the patient and keep him unaware of issues that you were discussing. I don't think this is unique to medicine. I think this is a general phenomenon of professionalization. [Learning the language] was a matter of establishing some common ground with people you were going to be relating to on a professional basis for the rest of your life (Interview: Spring, third year).

... you just can't survive if you don't learn the jargon. It's not so much an effort to identify as it is an effort to survive. People in medicine have a world unto themselves and a language unto themselves. It's a world with a vocabulary ... and a vocabulary that, no question about it, creates a fraternity that excludes the rest of the world and it's a real tyranny to lay persons who don't understand it.... (Interview: Spring, third year).

In sum, the adoption of special props, costume and language reinforces the students' identification with, and commitment to medicine while it enables them to project an image of having adopted a new and special role. Having learned how to manipulate the symbols to reflect audiences' expectations, they begin to shape and control their professional relationships.

The manipulation of symbolic language and props does more than shape and control professional relationships, it actually changes the neophyte's own perception of himself or herself. Because students wear and manipulate the symbols of their trade, they are presumed by others to possess special knowledge. Not only this, but students, because of a developing facility to manipulate symbols, eventually convince themselves that indeed they are special. One student thoughtfully comments on the dynamic nature of the relationship existing between the symbol system and his own self-image:

When you wore the jacket, especially in the beginning, people were impressed. After all, it told everyone, including yourself, that you were studying to be a doctor.... *The other thing about wearing the white jacket is that it does make things more obvious. You know what you are, what you are doing sort of thing. You know, it is sort of another way of identifying. There were very few ways that people had to identify with the medical profession and one of the ways was to begin to look like some of the doctors (Interview: Spring, second year).*

MANAGING THE SITUATION

It must be noted, however, that while appropriate medical accoutrements help new clerks manage their new roles, they remain acutely aware of their limitations, and are highly sensitive to a perceived need that they must meet a variety of role expectations. Their short-term goal is to convince their audience of their competence without inviting criticism: they must gain the confidence of those who can affect their reputation. One student discussed the importance of impression management in relation to varying audience expectations in these terms:

The first day you've got to make a good impression. If you make a bad impression the first day, then that's it. You've got to spend the whole rest of the rotation redeeming yourself for making a boo-boo. Maybe it's just an insignificant thing, but if you do that the first day, then you've had it (Field notes: Fall, second year).

In their attempt to control their audiences' impressions of them, students usually use two broadly based but intricately related strategies: the first is covering up, a strategy intended to provide protection from charges of incompetence; the second is the necessity of taking initiative. Both strategies are designed to convince others that they are developing the necessary attribute of trustworthy competence. Both strategies require considerable skills in self-presentation. A student describes one of these strategies as a form of initiative taking that provides protection from divergent medical approaches taken by senior personnel:

Like Dr. Jones who was my advisor or boss for medicine, he always came and did rounds on Tuesday mornings.... His interest was in endocrinology and ... he was going to pick up that endocrine patient to talk about, and so of course any dummy can read up Monday night like hell on the new American Diabetic Association standards for diabetes or hyperglycemia.... So the next day you seem fairly knowledgeable.... But I just wonder how much you remember when you try to read over in a hurry and you try to be keen just for the next day. Because that afternoon you forget about it because you figure Wednesday morning hematology people make their rounds and, of course, you have to read hematology Tuesday night (Interview: Winter, second year).

The constant need to create and manage the image of a competent self through the process of impression management is sometimes at odds with a basic tenet of the school's philosophy that encourages learning through problem-solving, and the complementary development of a questioning attitude. In order to deal with this contradiction students attempt to manage an appearance of competence while at the same time they control others' impressions of it. This student expresses his handling of the problem this way:

The best way of impressing others with your competence is asking questions you know the answers to. Because if they ever put it back on you, "Well what do you think?" then you tell them what you think and you'd give a very intelligent answer because you knew it. You didn't ask to find out information. You ask it to impress people (Interview: Winter, third year).

The same contradiction gives rise to another strategy that students employ designed to mask uncertainty and anxiety with an image of self-confidence. Projection of the right image is recognized by students as being as important as technical competence. As one student remarks: "We have to be good actors, put across the image of self-confidence, that you know it all...." Another student, referring to the importance of creating the right impression, claims:

It's like any fraternity. You've got to know. You've got to have a certain amount of basic knowledge before they think it's worth talking to you. If you display less than that basic knowledge their reflexes come into play and they think this person is an idiot. Let's find out exactly how much they don't know, rather than building on what you do know. That's a different maneuver. Being out in the pale, not worth talking to, or within the pale and well-worth talking to. There is image management in every profession. It's very unfortunate because the people who precisely need the help are those who are willing to admit their ignorance, and I've been in tutorials where people who are really willing to admit their ignorance tend to get put down for it. After a while they stop asking questions. That's very unfortunate (Interview: Spring, third year).

Clinical clerks believe that they must always be aware of the expectations of their audience before they carefully balance a self-confident demeanor with an attitude and gestures of proper deference in the face of those who control their career:

Student A: Sometimes there is a lot of politics involved ... in speaking up because you are aware of your position.... You don't want to seem too smart. You don't want to show up people. If you happen to know something, you know, that say the resident doesn't know, you have to be very diplomatic about it because some of these guys are very touchy.
Student B: And you don't want to play the game either of just "I'll be student and you be teacher."
Student A: Yeah, and at the same time you don't want to come off as appearing stupid. If you happen to believe something ... you try to defend yourself but in a very diplomatic manner, all the time being careful not to step on anybody's toes (Interview: Spring, third year).

The use of presentational skills can only be understood in terms of students' perceptions that impression management offers the most appropriate tactics for successfully negotiating the evaluation system they face (Becker et al., 1961; 1968). Most are quite frank about the importance of consciously impressing others. Two students comment:

In that context [with the clinical skills preceptor] I try to shine. I try to outdo others. It's also good if you raise your hand and give a sidepoint.... You guess with confidence. If you don't know, no matter what, you say it with confidence. You'll be much better on rounds if you do that.... (Interview: Spring, second year).

If you want to establish a reputation as a great staff man or whatever one of the things is that you know a lot and this is one of the ways you establish your reputation.... Some people will cover up by bull-shitting very skillfully. People usually don't make the effort to prove them wrong. And it always helps to be ready with a
quick snappy answer which is right.... And what I usually do is I say I don't know, but I usually say it with a very aggressive air, you know, but not in a put-down way (Interview: Fall, third year).

The relationship between verbal or interactional skills and reputation-making is highlighted during these student interviews:

Well, I know people who came across as knowing a lot and they don't do it purposely or they don't do it arrogantly or anything, they just talk a lot. And usually most of these people do know a lot and they talk a lot. But a fair amount of it is also they are just good talkers. They are good with words and if you were to sort of compare them with someone who is less flashier in a different setting, in other words, ask them to do a write-up or ask them to do a written assessment of the patient, the quieter one would probably do just as well. These people are better on their feet so they come across all right. There is definitely that aspect and you see that even more when you get into clinical medicine and really much of what gives a person a reputation is not really how much he knows, although he's got to know a fair amount, he's got to know certainly above average, but really how much of a performer he is (Interview: Spring, third year).

The way reputations are established on a ward, be it for clinical clerks, interns, residents, or staff is largely on the basis of verbal discussions that occur all over the place. They occur at rounds ... they occur at seminars and so on. And these are all verbal, that's the big thing about them. At these sorts of goings on, it's people who were quick, who jumped in with a diagnosis when only two symptoms were known and were right, who are good with words and that sort of thing — these sort of people are the ones who tend to establish reputations. Rarely are reputations made on the basis of reading written products of their work. Residents, they do write things. You know, they write discharge summaries, they write admitting histories and physicals. And often times, especially if the patient comes back, these things will be read by another person. In that sense you may get an idea of what the person has done at a quieter time when he hasn't had to perform verbally. By and large, that's a lesser aspect of it than what happens at these sessions.

It's really the people who are verbal and sort of aggressive in that way who are known as being good. (Interview: Spring, third year).

Even as they pursue good evaluations through good interactional performances, the students do not ignore their long-term goal of achieving competence. One aptly sums up the relationship of meeting the expectations of frequently changing audiences, and the necessity of impression management, with a lesser but, nonetheless, important concern about his future role as a decision maker:

This week I was at all different places, some of which I had never been to. You're having a constant turnover of patients and a constant turnover of staff people that you run into. Each of them has different expectations towards you, and you're always on guard. You're never exactly sure how each of them wants you to act, so it puts you in a kind of tension situation. I know when I leave work I really feel a big relief that I can finally let my hair down. Most of us present this image that we are comfortable and confident. That's the image you have to present.... I figure to myself as a doctor you shouldn't have to feel this way, but I think one thing medical school does to you is by the time you graduate you realize how little you do know and how much there is to know. And it's so overwhelming to see your finiteness and limitations, and to recognize when you get the degree, all of a sudden you're going to be expected to know. You're going to be expected to make decisions (Interview: Winter, third year).

Performance Success and Professionalizing Confidence and Identification

As they advance through the program, students continually observe doctors' working habits, listen to their philosophies of medical practice, take note of their competencies and incompetencies, and reflect upon the nature of their own present and future relationships with patients. The physicians with whom they practice their clinical skills become models after which students pattern their own beliefs and behavior:

... certainly there are people who impress me ... certain aspects of their personality that I would want to incorporate in some way in my practice. It is easy to model yourself after people you see on

the wards.... You don't know anything and you start watching them and before too long you find yourself in a position where you tend to model yourself after these people....

Through observation, role-playing, and practice, students begin to identify with the organization and practice of the medical profession.

As students observe and experience the problems of medical care and practice, they develop an understanding of, and learn to identify with, the profession and the means by which its members confront their problems. Consequently, students become less able to voice criticisms of what they see as they adopt the role of those they will emulate in the future. As they assume increased responsibilities and make medical judgments for which they must account to a variety of professionals, they develop an increasingly sympathetic outlook towards their future profession.

Students gain clinical and interactional experience in ward settings that allows them to increase their repertoire of roles played for various audiences and in different situations. A student describes her experiments with various scripts when she says:

Every patient I see gives me more experience. I'll see as many patients as I can because I can learn from seeing them. Like I can try out a different approach and see the reaction that I get. I found that every time I see a patient, I try to ask questions in a different way and test out different approaches. It's like going to see a play that you've already seen many times, but every time you see it you notice something different. In a sense it's the same with the patients. You gain a little more experience every time, and that is really important (Interview: Spring, second year).

It would appear that nothing succeeds like success; and as the students gain confidence they learn that the projection of a successful image is an effective way of controlling others' impressions of their developing professionalism. A student describes the importance of impression-management skills in easing their relationships with patients, particularly in dealing with the sensitive areas of the physical examination:

I think it's largely a matter of how you present yourself. Now if I go in all shaky and flushed and nervous about it, the patient is going to pick up on this and is going to respond. So I think you have to go in with a confident manner and know your business and go about it in a very clear cut way, so the patient does not know you have any fears of the situation and therefore you don't transfer those fears to the patient (Interview: Winter, third year).

Another student graphically describes the ambiguous nature of interactional evaluation and the skills required to handle the ambiguity. Students believe they can deflect others from evaluating cognitive or performance competence negatively:

You see the kind of student that they [faculty] want to see is the strong and the assertive-type person. Medical people like to see people who state their position and take a stand ... a go-getter, an individual who can relate, an individual who on their own can lead a tutorial group, who can take patients and follow them through, who can take initiatives.... If they see you being decisive and confident and they see you can do something, then they think you're good. I think it's very easy for you to slide by on personality. Sometimes I think I'm at fault ... because I think I have the personality that I can put others in the situation where they won't go and find out if I'm weak in some areas. That's the problem with this place: that they never really separate personality from academics (Interview: Winter, second year).

As students gain confidence they learn that skillful methods of communication provide an effective way of controlling others' impressions of their professionalism. The intimate relationship between developing confidence and professional success through the projection of confident performances that convey success is indicated in the following student's comments:

If you act like you know, they treat you like you know. If you act like you don't know what is happening, then that's the way they treat you. It might sound really strange, but that is the way it is. You've got to let them know that you know what you are doing (Field notes: Fall, third year).

Confidence is often bolstered by the comparisons that students inevitably make with their peers and practicing professionals; the clerks realize that other players too, are involved in the game of impression management. Lack of knowledge and even incompetence are easy to hide in a milieu that emphasizes appearance.[3] A student makes this point:

The comforting thing about clerkship is that you see that specialists and interns and residents don't know everything. That's kind of reassuring to

know that first of all you don't have to know everything and secondly that a lot of people who are beyond you in their training don't know everything (Field notes: Spring, third year).

Clerks are in continuous contact with other members of the medical hierarchy and thus have ample opportunity to imitate them. Conforming to the model of their evaluators makes them aware that professional practice is a mixture of both science and art. The art of impression management when mastered allows the clerks to increase their identification with the practice, and allows them to gain confidence about their ability to demonstrate professional competence. Eventually, successful completion of the clerkship provides a social badge of legitimation, which affirms they have taken another step in the transition from student to professional.

In summary, the students come to realize that, as practicing professionals, they will continue to place emphasis on the symbolic communication of competence. Effective reputation-making, for practitioners as well as for students, depends on the successful control and manipulation of symbols, ideas, and legitimators in professional rituals and situations. Donald Light astutely points out the outcome of what amounts to a ritual ordeal in the study of psychiatric residents when he notes:

By structuring them (training programs) so that the trainees experience feelings of intense anxiety, ignorance, and dependence, such programs may be teaching professionals to treat clients as they have been treated. And by exaggerating their power and expertise, mentors establish a model of omnipotence that their students are fated to repeat. To the extent that laymen accept this mythology, omnipotent tendencies become reinforced in daily life. To the extent they challenge it, professionals like physicians or psychiatrists become embattled and defensive (1980: 307).

A key factor in the professionalization process is that students learn authoritativeness. It is communicated by means of body language, demeanor, and carefully managed projections of the self-image. They believe that to be a good student-physician is either to be or appear to be competent. They observe that others react to their role playing. A student describes this process when he says:

To be a good GP, you've got to be a good actor, you've got to respond to a situation. You have to be quick, pick up the dynamics of what is going on at the time and try to make the person leave the office thinking that you know something. And a lot of people, the way they handle that is by letting the patient know that they know it all and only letting out a little bit at a time, and as little as possible. I think that they eventually reach a plateau where they start thinking to themselves they are really great and they know it all, because they have these people who are worshipping at their feet (Interview: Spring, third year).

The self-fulfilling nature of the conversion process, whereby newcomers attain the higher moral status of a professional, is captured in two separate interview comments:

People expect you to be the healer and so you have to act like the healer. (Field notes: Spring, third year.)

You know a large part of our role is a God role. You have to act like God. You're supposed to be like God. If you don't inspire confidence in your patients, they are not going to get better even if you know the correct diagnosis and have the correct treatment. If they don't have faith in you, they are not going to get better (Interview: Winter, second year).

The perception of exaggerated expectations from their audience and the ritual ordeal nature of the professionalization process contribute to the model of omnipotence that students believe is helpful for performance success. There is, however, a fine line and tension between confident acting and audience perceptions of arrogance and abuse of authority. The root of this dilemma is reflected in Lord Acton's famous dictum, "Power tends to corrupt and absolute power tends to corrupt absolutely." A clinical clerk describes the corruptive tendency of the professionalizing process when he says:

They [the nurses] expect you to act that way [abusively]. If you don't, they won't respect you. They need to know you're the boss or they won't respect you (Field notes: Spring, third year).

The process of adopting the cloak of competence is ultimately justified by students as being helpful to the patient. A student summarizes the relationship between acting competently and patients responding to such a performance by getting well when he says:

You know the patients put pressure on you to act as if you are in the know. If you know anything about the placebo effect, you know that a lot of the healing and curing of patients does not involve doing anything that will really help them, but rather creating confidence in the patient that things are being done and will be done. We know that the placebo effect for example has even cured cancer patients. If they have the confidence in the doctor and what doctor and what treatment they are undergoing, they are much more likely to get well, irrespective of the objective effects of the treatment (Interview: Spring, second year).

CONCLUSION

Students learn the practical importance of assuming the cloak of competence.[4] The cloak allows patients to trust, without question, both the health professional and the prescribed treatment. Successful negotiations of the trial by ordeal through proper performances helps newcomers gain control or dominance (Freidson, 1970) which is basic to professionalism. The process has a self-fulfilling quality as neophyte professionals move up the professional ladder. Students recognize the importance of appearing authoritative in professional situations. In turn, as they perceive themselves to be successful, they come to believe in their competence in professional matters. The changing nature of the definition of self and the fragility of control over others' perceptions and reactions leads students to develop and maintain a protective shield.

The posture of authoritativeness in professional matters is an expected outcome of the trial by ordeal. The special status and role of professional is enveloped in a set of expectations that require special demonstrations of "possessed" competence. Practicing at playing the role eventually results in its adoption and identification. Newcomers model and imitate their mentors (who are also responsible for evaluating them) and the self-perpetuation of the notion of their having a special authoritativeness proceeds.

Neophytes and professionals are similarly involved in careers based on reputational control. Indeed, many laypeople are not only aware that the professionals they deal with are almost constantly engaged in playing a part, in projecting the "proper" image, they demand it. The interactional basis for this adaptation to a lifetime role is summarized by Halmos when he says:

We must conclude that the role-playing of being a professional is a hard social fact, and a potent behavioural model for the nonprofessionals, and thus for society at large.... The strange thing is that the world cannot afford to dispense with being systematically conned! Of course, the truth is that the world is not being deceived: it demands the professing of values and their embodiment in a culturally defined style and ritual (1970: 180–81).

In his study of the mentally retarded, Edgerton (1967) maintains that the central and shared commonality of the mentally retarded released from institutions was for them to envelop themselves in a cloak of competence to deny the discomforting reality of their stigma. The development of a cloak of competence is, perhaps, most apparent for those who must meet exaggerated expectations. The problem of meeting others' enlarged expectations is magnified for those uncertain about their ability to manage a convincing performance. Moreover, the performer faces the personal problem of reconciling his or her private self-awareness and uncertainty with his or her publicly displayed image. For those required to perform beyond their capacities, in order to be successful, there is the constant threat of breakdown or exposure. For both retardates and professionals the problem and, ironically, the solution, are similar. Expectations of competence are dealt with by strategies of impression management, specifically, manipulation and concealment. Interactional competencies depend on convincing presentations and much of professionalism requires the masking of insecurity and incompetence with the symbolic-interactional cloak of competence.

As Hughes has observed, "... a feature of work behavior found in one occupation, even a minor or odd one, will be found in others" (1952: 425). In fact, the basic processes of social life operate throughout the social structure. All social groups create boundaries and differences, view themselves in the most favorable ways.[5] All individuals and groups strive to protect themselves from ridicule and charges of incompetence. Our analysis has captured what is and has been a "taken-for-granted" understanding of social life: much behavior is performance designed to elicit certain reactions. In fact, as we maintain, professional behavior is, or can be, understood as performance.[6]

NOTES

1. Ernest Becker (1975) argues that man's innate and all-encompassing fear of death drives him to attempt to transcend death through culturally standardized hero systems and symbols.

2. The complaint that physicians avoid patient death and dying is partly explained in the the basic human fear of death (Becker, 1975). Although they may grow more desensitized to others' death and dying, they are, at the same time, more often reminded of their own mortality. Moreover, the doctor facing such a situation of telling patient and/or family of impending death is vulnerable to charges of incompetence or failure and it is competence or its appearance that defines the doctor's role.

3. One merely has to note the numerous and apparently increasing number of imposters who have been discovered in medical practice. See, for example, *New York Times*, February 20, 1983, p. 24. See also Frank Abnagale, Jr. (1982) for a discussion of how the author posed successfully as a member of various professions.

4. The genre of this script is certainly not unique to the professionalization of medical practictioners. For an analogous example of an occupational group that uses collective adoption of a cloak of competence to deal with anxiety about fateful matters, see Haas, 1977. See also Edgerton's analysis of mental retardates' attempts to pass in conventional society by adoption of such a cloak of competence (1967). These examples suggest that the demand for credible performance is accented in those social roles that are perceived as bearing exaggerated expectations about competence.

5. For an example of an occupation where members shroud themselves in a cloak of competence, see Haas (1972, 1974, 1977). High steel ironworkers, like physicians, must act competently and confidently in fateful matters. Ironworker apprentices, like student-physicians, were observed attempting to control others' definitions of them by acting competently and not revealing their fear or ignorance. In both situations we find neophytes reluctant to reveal their incompetence.

6. Ernest Becker reminds social scientists about their most important question and responsiblity when he says: "how do we get rid of the power to mystify? The talent and processes of mesmerization and mystification have to be exposed. Which is another way of saying that we have to work against both structural and psychological unfreedom in society. The task of science would be to explore both of these dimensions" (1975: 165). Our analysis suggests that demystification requires an appreciation of the interactive, collaborative and symbolic nature of professional-client relations and definitions of the situation.

REFERENCES

Abnagale, F., Jr. 1982. *Catch Me If You Can*. New York: Pocket Books.

Apple, M. 1971. "The hidden curriculum and the nature of conflict." *Interchange* 2: 27–40.

Ball, D. 1967. "The ethnography of an abortion clinic." *Social Problems* 14: 293–301.

Becker, Ernest. 1975. *Escape from Evil*. New York: The Free Press.

Becker, H.S. 1960. "Notes on the concept of commitment." *American Journal of Sociology* 66: 32–40.

———. 1962. "The nature of a profession." Pp. 27–46 in *Education for the Professions*, Sixty-first Yearbook of the National Society for the Study in Education, Part II. University of Chicago Press.

———. 1964. "Problems in the publication of field studies." Pp. 267–84 in Arthur J. Vidich, Joseph Bensman, and Maurice R. Stein, eds., *Reflections on Community Studies*. New York: John Wiley and Sons.

Becker, H.S. and B. Geer. 1958. "The fate of idealism in medical school." *American Sociological Review* 23: 50–56.

Becker, H.S., B. Geer, and E.C. Hughes. 1963. *Making the Grade: The Academic Side of College Life*. New York: John Wiley and Sons.

Becker, H.S., B. Geer, E.C. Hughes, and A.L. Strauss. 1961. *Boys in White: Student Culture in Medical School*. Chicago: University of Chicago Press.

Blackenship, R.L., ed. 1977. *Colleagues in Organizations: The Social Construction of Professional Work*. New York: John Wiley and Sons.

Bloom, S. 1973. *Power and Dissent in the Medical School*. New York: Macmillan.

Bogdan R. and S.J. Taylor. 1975. *Introduction to Qualitative Research Methods: A Phenomenological Approach to the Social Sciences*. New York: John Wiley.

Bourdieu, P. 1973. "Cultural reproduction and social reproduction." Pp. 71–112 in R. Brown, ed., *Knowledge, Education, and Cultural Change*. London: Tavistock.

Bramson, R. 1973. "The secularization of American medicine." *Hastings Center Studies* 1: 17–28.

Broadhead, R. 1983. *The Private Lives and Professional Identity of Medical Students*. New Brunswick, NJ: Transaction, Inc.

Bucher, R. and J. Stelling. 1977. *Becoming Professional*. Beverly Hills, CA: Sage.

Collins, R. 1982. *Sociological Insight: An Introduction to Non-Obvious Sociology*. New York: Oxford University Press.

Coombs, R.H. 1978. *Mastering Medicine: Professional Socialization in Medical School*. New York: Macmillan.

Coombs, R.H. and B.P. Boyle. 1971. "The transition to medical school: Expectations versus realities." Pp. 91–109 in R.H. Coombs and C.E. Vincent, eds., *Psychosocial Aspects of Medical Training*. Springfield, IL: Charles C. Thomas.

Coombs, R.H. and P.S. Powers. 1975. "Socialization for death: the physician's role." *Urban Life* 4: 250–71.

Daniels, M.J. 1960. "Affect and its control in the medical intern." *American Journal of Sociology* 66: 259–67.

Davis, F. 1968. "Professional socialization as subjective experience: the process of doctrinal conversion among student nurses." Pp. 235–51 in H.S. Becker et al., eds., *Institutions and the Person*. Chicago: Aldine Publishing Company.

Douglas, J. 1976. *Investigative Social Research: Individual and Team Field Research*. Beverly Hills, CA: Sage.

Edgerton, R.B. 1967. *The Cloak of Competence: Stigma in the Lives of the Mentally Retarded*. Berkeley: University of California Press.

Emerson, J.P. 1970. "Behavior in private places: sustaining definitions of reality in gynecological examinations." Pp. 73–97 in H.P. Dreitzel, ed., *Recent Sociology*. New York: The Macmillan Company.

Etzioni, A. 1975. *A Comparative Analysis of Complex Organizations: On Power, Involvement and Their Correlates*. New York: The Free Press.

Filstead, W., ed. 1970. *Qualitative Methodology: Firsthand Involvement with the Social World*. Chicago: Markham.

Fox, R. 1957. "Training for Uncertainty." Pp. 207–41 in Robert K. Merton, George G. Reader and Patricia L. Kendal, eds., *The Student Physician*. Cambridge, MA: Harvard University Press.

———. 1974. "Is there a 'new' medical student?" Pp. 197–227 in L.R. Tancred, ed., *Ethics of Health Care*. Institute of Medicine: National Academy of Science.

Fredericks, M.A. and P. Mandy. 1976. *The Making of a Physician*. Chicago: Loyola University Press.

Freidson, C. 1970. *Profession of Medicine*. New York: Dodds Mead and Company.

———. 1975. *Doctoring Together*. New York: Elsevier.

Fullan, M. 1972. "Overview of the innovative process and the user." *Interchange* 3: 1–46.

Gans, H. 1968. "The participant-observer as a human being: observations on the personal aspects of field work." Pp. 300–17 in H.S. Becker et al., eds., *Institutions and the Person*. Chicago: Aldine.

Garfinkel, H. 1956. "Conditions of successful degradation ceremonies." *American Journal of Sociology* 61: 420–24.

Geer, B. 1964. "First days in the field." Pp. 322–344 in P. Hammond, ed., *Sociologists at Work: Essays on the Craft of Social Research*. Garden City, NY: Doubleday Company.

———. 1972. *Learning to Work*. Beverly Hills, CA: Sage Publications, Inc.

Geer, B., J. Haas, C. Vivona, S.J. Miller, C. Woods, and H.S. Becker. 1968. "Learning the ropes: situational learning in four occupational training programs." Pp. 209–33 in I. Deutscher and E.J. Thompson, eds., *Among the People: Encounters with the Poor*. New York: Basic Books, Inc.

Gerth, H. and C.W. Mills. 1953. *Character and Social Structure: The Psychology of Social Institutions*. New York: Harcourt Brace Jovanovich.

Glaser, B. and A.L. Strauss. 1964. "Awareness contexts and social interaction." *American Sociological Review* 29: 659–79.

———. 1971. *Status Passage*. Chicago: Aldine.

Goffman, L. 1959. *The Presentation of Self in Everyday Life*. Garden City, NY: Doubleday-Anchor.

———. 1961. *Asylums*. New York: Doubleday.

———. 1963. *Stigma: Notes on the Management of Spoiled Identify*. Baltimore: Penguin.

Golde, P., ed. 1970. *Women in the Field: Anthropological Experiences*. Chicago: Aldine.

Goode, W.J. 1957. "Community within a community: the professions." *American Sociological Review* 22: 194–200.

Haas, J. 1972. "Binging: educational control among high-steel ironworkers." *American Behavioral Scientist* 16: 27–34.

———. 1974. "The stages of the high-steel ironworkers apprentice career." *The Sociological Quarterly* 15: 93–108.

———. 1977. "Learning real feelings: a study of high-steel ironworkers' reactions to fear and danger." *Sociology of Work and Occupations* 4: 147–70.

Haas, J., V. Marshall, and W. Shaffir. 1981. "Initiation into medicine: neophyte uncertainty and the ritual ordeal of professionalization." Pp. 109–23 in L. Lundy and B. Warme, eds., *Work in the Canadian Context: Continuity Despite Change*. Toronto: Butterworths.

Haas, J. and W. Shaffir. 1978. "Do new ways of professional socialization make a difference?: a study of professional socialization." Paper presented at the Ninth World Congress of Sociology, Uppsala, Sweden.

———. 1977. "The professionalization of medical students: developing competence and a cloak of competence." *Symbolic Interaction* 1: 71–88.

———. 1982a. "Taking on the role of doctor: a dramaturgical analysis of professionalization." *Symbolic Interaction* 5: 137–203.

———. 1982b. "Ritual evaluation of competence: the hidden curriculum of professionalization in an innovative medical school program." *Work and Occupations* 9: 131–54.

Habenstein, R. 1970. *Pathways to Data: Field Methods for Studying Ongoing Social Organizations*. Chicago: Aldine.

Halmos, P. 1970. *The Personal Service Society*. New York: Schocken.

Hamilton, J.D. 1972. "The selection of medical students at McMaster University." *Journal of the Royal College of Physicians of London* 6: 348–51.

Hammond, P., ed. 1964. *Sociologists at Work: Essays on the Craft of Social Research*. Garden City, NY: Doubleday and Company.

Henslin, J. 1968. "Trust and the cab driver." Pp. 138–58 in M. Truzzi, ed., *Sociology and Everyday Life*. Englewood Cliffs, NJ: Prentice-Hall.

Hughes, E.C. 1945. "Dilemmas and contradictions of status." *American Journal of Sociology* 50: 353–59.

———. 1951a. "Work and self." In J.H. Rohrer and M. Sherif, eds. *Social Psychology at the Crossroads*. New York: Harper & Row.

———. 1951b. "Mistakes at work." *Canadian Journal of Economics and Political Science* 17: 320–27.

———. 1952. "The sociological study of work: an editorial foreword." *The American Journal of Sociology* 62.

———. 1956. "The making of a physician." *Human Organization* 14: 21–25.

———. 1959. "The study of occupations." In R.K. Merton, L. Broom, and L.S. Cottrell, Jr., eds., *Sociology Today*. New York: Basic Books.

———. 1963. "Professions." *Daedalus* 92 (Fall): 655–58.

Johnson, J. 1975. *Doing Field Research*. New York: Free Press.

Junker, B. 1960. *Field Work: An Introduction to the Social Sciences*. Chicago: University of Chicago Press.

Kadushin, C. 1962. "Social distance between client and professional." *American Journal of Sociology* 67: 517–31.

Kamens, D.H. 1977. "Legitimating myths and educational organization: the relationship between organizational ideology and formal structure." *American Sociological Review* 42: 208–19.

Larson, M.S. 1977. *The Rise of Professionalism: A Sociological Analysis*. Berkeley: University of California Press.

Lesson, J. and J. Gray. 1978. *Women and Medicine*. London: Tavistock Publications

Liebow, E. 1976. *Tally's Corner*. Boston: Little, Brown and Company.

Lief, H.I. and R. Fox. 1963. "Training for 'detached concern' in medical students." Pp. 12–35 in H.I. Lief et al., eds., *The Psychological Basis of Medical Practice*. New York: Harper & Row.

Light, D.W., Jr. 1972. "Psychiatry and suicide: the management of a mistake." *American Journal of Sociology* 77: 821–83.

———. 1980. *Becoming Psychiatrists: The Professional Transformation of Self*. New York: W.W. Norton and Company.

Lofland, J. 1967. "Notes on naturalism in sociology." *Kansas Journal of Sociology* 3: 45–61.

———. 1971. *Analyzing Social Settings: A Guide to Qualitative Observation and Analysis*. Belmont, CA: Wadsworth.

———. 1976. *Doing Social Life: The Qualitative Study of Human Interaction in Natural Settings*. New York: Wiley.

Lortie, D. 1958. "Shared ordeal and induction to work." Pp. 252–64 in H.S. Becker et al., eds., *Institution and the Person*. Chicago: Aldine.

Mackenzie, N. 1962. *Secret Societies*. New York: Holt, Rinehart and Winston.

Martin, W.B. 1976. *The Negotiated Order of the School*. Toronto: Macmillan of Canada.

Maurer, D. 1962. *The Big Con*. New York: New American Library.

Mayer, J.E. and A. Rosenblatt. 1975. "Encounters with danger: social workers in the ghetto." *Sociology of Work and Occupations* 2: 227–45.

Mechanic, D. 1962. *Students Under Stress: A Study in the Social Psychology of Adaptation*. New York: Macmillan.

Mendelsohn, R. 1979. *Confessions of a Medical Heretic*. Chicago: Contemporary Books.

Merton, R.K., G.C. Reader, and P.L. Kendall, eds. 1957. *The Student Physician*. Cambridge, MA: Harvard University Press.

Millman, M. 1976. *The Unkindest Cut.* New York: William Morrow.

Mills, C.W. 1940. "Situated actions and vocabularies of motive." *American Sociological Review* 5: 904–13.

Montagna, P.D. 1977. "The professions: approaches to their study." Pp. 195–219 in P.D. Montagna, ed., *Occupations and Society: Toward a Sociology of the Labor Market.* New York: John Wiley.

Neufeld, V.R. and H.S. Barrows. 1974. "The 'McMaster philosophy': an approach to medical education." *Journal of Medical Education* 49: 1040–50.

Oakley, A. 1976. "Wisewoman and medicine man: changes in the management of childbirth." Pp. 17–58 in J. Mitchell and A. Oakley, eds., *The Rights and Wrongs of Women.* Middlesex: Penguin Books.

Olesen, V.L. and E.W. Whittaker. 1968. *The Silent Dialogue: A Study in the Social Psychology of Professional Socialization.* San Francisco: Jossey-Bass.

Orth, C.D., III. 1963. *Social Structure and Learning Climate: The First Year at the Harvard Business School.* Boston: Division of Research, Graduate School of Business Administration, Harvard University.

Parsons, T. 1951. *The Social System.* London: Routledge & Kegan Paul.

Pelio, P.J. 1970. *Anthropological Research.* New York: Harper & Row.

Popper, H., ed. 1967. *Trends in Medical Schools.* New York: Grune and Stratton.

Postman, N. and C. Weingartner. 1969. *Teaching as a Subversive Activity.* New York: Dell Publishing Co.

Powdermaker, H. 1966. *Stranger and Friend: The Way of an Anthropologist.* New York: W.W. Norton and Company, Inc.

Prus, R. and C.D. Sharper. 1979. *Road Hustler.* Toronto: Gage.

Riemer, J.W. 1977. "Varieties of opportunistic research." *Urban Life and Culture* 5: 461–77.

Roethlisberger, F.J. and W.J. Dickson. 1939. *Management and the Worker.* Cambridge, MA: Harvard University Press.

Rosenthal, R. and R. Rosnow, eds. 1970. *Sources of Artifact in Social Research.* New York: Academic Press.

Ross, A.D. 1961. *Becoming a Nurse.* Toronto: Macmillan Company of Canada.

Roth, J. 1957. "Ritual and magic in the control of contagion." *American Sociological Review* 22: 310–14.

———. 1966. "Hired hand research." *American Sociologist* 1: 190–96.

Roy, D. 1952. "Quota restriction and goldbricking in a machine shop." *American Journal of Sociology* 57: 427–42.

Rueschemeyer, D. 1964. "Doctors and lawyers: a comment on the theory of the professions." *Canadian Review of Sociology and Anthropology* 1: 17–30.

Rüzer, G. 1977. *Working: Conflicts and Change.* Second Edition. Englewood Cliffs, NJ: Prentice-Hall, Inc.

Schanck, R.L. 1932. "A study of a community and its groups and institutions conceived of as behavior of individuals." *Psychological Monographs* 43, 2.

Schatzman, L. and A.L. Strauss. 1973. *Field Research: Strategies for a Natural Sociology.* Englewood Cliffs, NJ: Prentice-Hall.

Scott, M.B. 1963. *The Racing Game.* Chicago: Aldine.

Shaffir, W., V. Marshall, and J. Haas. 1980. "Competing commitments: unanticipated problems of field research." *Qualitative Sociology* 2: 56–71.

Shibutani, T. 1966. *Improvised News: A Sociological Study of Rumor.* Indianapolis: Bobbs-Merrill.

Shipman, M., ed. 1976. *The Organization and Impact of Social Research.* London: Routledge & Kegan Paul.

Siegler, M. and H. Osmond. 1973. "Aesculapian authority." *Hastings Center Studies* 1: 41–52.

Simmel, G. 1956. "The triad." In K.H. Wolff, ed., *The Sociology of Georg Simmel.* New York: Free Press.

Simpson, M. 1972. *Medical Education: A Critical Approach.* London: Butterworth.

Spaulding, W.B. 1969. "The undergraduate medical curriculum (1969 model): McMaster University." *Canadian Medical Association Journal* 109: 659–64.

Strauss, A.L., L. Schatzman, R. Bucher, D. Ehrlich, and M. Sabshin. 1954. *Psychiatric Ideologies and Institutions.* New York: Free Press.

Sweeney, G.D. and D.L. Mitchell. 1975. "An introduction to the study of medicine: phase I of the McMaster M.D. program." *Journal of Medical Education* 50: 70–77.

Turner, V. 1970. *The Ritual Process: Structure and Anti-Structure.* Chicago: Aldine.

Valentine, C. 1968. *Culture and Poverty.* Chicago: University of Chicago Press.

Vancy, W.L. and L. Rainwater. 1979. "Problems in the ethnography of the urban under-class." Pp. 245–69 in R. Habenstein, ed., *Pathways to Data: Field Methods for Studying On-going Social Organizations.* Chicago: Aldine.

Vidich, A.J., J. Bensman, and M.R. Stein, eds. 1964. *Reflections on Community Studies.* New York: Harper & Row.

Walsh, W.J. 1978. "The McMaster programme of medical education, Hamilton, Ontario, Canada: developing problem-solving abilities." Pp. 69–79 in F.M. Katz and T. Fulop, eds., *Personnel for Health Care: Case Studies of Educational Programmes.* Public Health Papers 70. World Health Organization, Geneva.

Watson, J.D. 1969. *The Double Helix: A Personal Account of the Discovery of the D.N.A.* New York: New American Library.

Whyte, W.F. 1955. *Street Corner Society.* Chicago: University of Chicago Press.

Wilensky, H.R. 1964. "The professionalization of everyone?" *American Journal of Sociology* 70 (2): 137–58.

Zimmerman, D.H. and D.L. Wieder. 1977. "The diary: diary-interview method." *Urban Life* 5: 479–98.

PART 2B

CULTURE

In Chapter 5, Daniel Albas and Cheryl Albas of the University of Manitoba demonstrate that culture is a human invention that is created to fulfil human needs. They make their case by analyzing a situation that generates high anxiety —writing exams in university — and showing that many students invent magical practices in order to cope with the stress. One student they interviewed, for example, felt that she would do well only if she ate a sausage and two eggs sunny-side-up on the morning of each exam, and only if the sausage were arranged vertically on the left side of her plate and the eggs placed beside the sausage to form the "100" percent grade for which she was striving. Naturally, the ritual had more direct influence on her cholesterol level than on her grade. But indirectly it may have had something of the desired effect: to the degree that it helped relieve her anxiety and relax her, she may have performed better in exams.

Rites such as those described by Albas and Albas are invented by individuals without the benefit of a pre-existing cultural "script." Therefore, there are nearly as many different magical practices surrounding the writing of exams as there are individuals; and what is good luck for one person (e.g., wearing a pink sweatshirt) may be bad luck for another.

Shared cultures eliminate some of this variety and ambiguity, to some degree establishing standardized practices for groups of individuals. In fact, Albas and Albas note the existence of a continuum ranging from high cultural uniformity to high cultural diversity. At one end of the continuum, cultural beliefs and practices are virtually homogeneous for all members of a group. For example, in preliterate societies, most religious rituals are practised communally by all tribal members and no variation from prescribed practice is allowed. At the other extreme are the highly individualized and unscripted magical rites of students writing exams, soldiers going off to war, and athletes preparing to compete. Between the extremes of standardized culture and individualized magic lie contemporary religions, ethnic customs, political ideologies, professional beliefs, and so forth.

Historically, culture has tended to become more diverse as the variety of occupational roles (or the **division of labour**) has increased, as members of different ethnic groups migrate and come into contact with each other, as cheap global communications and accessible mass media make contact between diverse cultures easier, and as new political and intellectual movements crystallize. In general, people are now less obliged to accept the culture into which they are born and freer to choose and combine elements of culture from a wide variety of historical periods and geographical settings. In a sense, contemporary culture compresses time and space. It also undermines truths that were formerly felt to be universally valid, making them seem less certain or specific only to certain groups. This condition of ambiguity is called **postmodernism**. For example, it was widely believed in the last century that progress was desirable and inevitable, that the forces of history were pushing people to become more rational, scientific, and humane. As it turned out, science and rationality did benefit humankind; but they also helped foster genocide, nuclear war, and environmental ruin. On average, nearly a million people have been killed each year of this century due to war, so is it any wonder that people are less inclined now than they were a century ago to believe in progress? Such pessimism is, in any case, one symptom of postmodernism.

In Chapter 6, Reginald Bibby of the University of Lethbridge shows how the freedom to choose and combine elements of culture operates in contemporary Canadian religions. His surveys demonstrate that Canadians often supplement Judeo-Christian beliefs and practices with less conventional ideas about astrology, psychic powers, communication with the dead, and so forth. People who attend church regularly are just as likely to hold such unconventional beliefs as non-attenders. Despite the widespread acceptance of unconventional beliefs, however, the overwhelming majority of Canadians still turn to established religions for **rites of passage**, or ceremonies that mark the transition from one stage of life to another (e.g., baptisms, confirmations, weddings) or from life to death (funerals). Individuals thus choose their own mix of unconventional and conventional beliefs and practices; they draw on religions much like consumers shop in a mall; they practise religion à la carte. Meanwhile, the churches in Canada have diversified their menus in order to appeal to the spiritual, leisure, and social needs of religious consumers and retain their loyalties in the competitive market for congregants and parishioners.

Sometimes the cultural practices of people outside our own social groups appear irrational and bizarre. When confronted with the exotic, we may express amazement at the "inexplicable diversity of human nature" and take comfort in the "fact" that we are so much more sensible than others. When we do so, we are failing to think sociologically; we are ignoring the degree to which all of culture — even the most enigmatic elements of the most alien culture — is rooted in real human needs. The American anthropologist, Marvin Harris, elaborates this point in Chapter 7. He focusses on the apparently irrational practice of cow worship in India. Harris shows that it is not ignorance, fear, spirituality, stupidity, or a lack of love for life that makes millions of hungry Indian peasants refuse to kill cows and eat beef, allowing the animals to block traffic and sleep on railway tracks. Rather, Indian cow worship is rooted in an economic logic that Harris explains in detail but that ethnocentric Westerners (and many Indians themselves) fail to see. The broader implication of Harris's point is clear: a social scientific understanding of the practical facts of everyday life goes a long way toward clarifying elements of cultural practice that are otherwise inscrutable.

GLOSSARY

The **division of labour** is the variety of occupational roles in a society; the greater the division of labour, the greater the variety of occupational roles.

Postmodern culture compresses time and space and makes truths which formerly appeared to be universally valid seem either less certain or specific to particular groups.

Rites of passage are public ceremonies that mark the transition from one stage of life to the next or from life to death.

Chapter 5

STUDENTS' USE OF MAGIC DURING EXAMINATIONS

Daniel Albas and Cheryl Albas

MAGIC AND SUCCESS: THE CASE OF EXAMINATIONS

In a comprehensive study of university student life (Albas and Albas 1984), still ongoing, we identify a number of practices designed to allay anxiety and so increase chances for success in examinations. We set out to analyze these common but yet to be systematically studied unusual practices as a kind of "modern day" magic.

Magic seems inevitably to be associated with anxiety-causing events, whether its function is to allay the anxiety, as Malinowski suggests, or to generate anxiety where it does not exist and for societal reasons should, as Radcliffe-Brown suggests (Homans 1941). Examinations are highly tense and anxiety-causing events, and the practices described in this chapter as magic are essentially anxiety-coping mechanisms.

The examination arena is one in which students, no matter how well prepared, encounter a number of uncertainties. These include, for example, whether they have interpreted the questions correctly; whether the professors will interpret their answers as they intend them; and not least, whether they themselves are "up" for the contest in terms of the sharpness of their memories, organizational abilities, and ability to complete the task on time. Accordingly, it is not surprising to find surrounding the examination a number of practices by students that are clearly intended as uncertainty-coping mechanisms and which could be called magic, if magic is defined as an *action directed toward the achievement of a particular outcome with no logical relationships between the action and the outcome or, indeed, any empirical evidence that the one produces the other*. In effect, this is nonrational behavior in a setting where one might expect maximum rationality. Clearly we are not dealing with the magic of the sleight-of-hand professional magicians intend for entertainment, nor with that of preliterate shamans or urban gypsies (i.e., cultic magic). Such behavior is directed toward achieving an outcome, involves many everyday and commonplace acts, yet does seem to rely for the achievement of the outcome on some mystical element.

In this chapter we attempt to depict and analyze magical practices students use to allay anxiety and so increase their chances for success. It must be clearly understood that what we are describing as "magic" is behavior that falls on a continuum between the "heavy magic" of preliterate peoples and superstition (Jahoda 1969). Student magic is more like the kind of superstition practiced by athletes (Gmelch 1971), soldiers under battle conditions (Stouffer et al. 1949), miners (Wilson 1942), and gamblers (Henslin 1967). It is being described here for its ethnographic interest. We realize that magic among students has been observed in the past, but we are not aware of any previous effort to examine it systematically.

A description of how the study was carried out is followed by a discussion of general and specific characteristics of student magic. In the final section we suggest implications of this modern adaptation of an ancient technique for the wider societal context.

Source: "Modern Magic: The Case of Examinations," *The Sociological Quarterly* 30, 4 (1989): 603–13. © 1989 by Midwest Sociology Society. Reprinted by permission of the publisher and the authors.

METHOD

We gathered the data over the last thirteen years from over 300 students in our own and others' classes in the province's largest university (now enrolling 24,000 students). The sample represents a complete spectrum of student background as to age, sex, marital status, and social class. We observed and interacted with students as they studied in libraries, took study breaks, and made last-minute preparations before making their way to their respective exam sites. We continued our tracking as students gathered outside the exam centers, entered, chose their seats, and wrote their exams. Finally, we monitored students as they again congregated outside the exam sites and even as they gathered in pubs and local restaurants for the traditional "post-mortems." As a result we were able to record the increased frequency of magical practices as they neared culmination on the day of the exam and dropped dramatically (though not entirely) immediately upon completion of the exam.

The methodological process involved triangulation: data of different kinds were collected from a variety of sources in such a way that the weaknesses of one data-collecting technique were compensated for by the strengths of another, thus better ensuring reliability and validity. The four sources employed were: (1) exam logs, (2) surveys, (3) observation and probing for meaning, and (4) student accounts to explain failures.

The Logs

A source of data that proved rich in subjective detail was the exam logs which students were asked to keep over the thirteen-year period. These logs included descriptions of thoughts, sentiments, and behavior that they considered significant, from the first day of classes up to and including the return of their examination grades. Over time, such logs were collected from approximately 300 students of all ages, grade levels, achievement levels, and marital statuses. These records served as a valuable source of information about the inner-life of students and other aspects that we were in no position to observe. Although the word magic was never mentioned, approximately one-fifth of the students mentioned practices that could be classified as magical.

The Survey (Interviews)

In checking these accounts, we asked different students who had never submitted logs whether they had employed any of the forms of magic that were listed in the logs provided by other students. The general form of the question was, "Do you engage in any practices designed to enhance 'good luck' or to ward off 'bad luck'?" About one-third of the approximately 65 students interviewed indicated that they had done so at one time or another.

Observations and Probes

Sensitized to the variety and prevalence of magic, we "probed" by asking for explanations whenever we observed some unusual behavior. A student suddenly breaking the rhythm and length of his stride as he walked into the exam room was avoiding walking on a line (of the basketball court in the gym). Another, rolling his study notes into a cylinder and squeezing them, sought to wring knowledge from his notes. We did not code all explanations given for unusual behaviors as descriptions of magic in our sense. Where explanations showed any sort of plausible empirical connection between the practice and the result sought, the practice was not coded as magical.

Additional Student Accounts (Written and Verbal)

Another data source was the accounts given by students in about a dozen counseling sessions subsequent to the exams to explain their failures on examinations. On such occasions some students would sheepishly admit to having neglected some important practice which they had come to regard as necessary for success.

GENERAL CHARACTERISTICS OF STUDENT MAGIC

We found that from one-fifth to one-third of our students used magic, predominantly of the kind intended to bring good luck rather than to ward off bad luck. In Frazer's (1958) terms, it was largely "contagious" magic rather than "imitative" (no more than half a dozen cases of the latter), and there was only a handful of cases in which "omens" were given credence. The descriptions of magical behaviors and material items employed by students fall into the two major categories of Material Items (Figure 5.1) and Behavior (Figure 5.2). In turn, these categories are further divided into Prescribed for Luck, on the one hand, and Unlucky or Tabooed, on the other. Focusing first on Material Items Prescribed for Luck, these can be sub-classified as Favorite Oldies and Oddities, Lucky Locations, and Miscellaneous. Favorite Oldies and Oddities

Figure 5.1 Areas of Magic: Material Items

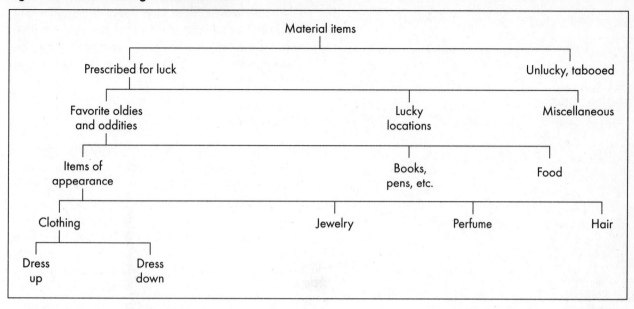

Figure 5.2 Areas of Magic: Behaviors

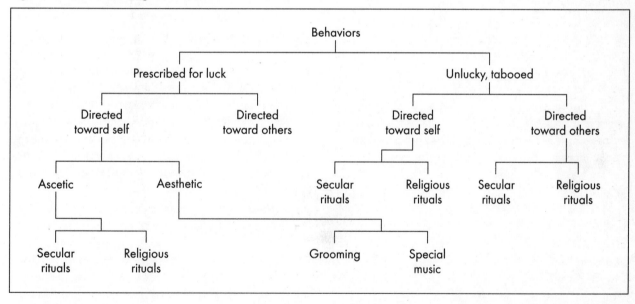

are represented by Items of Appearance, Books and Pens, and Food. Items of Appearance include not only Clothing but also Jewelry, Perfume, and Modes of Wearing the Hair. Thus, Items Prescribed for Luck exhibit a variety of at least seven different classes of items. If one distinguishes between Dressing Up and Dressing Down, the number of different classes of Items Prescribed for Luck increases to eight. It did not seem feasible to classify Unlucky Items. Accordingly, the total variety of classes into which magical Material Items fall is nine — eight Prescribed for Luck and an unclassified miscellany of Unlucky Items.

Within the other major category, Behavior, there are five distinct classes prescribed for Luck: Secular Rituals, Religious Rituals, Grooming, Special Music, and a Miscellany of Behavior Directed Toward Others. Under Tabooed Behavior, in regard to both Behavior Directed Toward Self and Behavior Directed Toward Others, is the twofold classification of Secular Rituals and Religious Rituals. This brings the total number of distinct classes of magical Behavior to nine. We now turn to specific descriptions of bottom-line Items and Behavior (those that appear on the bottom line of each of the two figures are not further subclassified).

Magical Items

Items Prescribed for Luck

In regard to Clothing, most students at exam time dress down (i.e., untidily, sloppily), though there are a few who dress up. Among the notable down dressers were: a young woman who always wore to exams her boyfriend's sweatshirt "which was in a deplorable condition with holes everywhere, stretched out of shape and much too big for me"; a science student who always wore an ancient scarf that he insisted "carries parts of my brain in it"; and an engineering student who wore a pink sweatshirt with purported magical qualities. An example of dressing up is the case of a student who always wore a three-piece suit that he had found particularly efficacious when he wore it on one occasion to a job interview. As he indicates, "It's not a very logical thing to wear to an exam because it's hot and restricting." Nevertheless he persists because of his belief in the continuing efficacy of his suit.

Notable items of Jewelry listed by students as bringing them luck were mother's wedding ring, mother's R.N. pin, and father's class ring. In all of these cases, the students mentioned that the parent was particularly bright and successful, thus implying a faith in magic by contagion.

Under the heading of Perfume, which includes one case of burning incense, all of the accounts suggest a conviction on the part of the students that association with success has the magical power to produce success. One woman wears the perfume that she wore when she met her boyfriend (a lucky event) — "I feel it brings me good luck, as it was luck that brought us together."

Hair is felt by our sample population to possess magical qualities both by its presence and by its absence. One student always has his hair cut short before an exam to permit, as he says, "knowledge to flow freely around my head." Another student, like Sampson, always allows his hair to grow long before exams "in order to keep the knowledge in."

The general impression is that certain favorite items provide a "security blanket" even if students can only see them (e.g., at the front of the room on the floor) and not actually handle them during the examination. Some "special pens" have written previous successful examinations and, without them, students would have less confidence in their ability to do well. For example, an advertisement in a student newspaper read, "Help! I've lost my silver Cross pen. Deep psychological and sentimental value; never written an exam without it. Lost last Friday. If found contact Anna (phone number)." In another instance, the pen

had been used to write all of the notes for the course and the student believed that it "knew" the material. Books and notes, although strictly prohibited from use during the exam, are often placed in heaps at the front and along the walls of the room, where students can see them. Many students claim that, in merely looking at the books, "summaries come up through the covers" to them. One student said that on the infrequent occasions she is allowed to take her books with her to her seat, she puts them on the floor and then puts her feet on them. She swears that the knowledge comes up to her through her legs. She adds the disclaimer that she is not crazy and that "it is true."

The magical properties of certain foods or food eaten in a special way at a special time or bought from some particular vendor — all have been claimed to bring good luck. One student insists that the purchase of a *carrot muffin* (no other kind) at the "*patty wagon*" (no other vendor) on the way to the examination room is most potent. Failure to secure the right muffin at the right place is an ill omen for her. Another student insists that on examination days she has to have the following breakfast in the following manner: one sausage placed vertically on the left of the plate and beside it two eggs sunny side up to make the configuration "100" (percent). Still another student stirs his coffee exactly 20 times on examination days. His rationale was that he was taking 5 courses and aspired to an A in each (which is the equivalent of 4 grade points), and 5 times 4 equals 20. This student attained a straight A average over his university career. These student practices resemble what Frazer (1958) refers to in *The Golden Bough* as imitative magic, where the magical method imitates the desired effect.

Examples of Lucky Locations are specific zones of the examination room and may include the back, sides, front, or middle. Students arrive early to secure these Lucky Locations because to sit anywhere else is to court confusion and disaster. Some students insist on a specific seat number that has proved lucky in the past. Some are not particular about the region of the room or a specific seat but they feel they must be in the same cluster with, and close to, those with whom they studied during the term.

Miscellaneous Items include the usual rabbit's feet, dice, coins, as well as tiny teddy bears, kangaroos, and other cuddly toys. One young medical student, very much a positivist in other areas of her life, must, like Christopher Robin, have "Roo" along when she writes her examinations. A young male student is reluctant to write an exam unless he has "found" a coin, which he takes as a sign of "luck." He searches for a coin on the day of the exam, often using up precious study time by "scrounging around bus stops" until he is successful, even at the risk of being late. Another student carries around a lock of his ex-girlfriend's hair in the hope that her extraordinary brightness will illuminate his own efforts.

Unlucky, Tabooed Items

Unlucky Items, interestingly enough, often turn out to be Oldies and Oddities once thought to be lucky but which have failed the owner and so become Tabooed Items. For example, a pink shirt (not the same one mentioned earlier) that had been a lucky talisman was found to be unlucky and thus shunned ever after. What is more, any other student at the same exam who wore a pink shirt was also to be shunned. Another example is the student who reported that in high school he once "crammed" for an exam at home the same day he was to write it and, when he was hungry, heated up a frozen TV dinner. He did unusually well on that exam, so he repeated the pattern of "cramming" at home the day of the exam and eating frozen waffles for breakfast and a TV dinner for lunch. However, when this student arrived at the university he found that studying only on the day of the exam was woefully inadequate and his performance was dreadful. Instead of changing his study habits he changed his "faith" in his lucky food: "It was to the point that even if I ate a whole freezer full of frozen food I would still do poorly on the exam.... I not only stopped eating frozen TV dinners before exams, I now make a point of always avoiding them." Other items, such as a bra (which the student believed to be repressive) and anything new or borrowed, are avoided. (Note the inconsistencies across the sample: one student always borrows her boyfriend's sweatshirt while another will not borrow even a pen.)

Magical Behaviors

Turning now to Magical Behavior, by far the most prevalent practices — whether directed toward self or others, whether lucky or unlucky — are those which could be termed *rituals*. In turn, these rituals can be subclassified as secular or religious.

Behaviors Directed Toward Self Prescribed for Luck

Examples of Secular Rituals Directed Toward Self include: knocking on the exam room door three times before entering the room (cf. knocking on wood); stepping over the threshold of the exam room with the right foot first (right in both senses); and making a circuit of the exam building, whatever the weather. However, Behaviors Directed Toward Self Prescribed For Luck consist almost entirely of prayer, even in cases where students by their own admission are not particularly religious. Such students nevertheless express a dread of offending God, particularly around examination time, and become compulsively scrupulous in their prayer life and penitent if they forget this duty. There is also, at exam time, an emphasis on virtuous behavior, particularly toward members of the immediate family, but often also even toward people met on the street. There is a distinct "minding of p's and q's" in the fear that any deviation from the path of righteousness (no matter how occasionally trodden) will be punished. Accordingly, whatever the strength of one's belief, it is not worth taking chances with inexorable fate.

Both the Secular and Religious Rituals Directed Toward Self described above could be classified together as being Ascetic in that they involve an element of sacrifice and self-discipline, however unusual. The two other behavior practices directed toward self, namely Grooming and Special Music, may be classified as Aesthetic in that they have to do with effects that are pleasing to the senses.

Another example of Behavior Directed Toward Self Prescribed for Luck involves students who report that being well groomed contributes to good performance. This in itself may not be magical even by our broad definition. However, when one student states that she puts special care into the manicuring of the three fingers that hold her pen, this begins to seem like magic, certainly the *imitative magic* described by Frazer (i.e., polished fingernails produce polished answers).

A number of students report a Behavior Directed Toward Self Prescribed For Luck which involves "lucky tunes" to which they always listen prior to writing examinations: "... then twenty minutes before the exam I drive to school listening to 'Money Changes Everything.' I consistently follow this strategy before I write any exam." The following account is worthy of mention, though not technically a tune nor even magic according to our definition (in that there is clearly a thread of empirical connectedness between the act and expected result). One student states that before every exam he listens to a tape by Martin Luther King in which the Reverend King speaks about "his dream" and reiterates the refrain "We shall overcome." Clearly the dream for the student is life success and overcoming this particular exam.

Behaviors Directed Toward Others Prescribed for Luck

The category, Behaviors Prescribed For Luck Directed Toward Others, might better be described as behavior required of others by the student. However, since in most cases students go to great ends to elicit such behavior from family and friends, they may be said indeed to engineer specific forms of behavior in others. Examples of this are students who insist that before leaving for an examination they be wished good luck by various members of their families according to a formula of specific wording and at a high volume. Quite often it is not sufficient for the formula of the wishes to be secular, they must be invoked by prayer. "At the moment before I walk out of the door I make sure that my parents wish me good luck and especially add 'God Bless You.' The good luck part I could probably do without, but not hearing 'God Bless You' leaves me feeling I'm not getting all the help I could for an exam." In some cases the others who are expected to tender good luck wishes are non-human others. For one student, it was essential for her dog to sit upon his haunches, offer a paw, and "woof" her good luck.

Much as in the case of Lucky Locations, some students seek out lucky people to sit near during the examination (i.e., people whom they think are likely to be star performers). One interesting case of this is a student who stated that he always sought out the ugliest girl to sit next to. By his reasoning, she would not have a boyfriend and would devote all her time to study and be thoroughly well prepared which, in turn, would rub off on him. The magic, of course, is implied in the term "rubbing off" and could best be classified as magic by contagion.

Tabooed Behaviors Directed Toward Others

Secular examples of this include refraining from sexual intercourse even, in some cases, by married partners; refraining from discussing the exam, particularly joking about it; and, above all, in this context, avoiding well-wishing. This is particularly interesting since it seems to contradict the notion of imitative magic that we saw in the case of the student with the manicured pen fingers. Some students avoid others, even lovers and spouses, who are liable to wish them luck. One student who followed this taboo emphatically avowed that he did not believe in luck. He was nevertheless very upset if someone wished him good luck, and he therefore went out of his way to avoid being so wished.

A few activities were classified as rituals tabooed for religious reasons; for example, refraining from gossip about other people because it is offensive to God, and staying away from entertainment and other secular pursuits because by so doing one acquires virtue which will be rewarded. These practices, in regard to both items and behavior, would seem to be most intense when anxiety for the student is at its highest. Similarly, the magic wanes and disappears as the cause for anxiety passes.

DISCUSSION

Examining Figures 5.1 and 5.2 suggests that, among our college students, luck-bringing magic is more prevalent than magic to ward off bad luck. This is particularly the case in Figure 5.1. It is not as immediately apparent in Figure 5.2, but does emerge when one notes that most of the tabooed behavior described is really directed toward bringing luck rather than warding off misfortune. The point becomes especially clear when we note the prevalence of active manipulative behavior over passive behavior, implying the existence of a feeling among the students of being in command of their destinies rather than succumbing to the fate of omens. Of all the accounts of Magical Items and Behaviors, only about 10 mentioned the significance of omens. This aspect of student magic is in strong contrast to preliterate magic where so much credence is placed in omens. Another contrast is that whereas Frazer found imitative magic to be the more prevalent form among preliterates, we found that among students contagious magic is more prevalent.

Another pattern that emerges from these accounts is that items employed and behaviors exhibited are highly private and idiosyncratic. That is, what may be used and considered efficacious by one student may be tabooed by another (e.g., the pink shirts mentioned earlier and careful grooming versus the disheveled look). This in turn would seem to be related to the fact that student magic is largely invented by the practitioners themselves. It is not traditional or socially shared as is preliterate magic. Student magic is, above all, entirely directed toward self enhancement, and there is not a single case of magic directed toward the detriment of another, quite unlike the cultic magic of preliterates. Finally, student magic, quite unlike that of preliterate groups, is pragmatic, in that students are willing to abandon any item or behavior that does not work.

Toward a Theory

On the basis of our information, it appears that student magic can be thought of as being at one end of a continuum that began with preliterate magic and emerged through other forms such as those practiced by soldiers in warfare, miners, and sports competitors. At the preliterate-magic end of the continuum, magic is a communal, co-operative enterprise in which the participants have shared meanings in regard to the practices and are motivated by a strong collectivity orientation. Among the soldiers, miners, and athletes, magic is still practiced in a community in which there are, to some extent, shared meanings and also, to some extent, but considerably less than among preliterate peoples, a collectivity orientation. When we come to students writing exams, we have reached the near end of the continuum of magical practices. Here we find magic practiced individually and in isolation, without shared meaning (even, to some extent, with contradictory meanings), and completely self-oriented in its motivation. In an attempt to understand these differences along the continuum, it might be suggested that for preliterate peoples living in a less complex and completely homogeneous society, one would expect shared meanings in a way that is not to be expected among heterogeneous, largely anonymous groups of students in contemporary urban society. However, even in contemporary society it is reasonable to expect that, within a group of soldiers who have been trained together to act in unison and whose very lives depend upon the actions of every other one in the group, there would tend to be more of a collectivity orientation than among university students writing exams (although perhaps not as much as within more homogeneous, proliferate groupings). The phenomenon of shared meanings would also be expected to be in an intermediate position, since even though soldiers, miners, and athletes are the products of a heterogeneous socialization compared to preliterate peoples, they nevertheless work together and constitute communities to a greater degree than do exam-writing students. As such, this "middle category" has developed many well-known agreed-upon magical rituals such as "break a leg," "three on a match," not referring to a "winning streak," and "the fatal last shift." In effect then, the particular aspects of student magic that we described earlier, which may seem atypical of magic in the past and in some ways inexplicable, maybe partially explained in terms of increasing societal complexity and heterogeneity as well as shifts in cultural values.

In sum, as society moves from prelilerate to contemporary, increasing in complexity as well as scientific sophistication, we might expect magic to be transformed from: (1) being publicly performed to being privately and individually performed; (2) being culturally transmitted to being spontaneously generated; (3) being completely shared by the whole community to being utilized privately by individuals; and (4) being unvaryingly uniform and consistent in its rituals to being highly variable and even contradictory. Clearly, with an ideal-type polar construct of this kind, no actual case of magic (including student magic) will in all respects conform to the characteristics of either pole. The burden of this article, however, is that students' magic falls rather toward the latter end of each of these four continua.

REFERENCES

Albas, D., and C. Albas. 1984. *Student Life and Exams: Stresses and Coping Strategies.* Dubuque, IA: Kendall/Hunt.

Frazer, J. 1958. *The Golden Bough: A Study in Magic and Religion.* New York: Macmillan.

Gmelch, G. 1971. "Baseball Magic." *Society* 8(8): 39–41.

Henslin, J. 1967. "Craps and Magic." *The American Journal of Sociology* 73: 316–30.

Homans, G. 1941. "Anxiety and Magic." *American Anthropologist* 43: 164–72.

Jahoda, G. 1969. *The Psychology of Superstition.* London: The Penguin Press.

Stouffer, S., A. Lumsdaine, M. Lumsdaine, R. Williams, Jr., M. Smith, I. Janis, and L. Cottrell, Jr. 1949. *Studies in Social Psychology in World War II: The American Soldier, Combat and Its Aftermath.* Princeton, NJ: Princeton University Press.

Wilson, W. 1942. "Miners' Superstitions." *Life and Letters Today* 32: 86–93.

Chapter 6

FRAGMENTED GODS: RELIGION IN CANADA

REGINALD W. BIBBY

If Sigmund Freud could have been at Exhibition Place in Toronto in the first week in February 1987, I suspect he would have been astonished — perhaps disappointed, maybe troubled. For there was advanced technology at its glorious best, aiding and abetting, rather than destroying and replacing, supernatural ideas. The occasion: the annual "Psychics, Mystics and Seers Fair." The fair, like many others elsewhere in the country, was jammed with more than 150 exhibitors, showcasing numerology, New-Age thought, iridology, reincarnation, and tarot-card, crystal-ball, palmist, and psychic readers. Broadcaster and lecturer Henry Gordon (1987: H7) comments,

> But high tech has really taken over. The computer and the printed readout dominate. And that's where the real bargains are. A mere $3 will satisfy your curiosity. At most of the comput-

erized booths, you need only fill in a card with your name and birth date and you get an immediate reading.... Three bucks in 15 seconds — seems like a fairly profitable operation.

In Canada, an abundance of Judeo-Christian beliefs and practices are supplemented by a wide array of less conventional ideas and behaviour. Just under 25% think it is possible to communicate with the dead; 35% say they believe in astrology; more than 60% in ESP; the same proportion believe some people have psychic powers (see Table 6.1).

Interest does not stop at beliefs, but extends to practices and experiences. Horoscope readers easily outnumber the nation's Bible readers. Some 75% say they read their horoscopes at least occasionally, easily above the 45% level for Bible-reading; the daily proportions are 13% and 4%, respectively (see Table 6.2).

Table 6.1 Less Conventional Beliefs (In %s)

"Do you believe:"	N	Yes, I Definitely Do	Yes, I Think So	No, I Don't Think So	No, I Definitely Do Not
• That it is possible to communicate with the dead	1163	7	15	41	37
• In astrology	1147	9	26	38	27
• In ESP (extra-sensory perception)	1139	24	37	24	15
• That some people have psychic powers, enabling them to predict events	1160	21	42	23	14

Source: Project Can85.

Source: Fragmented Gods: The Poverty and Potential of Religion in Canada (Toronto: Irwin, 1987), pp. 73–84. Reprinted by permission of the publisher.

Table 6.2 Less Conventional Practices and Experiences (In %s)

"How often do you read your horoscope?"
Daily | 13
Occasionally | 62
Never | 25
I'm not sure what a horoscope is | 0

"Have you ever had any experience that you think is an example of mental telepathy (awareness of others' thoughts)?"
Yes, I'm sure I have | 19
Yes, I think I have | 32
No | 49

"Have you ever had any experience that you think is an example of premonition (anticipation of a coming event)?"
Yes, I'm sure I have | 20
Yes, I think I have | 38
No | 42

Source: Project Can80.

For many, horoscope reading seems merely a form of entertainment. A number of respondents comment that they turn to the "sign column" in the newspaper "just for the fun of it." One respondent from a small Alberta community said, "My newspaper arrives a day late. I like to read my horoscope to find out what was supposed to have happened to me yesterday." An Ontario respondent reminds us, however, that for some, like herself, "astrology is a science."

As for experiences, about one in two Canadians think they have personally experienced mental telepathy. Even more — some 60% — maintain they have experienced premonition (the anticipation of a future event). A 45-year-old Regina woman tells us:

> Many times I have a fleeting glimpse of something. Then, when it happens, I recall that instant vision that seemed to have passed. Usually it turns out to be a tragedy. It passes through my mind and it happens weeks or months later. Feelings really seem to warn me. Really weird, yet these forewarnings happen.

As the 60% figure indicates, her claim is far from rare. In exploring such experiences informally with people over the past decade or so, I have found they are innumerable. My mother, a devout Christian, recalls the night when she had a nightmare that my father, returning home from a trip, had slid off the icy highway into the ditch. Awakening suddenly, she looked at the clock beside her bed — it was 2:15 A.M.. She learned within the hour that my father had indeed gone off the highway, at precisely 2:15 A.M.

As a result of such experiences and exposure to the claims of others, Canadians seem to embrace fairly readily both conventional and less conventional ideas about the supernatural. People who attend religious services weekly are only slightly less inclined than others to believe in astrology, ESP, and psychic powers (see Table 6.3). Those who "never" attend services are just as likely to hold such beliefs as other people.

Bryan Wilson (1982: 172) observes that people "might go through the motions of accepting orthodoxy, but they may not always accept that orthodoxy is enough." Supplementation of conventional ideas among Canadians is common.

THE RIGHT TO RITES

The national surveys have also found that Canadians continue to look to the churches for an array of services such as baptisms, confirmations, marriages, and funerals. These are commonly referred to as "rites of passage," because they surround the critical life stages of birth, adulthood, marriage, and death.

Approximately seven in ten Canadians indicate that the church (or synagogue) has carried out baptisms and marriages for them in the past, while some five in ten have had confirmations and funerals performed (see Table 6.4). Reflecting the age structure of the Canadian population, about 15% expect to have future baptisms and confirmations carried out, and 20% expect church weddings. Almost 50% expect to have church funerals. The market for rites of passage continues to be extensive.

Table 6.3 Less Conventional Traits and Service Attendance (% Positive)

Attendance Level	N	Commun Dead	Astrol	Horo Read	Psychic Powers	ESP	Precog	Telep
Weekly	369	24	27	33	56	48	47	42
Monthly	113	21	45	41	72	64	61	57
Yearly	571	23	36	42	65	63	61	55
Never	242	22	37	33	63	68	49	52

Source: Project Can80.

People who worship irregularly are almost as likely as weekly attenders to expect to be "serviced" by the nation's religious groups, also primarily in times of birth, marriage, and death (see Table 6.4).

Data from the aforementioned 1986 analysis of the Toronto Anglican diocese has helped to clarify the thoughts of some Canadians on passage rites (Bibby 1986). For starters, inactive Anglicans are just as likely as active Anglicans to expect to have these rites carried out for them. It is also clear that inactives are not just thinking of rote performances. One 30-year-old inactive mother in Toronto comments:

> I have witnessed public Baptisms which seemed almost assembly line (eight children at once). I think this many at once takes away from the specialness of this event for each individual child. To have so many children and parents lining up seemed somehow "not the Anglican way." If I am to be honest here, at the end of this service (at which I was a Godmother), there was no longer awe — only boredom.

Given this demand for professional services on the part of infrequent attenders, the obvious question facing Anglicans and other religious groups is how to respond. Anglican inactives, for example, have very strong feelings about their "right to rites." In the Toronto diocese, some 90% or more maintain they should be allowed to have church burials, marriages, and baptisms. The logic involved is diverse. A 40-year-old Brampton inactive argues, "Just because people don't attend Church doesn't mean they don't believe in God and shouldn't be able to be baptized, married, and buried in a church, which represents God."

It is important to note that religious inactives have allies in their expectations. More than 80% of active Anglicans, according to the Toronto study, say inactives should be allowed church marriages and baptisms, and 94% support their right to church burials. One 63-year-old active, for example, says:

> I'm against making young people go to church regularly to have their babies baptized. I feel we are turning our young married couples away from the church by demanding they come. I feel no child should be refused.

A 32-year-old illustrates the support of younger actives as well. In agreeing that rites should be extended to inactives, she adds, "Perhaps they will return in the future. Why alienate them?" And finally, concerning burials specifically, one active offers this rationale: "God wouldn't deny it, so why should we?"

Some religious leaders have argued for a tough stance. It is not uncommon, both in conservative and in more liberal churches, for couples to be required to complete pre-marriage counselling classes. In a few cases, couples are refused ceremonies if they are not prepared to profess commitment.

What would the costs be if religious organizations collectively denied rites of passage to their inactive affiliates? In the case of weddings, many people would probably turn elsewhere and thereby be lost to the religious groups. It is possible that quasi-religious rites-of-passage "businesses" would come into being to meet the new marriage-market need. One can readily imagine the emergence of "religious-like retail outlets," providing weddings — perhaps even additional services — in attractive settings with congenial and competent personnel.

The somewhat brash comment of one 38-year-old Anglican woman puts the consumer outlook in blunt terms: "I'm inactive! If I weren't married, baptized, confirmed, and allowed to attend when I wish, I wouldn't be an Anglican, and that would be your loss."

RELIGIOUS SELF-IMAGES

Beyond relying on responses to questions about belief, practice, experience, and knowledge in probing religious commitment, another obvious method is to let people speak for themselves. The Project Canada surveys have done so, asking people to describe the nature of their religion. A number of options have been offered to them, with an opportunity to write in more applicable responses if they so desire.

The results: some 40% of Canadians say they regard themselves as committed Christians, with about

Table 6.4 Previous and Expected Professional Services by Attendance (In %s)

"Which of the following have been performed for you by the church (1) in the past or, as you see it, (2) will probably be carried out for you by the church (or synagogue) in the future?"

		N	Bapt	Confirm	Wed	Fun'l
Past	Nationally	1201	71	52	66	46
	Weekly	299	81	67	72	51
	<Weekly	892	67	47	64	45
Future	Nationally	1201	14	13	20	45
	Weekly	299	12	11	17	51
	<Weekly	892	15	13	21	43

Note: At least one in the past, 84%; in the future, 52%; in either, 92%.

Source: Project Can85.

2% indicating they are committed to other faiths (see Table 6.5). Almost another 40% are uncommitted, either seeing themselves as interested in religion but not strongly committed, or as religious in somewhat unconventional ways. The remaining 20% do not regard themselves as religious.

To be sure, the content of Christian faith for the four in ten who profess to be committed Christians varies dramatically. Only about one-third, for example, exhibit the aforementioned traditional style of commitment — believing in God, the divinity of Jesus, and life after death, praying privately, experiencing God, and having some knowledge of the Christian tradition.

The other two-thirds of the committed Christians exhibit fragments — to varying degrees not holding

conventional beliefs about God, Jesus, and immortality, not praying, not claiming to have experienced God, or having a limited knowledge of Christianity.

The religion of most of the remaining 60% of Canadians seems to be characterized by specialized consumption rather than religious commitment (see Table 6.6). They readily adopt "religious fragments" — isolated beliefs, isolated practices, and isolated professional services. But they make no pretense that religion informs their lives.

RELIGIOUS FRAGMENTS

Canadians give little indication of abandoning their ties with the established religious groups. Nonetheless, things have changed. As the century draws to a close, people in greater and greater numbers are drawing upon religion as consumers, adopting a belief here and a practice there. Additionally, they are calling on clergy to perform various rites of passage relating primarily to birth, marriage, and death.

At the same time, Canadians appear to be moving away from Christianity or other religions as meaning systems addressing all of life. They are opting for Judeo-Christian fragments. To borrow a phrase one of France's sociologists used in telling me about religion in his country, Canadians are into "religion à la carte." The national drop-off in attendance at services is merely a symptom of the increasing tendency of Canadians to consume religion selectively.

It appears that a major shift in religious styles has been taking place in Canada during the twentieth century, involving the increasing movement from religious commitment to religious consumption.

Invariably people raise the questions, "But are things really any different now than they were in the past? Haven't most people always been adopting religious fragments?"

Table 6.5 Self-Reported Nature of One's Religion (In %s)

"Which of the following statements comes closest to describing the nature of your religion?"

I regard myself as a committed Christian	42
I have a mild interest in Christianity and an inquisitive interest in other religions, but I hardly regard myself as a strongly religious person	24
I am not a religious person	19
I find myself interested in a variety of religions, but not committed to any particular one	4
I am deeply committed to a religion other than Christianity	1
Write-in Regard self as Christian, practice irregularly (5) Other (5)	10

Source: Project Can85

Table 6.6 Self-Reported Commitment Styles and Select Beliefs and Services (In %s)

	N	Tradit Commit	Astrol	ESP	Weds Future	Fun'ls Future
Committed						
To Christianity	494	35	33	55	20	47
To other religions		—	17	23	14	42
Uncommitted	383	9	39	70	24	47
Non-religious	224	2	32	54	15	38
Other	53	27	48	77	17	57

Source: Project Can85.

Four quick responses: First, yes, fragments are not new. But there are indications that the extent of their adoption is. What is different from the past is our current cultural reality — a highly specialized, consumption-oriented Canada. That culture is dramatically eroding religion as a system addressing all of life.

Second, we need only look at Quebec to see how religion at one time coloured culture and the structure of society. As historian Ian Rennie (1986: 37) concludes in examining the question, "Was Canada Ever Christian?", those people who settled and governed early French and English Canada "developed its laws and governing policies on the basis of what they conceived to be a Christian world view." That religious tone is largely gone.

Third, the fact of the matter is that there has been a downward turn in service attendance over time. As we will see shortly, there also is a much greater tendency for older Canadians to profess commitment, and for younger people to adopt fragments. Such findings suggest that, at least since the turn of this century, there has indeed been an increase in the tendency of Canadians to order off the religion à la carte menu.

Fourth, in some ways the question is academic. In the minds of many proponents of religion, the important issue is not how recent widespread fragment adoption is, but rather, how pervasive the pattern is at present. Whether new or ongoing, fragment selection is not what religion has been all about.

According to John Webster Grant (1972), a consumer attitude towards Christianity was prevalent by at least the 1950s. Grant writes:

> [People] were selective in what they took. They crowded church buildings on Sunday morning, but except for conservative evangelicals, stayed home to watch [television] in the evening.... Newly active members sought a product called religion in buildings that increasingly resembled attractive retail outlets. They went to church not so much to express convictions as to seek answers to questions, solutions to problems, and guidance in decisions.

The social forecaster John Naisbitt (1984: 260) has written that society, in a relatively short time, "has fractionalized into many diverse groups of people with a wide array of differing tastes and values." The idea of "a multiple-option society," he says, has spilled over into a number of areas, including the family, music, food, entertainment, and religion.

In Canada, increasing institutional specialization has been associated with the tendency for people to look to the Church to provide very specific commodities. These include isolated beliefs and practices. Thus it is that Canadians believe in God but are not sure about the divinity of Jesus or the nature of life after death. They find themselves praying once in a while, even if they seldom read a Bible or say grace. Indeed, as we have seen, a higher proportion of Canadians say they pray (77%) than say they believe in a personal God (66%). They attend services occasionally, but hardly weekly. And, of course, they look to the Church to provide the critical rites of passage.

Canadians tend to pick and choose religious fragments at will. An Anglican housewife and mother in a small New Brunswick community comments, "I believe in God but do not believe in the divinity of Jesus." From an Edmonton science administrator comes the acknowledgement, "I believe in Jesus Christ but have doubts about immortality." And a pragmatic, retired Roman Catholic living in rural British Columbia attends services only infrequently, but quips, "I have to believe in God — I'm too old to take a chance!"

Canadians also readily supplement their conventional Christian menu with an assortment of other supernatural beliefs and practices, including astrology, psychic phenomena, auras, bio-rhythms, demon possession, and communication with the dead.

Significantly, however, beyond a certain investment of time and money, the returns are diminishing. Attendance at services is a case in point. The fact that decreasing numbers of Canadians attend services every week suggests that many feel weekly attendance is unnecessary for experiencing what religious groups have to offer. Less than once a week is sufficient. Aldous Huxley seemed to know what was coming. In *Brave New World* (Huxley 1932: 52), Barnard attends his "Solidarity Service" only twice a month.

The same principle seems to hold for money — putting a little in the offering plate is fine, but putting in a lot is too much. When Canadians are asked why they are no longer as involved in churches as they once were, the dominant response is not that they are "down" on the Church or opposed to contributing; it is simply that they prefer to spend more of their time on other things.

Some, of course, solidly endorse religious groups. A 67-year-old Mulgrave, Nova Scotia, man, for example, says, "For me there's no substitute for the Roman Catholic Church." But many are quick to deny the necessity of involvement in religious groups. A Toronto man working in public relations comments, "I object to the assumption that any person not subscribing to an organized religion is not religious. Anyone can develop their own religious attitudes." A young rural Alberta mother with United Church ties says,

> I've been through a great deal in life and my faith is very strong. But I believe that one is closer to God in their own home and garden than a church. I see going to church these days as "keeping up with the Joneses."

A 30-year-old man in St. John's notes, "I have no specific denomination, but I consider myself to be a Christian." A similar view is offered by a Montreal man, 48, who says, "I believe in a supreme power or force, but I am not involved in organized religion."

But even if such people are not attending, few are disenchanted and turning elsewhere. In the words of Raymond Currie (1976), a sociologist at the University of Manitoba, belonging exceeds commitment. Canadians are not "dropping out." As a student in one of my classes pointed out, it probably would be more accurate to describe them as "dropping in."

REFERENCES

Gordon, Henry. 1987. *The Toronto Star* (February 8).

Wilson, Bryan. 1982. *Religion in Sociological Perspective.* London: Oxford University Press.

Bibby, Reginald W. 1986. *Anglitrends: A Profile and Prognosis.* Toronto: Anglican Diocese of Toronto.

Rennie, Ian. 1986. *Faith Today* (July–August).

Grant, John Webster. 1972. *The Church in the Canadian Era.* Toronto: McGraw-Hill Ryerson.

Naisbitt, John. 1984. *Megatrends.* New York: Warner Books.

Huxley, Aldous. 1932. *Brave New World.* New York: Harper and Row.

Currie, Raymond. 1976. "Belonging, Commitment, and Early Socialization in a Western City." In Stewart Crysdale and Les Wheatcroft, eds., *Religion in Canadian Society.* Toronto: Macmillan.

Chapter 7

HOLY COW

MARVIN HARRIS

Ours is an age that claims to be the victim of an overdose of intellect. In a vengeful spirit, scholars are busily at work trying to show that science and reason cannot explain variations in human lifestyles. And so it is fashionable to insist that the riddle examined in the material to come has no solution. The ground for much of this current thinking about lifestyle enigmas was prepared by Ruth Benedict in her book *Patterns of Culture*. To explain striking differences among the cultures of the Kwakiutl, the Dobuans, and the Zuni, Benedict fell back upon a myth which she attributed to the Digger Indians. The myth said: "God gave to every people a cup, a cup of clay, and from this cup they drank their life.... They all dipped in the water but their cups were different." What this has meant to many people ever since is that only God knows why the Kwakiutl burn their houses. Ditto for why the Hindus refrain from eating beef, or the Jews and Moslems abhor pork, or why some people believe in messiahs while others believe in witches. The long-term practical effect of this suggestion has been to discourage the search for other kinds of explanations. For one thing is clear: If you don't believe that a puzzle has an answer, you'll never find it.

To explain different patterns of culture we have to begin by assuming that human life is not merely random or capricious. Without this assumption, the temptation to give up when confronted with a stubbornly inscrutable custom or institution soon proves irresistible. Over the years I have discovered that lifestyles which others claimed were totally inscrutable actually had definite and readily intelligible causes. The main reason why these causes have been so long overlooked is that everyone is convinced that "only God knows the answers."

Another reason why many customs and institutions seem so mysterious is that we have been taught to value elaborate "spiritualized" explanations of cultural phenomena more than down-to-earth material ones. I contend that the solution to the riddle examined in this chapter lies in a better understanding of practical circumstances. I shall show that even the most bizarre-seeming beliefs and practices turn out on closer inspection to be based on ordinary, banal, one might say "vulgar" conditions, needs, and activities. What I mean by a banal or vulgar solution is that it rests on the ground and that it is built up out of guts, sex, energy, wind, rain, and other palpable and ordinary phenomena.

This does not mean that the solutions to be offered are in any sense simple or obvious. Far from it. To identify the relevant material factors in human events is always a difficult task. Practical life wears many disguises. Each lifestyle comes wrapped in myths and legends that draw attention to impractical or supernatural conditions. These wrappings give people a social identity and a sense of social purpose, but they conceal the naked truths of social life. Deceptions about the mundane causes of culture weigh upon ordinary consciousness like layered sheets of lead. It is never an easy task to circumvent, penetrate, or lift this oppressive burden.

In an age eager to experience altered, nonordinary states of consciousness, we tend to overlook the extent to which our ordinary state of mind is already a profoundly mystified consciousness — a consciousness surprisingly isolated from the practical facts of life. Why should this be?

For one thing, there is ignorance. Most people achieve awareness of only a small portion of the range of lifestyle alternatives. To emerge from myth and legend to mature consciousness we need to compare the full range of past and present cultures. Then there is fear. Against events like growing old and dying, false consciousness may be the only effective defense. And finally, there is conflict. In ordinary social life, some persons invariably control or exploit others. These inequalities are as much disguised, mystified, and lied about as old age and death.

Ignorance, fear, and conflict are the basic elements of everyday consciousness. From these elements, art and politics fashion that collective dreamwork whose function it is to prevent people from understanding what their social life is all about. Everyday consciousness, therefore, cannot explain itself. It owes its very existence to a developed capacity to deny the facts that explain its existence. We don't expect dreamers to explain their dreams; no more should we expect lifestyle participants to explain their lifestyles.

Some anthropologists and historians take the opposite view. They argue that the participants' explanation constitutes an irreducible reality. They warn that human consciousness should never be treated as an "object," and that the scientific framework appropriate to the study of physics or chemistry has no relevance when applied to the study of lifestyles. Various prophets of the modern "counter-culture" even blame the inequities and disasters of recent history on too much "objectification." One of them claims that objective consciousness always leads to a loss of "moral sensitivity," and thereby equates the quest for scientific knowledge with original sin.

Nothing could be more absurd. Hunger, war, sexism, torture, and exploitation have occurred throughout history and prehistory — long before anybody got the idea of trying to "objectify" human events.

Some people who are disillusioned with the side effects of advanced technology think that science is "the commanding lifestyle of our society." This may be accurate with respect to our knowledge of nature, but it is terribly wrong with respect to our knowledge of culture. As far as lifestyles are concerned, knowledge can't be original sin because we are still in our original state of ignorance.

Whenever I get into discussions about the influence of practical and mundane factors on lifestyles, someone is sure to say, "But what about all those cows the hungry peasants in India refuse to eat?" The picture of a ragged farmer starving to death alongside a big fat cow conveys a reassuring sense of mystery to Western observers. In countless learned and popular allusions, it confirms our deepest conviction about how people with inscrutable Oriental minds ought to act. It is comforting to know — somewhat like "there will always be an England" — that in India spiritual values are more precious than life itself. And at the same time it makes us feel sad. How can we ever hope to understand people so different from ourselves? Westerners find the idea that there might be a practical explanation for Hindu love of cow more upsetting than Hindus do. The sacred cow — how else can I say it? — is one of our favorite sacred cows.

Hindus venerate cows because cows are the symbol of everything that is alive. As Mary is to Christians the mother of God, the cow to Hindus is the mother of life. So there is no greater sacrilege for a Hindu than killing a cow. Even the taking of human life lacks the symbolic meaning, the unutterable defilement, that is evoked by cow slaughter.

According to many experts, cow worship is the number one cause of India's hunger and poverty. Some Western-trained agronomists say that the taboo against cow slaughter is keeping one hundred million "useless" animals alive. They claim that cow worship lowers the efficiency of agriculture because the useless animals contribute neither milk nor meat while competing for croplands and foodstuff with useful animals and hungry human beings. A study sponsored by the Ford Foundation in 1959 concluded that possibly half of India's cattle could be regarded as surplus in relation to feed supply. And an economist from the University of Pennsylvania stated in 1971 that India has thirty million unproductive cows.

It does seem that there are enormous numbers of surplus, useless, and uneconomic animals, and that this situation is a direct result of irrational Hindu doctrines. Tourists on their way through Delhi, Calcutta, Madras, Bombay, and other Indian cities are astonished at the liberties enjoyed by stray cattle. The animals wander through the streets, browse off the stalls in the market place, break into private gardens, defecate all over the sidewalks, and snarl traffic by pausing to chew their cuds in the middle of busy intersections. In the countryside, the cattle congregate on the shoulders of every highway and spend much of their time taking leisurely walks down the railroad tracks.

Love of cow affects life in many ways. Government agencies maintain old age homes for cows at which owners may board their dry and decrepit animals free of charge. In Madras, the police round up stray cattle that have fallen ill and nurse them back to health by letting them graze on small fields adjacent to the station house. Farmers regard their cows as members of the family, adorn them with garlands and tassels, pray for them when they get sick, and call in their neighbors and a priest to celebrate the birth of a new calf. Throughout India, Hindus hang on their walls calendars that portray beautiful, bejeweled young women who have the bodies of big fat white cows. Milk is shown jetting out of each teat of these half-woman, half-zebu goddesses.

Starting with their beautiful human faces, cow pinups bear little resemblance to the typical cow one sees in the flesh. For most of the year their bones are their most prominent feature. Far from having milk gushing from every teat, the gaunt beasts barely manage to nurse a single calf to maturity. The average yield of whole milk from the typical humpbacked breed of zebu cow in India amounts to less than 500 pounds a year. Ordinary American dairy cattle produce over 5,000 pounds, while for champion milkers, 20,000 pounds is not unusual. But this comparison doesn't tell the whole story. In any given year about half of India's zebu cows give no milk at all — not a drop.

To make matters worse, love of cow does not stimulate love of man. Since Moslems spurn pork but eat beef, many Hindus consider them to be cow killers. Before the partition of the Indian subcontinent into India and Pakistan, bloody communal riots aimed at preventing the Moslems from killing cows became annual occurrences. Memories of old cow riots — as, for example, the one in Bihar in 1917 when thirty people died and 170 Moslem villages were looted down to the last doorpost — continue to embitter relations between India and Pakistan.

Although he deplored the rioting, Mohandas K. Gandhi was an ardent advocate of cow love and wanted a total ban on cow slaughter. When the Indian constitution was drawn up, it included a bill of rights for cows which stopped just short of outlawing every form of cow killing. Some states have since banned cow slaughter altogether, but others still permit exceptions. The cow question remains a major cause of rioting and disorders, not only between Hindus and the remnants of the Moslem community, but between the ruling Congress Party and extremist Hindu factions of cow lovers. On November 7, 1966, a mob of 120,000 people, led by a band of chanting, naked holy men draped with garlands of marigolds and smeared with white cow-dung ash, demonstrated against cow slaughter in front of the Indian House of Parliament. Eight persons were killed and forty-eight injured during the ensuing riot. This was followed by a nationwide wave of fasts among holy men, led by Muni Shustril Kumar, president of the All-Party Cow Protection Campaign Committee.

To Western observers familiar with modern industrial techniques of agriculture and stock raising, cow love seems senseless, even suicidal. The efficiency expert yearns to get his hands on all those useless animals and ship them off to a proper fate. And yet one finds certain inconsistencies in the condemnation of cow love. When I began to wonder if there might be a practical explanation for the sacred cow, I came across an intriguing government report. It said that India had too many cows but too few oxen. With so many cows around, how could there be a shortage of oxen? Oxen and male water buffalo are the principal source of traction for plowing India's fields. For each farm of ten acres or less, one pair of oxen or water buffalo is considered adequate. A little arithmetic shows that as far as plowing is concerned, there is indeed a shortage rather than a surplus of animals. India has 60 million farms, but only 80 million traction animals. If each farm had its quota of two oxen or two water buffalo, there ought to be 120 million traction animals — that is, 40 million more than are actually available.

The shortage may not be quite so bad since some farmers rent or borrow oxen from their neighbors. But the sharing of plow animals often proves impractical. Plowing must be coordinated with the monsoon rains, and by the time one farm has been plowed, the optimum moment for plowing another may already have passed. Also, after plowing is over, a farmer still needs his own pair of oxen to pull his oxcart, the mainstay of bulk transport throughout rural India. Quite possibly private ownership of farms, livestock, plows, and oxcarts lowers the efficiency of Indian agriculture, but this, I soon realized, was not caused by cow love.

The shortage of draft animals is a terrible threat that hangs over most of India's peasant families. When an ox falls sick a poor farmer is in danger of losing his farm. If he has no replacement for it, he will have to borrow money at usurious rates. Millions of rural households have in fact lost all or part of their holdings and have gone into sharecropping or day labor as a result of such debts. Every year hundreds of thousands of destitute farmers end up migrating to the cities, which already teem with unemployed and homeless persons.

The Indian farmer who can't replace his sick or deceased ox is in much the same situation as an American farmer who can neither replace nor repair his broken tractor. But there is an important difference: tractors are made by factories, but oxen are made by cows. A farmer who owns a cow owns a factory for making oxen. With or without cow love, this is a good reason for him not to be too anxious to sell his cow to the slaughterhouse. One also begins to see why Indian farmers might be willing to tolerate cows that give only 500 pounds of milk per year. If the main economic function of the zebu cow is to breed male traction animals, then there's no point in comparing her with specialized American dairy animals, whose main function is to produce milk. Still, the milk produced by zebu cows plays an important role in meeting the nutritional needs of many poor families. Even small amounts of milk products can improve the health of people who are forced to subsist on the edge of starvation.

When Indian farmers want an animal primarily for milking purposes they turn to the female water buffalo, which has longer lactation periods and higher butterfat yields than zebu cattle. Male water buffalo are also superior animals for plowing in flooded rice paddies. But oxen are more versatile and are preferred for dry-field farming and road transport. Above all, zebu breeds are remarkably rugged, and can survive the long droughts that periodically afflict different parts of India.

Agriculture is part of a vast system of human and natural relationships. To judge isolated portions of this "ecosystem" in terms that are relevant to the conduct of American agribusiness leads to some very strange impressions. Cattle figure in the Indian ecosystem in ways that are easily overlooked or demeaned by observers from industrialized, high-energy societies. In the United States, chemicals have almost completely replaced animal manure as the principal source of farm fertilizer. American farmers stopped using manure when they began to plow with tractors rather than mules or horses. Since tractors excrete poisons rather than fertilizers, a commitment to large-scale machine farming is almost of necessity a commitment to the use of chemical fertilizers. And around the world today there has in fact grown up a vast integrated petrochemical-tractor-truck industrial complex that produces farm machinery, motorized transport, oil and gasoline, and chemical fertilizers and pesticides upon which new high-yield production techniques depend.

For better or worse, most of India's farmers cannot participate in this complex, not because they worship their cows, but because they can't afford to buy tractors. Like other underdeveloped nations, India can't build factories that are competitive with the facilities of the industrialized nations nor pay for large quantities of imported industrial products. To convert from animals and manure to tractors and petrochemicals would require the investment of incredible amounts of capital. Moreover, the inevitable effect of substituting costly machines for cheap animals is to reduce the number of people who can earn their living

from agriculture and to force a corresponding increase in the size of the average farm. We know that the development of large-scale agribusiness in the United States has meant the virtual destruction of the small family farm. Less than 5 percent of U.S. families now live on farms, as compared with 60 percent about a hundred years ago. If agribusiness were to develop along similar lines in India, jobs and housing would soon have to be found for a quarter of a billion displaced peasants.

Since the suffering caused by unemployment and homelessness in India's cities is already intolerable, an additional massive build-up of the urban population can only lead to unprecedented upheavals and catastrophes.

With this alternative in view, it becomes easier to understand low-energy, small-scale, animal-based systems. As I have already pointed out, cows and oxen provide low-energy substitutes for tractors and tractor factories. They also should be credited with carrying out the functions of a petrochemical industry. India's cattle annually excrete about 700 million tons of recoverable manure. Approximately half of this total is used as fertilizer, while most of the remainder is burned to provide heat for cooking. The annual quantity of heat liberated by this dung, the Indian housewife's main cooking fuel, is the thermal equivalent of 27 million tons of kerosene, 35 million tons of coal, or 68 million tons of wood. Since India has only small reserves of oil and coal and is already the victim of extensive deforestation, none of these fuels can be considered practical substitutes for cow dung. The thought of dung in the kitchen may not appeal to the average American, but Indian women regard it as a superior cooking fuel because it is finely adjusted to their domestic routines. Most Indian dishes are prepared with clarified butter known as *ghee*, for which cow dung is the preferred source of heat since it burns with a clean, slow, long-lasting flame that doesn't scorch the food. This enables the Indian housewife to start cooking her meals and to leave them unattended for several hours while she takes care of the children, helps out in the fields, or performs other chores. American housewives achieve a similar effect through a complex set of electronic controls that come as expensive options on late-model stoves.

Cow dung has at least one other major function. Mixed with water and made into a paste, it is used as a household flooring material. Smeared over a dirt floor and left to harden into a smooth surface, it keeps the dust down and can be swept clean with a broom.

Because cattle droppings have so many useful properties, every bit of dung is carefully collected. Village small fry are given the task of following the family cow around and of bringing home its daily petrochemical output. In the cities, sweeper castes enjoy a monopoly on the dung deposited by strays and earn their living by selling it to housewives.

From an agribusiness point of view, a dry and barren cow is an economic abomination. But from the viewpoint of the peasant farmer, the same dry and barren cow may be a last desperate defense against the moneylenders. There is always the chance that a favorable monsoon may restore the vigor of even the most decrepit specimen and that she will fatten up, calve, and start giving milk again. This is what the farmer prays for; sometimes his prayers are answered. In the meantime, dung-making goes on. And so one gradually begins to understand why a skinny old hag of a cow still looks beautiful in the eyes of her owner.

Zebu cattle have small bodies, energy-storing humps on their back, and great powers of recuperation. These features are adapted to the specific conditions of Indian agriculture. The native breeds are capable of surviving for long periods with little food or water and are highly resistant to diseases that afflict other breeds in tropical climates. Zebu oxen are worked as long as they continue to breathe. Stuart Odend'hal, a veterinarian formerly associated with Johns Hopkins University, performed field autopsies on Indian cattle which had been working normally a few hours before their deaths but whose vital organs were damaged by massive lesions. Given their enormous recuperative powers, these beasts are never easily written off as completely "useless" while they are still alive.

But sooner or later there must come a time when all hope of an animal's recovery is lost and even dung-making ceases. And still the Hindu farmer refuses to kill it for food or sell it to the slaughterhouse. Isn't this incontrovertible evidence of a harmful economic practice that has no explanation apart from the religious taboos on cow slaughter and beef consumption?

No one can deny that cow love mobilizes people to resist cow slaughter and beef eating. But I don't agree that the anti-slaughter and beef-eating taboos necessarily have an adverse effect on human survival and well-being. By slaughtering or selling his aged and decrepit animals, a farmer might earn a few more rupees or temporarily improve his family's diet. But in the long run, his refusal to sell to the slaughterhouse or kill for his own table may have beneficial consequences. An established principle of ecological analysis states that communities of organisms are adapted not to average but to extreme conditions. The relevant situation in India is the recurrent failure of the monsoon rains. To evaluate the economic significance of the anti-

slaughter and anti-beef-eating taboos, we have to consider what these taboos mean in the context of periodic droughts and famine.

The taboo on slaughter and beef eating may be as much a product of natural selection as the small bodies and fantastic recuperative powers of the zebu breeds. During droughts and famines, farmers are severely tempted to kill or sell their livestock. Those who succumb to this temptation seal their doom, even if they survive the drought, for when the rains come, they will be unable to plow their fields. I want to be even more emphatic: Massive slaughter of cattle under the duress of famine constitutes a much greater threat to aggregate welfare than any likely miscalculation by particular farmers concerning the usefulness of their animals during normal times. It seems probable that the sense of unutterable profanity elicited by cow slaughter has its roots in the excruciating contradiction between immediate needs and long-run conditions of survival. Cow love with its sacred symbols and holy doctrines protects the farmer against calculations that are "rational" only in the short term. To Western experts it looks as if "the Indian farmer would rather starve to death than eat his cow." The same kinds of experts like to talk about the "inscrutable Oriental mind" and think that "life is not so dear to the Asian masses." They don't realize that the farmer would rather eat his cow than starve, but that he will starve if he does eat it.

Even with the assistance of the holy laws and cow love, the temptation to eat beef under the duress of famine sometimes proves irresistible. During World War II, there was a great famine in Bengal caused by droughts and the Japanese occupation of Burma. Slaughter of cows and draft animals reached such alarming levels in the summer of 1944 that the British had to use troops to enforce the cow-protection laws. In 1967 *The New York Times* reported:

> Hindus facing starvation in the drought-stricken area of Bihar are slaughtering cows and eating the meat even though the animals are sacred to the Hindu religion.

Observers noted that "the misery of the people was beyond imagination."

The survival into old age of a certain number of absolutely useless animals during good times is part of the price that must be paid for protecting useful animals against slaughter during bad times. But I wonder how much is actually lost because of the prohibition on slaughter and the taboo on beef. From a Western agribusiness viewpoint, it seems irrational for India not to have a meat-packing industry. But the actual potential for such an industry in a country like India is very limited. A substantial rise in beef production would strain the entire ecosystem, not because of cow love but because of the laws of thermodynamics. In any food chain, the interposition of additional animal links results in a sharp decrease in the efficiency of food production. The caloric value of what an animal has eaten is always much greater than the caloric value of its body. This means that more calories are available per capita when plant food is eaten directly by a human population than when it is used to feed domesticated animals.

Because of the high level of beef consumption in the United States, three-quarters of all our croplands are used for feeding cattle rather than people. Since the per capita calorie intake in India is already below minimum daily requirements, switching croplands to meat production could only result in higher food prices and a further deterioration in the living standards for poor families. I doubt if more than 10 percent of the Indian people will ever be able to make beef an important part of their diet, regardless of whether they believe in cow love or not.

I also doubt that sending more aged and decrepit animals to existing slaughterhouses would result in nutritional gains for the people who need it most. Most of these animals get eaten anyway, even if they aren't sent to the slaughterhouse, because throughout India there are low-ranking castes whose members have the right to dispose of the bodies of dead cattle. In one way or another, twenty million cattle die every year, and a large portion of their meat is eaten by these carrion-eating "untouchables."

My friend Dr. Joan Mencher, an anthropologist who has worked in India for many years, points out that the existing slaughterhouses cater to urban middle-class non-Hindus. She notes that "the untouchables get their food in other ways. It is good for the untouchable if a cow dies of starvation in a village, but not if it gets sent to an urban slaughterhouse to be sold to Muslims or Christians." Dr. Mencher's informants at first denied that any Hindu would eat beef, but when they learned that "upper-caste" Americans liked steak, they readily confessed their taste for beef curry.

Like everything else I have been discussing, meat eating by untouchables is finely adjusted to practical conditions. The meat-eating castes also tend to be the leather-working castes, since they have the right to dispose of the skin of the fallen cattle. So despite cow love, India manages to have a huge leathercraft industry. Even in death, apparently useless animals continue to be exploited for human purposes.

I could be right about cattle being useful for traction, fuel, fertilizer, milk, floor covering, meat, and leather, and still misjudge the ecological and economic significance of the whole complex. Everything depends on how much all of this costs in natural resources and human labor relative to alternative modes of satisfying the needs of India's huge population. These costs are determined largely by what the cattle eat. Many experts assume that man and cow are locked in a deadly competition for land and food crops. This might be true if Indian farmers followed the American agribusiness model and fed their animals on food crops. But the shameless truth about the sacred cow is that she is an indefatigable scavenger. Only an insignificant portion of the food consumed by the average cow comes from pastures and food crops set aside for their use.

This ought to have been obvious from all those persistent reports about cows wandering about and snarling traffic. What are those animals doing in the markets, on the lawns, along the highways and railroad tracks, and up on the barren hillsides? What are they doing if not eating every morsel of grass, stubble, and garbage that cannot be directly consumed by human beings and converting it into milk and other useful products! In his study of cattle in West Bengal, Dr. Odend'hal discovered that the major constituent in the cattle's diet is inedible by-products of human food crops, principally rice straw, wheat bran, and rice husks. When the Ford Foundation estimated that half of the cattle were surplus in relation to feed supply, they meant to say that half of the cattle manage to survive even without access to fodder crops. But this is an understatement. Probably less than 20 percent of what the cattle eat consists of humanly edible substances; most of this is fed to working oxen and water buffalo rather than to dry and barren cows. Odend'hal found that in his study area there was no competition between cattle and humans for land or the food supply: "Basically, the cattle convert items of little direct human value into products of immediate utility."

One reason why cow love is so often misunderstood is that it has different implications for the rich and the poor. Poor farmers use it as a license to scavenge while the wealthy farmers resist it as a rip-off. To the poor farmer, the cow is a holy beggar; to the rich farmer, it's a thief. Occasionally the cows invade someone's pastures or planted fields. The landlords complain, but the poor peasants plead ignorance and depend on cow love to get their animals back. If there is competition, it is between man and man or caste and caste, not between man and beast.

City cows also have owners who let them scrounge by day and call them back at night to be milked. Dr. Mencher recounts that while she lived for a while in a middle-class neighborhood in Madras her neighbors were constantly complaining about "stray" cows breaking into the family compounds. The strays were actually owned by people who lived in a room above a shop and who sold milk door to door in the neighborhood. As for the old age homes and police compounds, they serve very nicely to reduce the risk of maintaining cows in a city environment. If a cow stops producing milk, the owner may decide to let it wander around until the police pick it up and bring it to the precinct house. When the cow has recovered, the owner pays a small fine and returns it to its usual haunts. The old age homes operate on a similar principle, providing cheap government-subsidized pasture that would otherwise not be available to city cows.

Incidentally, the preferred form of purchasing milk in the cities is to have the cow brought to the house and milked on the spot. This is often the only way that the householder can be sure that he is buying pure milk rather than milk mixed with water or urine.

What seems most incredible about these arrangements is that they have been interpreted as evidence of wasteful anti-economic Hindu practices, while in fact they reflect a degree of economizing that goes far beyond Western, Protestant standards of savings and husbandry. Cow love is perfectly compatible with a merciless determination to get the literal last drop of milk out of the cow. The man who takes the cow door to door brings along a dummy calf made out of stuffed calfskin which he sets down beside the cow to trick it into performing. When this doesn't work, the owner may resort to *phooka*, blowing air into the cow's uterus through a hollow pipe, or *doom dev*, stuffing its tail into the vaginal orifice. Gandhi believed that cows were treated more cruelly in India than anywhere else in the world. "How we bleed her to take the last drop of milk from her," he lamented. "How we starve her to emaciation, how we ill-treat the calves, how we deprive them of their portion of milk, how cruelly we treat the oxen, how we castrate them, how we beat them, how we overload them."

No one understood better than Gandhi that cow love had different implications for rich and poor. For him the cow was a central focus of the struggle to rouse India to authentic nationhood. Cow love went along with small-scale farming, making cotton thread on a hand spinning wheel, sitting cross-legged on the floor, dressing in a loincloth, vegetarianism, reverence for life, and strict nonviolence. To these themes Gandhi owed

his vast popular following among the peasant masses, urban poor, and untouchables. It was his way of protecting them against the ravages of industrialization.

The asymmetrical implications of *ahimsa* for rich and poor are ignored by economists who want to make Indian agriculture more efficient by slaughtering "surplus" animals. Professor Alan Heston, for example, accepts the fact that the cattle perform vital functions for which substitutes are not readily available. But he proposes that the same functions could be carried out more efficiently if there were 30 million fewer cows. This figure is based on the assumption that with adequate care only 40 cows per 100 male animals would be needed to replace the present number of oxen. Since there are 72 million adult male cattle, by this formula, 24 million breeding females ought to be sufficient. Actually, there are 54 million cows. Subtracting 24 million from 54 million, Heston arrives at the estimate of 30 million "useless" animals to be slaughtered. The fodder and feed that these "useless" animals have been consuming are to be distributed among the remaining animals, who will become healthier and therefore will be able to keep total milk and dung production at or above previous levels. But whose cows are to be sacrificed? About 43 percent of the total cattle population is found on the poorest 62 percent of the farms. These farms, consisting of five acres or less, have only 5 percent of the pasture and grazing land. In other words, most of the animals that are temporarily dry, barren, and feeble are owned by the people who live on the smallest and poorest farms. So that when the economists talk about getting rid of 30 million cows, they are really talking about getting rid of 30 million cows that belong to poor families, not rich ones. But most poor families own only one cow, so what this economizing boils down to is not so much getting rid of 30 million cows as getting rid of 150 million people — forcing them off the land and into the cities.

Cow-slaughter enthusiasts base their recommendation on an understandable error. They reason that since the farmers refuse to kill their animals, and since there is a religious taboo against doing so, therefore it is the taboo that is mainly responsible for the high ratio of cows to oxen. Their error is hidden in the observed ratio itself: 70 cows to 100 oxen. If cow love prevents farmers from killing cows that are economically useless, how is it there are 30 percent fewer cows than oxen? Since approximately as many female as male animals are born, something must be causing the death of more females than males. The solution to this puzzle is that while no Hindu farmer deliberately slaughters a female calf or decrepit cow with a club or a knife, he can and does get rid of them when they become truly useless from his point of view. Various methods short of direct slaughter are employed. To "kill" unwanted calves, for example, a triangular wooden yoke is placed about their necks so that when they try to nurse they jab the cow's udder and get kicked to death. Older animals are simply tethered on short ropes and allowed to starve — a process that does not take too long if the animal is already weak and diseased. Finally, unknown numbers of decrepit cows are surreptitiously sold through a chain of Moslem and Christian middlemen and end up in the urban slaughterhouses.

If we want to account for the observed proportions of cows to oxen, we must study rain, wind, water, and land-tenure patterns, not cow love. The proof of this is that the proportion of cows to oxen varies with the relative importance of different components of the agricultural system in different regions of India. The most important variable is the amount of irrigation water available for the cultivation of rice. Wherever there are extensive wet rice paddies, the water buffalo tends to be the preferred traction animal, and the female water buffalo is then substituted for the zebu cow as a source of milk. That is why in the vast plains of northern India, where the melting Himalayan snows and monsoons create the Holy River Ganges, the proportion of cows to oxen drops down to 47 to 100. As the distinguished Indian economist K.N. Raj has pointed out, districts in the Ganges Valley where continuous year-round rice-paddy cultivation is practiced have cow-to-oxen ratios that approach the theoretical optimum. This is all the more remarkable since the region in question — the Gangetic plain — is the heartland of the Hindu religion and contains its most holy shrines.

The theory that religion is primarily responsible for the high proportion of cows to oxen is also refuted by a comparison between Hindu India and Moslem West Pakistan. Despite the rejection of cow love and the beef-slaughter and beef-eating taboos, West Pakistan as a whole has 60 cows for every 100 male animals, which is considerably higher than the average for the intensely Hindu Indian state of Uttar Pradesh. When districts in Uttar Pradesh are selected for the importance of water buffalo and canal irrigation and compared with ecologically similar districts in West Pakistan, ratios of female to male cattle turn out to be virtually the same.

Do I mean to say that cow love has no effect whatsoever on the cattle sex ratio or on other aspects of the agricultural system? No. What I am saying is that cow love is an active element in a complex, finely articulated material and cultural order. Cow love mobilizes the latent capacity of human beings to persevere in a low-energy ecosystem in which there is little room for waste or indolence. Cow love contributes to the adaptive resilience of the human population by preserving temporarily dry or barren but still useful animals; by discouraging the growth of an energy-expensive beef industry; by protecting cattle that fatten in the public domain or at landlord's expense; and by preserving the recovery potential of the cattle population during droughts and famines. As in any natural or artificial system, there is some slippage, friction, or waste associated with these complex interactions. Half a billion people, animals, land, labor, political economy, soil, and climate, are all involved. The slaughter enthusiasts claim that the practice of letting cows breed indiscriminately and then thinning their numbers through neglect and starvation is wasteful and inefficient. I do not doubt that this is correct, but only in a narrow and relatively insignificant sense. The savings that an agricultural engineer might achieve by getting rid of an unknown number of absolutely useless animals must be balanced against catastrophic losses for the marginal peasants, especially during droughts and famines, if cow love ceases to be a holy duty.

Since the effective mobilization of all human action depends upon the acceptance of psychologically compelling creeds and doctrines, we have to expect that economic systems will always oscillate under and over their points of optimum efficiency. But the assumption that the whole system can be made to work better simply by attacking its consciousness is naïve and dangerous. Major improvements in the present system can be achieved by stabilizing India's human population, and by making more land, water, oxen, and water buffalo available to more people on a more equitable basis. The alternative is to destroy the present system and replace it with a completely new set of demographic, technological, politico-economic, and ideological relationships — a whole new ecosystem. Hinduism is undoubtedly a conservative force, one that makes it more difficult for the "development" experts and "modernizing" agents to destroy the old system and to replace it with a high-energy industrial and agribusiness complex. But if you think that a high-energy industrial and agribusiness complex will necessarily be more "rational" or "efficient" than the system that now exists, forget it.

Contrary to expectations, studies of energy costs and energy yields show that India makes more efficient use of cattle than the United States does. In Singur district in West Bengal, Dr. Odend'hal discovered that the cattle's gross energetic efficiency, defined as the total of useful calories produced per year divided by the total calories consumed during the same period, was 17 percent. This compares with a gross energetic efficiency of less than 4 percent for American beef cattle raised on Western range land. As Odend'hal says, the relatively high efficiency of the Indian cattle complex comes about not because the animals are particularly productive, but because of scrupulous product utilization by humans: "The villagers are extremely utilitarian and nothing is wasted."

Wastefulness is more a characteristic of modern agribusiness than of traditional peasant economies. Under the new system of automated feed-lot beef production in the United States, for example, cattle manure not only goes unused, but it is allowed to contaminate ground water over wide areas and contributes to the pollution of nearby lakes and streams.

The higher standard of living enjoyed by the industrial nations is not the result of greater productive efficiency, but of an enormously expanded increase in the amount of energy available per person. In 1970 the United States used up the energy equivalent of twelve tons of coal per inhabitant, while the corresponding figure for India was one-fifth ton per inhabitant. The way this energy was expended involved far more energy being wasted per person in the United States than in India. Automobiles and airplanes are faster than oxcarts, but they do not use energy more efficiently. In fact, more calories go up in useless heat and smoke during a single day of traffic jams in the United States than is wasted by all the cows of India during an entire year. The comparison is even less favorable when we consider the fact that the stalled vehicles are burning up irreplaceable reserves of petroleum that it took the earth tens of millions of years to accumulate. If you want to see a real sacred cow, go out and look at the family car.

PART 2C

SOCIAL STRUCTURE

Perhaps the best way to gain an appreciation of the importance of social structure is to observe how people live without it. The Ik tribe are about as close as one can get to that state of affairs. Until the 1930s, the Ik were a nomadic people who hunted and gathered food as they roamed throughout Uganda, Kenya, and Sudan. Before World War II, however, they were encouraged by the British colonial authorities to settle permanently in the mountainous northeast corner of Uganda. Once the Ik were settled, the authorities turned their major hunting territory into a national park. Hunting and gathering were forbidden. By the time American anthropologist Colin Turnbull spent nearly two years studying the Ik in the 1960s, drought had nearly finished them off. They were not just starving. Most of their social structures — involving family organization, economic co-operation, political institutions, and more — had been destroyed as they engaged in a highly individualized fight for survival. Children were cast out of their homes at the age of three or four; the elderly were abandoned and beaten; the best of "human nature" was jettisoned. The Ik, writes Turnbull, "were as unfriendly, uncharitable, inhospitable and generally mean as any people can be." One may conclude that there is no "human nature," or at least that human nature is so plastic that, under certain conditions, almost anyone can behave "inhumanly." We learn from Turnbull's discussion of the Ik in Chapter 8 that there can be little love, co-operation, and human decency without social structure.

Turnbull believes that people living in the rich industrialized countries are in danger of losing some of their humanity too because "family, economy, government and religion, the basic categories of social activity and behaviour, no longer create any sense of social unity involving a shared and mutual responsibility among all members of our society." But I think Turnbull exaggerates. He underestimates both the degree to which preindustrial societies were torn by conflict and discord, and the degree to which human community exists today in countries like Canada.

Turnbull's mistake rests partly on his failure to see the new forms of social structure that are emerging to replace the old. In Chapter 9, Barry Wellman of the University of Toronto and his colleagues analyze one such new structure: the "personal community." (See also Benjamin Barber's analysis of new political structures in Chapter 21.) A **traditional community** is a group of people who live in households that are situated close to each other and who engage in frequent, face-to-face, mutually supportive interaction. In contrast, **formal organizations** (also known as *secondary associations*) are large, impersonal, bureaucratic associations that exist for specific and clearly defined economic or political purposes. Before the 1970s, many urban sociologists debated the degree to which communities were being saved or lost as more and more individuals moved to big cities and found their lives shaped by faceless bureaucracies and anonymous factories. More recently, sociologists have asked whether a new, "liberated" form of community is emerging, in which fast and inexpensive transportation and communication allow people to become members of many geographically dispersed associations based on shared interest. For example, the Internet has encouraged the creation of thousands of "virtual communities." Each such community is an association of people, scattered across the country, continent, or planet, who communicate by means of computer and modem about a subject of common interest.

Wellman and his colleagues treat saved, lost, and liberated communities as community forms that may co-exist to varying degrees. Their survey data from East York (a Toronto borough) show that each individual sits at the centre of a **personal community** (see Figure 2C.1). The personal community is a **network**, a set of social ties linking people. Material and emotional resources flow through the ties. The individual's personal community connects him or her to densely knit groups (saved communities), formal organizations (lost communities), and specialized, geographically dispersed, informal groups (liberated communities). The relative importance of the three types of community for any particular individual depends on where he or she is located in the class structure — whether the individual is unemployed, a homemaker, middle-class, working-class, etc. But regardless of the individual's economic location, two things are apparent. First, a new social structure, a complex network of social relations, has replaced the traditional community. Second, the new social structure is not

Figure 2C.1 The Personal Community of a Typical Urban North American

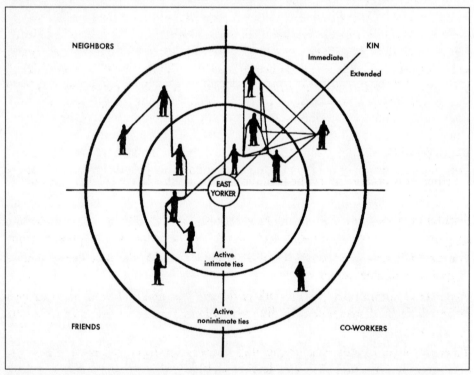

Note: Each person portrayed in Figure 2C.1 is regarded by the individual in the centre as a significant person in his or her life. The individual in the centre is aware of the social ties linking many network members to one another (indicated by lines joining individuals in the network). The individual is also aware of a tightly knit cluster of kin, three of whom he or she thinks of as intimates, and less dense ties among six friends and neighbours. One close work mate is an isolate, connected only to the individual in the centre. This reflects the fact that the individual in the centre separates employed and social life, and uses interpersonal ties to deal with domestic concerns and not problems of earning a living.

Source: Barry Wellman, "Structural Analysis: From Method and Metaphor to Theory and Substance," in Barry Wellman and S.D. Berkowitz, eds., *Social Structures: A Network Approach* (Cambridge, UK: Cambridge University Press, 1988), pp. 27–28. © Cambridge University Press 1988. Reprinted with permission of Cambridge University Press.

as visible as traditional communities and formal organizations, which, after all, have names and addresses (e.g., Drumheller, Alberta; the Bank of Montreal). But initial appearances notwithstanding, social structures still govern urban life.

I do not use the term "govern" lightly. Social structures, it will be recalled, are not just created by people, they also regulate and constrain people's attitudes and behaviour. That is the main lesson one can learn from Chapter 10. In it, I analyze two important Canadian **social movements**, collective attempts by farmers and workers to challenge authority and improve the social conditions of their existence by forming new political parties and unions, and staging demonstrations and strikes.

Common sense suggests that social movements are most likely to emerge when and where people suffer most from low wages, poor working conditions, unemployment, and the like. The facts do not, however, support the common-sense view. The most deprived members of society rarely protest, and it is only under certain *social-structural* conditions that disadvantaged groups are able to turn their frustrations into action. Specifically, the capacity to protest is shaped by shifts in the distribution of power in society. **Power** is the probability of achieving one's aim even against opposition. The power of a group is a function of its size, level of social organization, and access to resources. As the history of Canadian social movements shows, disadvantaged groups are more likely to protest their lot in life and form social movements when they become more powerful due to the effects of industrialization, urbanization, the commercialization of agriculture, and the **business cycle** (the periodic rise and decline in the volume of economic activity). To be sure, successful social movements also require recruits who are frustrated with the status quo, competent leaders, and a **protest ideology**, a set of ideas that criticizes the existing social order, outlines a better social order, and explains how movement members can get from here to there. But even a compelling and skilfully articulated ideology will fail to mobilize potential recruits if the movement lacks enough power to sustain the struggle against its adversaries.

GLOSSARY

The **business cycle** refers to the periodic rise and decline in the volume of economic activity.

Formal organizations (also known as **secondary associations**) are large, impersonal, bureaucratic associations that exist for clearly defined economic or political purposes.

A **network** is a bounded set of individuals who are linked by the exchange of material and/or emotional resources.

A **personal community** is a network of densely knit groups, formal organizations, and specialized, geographically dispersed, informal groups to which an individual is attached.

Power is the probability of achieving one's aim even against opposition. The power of a group is a function of its size, level of social organization, and access to normative, material, and coercive resources.

A **protest ideology** is a set of ideas that criticizes the existing social order, outlines a better social order, and explains how social movement members can get from here to there.

Social movements are collective attempts to challenge authority and improve the social conditions of movement members.

A **traditional community** is a group of people who live in households that are situated close to one another and who engage in frequent, face-to-face, mutually supportive interaction.

Chapter 8

THE MOUNTAIN PEOPLE

COLIN TURNBULL

Atum ["the senior of all the Ik on Morungole"] was waiting for me. He said that he had told all the Ik that Iciebam [friend of the Ik] had arrived to live with them and that I had given the workers a "holiday" so they could greet me. They were waiting in the villages. They were very hungry, he added, and many were dying. That was probably one of the few true statements he ever made, and I never even considered believing it....

After [touring the Ik villages] Atum said we should start back and called over his shoulder to his village. A muffled sound came from within, and he said, "That's my wife, she is very sick — and hungry." I offered to go and see her, but he shook his head. Back at the Land Rover I gave Atum some food and some aspirin, not knowing what else to give him to help his wife....

While the Ik were working, their heads kept turning as though they were expecting something to happen. Every now and again one would stand up and peer into the distance and then take off into the bush for an hour or so. On one such occasion, after the person had been gone two hours, the others started drifting off. By then I knew them better; I looked for a wisp of smoke and followed it to where the road team was cooking a goat. Smoke was a giveaway, though, so they economized on cooking and ate most food nearly raw. It is a curious hangover from what must once have been a moral code that Ik will offer food if surprised in the act of eating, though they now go to enormous pains not to be so surprised.

I was always up before dawn, but by the time I got up to the villages they were always deserted. One morning I followed the little oror [gully] up from *oror a pirre'i* [Ravine of Pirre] while it was still quite dark

and I met Lomeja on his way down. He took me on my first illicit hunt in Kidepo. He told me that if he got anything he would share it with me and with anyone else who managed to join us but that he certainly would not take anything back to his family. "Each one of them is out seeing what he can get for himself, and do you think they will bring any back for me?"

Lomeja was one of the very few Ik who seemed glad to volunteer information. Unlike many of the others, he did not get up and leave as I approached. Apart from him, I spent most of my time, those days, with Losike the potter. She told me that Nangoli, the old lady in the adjoining compound, and her husband, Amuarkuar, were rather peculiar. They helped each other get food and water, and they brought it back to their compound to eat together.

I still do not know how much real hunger there was at that time, for most of the younger people seemed fairly well fed, and the few skinny old people seemed healthy and active. But my laboriously extracted genealogies showed that there were quite a number of old people still alive and allegedly in these villages, though they were never to be seen. Then Atum's wife died.

Atum told me nothing about it but kept up his demands for food and medicine. After a while the beady-eyed Lomongin told me that Atum was selling the medicine I was giving him for his wife. I was not unduly surprised and merely remarked that that was too bad for his wife. "Oh no," said Lomongin, "she has been dead for weeks." ...

Kauar [one of the Ik workers] always played and joked with the children when they came back from

Source: "The Mountain People," in Kurt Finsterbusch and Janet S. Schwartz, eds., *Sources: Notable Selections in Sociology* (Guilford, CT: The Dushkin Group, 1993), pp. 26–35, an edited version of material originally published in Colin M. Turnbull, *The Mountain People* (New York: Simon & Schuster, 1972). Copyright © by Colin M. Turnbull. Reprinted by permission of Simon & Schuster, Inc.

foraging. He used to volunteer to make the two-day walk into Kaabong and the even more tiring two-day climb back to get mail for me or to buy a few things for others. He always asked if he had made the trip more quickly than the last time.

Then one day Kauar went to Kaabong and did not come back. He was found on the last peak of the trail, cold and dead. Those who found him took the things he had been carrying and pushed his body into the bush. I still see his open, laughing face, see him giving precious tidbits to the children, comforting some child who was crying, and watching me read the letters he carried so lovingly for me. And I still think of him probably running up that viciously steep mountainside so he could break his time record and falling dead in his pathetic prime because he was starving....

Anyone falling down was good for a laugh, but I never saw anyone actually trip anyone else. The adults were content to let things happen and then enjoy them; it was probably conservation of energy. The children, however, sought their pleasures with vigor. The best game of all, at this time, was teasing poor little Adupa. She was not so little — in fact she should have been an adult, for she was nearly 13 years old — but Adupa was a little mad. Or you might say she was the only sane one, depending on your point of view. Adupa did not jump on other people's play houses, and she lavished enormous care on hers and would curl up inside it. That made it all the more jump-on-able. The other children beat her viciously.

Children are not allowed to sleep in the house after they are "put out," which is at about three years old, four at the latest. From then on they sleep in the open courtyard, taking what shelter they can against the stockade. They may ask for permission to sit in the doorway of their parents' house but may not lie down or sleep there. "The same thing applies to old people," said Atum, "if they can't build a house of their own and, of course, *if* their children let them stay in their compounds."

I saw a few old people, most of whom had taken over abandoned huts. For the first time I realized that there really was starvation and saw why I had never known it before: it was confined to the aged. Down in Giriko's village the old ritual priest, Lolim, confidentially told me that he was sheltering an old man who had been refused shelter by his son. But Lolim did not have enough food for himself, let alone his guest; could I ... I liked old Lolim, so, not believing that Lolim had a visitor at all, I brought him a double ration that evening. There was a rustling in the back of the hut, and Lolim helped ancient Lomerani-

ang to the entrance. They shook with delight at the sight of the food.

When the two old men had finished eating, I left; I found a hungry-looking and disapproving little crowd clustered outside. They muttered to each other about wasting food. From then on I brought food daily, but in a very short time Lomeraniang was dead, and his son refused to come down from the village above to bury him. Lolim scratched a hole and covered the body with a pile of stones he carried himself, one by one.

Hunger was indeed more severe than I knew, and, after the old people, the children were the next to go. It was all quite impersonal — even to me, in most cases, since I had been immunized by the Ik themselves against sorrow on their behalf. But Adupa was an exception. Her madness was such that she did not know just how vicious humans could be. Even worse, she thought that parents were for loving, for giving as well as receiving. Her parents were not given to fantasies. When she came for shelter, they drove her out; and when she came because she was hungry, they laughed the Icien laugh, as if she had made them happy.

Adupa's reactions became slower and slower. When she managed to find food — fruit peels, skins, bits of bone, half-eaten berries — she held it in her hand and looked at it with wonder and delight. Her playmates caught on quickly; they put tidbits in her way and watched her simple drawn little face wrinkle in a smile. Then as she raised her hand to her mouth, they set on her with cries of excitement, fun and laughter, beating her savagely over the head. But that is not how she died. I took to feeding her, which is probably the cruelest thing I could have done, a gross selfishness on my part to try to salve my own rapidly disappearing conscience. I had to protect her, physically, as I fed her. But the others would beat her anyway, and Adupa cried, not because of the pain in her body but because of the pain she felt at the great, vast, empty wasteland where love should have been.

It was *that* that killed her. She demanded that her parents love her. Finally they took her in, and Adupa was happy and stopped crying. She stopped crying forever because her parents went away and closed the door tight behind them, so tight that weak little Adupa could never have moved it.

The Ik seem to tell us that the family is not such a fundamental unit as we usually suppose, that it is not essential to social life. In the crisis of survival facing the Ik, the family was one of the first institutions to go, and the Ik as a society have survived.

The other quality of life that we hold to be necessary for survival — love — the Ik dismiss as idiotic and highly dangerous. But we need to see more of the Ik before their absolute lovelessness becomes truly apparent.

In this curious society there is one common value to which all Ik hold tenaciously. It is *ngag*, "food." That is the one standard by which they measure right and wrong, goodness and badness. The very word for "good" is defined in terms of food. "Goodness" is "the possession of food," or the "*individual* possession of food." If you try to discover their concept of a "good man," you get the truly Icien answer: one who has a full stomach.

We should not be surprised, then, when the mother throws her child out at three years old. At that age a series of *rites de passage* begins. In this environment a child has no chance of survival on his own until he is about 13, so children form age bands. The junior band consists of children between three and seven, the senior of eight- to twelve-year-olds. Within the band each child seeks another close to him in age for defense against the older children. These friendships are temporary, however, and inevitably there comes a time when each turns on the one that up to then had been the closest to him; that is the *rite de passage*, the destruction of that fragile bond called friendship. When this has happened three or four times, the child is ready for the world.

The weakest are soon thinned out, and the strongest survive to achieve leadership of the band. Such a leader is eventually driven out, turned against by his fellow band members. Then the process starts all over again; he joins the senior age band as its most junior member.

The final *rite de passage* is into adulthood, at the age of 12 or 13. By then the candidate has learned the wisdom of acting on his own, for his own good, while acknowledging that on occasion it is profitable to associate temporarily with others....

There seemed to be increasingly little among the Ik that could by any stretch of the imagination be called social life, let alone social organization. The family does not hold itself together; economic interest is centered on as many stomachs as there are people; and co-operation is merely a device for furthering an interest that is consciously selfish. We often do the same thing in our so-called "altruistic" practices, but we tell ourselves it is for the good of others. The Ik have dispensed with the myth of altruism. Though they have no centralized leadership or means of physical coercion, they do hold together with remarkable tenacity.

In our world, where the family has also lost much of its value as a social unit and where religious belief no longer binds us into communities, we maintain order only through coercive power that is ready to uphold a rigid law and through an equally rigid penal system. The Ik, however, have learned to do without coercion, either spiritual or physical. It seems that they have come to a recognition of what they accept as man's basic selfishness, of his natural determination to survive as an individual before all else. This they consider to be man's basic right, and they allow others to pursue that right without recrimination....

[The oldest and greatest Icien ritual priest] Lolim became ill and had to be protected while eating the food I gave him. Then the children began openly ridiculing him and teasing him, dancing in front of him and kneeling down so that he would trip over them. His grandson used to creep up behind him and with a pair of hard sticks drum a lively tattoo on the old man's bald head.

I fed him whenever I could, but often he did not want more than a bite. Once I found him rolled up in his protective ball crying. He had had nothing to eat for four days and no water for two. He had asked his children, who all told him not to come near them.

The next day I saw him leaving Atum's village, where his son Longoli lived. Longoli swore that he had been giving his father food and was looking after him. Lolim was not shuffling away; it was almost a run, the run of a drunken man, staggering from side to side. I called to him, but he made no reply, just a kind of long, continuous and horrible moan. He had been to Longoli to beg him to let him into his compound because he knew he was going to die in a few hours, Longoli calmly told me afterward. Obviously Longoli could not do a thing like that: a man of Lolim's importance would have called for an enormous funeral feast. So he refused. Lolim begged Longoli then to open up Nangoli's *asak* for him so that he could die in *her* compound. But Longoli drove him out, and he died alone....

If there was such a thing as an Icien morality, I had not yet perceived it, though traces of a moral past remained. But it still remained a possibility, as did the existence of an unspoken, unmanifest belief that might yet reveal itself and provide a basis for the reintegration of society. I was somewhat encouraged in this hope by the unexpected flight of old Nangoli, widow of Amuarkuar.

When Nangoli returned and found her husband dead, she did an odd thing: she grieved. She tore down what was left of their home, uprooted the stockade, tore up whatever was growing in her little field. Then she fled with a few belongings.

Some weeks later I heard that she and her children had gone over to the Sudan and built a village there. This migration was so unusual that I decided to see whether this runaway village was different.

Lojieri led the way, and Atum came along. One long day's trek got us there. Lojieri pulled part of the brush fence aside, and we went in and wandered around. He and Atum looked inside all the huts, and Lojieri helped himself to tobacco from one and water from another. Surprises were coming thick and fast. That households should be left open and untended with such wealth inside ... That there should have been such wealth, for as well as tobacco and jars of water there were baskets of food, and meat was drying on racks. There were half a dozen or so compounds, but they were separated from each other only by a short line of sticks and brush. It was a village, and these were homes, the first and last I was to see.

The dusk had already fallen, and Nangoli came in with her children and grandchildren. They had heard us and came in with warm welcomes. There was no hunger here, and in a very short time each kitchen hearth had a pot of food cooking. Then we sat around the central fire and talked until late, and it was another universe.

There was no talk of "how much better it is here than there"; talk revolved around what had happened on the hunt that day. Loron was lying on the ground in front of the fire as his mother made gentle fun of him. His wife, Kinimei, whom I had never seen even speak to him at Pirre, put a bowl of fresh-cooked berries and fruit in front of him. It was all like a nightmare rather than a fantasy, for it made the reality of Pirre seem all the more frightening....

[Back at Pirre, the days of drought wore on into weeks and months and, like everyone else, I became rather bored with sickness and death. I survived rather as did the young adults, by diligent attention to my own needs while ignoring those of others.

More and more it was only the young who could go far from the village as hunger became starvation. Famine relief had been initiated down at Kasile, and those fit enough to make the trip set off. When they came back, the contrast between them and the others was that between life and death. Villages were villages of the dead and dying, and there was little difference between the two. People crawled rather than walked. After a few feet some would lie down to rest, but they could not be sure of ever being able to sit up again, so they mostly stayed upright until they reached their destination. They were going nowhere, these semi-animate bags of skin and bone; they just wanted to be

with others, and they stopped whenever they met. Perhaps it was the most important demonstration of sociality I ever saw among the Ik. Once they met, they neither spoke nor did anything together.

Early one morning, before dawn, the village moved. In the midst of a hive of activity were the aged and crippled, soon to be abandoned, in danger of being trampled but seemingly unaware of it. Lolim's widow, Lo'ono, whom I had never seen before, also had been abandoned and had tried to make her way down the mountainside. But she was totally blind and had tripped and rolled to the bottom of the *oror a pirre'i*; there she lay on her back, her legs and arms thrashing feebly, while a little crowd laughed.

At this time a colleague was with me. He kept the others away while I ran to get medicine and food and water, for Lo'ono was obviously near dead from hunger and thirst as well as from the fall. We treated her and fed her and asked her to come back with us. But she asked us to point her in the direction of her son's new village. I said I did not think she would get much of a welcome there, and she replied that she knew it but wanted to be near him when she died. So we gave her more food, put her stick in her hand and pointed her the right way. She suddenly cried. She was crying, she said, because we had reminded her that there had been a time when people had helped each other, when people had been kind and good. Still crying, she set off.

The Ik up to this point had been tolerant of my activities, but all this was too much. They said that what we were doing was wrong. Food and medicine were for the living, not the dead. I thought of Lo'ono. And I thought of other old people who had joined in the merriment when they had been teased or had a precious morsel of food taken from their mouths. They knew that it was silly of them to expect to go on living, and, having watched others, they knew that the spectacle really was quite funny. So they joined in the laughter. Perhaps if we had left Lo'ono, she would have died laughing. But we prolonged her misery for no more than a few brief days. Even worse, we reminded her of when things had been different, of days when children had cared for parents and parents for children. She was already dead, and we made her unhappy as well. At the time I was sure we were right, doing the only "human" thing. In a way we were — we were making life more comfortable for ourselves. But now I wonder if the Ik way was not right, if I too should not have laughed as Lo'ono flapped about, then left her to die....

And now that all the old are dead, what is left? Every Ik who is old today was thrown out at three and has survived, and in consequence has thrown his own children out and knows that they will not help him in his old age any more than he helped his parents. The system has turned one full cycle and is now self-perpetuating; it has eradicated what we know as "humanity" and has turned the world into a chilly void where man does not seem to care even for himself, but survives. Yet into this hideous world Nangoli and her family quietly returned because they could not bear to be alone.

For the moment abandoning the very old and the very young, the Ik as a whole must be searched for one last lingering trace of humanity. They appear to have disposed of virtually all the qualities that we normally think of as differentiating us from other primates, yet they survive without seeming to be greatly different from ourselves in terms of behavior. Their behavior is more extreme, for we do not start throwing our children out until kindergarten. We have shifted responsibility from family to state, the Ik have shifted it to the individual.

It has been claimed that human beings are capable of love and, indeed, are dependent upon it for survival and sanity. The Ik offer us an opportunity for testing this cherished notion that love is essential to survival. If it is, the Ik should have it.

Love in human relationships implies mutuality, a willingness to sacrifice the self that springs from a consciousness of identity. This seems to bring us back to the Ik, for it implies that love is self-oriented, that even the supreme sacrifice of one's life is no more than selfishness, for the victim feels amply rewarded by the pleasure he feels in making the sacrifice. The Ik, however, do not value emotion above survival, and they are without love....

When the rains failed for the second year running, I knew that the Ik as a society were almost certainly finished and that the monster they had created in its place, that passionless, feelingless association of individuals, would spread like a fungus, contaminating all it touched. When I left, I too had been contaminated....

I departed with a kind of forced gaiety, feeling that I should be glad to be gone but having forgotten how to be glad. I certainly was not thinking of returning within a year, but I did. The following spring I heard that rain had come at last and that the fields of the Ik had never looked so prosperous, nor the country so green and fertile. A few months away had refreshed me, and I wondered if my conclusions had not been excessively pessimistic. So early that summer, I set off to be present for the first harvests in three years.

I was not surprised too much when two days after my arrival and installation at the police post I found

Logwara, the blind man, lying on the roadside bleeding, while a hundred yards up other Ik were squabbling over the body of a hyena. Logwara had tried to get there ahead of the others to grab the meat and had been trampled on.

First I looked at the villages. The lush outer covering concealed an inner decay. All the villages were like this to some extent, except for Lokelea's. There the tomatoes and pumpkins were so carefully pruned and cleaned, so that the fruits were larger and healthier. In what had been my own compound the shade trees had been cut down for firewood, and the lovely hanging nests of the weaver birds were gone.

The fields were even more desolate. Every field without exception had yielded in abundance, and it was a new sensation to have vision cut off by thick crops. But every crop was rotting from sheer neglect.

The Ik said that they had no need to bother guarding the fields. There was so much food they could never eat it all, so why not let the birds and baboons take some? The Ik had full bellies; they were good. The *di* at Atum's village was much the same as usual, people sitting or lying about. People were still stealing from each other's fields, and nobody thought of saving for the future.

It was obvious that nothing had really changed due to the sudden glut of food except that interpersonal relationships had deteriorated still further and that Icien individualism had heightened beyond what I thought even Ik to be capable of.

The Ik had faced a conscious choice between being humans and being parasites and had chosen the latter. When they saw their fields come alive, they were confronted with a problem. If they reaped the harvest, they would have to store grain for eating and planting, and every Ik knew that trying to store anything was a waste of time. Further, if they made their fields look too promising, the government would stop famine relief. So the Ik let their fields rot and continued to draw famine relief.

The Ik were not starving any longer; the old and infirm had all died the previous year, and the younger survivors were doing quite well. But the famine relief was administered in a way that was little short of criminal. As before, only the young and well were able to get down from Pirre to collect the relief; they were given relief for those who could not come and told to take it back. But they never did — they ate it themselves.

The Ik teach us that our much vaunted human values are not inherent in humanity at all but are associated only with a particular form of survival called society and that all, even society itself, are luxuries that can be dispensed with. That does not make them any less wonderful, and if man has any greatness, it is surely in his ability to maintain these values, even shortening an already pitifully short life rather than sacrifice his humanity. But that too involves choice, and the Ik teach us that man can lose the will to make it. That is the point at which there is an end to truth, to goodness and to beauty, an end to the struggle for their achievement, which gives life to the individual and strength and meaning to society. The Ik have relinquished all luxury in the name of individual survival, and they live on as a people without life, without passion, beyond humanity.

Chapter 9

NETWORKS AS PERSONAL COMMUNITIES

BARRY WELLMAN, PETER J. CARRINGTON, AND ALAN HALL

THE COMMUNITY QUESTION

Until the 1960s, debates about the overall tenor of community life were focused on the extent to which neighborhoods and kinship groups had remained solidary and supportive. Many scholars feared that large-scale social changes had created an environment in which community could not survive. They looked out their windows and saw the same sort of empty streets and bureaucratic services that we found in East York. They believed that community ties were now few in number, weak, narrowly specialized, transitory, and fragmented. They argued that individuals had become isolated atoms in a "mass society" — dependent on large bureaucracies for care and control (Kornhauser, 1959). These scholars feared that community had been "lost," and they worried that antisocial people would injure themselves and others when freed from nurturing and restraining communal bonds.[1]

Others argued that people gregariously form and retain communities in all social settings. They went out to look for community: hanging out on street corners, ringing doorbells for surveys, and sipping tea while conducting interviews. By the 1960s, their "Community Saved" argument had had much the better of the debate empirically. Hordes of social scientists had demonstrated convincingly that neighborhood and kinship groups continued to be abundant and strong. Rather than withering away in the face of the Industrial Revolution, such groups had acted as buffers against large-scale forces, filled gaps in contemporary

social systems by providing flexible, low-cost aid, and provided secure bases from which residents could powerfully engage the outside world.[2]

This demonstration that communities have persisted has been convincing but not complete. Both the "Lost" and the "Saved" arguments define community as a solidary, local, kinshiplike group. They disagree only about whether or not such communities still flourish. Thus, both assume that a flourishing community can only be one that replicates the standard image of preindustrial communities: densely knit, tightly bounded, and mutually supportive villages: But such bucolic imagery not only disregards widespread preindustrial individualism, exploitation, cleavage, and mobility (see, for example, Laslett, 1971; Mayer with Mayer, 1974; Williams, 1975; LeRoy Ladurie, 1975; Macfarlane, 1978), it also restricts the criteria by which analysts can evaluate contemporary communities. For if neighborhood and kinship ties make up only a portion of community ties, then studies restricted to neighborhood and kinship groups give a distorted picture of community that can lead analysts to label people as "lost" if they have many far-flung, sparsely knit, community ties.

Scholars who have avoided this mislabeling have been fascinated by the possibilities offered by cheap, effective, long-distance transportation and communication facilities for maintaining relationships beyond local areas. Such scholars argue that large-scale specialization and personal mobility have "Liberated" community — encouraging membership in multiple, interest-based communities predominantly composed

---

Source: Excerpted from "Networks as Personal Communities," in Barry Wellman and S.D. Berkowitz, eds., *Social Structures: A Network Approach* (Cambridge, UK: Cambridge University Press, 1988), pp. 130–84. © Cambridge University Press 1988. Reprinted with permission of Cambridge University Press.

of long-distance friendship ties.[3] Their argument implies that people are not so much antisocial or gregarious beings as they are *operators* who are willing to forgo a secure source of fruit for a chance to connect with more of the world. Perhaps East York's streets were deserted because East Yorkers were driving to friends' homes or were on the telephone chatting with physically distant, but socially close kinfolk!

Whatever side they take in this debate, most commentators have seen the Lost, Saved, and Liberated arguments either as alternative "true" descriptions of contemporary life or as evolutionary successors — with preindustrial Saved communities giving way to Lost, superseded by postindustrial Liberated. By contrast, we see them as alternative structural models. Each model speaks to a different means of obtaining and retaining resources: direct use of formal organizations (Lost); membership in densely knit, all-encompassing, solidary groups (Saved); or selective use of specialized, diversified, sparsely knit social nets (Liberated). Although one or the other may predominate in a social system, all three models are likely to be reflected in current realities to some extent. Indeed, a single personal community may well be a composite of a densely knit core cluster and some more sparsely knit ties reaching out to connect with other groups and their resources.

TWO-PERSON TIES

The composition of East Yorkers' ties provides a good indication of why analysts have been unable to decide whether contemporary communities are Lost, Saved, or Liberated. There is no one correct view. Rather, the view analysts hold depends on where they focus their attention in a complex, three-dimensional picture of East Yorkers' ties (see Table 9.1).

To some extent, the foreground of the picture supports contentions that many urbanites have lost community. Most East Yorkers have only a few ties with whom they are routinely in touch — by telephone or face to face. In their day-to-day lives, most deal only with three or fewer ties — only one of whom is a socially close intimate — and have less frequent contact with other network members. Although they may encounter many acquaintances, only a small proportion of East Yorkers are in routine touch with more than a handful of significant ties.

Yet, to look only at the foreground is to ignore most of the picture: most East Yorkers have a good number of stable, traditional ties at the core of their networks. Most ties have endured for 19 years or more. Even routine ties — primarily with neighbors and coworkers — have usually lasted for at least 8 years. About two-thirds of the ties have developed from traditional communal sources — kin, childhood friends, the neighborhood — and almost all were formed under the auspices of some social institution. Kin loom large in East Yorkers' worlds by all criteria except frequency of contact, and ties with parents and siblings are especially important for socially close intimate relations. Most network members are readily at hand, if not in the neighborhood or at work, then by a quick, low-cost drive or telephone call in the

Table 9.1 Three Expectations for the Size, Composition, and Accessibility of Ties Compared with the East Yorkers' Data

	Lost	Saved	Liberated	East Yorkers
Size of network	Very small	Very large	Large	1 active, 3 routine, 4 intimate
Origins	Friends, organizations	Kin, neighborhood	Friends, workplace	Kin, neighborhood, workplace
Duration	Short	Long	Mostly short	8–20 + years
Roles	Acquaintances	Kin, neighbors	Friends, coworkers	Kin, friends
Sociophysical context	Public, private	Communal spaces	Private spaces	Private (home, phone)
Residential separation	Somewhat dispersed	Local	Highly dispersed	10 miles; 1/4 within 1 mile, 1/3 more than 30 miles
Frequency of contact	Low	High (much in person)	High (much phone use)	Once a week; equal phone and face to face

metro Toronto area. Although some East Yorkers are socially isolated — their small networks do not keep in touch very much — they seem more assuredly self-reliant than abandoned or lost.

The stable ties at the center still do not complete the picture. In some important ways, these networks provide support for the Liberated argument. Many ties have formed within the past decade, most since adulthood. Only a minority of ties are with kin. Friends are present to a significant degree in almost all networks. Almost all networks contain a variety of friends, kin, neighbors, coworkers, and, perhaps, organizational ties. More than three-quarters of all active network members live more than a mile away in walking distance, and intimates are even more likely to live outside the neighborhood. Indeed, network members tend to use telephones more often than face-to-face encounters to maintain contact — although they spend more time interacting face to face.

Networks, however, are more than the sum of discrete two-person ties, floating free in physical and social space. They are structures that help to determine which persons are available for interaction, what resources are available for use, and the extent to which these resources can flow to network members. In the next section, we examine the extent to which the East Yorkers' networks resemble disconnected sets of isolates predicted by the Lost argument, the densely knit solidarities foreseen by the Saved argument, or the multiple sets of specialized clusters implicit in the Liberated argument.

NETWORK STRUCTURES

East Yorkers' networks rarely correspond to the densely knit solidarities suggested by the Saved argument or to the disconnected fragments envisioned by the Lost argument. Of 90 possible links between 10 network members, 30 actually existed. Such links are neither evenly nor randomly distributed: They clump together within the denser-knit networks roughly corresponding to such principal foci of East Yorkers' lives as kinship and work (Feld, 1981).[4]

Despite the sparseness of most networks, they are well connected in certain respects. In addition to one or two isolates or dyads, there is typically one large-core *component* of about eight members, all of whom are directly or indirectly linked with one another, for example, as "friends of friends." These components form the boundaries of the channels through which information and other resources can flow without involving the focal East Yorkers.

The network structures themselves tend to complement the analytic patterns we found above at the level of ties (see Table 9.2). Only two networks are so fragmented that they lack clusters, and only three are simply one large cluster. Instead, East Yorkers are members of networks that are simultaneously decentralized into several clusters, dyads, and isolates and are centralized through high-density clusters and links between clusters. Their overall decentralization means that East Yorkers must obtain assistance from distinct, somewhat disconnected sources within their networks and cannot assume that information about their needs flows easily to all members. However, the high density of clusters and the moderate density of the large core components facilitates a substantial coordination of activity within most networks.

The information on the nature of East Yorkers' networks tends to resolve the paradox of community ties manifestly visible in surveys and interviews but not

Table 9.2 Three Expectations for Network Structure Compared with the East Yorkers' Data

	Lost	Saved	Liberated	East Yorkers
Structural embeddedness	None	Very high	High	High
Network context	Dyads	Large group	Small clusters	Clusters, dyads, couples
Density	Very low	Very high	Moderate overall, with dense clusters	Moderate overall, with higher density component, and even higher density clusters
Cluster overlap	Low	1 big cluster	Low	Moderate (0.43)
Number of network pieces (components + isolates)	Many small fragments and isolates	1 big cluster, no isolates	Several small clusters and isolates	1 big component containing 1 cluster; 1 isolate
Cluster dominance	No	Yes, by 1	Yes, by several	Moderate (0.50)

visible to the naked eye. Certainly these ties exist and are well structured. But they exist in small clusters — through meetings in private homes and on the telephone — and not in large, palpable bodies gathering in public squares, cafes, and meeting halls. Indeed, the very privacy of their operation may help to account for the stability of these networks: It is quite difficult for East Yorkers to meet many new persons unless they change homes, jobs, or spouses.

NETWORK RESOURCES

Networks are not just structures without content. They convey resources. Indeed, the resources they carry largely determine the nature, and very existence of, ties. East Yorkers report that ties that do not do anything quickly fade into faint memory. Most East Yorkers say they want their networks to bring them two sorts of resources (Leighton, 1986): companionship ("people who I enjoy being with"), and aid ("people who understand me, who I can count on in a crisis"). But what do East Yorkers actually get from their ties and networks? Although the Lost argument holds that they do not get much of anything, the Saved argument maintains that most ties in most networks provide a wide spectrum of companionship and aid, and the Liberated argument implies that people can get a wide spectrum of aid, but only by selectively using specialized ties.

Our findings clearly take issue with the large health care literature that assumes that all interpersonal ties provide a generalized something called "support."[5] Most East Yorkers' ties are quite specialized in the kinds of resources they carry, and the kinds of supportive resources vary greatly between ties (see Table 9.3). Thus, East Yorkers often obtain even the most widely available resources — forms of emotional aid and small services — from different ties, and they are fortunate if any of their ties give them large services, amounts of money, or specialized information for dealing with organizations, jobs, and housing. Nor is support always a two-way street: Many strands flow only in one direction, especially those that transfer significant amounts of material resources or services.

Yet, overall, these networks are reciprocal and supportive. The few East Yorkers who do not get — or give — much help are making a virtue of self-reliance rather than being involuntarily disconnected. Although East Yorkers do not get many kinds of resources from most ties, almost all can get a wide range of help from somewhere in their network (Wellman and Goldman, 1986). Their diversified portfolios of ties provide access to a wide range of network members and resources. The ramifying, multiple pieces of their networks means that network members, in the aggregate, have further access to the resources of other social circles.

INDIVIDUAL NETWORKS AND THE DIVISION OF LABOR IN SOCIETY

The nature of individual networks varies greatly according to the ways in which East Yorkers are located in large-scale divisions of labor. For instance, about half a dozen East Yorkers have small networks, in which there are few links between members and low levels of aid exchanged. However, of these, only two unemployed single young men appear to be Lost: drifting through short-term ties and getting most of their resources from government and commercial organizations. They lack the kinship ties that marriage brings, the coworker ties a job brings, and the neighborhood

Table 9.3 Three Expectations for the Contents of Ties and Networks Compared with the East Yorkers' Data

	Lost	Saved	Liberated	East Yorkers
Abundance of aid	Low	High	Moderate	Moderate to low
Variety of aid	Low	High	High	Low to moderate
Articulation with large-scale social system	Little (companionship only)	Defensive coping with demands; companionship	Ways of accessing resources; companionship	Companionship; use of emotional aid; small services as defensive coping; some external articulation
Specialization	Specialized ties	Multistranded ties	Specialized ties	Specialized ties; somewhat more multistranded for intimate, routine ties
Reciprocity	Low; only dyadic	High; communal	High within circles	High; communal, dyadic

ties child care brings. The others with small networks are skilled tradesmen (and one woman married to such a person) who value an "inner-directed" (Riesman, Glazer, and Denny, 1950), self-reliant lifestyle. Their life, like their work, is based on the exchange of artisanal skills and services. They look forward to retirement in a rural cottage where they can putter around endlessly, without "disturbing" social obligations.

Even more of the East Yorkers' personal networks closely correspond to what we would expect given the Saved model of densely knit, traditional community solidarities. Several are working-class people, heavily involved with hometown kin and workmates. Their kin tend to live near one another — thus, group contact is facilitated — and their jobs tend to foster contact with coworkers. In all cases, it is the women who maintain relations with kin (their own families and their in-laws) and the men with workmates.

Several other women's personal networks fit the Saved model by being heavily involved with neighborhood support groups. They are all homemakers who have changed neighborhoods and lifestyles as their husbands have changed jobs. Upon arriving in a new neighborhood, these suburbanites plunge heavily into local ties and institutions in order to obtain companionship and aid (Clark, 1966; Gans, 1967). Their community ties are more local in origin than in practice, since they have kept some long-distance ties with friends in their former neighborhoods.

Several middle-class men have personal networks that fit with the Liberated model: They are heavily involved in multiple clusters of ties and use their coworker ties for job survival, advancement, and sociability. Three of these men have moved quickly up occupational ladders, in large part because patrons have shown them the ropes and sponsored their advancement.

Yet even those networks that best epitomize the Lost, Saved, and Liberated models do not fit these types exactly, and many networks contain elements of both models. This is because the diversity of the overall patterns of East Yorkers' ties and networks is a product of diversity within individual networks as well as of differences between them. Most networks contain kin and friends, local and long-distance ties, clusters and isolates, multistranded and specialized ties, and so on. Indeed, close scrutiny of these networks often reveals the comfortable coexistence of Saved kinship clusters and Liberated friendship ties. Although this diversity makes for low communal solidarity, it has its own payoffs: Densely knit clusters within networks provide bases for cooperative activity,

and the variety of ties organized into multiple clusters gives East Yorkers direct and indirect access to a wide spectrum of resources.

COMMUNITY?

East Yorkers are clearly coping and, to some extent, thriving in modern times. But do they have community? We have called their networks "personal communities" to demonstrate that they do many of the things that communities are supposed to do. But, in the traditional sense, these networks are not communities: Only those East Yorkers who spend a good deal of time around the house — homemakers and retirees — tend to know many of the people in their neighborhoods. Only a minority are members of densely knit Solidarities. Thus, we have not found communities in the traditional sense. But we have surely found networks, and they seem to have satisfied most East Yorkers.

NOTES

1. The classic arguments are in Tönnies ([1887] 1955), the first two-thirds of Simmel ([1902–3] 1950), and Wirth (1938). For more contemporary statements, see Stein (1960), Kornhauser (1968), Nisbet (1969), and Slater (1970).

2. Key early works include Jacobs (1961), Gans (1962, 1967), and Greer (1962, 1972). For more contemporary statements, see Bell and Newby (1971, 1976), Frankenberg (1966), Palm (1973), Craven and Wellman (1973), Wellman and Whitaker (1974), R. Warren (1978), D. Warren (1981), and Greenbaum (1982).

3. Some key works are Webber (1964), Kadushin (1966), Wellman (1972), Granovetter (1973), Fischer (1975, 1976, 1982), Fischer et al., 1977, and Hiltz and Turoff (1979).

4. To cluster these ties within the thirty-three communities, we used the SOCK/COMPLT computer package (Alba, 1973). We thank Richard Alba for his generosity in making these programs available and his advice when we were using them. This is the first time to our knowledge that this sort of clustering has been done for such a large, naturally occurring sample of egocentric networks. Because of the time and cost involved, we have not clustered the less inclusive intimate and routine subsets of these networks.

We caution that these are respondent-reported data. The problem is compounded here because the East Yorkers are reporting about ties between two other persons. For that reason, we did not ask them to report about the directionality of the tie; i.e., we assumed all ties were symmetric. We did not ask them to report about any subtle qualities of the relationship other than that the two persons were "in touch" with each other, the same phrase we used to define the East Yorkers' own nonintimate ties.

5. The "support system" literature is reviewed and critiqued in Gottlieb (1983), Cohen and Syme (1985), and Sarason and Sarason (1985).

REFERENCES

Alba, Richard. "A Graphic-Theoretical Definition of a Sociometric Clique." *Journal of Mathematical Sociology* 3 (1973): 113–26.

Bell, Colin, and Howard Newby. *Community Studies.* London: Allen and Unwin, 1971.

Clark, S.D. *The Suburban Society.* Toronto: University of Toronto Press, 1966.

Cohen, Sheldon, and S. Leonard Syme, eds. *Social Support and Health.* New York: Academic Press, 1985.

Craven, Paul, and Barry Wellman. "The Network City." *Sociological Inquiry* 43 (1973): 57–88.

Feld, Scott. "The Focussed Organization of Social Ties." *American Journal of Sociology* 86 (1981): 1015–35.

Fischer, Claude S. "Toward a Subcultural Theory of Urbanism." *American Journal of Sociology* 80 (1975): 1319–41.

———. *The Urban Experience.* New York: Harcourt Brace Jovanovich, 1976.

———. *To Dwell among Friends.* Chicago: University of Chicago Press, 1982.

Fischer, Claude S., Robert Max Jackson, C. Ann Steuve, Kathleen Gerson, and Lynne McCallister Jones, with Mark Baldassare. *Networks and Places.* New York: Free Press, 1977.

Frankenberg, Ronald. *Communities in Britain.* Harmondsworth, England: Penguin, 1966.

Gans, Herbert. *The Urban Villagers.* New York: Free Press, 1962.

———. *The Levittowners.* New York: Pantheon, 1967.

Gottlieb, Benjamin. *Social Support Strategies.* Beverly Hills, Calif.: Sage, 1983.

Granovetter, Mark. "The Strength of Weak Ties." *American Journal of Sociology* 78 (1973): 1360–80.

Greenbaum, Susan. "Bridging Ties at the Neighborhood Level." *Social Networks* 4 (1982): 367–84.

Greer, Scott. *The Emerging City.* New York: Free Press, 1962.

Hiltz, S. Roxanne, and Murray Turoff. *The Network Nation.* Reading, Mass.: Addison-Wesley, 1979.

Jacobs, Jane. *The Death and Life of Great American Cities.* New York: Random House, 1961.

Kadushin, Charles. "The Friends and Supporters of Psychotherapy: On Social Circles in Urban Life." *American Sociological Review* 31 (1966): 786, 802.

Kornhauser, William. "Mass Society." *International Encyclopedia of the Social Sciences* 10 (1968): 58–64.

Laslett, Peter. *The World We Have Lost.* London: Methuen, 1971.

Leighton, Barry. "Experiencing Personal Communities." Ph.D. Thesis, Department of Sociology, University of Toronto, 1986.

LeRoy Ladurie, Emmanuel. *Montaillou.* Translated by Barbara Bray. New York: Braziller, [1975] 1978.

Macfarlane, Alan. *The Origins of English Individualism.* Oxford: Basil Blackwell, 1978.

Mayer, Philip, with Iona Mayer. *Townsmen or Tribesmen.* 2nd ed. Capetown: Oxford University Press, 1974.

Nisbet, Robert A. *The Quest for Community.* New York: Oxford University Press, 1969.

Palm, Risa. "Factorial Ecology and the Community of Outlook." *Annals of the Association of American Geographers* 63 (1973): 341–46.

Riesman, David, with Nathan Glazer and Reuel Denny. *The Lonely Crowd.* New Haven, Conn.: Yale University Press, 1950.

Sarason, Irwin, and Barbara Sarason, eds. *Social Support: Theory, Research and Applications.* The Hague: Martinus Nijhoff, 1985.

Simmel, Georg. "Group Expansion and the Development of Individuality." Translated by Richard P. Albanes. In Donald N. Levine, ed., *Georg Simmel on Individuality and Social Forms.* Chicago: University of Chicago Press, [1908] (1971).

Slater, Philip. *The Pursuit of Loneliness.* Boston: Beacon Press, 1970.

Stein, Maurice. *The Eclipse of Community.* Princeton, N.J.: Princeton University Press, 1960.

Tönnies, Ferdinand. *Community and Association.* Translated by Charles Loomis. London: Routledge and Kegan Paul, [1887] 1955.

Warren, Donald. *Helping Networks.* Notre Dame, Ind.: University of Notre Dame Press, 1981.

Warren, Roland. *The Community in America.* Chicago: Rand McNally, 1978.

Webber, Melvin. "The Urban Place and the Nonplace Realm," in Melvin Webber et al., eds. *Explorations into Urban Structure.* Philadelphia: University of Pennsylvania Press, 1964.

Wellman, Barry. "Who Needs Neighbourhoods?" In Allan Powell, ed. *The City: Attacking Modern Myths.* Toronto: University of Toronto Press, 1972.

Wellman, Barry, and Paula Goldman. "The Network Basis of Support." Paper presented to the Annual Meeting of the American Sociological Association, New York City, September 1986.

Wellman, Barry, and Marilyn Whitaker, eds. *Community-Network-Communication: An Annotated Bibliography.* University of Toronto, Centre for Urban and Community Studies Bibliographic Paper 4. Toronto, 1974.

Williams, Raymond. *The Country and the City.* London: Paladin, 1975.

Wirth, Louis. "Urbanism as a Way of Life." *American Journal of Sociology* 44 (1938): 3–24.

Chapter 10

THE FARMERS' AND WORKERS' MOVEMENTS IN CANADA

ROBERT J. BRYM

THE FARMERS' MOVEMENT IN CANADA

Assuming the existence of discontent, ideology, and leadership, the spread of an embryonic social movement is closely tied to its access to power resources. Such resources fall under three broad headings: (1) the *size* of the movement and its allies, (2) the level of *social cohesion* of movement recruits, and (3) various *means of influencing people's beliefs and actions*, including newspapers and schools, money and jobs, and police and military forces. All else the same, movements will be more successful if they have more power resources. Note, however, that authorities also have access to fewer or greater power resources. Properly speaking, therefore, we should say *that social-movement strength is partly a response to the distribution of power resources between authorities and movement partisans.*

At one extreme, power resources may be very heavily skewed in favor of the authorities. In that case, established political norms will be so firmly ingrained in the public mind through various propaganda organs that potential partisans of change will scarcely be able to conceive of the possibility of improving their life situation. One is reminded here of the totalitarian society depicted in George Orwell's *Nineteen Eighty-Four*, in which a virtually new language, "Newspeak," was created by the authorities for such political ends: "It was intended that when Newspeak had been adopted once and for all and Oldspeak forgotten, a heretical thought ... should be

literally unthinkable, at least so far as thought is dependent on words."[1] Similarly, where authorities are very powerful they can buy off or co-opt potential troublemakers by giving them jobs or threatening to take away their jobs and preventing them from finding employment elsewhere. If necessary they can also call troops into action and suppress dissent violently. However, where authorities have access to relatively fewer means of influence, are less well-organized, or are able to win over fewer supporters, the probability increases that movements for change will spread.

These principles illuminate the evolution of the farmers' movement in Canada. Beginning in the 1900s, Canadian farmers formed movements for economic co-operation that stimulated the growth of "third parties" such as the Co-operative Commonwealth Federation (CCF), which became the government of Saskatchewan in 1944. The farmers' movement was politically most successful in the West, where farmers were more numerous, socially cohesive, and had access to more resources than primary producers elsewhere in the country. The following thumbnail sketch demonstrates that point quite conclusively.

The Prairies have aptly been called an "internal colony" of Canada. Since the time of Confederation, Montreal and Toronto financiers and industrialists dreamed about settling the West with immigrants. There they wished to establish a market for the manufactured goods of central Canada and a source of agricultural exports that would earn revenue for the

Source: "The Farmers' Movement in Canada" and "Strikes and the Workers' Movement," in Irving M. Zeitlin with Robert J. Brym, *The Social Condition of Humanity*, Canadian ed. (Toronto: Oxford University Press, 1991), pp. 242–52. © Oxford University Press Canada 1991. Reprinted by permission of the publisher.

new Dominion. To achieve those aims, they — or, more accurately, the federal government which they largely controlled — placed high tariffs on manufactured goods. That protected central Canadian manufacturers and their employees from foreign competition. From the point of view of the Prairie farmer, however, it made ploughs and tractors, saws and hammers, shoes and automobiles, more expensive. Moreover, the federal government set freight rates to ensure that the West would remain an agricultural frontier: the cost of shipping grain out of the region, and of shipping manufactured goods in, were kept low. Finally, large central Canadian business interests controlled the marketing of grain and the availability of credit. Western farmers felt that the noncompetitive business environment enabled eastern businessmen to set low prices for grain and high interest rates for loans.

Western farmers were thus deeply discontented, and they directed their anger squarely against eastern business interests. The protective tariff, freight rates policy, and price-setting were the issues that finally galvanized the farmers into collective action. As early as 1906 they formed a company to collect wheat in a collectively-owned grain elevator system and sell it directly to the central wheat exchange without using the services of middlemen. That was only one of the many important marketing and consumer co-operatives that the farmers created in order to lower their costs of production and increase their incomes.

In the 1910s, however, two developments demonstrated the limits of collective economic action. The price of wheat fell sharply on the world market. Freight rates and the cost of manufactured goods rose. The farmers, caught in a cost-price squeeze, decided that *political* action was necessary. They calculated that by electing Members of Parliament to represent their interests it might be possible to force the government to lower the tariff on manufactured goods, temporarily buy grain that could not be sold immediately to consumers, establish a floor price for wheat, and take other actions that would ease the hardships faced by the agricultural sector.

After an abortive attempt to form a truly independent political party in the 1920s, the farmers created the CCF in 1933 in alliance with the small Independent Labour Party. In order to gain broad appeal the CCF soon abandoned its most radical principles, notably the idea that the government should own all land for the benefit of the population as a whole. Most farmers considered state ownership of farm land no different from robbery and therefore rejected it out of

hand. But even with this watering down of principles, it was only in 1944 that the CCF was able to become the government of the province. Thereafter the CCF remained a party that stood for the reform and humanization of the capitalist system, and it championed progressive reforms at the provincial and federal levels: unemployment insurance, universal health care, and so forth. It also remained a highly democratic party that stood for the protection of individual and minority rights.

The rise of the CCF owed much to the large number of farmers in Saskatchewan, their social cohesiveness, and their access to means of influencing opinion. The simple fact that there were so many farmers in the province promoted the growth of the movement. Saskatchewan's huge agricultural sector employed nearly 60 percent of the work force in 1941. As a result, a comparatively large mass of people on the Prairies faced an easily identifiable group in the East that was widely seen as the major source of the population's disadvantaged position.

Social cohesiveness within the farming community also fostered protest. Insofar as the farmers faced similar economic problems they started taking part in co-operative ventures early in this century. That experience taught them much about how to mobilize people and about the benefits of joint action. That the pre-existing dense network of ties among farmers in the co-operative movement facilitated their participation in the CCF is evident from Seymour Martin Lipset's analysis of early movement activists. Most of them had been co-operative movement organizers before the CCF was formed. A smaller contingent of early activists were blue-collar workers who had had previous experience as trade-union leaders.[2]

It is also noteworthy that the CCF was unable to take office until a large number of farmers had access to the material resources needed for political action. During the Great Depression and Dust Bowl of the 1930s most people were too busy worrying about their sustenance to give much thought to political organization. By 1944, however, when the CCF became the government of Saskatchewan, the drought and depression had ended and farm incomes rose substantially. Many farmers were finally able to direct their energies and resources into the election of an anti-establishment party. We thus see the importance of all the power resources mentioned above — size, cohesion, and access to means of influence — in explaining the rise of the CCF.

If third parties thrived on the Prairies, they withered as soon as activists tried to transplant them to

Atlantic Canada. How can that contrast be explained? On average, Atlantic Canadians were more disadvantaged than Westerners. And ever since social scientists began conducting polls on the subject, Atlantic Canadians have expressed more discontent with their governments than any other regional group of Canadians. Why did their disadvantages and dissatisfactions not lead them to protest?

Atlantic Canadians did not rebel because the distribution of power in the region was highly skewed in favor of ruling circles. Potential partisans of change were relatively weak for several reasons. First, primary producers — mainly farmers and fishermen — tended to be less socially cohesive than primary producers elsewhere in the country because they produced less for the market and more for their own subsistence. Thus they did not find it necessary to form many of the economic co-operatives that greatly increased the social cohesion and solidarity of Prairie farmers and served as a vitally important mobilizing force out West. Less production for the market also meant less money income, and therefore less of one of the most valuable resources needed for political activism.

An analogous argument holds for blue-collar workers who formed an important ally of the farmers in the CCF. Atlantic Canada's blue-collar workers were less socially cohesive and had less access to resources than blue-collar workers in other regions because they suffered from especially high rates of unemployment and because when they were employed they tended to work in small establishments. Those facts are significant because employed workers, and especially workers employed where they have close contact and communication with other workers, recognize that they are similarly disadvantaged and can decide to take collective action to improve their conditions. But the Atlantic region was economically underdeveloped. High levels of unemployment and relatively small-scale industrial establishments constrained political mobilization.

For all those reasons, Atlantic Canadians were less likely to form social movements and third parties than Westerners before World War II. True, there were a few instances of third-party candidates winning seats in Atlantic Canada. Significantly, however, that tended to occur in areas where unusually high levels of capital investment created relatively solidary and prosperous groups of farmers, fishermen, and blue-collar workers — and at times when the establishment parties were temporarily disunited.[3] In Atlantic Canada as on the Prairies, the distribution of power clearly helped decide the level of protest activity.

STRIKES AND THE WORKERS' MOVEMENT

Only about 5 percent of the Canadian labor force are now engaged in agriculture and fishing, while more than 75 percent are employed as blue-collar and white-collar wage-laborers. Understandably, the composition of third-party supporters reflects the massive change in class structure implied by these figures. Workers, particularly union members, have become major forces in such Canadian third parties as the NDP and the *Parti québécois*. If third parties were first founded largely as a response to farmers' demands, the subsequent consolidation and growth of third parties have been partly in response to workers' increasingly important role in Canadian society. Through third parties, workers have tried to get their interests established as rights. They have, for example, sought to influence governments to redistribute income more equitably, provide more protection against market forces, make public daycare widely available, and so forth.

Apart from using third parties, workers have sought to achieve their goals through unions and the strike weapon. By withholding their labor, workers generally aim to extract higher wages or better working conditions. On rare occasions strikes have taken on a political character, with workers demanding that governments be reformed or thrown out of office altogether.

Like the incidence of social movement and third-party formation, patterns of strike activity reflect the distribution of power in Canada. Researchers have shown that since World War II changes in both the frequency of strikes and the amount of time lost due to strikes have been closely related to fluctuations in the business cycle. In prosperous times there are more strikes and more time is lost due to strikes.[4] Why? Largely, it seems, because workers are more powerful under good business conditions and weaker under poor business conditions. In prosperous times — when unemployment is low and real wages are steadily increasing — workers are in a better position to press their demands. Employers are anxious to maintain high production levels since profits are up. Workers have more personal and union financial reserves to sustain them while on strike, and there are likely to be alternative job opportunities to which they can turn if necessary. However, during economic slowdowns employers are less anxious to settle disputes. In fact, during troughs in the business cycle employers welcome work stoppages because they prevent the buildup of large inventories that cannot be sold. Workers know that, and are therefore inclined to avoid strikes in less prosperous times. Workers also find strikes less desirable during economic downturns because they have less money and fewer alternative job opportunities.

Long-run trends in strike activity can be interpreted in similar terms.[5] Figure 10.1 shows the volume of strike activity in Canada from 1901–80. The graph reveals a strong upward trend. It also shows that peaks in the volume of strike activity have occurred more frequently with the passage of time. Both tendencies may be viewed as results of increasing working-class power. The *size* of the non-agricultural labor force has increased greatly since the beginning of the century, both in absolute terms and as a percentage of the entire labor force. (In 1911, 66 percent of the 2.7 million people in the labor force were non-agricultural workers, compared with 95 percent of 9.3 million people in the labor force in 1975.) Working-class *cohesion* has also increased: workplaces are on average much larger and a steadily increasing proportion of the labor force has become unionized. (In 1923, 13 percent of the non-agricultural paid labor force was unionized. In 1983, the figure reached 40 percent.) And the *material resources* of workers have also increased markedly. (After taking inflation into account, there was a 119 percent increase in real average weekly wages and salaries from 1939 to 1980.)

It is also instructive to examine historical tendencies in the *shape* of Canadian strikes. In Figure 10.2, strike shapes for four 20-year periods are shown. The boxes are formed by three dimensions: (1) the *weighted frequency* of strikes, or strike frequency divided by the number of people in the non-agricultural work force per year; (2) the *average size* of strikes, or the number of strikers divided by the strike frequency per year; and (3) the *average duration* of strikes, or time lost due to strikes divided by the number of strikers per year. Figure 10.2 demonstrates that between 1901 and 1980 there was a tendency for strikes to occur more frequently and a strong tendency toward bigger strikes. Strikes also tended to be of shorter duration.

Although there were wide variations from country to country in these dimensions of strike activity, there was a tendency in all the advanced capitalist countries toward more frequent, bigger strikes of shorter duration. In general, industrialization and urbanization

Figure 10.1 The Volume of Strike Activity in Canada, 1901–1985

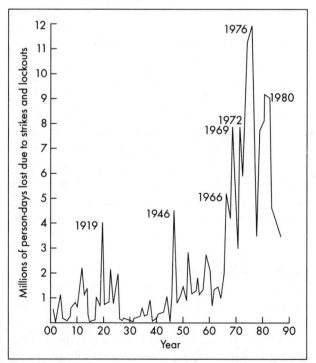

Figure 10.2 The Shape of Strikes in Canada, 1901–1980

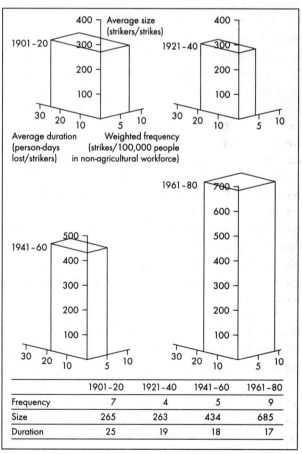

	1901–20	1921–40	1941–60	1961–80
Frequency	7	4	5	9
Size	265	263	434	685
Duration	25	19	18	17

Source: Adapted from *Report on Strikes and Lockouts in Canada, 1901–1916* (Ottawa: Department of Labour, 1918); *Strikes and Lockouts in Canada* (Ottawa: Department of Labour, annual, 1917–86).

caused working-class power to grow, so that while strikes were at first tests of endurance they became shows of strength.

Despite that general tendency, Canadian strikes tended to last longer than those of any other country in the Western industrialized world. That is the main reason why in the 1970s Canada placed first among the advanced capitalist countries in person-days lost due to strikes per 1,000 workers, and why from 1980 to 1985 Canada placed second, next to Italy.[6] Here we arrive at a fascinating paradox. Above, the pattern of strike activity in Canada was interpreted as a sign of how working-class power *increased over time*. But it may also be suggested that *when Canada is compared to most other Western countries*, its working class is *weak*: a smaller proportion of the working class is unionized and trade-union structure is highly decentralized. In most Western European countries, strikes by large, powerful, and unified trade-union movements can cripple the entire nation's economy, so disputes are settled quickly and the overall volume of strike activity is consequently low. Not so in Canada, where strikes are more likely to be bitter, protracted affairs.[7]

All this is interesting because there is a strong relationship between strike activity and democratic-socialist party strength: where democratic-socialist parties form governments for long periods of time, strike volume is lowest.[8]

The advanced capitalist countries with the highest levels of strike activity since World War II — Canada, Italy, and the U.S. — are also the countries that have had little or no democratic-socialist representation in federal cabinets. The countries with the lowest levels of strike activity — the Scandinavian nations — have the longest histories of democratic-socialist rule. This does not mean that fights over the distribution of rewards in society cease when democratic-socialist governments get elected. They continue; but their locus shifts. Conflict tends to occur in parliament, or at the government-sanctioned negotiating table, not on the picket line.

It is uncertain whether Canada will eventually follow the Western European model, whether its democratic-socialist party, the NDP, will grow beyond minor party status, form the federal government, and eventually exert a dampening influence on strike levels. There are forces leading in that direction, but countervailing tendencies also exist, and they now seem to predominate.

Among the major developments pushing Canada toward the Western European pattern is the "nationalization" of the trade-union movement. Until the mid-1970s the great majority of trade unionists in Canada were members of American-dominated unions with American and Canadian members, usually in the ratio 10:1. These "internationals" are "business unions." They stand for the idea that workers should use their votes to punish their political enemies and reward their political friends without, however, forming an independent labor party. The idea of an independent labor party was thus slow to take root in Canada: American labor leaders opposed it and the right to support such a party was expressly denied in some international union charters. Consequently, the trade-union movement in Canada has historically had weaker ties to the CCF/NDP than union movements in Western Europe have had to their respective labor parties.

Over the past fifteen years this picture has changed somewhat. In the mid-1970s, some Canadian unionists who were involved in protracted strikes were angered to watch their co-unionists in the U.S. work extra shifts to make up for lost production in Canadian plants. The feeling also grew that union funds were being drained from Canadian locals to head offices in the U.S., and there was a general rise of nationalist feeling in Canada. These factors all contributed to the so-called "breakaway movement": the resignation of Canadian members from international unions and the formation of independent Canadian unions. By 1977, for the first time in Canadian history, a majority of trade unionists were not members of internationals, and this trend is continuing. Important gains in Canadianization have also been registered since the mid-1970s because of the continuing first-time unionization of white-collar workers (public service employees, nurses, etc.).[9]

The Canadianization movement has brought about a strengthening of ties between trade unions and the NDP: increased financial support, election campaigning, and so forth. That is reminiscent of the strong ties that unite Western European trade unions and labor parties. At the federal level, support for the NDP has risen slowly and unevenly to 20 percent of the popular vote in the 1988 election. Over the next few decades the weakening influence of American trade-union political practice may result in increased popular support for the democratic left in Canada, as has already occurred with the NDP victory in the 1990 Ontario provincial election.

One must quickly add, however, that strong countervailing forces are being unleashed by the free-trade deal which Canada and the U.S. signed at the end of the 1980s. Consider the following scenario, sketched by one Harvard economist.[10] Imagine that under free trade a firm wants to build a new plant in North America. Its owners will know that, as a general rule, strong unions are able to extract wage concessions from employers. The owners will also know that proportionately more than twice as many workers belong to unions in Canada as in the U.S. They will therefore be inclined to establish the new plant in the relatively non-unionized U.S. — unless Canadian workers are able to offer concessions by accepting lower wages, a more modest package of social benefits, and/or a reduced level of unionization. At the beginning of the 1990s there were already some cases of workers agreeing to wage freezes and pay cuts in order to avoid having plants shut down and moved to the U.S.[11] By the mid-1990s, wage levels were falling, unemployment was up, social benefits were being cut on a wide scale, and labour unrest, as measured by strike activity, has dropped markedly.

The material resources (wages, welfare state benefits) and level of social cohesion (unionization) of Canadian workers are thus declining under the impact of free trade. Although the Canadianization movement is pushing workers in a more radical direction, the free-trade environment is the dominant force, lowering the level of working-class power and resulting in less support for the NDP.

NOTES

1. George Orwell, *Nineteen Eighty-Four* (Harmondsworth, Eng.: Penguin, 1954 [1949]), 241.
2. Seymour Martin Lipset, *Agrarian Socialism: The Cooperative Commonwealth Federation in Saskatchewan*, rev. ed. (Berkeley, Cal.: University of California Press, 1968 [1950]); see also C.B. Macpherson, *Democracy in Alberta: Social Credit and the Party System*, 2nd ed. (Toronto: University of Toronto Press, 1962 [1953]).
3 Robert J. Brym, "Political Conservatism in Atlantic Canada," in Robert J. Brym and R. James Sacouman, eds., *Underdevelopment and Social Movements in Atlantic Canada* (Toronto: New Hogtown Press, 1979), 59–79; Robert J. Brym, "Canada's Regions and Agrarian Radicalism," in James Curtis and Lorne Tepperman, eds., *Images of Canada: The Sociological Tradition* (Scarborough, Ont.: Prentice-Hall of Canada, 1990), 121–31; Robert J. Brym and Barbara Neis, "Regional Factors in the Formation of the Fishermen's Protective Union of Newfoundland," *Canadian Journal of Sociology*, 3 (1978): 391–407.
4. Douglas A. Hibbs, "Industrial Conflict in Advanced Industrial Societies," *American Political Science Review*, 70 (1976): 1033–58; Walter Korpi and Michael Shalev, "Strikes, Power, and Politics in the Western Nations, 1900–1976," *Political Power and Social Theory*, 1 (1980): 301–34; Michael R. Smith, "Industrial Conflict in Post-war Ontario or One Cheer for the Woods Report," *Canadian Review of Sociology and Anthropology*, 18 (1981): 370–92.
5. Douglas A. Hibbs, "On the Political Economy of Long-run Trends in Strike Activity," *British Journal of Political Science*, 8 (1978): 153–75; Korpi and Shalev, "Strikes, Power, and Politics"; Edward Shorter and Charles Tilly, "The Shape of Strikes in France, 1830–1960," *Comparative Studies in Society and History* (1971): 60–86.
6. Bruce Ward, "Coyote Condition Makes Our Strikes Long, Spiteful Battles," *The Toronto Star*, August 5, 1981, p. A20; International Labour Organisation. *Yearbook of Labour Statistics*, 1986 (Geneva: 1987).
7. Cf. Geoffrey K. Ingham, *Strikes and Industrial Conflict: Britain and Scandinavia* (London: Macmillan, 1974). At the same time, the capitalist class in Canada is powerful by international standards, as ownership concentration figures and other indices show. See Michael D. Ornstein, "The Social Organization of the Canadian Capitalist Class in Comparative Perspective," *Canadian Review of Sociology and Anthropology*, 26 (1989): 151–77.
8. Douglas A. Hibbs, "On the Political Economy of Long-run Trends in Strike Activity." *British Journal of Political Science*, 8 (1978): 153-75.
9. Robert Laxer, *Canada's Unions* (Toronto: James Lorimer, 1976): Stuart Jamieson, *Industrial Relations in Canada*, 2nd ed. (Toronto: Macmillan, 1973).
10. "Unions May Scare Off U.S. Investment: Harvard," *The Globe and Mail*, December 1, 1988, p. B9.
11. Stevie Cameron, "Post-election Days Just Full of Coincidences for Canadians to Ponder," *The Globe and Mail*, December 1, 1988, A2.

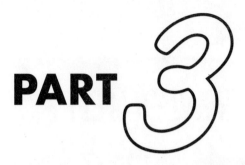

PART 3

SOCIAL INEQUALITY

SOCIAL INEQUALITY IS a core — some would say the central — sociological problem. It has provoked and confounded analysts since the founding of the discipline.

For example, the simplification of the capitalist class system forecast by Marx (see Chapter 2) never took place. Instead of polarizing around a large class of impoverished workers and a tiny class of wealthy capitalists, the stratification system became more complex. Small business owners did not disappear. In recent years they have actually become more numerous as a proportion of the economically active population. What C. Wright Mills called an "occupational salad" of "white-collar" personnel — professionals, educated office holders, clerks, and so forth — became the largest component of the stratification system. Manual or "blue collar" workers experienced a rising standard of living (at least until the early 1970s) while their numbers as a proportion of the total labour force shrunk. The revolution that Marx expected never happened.

Also complicating the stratification picture are the effects of gender. On the one hand, most adult women now work for a wage in the paid labour force, a development totally unforeseen by Marx (and, for that matter, Weber and others). On the other hand, women tend to be segregated in "pink collar" jobs — occupations that are analogous to women's traditional family roles as servers, teachers, and nurturers. Even today, it is uncommon for women to have authority over men.

Another unanticipated development in the realm of social stratification concerns the tenacity of ethnic and racial inequality, which the founders of sociology expected to disappear under capitalism. They believed that large factories and bureaucracies would, in effect, homogenize people, forcing them to work together, treating them all the same, and making cultural differences between them less pronounced. Actually, although ethnic and racial stratification have declined in Canada and elsewhere, different ethnic and racial groups still tend to occupy definite niches in the social hierarchy.

Which positions are expanding and which are contracting? How are social rewards (income, prestige, power) distributed, and how does the distribution change over time? How do class, gender, race, and ethnicity interact to produce the patterns of stratification we see today? These are some of the key problems in stratification research and some of the chief issues examined in the chapters that follow.

PART 3A

CLASS AND GENDER INEQUALITY

Since the early 1970s, the average real income (or "purchasing power") of Canadians has fallen, reversing the post-World War II trend to higher real incomes. Also since the early 1970s, income inequality has increased: the richest 20 percent of Canadians earn a larger share of total national income than they did 20 years ago, the middle 60 percent earn less, and the poorest 20 percent earn about the same. The share of total after-tax national income earned by the richest 20 percent of Canadians is now about 42 percent. The middle 60 percent of Canadians earn about 50 percent of total after-tax national income. The share of total after-tax national income earned by the bottom 20 percent of Canadians is about 8 percent.

Little wonder, then, that poverty remains a serious and persistent problem, as Ann Duffy of Brock University and Nancy Mandell of York University show in Chapter 11. The **poverty rate** is usually defined as the proportion of Canadian families whose members spend more than 58.5 percent of their gross income on the necessities of food, clothing, and shelter. Using that standard, the poverty rate fell between the end of World War II and the early 1970s but has remained fairly steady at about one-eighth of the population since then (although in 1993, the most recent year for which data are available, the poverty rate jumped to over one-sixth of the population). Most poor people work for a living, but more of the poor are lone women and their small children than used to be the case. As Duffy and Mandell document, the social and personal costs of poverty remain staggering.

In Chapter 12, Wallace Clement of Carleton University and John Myles of Florida State University analyze the gendered nature of the working and professional/managerial classes in postindustrial societies. They derive their data from a large sociological survey conducted in Canada, the United States, Sweden, Norway, and Finland. **Postindustrial society** is characterized by a small and shrinking blue-collar or manual working class and a large and expanding service sector that employs white-collar workers. Clement and Myles argue that the decline of the manual working class is attributable to both an increasingly efficient manufacturing sector (which requires less manual labour) and the entry of most adult women of working age into the paid labour force (especially the service sector). This pattern of recruitment of women into the paid work force suggests that the capitalist labour market is not gender-blind. One reaches the same conclusion if one considers the consequence of women's labour force recruitment: once in the paid work force, women start to make gender-specific demands for labour market reform, such as expanded day-care facilities and pay equity with men.

It is in the category of clerical and related occupations that one finds the biggest gender discrepancy in employment patterns between men and women. In 1991, 31.6 percent of women in Canada's paid labour force worked in clerical and related occupations, compared with just 7.0 percent of men. This pattern repeats itself, although to a lesser degree, in all occupational categories; a gender division of labour is pervasive, and in general women get jobs with less income, less status, and less authority.

In all of the countries analyzed by Clement and Myles, women are much more likely to hold authority and decision-making positions in the service sector than in the manufacturing sector. However, even in the service sector, the proportion of women in authority and decision-making positions is less than the overall proportion of women in that sector. In fact, for most industries, the gender gap between men in authority and women in subordinate roles is bigger in services than in manufacturing! Thus, postindustrialism has so far consolidated, not eroded, the traditional sexual division of labour. True, women have been gaining ground in middle management positions, where they have authority mainly over other women. But they have been losing ground in upper management positions, where male authority is even more entrenched than it used to be a couple of decades ago.

Women's progress in the labour market is hampered by their disproportionately large share of domestic responsibilities. Without an affordable and accessible day-care system, for example, women continue to shoulder most of the responsibility for raising children. They therefore tend to have less energy, time, and emotion to invest in paid work than do men. Nonetheless, Clement and Myles demonstrate that the greater the share of women's contribution to family income, the more decision-making power women have at home. In addition, they discuss national and class differences in the level of household equality.

Fifteen years ago, American writer Alison Lurie wrote a fascinating social history of clothing, a chapter of which is reprinted here as Chapter 13. With Lurie we move from the economic side of social inequality to its culture and symbols — in Weber's terms, Lurie focusses on how people use clothing to demonstrate their social status and thereby evoke esteem and gain prestige. By wearing clothes made of expensive materials, sporting many different outfits, keeping up with style changes dictated by expensive fashion houses, and conspicuously displaying labels, the better-off are able to demonstrate their perceived superiority (and the less-well-to-do are sometimes able to pass for something they are not). Lurie argues that many of the clothes we wear are uncomfortable, poorly designed for the activities that occupy us, wasteful of materials, and priced far above reasonable profit margins. But if they convey high status we put them on, put up with them, and even come to regard them as beautiful. That is because clothes are an important vehicle for the presentation of self in everyday social interaction, the conscious manipulation of how others see us and how we see ourselves. Because clothing performs this function, personality shifts often accompany a change in costume; people dress to look and feel sexy, athletic, casual, formal, rich, etc.

GLOSSARY

Postindustrial society is characterized by a shrinking blue-collar or manual working class and an expanding service sector that employs white-collar workers.

The **poverty rate** is the proportion of Canadian families whose members spend more than 58.5 percent of their gross income on the necessities of food, clothing, and shelter.

Chapter 11

POVERTY IN CANADA

ANN DUFFY AND NANCY MANDELL

THE POOR IN CANADA TODAY

Any discussion of poverty inevitably must confront the contentious issues of definition and measurement. It is easy to see that homeless, starving children in nineteenth-century Montreal were poor; it is more difficult to identify those contemporary Canadians who have too little to get by and who are unable to participate in any meaningful fashion in the social, political, educational, or spiritual life of the nation. While these individuals are not (necessarily) starving or homeless, they are "relatively deprived" in the nation and community in which they live.

For years, government agencies, social researchers, and advocacy groups have struggled to arrive at objective standards of impoverishment — level of family income, costs of housing, food, clothing, fuel, etc. — that distinguish the poor. To date Canada has not arrived at an "official" definition of poverty. Statistics Canada, the Canadian Council on Social Development, the Senate's Special Committee on Poverty, various metropolitan centres, and other groups and organizations have all devised independent measures.

The best-known measure is the Statistics Canada definition (adopted in 1973) that establishes income cut-offs below which people are considered to live in "straitened circumstances." The cut-offs are based on the notion that poor families are those who spend more than 58.5 per cent of their gross income on food, clothing, and shelter, leaving few or no funds for transportation, health, personal care, education, household operation, recreation, or insurance. These income cut-offs vary in terms of the size of the household and the size of the area of residence (more than 500,000, 100,000–499,999, and so on). For example, a single person living in Toronto on less than $13,414 in 1989, by StatsCan definition, was considered poor, while a single person living on less than $9,135 in a rural area was poor (Ross and Shillington, 1989: 5–7; see also National Council of Welfare, 1989).

It is important to keep in mind that the sources of income for the poor are varied. Many are poor because the social assistance they receive is below the low-income cut-offs. An Ontario couple with two children in 1989 would have received $16,478 in total welfare income (including basic social assistance, additional benefits, family allowances, child tax credit, child-related benefits, federal sales tax credit, and provincial tax credits). This income placed them $10,323 *below* Statistics Canada's low-income cut-off. In general, incomes from welfare payments for two-parent families with two children ranged between 44 per cent and 78 per cent of the poverty line; for single-parent families they constituted 50 to 75 per cent of the poverty line (National Council of Welfare, 1990b: 29, 31).

Many other Canadians are poor because their earnings from employment are below the low-income cut-offs. The overwhelming majority (98 per cent) of poor families have members who are in the labour force for some period during the year (Economic Council of Canada, 1992: 14; see also National Council of Welfare, 1988a: 78).[1] When the worker lives alone or is a single parent, when only the husband in the family is employed, when the work is part-time, contract, short-term, irregular, low-wage, unskilled (young, immigrant, and/or poorly educated workers),

Source: Excerpted from "The Widening Gap: Social Inequality and Poverty," in Dan Glenday and Ann Duffy, eds., *Canadian Society: Understanding and Surviving in the 1990s* (Toronto: McClelland & Stewart, 1994), pp. 49–85. Reprinted by permission of the Canadian Publishers, McClelland & Stewart.

and when there are dependent children in the home, employment frequently fails to provide an escape from poverty (Ross and Shillington, 1989: 57–64; Gunderson, Muszynski, and Keck, 1990: 68–71).

There are serious shortcomings with the Statistics Canada measure of Canadian poverty. It leaves out all Natives living on reserves, institutional inmates, residents of the Yukon and Northwest Territories, and the homeless. It tells us nothing about the duration or depth of poverty; that is, how long any one individual is poor and how poor he/she is. There is considerable debate about the locational adjustments, which assume it costs less (as much as 32 per cent less) to live in rural areas than in a large metropolitan area. Others argue that with the increasing tax bite, income cut-offs should be based on after-tax income. Finally, the measure ignores differences in the actual level of need in the household. For example, severe disability and lack of access to subsidized services may significantly increase household needs (Ross and Shillington, 1989).

Despite these flaws, the low-income cut-offs provide a sobering portrait of poverty in Canada today. In all, 13.1 per cent of Canadian families in 1991 (949,000 families) were poor.[2] Among unattached individuals, 36.5 per cent (1.26 million individuals) lived below the low-income cut-offs. Predictably, there is a distinct regional dimension to Canadian poverty. In 1991, only 13.5 per cent of Ontario families were poor, while poverty was a fact of life for 21.1 per cent of Manitoba families. Almost 40 per cent (1990) of families headed by young people (under twenty-five years of age) and more than 50 per cent of unattached young people are poor. Families and individuals with low levels of education are more likely to be poor, as are families with only one wage-earner (National Council of Welfare, 1992, 1993; Ross and Shillington, 1989: 21–29).

The Feminization of Poverty

Canadian women are particularly at risk of being poor. This "feminization of poverty" refers to the fact that women in many of the industrialized Western nations are more likely to be poor than men (Pearce, 1984; Goldberg, 1990). Though Canadian women are better off than their American counterparts (as a result of lower rates of single parenthood and more expansive social policies), over 15 per cent of Canadian women and only 11 per cent of Canadian men lived in poverty in 1987. Women constitute 59 per cent of the Canadian adults who are poor (National Council of Welfare, 1990a). Nor is this a new problem; the ranks of the poor have long been populated by women who were deserted, widowed, or orphaned (Katz, 1975: 60; Simmons, 1986).[3] Evidence suggests, too, that women figure among the poorest of the poor. For example, the largest poverty gap for poor families (how far below the poverty line an individual or family lives) is found among female-headed single-parent families (National Council of Welfare, 1993: 14; 1990a: 9–14; Ross and Shillington, 1989: 54).

While the reasons behind women's impoverishment are complex they have much to do with traditional gender ideologies, inequities in the labour force, and flaws in our family law and responses to marriage breakdown. For generations, women have been expected to devote their lives to their unpaid duties in marriage and motherhood. Although many wives and mothers also worked for pay, this was generally seen as undesirable. Lower pay rates for women, rules against the employment of married women, and the peripheralization and stigmatization of "women's work" all reinforced the notion that women's place was in the home (Duffy and Pupo, 1992: 13–40).

Throughout the twentieth century, however, these notions have come under increasing attack. The first and second waves of the women's movement, advanced education for women, and the reduction in family size, among other factors, have undermined the traditional sexual division of labour. In particular, increasing numbers of Canadians have found that they simply cannot survive on the uncertain income of a single male (or female) breadwinner. The failure of wages to keep pace with inflation, increases in taxation, high rates of unemployment, and the loss of high-paying industrial and resource extraction jobs have made the male-breadwinner family increasingly anachronistic.[4] Today, 59 percent (1988) of married women and 62 per cent of wives with pre-school children are in the paid work force (Statistics Canada, 1990: 74, 80). Indeed, the poverty rate among two-parent families would double (to 16 per cent of Canadian families) if these wives and mothers were not in the paid labour force (National Council of Welfare, 1990a: 40).[5]

While much has changed, much remains the same. Women are still encouraged to focus their energies on marriage and motherhood; women's employment is still less well paid than men's, with full-time women workers earning about 65 per cent of male wages; patterns of sexual and gender harassment continue to maintain female job ghettos. Women are still occupationally segregated into work with lower wages, less prestige, and less opportunity for advancement.

Women workers are less likely to be protected by union organizations in their places of employment. Finally, and most importantly, women are still considered responsible for most child care and housework. In the absence of adequate child-care and parental leave policies, juggling the conflicting demands of child care, housework, and paid work often means costly interruptions[6] in labour force participation and/or peripheral employment as a part-time, casual, or contract employee (Gunderson, Muszynski, and Keck, 1990). Being employed in "women's work" or taking several years off to care for young children can translate into disaster when marriages end in divorce, when women face long years of widowhood, or when women opt for unmarried, single parenthood.

An astounding 75 per cent of never-married single-parent mothers and 52 per cent of women who head single-parent families because of divorce, death, or desertion are poor (National Council of Welfare, 1990a: 9).[7] Without a male breadwinner in the family and with inadequate or non-existent support payments, many women cannot provide sufficient income for their families. The Economic Council of Canada's five-year survey of Canadian incomes found women's incomes (adjusted for family size) dropped by about 39 per cent when they separated or divorced and there after rose only slightly. Three years after the marriage breakup, women's incomes were still 27 per cent below their earlier level. Men's income (adjusted for family size), in contrast, increased by an average of 7 per cent. Along with the labour force inequalities discussed above, inadequate support payments produce the inequity. Only 68 per cent of divorces involving dependent children (1989) resulted in a child-support order, and those orders averaged a scant $250 per child per month (Economic Council of Canada, 1992: 49).[8]

Similarly, elderly women (sixty-five and over) who are widowed, divorced, or never married face high rates of poverty. In 1990, almost half (47.1 per cent), compared with 33.6 per cent for unattached elderly men, lived below the low-income cut-offs.[9] As these women age, their rate of impoverishment increases; 50 per cent of unattached women seventy-five or over are poor.[10] While being unattached jeopardizes both male and female seniors, women are particularly at risk because they are less likely to receive income from occupational pension plans, the Canada/Quebec Pension Plan, and investments. The traditional patterns of women's work, with its work interruptions to take care of family responsibilities, work in low-paying, poorly benefited jobs, along with high rates of part-time and contractual work, contribute to high rates of female impover-

ishment whenever women find themselves without a spouse (National Council of Welfare, 1992: 68; 1990a: 98–103).[11]

Based on current trends in marriage, divorce, and life expectancy, an estimated 84 per cent of all Canadian women can expect to spend some portion of their adult lives without a male breadwinner in the home[12] — as pregnant teens, single mothers, divorced middle-aged workers, and/or elderly widows (National Council of Welfare, 1990a: 17). In these situations they will have to support themselves and, possibly, their children. Yet, few Canadian women live with these expectations, and fewer still plan their work and marital lives to bring them financial independence and solvency (Duffy, Mandell, and Pupo, 1988). In a society that perpetuates unrealistic notions of romantic love, marital life, and parenting, and in an economy premised on the peripheralized, low-wage, ghettoized work of women, many women continue to be set up for poverty.

Predictably, certain groups of women — immigrant women, the disabled, minority women, and Native Canadians — are at greater risk. Native women, for example, have lower than average labour force participation rates, lower than average earnings, and substantially higher rates of unemployment, partly because of the remote, rural areas in which many live (Abella, 1984). Visible minority and immigrant women frequently find that racial and ethnic discrimination, along with language difficulties and inadequate government policy, translate into long hours of low-wage work (National Council of Welfare, 1990a: 118–27). Foreign-born elderly women (sixty-five and over), in all marital categories, have lower average incomes than their Canadian-born counterparts. Elderly women who are recent immigrants and/or who come from the Third World receive particularly low incomes (Boyd, 1989). Although the majority (57 per cent) of the disabled are poor, disabled women are, generally, worse off than their male counterparts (Ross and Shillington, 1989: 28; Barile, 1992).

The Poverty of Children

Hand in hand with the impoverishment of women and families has gone the poverty of children. More than 1.2 million children[13] are growing up poor (1991), and Canadian children are more likely to be poor than adults aged 16–64 (National Council of Welfare, 1993: 4; Cregheur and Devereaux, 1991: 4). Children constitute more than one-quarter of our poor[14] and the child poverty rate in Canada is the second highest in the industrialized world, topped only by that of the United States (Kitchen et al., 1991: 2, 15).

Although most (56 per cent) poor children are growing up in two-parent families, an increasing proportion live in lone-parent (usually mother-led) families (Kitchen et al., 1991: 17). Today (1991), when almost two-thirds (61.9 per cent) of female-headed single-parent families (along with one-quarter of the many fewer male-headed single-parent families) are poor, one child in eight is growing up in a lone-parent family (National Council of Welfare, 1993: 8; Economic Council of Canada, 1992: 47).

THE CHANGING FACE OF POVERTY

Poverty patterns are not static. In the last quarter-century there have been significant reductions in the rate and depth of poverty (Economic Council of Canada, 1992: 2). Progress slowed during the 1970s, and since 1973 the poverty rate has tended to fluctuate with the health of the economy[15] (Ross and Shillington, 1989: 21; National Council of Welfare, 1988a: 1). Although the rate of family poverty has remained about the same from 1973 to 1986, the rate among unattached individuals "dropped considerably" between 1979 and 1986. The regional distribution of poverty has also shifted, with less poverty in Atlantic Canada, Ontario, and the Prairies and more in Quebec and British Columbia between 1973 and 1986.[16] Also, poverty has increasingly become an urban phenomenon. Predictably, a weakened economy resulted in higher figures overall in the early 1990s.

An increasing proportion of poor families are headed by young people[17] and more and more poor families are headed by a single parent, most frequently a woman.[18] From 1973 to 1986 there was also an increase in the number of poor families with two or more earners. This reflects, in part, the failure of real family wages to keep pace with rising costs, along with a failed commitment to maintain an adequate minimum wage. In 1973 minimum-wage legislation meant that a worker who worked forty hours a week over fifty-two weeks could earn a yearly income 20 per cent over the poverty line. By 1991 the same worker would have to work fifty hours a week for fifty-two weeks simply to reach the poverty line (Kitchen et al., 1991: 36). During this same period, education has become less of a barrier to impoverishment; by 1990, 6 per cent of poor families were headed by a person with a university degree (National Council of Welfare, 1992: 37).

The poverty success story has been the marked decrease in poverty among the elderly. Policy changes, including the federal Guaranteed Income Supplement, have meant that instead of 33.6 per cent of seniors being poor (1980), only 20.0 percent have low incomes (1991). Similarly, the poverty rate for families headed by individuals sixty-five or older went from 41.4 per cent in 1969 to 9.0 per cent in 1991 (National Council of Welfare, 1988a: 14; 1993: 6, 8).

Finally, important recent research has given us a better understanding of Canadian poverty and cleared up a variety of misconceptions. Poor families are not necessarily mired in an endless cycle of poverty. By tracking the income of a sample of Canadians for a five-year period (1982–86), the Economic Council of Canada determined that more than 27 per cent of Canadians who were poor one year were not poor the next year. However, for every Canadian escaping poverty, another fell into poverty (1992: 22; see also Bouchard, 1988: 9). It appears that poverty is much more volatile than commonly assumed and the line between "us" and "them" is much murkier. Some families and individuals fall in and out of poverty several times over a five-year span. Indeed, almost one-third of all Canadians will experience at least one episode of poverty during their working lives.

Any number of common events can precipitate poverty for a family or individual: family breakdown, disability, job loss, death of wage-earner. The duration of that impoverishment will depend on a number of individual, societal, and economic factors. Those who are particularly disadvantaged, such as the disabled, lone-parent families, and older single individuals, are more likely to experience longer durations of poverty. For example, it is estimated that lone-parent families average in excess of six years of poverty (Economic Council of Canada, 1992: 19–27, 47).

STRUGGLING WITH POVERTY: THE PERSONAL EXPERIENCE

Being poor has always meant much more than getting by at some arbitrary level of income, and understanding poverty demands more than a statistical overview. Poverty often affects people's lives, their sense of self, and their most important relationships with others. The emotional, physical, and social toll that poverty frequently takes is most apparent among children.

For children and their families, poverty still generally translates into inadequate housing. In Calgary, Edmonton, Vancouver, and Toronto, poor children are likely to live with sub-standard heating, too little hot water, improper ventilation, generally unsafe conditions (exposed wiring and electrical outlets, and so on), and too little space in which to play or study. Housing problems are frequently compounded by neighbourhoods plagued with high rates of crime and vandalism, inadequate play facilities, and/or hazardous traffic conditions (Marsden, 1991: 8; Kitchen et al., 1991: 6). Echoing nineteenth-century Montreal, recent research indicates that there are New Brunswick children living in Third World conditions in dwellings with mud floors, leaking roofs, and no running water (Spears, 1991: A21).

Housing problems combine with inadequate nutrition. Poor families often lack the income to maintain a nutritious diet. High housing costs and the spectre of homelessness mean that food budgets are stretched to the limit:

> Juice wars we have at our place. "You can't have that extra glass of juice." They bring somebody in the house and the three of them are having a glass of juice and that's all the juice there is for the rest of the week. And there they are just drinking it down, and you're going, "Oh my God, don't they understand anything?" (Women for Economic Survival, 1984: 13)

While Canada's many food banks[19] and soup kitchens provide a stop-gap solution for many families, many poor children clearly get by on too little or low-quality (high fat-sugar content) food (Kitchen et al., 1991: 7).

Predictably, dangerous neighbourhoods, inadequate housing, and insufficient nutrition take a toll on the health of poor children. As in the past, the youngest are the most vulnerable. Infants born into Canada's poorest families are twice as likely to die during the first year of life than infants born into our wealthiest families (Boyle, 1991: 100). Surviving infancy means that poor children will face higher rates of disability and physical and mental health problems than other Canadian children. For example, they are twice as likely to suffer chronic health problems and more than twice as likely to have a psychiatric disorder (Boyle, 1991: 105; Kitchen et al., 1991: 7; Offord, 1991: 10).

Certain groups of economically disadvantaged children are particularly at risk. The infancy death rate among Native Canadians is five times higher than it is for non-Native children. At each age level beyond infancy, Native children are four times more likely to die than other Canadian children. Being forced to live on the economic and social periphery exacts a heavy psychological toll as well as a physical cost. Native children (aged 10–19) are between five and seven times more likely to commit suicide than the total Canadian population (Boyle, 1991: 99–100).

The psychological health of poor children, in turn, reflects the painful social and emotional environment in which many live. The pressure of poverty contributes to family breakdown and dislocation. Some evidence suggests that poorer families are more subject to family violence, including child abuse and neglect (MacLeod, 1987: 20–21; Gelles and Cornell, 1990: 14–15).[20] Growing up poor often means coping with a parent or parents who are themselves struggling with fear, anger, frustration, isolation, and despair.

The emotional and psychological realities of poverty are complex, and reactions to poverty reflect the particular personal circumstances and history of each individual. Many poor adults and children cope with courage, resourcefulness, and a sense of humour, and many poor children grow up with positive adult role models and a strong sense of family loyalty. However, most poor children do not live on Walton Mountain and the adults in their lives are also often deeply troubled by their economic straits.

Poverty typically means more than doing without; it means feeling cut off from the mainstream of our consumer society. With a few exceptions, the lives and experiences of the poor are not reflected on television or in the movies: the advertisements in magazines and on subway trains simply underscore the insufficiencies of their lifestyle. Life becomes an observer sport: watching other people get new jobs, buy new houses, or take their families to Disneyland. A fifty-year-old woman, on her own, who had been looking for work for five months, voiced the alienation felt by so many: "I need a job. I want to work. I want to be able to pay my bills. I want to be solvent. I want to live!" (Burman, 1988: 54).

Each day small and large events underscore the poor person's marginalization in society. When the school organizes a bike hike, any children without bikes have to sit in the classroom and do worksheets. Frustrated parents see their children left out and humiliated: "It visually stamps them as poor. You can hide many things, but when visually you're made poor, then something's bloody wrong" (Women for Economic Survival, 1984: 16). A woman buys food with a food voucher at her local grocery store and when change is owed, the cashiers engage in a loud conversation about whether "you're supposed to give them any money." Not surprisingly, the woman ends up feeling "like they were talking about somebody who wasn't a person. I just wanted to tell them to forget about it, keep the damn change" (Carniol, 1987: 90). Day by day and incident by incident, the chasm grows between being poor and "normal life," leaving poor adults and their children feeling more isolated, stereotyped, and rejected:

> I could read their mind, right, so that I know what they're saying, "Well he's unemployed, he's getting nowhere," right? Because that's what I'm doing right now, getting nowhere. (Burman, 1988: 204)

> People never really think of what it's like to be poor until they are poor themselves. It's a sad fact but it's true.... They have to live it. My husband is not one of those "welfare bums." He tries; he tries really hard. (Baxter, 1988: 41)

When people become poor themselves, it comes as a shock that the negative stereotype now applies to them:

> When I went down there, I felt that I just stuck right out. I thought, "Oh my God, people think I'm on welfare." Typical stereotype I guess you're led to believe. You used to think, "It's those people who are on welfare," and now you discover you're one of those people. (Burman, 1988: 86)

Being one of *those* people often means living with a stigma. Many poor are ashamed of their identity as poor, seek to hide it whenever possible, and feel there is something "wrong" with them:

> At the beginning [of being unemployed] I was feeling so good about myself that that was a lot easier.... Towards the end I was feeling like such a loser.... You portray this, it's written all over your face. (Burman, 1988: 196)

> I need to move to a better place. There are so many losers living around me but being on welfare people think you're a loser anyway. (Baxter, 1988: 165).

Coping with stigmatization may mean being filled with anger at the injustices of a social system that seems to benefit so many other people:

> I walked down the street one day — God, how do people buy their clothes, where are they getting their money, how come they have a job? ... Like, I just thought shit! (Burman, 1988: 203)

For some, when the impoverishment seems to grind on endlessly or when their personal situations deteriorate, anger and frustration give way to despair and depression. Over and over poor people talk of periods of hopelessness and of suicidal depression.

Being poor and being on welfare can be a double whammy. Many of the poor, who must rely on social assistance for all or part of their income, report that dealing with the social work apparatus compounds feelings of stigmatization and vulnerability. Even when individual welfare workers are helpful and supportive, the relationship between worker and client is structured to erode the autonomy, power, and privacy of the poor. The negativity of some welfare workers merely exacerbates a bad situation:

> Social assistance is based on the notion that women need help and can't make decisions. The system makes you feel like you failed at your role in life. (Blouin, 1992)

> My worker is very strict. It's like being with my parents when I was younger ... the worker controls my life. I hate it. (Blouin, 1992)

> They have a real looking-down-on-you attitude, and my back just gets right up. I don't find them very pleasant people. I keep thinking how people less assertive than me deal with that. I bet there's a lot of people that cry. (Burman, 1988: 85)

Home visits by welfare workers, personal questions from workers, and the constant fear of being "reported to welfare" for having not followed all the rules tend to undermine clients' sense of personal power and self-confidence:

> I never want to go back on welfare. Self-esteem while you are on welfare is really low. You end up being dependent on somebody you don't want to be dependent on. You don't have any say or any control over your own life. When I was a single parent on welfare and my kids were here, welfare was always checking up on me, social workers were pulling these short-notice visits, like five minutes notice, to see who was living at my house. (Baxter, 1988: 31)

Problems with the welfare apparatus are further complicated by the negative reactions of the general public to welfare recipients. Commonly, landlords will not rent to individuals on welfare, and women on welfare may find themselves labelled as desperate and available: "He wants to go to bed with me! I refuse and he says, 'You'll be sorry.' He figures I'm on welfare, I'm a single parent — I'm fair game" (Carniol, 1987: 86–87). Most commonly, the social assistance recipient has to confront the still popular belief, held by much of the general public as well as many social assistance workers, that people on welfare cheat (Blouin,

1992). Informed by the historical notions that many of the poor are not deserving and/or should be punished for their plight, attitudes toward the provision of adequate social assistance remain ambivalent at best.

As welfare cases soar in the recession of the early 1990s, public preoccupation with welfare fraud has intensified. In 1991 *The Toronto Star* ran at least two major stories on welfare cheating, followed in 1992 by a front-page article on welfare abuse. Although a survey of welfare fraud by independent researchers indicated that less than 3 per cent of the welfare caseload involved cheating, prominent members of the community continue to protest that the welfare rules on eligibility are too lax and that penalties for welfare abusers are too lenient (Armstrong, 1992: A18; Sweet, 1991: B1). The poor, who after all receive welfare benefits that leave them below the low-income cut-offs, must face the knowledge that numerous Canadians (some 20 per cent of whom admit to cheating on their income tax) think of them as cheats.[21] Even when the issue of cheating is left aside, many Canadians continue to evidence a harsh and unsympathetic attitude toward welfare recipients. Despite the proliferation of food banks and homeless, a full one-third of the Canadian public think the government spends too much money on welfare, and one-quarter feel that most people on welfare could get along without it if they tried (*The Toronto Star*, January 10, 1991: A12).

Being poor means living with the knowledge that in many ways one is despised or pitied by our consumer society, or, at best, considered to be irrelevant. Not surprisingly, this takes a heavy toll on personal and family life:

> There are times when I am so scared that I'm not going to find a job, I think, "What the hell is wrong with me?" ... I can get scared to death.... I'll have periods of insomnia. I'll get very short-tempered with my husband and with the children. (Burman, 1988: 195)

> My husband and I are very close. In the past year with the pressure of his job when he suddenly turned 55, he's got very sharp with me. He yelled at me twice and he's never yelled at me in his life. We're fighting for our relationship and we're fighting to survive. What's happening financially can destroy couples that are so close. (Women for Economic Survival, 1984: 14)

> If I say "no" to the children, they feel very depressed when they see other children taking things to school. The children feel very disappointed. They kind of lose love for you. They

> think that you don't love them. (Women for Economic Survival, 1984: 23)

The child, lacking the life experience and acquired coping skills of adults, is often most deeply wounded by poverty and its personal and familial consequences. When the adults in his/her life are filled with confusion, frustration, anger, rage, humiliation, and fear, when their lives seem beyond their control and beyond hope, the child grows up truly impoverished.

The burdens placed on many poor children serve to perpetuate poverty and economic vulnerability. Predictably, poor children tend to do more poorly in school. By age eleven, one in three girls from families on social assistance evidences poor school performance (for example, repeating a grade or being placed in a special class). Four of ten children (aged 12–16) living in subsidized housing have poor school performance (Offord, 1991).[22]

Inevitably, children who do not do well in school are more likely to drop out, and dropouts are more likely to come from single-parent, minority group, and/or poorly educated families (Denton and Hunter, 1991: 133). Children from poor families are almost twice as likely to drop out of school as non-poor children. While children of average and low ability from well-to-do families are likely to stay in school, even children of high ability from poor families are likely to succumb to the pressures. Without a private place to study, with parents who are preoccupied with their economic plight, and with the ever-apparent need for more family income, students from poor families often see immediate employment as the best option (Kitchen et al., 1991: 10–11). Unfortunately, in the long run their lack of education and skills may simply perpetuate their own and, later, their children's economic and social marginalization.

NOTES

1. Kitchen et al. report that in 1987, 32 per cent of poor families had one or more earners (1991: 20).
2. Research suggests that few of the poor are destitute; that is, with no yearly income at all. Under 5 per cent of the poor fall into this category; an additional 6 per cent are "marginally employed"; that is, they earn 50 per cent or less of the low-income cut-offs (Economic Council of Canada, 1992: 14).
3. It is interesting to note, for example, that the proportion of single-parent families was about the same fifty years ago. In the 1940s most of these families were headed by widows (66 per cent); today, most are headed by separated, divorced, or never-married women (Economic Council of Canada, 1992: 16).

4. Despite the mass movement of women into paid employment, real family wages have not increased significantly since the mid-1970s (Kitchen et al., 1991: 19).

5. The dramatic increase in two-earner families has produced only a slight decline in the incidence of poverty in intact families (Economic Council of Canada, 1992: 17). However, if wives had not participated in the paid labour force (1990), the number of poor families would have more than doubled (National Council of Welfare, 1992: 70).

6. While women today are "dropping out" of the labour force less frequently and for shorter periods of time, the majority of women still interrupt their paid labour at least once (Robinson, 1986). A recent federal government study indicates that when women stay home to raise their children, they lose tens of thousands of dollars of earning capacity resulting in significant and long-term earning losses." In the event of divorce, these losses are rarely compensated (*The Toronto Star*, July 7, 1992: A9).

7. In 1986, 11 per cent of Canadian families were lone-parent families. Of this group, 83 per cent were led by women (Statistics Canada, 1990: 15). The poverty rate in female-headed lone-parent families is considerably higher than that in other types of families. Only about 10 per cent of two-parent families and 23 per cent of male-headed, single-parent families are poor (Ross and Shillington, 1989: 44).

8. The problem has often been further compounded by the half to three-quarters of spouses who default on support orders. While enforcement measures have improved, they do not solve the problem of spouses who cannot be found or simply cannot afford to pay (Kitchen et al., 1991: 17).

9. In 1979 two-thirds of elderly widows were living in poverty. Improvements in these rates have been effected by Guaranteed Income Supplements and other measures (National Council of Welfare, 1979: 13).

10. Even middle-aged (55–64) women who find themselves on their own (because of divorce, separation, widowhood, or never marrying) report incomes 24 per cent below those of comparable men and 56 per cent lower than incomes of all families and unattached individuals (Burke and Spector, 1991: 16).

11. Further, an unfair tax structure functions to reinforce women's economic disadvantages. For example, women earn 32 per cent of all pre-tax income and men earn 68 per cent. After all taxes are taken into account, women earn only 26.8 per cent of post-tax income and men's share increases to 73.2 percent (Lahey, 1992).

12. As the divorce rate increases, the probability of women being without a spouse is also increasing (National Council of Welfare, 1990a: 17).

13. Not included in these figures are the 51 per cent of Native children (living on and off reserves) who are poor (Kitchen et al., 1991: 15).

14. This is down from 1971, when children comprised 36 per cent of all poor Canadians (National Council of Welfare, 1975).

15. However, since the overall population has grown, the number of poor in Canada increased between 1973 and 1986 to 2.03 million (Ross and Shillington, 1989: 22). An estimated 3.8 million were poor by 1990 (National Council of Welfare, 1992: 71).

16. Currently (1991), poverty rates are highest in the Prairie provinces, Quebec, and Newfoundland, and lowest in Ontario and P.E.I. (National Council of Welfare, 1993: 10).

17. Between 1973 and 1986 the poverty rate among families headed by someone twenty-five or under almost doubled (Ross and Shillington, 1989: 43).

18. Female lone-parents who are poor are typically younger, less educated, less likely to be employed, have more and younger children, and are more likely to live in cities than non-poor lone-parent mothers (Ross and Shillington, 1989: 45–47).

19. In Metropolitan Toronto, 40 per cent of the 124,000 people who rely on food banks each month are children (Reid, 1991: A10).

20. Higher rates of reported violence among poorer families may reflect, at least in part, the greater vulnerability of many poor families to public scrutiny and the stigmatization of the poor.

21. It is estimated that the federal government loses about $90 billion per year as a result of tax evasion and the underground economy (McCarthy, 1992: A1).

22. Research now suggests that poverty, not separation and divorce, is the key factor contributing to children's low self-esteem and behaviour problems, which are then clearly implicated in educational difficulties (Cox, 1991: C1).

REFERENCES

Abella, R.S. (1984). *Equality in Employment: A Royal Commission Report.* Ottawa: Ministry of Supply and Services.

Armstrong, Jane (1992). "Is our welfare system being abused?" *The Toronto Star*, March 7: A1, A18.

Barile, Maria (1992). "Dis-Abled Women: An Exploited Genderless Underclass," *Canadian Woman Studies* (Summer): 32–33.

Baxter, Sheila (1988). *No Way to Live: Poor Women Speak Out.* Vancouver: New Star Books.

Blouin, Barbara (1992). "Welfare Workers and Clients: Problems of Sexism and Paternalism," *Canadian Women Studies* (Summer): 64–65.

Bouchard, Camil (1988). "Poverty: A Dangerous Curve," *Transition*, Vanier Institute of the Family (September): 9–12.

Boyd, Michael (1991). "Child Health in Ontario," in Richard Barnhorst and Laura C. Johnson, eds., *The State of the Child in Ontario.* Toronto: Oxford University Press.

Boyle, Michael (1991). "Child Health in Ontario," in Richard Barnhorst and Laura C. Johnson, eds., *The State of the Child in Ontario.* Toronto: Oxford University Press.

Bradbury, Bettina (1982). "The Fragmented Family: Family Strategies in the Face of Death, Illness, and Poverty, Montreal, 1860–1885," in Joy Parr, ed., *Childhood and Family in Canadian History.* Toronto: McClelland and Stewart.

Braun, Denny (1991). *The Rich Get Richer: The Rise of Income Inequality in the United States and the World.* Chicago: Nelson-Hall.

Burke, Mary Anne, and Aron Spector (1991). "Falling Through the Cracks: Women Aged 55–64 Living On Their Own," *Canadian Social Trends* (Winter): 14–17.

Burman, Patrick (1988). *Killing Time, Losing Ground: Experiences of Unemployment.* Toronto: Wall and Thompson.

Carniol, Ben (1987). *Case Critical: The Dilemma of Social Work in Canada.* Toronto: Between the Lines.

Cox, Bob (1991). "Poverty, not divorce, blamed for youth's bad behavior," *Toronto Star*, August 15: C1.

Cregheur, Alain, and Mary Sue Devereaux (1991). "Canada's Children," *Canadian Social Trends* (Summer): 2–5.

Denton, Margaret and Alfred Hunter (1991). "Education and the Child," in Richard Barnhorst and Laura C. Johnson, eds., *The State of the Child in Ontario.* Toronto: Oxford University Press.

Duffy, Ann, Nancy Mandell, and Norene Pupo (1988). *Few Choices: Women, Work and Family.* Toronto: Garamond.

Duffy, Ann and Norene Pupo (1992). *Part-Time Paradox: Connecting Gender, Work, and Family.* Toronto: McClelland & Stewart.

Duncan, Kenneth (1974). "Irish Famine Immigration and the Social Structure of Canada West," in Michiel Horn and Ronald Sabourin, eds., *Studies in Canadian Social History.* Toronto: McClelland and Stewart.

Economic Council of Canada (1992). *The New Face of Poverty: Income Security Needs of Canadian Families.* Ottawa: Ministry of Supply and Services.

Fuchs, Rachel Ginnis (1984). *Abandoned Children: Foundlings and Child Welfare in Nineteenth-Century France.* Albany: State University of New York Press.

Gelles, Richard J. and Claire P. Cornell (1990). *Intimate Violence in Families*, 2nd ed. Newbury Park, Calif.: Sage Publications.

Goldberg, Gertrude Schaffner (1990). "Canada: Bordering on the Feminization of Poverty," in Gertrude Schaffner Goldberg and Eleanor Kremen, eds., *The Feminization of Poverty: Only in America?* New York: Praeger.

Gunderson, Morley and Leon Muszynski with Jennifer Keck (1990). *Women and Labour Market Poverty.* Ottawa: Canadian Advisory Council on the Status of Women.

Katz, Michael B. (1975). *The People of Hamilton, Canada West: Family and Class in a Mid-Nineteenth Century City.* Cambridge, Mass.: Harvard University Press.

Kitchen, Brigitte, Andrew Mitchell, Peter Clutterbuck, and Marvyn Novick (1991). *Unequal Futures: The Legacies of Child Poverty in Canada.* Toronto: Child Poverty Action Group and the Social Planning Council of Metropolitan Toronto.

Lahey, Kathleen A. (1992). "The Impoverishment of Women in Canada: The Role of Taxation," *Canadian Woman Studies* (forthcoming).

MacLeod, Linda (1987). *Battered But Not Beaten: Preventing Wife Battering in Canada.* Ottawa: Canadian Advisory Council on the Status of Women.

Marsden, Lorna, chair (1991). *Children in Poverty: Toward a Better Future.* Standing Senate Committee on Social Affairs, Science and Technology. Ottawa: Ministry of Supply and Services.

McCarthy, Shawn (1992). "Ottawa missing $90 billion a year as cheaters use cash to dodge taxes," *Toronto Star*, April 30: A1, A32.

National Council of Welfare (1979). *Women and Poverty.* Ottawa: Ministry of Supply and Services.

———. (1988). *Poverty Profile 1988.* Ottawa: Ministry of Supply and Services.

———. (1990a). *Women and Poverty Revisited.* Ottawa: Ministry of Supply and Services.

———. (1990b). *Welfare Incomes 1989.* Ottawa: Ministry of Supply and Services.

———. (1992). *Poverty Profile 1980–1990.* Ottawa: Ministry of Supply and Services.

———. (1993). *Poverty Profile Update for 1991.* Ottawa: Ministry of Supply and Services.

Offord, Dan (1991). "Growing Up Poor in Ontario," *Transition*, Vanier Institute of the Family, June: 10–11.

Pearce, Diana (1978). "The Feminization of Poverty: Women, Work and Welfare," *Urban and Social Change Review*, 11 (February): 28–36.

Reid, Susan (1991). "Facing up to poverty in Metro," *Toronto Star*, November 5: A10.

Robinson, Patricia (1986). Ottawa: Ministry of Supply and Services.

Ross, David and Richard Shillington (1989). *The Canadian Fact Book on Poverty.* Ottawa: Canadian Council on Social Development.

Simmons, Christina (1986). "'Helping the Poorer Sisters': The Women of the Jost Mission, Halifax, 1905–1945," in Veronica Strong-Boag and Anita Clair Fellman, eds., *Rethinking Canada: The Promise of Women's History.* Toronto: Copp Clark Pitman.

Spears, John (1991). "N.B. Seeks Answer to Childhood Poverty." *The Toronto Star*, May 31: A21.

Special Senate Committee on Poverty (1976). *Poverty in Canada.* Ottawa: Ministry of Supply and Services.

Statistics Canada (1990). *Women in Canada: A Statistical Report*, 2nd ed. Ottawa: Ministry of Supply and Services.

Sweet, Lois (1991). "Is Welfare Cheating Running Wild?" *The Toronto Star*, June 2: B1, B7.

Women for Economic Survival (1984). *Women and Economic Hard Times: A Record.* Victoria: Women for Economic Survival and the University of Victoria.

Chapter 12

GENDER, CLASS, AND POSTINDUSTRIALISM IN CANADA, SCANDINAVIA, AND THE USA

WALLACE CLEMENT AND JOHN MYLES

There are two reasons why the male blue-collar worker is no longer symbolic of the class structure of the advanced capitalist economies. The first is the revolution in the forces of production that makes the direct producer of most goods increasingly redundant. The second, and equally important, reason has been the incorporation of women into the paid labour force. The massive entry of women into paid work in the latter part of the twentieth century has been as dramatic as the changes in industry composition and virtually inseparable from it. As Table 12.1 shows, from about the end of the Second World War until 1982 (about the time of our surveys), women increased their share of employment from approximately one-quarter to over two-fifths of the labour force. Finland is the exception to this pattern. By 1950 women already made up over two-fifths of the Finnish labour force, compared with a quarter or less of the labour force of the other countries.

As Table 12.2 indicates, the labour force participation of women tends to be rather higher in the Nordic countries than in North America. In the mid-1970s, the Norwegian level was closer to the North American pattern than to that of Sweden or Finland. By the early 1980s, however, Norway had drawn closer to the Swedish-Finnish levels.

Almost all of this growth in female employment occurred in services.[1] Indeed, if unpaid domestic labour were counted as an industry in the usual classifications, we might describe postindustrialism more in terms of the shift from unpaid to paid service work and put less emphasis on the "goods to services" metaphor. Most

Table 12.1 Women's Share of the Labour Force, 1950 and 1982

	1950	1982
United States	28	42
Canada	21	40
Norway	27	42
Sweden	26	46
Finland	41	47

Source: Compiled from data inOECD, *The Integration of Women into the Economy* (Paris: OECD, 1985), 14.

Table 12.2 Labour-Force Participation by Sex

	Women		Men	
	1975	1983	1975	1983
United States	53	62	85	85
Canada	50	60	86	85
Norway	53	67	86	86
Sweden	68	77	89	86
Finland	66	74	80	83

Source: Compiled from data in OECD, *The Integration of Women into the Economy* (Paris: OECD, 1985), 13.

Source: Relations of Ruling: Class and Gender in Postindustrial Societies (Montreal/Kingston: McGill-Queen's University Press, 1994), pp. 33–37, 135–40, and 207–10. Reprinted by permission of the publisher.

men (56 per cent or more) continue to be employed in the traditional sectors associated with an "industrial" economy: goods and distribution. Most women — approximately two-thirds — are employed in the growing postindustrial sectors of the labour market, especially personal/retail, business, and social services.

As a result, the "new" — postindustrial — working class is predominantly female labour employed in clerical, sales, and service occupations in the service industries (see Table 12.3). And consequently the working class now has two prototypes rather than one: the traditional blue-collar male and the postindustrial female service worker. Moreover, variations in postindustrial employment patterns are experienced mainly by women. The large welfare states of Sweden and Norway, in particular, result in the fact that most women workers are employed by the state in those countries. Half of all employed Swedish women are in social services, compared with only a quarter of American women.

The significant fact about the postindustrial division of labour, then, is not so much that the working class of industrial capitalism has come to an end. Rather, a new working class employed in services has grown up alongside it. And superimposed on this material division of labour is a social division based on gender.

As we show in Figure 12.1, the working class in advanced capitalism has two sexes. In all five countries,

Table 12.3 Selected Characteristics of Working-Class Women

Percentage of Working-Class Women Who Are in:	United States	Canada	Norway	Sweden	Finland
Clerical, sales, and service occupations	66	64	60	66	66
Goods & distributive industries	34	24	28	26	40
State employment	31	38	55	63	38
Unskilled jobs	86	79	81	77	83

Figure 12.1 Class Distributions by Sex and Nation

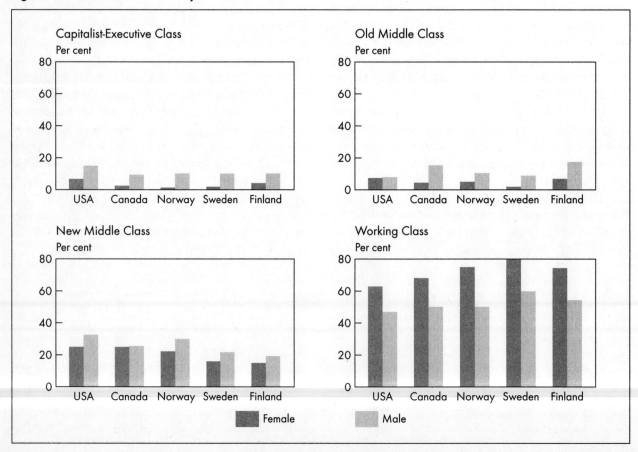

women are more likely to be working class than men and less likely to be in any of the other three classes that exercise significant powers over production. In all five countries, women make up 50 per cent or more of the working class and a minority of all other classes. But just what historical, social, or political significance should we attach to this fact?

Since the 1970s, it has been commonplace for feminist scholars to comment upon the "gender-blind" character of conventional class theory, but such a charge has had two rather different meanings. Sometimes the charge implies that the "male" preoccupation with class relations results in a disciplinary bias leading to the systematic neglect of gender relations — structured relations of domination and inequality between the sexes. To such a charge, class analysts can plead guilty without necessarily conceding that there are serious flaws in their theories or empirical claims *about* classes. There is no inherent reason why theories about classes must explain all forms of social domination and inequality.

The charge of being gender-blind, on the other hand, can also mean that analyses of classes and processes of class formation which overlook the gendered structure of class relations are both incomplete and incorrect. In short, class analyses that are gender-blind are incomplete on their own terms, not just when measured against the criteria of an alternative problematic. Capitalism and the labour market are not inherently gender-blind, as the conventional wisdom of both neoclassical and Marxian economic theory would have it.

The fact that a "worker" is female rather than male, that she comes to work in a skirt and blouse rather than in overalls, alters the relation between capital and labour in fundamental ways.[2] An example will suffice to illustrate.

The patriarchal organization of households means that most women sell their labour under very different conditions from those of most men. The burden of the "double day" of paid labour and unpaid domestic labour circumscribes both how much labour power women can sell in the market and the timing of its availability. One result is to transform the conditions under which the capital–labour wage relation is negotiated and the agenda of labour when it confronts capital at the bargaining table. The focus of "class struggle" now expands to include new labour-force practices and state policies such as pay equity and day care. In effect, the struggle over the price of labour and the conditions of its employment is transformed as a result of the conditions and extra-market social relations of the persons (women) who offer their labour for sale in the market. And the upshot is irrevocably to alter the trajectory of class formation in *postindustrial* capitalism. Employers are faced with novel demands about the form of the pay packet, work schedules, and the fringe benefits they must negotiate. The state is faced with new demands for legislation and social programs to protect women against the market. As a result, labour unions and labour parties that fail to take up these demands, to incorporate the material interests of a working class that is predominantly female, become doomed to extinction. Likewise, a *class* analysis that does not take account of the changed conditions of the class struggle is doomed to failure.

Numerically, the labour force of traditional industrial labour markets was and is predominantly male (Table 12.4). In contrast, the labour force of the postindustrial sectors is dominated by women. Men are in the majority in both goods production (manufacturing, construction) and distribution (transport, utilities, communication, and wholesale trade), the sectors associated with both the first and the second "industrial revolutions." Here we would expect few women to achieve significant positions within capitalist relations of ruling. In contrast, women dominate in the more "modern" business, consumer, and public services. Female-dominated work sites are more numerous (schools, health-care agencies), and there is less likelihood that women in authority will be required to exercise their authority over male subordinates.

Table 12.4 Per Cent Female by Industry Sector, Employed Labour Force, Full-Time and Part-Time Employees

Sectors	United States	Canada	Norway	Sweden	Finland
GOODS & DISTRIBUTION	31	24	24	24	35
Goods	32	21	24	23	36
Distributive services	28	31	23	25	33
POSTINDUSTRIAL SERVICES	61	61	57	67	68
Business, personal, & retail services	60	61	52	60	63
Social services & public administration	62	60	60	70	71

There are reasons other than numbers to expect that gender differences in the distribution of positions of power and authority might abate in postindustrial labour markets. The first is the very "modernity" of the service industries. The growth of personal, business, and social services is a contemporary phenomenon, and, as Stinchcombe has shown, the organization of labour within firms, industries, and occupations tends to bear the imprint of the historical period of their foundation and growth.[3] Baron and Newman, for example, show that wage differentials between men and women are greater in "old" than in "new" job categories.[4] Second, state employment is more prevalent in the service sector, and studies of earnings differentials between men and women have shown that the gender gap narrows in the public sector, a result of both public policy and stronger labour unions.[5] Finally, postindustrial labour markets — and especially social and business services — tend to be not only "knowledge-intensive" but also "credential-intensive." Job-relevant skills in services tend to be acquired through the educational system rather than through on-going training and apprenticeship programs. This should benefit women, who are typically excluded from on-the-job training programs but who tend to have high levels of formal education.[6]

There is little question that postindustrialism has brought women into the exercise of economic power to a degree unprecedented in history (Table 12.5). In the United States, for example, women in postindus-trial services fill almost half of all positions with power and authority, compared with less than 20 per cent of such positions in goods and distribution. And as the pattern of consistently positive signs in Table 12.5 indicates, women in all countries have greater access to positions of power and authority in postindustrial services than in the traditional industrial core. But the question remains as to whether postindustrialism also means that the rules of the game have changed. Have postindustrial work sites been "degendered"? Does women's *representation* in positions of power and authority more closely reflect their numbers? Has the law of anti-matriarchy been eroded?

The answer to the first of these questions is a clear no. In general, our results for all five countries do not support our postindustrial expectations. Women have not closed the gender gap in the more "modern" sectors of the economy. Of the twenty possible contrasts in Table 12.6, only three indicate that women are better represented in postindustrial services, four indicate no difference between sectors, and thirteen indicate that women's under-representation is greater in the postindustrial, than in the industrial, sector of the economy. In Sweden and the United States, postindus-trial services provide somewhat more scope for women to participate in decision making, but these gains are not reflected in greater access to the formal managerial hierarchy. Rather than eroding the traditional sexual division of power, postindustrial labour markets appear

Table 12.5 Women's Share of Decision-Making and Authority Positions by Industry, Full-Time Employees Only (Percentages)

Positions & Sectors	United States	Canada	Norway	Sweden	Finland
MIDDLE AND UPPER MANAGEMENT					
Goods & distribution	18	19	5	5	15
Postindustrial services	46	44	20	35	52
Difference	+28	+25	+15	+20	+37
DECISION-MAKERS					
Goods & distribution	9	13	7	8	27
Postindustrial services	45	39	22	38	57
Difference	+36	+26	+15	+30	+30
SANCTIONING AUTHORITY					
Goods & distribution	19	24	5	4	16
Postindustrial services	47	43	19	36	50
Difference	+28	+19	+14	+32	+24
TASK AUTHORITY					
Goods & distribution	19	15	8	6	16
Postindustrial services	46	47	24	37	53
Difference	+27	+32	+16	+31	+37

Table 12.6 Women's Representation in Decision-Making and Authority Positions by Industry, Full-Time Employees Only*

Positions & Sectors	United States	Canada	Norway	Sweden	Finland
MIDDLE AND UPPER MANAGEMENT					
Goods & distribution	–12	–4	–16	–17	–27
Postindustrial services	–16	–20	–24	–27	–27
DECISION-MAKERS					
Goods & distribution	–17	–7	–10	–11	–10
Postindustrial services	–9	–15	–14	–6	–17
SANCTIONING AUTHORITY					
Goods & distribution	–10	–7	–11	–13	–21
Postindustrial services	–10	–13	–19	–17	–22
TASK AUTHORITY					
Goods & distribution	–11	–7	–8	–11	–22
Postindustrial services	–11	–9	–14	–16	–19

*Calculation of representation is simply per cent female within a class subtracted from the female share of the total labour force. Calculated scores may show slight discrepancies; these are the result of rounding procedures.

to be the site of its consolidation (in the United States and Finland) and even growth (in Canada, Sweden, and Norway).

Some of the reasons for these results can be interpolated from closer inspection of differences among service industries. In those sectors of the service economy characterized by an unusual number of "good jobs," men have tended to appropriate an even larger share of power and authority, so that gender differences are augmented rather than diminished. Women's gains in postindustrial services are largely confined to the low-wage and unskilled sectors of the service economy.

To demonstrate the point, we divide the postindustrial sector into high-end (business and public) services, where wages and job skills are above average, and low-end (personal and retail) services, characterized by low wages and limited job skills. As the results in Table 12.7 show (Finland is excluded because of small sample size), women do comparatively well in the low end of the service economy but very poorly in high-end business and public services.

Here, however, our conclusions run into technical limitations imposed by the relatively small size of our national samples. Although our data *suggest* that

Table 12.7 Women's Representation in Decision-Making and Authority Positions by Postindustrial Service Sector, Full-Time Employees Only

Positions & Sectors	United States	Canada	Norway	Sweden
MIDDLE AND UPPER MANAGEMENT				
Personal & retail services	–6	–2	(–7)	(–13)
Business & public services	–11	–16	–22	–20
DECISION-MAKERS				
Personal & retail services	–4	–11	(–2)	(+8)
Business & public services	–11	–16	–18	–9
SANCTIONING AUTHORITY				
Personal & retail services	–6	–7	(–12)	(–5)
Business & public services	–11	–16	–22	(–22)
TASK AUTHORITY				
Personal & retail services	–5	–5	(–7)	(+1)
Business & public services	–13	–11	–17	–21

( ) indicates estimates based on an underlying industry sample of less than 50. For Sweden, cell counts in personal & retail services are based on less than 20 cases. All other ( ) cells are based on 38 or more cases.

gender differences are larger in postindustrial services than in goods and distribution, the number of cases involved is not sufficient to provide statistically robust evidence for this conclusion.[7] Quite simply, it may be that our conclusions are a result of sampling error. To test this assumption, Boyd, Mulvihill, and Myles examined Canadian census data to determine if similar results could be reproduced using census occupations.[8] The results were remarkably similar. For example, the "gender gap" — the percentage difference between men and women — in upper-management occupations in 1981 (the time of our survey) was largest in business services (–6.6), followed by social services (–5.0), public services (–3.3), distributive services (–2.9), retail services (–1.8), manufacturing (–1.5), and personal services (–0.6).

None of this implies that women have not been gaining ground in the class hierarchy, but there have been two offsetting trends in the labour market: women have been improving their position relative to men in lower-level management and supervisory jobs but losing ground relative to men in upper-level management. As Boyd, Mulvihill, and Myles show, the gender gap has fallen among middle managers and supervisors in all industries except retail trade since 1971. In contrast, the gender gap in senior-management occupations has risen in all industries except social services.

Bringing these results together suggests the following. As women have entered the labour force in ever larger numbers, a rising share of supervisory and middle-management positions have also opened to them. Women have acquired real economic powers in the public sphere to a degree unprecedented in Western history. Our Canadian results indicate that women encounter the "glass ceiling" to further advancement near the top of the class pyramid, where they begin to compete for positions that involve the exercise of significant authority over men, particularly over senior men. The result, as Mann suggests, is a form of neo-patriarchy, an economy ruled by senior males in which women may rule women but not men. Postindustrialism matters for women because the concentration of women in postindustrial services provides many more opportunities for the exercise of power over other women but not because the glass ceiling has been broken. Indeed, despite their small numbers in services, men have, if anything, been more effective at appropriating class powers in postindustrial, than in traditional industrial, work sites.

The division of domestic responsibilities is intimately associated with people's relationship to the labour force. For women, this has meant that these responsi-

bilities have inhibited their paid working lives, while men have benefited both within the household by being relieved of an equitable responsibility for domestic work *and* within the paid labour force, where they have been advantaged over women burdened by their household duties. Employers have used women's weaker labour-market positions to keep wages down, thus further weakening women's economic power within the household. This entire system is reinforced by patriarchal ideologies and practices that privilege men over women.

Still, there are important gender differences within this broad pattern based upon nation, class, and status. The more economic clout a woman has within the household, as determined by her relative income contribution, the more say she has in making key financial and budgetary decisions. This economic clout is closely associated with her class position, especially for a few capitalist-executive women but more notably for a substantial number of new-middle-class women. There are some key national differences that transcend class and gender. Overall, the Nordic countries are much more equitable in their household decision making than is the United States, with Canada suspended in the middle. This pattern holds across classes and between sexes, whether in conventional or unconventional households, as indicated by spouse's income contribution.

In terms of actual practices, Swedish men stand out as the least progressive in sharing child-care responsibilities, while U.S. men resemble Canadian men. Norwegian men are the most equitable. For household tasks, however, Swedish men become more involved and U.S. men are the least likely to share responsibilities. Nevertheless, women in all these countries overwhelmingly carry the greatest load of domestic responsibilities.

Men in the propertied classes have made the least contribution to domestic work, while new-middle-class women were able to command greater sharing than those from other classes. Most sharing occurs when both partners are working class or a new-middle-class woman is living with a working-class man. The least occurs when women are housewives. These general patterns were upheld for all four countries, but again the overwhelming share of domestic work falls to women in every case.

Household responsibilities disrupt women's labour-force participation in Canada, especially for those currently other than full-time workers. A majority of women in all age groups had some disruption. Number of children affected the experience of disruptions, but even women without children were much more likely to be disrupted in their careers than all types of men by a margin of 43 per cent to 17 per cent. These disruptions affected women from all classes, although working-class women were most severely impacted. Progressive households where there is a more equal sharing of household tasks have the twin effects of decreasing women's labour-force disruptions rather substantially (by –13 percentage points) and increasing men's disruptions by a like amount (+11 percentage points).

Canadian men in unconventional households have attitudes toward traditional families very similar to the progressive attitudes of Nordic men and women; indeed, men in these unconventional income positions (where their wives earn as much or more than they do) are more progressive in some ways than Canadian women. Canadian women, while more progressive than U.S. women, are not as progressive as Nordic women on a variety of gender-related issues. Canadian men in unconventional income situations are therefore a key bridgehead for progressive gender issues.

The employment status of men matters little to their gender attitudes, but status matters a great deal for women, especially since many women are housewives (the least progressive women's status), while women employed full time are the most progressive. Full-time working Canadian women more closely resemble Nordic women working full time in terms of their gender attitudes than do their U.S. counterparts. The greater a woman's attachment to the labour force, the more her attraction to feminism.

Women are empowered *inside* the home when their class power exceeds men's (as in households with working-class men and new-middle-class women). When partners are of the same class, there are different effects: both working class is more liberating for women than both new middle class. When both have new-middle-class careers, it is the man's that takes priority.

Women with relatively more class power than men have a positive influence on their partner's attitudes towards gender issues, and, inversely, men with relatively more power have a reverse effect on women's attitudes. More powerful men tend to dampen women's feminist expectations.

Household-class combinations strongly influenced the attitudes of men toward traditional families, while men living with women working outside the home are much more progressive than those living with housewives. Housewives everywhere tend to be the least progressive women on gender issues. Again, men are more homogeneous in their views and women more diverse with respect to gender attitudes. The lack of unity on the part of women follows from their much more diverse statuses since some women obviously are housewives and others much more likely to be part-time workers, while men are concentrated in full-time status. At the foundation of the differences between men and women, however, is their radically distinct attachment to household responsibilities both on a day-to-day domestic level and at the broader level of careers. The basic gender difference in the intersection between domestic and paid work is fundamental to an understanding of work performed by both sexes.

So, how are families changing? We summarized the changes in income and domestic labour contributions into household types. For women we were able to examine three types: "traditional," where the woman does most of the domestic work and the man brings in most of the money; "transitional," where the woman contributes equally to the household income but there is no reciprocity in men's contribution to domestic labour; and "modern," where there is basic equality in both income and domestic work. It was more difficult to identify "modern" men because they are more reluctant than women to state that their wives contributed as much financially as they do. Still, it was possible to highlight some directions of change. The most modern relationships occur when a working-class man is with a new-middle-class woman, followed by homogeneous working-class families.

Men's gender attitudes are especially influenced by household types, with a major increase in support for feminist issues in all four countries in transitional situations. Women tend to be more strongly influenced by modern arrangements when they are most feminist.

Households are complex sites, where class and gender relations meet to mediate a variety of demands on an individual's behaviour and attitudes. These demands greatly influence the way Nordic and North American women experience the world since households tend to weaken their powers while enhancing men's. We have shown that the more women are attached to the labour force, the more progressive they are on feminist issues and the more influence they exert on their husbands' ideas and — however gradually — their practices in sharing domestic responsibilities. Age and, to some extent, education appear to work toward a more favourable approach to feminist issues, but the way remains contested by traditional men, who have the most power to lose. Before equality can be achieved in the paid labour-force, much more attention to equality in the domestic sphere will be required. The point will not only be to change the attitudes of men but their domestic practices. The ongoing sites of struggle include the workplace and the household. In every case, it is the combination of class and gender factors that mediates the practice of inequality.

NOTES

1. For detailed analysis of the Canadian case see Monica Boyd, Mary Ann Mulvihill, and John Myles, "Gender, Power and Postindustrialism," *Canadian Review of Sociology and Anthropology* 28, 4 (1991): 407–36.
2. See Joan Acker, "Gender, Class and the Relations of Distribution," *Signs* 13, 3 (1988): 473–97.
3. A.L. Stinchcombe, "Social Structure and Organizations," in *Handbook of Organizations*, J.G. March, ed. (Chicago: McNally, 1965).
4. James Baron and Andrew Newman, "For What It's Worth: Organizations, Occupations and the Value of Work Done by Women and Nonwhites," *American Sociological Review* 55 (1990): 155–75.
5. See Monica Boyd and Elizabeth Humphreys, *Labour Markets and Sex Differences in Canadian Incomes*, Discussion Paper no. 143 (Ottawa: Economic Council of Canada, 1979); Margaret Denton and Alfred A. Hunter, *Equality in the Workplace Economic Sectors and Gender Discrimination in Canada*, Discussion Paper, Ser. A., no. 6 (Ottawa: Labour Canada, Women's Bureau, 1982).
6. See John Myles and Gail Fawcett, *Job Skills and the Service Economy*, Working Paper no. 4 (Ottawa: Economic Council of Canada, 1990).
7. In technical terms, tests for interactions across industrial sectors are not statistically significant.
8. Boyd, Mulvihill, and Myles, "Gender, Power and Postindustrialism."

Chapter 13

THE CLASS LANGUAGE OF CLOTHES

ALISON LURIE

Clothing designed to show the social position of its wearer has a long history. Just as the oldest languages are full of elaborate titles and forms of address, so for thousands of years certain modes have indicated high or royal rank. Many societies passed decrees known as *sumptuary laws* to prescribe or forbid the wearing of specific styles by specific classes of persons. In ancient Egypt only those in high position could wear sandals; the Greeks and Romans controlled the type, color and number of garments worn and the sorts of embroidery with which they could be trimmed. During the Middle Ages almost every aspect of dress was regulated at some place or time — though not always with much success. The common features of all sumptuary laws — like that of edicts against the use of certain words — seem to be that they are difficult to enforce for very long.

Laws about what could be worn by whom continued to be passed in Europe until about 1700. But as class barriers weakened and wealth could be more easily and rapidly converted into gentility, the system by which color and shape indicated social status began to break down. What came to designate high rank instead was the evident cost of a costume: rich materials, superfluous trimmings and difficult-to-care-for styles; or, as Thorstein Veblen later put it, Conspicuous Consumption, Conspicuous Waste and Conspicuous Leisure. As a result, it was assumed that the people you met would be dressed as lavishly as their income permitted. In Fielding's *Tom Jones*, for instance, everyone judges strangers by their clothing and treats them accordingly; this is presented as natural. It is a world in which rank is very exactly indicated by costume, from the rags of Molly the gamekeeper's daughter to Sophia Western's riding habit "which was so very richly laced" that "Partridge and the post-boy instantly started from their chairs, and my landlady fell to her curtsies, and her ladyships, with great eagerness." The elaborate wigs characteristic of this period conferred status partly because they were both expensive to buy and expensive to maintain.

By the early eighteenth century the social advantages of conspicuous dress were such that even those who could not afford it often spent their money on finery. This development was naturally deplored by supporters of the status quo. In Colonial America the Massachusetts General Court declared its "utter detestation and dislike, that men or women of mean condition, should take upon them the garb of Gentlemen, by wearing Gold or Silver lace, or Buttons, or Points at their knees, or to walk in great Boots; or Women of the same rank to wear Silk or Tiffiny hoods, or Scarfes...."[1] What "men or women of mean condition" — farmers or artisans — were supposed to wear were coarse linen or wool, leather aprons, deerskin jackets, flannel petticoats and the like.

To dress above one's station was considered not only foolishly extravagant, but deliberately deceptive. In 1878 an American etiquette book complained,

It is ... unfortunately the fact that, in the United States, but too much attention is paid to dress by those who have neither the excuse of ample

Source: The Language of Clothes (New York: Random House, 1981), pp. 115–39. Copyright © 1981 by Alison Lurie. Reprinted by permission of Melanie Jackson Agency.

means nor of social claims.... We Americans are lavish, generous, and ostentatious. The wives of our wealthy men are glorious in garb as are princesses and queens. They have a right so to be. But when those who can ill afford to wear alpaca persist in arraying themselves in silk ... the matter is a sad one.[2]

CONTEMPORARY STATUS: FINE FEATHERS AND TATTERED SOULS

Today simple ostentation in dress, like gold or silver lace, is less common than it used to be; but clothes are as much a sign of status as ever. The wives of our wealthy men are no longer praised for being glorious in garb; indeed, they constantly declare in interviews that they choose their clothes for ease, comfort, convenience and practicality. But, as Tom Wolfe has remarked, these comfortable, practical clothes always turn out to have been bought very recently from the most expensive shops; moreover, they always follow the current rules of Conspicuous Consumption, Waste and Leisure.

At the same time, as high-status clothes have become superficially less gorgeous they have increasingly tended to take on an aura of moral virtue. A 1924 guide to good manners clearly suggests this:

> *An honest heart may beat beneath the ragged coat, a brilliant intellect may rise above the bright checked suit and the yellow tie, the man in the shabby suit may be a famous writer, the girl in the untidy blouse may be an artist of great promise, but as a general rule, the chances are against it and such people are dull, flat, stale and unprofitable both to themselves and to other people.*[3]

The implication is that an ill-dressed person is also probably dishonest, stupid and without talent. Today this idea is so well established that one of our foremost historians of costume, Anne Hollander, has refused to admit that true virtue can shine through ugly or ragged clothes, as in the tale of Cinderella:

> *In real life ... rags obviously cannot be "seen through" to something lovely underneath because they themselves express and also create a tattered condition of soul. The habit of fine clothes, however, can actually produce a true personal grace.*[4]

In a society that believes this, it is no wonder that many of those who can ill afford to wear alpaca — or its modern equivalent, polyester — are doing their best to array themselves in silk. Popular writers no longer complain that those of modest means wear clothes above their rank; instead they explain how best to do so: how to, as the title of one such book puts it, *Dress for Success*. At the moment there are so many such guidebooks it may seem surprising that their advice is not followed by more people. However, as my friend the lady executive remarks, "wardrobe engineering won't do much for you if your work is lousy ... or if you're one of an army of aspirants in impeccable skirted suits all competing for the same spot. As with investment advice, once everyone agrees that it's the thing to do, it's time to look for value somewhere else."

There are other problems with dressing to advance your status professionally. First and most obviously, it is very expensive. The young executive who buys a high-priced suit instead of a stereo system or a week's vacation in Portugal or the Caribbean is giving up certain present pleasure for possible future success in a society that regards hedonistic self-fulfillment as a right. Second, there are one's colleagues to consider. For many people, agreeable working conditions and well-disposed birds are worth more than a possible promotion in the bush. The clerk who dresses like his boss is apt to be regarded by other clerks as a cold fish or an ass-kisser; the secretary in her severe skirted suit is seen as snotty and pretentious: Who does she think she is, in that getup? Moreover, somebody who is distrusted and disliked by his or her equals is very unlikely ever to become their superior. It is also a rare boss who wants to have employees who dress exactly as he or she does — especially since they are usually younger and may already have the edge in appearance. Fortunately for the manufacturers, however, there are more ways than one of advertising high status. Today, "simple," "easy-care" and "active" may be the bywords of fashion copy; but fashionable luxury, waste and inconvenience continue to flourish in new forms.

CONSPICUOUS ADDITION: EATING AND LAYERING

The most primitive form of Conspicuous Consumption is simply to consume so much food that one becomes conspicuous by one's bulk, a walking proof of having dined often and well. Fatness, frequently a sign of high status in primitive tribes, has also been admired in more civilized societies. In late nineteenth-century Europe and America it was common among well-to-do men, who often, as Robert Brain has remarked, "were as proud of their girth as a Bangwa chief, the big belly being a sign of imposing male power. It was a culture trait among German men, for whom fatness reflected wealth and status."[5] The late-Victorian woman, too, was often as handsomely solid and well-upholstered as her furniture.

In general, the fashionable size seems to vary according to real or imagined scarcity of food. When a large proportion of the population is known to be actually going hungry, it is chic to be well-padded and to dine lavishly. When (as in England and America in the 1960s) there seems to be at least enough starchy food to go around, it becomes chic to be thin, thus demonstrating that one is existing on an expensive protein diet rather than on proletarian bread, potatoes, franks and beans. Today, when food prices are rising astronomically and the facts of world hunger have come to the attention even of cafe society, it is again no longer necessary to be very thin in order to be chic.

Another simple and time-honored way of consuming conspicuously is to wear more clothes than other people do. "More" of course is relative: when most people went naked, the mere wearing of garments conferred prestige. In ancient Egypt, for instance, slaves and servants often wore nothing, or at most a brief loincloth; aristocrats put on clothes not out of modesty or for warmth, but to indicate rank. Even in colder climates and more Puritanical societies it has generally been true that the more clothes someone has on, the higher his or her status. This principle can be observed in medieval and Renaissance art, where peasants wear relatively few garments, while kings and queens (including the King and Queen of Heaven) are burdened with layers of gowns and robes and mantles, even in indoor scenes. The recent fashion for "layered" clothes may be related, as is sometimes claimed, to the energy shortage; it is also a fine way of displaying a large wardrobe.

In any contemporary gathering, no matter what its occasion, the well-to-do can be observed to have on more clothes. The men are more likely to wear vests; the women are more apt to wear panty hose, superfluous scarves and useless little wraps. Even in hot weather the difference is plain. At an outdoor restaurant on a summer day the customers who have more money and have had it longer will be the ones in jackets and/or long-sleeved shirts and dresses. If it gets frightfully hot they may roll up their sleeves, but in such a way that there is no doubt about their actual length. On the beach, though the rich may splash into the waves in suits as skimpy as anyone else's, the moment they emerge they will make a dash for the conspicuous raw-silk beach kimono, terry swim dress or linen shirt that matches their bathing suit and restores the status quo.

CONSPICUOUS DIVISION

It is also possible to advertise one's rank by wearing more clothes consecutively rather than simultaneously. Traditionally, the more different outfits one can display, the higher one's status; high society in the past has made this sort of display possible by the division of daily life into many different types of activity, each of which demands a special costume. As a 1924 book on etiquette puts it:

> In the world of good society, dress plays an important part in the expression of culture. There is proper dress for afternoon wear, and another for evening functions. There are certain costumes for the wedding, and others for the garden fête. The gentlemen wears one suit to business, and another to dinner. Where civilization has reached its highest point, there has dress and fashion reached its finest and most exquisite development.[6]

The contemporary man does not need to have a morning coat, a frock coat, a dress coat and a dinner jacket (and the appropriate trousers, shirts and shoes) as he did in the 1900s. Nor must the contemporary woman possess morning costumes, walking costumes, afternoon costumes, tea gowns, motoring outfits and evening dresses — all of which it would have been considered extremely improper and embarrassing to wear at the wrong time or place. Today, the conspicuous multiplication of clothing continues to thrive, but now the emphasis is on sports rather than on social life. The truly fashionable person will have separate getups for tennis, jogging, hiking (winter and summer), bicycling, swimming, skiing, golf and that anonymous and disagreeable sport known simply as "exercise." If he or she also goes in for team sports or dancing (ballet, modern, tap, folk or disco) yet more costumes must be acquired, each one unique. From a utilitarian point of view there is no reason not to play golf in jogging clothes, or ride your bike in a bathing suit on a hot day — except of course that it would cause a drastic loss of prestige.

In order to maintain (or better yet to advance) status, it is not merely necessary to have separate costumes for each sporting activity; one must also have costumes — and where relevant, equipment — of properly high prestige. Just any jogging shoes, tennis racket or leotards will not do; they must bear the currently correct brand and model names, which tend to change so fast that if I were to list them here they would be out of date by the time this book appears.

CONSPICUOUS MULTIPLICATION

Wearing a great many clothes at once is a burdensome and often unpleasantly hot form of Conspicuous Consumption; changing into different outfits for different activities is a nuisance. An alternative or supplementary way of demonstrating high status is to own many similar garments, so that you almost never wear exactly the same costume. The extreme case of this is the person who — like Marie Antoinette — never wears the same thing twice. Today such extravagance is rare and felt to be excessive, but the possession of a very large wardrobe is still considered charming by those who follow what Veblen called "pecuniary canons of taste."

F. Scott Fitzgerald, in a famous scene, describes the effect of Jay Gatsby's extensive collection of shirts on Daisy Buchanan:

> He took out a pile of shirts and began throwing them, one by one, before us, shirts of sheer linen and thick silk and fine flannel, which lost their folds as they fell and covered the table in many-colored disarray. While we admired, he brought more and the soft rich heap mounted higher — shirts with stripes and scrolls and plaids in coral and apple-green and lavender and faint orange, with monograms of Indian blue. Suddenly, with a strained sound, Daisy bent her head into the shirts and began to cry stormily. "They're such beautiful shirts," she sobbed, her voice muffled in the thick folds. "It makes me sad because I've never seen such — such beautiful shirts before."

The particular type of Conspicuous Consumption that consists in the multiplication of similar garments is most common among women. In men it is more rare, and usually associated either with dandyism or with great and rapidly acquired wealth, as in the case of the bootlegger Gatsby. A man who gets a raise or a windfall usually buys better clothes rather than more of them, and he has no need to wear a different outfit each day. Indeed, if he were seen to vary his costume as often as his female colleagues do he would be thought vain and capricious — perhaps even unstable. Monotony of dress is only a minor fault, though a man who wore the same tie to the office every day for a week would probably be considered a dull fellow.

For a woman, on the other hand, variety in dress is essential, and the demand for it starts very early. In America many girls in secondary school or even younger feel acute embarrassment about wearing the same outfit twice in the same week — let alone on consecutive days. Even if they own relatively few garments they will go to great lengths to combine them differently and to alter the total effect with accessories. So strong is this compulsion that quantity is usually preferred to quality, and shoddy new garments to well-made old ones. In terms of the struggle for status, this may be the right decision: young girls may not be able to recognize good clothes, but they can certainly count.

This female sense of the shamefulness of repetition persists into adult life. One of the most double-edged compliments one woman can give another is "Oh, you're wearing that pretty dress *again!*" (Men, who know no better, are forgiven such remarks.) Often the compulsion continues into old age: my mother, when nearly ninety, still liked to appear in a different outfit each day "so as not to be boring." But it seems to be strongest among women in offices, for whom the fact that a colleague arrives at work on Tuesday in the same costume she was wearing on Monday is positive proof that she spent the intervening night unexpectedly at somebody else's apartment.

The constant wearing of new and different garments is most effective when those you wish to impress see you constantly — ideally, every day. It is also more effective if these people are relative strangers. If you live and work in an isolated country village, most of the people you meet will already have a pretty good idea of your rank and income, and they will not be much impressed if you keep changing your clothes. If you live in or near a city and work in a large organization, however, you will be seen often by the same people, but most of them will know little about you. Having a large and up-to-date sartorial vocabulary then becomes a matter of the first importance, especially if you have not yet established yourself socially or professionally. For this reason, it is not surprising that the most active supporters of the fashion industry today are young women in places like London and New York.

What is surprising, though, is the lengths to which this support can go. Many young working women now seem to take it for granted that they will spend most of their income on dress. "It's awfully important to look right," a secretary in a London advertising agency explained to me. "If a girl lives at home it'll be her main expense. If she's living in town, even sharing a flat, it's much harder. I'm always in debt for clothes; when I want something I just put it on my credit card. I know things cost more that way. But, well, take these boots. They were eighty-nine pounds, but they were so beautiful, I just had to have them, and they make me feel fantastic, like a deb or a film star. All my friends are the same."

CONSPICUOUS MATERIALS: FUR AND LEATHER

Through the centuries, the most popular form of Conspicuous Consumption has been the use of expensive materials. For a long time this meant heavy damasked satins, patterned brocades and velvets that were hand-woven at tremendous expense of time and labor. Today, when the machine-weaving of such fabrics is relatively simple, but hand labor and natural resources scarce, the desirable materials are wool, silk, leather and hand-knits. When "artificial silk" (rayon) and nylon first appeared they were expensive and highly fashionable. But since the prestige of any fabric tends to vary in direct relation to its price per yard, the synthetic materials lost distinction as they became cheaper to produce; today "polyester" is a dirty word in many circles. "Natural" fabrics are chic now not only because of the current prestige of nature, but because they cost more than the man-made alternatives.

The wearing of the skins and pelts of animals to indicate wealth has a varied history. In the past, when the world population of beasts was larger in proportion to that of people, only the furs of the least common animals conferred prestige. Those who had been enriched by their rapacity in war or trade might cover their floors or their beds with rugs made from the skins of the larger and more rapacious beasts, such as the tiger and the bear; or they might on formal occasions wear garments decorated or lined with the pelts of rare animals. Merchants wore robes trimmed with beaver, noblemen preferred sable; kings and queens (as they still do on ceremonial occasions) decked themselves in ermine. But common hides and furs were the dress of the common people. A leather jerkin meant a peasant, a sheepskin jacket a shepherd; the furs of common wild animals like the fox and the rabbit were associated with hunters and outlaws.

In the nineteenth century, however, as wildlife grew rarer, fur collars and cuffs began to appear on outdoor clothing, and fur muffs and tippets became popular. In the 1880s it suddenly became fashionable to decorate women's costumes and accessories with real or imitation dead animals, birds and even insects, and little capes of opossum, raccoon and marten fur were worn. By the 1890s an entire coat made of or lined with fur had begun to suggest a large bank account rather than too great a familiarity with life in the backwoods.

The first fur coats were usually worn by men; it was not until the turn of the century that they were generally seen on women. For a while the fashion was unisexual; a stylish couple, for instance, might appear in public in identical raccoon coats. After the Depression, however — in spite of the efforts of manufacturers and fashion columnists — a fur coat on a man was a sign either of personal eccentricity or of sports or entertainment stardom — often of both. On a woman it was a conventional way of displaying wealth, with the rarer and more expensive furs such as mink and sable naturally ranking above the pelts of more common beasts.

Leather, particularly that of domestic animals like the cow and the sheep, took somewhat longer to become fashionable. Even today, garments made of hide only have real status if they come from rare and disagreeable animals like the llama and the alligator, or if they can be seen at a glance to have necessitated much tedious hand labor (dyeing, piecing, tooling, etc.).

In the sixties and seventies, when it became clear that many species of animals were threatened with extinction, fur coats became less popular. Many women refused to buy them, and hid any furs they already owned in the closet. Today, though coats made of the skins of rare wild beasts continue to be sold and worn, they have become associated with disregard for environmental values and a slightly murderous disposition. Wearing the fleece of sheep or the skins of cattle, on the other hand, is thought to be consistent with humanitarian views, and is still acceptable except to vegetarians.

CONSPICUOUS WEALTH: WEARING MONEY

Another primitive and simple way of displaying wealth is the wearing of actual money. In the past sharks' teeth, wampum and coins, as well as many other forms of legal tender, have been made into jewelry or used to trim garments. Today, even in parts of the world where they cannot be used to buy lunch, such pieces retain some of their original prestige, and are often worn as accessories to high-fashion dress, to which they are believed to lend a barbaric glamour. Contemporary currency, which has no intrinsic value, is seldom or never made into jewelry, though the silver dimes and sixpences that have now been replaced by cheaper alloys are occasionally attached to bracelets and necklaces.

More common today, as well as in the past, is the decoration of the person with lumps of high-priced rock and metal. This method of announcing one's wealth also has the advantage of simplicity, since more people are aware of the approximate cost of such substances, especially when the local currency is based on them. The recent rise in the price of gold has made gold jewelry far more chic than it used to be, and diamonds, though their rise has not been so spectacular, retain their appeal. Materials such as rubies and emeralds, whose market price is less well-known, or which can more easily be imitated, are naturally less popular. Instant identification is desirable: platinum, though more costly than gold, never really caught on because most people couldn't tell it from silver or aluminum.

IN-GROUP SIGNALS

Sheer bulk and the wearing of many or obviously expensive garments and decorations are signs of status that can be read by almost anyone. More subtle sorts of Conspicuous Consumption are directed toward one's peers rather than toward the world in general; they are intended not to impress the multitude but to identify one as a member of some "in" group.

The costume of the upper-class British male, for example, is a mass of semiotic indicators. According to my informants,[7] he customarily wears striped shirts, sometimes with white collars, leaving plenty of cuff showing and always fastening at the wrist with cuff links. The shirt collars must be neither too long and pointed nor too round, and never button-down: "In fact, the obsession of the gentleman is to avoid all extremes at all times." His suits, made by a "good" — i.e., superb — Savile Row tailor, are embellished in a number of small ways that will be noted by observant people: for instance, they may have extra buttons on the jacket cuff that can actually be buttoned, and a ticket pocket. The trousers will be cut fairly high in the waist and usually provided with buttons to which to attach braces or suspenders: "Wearing a belt is not done except with country suits, sometimes in the City called 'Friday suits,' since they are worn preparatory to going out of town. Older public-school men prefer to wear a tie around the waist rather than a belt." Ideally, the suit will be a dark pin stripe with a vest. The latter must never have lapels, which are "flashy" and "suggest the dandy or even the pouf." Recently, when one British politician became involved in a homosexual scandal, my informants remarked to one another that they were not really all that surprised: though his suit, hat and watch chain were very reputable, "the lapels on his waistcoats were a nasty giveaway."

It is not only the clothes themselves that must be correct, but the haircut and the accessories. "A gentleman practically never wears sideburns or a hairstyle that covers his ears"; if he has a mustache it must be of moderate size. His eyeglasses must be of real tortoise shell or gold-rimmed, and he must carry the right umbrella. "Umbrellas are as talismanically magic as fairies' wands. They must be tightly rolled, and preferably never unrolled even in heavy rain." Old Etonians, however, always carry an unrolled umbrella.

Though the ordinary casual observer might miss or misinterpret these details, those in the know will recognize proper London tailoring — just as they will recognize the accent that means someone has gone to the right (i.e., sufficiently expensive) sort of school. Since they too have shopped abroad, they will also notice expensive foreign-made clothes, just as they would notice foreign words that happened to be dropped in conversation. To be acceptable, these must be the right sort of clothes, and from a currently fashionable country. Ideally, they should not be available at home; foreign fashions, like foreign words, are most prestigious when not too familiar. Once they have become naturalized they are no longer very chic — like the word chic itself. French T-shirts and Italian sandals, once high fashion, now cause no more thrill than the words boutique and espresso.

A similar law of diminishing returns affects foreign *types* of garment. The triangular head scarf tied under the chin, originally featured in *Vogue* as an exotic accessory, was so useful and soon became so familiar that it was a negative status indicator. The Oriental kimono, a glamorous import at the turn of the century, was by the 1930s associated with slatternly females of easy virtue, and today is one standard pattern for terry-cloth bathrobes. If such styles are to retain any of their initial prestige they must be made up in very costly materials: the head scarf must be of hand-woven wool and sprout hand-printed roses; the kimono must be of silk embroidered with golden dragons.

CONSPICUOUS LABELING

Not long ago, expensive materials could be identified on sight, and fashionable men and women recognized Savile Row tailoring or a Paris designer dress at a glance. In the twentieth century, however, synthetics began to counterfeit wool, silk, linen, leather, fur, gold and precious stones more and more successfully. At the same time, manufacturing processes became more efficient, so that a new and fashionable style could be copied in a few months and sold at a fraction of its original price. Meanwhile, the economic ability to consume conspicuously had been extended to millions of people who were ignorant of the subtleties of dress, who could not tell wool from Orlon or Schiaparelli from Sears Roebuck. As a result there was a world crisis in Conspicuous Consumption. For a while it seemed as if it might actually become impossible for most of us to distinguish the very rich from the moderately rich or the merely well-off by looking at what they were wearing.

This awful possibility was averted by a bold and ingenious move. It was realized that a high-status garment need not be recognizably of better quality or more difficult to produce than other garments; it need only be recognizably more expensive. What was necessary was somehow to incorporate the price of each garment into the design. This was accomplished very simply: by moving the maker's name from its former modest inward retirement to a place of outward prominence. Ordinary shoes, shirts, dresses, pants and scarves were clearly and indelibly marked with the names, monograms or insignia of their manufacturers. The names or trademarks were then exhaustively publicized — a sort of saturation bombing technique was used — so that they might become household words and serve as an instant guide to the price of the clothes they adorned. These prices were very high, not because the clothes were made of superior materials or constructed more carefully, but because advertising budgets were so immense.

When this system was first tried, certain critics scoffed, averring that nobody in their right mind would pay sixty dollars for a pair of jeans labeled Gloria Vanderbilt when a more or less identical pair labeled Montgomery Ward could be purchased for twelve. Others claimed that consumers who wanted a monogram on their shirts and bags would want it to be their own monogram and not that of some industrialist they had never met. As everyone now knows, they were wrong. Indeed, it soon became apparent that even obviously inferior merchandise, if clearly labeled and known to be extravagantly priced, would be enthusiastically purchased. There was, for instance, a great boom in the sale of very ugly brown plastic handbags, which, because they were boldly stamped with the letters "LV," were known to cost far more than similar but less ugly brown leather handbags. Cotton T-shirts that faded or shrank out of shape after a few washings but had the word Dior printed on them were preferred to better-behaved but anonymous T-shirts. Those who wore them said (or were claimed in advertisements to say) that they felt "secure." After all, even if the shirt was blotchy and tight, everyone knew it had cost a lot of money, and if it got too bad you could always buy another

of the same kind. Thus Conspicuous Consumption, as it so often does, merged into Veblen's second type of sartorial status.

CONSPICUOUS WASTE: SUPERFLUOUS DRAPERY

Historically speaking, Conspicuous Waste has most often involved the use of obviously unnecessary material and trimmings in the construction of clothing. The classical toga portrayed in Greek and Roman sculpture, for instance, used much more fabric than was really needed to cover the body, the excess being artistically if inconveniently draped over one arm.

Anne Hollander has written most perceptively about the use of superfluous draped cloth in medieval, Renaissance and Baroque art. In preindustrial Europe, as she points out, cloth was the most important manufactured commodity, "the primary worldly good." Beautiful material was as admirable as gold or blown glass, and occupied far more space. The ownership of elaborate and expensive clothing was an important proof of social dominance. A single aristocrat sitting for his portrait, however, could only wear one luxurious outfit at a time. The display of many yards of velvet or satin behind him would suggest that he owned more such stuff and was able, in modern terms, to fling it around. Even after immensely full and trailing garments ceased to be worn, at least by men, excess drapery survived in art: it is notable for example in the paintings of Hals and Van Dyck and the sculptures of Bernini. The Frick Collection portrait of the Earl of Derby and his family "shows the family out of doors, standing on bare earth with shrubbery in the foreground and trees behind. But on the right side of the painting, behind the earl, next to a column that might conceivably be part of a house, fifty yards of dark red stuff cascade to the ground from nowhere. So skillfully does Van Dyck fling down these folds that their ludicrous inconsequence is unnoticeable...."[8]

Traditionally, as Ms. Hollander remarks, superfluous drapery has been a sign not only of wealth and high rank but of moral worth: angels, saints, martyrs and Biblical characters in medieval and Renaissance art often wear yards and yards of extra silk and velvet. Drapery derived additional prestige from its association with classical art, and thus with nobility, dignity and the ideal. Marble columns and togalike folds (occasionally, actual togas) were felt to transform the political hack into a national statesman and the grabby businessman into a Captain of Industry. As Ms. Hollander notes, Westminster Abbey and the Capitol in Washington, D.C., are full of such attempted metamorphoses, frozen into soapy marble.

Excess drapery survives today in middlebrow portrait painting, causing over-the-hill industrialists, mayors and society women to appear against stage backgrounds of draped velvet or brocade, the moral and economic prestige of which is somehow felt to transfer itself to them. Successful academics, I have noticed, are often painted in this manner: posed before velvet curtains, with their gowns and hoods and mortarboards treated in a way that recalls the idealized drapery and stiffened halos of Renaissance saints. (Appropriately, the halos of professors and college presidents are square rather than round.)

The use of superfluous fabric in costume never died out completely. During most of the period between 1600 and 1900, for instance, respectable middle-class and upper-class women wore a minimum of three petticoats; fewer than this was thought pathetic, and indicated negligence or poverty. Skirts were inflated with hoops or bustles to provide a framework on which to display great quantities of cloth, while overskirts, panniers, flounces and trains demanded additional superfluous fabric. A fashionable dress might easily require twenty or thirty yards of material. Elaborate trimmings of bows, ribbons, lace, braid and artificial flowers permitted yet more prestigious waste of goods. Men's clothing during the same period used relatively little excess fabric except in outerwear, where long, full coats and heavy capes employed yards of unnecessary cloth, adding greatly to their cost and to the apparent bulk of their wearers.

A glance through any current fashion magazine will show that the use of superfluous fabric today, though on a much more modest scale, is by no means outmoded. Expensive clothes are often cut more generously, and fashion photography tends to make the most of whatever extra material the designer provides, spreading it over prop sofas or blowing it about in the air. Even the most miserly excess of cloth may now be touted as a sign of prestige: a recent advertisement in *The New York Times* boasts of an extra inch in the back yoke of Hathaway shirts which, the manufacturer sobs, costs them $52,000 a year.

Wastage of material in the form of trimming, though less striking than it was in the past, still persists. Today, however, it is often thinly distinguished as practical. A prestigious shirt, for instance, has a breast pocket into which nothing must ever be put; the habit of filling it with pens and pencils is a lower-middle-class indicator, and also suggests a fussy personality. A related ploy, especially popular between the two World

Wars, was the custom of embroidering everything with the owner's initials. This may in some cases have had a practical function, as in the separation of laundry, but — and more importantly — it also added conspicuously to the cost of the garment.

SUPERFLUOUS PERSONALITIES

Changing styles, of course, are another and very effective form of Conspicuous Waste. Although I do not believe that fashions alter at the whim of designers and manufacturers — otherwise they would do so far more often — it is certainly true that, when social and cultural changes prompt a shift in the way we look, the fashion industry is quick to take advantage of it, and to hint in advertising copy that last year's dress will do our reputation no good. When new styles do not catch on, other ploys are tried. A recent one is to announce with disingenuous enthusiasm that fashion is dead; that instead of the tyranny of "this year's look" we now have a range of "individual" looks — which are given such names as Classic, Feminine, Sporty, Sophisticate and Ingenue. The task of the well-dressed liberated woman, the ads suggest, is to chose the look — or, much better and more liberated, *looks* — that suit her "life style." She is encouraged, for instance, to be sleek and refined on the job, glowingly energetic on holiday, sweetly domestic at home with her children and irresistibly sexy in the presence of what one department at my university has taken to calling her "spouse-equivalent." Thus, most ingeniously, life itself has been turned into a series of fashionable games, each of which, like jogging or scuba-diving or tennis, demands a different costume — or, in this case, a different set of costumes (winter/summer, day/night, formal/informal). The more different looks a woman can assume, the more fascinating she is supposed to be: personality itself has become an adjunct of Conspicuous Waste.

Men traditionally are not supposed to have more than one personality, one real self. Lately, however, they have been encouraged by self-styled "wardrobe engineers" to diversify their outward appearance for practical reasons. According to these experts, the successful businessman needs different sets of clothes in order to "inspire confidence in" (or deceive) other businessmen who inhabit different regions of the United States. This idea is not new, nor has it been limited to the mercantile professions. A former journalist has reported that as a young man he consciously varied his costume to suit his assignment. When sent to interview rich and powerful Easterners, he wore clothes to suggest that he was one of them: a dark-grey flannel

Savile Row suit, a shirt from André Oliver or Turnbull & Asser, a Cartier watch of a sort never available at Bloomingdale's and John Lobb shoes. "What you have to convey to rich people anywhere," he explained, "is that you don't have to try; so what you're wearing shouldn't ever be brand-new." New clothes, on the other hand, were appropriate when interviewing the *nouveau riche*; and since they might not recognize understated wealth, he (somewhat reluctantly, but a job is a job) would also put on a monogrammed shirt and Italian shoes with tassels.

When assigned to official Washington, this particular journalist took care to be three or four years behind current New York modes. "Washington hates fashion, especially New York fashion. The message should be, I am not attempting style; I am a man of the people, a regular fellow." He would therefore wear a somewhat rumpled pin-striped suit, a white shirt and a nondescript tie. Before leaving Manhattan he would get his hair cut shorter than usual. On the other hand, if he were sent to California, or were interviewing a writer, artist or musician anywhere in the country, he would try to let his hair grow or rumple it up a bit. He would wear slacks and a good tweed jacket over a turtleneck shirt; if the interviewee were financially successful he would add an expensive watch or pair of shoes to this costume. Still other getups were appropriate and available — for the Midwest, Texas, the South, Continental Europe and Britain.

When this system works it is no longer Waste; nor, since the clothes are deliberately chosen to blend into their surroundings, can they be called Conspicuous. But as the journalist himself remarked, clothes alone cannot disguise anyone, and the traveling salesman or saleswoman who engineers his or her wardrobe but not his or her voice, vocabulary or manners may simply be practicing Conspicuous Waste without its usual reward of enhanced status — let alone a rise in sales figures.

CONSPICUOUS LEISURE: DISCOMFORT AND HELPLESSNESS

Once upon a time leisure was far more conspicuous than it usually is today. The history of European costume is rich in styles in which it was literally impossible to perform any useful activity: sleeves that trailed on the floor, curled and powdered wigs the size, color and texture of a large white poodle, skirts six feet in diameter or with six-foot dragging trains, clanking ceremonial swords, starched wimples and cuffs and cravats that prevented their wearers from turning their heads or looking at anything below waist level, high-

heeled pointed shoes that made walking agony and corsets so tight that it was impossible to bend at the waist or take a normal breath. Such clothes proclaimed, indeed demanded, an unproductive life and the constant assistance of servants.

These conspicuously uncomfortable and leisurely styles reached an extreme in the late eighteenth century at the court of Versailles. The political and sartorial revolution that followed freed both sexes temporarily, and men permanently, from the need to advertise their aristocratic helplessness. Men's clothes became, and have remained ever since, at least moderately comfortable. Women's fashions on the other hand, after barely ten years of ease and simplicity, rapidly became burdensome again and continued so for the next hundred years.

Urban middle-class clothing today, though it does not usually cause pain, makes anything more than limited activity awkward. It is hard to run or climb in a business suit and slick-soled shoes; and the easily soiled white or pale-colored shirt that signifies freedom from manual labor is in constant danger of embarrassing its wearer with grimy cuffs or ring-around-the-collar. Urban women's dress is equally inconvenient. It should be pointed out, however, that inconvenience may be an advantage in some situations. A friend who often does historical research in libraries tells me that she always gets dressed up for it. If she is obviously handicapped by high heels, a pale, elegant suit and a ruffled white blouse, the librarians will search the stacks for the heavy volumes of documents and old newspapers she needs and carry them to her, dusting them on the way. If she wears a sweater, casual slacks and sensible shoes, they will let her do it herself. The same ploy would probably work for a man if he were middle-aged or older.

NOTES

1. Gerald Carson, *The Polite Americans: A Wide-Angle View of Our More or Less Good Manners over 300 Years* (Westport, Conn.: Greenwood Press, 1980), pp. 12–13.
2. Henrietta O. Ward, *Sensible Etiquette of the Best Society*, 18th ed. (Philadelphia: 1878), pp. 251–53.
3. Lillian Eichler, *Book of Etiquette*, Vol. II (Oyster Bay, N.Y.: Nelson Doubleday, 1921), p. 147.
4. Anne Hollander, *Seeing Through Clothes* (New York: Viking, 1978), p. 443.
5. Robert Brain, *The Decorated Body* (London: Hutchinson, 1979), p. 99.
6. Lillian Eichler, *Book of Etiquette*, p. 154.
7. The costume of the upper-class British male; I am indebted to Roland Gant and Nigel Hollis for this information.
8. Anne Hollander, *Seeing Through Clothes*, pp. 38–39.

PART 3B

ETHNIC AND RACIAL INEQUALITY

Ethnic groups are usually defined as social collectivities that are distinguished by ancestry and culture. **Races** have relatively unique ancestries and cultures too. In addition, races differ from ethnic groups and from each other in terms of visible physical characteristics, such as skin colour, that are socially defined as significant and that are significant in their social consequences.

Many people assume that cultural differences explain why some ethnic and racial groups are more economically and politically successful than others. In this view, only some groups are blessed with cultures that generate supportive families, respect for education, and an ethic of diligence and hard work. Other groups, culturally less well endowed, are condemned to broken families, low educational attainment, and limited occupational success. In Chapter 14, Stephen Steinberg of Queen's College in New York questions these easy assumptions about the role of culture in determining ethnic and racial fortunes. He focusses on the successes of Asians and Jews in American society, the presumed successes of West Indian blacks, and the failure of nearly 30 percent of American-born blacks to escape poverty. Steinberg shows that, as a result of a selective immigration policy in the United States, the successful groups in American society arrived with a head start compared with relatively unsuccessful groups: they came with occupational experiences, educational backgrounds, and, in some cases, capital that enabled them to achieve rapid movement up the socio-economic hierarchy. In sharp contrast, American-born blacks start their climb up the social hierarchy saddled with heavy historical and current liabilities: two hundred years of slavery, three hundred years of forced segregation, and continuing discrimination in employment, housing, and everyday life. Of course, there are cultural differences between American-born blacks and, say, Korean- and Japanese-Americans. But Steinberg's point is that these cultural differences are rooted in different historical and class experiences. In his judgement, culture is not an important *independent* cause of ethnic and racial success or failure.

In Chapter 15, Frances Henry of York University and her colleagues provide an overview of how discrimination affects members of Canada's racial minorities. (While **prejudice** refers to negative *attitudes* toward members of an ethnic or racial group, **discrimination** refers to *behaviour* that has negative consequences for such groups.) They first sketch the changing racial composition of Canadian society. By the year 2001, nearly 18 percent of Canadians will be members of racial minorities. The proportion will be much higher in large cities, reaching 25 percent in Montreal, Edmonton, Calgary, and Winnipeg, 40 percent in Vancouver, and nearly 50 percent in Toronto. Chinese, blacks, and South Asians will each account for roughly a fifth of the racial-minority population. Henry and her colleagues summarize government-sponsored studies and public opinion polls that have found evidence of widespread racism in Canada, concluding that somewhere between 30 and 55 percent of Canadians hold racist views. They also describe the several white supremacist hate groups that have sprung up in Canada and they report on field experiments and statistical census studies that demonstrate significant racial discrimination in employment, particularly against black Canadians.

Given such widespread racial discrimination, most of Canada's racial minorities have fared surprisingly well economically. (The glaring exception: Canada's aboriginal peoples; see Chapter 23.) This is a tribute to their resourcefulness and industry and it is largely a consequence of their social background. Thus, according to the 1986 census, the median annual income of black Canadians was 92.1 percent of the median annual income of Canadians of British origin. In stark contrast, the median annual income of black Americans was only 67.3 percent of the median annual income of white Americans in 1990. Of the twelve ethnic and racial groups in Canada with a population over 250 000, East Indians had the third-highest median income in 1986; the British ranked fourth. The economic achievement of most of Canada's racial minorities is due largely to the country's selective immigration policy, which favours immigrants with higher education and money. In brief, credentials and capital help to overcome the worst economic consequences of discrimination.

Nonetheless, there are persistent economic differences among racial and ethnic groups in Canada. These are explored in depth in Chapter 16, by Hugh Lautard of the University of New Brunswick and Neil Guppy of the University of British Columbia. Lautard and Guppy critically review past studies of ethnic and racial stratification in Canada and they analyze Canadian census data from 1931 to 1986. They conclude that occupational differences between ethnic and racial groups have decreased by 50 percent over the 55-year period they studied but that they still remain substantial. How substantial? Occupational differences among ethnic and racial groups are about 40 percent as large as occupational differences between men and women. Why are the differences so large? Mainly because some groups continue to be augmented by substantial numbers of immigrants, and immigrants suffer more disadvantages that native-born Canadians. For example, immigrants may lack English and French language skills and contacts in the wider community that could help them find better jobs. The Canadian-born children of immigrants are less disadvantaged in this regard, and their movement up the stratification system is therefore somewhat easier, even though discrimination persists, especially for members of racial minority groups.

The results of a recent study based on the 1986 Canadian census illustrate the effect of immigration status on income. Samples of immigrant and Canadian-born adults were first matched. That is, the members of both groups who were compared had the same distribution of ages, areas of residence, marital statuses, educational levels, occupations, full-time and part-time work statuses, and number of weeks worked in the preceding year. Next, the annual incomes of Canadian-born and foreign-born men and women, both visible-minority and non-visible-minority, were calculated. Table P3B.1 shows the results, expressed in dollars above or below the national average for men and women. Examine the left-hand column first. Note that all immigrants earned below-average incomes and that visible-minority immigrants earned less than non-visible-minority immigrants. Turn now to the right-hand column, which contains data on Canadian-born adults. There we see that the group differences are much smaller than in the left-hand column. Moreover, three of the four Canadian-born groups earned more than the national average. Among Canadian-born adults, visible-minority women actually earned more than non-visible-minority women. Only Canadian-born, visible-minority men earned less than the national average for men. But even for them, substantial improvement is evident; while the immigrant generation of visible-minority men earned 19.6 percent less than the average for men, the Canadian-born generation of visible-minority men earned only 2.3 percent less than the average for men. Clearly, being an immigrant carries with it an economic liability. Just as clearly, the liability diminishes for the first Canadian-born generation.

Table P3B.1 Annual Income by Immigration Status, Sex, and Visible-Minority Status for Canadians Age 25–64 in 1986 (Deviations from Male and Female Averages in Dollars)

	Immigrant	Canadian-born	Average
MEN			
Visible minority	–5,307	–627	27,019
Non-visible minority	–424	436	
WOMEN			
Visible minority	–1,634	474	15,080
Non-visible minority	–198	154	

Source: Adapted from Monica Boyd, "Gender, Visible Minority, and Immigrant Earnings Inequality: Reassessing an Employment Equity Premise," in Vic Satzewich, ed., *Deconstructing a Nation: Immigration, Multiculturalism and Racism in '90s Canada* (Halifax: Fernwood, 1992), p. 298.

GLOSSARY

Discrimination refers to behaviour that has negative consequences for members of an ethnic or racial group.

Ethnic groups are social collectivities that are distinguished by relatively unique ancestry and culture.

Prejudice refers to negative attitudes toward members of an ethnic or racial group.

Races have relatively unique ancestries and cultures but they also differ from ethnic groups and from each other in terms of physical characteristics (e.g., skin colour) that are socially defined as important and that are important in their social consequences.

Chapter 14

ETHNIC HEROES AND RACIAL VILLAINS

STEPHEN STEINBERG

Myths die hard, as the saying goes. To be sure, myths about race and ethnicity are deep-seated and often appear immune to change, but this is not because of some inherent potency or appeal. Myths are socially constructed. They arise in specific times and places, in response to identifiable circumstances and needs, and they are passed on through processes that can be readily observed. Whether a myth prospers or withers is always problematic; most, in fact, are relinquished or forgotten. To explain why some myths persist, we have to explore the relationship that these myths have to larger social institutions that promote and sustain them, and that in turn are served by them.

This chapter deals with myths that purport to explain why racial and ethnic groups occupy higher or lower places in the class system — why, in the popular idiom, "we have made it and they have not." The popular explanation, translated into respectable academic language by mainstream social scientists, is that "we" had the cultural virtues and moral fiber that "they" are lacking. If this theory were predicated on fact alone, it would be fairly easy to dispense with — for example, by showing that Jews, the archetype of ethnic success, arrived with occupational experiences and skills that gave them a headstart relative to other immigrants from eastern and southern Europe, that these latter groups were favorably positioned relative to blacks, who were excluded from industrial employment altogether during the critical early phases of industrialization, and that racial minorities — blacks in particular — have been encumbered by discriminatory barriers across gen-

erations that constitute the chief reason for their current economic plight. However compelling these facts might be, even when fully documented and analyzed, they are overpowered by other assumptions and beliefs that are almost universally shared in American society and that pervade American social science as well.

My point is that racial and ethnic myths about "making it" are embedded in a larger "success myth," one that is deeply rooted in American history and culture, and not easily countervailed. As Richard Weiss writes at the outset of his book on *The American Myth of Success*:

> ... the idea that ours is an open society, where birth, family, and class do not significantly circumscribe individual possibilities, has a strong hold on the popular imagination. The belief that all men, in accordance with certain rules, but exclusively by their own efforts, can make of their lives what they will has been widely popularized for well over a century. The cluster of ideas surrounding this conviction makes up the American myth of success.[1]

As Weiss goes on to say, the word "myth" does not imply something entirely false. The success myth was forged when the United States was a nation of yeomen and artisans, and it was sustained through two centuries of virtually uninterrupted territorial expansion and economic growth. There is much in our national experience to sustain notions of America as an open society where the individual can surmount impediments of "birth, family, and class." The problem arises when this simple schema glosses over major contradictions.

To wit, colonial America was not just a nation of yeomen and artisans — one-fifth of its inhabitants were slaves, and the wealth that flowed from slavery had a great deal to do with the expanding opportunities for those early Americans who exemplified Puritan virtues of industry, frugality, and prudence. A problem also arises when success is equated with virtue, and failure with sin and personal inadequacy. Not only does this individualize success or failure, thus obscuring the whole issue of social justice, but it also treats virtue and its opposite as a matter of personal endowment, rather than as traits that need to be explained in terms of their historical and social sources.

It has never been easy to accommodate the success myth to the embarrassing realities of racial inequality. If the United States is an open society where the individual is not irreparably handicapped by "birth, family, and class," then how is racial hierarchy to be explained? When Gunnar Myrdal suggested in the 1950s that racism constituted an unhappy contradiction between American ideals and practices, this was heralded as a major advance. Indeed, the thrust of previous research had been to find in the cephalic index or in intelligence tests clear evidence of a biological inferiority that predestined blacks to subordinate status. The discrediting of scientific racism is unquestionably one of the great triumphs of liberal social science. However, subsequent theorists developed a social-scientific variant of scientific racism that essentially substituted culture for genes. Now it was held that groups that occupy the lowest strata of society are saddled by cultural systems that prevent them from climbing the social ladder. As before, failure is explained not in terms of societal structures, but in terms of traits endemic to the groups themselves.

For the exponents of social-scientific racism, furthermore, culture is almost as immutable as the genes themselves. Thus, for example, Thomas Sowell writes:

> Specific skills are a prerequisite in many kinds of work. But history shows new skills being rather readily acquired in a few years, as compared to the generations — or centuries — required for attitude changes. Groups today plagued by absenteeism, tardiness, and a need for constant supervision at work or in school are typically descendants of people with the same habits a century or more ago. The cultural inheritance can be more important than biological inheritance, although the latter stirs more controversy.[2]

As Sowell contends in this passage and his more extended disquisitions, a defective culture is the chief reason that blacks have not followed in the footsteps of immigrants in their pursuit of the American Dream. Jews, on the other hand, are the perfect counter example — "the classic American success story — from rags to riches against all opposition."[3] Their formula for success amounts to having a certain cultural magic, called "human capital." To quote Sowell again:

> Whether in an ethnic context or among peoples and nations in general, much depends on the whole constellation of values, attitudes, skills, and contacts that many call a culture and that economists call "human capital." ... The importance of human capital in an ethnic context is shown in many ways. Groups that arrived in America financially destitute have rapidly risen to affluence, when their cultures stressed the values and behavior required in an industrial and commercial economy. Even when color and racial prejudices confronted them — as in the case of the Chinese and Japanese — this proved to be an impediment but was ultimately unable to stop them.[4]

In the hands of Thomas Sowell, "human capital" is little more than an obfuscation for writing a morality tale whereby groups — notably Jews and Asians — who have "the right stuff" overcome every impediment of race and class to reach the economic pinnacle. Other groups — especially blacks — suffer from historically conditioned cultural defects that condemn them to lag behind in the economic competition. Of course, Sowell's morality tale is not an original creation. His ethnic heroes and racial villains are merely an updated version of traditional folklore that pitted rugged cowboys against treacherous Indians (which also had racist overtones).

Nor is this racist folklore, masked as social science, politically innocent. Its covert ideological function is to legitimize existing racial inequalities. By placing cultural blame on the victims, the nation's vaunted ideals are reconciled with patently undemocratic divisions and inequities. By projecting collective Horatio Algers, in the unlikely forms of Jews and Asians, it is demonstrated that "success" is attainable to everyone, without regard to "birth, family, and class." Like all myths, the ethnic myth has an implicit morale: "we" are not responsible, morally or politically, for "their" misfortune.

NEW HEROES: ASIANS AND WEST INDIANS

Social science's enchantment with the success myth, replete with its cast of heroes and villains, has been renewed in recent years with the arrival of millions of immigrants, the majority of whom are Asians, West

Indians, and Hispanics. That these new immigrants have generally settled in cities with large concentrations of poverty-stricken blacks has only highlighted the contrast between upwardly mobile immigrants and inner-city blacks. Invidious comparisons have been common in the popular press, and social scientists have churned out more spurious scholarship extolling cultural virtue and reciting the stock tale of triumph over adversity. That these new heroes — Asians and West Indians — belong to racial minorities has thickened the plot, since it demonstrates, according to these scholars, that "race" is not an insurmountable obstacle and cannot explain why so many blacks are still mired in poverty.

Thomas Sowell is prominent among those who have advanced this point of view. In the passage quoted earlier, Sowell notes that Chinese and Japanese confronted "color and racial prejudices," but asserts that this "was ultimately unable to stop them." It is the West Indians, however, who provide Sowell with the clincher to his argument that it is culture, not race, that explains why blacks languish in poverty:

> While not racially distinct from American Negroes, West Indians have had a different cultural background.... These differences provide some clues as to how much of the situation of American Negroes in general can be attributed to color prejudice by whites and how much to cultural patterns among blacks.[5]

Several pages later Sowell is less equivocal:

> The contrast between the West Indians and American Negroes was not so much in their occupational backgrounds as in their behavioral patterns. West Indians were much more frugal, hard-working, and entrepreneurial. Their children worked harder and outperformed native black children in school.[6]

The passages above are examples of a unique logical fallacy, which might be called a "Sowellgism." It goes as follows:

> Premise 1: Blacks, Asians, and West Indians are all races.
> Premise 2: Asians and West Indians have succeeded.
> Conclusion: Race cannot explain why blacks have not succeeded.

The trouble with this reasoning is that it uses an overgeneralized abstraction, "race," to gloss over crucial differences among the racial groups being compared with one another. Only in the most general sense can it be claimed that Asians, West Indians, and African Americans are all "races" that have been victims of racial stereotyping and discrimination. Although true, this proposition obscures the unique oppression that blacks have endured throughout American history, beginning with two centuries of slavery and another century of official segregation, reinforced by the lynch mob and systematically unequal treatment in all major institutions. West Indians, of course, were also slaves, but living in island homelands that were predominantly black, they have been insulated from the legalized and all-encompassing segregation that is unique to the African American experience.

Nor can this be dismissed as "history" that has no bearing on the present generation. If mobility is placed in correct sociological perspective, and regarded not as an individual event but as a process that occurs incrementally across generations, it becomes clear that America's legacy of racism has had a significant impact on the life chances even of today's black youth. To say this is not to engage in "comparative suffering." It is merely to acknowledge the unique oppression that blacks have experienced on American soil. Otherwise it is scarcely possible to explain why blacks have been a perennial underclass in American society, and why they continue to lag behind other "racial" minorities.

THE MYTH OF ASIAN SUCCESS

In 1986 the five top recipients of the prestigious Westinghouse Science Talent Search were of Asian descent. This prompted a spate of articles in magazines and newspapers seeking to explain how a tiny minority, representing less than 2 percent of the national population, could achieve such bewildering success. The question, as framed by Malcolm Browne in an op-ed piece in the New York Times, is: "Do Asians have genetic advantages, or does their apparent edge in scientific skills stem from their special cultural tradition?"[7] Thus are we offered a choice between genes and culture as explanations for the academic excellence among Asians. Browne rejects genetic determinism, but has no such qualms with respect to cultural determinism. Paraphrasing an unnamed Westinghouse spokesman, he writes: "Tightly-knit families and high respect for all forms of learning are traditional characteristics of Asian societies ... as they are for Jewish societies; in the past a very high proportion of top Westinghouse winners were Jewish." Of course, as Browne himself remarks, "the odd thing is that until the twentieth century, real science scarcely existed in Asia." Undaunted by this apparent contradiction, he argues that Asian children are endowed with "an underlying devotion to scholarship — the kind of devotion imprinted on Asian children by a pantheon of ancestors" — that has made them receptive to Western scientific thought. Thus is a theory bent to accommodate inconvenient facts.

Two years later the *New York Times* ran another piece under the heading, "Why Do Asian Pupils Win Those Prizes?"[8] The author, Stephen Graubard, a professor of history at Brown University and editor of *Daedalus*, opines that Asians, who were eleven of the fourteen Westinghouse finalists from Cardozo High School in Queens, New York, have the advantage of stable families and Asian mothers who rear their children for success. With an air of resignation, he then turns the question onto blacks and Puerto Ricans: "What is to be done for those hundreds of thousands of other New York children, many of illegitimate birth, who live with one parent, often in public housing, knowing little outside their dilapidated and decaying neighborhoods?" Since Graubard does not believe that the schools can do much to compensate for the defective culture of children from poverty backgrounds, these children are presumably condemned to languish in the cultural wasteland.

The same single-minded preoccupation with culture is found in yet another article in *The New York Times Magazine* on "Why Asians Succeed Here." The author, Robert Oxnam, president of the prestigious Asia Society, writes as follows:

> The story of these new immigrants goes far beyond the high school valedictorians and Westinghouse Science scholars we read about in our newspapers. It is the story of a broader cultural interaction, a pairing of old Asian values with American individualism, Asian work ethics with American entrepreneurship. And, where those cultural elements have collided, it has also been a story of sharp disappointments and frustration.[9]

Once again, culture is the fulcrum of success. Like the other writers quoted above, Oxnam identifies "the strong family ties and powerful work ethics of Asian cultures" as "key factors in Asian-American achievement."

This theory of Asian success is a new spin on earlier theories about Jews, to whom Asians are explicitly compared. As with the theory of Jewish success, there are a number of conceptual and empirical problems that throw the theory into question:

1. The theory of "Asian" success lumps together some twenty-five nationalities that are very disparate in history and culture. It is only in the United States that they are assumed to share a common "Asian" heritage. Little or no evidence is put forward to substantiate claims that they share common values with respect to family and work, that these values are significantly different from those found among non-Asian groups, or that these values are the key factors in explaining which Asians get ahead or why more Asians do so than others. Here is a classic case of circular reasoning. Values are not measured independently, but inferred from success, and then posited as the cause of success.

2. Theories of Asian success gloss over the fact that large segments of the Asian populations in the United States are far from prosperous. Alongside dramatic and visible success, touted in the popular media, are deep pockets of poverty, exploitation, and despair. Moreover, if successful Asians are presumed to owe their success to distinctively Asian values with respect to family and work, then are we to assume that less affluent Asians are deficient in these values? Are they therefore less "Asian"?

3. As in the case of Jewish success, the prevailing theory of Asian success overlooks the operation of premigration class factors that go a long way toward explaining the destinies of these immigrants after their arrival. The issue here has to do with selective migration — that is, with who decides to emigrate and who is permitted entry. As Ezra Vogel, a scholar of China and Japan, has noted, Asian immigrants "are a very biased sample, the cream of their own societies."[10] They are drawn disproportionately from the intellectual and professional elites that, for one reason or another, have restricted opportunity in their home countries. Many of then have been admitted under the occupational preferences built into the new immigration law. In short, they are "successful" even before their arrival in America.

Data collected by the Immigration and Naturalization Service demonstrate the class character of Asian immigration. Table 14.1 reports the percentage of immigrant workers classified as professionals.[11] In the case of Indians, over three-quarters of immigrants with occupations are professionals; this reached a high point in 1969–71 when nine out of every ten Indians with occupations were professionals. Among Filipinos, Koreans, and Japanese the figures range between half

Table 14.1 Percentage of Professionals Among Asian Immigrants with Occupations

	1961–65	1966–68	1969–71	1971–74	1975–77
China	31	35	47	37	31
India	68	67	89	84	73
Japan	44	50	45	37	28
Korea	71	75	70	51	38
Philippines	48	60	70	63	47
All Asians	40	52	62	54	44
All Immigrants	20	25	29	27	25

Source: Adapted from Morrison G. Wong and Charles Hirschman, "The New Asian Immigrants," in *Culture, Ethnicity, and Identity*, William McCready, ed. (New York: Academic Press, 1983), pp. 395–97.

and three-quarters; among Chinese, the figures are somewhat lower, but still much higher than for non-Asians. The influx of professionals of all nationalities reached a peak between 1969 and 1971, and declined thereafter. Nevertheless, the evidence is clear that a major segment of Asian immigration represents an educational and occupational elite.

Other data indicate that between 1965 and 1981 some 70,000 medical professionals — physicians, nurses, and pharmacists — came from the Philippines, South Korea, and India.[12] Another major source of immigrants has been students who enter the United States with student visas and then do not return to their home country. Of the 70,000 Chinese students from Taiwan between 1950 and 1983, it is estimated that 90 percent remained in the United States. The same is true of tens of thousands of students from Hong Kong, Korea, and other Asian countries. What these figures indicate is not a dramatic success story, but merely the transfer of intellectual and professional elites from less developed nations.

These immigrants start out with the educational and occupational resources that are generally associated with educational achievement in the next generation. To put the cultural theory to a fair empirical test, one would have to compare the children of Asian professionals with the children of other professionals. Only in this way could we assess the significance of distinctive ethnic factors. It is hardly valid to compare the children of upper-middle-class Asian professionals with the children of unemployed black workers, as is done when "Asians" are compared with "blacks."[13]

Not all Asian immigrants, however, come from advantaged backgrounds. Indeed, in recent years the flow of immigrants has included large numbers of uneducated and unskilled workers. These are the "downtown Chinese," as Peter Kwong calls them in his recent book, *The New Chinatown*.[14] These immigrants have difficulty finding employment in the racially segmented labor market outside of Chinatown, and are forced to accept jobs, commonly in sweatshops and restaurants, that match their nineteenth-century counterparts in their debasing exploitation. It has yet to be demonstrated that the children of these superexploited workers are part of an Asian success story. Indeed, the outbreak of gang violence among Chinatown youth has exploded another myth that had great currency in the 1950s; namely, that because of their close-knit families, delinquency is virtually nonexistent among the Chinese.[15]

In demystifying and explaining Asian success, we come again to a simple truth: that what is inherited is not genes, and not culture, but class advantage and disadvantage. If not for the extraordinary selectivity of the Asian immigrant population, there would be no commentaries in the popular press and the social science literature extolling Confucian values and "the pantheon of ancestors" who supposedly inspire the current generation of Asian youth. After all, no such claims are made about the Asian youth who inhabit the slums of Manila, Hong Kong, and Bombay, or, for that matter, San Francisco and New York.

THE MYTH OF WEST INDIAN SUCCESS

The mythical aspects of West Indian success, and the invidious comparisons between West Indians and blacks, predate the current wave of immigration. In *Beyond the Melting Pot*, published in 1963, Glazer and Moynihan wrote that "the ethos of the West Indians, in contrast to that of the Southern Negro, emphasized saving, hard work, investment and education."[16] Although Glazer and Moynihan offer no evidence to support their claims, their observations are consistent with those made by other observers over several decades.[17] The key issue, though, is not whether West

Indians in New York had the exemplary cultural traits that were ascribed to them. The issue is whether these cultural traits *explain* West Indian success, or whether, on the contrary, West Indians were more middle-class to begin with, and this explains their different attitudes with respect to "saving, hard work, investment and education."

As with Asians, the factor of selective migration must be considered. To begin with, we need to distinguish between two waves of West Indian immigration: the first, during the 1920s; the second, after the 1965 Hart-Celler Act. The first wave of immigrants were a highly selective group. According to immigration records, almost all of the adults — 89 percent — were literate, a figure far higher than that for West Indians who did not emigrate, or for the southern blacks to whom they are compared.[18] Over 40 percent of the West Indian immigrants were classified as skilled, and some of these were highly educated professionals. Thus, once again, in drawing overall comparisons between West Indians and African Americans, we are comparing groups that differ in their social class as well as their ethnicity. It has never been shown that West Indians are different in terms of "saving, hard work, investment, and education" when compared with their social class equals who are not West Indian.[19]

In other words, before generalizing about "West Indian cultural values," we need to be clear about which West Indians we have in mind. This is sharply illustrated by Nancy Foner's study of West Indians in New York City and London.[20] Since both groups have the same cultural heritage, this factor cannot explain why West Indians in New York have been more successful than those in Britain. Foner shows that the two immigrant pools are different in occupational background. Those who flocked to Britain during the 1950s were responding to labor shortages and an open-door immigration policy for Commonwealth nations. Although many were skilled workers, only about 10 percent were classified as white-collar. In contrast, among West Indian legal emigrants to the United States between 1962 and 1971, 15 percent were professional workers and another 12 percent worked in other white-collar occupations. For this reason alone, it is not surprising that West Indians in New York have been conspicuously more successful than those in London.[21]

The selective character of West Indian immigration to the United States, as already suggested, "stacks the deck" in terms of any comparisons to African Americans. Especially at a time when there was virtually no indigenous black middle class, the influx of a small West Indian elite of professionals, businessmen, and prominent individuals did in fact stand out, and seemed to support notions of West Indian cultural superiority. Two things have changed since the migration of the 1920s, however. In the first place, there is a sizable African American middle class. Second, West Indian migration has become more occupationally diverse than was previously the case. Therefore, we have to reconsider our assumptions regarding the social status of West Indians in relation to African Americans.

In a paper entitled "West Indian Success: Myth or Fact?" Reynolds Farley undertakes an extensive analysis of 1980 Census data.[22] He concludes that there is more myth than fact in suppositions about West Indian success.

Farley divided his sample into five groups: native whites, native blacks, black immigrants pre-1970, black immigrants post-1970, and blacks of West Indian ancestry (born in the United States but of West Indian parents or grandparents). On all relevant social and economic indicators, the four black cohorts differ little among themselves, and where differences exist, they are small in comparison to the differences between blacks and whites. For example, the figures below indicate the percentages of families that are female-headed:

Whites	11%
Native blacks	37%
Black immigrants pre-1970	33%
Black immigrants post-1970	25%
West Indian ancestry	38%

Except for recent immigrants, female-headed households are as prevalent among West Indians as among native blacks. Thus, the data do not support the widespread notion that West Indians have "strong families" in comparison to African Americans.

Nor do the data support the notion that West Indians are endowed with an entrepreneurial spirit that leads to business success. The following figures, adjusted for age, report the rate of self-employment among men:

Whites	87 per thousand
Native blacks	30
Black immigrants pre-1970	41
Black immigrants post-1970	22
West Indian ancestry	35

The rate of self-employment among recent West Indian immigrants is strikingly low (in contrast to what is found among recent Korean immigrants, for example). It is true that earlier West Indian immigrants and their descendants have a higher rate of self-employment than do native blacks, but the levels are still much lower than that for whites. In short, self-employment is not so pronounced among West Indians as to support crude popular notions concerning "Jew-maicans," or, for that matter, more refined claims of "ethnic enterprise" and "entrepreneurial spirit" supposedly endemic to West Indian culture.

Similar patterns are found with respect to education, occupation, and income. West Indians are generally higher on these measures of social class than native blacks, but the differences are not great and there is always the suspicion that they are an artifact of selective migration. For example, the figures below report the average earnings in 1979 of employed males between the ages of 25 and 64:

Whites	15,170
Native blacks	9,380
Black immigrants pre-1970	7,460
Black immigrants post-1970	11,170
West Indian ancestry	10,720

Again, West Indians are much closer to native blacks in their earnings than they are to whites, and recent West Indian immigrants have the lowest incomes of all five groups. On the basis of his analysis of these 1980 Census data, Farley reached the following conclusion:

> We have shown that black immigrants and West Indians in 1980 were quite similar to native blacks on the most important indicators of social and economic status. There is no basis now — and apparently there was none in the past — for arguing that the success of West Indians in the United States "proves" that culture, rather than racial discrimination, determines the current status of blacks.[23]

The critical role that premigration factors play in a group's "adjustment" is even more vividly illustrated by the two waves of Cuban immigration. The first wave, occurring in the aftermath of the Cuban Revolution, consisted largely of Cuba's economic elites — professionals, businessmen, shopkeepers, and others disenchanted with Cuban socialism. The second wave, "the Mariel invasion," consisted of ordinary Cubans, including a small number of criminals and mental patients whom the Cuban government cynically placed aboard the boats. The first wave was welcomed, especially in southern Florida's depressed economy, and inspired exuberant articles, like the one in *Fortune* magazine on "Those Amazing Cuban Emigrants."[24] The second wave received a far less hospitable reception, and were besmirched by sensational press reports

suggesting that the Mariel Cubans were mostly criminals, lunatics, and degenerates.[25] The Cuban cultural magic seemed to have vanished.

In the final analysis, the attempt to use Asians and West Indians to prove that "race" cannot explain the plight of black America is fallacious at best, and sinister at worst. It is based on an untenable juxtaposition of groups that look alike in terms of a simplistic racial classification (they are all "racial" minorities), but who are very different in terms of their social class origins, in terms of the structures of opportunity they encounter after their arrival, and even in terms of the depth of racism that limits access to these opportunities. This is not to deny that Asians and West Indian immigrants confront a difficult situation, one that calls forth all their cultural and personal resources. Nor is it to deny that both groups encounter racist barriers in their quest for a better life. It does not do them or ourselves any good, however, to use these struggling minorities to make specious comparisons to African Americans, and to minimize the significance of racism.

NOTES

1. Richard Weiss, *The American Myth of Success* (New York: Basic Books, 1969).
2. Thomas Sowell, *Ethnic America* (New York: Basic Books, 1981), p. 284. Italics added.
3. Ibid., p. 98.
4. Ibid., p. 282. For another view, see Stephen Steinberg, "Human Capital: A Critique," *The Review of Black Political Economy* 14: 1 (Summer 1985), pp. 67–74.
5. Thomas Sowell, op. cit., p. 216.
6. Ibid., p. 219. For a similar popular account, see "America's Super Minority," *Fortune* 114 (November 24, 1986), p. 148.
7. Malcolm W. Browne, "A Look at Success of Young Asians," *New York Times* (March 25, 1986), p. A31.
8. Stephen G. Graubard, "Why Do Asian Pupils Win Those Prizes?" *New York Times* (January 29, 1988), p. A35.
9. Robert B. Oxnam, "Why Asians Succeed Here," *New York Times Magazine* (November 30, 1986), p. 70.
10. Quoted in Fox Butterfield, "Why Asians Are Going to the Head of the Class," Education Supplement, *New York Times* (August 3, 1986), section 12, p. 20.
11. These percentages are based on the number of immigrants who report having a job, thereby excluding non-working women, as well as the old and young.
12. Illsoo Kim, "Ethnic Class Division among Asian Immigrants: Its Implications for Social Welfare Policies," unpublished paper presented at the Conference on Asian American Studies, Cornell University, October 24, 1986, p. 3.

13. If there is a distinctively ethnic factor in patterns of Asian mobility, it is that, like Jews of earlier generations, Asians realize that their channels of opportunity are restricted by prejudice. Closed off from the corporate fast lane, they are drawn to the professions. The sciences are particularly attractive to individuals who lack fluency in English. Data reporting SAT scores indicate that Asian American students score far above average on the math test, but far below average on the verbal test. *New York Times*, section 12: "Education Life" (August 3, 1986), p. 3.

14. Peter Kwong, *The New Chinatown* (New York: Hill & Wang, 1987), pp. 5–6.

15. For example, see Henry Beckett, "How Parents Help Chinese Kids Stay Out of Trouble," series in the *New York Post* (July 11–13, 1955), and Betty Lee Sung, *The Story of the Chinese in America* (New York: Collier, 1971), p. 156.

16. Nathan Glazer and Daniel Patrick Moynihan, *Beyond the Melting Pot* (Cambridge: MIT Press, 1963), p. 35.

17. For example, Ira Reid, *The Negro Immigrant* (New York: Arno Press, 1969), originally published in 1939; James Weldon Johnson, *Black Manhattan* (New York: Knopf, 1930).

18. Nancy Foner, "West Indians in New York City and London. A Comparative Analysis," in Constance R. Sutton and Elsa M. Chaney, eds., *Caribbean Life in New York City* (New York Center for Migration Studies, 1987), p. 123.

19. In their study of Jamaican and black American migrant farm workers, Nancy Foner and Richard Napoli observed differences between the two groups that, at first glance, appear to support the cultural thesis. The black America farm workers were frequently apathetic on the job, and squandered part of their wages on liquor and gambling. In contrast, the Jamaican workers "worked very hard, were extremely productive, and saved most of their earnings" (p. 492).

To their credit, Foner and Napoli probe beneath surface behavior, and show that the two groups have different origins and are recruited through different procedures. For black Americans, migrant labor was a last resort and a dead end, whereas for Jamaicans the wages meant a higher living standard when they returned home, and the possibility of purchasing land or establishing a small business. Thus, the same work attracted a different calibre of worker, and the same pay provided different incentives.

Second, as offshore workers, Jamaicans were recruited under a program that not only included a physical exam, but also considered their previous work record. They also had to meet a work quota to remain in the camp and to ensure that they would be hired again. In these ways the Jamaican recruiting system "seemed to weed out the kinds of workers who frequently travelled North in the black American migrant stream" (p. 501). Nancy Foner and Richard Napoli, "Jamaican and Black-American Migrant Farm Workers: A Comparative Analysis," *Social Problems* 25 (June 1978), p. 491–503.

20. Nancy Foner, "West Indians in New York City and London: A Comparative Analysis," in Sutton and Chaney, eds., *Caribbean Life in New York City*, op. cit. Also, see Roy Simon Bryce-Laporte, "New York City and the New Caribbean Immigration: A Contextual Statement," *International Migration Review* 13: 2 (1979), pp. 214–34.

21. Ibid., p. 123. In addition to differences in the occupational background of the two West Indian cohorts, Foner cites two other factors that help to explain why West Indians have fared better in the United States: (1) the migration spans a much longer period, and is already into the second generation, and (2) they benefited from having a preexisting black community that provided patronage for West Indian professionals and entrepreneurs, and that allowed West Indians to be cast into a privileged intermediary position between black and white America (comparable in some ways to the position of the coloreds in South America).

22. Reynolds Farley, "West Indian Success: Myth or Fact," unpublished manuscript (Ann Arbor, Mich.: Population Studies Center, University of Michigan, 1987). Statistical data are taken from pp. 8, 11, and 13. Also see Reynolds Farley and Walter R. Allen, *The Color Line and the Quality of Life in America* (New York: Russel Sage, 1987), chapter 12.

23. Ibid., p. 15.

24. Tom Alexander, "Those Amazing Cuban Emigres," *Fortune* 74 (October 1966), pp. 144–49.

25. Actually, less than 5 percent of the Mariel migrants were hardened criminals, mental patients, or other undesirables. See Robert L. Bach, Jennifer B. Bach, and Timothy Triplett, "The Flotilla 'Entrants': Latest and Most Controversial," *Cuban Studies* 11 (1981), pp. 29–48.

Chapter 15

THE VICTIMIZATION OF RACIAL MINORITIES IN CANADA

FRANCES HENRY, CAROL TATOR, WINSTON MATTIS, AND TIM REES

A significant shift has occurred in the composition of Canadian society. This changing demographic pattern is largely the result of the ending of the most overt forms of racism in immigration policies and the opening up of immigration to Third World countries (Samuals, 1992).

Canada's population has become increasingly racially diverse. From what was a country largely inhabited by Whites and Aboriginal peoples, the population has changed to include people from more than 70 countries. In addition, the source countries from which immigrants come have dramatically altered. In 1961, 90 percent of Canada's immigrants came from European countries; between 1981 and 1991, this figure declined to 25 percent. Almost half of all immigrants who came to Canada between 1981 and 1991 were Asian-born.

By 1986, 38 percent of Canadians had at least one ancestor who was neither French nor English. In the same year, racial minorities accounted for 6.3 percent, or 1.6 million, of Canada's population. In 1991, the figure had increased to 9.6 percent, or 2.6 million. Recent projections indicate that the racial minority population will rise to 17.7 percent — 5.7 million people — in the year 2001.

More than two-thirds of racial-minority immigrants to Canada come from Asia. Chinese comprise the most numerous group, with 1.3 million people, followed by South Asians (East Indians, Pakistanis, Sri Lankans, and Bangladeshis) and Blacks, with 1.1 million each. The next most numerous groups are West Asians and Arabs, Filipinos, Southeast Asians (Indochinese), and Latin Americans. The number of Latin American immigrants is expected to grow fourfold by the turn of the century.

By 2001, about half the population of Toronto and two-fifths of the population of Vancouver are expected to be racial minorities. About one-quarter of the popu-

Table 15.1 Provincial Distribution of Racial Minorities, 1986–2001

Provinces/Territories	1991	2001
Newfoundland	5 200	11 400
Prince Edward Island	2 600	5 700
Nova Scotia	38 800	85 200
New Brunswick	12 900	28 400
Quebec	367 300	806 800
Ontario	1 270 300	2 789 900
Manitoba	90 500	198 900
Saskatchewan	38 800	85 200
Alberta	274 200	602 300
British Columbia	483 800	1 062 500
Yukon & Northwest Territories	2 600	5 700
Total	2 587 000	5 682 000

Source: T.J. Samuals, *Visible Minorities in Canada: A Projection.* Toronto: Race Relations Advisory Council on Advertising, Canadian Advertising Foundation, 1992.

Source: Adapted from *The Colour of Democracy: Racism in Canadian Society* (Toronto: Harcourt Brace, 1995), pp. 78–104. Used by permission of the publisher.

Figure 15.1 Ethnicity of Racial Minorities, 2001

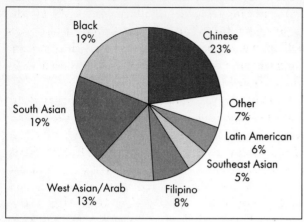

Source: T.J. Samuals, *Visible Minorities in Canada: A Projection.* Toronto: Race Relations Advisory Council on Advertising, Canadian Advertising Foundation, 1992.

lations of Montreal, Edmonton, Calgary, and Winnipeg are expected to be racial minorities. In Ottawa-Hull and Windsor, one-sixth of the populations will consist of racial minorities. Halifax, Kitchener, Hamilton, Victoria, and Regina will have 10–14 percent.

There are many kinds of data one can turn to in assessing the impact of these changes in the composition and complexion of immigrants to Canada. One of the most important and reliable sources of data on racism is the direct experiences of the victims. This

evidence is found in the numerous reports of task forces, commissions, and surveys, often conducted by academics, public authorities, and ad hoc advisory committees. It is also found in the oral histories of people of colour. A growing body of literature documents the experiences of racial minorities. Although these kinds of data are sometimes dismissed as being too subjective, they are critical to the understanding of racism.

Another source of data consists of the polls and surveys that seek to measure racist attitudes among individuals or groups. In the past two decades, many such surveys have been initiated by government agencies, politicians, the media, and academics.

A third source is the research findings of academics and commissioned studies by universities and other public sector agencies.

The final sections of this chapter examine the evidence of employment discrimination. Employment discrimination has been singled out for special attention because it is perhaps the single most important arena in which racism flourishes. Barriers to access and equity in the workplace ultimately affect all other areas of social functioning.

VICTIMS' MANIFESTATIONS

Evidence of racism in Canada, particularly over the past two decades, can be found in a number of

Figure 15.2 Racial Minorities in Selected CMAs, 1991 and 2001 (Projected)

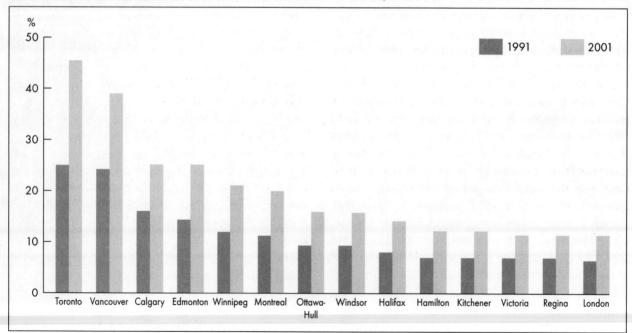

Source: T.J. Samuals, *Visible Minorities in Canada: A Projection.* Toronto: Race Relations Advisory Council on Advertising, Canadian Advertising Foundation, 1992.

government-sponsored inquiries, task forces, and commissions, which have usually been established after a series of highly publicized events or incidents involving members of racial-minority communities. For example, in 1975, the Nova Scotia Human Rights Commission received more than 800 complaints of racial discrimination in the educational system. Most were from Black residents in several largely segregated Black communities.

In 1977, Walter Pitman, then President of Ryerson Polytechnical Institute, was appointed by the Municipality of Metropolitan Toronto to lead an inquiry into the reasons for an increase in the number of racial-minority persons being assaulted in Metropolitan Toronto.

The Pitman Task Force found sufficient evidence of racism in the city to warrant action. While subway attacks were the most obvious examples of racial violence, the task force found that there were numerous instances of racial violence in parks and recreation areas, in public housing complexes, in school playgrounds, on the streets, and in shopping plazas.

Its report described the vicious and continuous harassment of South Asian businesspeople, the verbal and physical harassment of children, and repeated attacks on the homes of racial-minority members and houses of worship belonging to the South Asian community. The task force found that a substantial number of Toronto's citizens lived in fear, were unwilling to use the subway, and felt uncomfortable and threatened in their own neighbourhoods. While the report dealt with individual racist attacks, it also pointed to the failure of a number of institutions to respond to the problem, including municipal governments, the police, schools, the media, and social agencies.

In the same year, the Ontario Human Rights Commission Annual Report raised concerns about the dramatic increase in reported incidents of assaults and verbal abuse against racial minorities. Another report that year, documenting a series of case histories of racial incidents as related by South Asian victims, indicated that the individuals responsible belonged to all groups and socioeconomic categories and even included police and immigration officers. Like Pitman, Ubale identified racism as the root cause and suggested that it was linked to the racial bias and discrimination of Canadian institutions (Ubale, 1977).

Wilson Head (1981) conducted a study on the adaptation of racial-minority immigrants in Canadian society by analyzing their perceptions of discriminatory treatment in the areas of housing, employment, and access to community services. He identified a number of barriers that prevented racial minorities from gaining suitable employment, such as the requirement for "Canadian experience." More than half of the respondents indicated that their present employment was not the type of work they were seeking or trained for.

In terms of community services, both respondents and community agency staff reported that the services were inadequate. The problem areas included the lack of training for staff; the need to hire staff from Black, South Asian, and other immigrant groups; and the need for more ethno-specific agencies. Several staff workers noted that although their Black clients were usually reluctant to talk about racial problems, this was a major concern for many clients.

When respondents were asked about their perceptions of the extent of racial discrimination in Metropolitan Toronto, almost 90 percent of Blacks and 72.2 percent of South Asians felt "some" or a "great deal" of discrimination. In contrast, only 35.3 percent of European respondents felt "some" or "a great deal" of discrimination. Most Blacks (63.7 percent) and South Asians (67.7 percent) reported having been subjected to racial discrimination in Toronto, while only 27.6 percent of the European-born respondents reported that they had experienced some form of ethnic discrimination.

Both Blacks and South Asians thought that racism was increasing. They felt only minimal acceptance by White Canadians and sensed that government agencies were reluctant to deal with racism. These perceptions were consistent with an earlier study carried out by Head (1975), which focussed on the impact of racism on the Black community in Canada.

In 1981, following the killing of a South Asian man in Vancouver, 1800 people demonstrated. The rally was a response to the growing incidence of violent attacks and the widespread racist activities of the Ku Klux Klan. During the rally, several people required hospitalization (Barrett, 1984).

In 1982, the federal government investigation into racial tensions in eleven urban communities across the country found that the racial climate was "tense." The study catalogued expressions of racism that ranged from the subtle acts of "polite racists" to the "sometimes violent" acts of racist zealots in each of these communities (Secretary of State, 1982).

In the same year, the Quebec Human Rights Commission investigated the violence between Haitian-born cabbies and Whites in the taxi industry that resulted from the firing of 20 Black taxi drivers from one company. The inquiry found that customers regularly asked for and were given White drivers only. Moreover, many taxi companies were refusing to hire Blacks. The widespread discrimination against Black taxi drivers was found to be only the latest in a series of racial incidents.

Continuing racial tension in the city of Vancouver resulted in the publication of an important survey documenting racist incidents involving South Asian Canadians in that city (Robson and Breems, 1985). It found that about half of Indo-Canadians (South Asians) had experienced at least one hostile incident in the two-year time frame of the study. The most frequently cited incidents involved name calling, verbal threats, and physical gestures, which occurred in cars, on the streets, in shopping malls, and in other public places. Graffiti was also frequently mentioned, and property damage was cited by 14 percent of the respondents; damage to cars and other stolen and damaged possessions were most often cited. Seven percent reported having suffered physical harm, and some of these respondents were in the company of young children when attacked.

Of particular interest in this study is the fact that over 70 percent of the South Asian respondents who reported incidents did nothing in response. The authors suggest that one reason for this is that there is no recourse or reporting mechanism in place for many of the more frequently experienced incidents, such as verbal harassment and graffiti. Another important finding of the study was that close contact between South Asians and members of the dominant culture had little impact. Members of the dominant culture who had the most racist attitudes were those living in areas with high concentrations of South Asian Canadians.

In the mid 1980s, the federal government established a parliamentary task force to examine the nature and extent of racism in Canadian society.

The catalyst for the task force was the cumulative effect of "racist incidents," which could no longer be ignored by the government. The report, *Equality Now*, was published in 1984. Authors of the briefs and witnesses who appeared before the task force described the devastating experiences and debilitating effects of racial prejudice and discrimination on the approximately two million people of colour living in Canada in 1984. The racial barriers identified include both the intentional discriminatory behaviour of racist individuals and the systematic and systemic barriers created by the major institutions in Canadian society, including education, employment, media, justice and law enforcement.

The invisibility of racial minorities was one of the recurring themes of the briefs, which repeatedly argued that people of colour are excluded from participation in political, social, and economic institutions. They are invisible in the official history of Canada. Racial bias is demonstrated by the recurring questions regarding who is really a Canadian. Participants argued that racism in Canada is unyielding; it does not disappear in one or two or even three generations. Dozens of witnesses argued that racist ideology is woven into Canada's public policies, entrenched in programs, and built into the systems and cultural networks of the whole society. The briefs not only focussed on individual racism, but also identified the important role of education, policing, justice, the media, and the human service delivery system in contributing to racism (*Equality Now*, 1984).

In the late 1980s, evidence of the growing intolerance and acts of discrimination were also documented in the annual reports of the Canadian Human Rights Commission. The 1989 report, for example, raised concerns about the nature of the controversy over whether Sikhs should be allowed to wear turbans in the Royal Canadian Mounted Police (RCMP). The issue resulted in petitions tabled in the Commons carrying the names of 250 000 Canadians who supported the proposition "that a handful of Sikhs wearing turbans would 'crack up the RCMP'" (Camp, 1990). Racist pins and calendars with depictions of turban-clad Mounties appeared across Canada.

The commissioner of the RCMP warned Canadians that "racial violence will cut to the heart of the Canadian soul unless something is done quickly to stop intolerance.... Violence in some form seems inevitable without a concerted effort to combat racism" (Watson, 1990). He also said that he wasn't as worried about the "few dedicated racists" as about the "significant population of well-meaning, intelligent and educated people who are among the opponents of the changes that a multi-racial society inevitably brings" (Watson, 1990).

In 1991, two major incidents in Nova Scotia drew attention to the racism directed at its Black community. In Cole Harbour, a community east of Dartmouth, a fight between a Black and a White youth attending a high school led to a larger confrontation involving about 50 Black and White students and nonstudents. The RCMP were called in to investigate, and charges were laid against eighteen people, ten of whom were Black. The parents unanimously protested the arrest of the students from these communities and decided to unite to ease racial tensions. Eventually the charges were dropped, except those against five Black plaintiffs.

Reactions to the incidents led to the mobilization of the Black community, and a series of studies and reports were commissioned to examine educational opportunities and labour participation rates among the residents of the three surrounding communities where Blacks lived. The findings of the studies led to the conclusion that the Black residents of the three areas were "significantly disadvantaged" compared with their White neighbours. A report of the Nova Scotia Advisory Group on Race Relations found that racism was rampant in the province and in all levels of the school system. The report also focussed on the racial implications of unemployment among Blacks (*Report of the Nova Scotia Advisory Group on Race Relations*, 1991).

In 1991, another incident in Nova Scotia escalated into a series of racial disturbances. After Black youths were refused entrance to a downtown Halifax bar, a brawl ensued in which a Black youth was stabbed. More than a thousand people participated in a march and rally following the incident, to demand action to combat racism in Nova Scotia. In July 1991, the federal, provincial, and municipal governments and representatives from the Black community agreed to form an advisory group on race relations to deal with racism and racial discrimination in education, employment, media policing, justice, and services.

The *Report of the Nova Scotia Advisory Group on Race Relations* (1991) provided the context for these incidents. It suggested that Blacks in the province had been excluded from all areas of mainstream life in communities in which they, their parents, grandparents, and great grandparents were born. Racist attitudes converged with racist policies and practices to deprive Blacks and other minorities from access to housing, education, employment, and other services that most White Canadians take for granted, such as access to bars and restaurants. Bridgal Pachai, executive director of the Nova Scotia Human Rights Commission, suggested that "the story of Nova Scotia is a story of denial of opportunity and broken promises to minorities ... who just happen to be Blacks, Aboriginal people and Acadians" (Murray, 1991).

The responses of the White and Black communities to incidents of racial unrest underscore how the two groups (one with power and privilege, the other deprived of fundamental rights) understand racism. Many Blacks readily speak of the explosion of racial tension as inevitable in a racist society, whereas White individuals express shock and anger at the threat of increased racial violence.

In the summer of 1992, the premier of Ontario, Bob Rae, appointed a former Canadian ambassador to the United Nations, Stephen Lewis, to lead a special inquiry on race relations following a disturbance in Toronto a few weeks before. A night of violence and looting followed a peaceful protest by a mixed-race crowd of more than two thousand people decrying the acquittal of Los Angeles police officers whose beating of a Black man was caught on videotape. While the rioters were of all races, the provincial government saw it as a symptom of racial unrest and called for an investigation.

Lewis consulted widely with individuals and groups from racial minorities, particularly the Black community, across the province. He concluded in his report that the root of the problem was anti-Black racism:

> While it is obviously true that every visible minority community experiences the indignities and wounds of systemic discrimination throughout Ontario, it is the Black community which is the focus. It is Blacks who are being shot, it is Black youth that is unemployed in excessive numbers, it is Black students who are being disproportionately streamed in schools, it is Black kids who are disproportionately dropping out.... It is Black employees, professional and non-professional, on whom the doors of upward mobility slam shut. (Lewis, 1992: 2)

POLLS AND SURVEYS

One of the first surveys of racist attitudes in Canada contained 57 attitudinal items pertaining to racial prejudice (Henry, 1978). The findings revealed that 16 percent of the White mainstream population was extremely intolerant and 35 percent somewhat racist. At least 18 percent had very liberal views about race, and a further 30 percent were somewhat liberal.

The attitudinal survey literature has been remarkably consistent over the 15 years since that first survey was done. Most of the surveys show that between 10 and 20 percent of Canadians are extremely intolerant of racial minorities. Another 20–35 percent are somewhat racist. Combining these two findings suggests that between 30 and 55 percent of the population could be characterized as racist.

A decade after the Henry study, another survey found that between 7 and 20 percent of Canadians could be described as strongly racist in their views (Environics, 1988). Evidence of "hard core" racism included the following findings: 19 percent of Canadians agreed with "research findings" that Orientals were superior to Whites who were, in turn, superior to Blacks. Moreover, 13 percent of Canadians would exclude non-White groups from immigrating to Canada, 7 percent would not vote for a Black political candidate, and 9 percent would not vote for a Chinese candidate.

A 1989 survey, conducted by researchers at the University of Toronto and York University, was designed to determine whether there was a significant difference between the racial attitudes of decision-makers — legislators, lawyers, administrators, and police officers — and those of the general population. The survey found that 23 percent of the "elite" Canadians thought minority groups needed to get rid of "harmful and irritating faults," compared with 39 percent of the general population who held the same view. Half of the decision-makers and 70 percent of the general population felt that immigrants often bring discrimination upon themselves; 16 percent of the "elites" and almost one-third of the general citizenry believed that "races are naturally unequal" (Gould, 1990).

A 1989 poll in British Columbia, which receives most racial-minority immigrants settling in the West, indicated that many residents believed that immigration does not bring economic advantages to the province. These perceptions were held despite the fact that shortly before, a highly publicized report by Employment and Immigration Canada found exactly the opposite. The report demonstrated that after 10 years in Canada, Third World immigrants paid more taxes per capita than did western European immigrants. These perceptions were also not shaken by the well-reported findings of the province's central statistics bureau, which showed that Asian entrepreneurial immigrants contributed $122.9 million to the B.C. economy and $5.4 million to the Alberta economy in 1988. Although entrepreneurial immigrants from Asia created 15 000 jobs in Canada in 1988, nearly half of B.C.'s population thought there were too many immigrants of colour moving into the province.

In a Toronto survey in 1992, when asked how well their racial or cultural group was accepted, 80 percent of those surveyed in the Black Canadian community, 63 percent in the Chinese Canadian community, and 62 percent of the East Indian–Pakistani Canadian community felt there was some prejudice toward them in Toronto. Seventy-three percent of Blacks, 48 percent of Chinese, and 47 percent of East Indians–Pakistanis felt discriminated against in obtaining work, compared with 31 percent of Jews, 16 percent of Portuguese, and 15 percent of Italians. In terms of discrimination in the legal or court system, the survey found that 49 percent of Blacks felt they were discriminated against. Twenty-one percent of East Indian–Pakistanis felt this way and 9 percent of Chinese (*The Toronto Star*, 1992).

A report by the Economic Council of Canada (1991) attempted to measure the changing attitudes toward prejudice over time by analyzing the results of 62 surveys taken from 1975 to 1990 by Gallup, Decima, Environics, and other polling organizations. The report found that respondents from communities with greater proportions of visible-minority immigrants were "likely to be more tolerant of racial and ethnic differences." The report also concluded that over time there were "diminishing levels of prejudice."

On the other hand, a survey by the federal immigration department of 1800 adults and fourteen focus groups showed a "growing acceptance" of attitudes and practices that show a dislike for "foreigners." One-third of the respondents agreed it was important to "keep out people who are different from most Canadians," while more than half were "really worried that they may become a minority if immigration is unchecked." Almost half admitted there were too many immigrants, even though most actually underestimated how many people were admitted (*The Globe and Mail*, 1992).

In a national survey undertaken by Decima Research in October 1993 for the Canadian Council of Christians and Jews, nearly three-quarters of the 1200 respondents rejected the concept of Canada as a multicultural mosaic, and 72 percent believed that different racial and ethnic groups should try to adapt to Canadian society rather than preserve their original cultures. The survey found that 41 percent of respondents thought that Canada's immigration policy "allows too many people of different cultures and races to come to Canada," and 53 percent agreed with the statement that "some racial and ethnic groups don't make enough of an effort to fit into Canada." Half agreed with the statement: "I am sick and tired of some groups complaining about racism being directed at them," and 41 percent agreed they are "tired of ethnic minorities being given special treatment."

The findings demonstrated some of the paradoxes of racism in Canadian society. For example, while Canadians generally saw themselves as tolerant of other cultures and racism, three-quarters believed that racism was a serious problem in Canada. These findings demonstrate that although many White people profess to be liberal, fair minded, and unbiased, they have two opposing and contradictory sets of racial attitudes — one expressed in positive terms, the other reflecting negative perceptions, attitudes, and assumptions.

HATE GROUPS

An ideology of White supremacy has long been considered within the bounds of respectable, defensible opinion in Canada. In the colonial era, Aboriginal peoples were portrayed by church and state as "heathens" and "savages" and somehow less than human. These images provided justification for the extermination, segregation, and subjugation of Aboriginal peoples. The dehumanizing impact of such blatant propaganda is clearly evident today in the conditions of many Aboriginal communities (Frideres, 1983).

The 1920s and the 1930s saw the development of racist organizations such as the Ku Klux Klan (KKK), which openly promoted hatred against Catholics, Jews, Blacks, and other minorities. The original Klan was founded in Tennessee in 1866. It established bases in Alberta, Manitoba, Saskatchewan, British Columbia, and Ontario, feeding on Canadian anti-Semitism and the fear of Blacks and southern Europeans. While the KKK in Canada today appears to have only a handful of members, a network of other groups peddle hate propaganda, including the Heritage Front, the Liberty Lobby, the Church of the Creator, the Church of Jesus Christ–Aryan Nation, the Aryan Resistance Movement, and the Western Guard. All these groups share an ideology that supports the view that the Aryan, or White, race is superior to all others morally, intellectually, and culturally and that it is Whites' manifest destiny to dominate society.

Barrett (1987) has made a significant contribution to understanding the recent activities of the extreme right in Canada. He found 130 organizations but under 600 members, many of whom belonged to more than one organization. Hate groups are usually coteries centred on a leader with a mailing list. Aside from holding meetings, they promote their ideology through distributing their literature widely. They hold rallies and parades, distribute buttons, paint slogans, establish dial-a-message telephone lines, demonstrate, and hold counter-demonstrations at the rallies of others. They may engage in paramilitary training, hold church services, or engage in political canvassing.

A recent strategy used by these groups is to defend their activities by presenting themselves as defenders of free expression. Since they consider themselves to be promoting the principles of civil libertarianism, any attempts to curb their activities are portrayed as censorship and therefore anti-democratic.

The extreme right wing in Canada today consists of three main groups: the Ku Klux Klan, the Western Guard, and a third group that includes a number of smaller organizations, such as the Canadian National Socialist Party. Barrett (1987) suggests that the main elements of White supremacist ideology are anti-communism, anti-liberalism, racism, and anti-Semitism. White Supremacists perceive themselves as the "saviours of the White race and Western Christian civilization" (Barrett, 1987: 90). They believe that the survival of White society in Canada is in jeopardy because of the practice of allowing "non-Aryans" into the country. The Ku Klux Klan suggests that one alternative to the problem of too many racial minorities in Canada is for the government to give "$35 000 to each coloured family as inducement to return to Pakistan, Africa, and elsewhere in the Third World" (Barrett, 1987). Jews too should be included in this form of "ethnic cleansing." The expansion of the White race should be encouraged by providing financial incentives for White parents to have more children.

Barrett concludes that the ideology of the radical right does, to some extent, reflect "what the majority of people think and feel privately, albeit often unconsciously." While hate groups and hate propaganda may be regarded as marginal phenomena, the impact of such extremists is, according to Barrett, disproportionate to their numbers. They gain notoriety and apparent influence by combining strong stances on sensitive policies (such as immigration), which are controversial and have a substantial popular base, with continuous racist appeals couched in emotional, inflammatory rhetoric and threats of violence.

Barrett suggests that most White Canadians hold racist attitudes, reflected in their comments about Blacks in the workplace, the peculiarity of Jews, or their choice of jokes. A relationship exists between many White supremacist beliefs and those of other White Canadians. "The two sets of beliefs ... constitute a continuum rather than a dichotomy" (Barrett, 1987: 97).

However, according to Barrett, it is important to distinguish between public and private beliefs. While a sizable portion of Whites may, in fact, share many of the less fanatical but nevertheless racist attitudes of the extreme right wing, they may never publicly express those views. This is consistent with the notion of "passive racisms." The radical right is articulating what a significant proportion of the dominant community is thinking and feeling, albeit sometimes unconsciously.

Since the publication of Barrett's pioneering work, right-wing groups have proliferated in Canada. KKK branches are active in all of Canada's major cities. Offshoot groups such as the Heritage Front, the Church of the Creator, the Knights for White Rights, and the Aryan Nation are flourishing. Their presence is felt in the many telephone "hot lines" established throughout the country that spew forth hate messages, many of which are directed at Aboriginal peoples and racial minorities. Multiculturalism and immigration policies are also frequently criticized. The messages hammer home the theme, "Keep Canada White."

In the past decade, the League for Human Rights of B'nai B'rith (1992) has monitored the number and types of anti-Semitic incidents that have occurred in all regions of Canada. The data file includes a large variety of incidents, ranging from non-violent ones — such as anti-Semitic graffiti — to more violent incidents that involve damage to persons or property and the desecration of synagogues. A recent analysis of this file showed a "significant increase ... in the numbers of incidents of all kinds." The report noted that this may reflect a "growing tendency of intolerance."

These racist incidents target not only the Jewish community. Hate-group activity and hate propaganda is directed at members of the Black, Chinese, and South Asian communities. Reports from various multicultural and antiracist organizations and networks, as well as the cases in the human rights commissions and courts, support the findings of the League for Human Rights of B'nai B'rith (BCOFR Report, 1992; Mock, 1992).

In the early 1990s, the Canadian Human Rights Commission began launching actions to prohibit telephone hate lines. In Vancouver, its action resulted in a tribunal ordering a telephone hate line disconnected. Similarly, in Toronto, the Heritage Front was issued with an injunction to stop producing hate messages. In Winnipeg, a human rights tribunal ordered the Manitoba Knights of the KKK to cease airing its messages. The tribunal found that "there is overwhelming uncontradicted evidence that the messages were likely to expose the persons involved to hatred and contempt by reason of their race, religion, national or ethnic origin, colour or sexual orientation." This decision included not only the Manitoba chapter of the KKK, but also "any other individuals who are member of or act in the name of the Knights of the Ku Klux Klan."

By 1992, racist violence was seen to be increasing in many Canadian urban centres. For example, over a period of a few weeks in 1993, three Tamil refugees were beaten in Toronto. One died as the result of the injuries inflicted by his White assailants, and one was paralyzed. These incidents must be studied in the context of a long history of racist attitudes toward immigrants and refugees (or those perceived to be "foreigners" by virtue of the colour of their skin). In 1987, Canadians vehemently reacted to the arrival of a few boatloads of Tamil and Sikh refugees who entered Canada without following the normal procedures, while at the same time expressing little concern about the equally unorthodox arrival of significant numbers of Polish refugees.

Thus, racist behaviour stretches along a wide continuum. At one end are the overt and covert daily acts of discrimination involving a significant proportion of the mainstream community. At the other end of the continuum, one finds far more explicit and extreme racist activity in the form of hate propaganda and racial violence perpetrated by a small minority of the population.

DISCRIMINATION IN THE WORKPLACE

One of the clearest demonstrations of racism in a society is the lack of access and equity experienced by people of colour in the workplace. A number of studies over the past two decades have documented the nature and extent of racial bias and discrimination in employment. One study, *Who Gets the Work?* (Henry and Ginzberg, 1984), examined access to employment. In this field research, matched Black and White job seekers were sent to apply for entry positions advertised in a major newspaper. An analysis of the results of several hundred applications and interviews revealed that Whites received job offers three times more often than did Black job applicants. In addition, telephone callers with accents, particularly those from South Asia and the Caribbean, were more often screened out when they phoned to inquire about a job vacancy.

A follow-up study to *Who Gets the Work?* focussed on the attitude, hiring, and management practices of large businesses and corporations in Toronto. *No Discrimination Here* documented the perceptions of employers and personnel managers in these organizations. In personnel interviews, recruitment, hiring, promotion, training, and termination practices, a high level of both racial prejudice and discrimination was demonstrated; 28 percent of the respondents felt that racial minorities did not have the ability to meet performance criteria as well as Whites (Billingsley and Muszynski, 1985).

Concern over employment discrimination against people of colour, women, persons with disabilities, and Aboriginal peoples led the federal government to establish a royal commission on equality in employment (Abella, 1984). Its task was to inquire into the employment practices of eleven designated Crown and government-owned corporations and to explore the most effective means of promoting equality in employment for four groups: women, Native peoples, disabled persons, and racial minorities. Its findings echoed the conclusions of the report *Equality Now* (1984) that racial bias and discrimination were a pervasive reality in the employment system. The commissioner, Judge Rosalie Abella, observed that "strong measures were needed to remedy the impact of discriminatory attitudes and behaviour." The remedy she recommended was employment equity legislation (Abella, 1984).

An analysis of the 1991 and 1992 annual reports of Employment and Immigration Canada shows that few gains have resulted from employment equity legislation. Of the four targeted groups, women made slightly more advances than the others. Aboriginal peoples and people with disabilities made the fewest gains. Although members of racial minorities had higher levels of education than the Canadian population and very high labour-force participation rates, they continued to be concentrated in certain occupational groups.

More than 70 percent of racial minority women were in the clerical categories, compared with 61.8 percent of all women; 24.9 percent of racial-minority men worked as clericals, compared with 14.6 percent of all men. In the banking sector, more than 40 percent of racial-minority men were employed in the clerical category, compared with only 19 percent of all men. More racial-minority men, however, were categorized as professionals (16 percent), compared with 6.3 percent of all men. This reflects the point system of immigration in which education and skills are rewarded.

Members of racial-minority groups have higher levels of education than do other Canadians. For example, 23 percent had university degrees, compared with 14 percent of other Canadians. Moreover, racial minorities had consistently higher levels of education than did other workers in the lower-paying occupations. In the category of "semi-professionals and technicians," for instance, 32.3 percent had university degrees, compared with 18.3 percent of others.

Despite higher levels of education, members of racial-minority groups were paid lower salaries than were other Canadians. In an important study, Reitz et al. (1981) demonstrated that there were considerable income disparities among various ethno-racial groups. People of colour, such as West Indians, and more recently arrived groups such as Portuguese, ranked lowest.

A decade later, the average salary for all levels of education for a member of a racial-minority in both the upper level and middle and other management occupations was approximately 18 percent lower than that of the total population (Employment and Immigration Canada, 57). Even in the "other manual workers" category, including all levels of education, members of racial minorities earned nearly 10 percent less than all other manual workers. With respect to the industries regulated by employment equity legislation, racial minorities made some gains. Their share of total hiring in the banking, transportation, and communications industries was 11.1 percent but their share of promotions was lower at only 9.5 percent. Promotions were highest in two groups — clerical and professional workers — both of which showed high visible-minority concentrations.

The overall representation of minorities was highest in the banking sector, where nearly two-thirds were clustered in the lower ranks and only 12.4 percent were in middle or upper management positions. Despite some slight improvement in the overall position of racial minorities in the employment regulated by the federal act, they are still concentrated in certain sectors; and despite higher levels of education, their earnings are lower than those of other Canadians. As the report notes, "the representation of members of visible minorities in the work force under the Act was lower than their representation in the Canadian labour force in seven of the 12 occupational groups including upper-level managers, semi-professionals, ... sales workers, service workers, ... other manual workers."

One of the key barriers preventing immigrants of colour from access and equity in the labour market is credentialism. Studies in Ontario (Ontario Ministry of Citizenship, 1989) and British Columbia (Fernando and Prasad, 1986) showed that there is little recognition in Canada of the professional qualifications, credentials, and experience of immigrants. Thousands of individuals find their university degrees and trade diplomas of little value in Canada. These barriers affect doctors, teachers, social workers, nurses, engineers, and others.

Public sector agencies also show a lack of representation of racial minorities. An audit done for the Ontario public service in 1986 showed that 77 percent of civil servants were White and only 11.9 percent were racial minorities, most of whom were clustered in lower-level positions. In 1989, racial minorities formed only 4 percent of the Metropolitan Toronto Police Force. Almost all of them were cadets, constables, or in training; only three had the rank of inspector (Small, 1992). Around the late 1980s, at the Toronto Board of Education, only 5 percent of the teaching staff were from racial minorities, but this figure increased to 8.5 percent with the inclusion of non-teaching staff. Only 6 percent were classified as managers. The Ontario Human Rights Commission has only one racial-minority director. The Metropolitan Toronto Housing Authority, which deals with large numbers of minority clients, has a minority contingent of only 16.7 percent, of whom 11 percent are at a middle or senior management level.

A survey of 672 corporate recruiters (Jain, 1988), hiring managers, and agency recruiters across Canada conducted by the Canadian Recruiters Guild concluded that there were gross deficiencies in Canada's recruitment and selection practices. It revealed that the moral, legal, and economic impact of recruitment was either not understood or simply ignored by recruiters.

A study undertaken by the Maritime School of Social Work at Dalhousie University in Halifax (Bambrough, Bowden, and Wein, 1992) tracked its racial-minority and Aboriginal graduates and found that minorities experienced considerable difficulty in obtaining employment after graduation. Acadian and Black graduates took several more weeks to find their first job, and Blacks had to apply to many more employers and undertake many more interviews to get a job offer. (In this respect, the study mirrors the results of *Who Gets the Work?*, which also found that Blacks and others had to make many more telephone calls than Whites to obtain an interview.)

The study also found that upon graduation, Blacks found less desirable jobs than others, including limited or term positions and more part-time jobs. Of particular interest was the fact that Blacks were more often in jobs in which the chances for advancement were relatively low, as were salaries. The report concluded that "Black graduates have been less successful than the Majority group in accessing the more prestigious social work jobs, such as those to be found in family counselling, hospital social work and in administrative/supervisory positions."

Harish Jain, who has done extensive research on employment discrimination in Canada, suggests that racial minorities, as well as women, Aboriginal peoples and people with disabilities, encounter both entry-level and post-employment discrimination in the workplace. He argues that the existence of human rights statutes across Canada have been ineffective in ensuring equality of opportunity in the workplace. Jain identifies numerous job barriers in the employment system, including narrow recruitment channels and procedures (e.g., word of mouth recruitment; inflated educational qualifications; biased testing; prejudice and stereotyping in the job interview process; poor performance evaluation; lack of promotions, transfers,

anchor salary increases, job ghettoization (Jain, 1985)). Unions are identified as another potential source of both racism and sexism (Leah, 1989).

Non-English-speaking and racial-minority immigrant women are part of a segregated and marginalized workforce and are employed mainly in three areas of work: private domestic service, service industries, and light manufacturing. Many immigrant racial-minority women working in the public sector are employed as cleaners, cafeteria workers, nurses' aides, and lower-level clerical workers (Vorst et al., 1989). Brand (1987) observes that most Black women work at low-status jobs in homes and institutions and do "Black women's work."

An ongoing research project on Caribbean communities in Toronto (Henry, 1994) has yielded some interesting results with respect to the continuing impact of racial discrimination on employment. More than one hundred in-depth interviews and many hundreds of hours of participant observation among persons of Caribbean origin in Toronto indicated that the community shows a fairly high level of institutional completeness, considering the recency of Caribbean migration to Canada. Although there are no financial institutions within the community, most service and retail sectors have developed to the extent that goods and services of many kinds can be obtained from Caribbean-owned and -managed businesses.

One of the main reasons for private entrepreneurship among the community was the racial discrimination experienced by job seekers and workers employed in mainstream-owned and -managed firms. Difficulty in obtaining employment was often cited as a major reason for dissatisfaction with living in Canada. In addition, racial harassment on the job and the inability to advance in the company was cited as a contributory factor to private entrepreneurship. Restaurateurs, clothiers, and variety-shop owners said they were "fed up" with racial harassment.

Employment Agencies

Allegations of racial discrimination in the operations of employment agencies in accepting and referring certain clients have been a concern for almost two decades. In 1975, the Canadian Civil Liberties Association (CCLA) conducted a survey of employment agencies. It randomly selected agencies, told their representatives that it represented an out-of-town firm planning to locate in their community, and asked whether, among the services provided, the agencies would agree to refer only White people for the jobs that had to be filled. Of the fifteen employment agencies in Metro Toronto that received discriminatory requests, eleven said they would screen out persons of colour.

The study was repeated in 1976, surveying employment agencies in Hamilton, Ottawa, and London. Again, eleven of the fifteen agencies indicated their willingness to fulfil discriminatory requests. In 1980, the CCLA surveyed ten agencies in Toronto, seven of whom expressed a willingness to abide by a "Whites only" restriction. In 1991, the CCLA repeated the survey for the fourth time, and of the fifteen agencies surveyed in four cities in Ontario, only three declared their unwillingness to accept discriminatory job orders.

Following are some examples of the agencies' responses.

> It is discrimination, but it can be done discreetly without anyone knowing. No problem with that.

> That's no problem, it's between you and me. I don't tell anyone; you don't tell anyone.

> You are paying to see the people you want to see.

> Absolutely — definitely ... that request is pretty standard here.

> That's not a problem. Appearance means a lot, whether it's colour or overweight people. (Rees, 1991)

While the role of employment agencies in colluding with discriminatory employers has long been known to those who monitor race relations in Canada, the publicity surrounding a complaint laid with the Ontario Human Rights Commission against two employment agencies in Toronto brought this issue into the public arena. Although the commission found discriminatory information about job applicants in some files, it maintained that the agencies did not have a deliberate policy of discriminating against job applicants. Accordingly, a settlement was reached in which the agencies agreed to develop written policies against accepting discriminatory job requests from employers and to provide training for their employees in race relations and employment equity.

Both agencies also said they would establish three-year employment equity plans, with goals and timetables that provided for the elimination of barriers in recruiting, referral, and placement services. The chief commissioner of the human rights commission was quoted as saying that this settlement "will provide a blueprint for all employment agencies in the province." A number of critics, however, noted that the settlement was fairly limited and did not adequately encompass all the aspects of this complex issue.

REFERENCES

Abella, R. (1984). *Report of the Commission on Equality in Employment.* Ottawa: Supply and Services Canada.

BC Organization to Fight Racism. (1992). Canada 125, Surrey: BCOFR.

Bambrough, J., W. Bowden, and F. Wein (1992). *Preliminary Results from the Survey of Graduates from the Maritime School of Social Work.* Halifax: Maritime School of Social Work, Dalhousie University.

Barrett, S. (1984). "White Supremists and Neo Fascists: Laboratories for the Analysis of Racism in Wider Society." O. McKague, ed., *Racism in Canada.* Saskatoon: Fifth House, 85–99.

———. (1987). *Is God a Racist? The Right Wing in Canada.* Toronto: University of Toronto Press.

Billingsley, B., and L. Muszynski. (1985). *No Discrimination Here.* Toronto: Social Planning Council of Metro Toronto and the Urban Alliance on Race Relations.

Brand, D. (1987). "Black Women and Work: The Impact of Racially Constructed Gender Roles on the Sexual Division of Labour." *Fireweed* (25): 35.

Camp, D. (1990). "Diefenbaker Would Have Backed Turbans in the RCMP." *The Toronto Star* (March 21): A25.

Economic Council of Canada. (1991). *Report.* Ottawa.

Employment and Immigration Canada. (1993). *Annual Report, Employment Equity Act, 1992.* Ottawa: Supply and Services.

Environics. (1988). Focus Canada Survey.

Equality Now: Report of the Parliamentary Task Force on the Participation of Visible Minorities in Canada. (1984). Ottawa: Queen's Printer.

Fernando, T., and K. Prasad. (1986). *Multiculturalism and Employment Equity: Problems Facing Foreign-Trained Professionals and Tradespeople in British Columbia.* Vancouver: Affiliation of Multicultural Societies and Service Agencies of British Columbia.

Frideres, J. (1983). *Native People in Canada: Contemporary Conflicts,* 2nd ed. Scarborough, ON: Prentice-Hall.

The Globe and Mail. (1992). (October 14).

Gould, T. (1990). "Who Do You Hate." *Toronto Life* (October).

Head, W. (1981). *Adaptation of Immigrants: Perceptions of Ethnic and Racial Discrimination.* North York, ON: York University.

———. (1975). *The Black Presence in the Canadian Mosaic: A Study of Perception and Practice of Discrimination Against Blacks in Metropolitan Toronto.* Toronto: Ontario Human Rights Commission.

Henry, F. (1994). *The Caribbean Diaspora in Toronto: Learning to Live with Racism.* Toronto: University of Toronto Press.

————. (1978). *Dynamics of Racism*. Ottawa: Secretary of State.

Henry, F., and E. Ginzberg. (1984). *Who Gets the Work? A Test of Racial Discrimination in Employment*. Toronto: Urban Alliance on Race Relations and the Social Planning Council of Toronto.

Jain, H. (1985). *Anti-Discrimination Staffing Policies: Implications of Human Rights Legislation for Employers and Trade Unions*. Ottawa: Secretary of State.

————. (1988). "Affirmative Action/Employment Equity Programmes and Visible Minorities in Canada." *Currents: Readings in Race Relations* 5(1): 3–7.

League for Human Rights of B'nai B'rith. (1992). *Annual Audit of Anti-Semitic Incidents*. Toronto.

Leah, R. (1989). "Linking the Struggles: Racism, Sexism and the Union Movement." In Vorst et al., eds. *Race, Class, Gender: Bonds and Barriers*. Toronto: Between the Lines.

Lewis, S. (1992). *Report on Race Relations to Premier Bob Rae*. Toronto. The quotation reproduced herein is reprinted with permission from the Queen's Printer for Ontario.

Mock, K. (1992). *Combatting Hate: Canadian Realities and Remedies*. Toronto: League for Human Rights, B'nai B'rith Canada.

Murray, M. (1991). *The Toronto Star* (June 23).

Ontario Ministry of Citizenship. (1989). *Access: Task Force on Access to Professions and Trades in Ontario*. Toronto: Ministry of Supply and Services.

Rees, T. (1991). "Racial Discrimination and Employment Agencies." *Currents: Readings in Race Relations* (Toronto) 7(2): 16–19.

Reitz, J., L. Calzavara, and D. Dasko. (1981). *Ethnic Inequality and Segregation in Jobs*. Toronto: Centre for Urban and Community Studies, University of Toronto.

Report of the Nova Scotia Advisory Group on Race Relations. (1991). Halifax.

Robson, R., and B. Breems. (1985). *Ethnic Conflict in Vancouver*. Vancouver: B.C. Civil Liberties Association.

Samuals, T.J. (1992). *Visible Minorities in Canada: A Projection*. Toronto: Race Relations Advisory Council on Advertising, Canadian Advertising Foundation.

Secretary of State. (1982). *Study of Racial Tensions in 11 Major Cities in Canada*. Ottawa: Secretary of State.

Small, P. (1992). "Promote Minorities, Report Tells Police." *The Toronto Star* (September 11): A6.

The Toronto Star. (1992). "Minority Community Survey."

Ubale, B. (1977). *Equal Opportunity and Public Policy: A Report on Concerns of the South Asian Community Regarding Their Place in the Canadian Mosaic*. Toronto: Ontario Ministry of the Attorney General.

Vorst, J., et al. (1989). *Race, Class, Gender: Bonds and Barriers*. Toronto: Between the Lines.

Watson, P. (1990). "RCMP Chief Fears Violence If Racism Continues to Grow." *The Toronto Star* (March 4): A1.

Chapter 16

ETHNIC INEQUALITY IN CANADA

HUGH LAUTARD AND NEIL GUPPY

John Porter's portrayal of Canadian society as a vertical mosaic is a powerful metaphor in contemporary social science research (Porter, 1965). Porter's image of the mosaic depicts Canada as a composite of enduring social groups defined principally by class and ethnicity, but also by language and religion. As well as delineating group boundaries, Porter demonstrated the vertical ranking of these communities on a series of inequality dimensions. In the context of ethnicity, the distinctive communities of the mosaic capture the potent force of ethnic identity, whereas the vertical alignment accentuates the hierarchy of ethnic inequality. It is an argument first of social differentiation, and second of social stratification.

The composition of the Canadian population has changed since Porter first wrote, but social cleavages based on ethnicity remain important. In the 1980s the imagery of a vertical mosaic has been reinterpreted in government circles (Abella, 1984; Boyer, 1985), where the subordinate positions of women, the disabled, Native Indians, and visible minorities have been highlighted. Responding to a growing human rights movement, new policies (e.g., the 1986 Employment Equity Act) have been enacted to facilitate equality and erode the vertical mosaic.

Ironically, at a time when governments are reacting to appeals concerning human rights, some sociologists have begun questioning the durability of ethnicity as an organizing principle in the vertical mosaic. Indeed, two decades after publication of *The Vertical Mosaic*, Porter himself co-authored a paper proclaiming "the collapse of the vertical mosaic" (Pineo and Porter, 1985: 390; see also Pineo, 1976; Darroch, 1979; Denis 1986).[1] This view is at odds with new government policy as well as with other sociological research demonstrating the continuance of intense ethnic antagonism and discriminatory behaviour (Henry and Ginzberg, 1985; Robson and Breems, 1986).

Sorting out the reasons for this divergence of opinion in the current literature is our starting point (see also Reitz, 1988). In reviewing that literature, we pay particular attention to research findings concerned with historical trends in the salience of ethnicity as a central component of the vertical mosaic. We then present new data, affording the longest historical perspective yet available on the association between ethnicity and occupation, using fifty-five years of census data, from 1931 to 1986. As did Porter before us, we stress both social differentiation and social stratification, although clearly the latter is the key to debates about the *vertical* mosaic.

THE DECLINING SIGNIFICANCE OF ETHNICITY?

In *The Vertical Mosaic* Porter offered three distinct observations about ethnic inequality. First, he argued that "charter status" groups, the French and English, commanded greater power and privilege than did "entrance status" groups (i.e., other immigrants) arriving later. Second, he noted an asymmetry of power favouring the English over the French. Third, he

Source: Excerpted from "The Vertical Mosaic Revisited: Occupational Differentials among Canadian Ethnic Groups," in Peter S. Li, ed., *Race and Ethnic Relations in Canada* (Toronto: Oxford University Press, 1990), pp. 189–208. Reprinted by permission of the authors.

claimed that among non-charter immigrant groups too, ethnic inequality persisted. These three aspects of inequality he saw as core features in the distribution of power and privilege in Canada.

Porter's most renowned evidence highlighted the economic elite, where he found that "economic power belong[ed] almost exclusively to those of British origin" (Porter, 1965: 286). While the French were significantly under-represented, members of non-charter minority groups were virtually absent among economic power-brokers. Clement's more recent (1975) sketch of the economic elite suggested a waning of British dominance, although of 775 elite members, 86.2 per cent still were English Canadian, 8.4 per cent were French Canadian, and only 5.4 per cent were of other ethnic origins.

Porter (1965) also presented data from the 1931, 1951, and 1961 censuses. Cross-classifying ethnic origin and occupation, he determined the extent to which various groups were over- and under-represented in different job categories. In the 1931 census he found British and Jewish groups ranked high (i.e., over-represented in professional and financial occupations, and under-represented in low-level, unskilled, and primary jobs); and, as he continued (ibid.: 81) the "French, German, and Dutch would probably rank next, followed by Scandinavian, Eastern European, Italian, Japanese, 'Other Central European,' Chinese, and Native Indian." He concluded (ibid.: 90) that by 1961 and "except for the French [who had slipped], the rough rank order [had] persisted over time."

Porter offered two complementary, although independent, explanations for the differential representation of ethnic groups by occupation level. First, immigrants compose a significant portion of the Canadian labour force (more than one in five as late as 1971), and traditionally Canada has attracted a polarized population of both the well educated and the poorly educated, with relatively few people in between.[2] New entrants to Canada reinforce traditional patterns of occupational inequality, since one difference between ethnic groups is the occupation level of their immigrants (Porter, 1965: 86; 1985: 40–51). For instance, new British immigrants acquire professional and financial jobs more often then do recent "Central European" immigrants, who disproportionately take up unskilled, lower-level positions.

Second, Porter also suggested that once in Canada ethnic groups differed in the extent to which they aspired to upward occupational mobility. Some ethnic groups valued achievement less than others, either because of cultural differences (e.g., less emphasis on material reward) or because of perceived or experienced discriminatory barriers (for a recent statement see Pineo and Porter, 1985: 360–61). However, to the extent that ethnic assimilation occurred, Porter reasoned that ethnic origin exerted less impact on individual occupational mobility. Conversely, in the face of continued ethnic affiliations, mobility was limited — a thesis of "ethnically blocked mobility."

Darroch (1979) has undertaken an ambitious revision of Porter's original interpretation. He suggests that Porter paid too much attention to the persistence of a "rough rank order" over the three censuses, and failed to note the diminishing strength of the association between ethnicity and occupation level. Quite simply, Porter was not sensitive enough to the fact that the occupational over- and under-representation of ethnic groups was much less in 1961 than had been the case in 1931. Darroch reviewed other evidence, including data from the 1971 census, to show that the salience of ethnicity for occupational allocation had diminished over time. He concluded (ibid.: 16) that the idea of blocked ethnic mobility had no foundation in fact and that we should be "skeptical of the idea that ethnic affiliations are a basic factor in generally limiting mobility opportunities in Canada."

These sentiments were echoed by Winn (1985) in the context of government policy debates. He was sharply critical of the Abella Commission's (1984: 4) call for the introduction of affirmative-action programs to augment mobility prospects for those groups whose progress had remained "unjustifiably in perpetual slow motion." Winn (1985: 689) reviewed data from the 1971 and 1981 censuses, concluding that his evidence provided "no empirical support for the premise that Canadian society is immobile and that visible or low prestige groups cannot make economic progress." Affirmative action was unnecessary, he said, because the ethnic inequality implied by the vertical mosaic was exaggerated.

A more pessimistic conclusion concerning the continuing salience of ethnicity as a basis for inequality appears in Lautard and Loree (1984). Using more detailed occupation data, they agreed with Darroch's finding that occupational inequality among ethnic groups had declined over time. But whereas Darroch (1979: 22) was willing to conclude that ethnicity was no longer a fundamental source of inequality, Lautard and Loree (1984: 342) maintained that "occupational inequality is still substantial enough to justify the use of the concept 'vertical mosaic' to characterize this aspect of ethnic relations in Canada."

Porter (1985: 44–51) repeated his earlier analysis with the 1971 census and, agreeing with Lautard and Loree, claimed that "ethnic stratification has persisted through to 1971" (ibid.: 48). Here he offers no hints about a "collapse" of the vertical mosaic. The census, however, contains data for both the foreign-born and the native-born, and so it confounds the two explanations that Porter offered for the association between ethnicity and occupation.

Working with Pineo (Pineo and Porter, 1985), Porter demonstrated that the strength of the association between ethnic origin and occupational status had attenuated in recent decades (up to 1973), at least for males from the major European ethnic groups.[3] They also showed that for native-born Canadian men, ethnic origin had no significant influence on individual occupational mobility. This latter finding suggests that the thesis of "blocked ethnic mobility" does not persist for second- and third-generation Canadian men (from the major European ethnic groups).

If, as these data show, occupational mobility is not limited by ethnic origin for many groups, then of Porter's two explanations for the ethnicity-occupation link, immigration would seem now to be the remaining factor. Boyd's (1985) research on the influence that birthplace exerts on occupational attainment supports this interpretation. For foreign-born men and women, she showed that ethnic origin had a definite effect on occupational attainment, even after controlling for differences in the average age, education, social origin, and place of residence of ethnic groups. For women she found evidence of a double negative for being female and foreign-born. Indeed, she concluded by noting the "importance of birthplace and sex as factors underlying the Canadian mosaic" (ibid.: 441).

A small part of the dispute over whether an ethnic component to the vertical mosaic has persisted in Canada is captured by the proverbial "is the glass half-full or half-empty?". Exactly how much inequality is enough to attribute it "fundamental" status? However, a far larger part of the dispute turns on matters of both theoretical definition and methodological procedure. For example, both Winn and Porter (in his early work) relied mainly on rank-ordered data, and Darroch was surely correct in contending that the size of the gap between ranks is crucial. But further, as Lautard and Loree insisted, the gap's size depends on the number of occupations considered, and so they improved the quality of evidence by looking at a wider range of occupation levels. In addition, the use of differing ethnic categories (especially notable in survey-based as opposed to census data), makes comparison and definitive conclusion precarious.

Key issues of theoretical and methodological dispute revolve around three aspects: the ethnic groups studied, the occupation levels considered, and the purity of historical comparability. These are reviewed in turn.

Ethnic groups. The definition of ethnicity remains contentious in social-science literature, and this debate touches directly on ethnic inequality and the vertical mosaic. Census data have been among the principal sources of evidence in evaluating the association between ethnic origin and occupation level. However, until 1981 the census definition of ethnicity relied on tracing ancestral male lineage, often a difficult task after several generations, especially given inter-ethnic marriages and historical changes around the world in national boundaries.

In addition, Statistics Canada is reticent about releasing detailed information for relatively small groups, and so ethnic categories have frequently been combined to form groups of mixed origin (e.g., Asian, Scandinavian). Typically the following ethnic categories have been used in the census: British (English, Irish, Scottish), French, German, Italian, Jewish, Dutch, Scandinavian, Eastern European (Polish, Ukrainian), Other European, Asian, and Native Indian.[4]

Occupations. Porter (1965) relied on five broad occupation groups and a residual category for his 1931 to 1961 census analysis: professional and financial, clerical, personal service, primary and unskilled, agriculture, and all others. By 1961 the residual category ("all others") had swollen to 58 per cent of the total. Darroch's (1979) reanalysis was forced to employ these crude groupings, but Lautard and Loree (1984) began afresh and used more refined occupation distinctions, amounting to hundreds of separate job categories for each census.

Also at issue here is how occupations are seen to be related. Attention can centre on whether or not ethnic groups tend to be concentrated in different occupations (a focus on the ethnic division of labour — i.e., social differentiation). Alternatively, if ethnic groups tend to congregate in different occupations, then there is a concern with the degree of status inequality between ethnic groups (a focus on the occupational prestige hierarchy — i.e., social stratification).

Historical comparability. Changes in the occupation structure and in the countries of origin of immigrants have meant that census procedures have had to be revised over the years. For occupation this has meant both the addition and deletion of job titles (e.g., computer programmer). For ethnicity one crucial change is in reporting procedures; for instance, in the early years when European groups dominated, little detail was made available for such visible minorities as Blacks or Indo-Pakistanis (even though both groups have a long history in Canada). Also, in 1981 the census questions for ethnicity changed (see Kralt, 1980).[5]

Since census definitions of occupations have changed over time there are advantages and disadvantages in the use of both broad and narrow occupation groups. The broad groups maximize comparability over time because most specific jobs are still classified in the same broad categories from one census to the next. However, the broad categories obscure crucial status gradations and are thus more useful in distinguishing social differentiation than social stratification, and the latter is the more important component in the current debate. Using more occupations gives a more refined calibration of inequality at any one point in time, although it does so by sacrificing comparability over time.

METHODS

We begin by reviewing the results reported by Lautard and Loree (1984) for 1931–71. We then present results for 1971, 1981, and 1986, based on unpublished census data, permitting an examination of seventeen ethnic groups.[6] To enhance comparability for the latter census years, we employ the 1971 occupational classification in both 1981 and 1986.

Although all of the nearly 500 detailed occupations of the 1971 classification are used in our full analysis of differentiation and stratification among ethnic groups, the broad occupational groups examined enabled us to see persisting aspects of the vertical mosaic. For example, British males and Jewish males and females are over-represented in managerial and administrative occupations, whereas Italians, Portuguese, Greeks, Yugoslavs, Chinese, Blacks, Native Indians and Métis, as well as South Asian (Indo-Pakistani) females are under-represented in this same occupational niche. Conversely, the British and the Jews are under-represented in service occupations, where there is an over-representation of Portuguese, Greeks, Chinese, and Blacks, as well as Yugoslav and Native Indian and Métis females.

Although we could continue to identify such differences, it is unlikely that doing so would give us a coherent sense of the overall differentials among the ethnic groups shown — there are simply too many possible comparisons. However, if we calculate the total of either the positive or the negative percentage differences between the occupational distribution of an ethnic group and the total labour force, we obtain a figure indicating the percentage of the members of the group who would have to have different occupations for that group's occupational distribution to be the same as that of the total labour force.[7] Called the index of dissimilarity, this measure allows us to compare occupational differentiation among groups.

For example, the index of dissimilarity for Black males is approximately 20, indicating that roughly one out of five Black men in the labour force would have to be in a different occupational category for there to be no difference between their occupational distribution and that of the total male labour force. The equivalent proportion for Native Indian and Métis men is approximately 28 per cent, indicating even greater differentiation.

Again, however, the broad occupational categories result in lower measures of dissimilarity than do the hundreds of more detailed occupations used for the results presented below. For example, although the percentage of British males in transport-equipment operating occupations is no different from that of the total male labour force, detailed occupational data indicate that British males are over-represented among air pilots and under-represented among taxi drivers.

Finally, measures such as the index of dissimilarity are most appropriately calculated for a group in comparison with the total labour force minus that group, to correct for the presence of the group itself in the total (Duncan and Duncan, 1955: 494). Accordingly, the results presented in the next section indicate the differentials between each ethnic group and the rest of the labour force, rather than between groups and the total labour force (as in the examples given above).

Dissimilarity, however, does not necessarily mean disadvantage. For example, the highest index of dissimilarity that can be calculated from the data is for Jewish males, at 43; this is the result of their over-representation in most of the categories in the upper half of the table and their corresponding under-representation in the remaining occupational categories. There is another measure, however — the index of net difference that may be calculated with occupational data ranked according to socio-economic scales. Related to the index of dissimilarity but more complicated in its calculation, the index of net difference provides a measure of the overall occupational ranking of a group in relation to the rest of the labour force. Indexes of net difference may be negative as well as positive, with a minus sign indicating comparatively lower occupational status, and a positive sign comparatively higher status; zero would indicate overall equality of occupational status.[8]

We now turn to the results of the analysis of ethnic occupational differentiation and stratification in Canada, using the indexes of dissimilarity and net difference.

RESULTS

Table 16.1 contains Lautard and Loree's (1984) indexes of occupational dissimilarity for the ethnic groups examined by Porter (1965) and Darroch (1979) for the census years 1931 through 1971. These indexes show the decline in occupational differentiation found by Darroch, although the levels of dissimilarity are considerably higher. The indexes for men in 1961, for example, include no values lower than 15 per cent, and the mean (29) is more than double that yielded by Darroch's analysis (14). By 1971 there is one value for men lower than 15 per cent, but again the mean (24) is nearly double that calculated by Darroch (14) for both sexes combined. After 1931, when the average dissimilarity for females is the same as that for

males (37 per cent), ethnic differentiation among women in the paid labour force is less than that among men, but even by 1971 only four groups (German, Dutch, Scandinavian, and Polish) have indexes of 15 per cent or less, and all these are above 10 per cent; the mean for women in 1971 is 21 per cent. Thus, on average, in 1971 a quarter of the male labour force and a fifth of the female labour force would have to have had different occupations in order for there to have been no occupational dissimilarity among ethnic groups. It is also evident from Table 16.1 that while the standard deviations, like the means, decline between 1931 and 1971, relative variation (V) undergoes a net increase for both sexes. The rankings of ethnic groups by degree of dissimilarity, moreover, remain remarkably stable, with the Italian, Jewish, Asian, and Native Indian groups tending to be more dissimilar from the rest of the labour force than other groups.

As noted in the previous section, occupational dissimilarity does not necessarily involve inequality of occupational status. Table 16.2 presents Lautard and Loree's (1984) indexes of net difference in

Table 16.1 Occupational Dissimilarity between Selected Ethnic Groups and the Rest of the Labour Force, by Sex: 1931, 1951, 1961, and 1971

Ethnic group	Male				Female			
	1931	1951	1961	1971	1931	1951	1961	1971
British	22	20	19	15	27	23	22	16
French	15	17	16	14	26	23	17	17
German[a]	24	23	17	15	20	14	13	11
Italian	48	34	40	35	39	24	45	38
Jewish	65	63	59	51	51	40	34	32
Dutch	21	20	17	17	14	17	15	15
Scandinavian	29	23	18	17	25	13	10	12
Polish	34[b]	23	18	15	45[b]	21	17	14
Ukrainian		28	21	15		22	21	16
Other European[c]	43	21	19	21	49	18	20	23
Asian[d]	61	46	45	36	50	25	20	25
Native Indian[e]	49	57	57	41	59	53	48	31
Mean (X)	37	31	29	24	37	24	24	21
Std. Dev. (s)	17	16	17	13	15	11	12	9
V (s/X)	.46	.52	.59	.54	.41	.46	.50	.43
(Number of occupations)	(388)	(278)	(332)	(496)	(265)	(226)	(277)	(412)

[a]Includes Austrian in 1931.

[b]Eastern European (Polish and Ukrainian combined).

[c]Other central European in 1931.

[d]Weighted average of Chinese and Japanese in 1931.

[e]Includes Eskimos in 1951.

Sources: 1931 (Dominion Bureau of Statistics, 1936: Table 49); 1951 (Dominion Bureau of Statistics, 1953: Table 12); 1961 (Dominion Bureau of Statistics, 1964: Table 21); 1971 (Statistics Canada, 1975: Table 4). Reproduced with permission from Lautard and Loree (1984: 338).

Table 16.2 Net Difference in Occupational Status between Ethnic Groups and the Total Labour Force, by Sex: 1951, 1961, and 1971

Ethnic group	Male			Female		
	1951	1961	1971	1951	1961	1971
British	.09	.11	.07	.11	.12	.07
French	−.11	−.10	−.04	−.11	−.07	−.01
German	−.03	−.06	−.07	−.13	−.11	−.09
Italian	−.15	−.28	−.21	−.08	−.37	−.34
Jewish	.41	.42	.35	.20	.21	.24
Dutch	−.10	−.09	−.09	−.15	−.12	−.10
Scandinavian	−.04	−.05	−.08	−.01	−.03	−.01
Polish	−.14	−.07	−.07	−.20	−.16	−.12
Ukrainian	−.11	−.10	−.09	−.20	−.19	−.12
Other European	−.12	−.11	−.11	−.17	−.19	−.20
Asian	−.14	−.03	−.10	−.06	−.05	−.01
Native Indian[a]	−.68	−.63	−.34	−.55	−.47	−.23
Mean (|X|)	.18	.17	.14	.16	.17	.13
Std. Dev. (s)	.19	.18	.11	.14	.13	.10
V (s/|X|)	1.06	1.06	.79	.88	.76	.77
(Number of occupational ranks)	(208)	(298)	(496)	(178)	(252)	(412)

[a]Includes Eskimo in 1951.

Sources: 1951 (Dominion Bureau of Statistics, 1953: Table 12); 1961 (Dominion Bureau of Statistics, 1964: Table 21); 1971 (Statistics Canada, 1975: Table 4). Reproduced with permission from Lautard and Loree (1984: 338).

occupational status between each ethnic group and the total labour force for 1951 through 1971.[9] The few positive indexes reflect the relatively high occupational rank of the British, Jewish, and, by 1971, Asian groups, as well as a slight advantage in 1951 and 1961 for Scandinavian females. The negative values indicate the relatively low status of the other groups. With one exception (women of Italian origin in 1971), the largest negative indexes are those for Native Indians, for whom even the 1971 indexes exceed −.30 for males and −.20 for females. Between 1951 and 1971, mean ethnic inequality declined, as did the standard deviations and the relative variation (V), but the latter remains very high for both sexes. The most pronounced shifts in the rank-order of the ethnic groups by relative occupational status include the Asian and Polish men, rising from a tie at third lowest in 1951 to second- and sixth-highest, respectively, in 1971; and Italian females dropping from fifth-highest in 1951 to lowest in 1971. Otherwise, the ranking of ethnic groups by relative occupational status is about as stable as that by occupational dissimilarity.

Table 16.3 contains indexes of dissimilarity for sixteen ethnic groups as of 1971, and seventeen as of 1981 and 1986. With the exception of the indexes for German, Dutch, and Polish males and Jewish females (which are slightly higher in 1986 than in 1971), and

those for French males and Polish females (which are the same in 1986 as in 1971), the figures in Table 16.3 indicate continuing declines in ethnic occupational differentiation. However, the replacement of "Other European" with Hungarian, Portuguese, Greek, and Yugoslav, and "Asian" with Chinese and South Asian, results in higher average dissimilarity for 1971 than in Table 16.1: 30 and 27 per cent, for males and females, respectively, compared with 24 and 21 per cent. As of 1986, a quarter of the males and a fifth of the females would have to have a different occupation in order for there to be no occupational differentiation among these ethnic groups. As well, relative variation remains around 50 per cent, with the British, French, Germans, Dutch, Scandinavians, Ukrainians, Polish, and Hungarians below the means and — except for Italian males and Yugoslavs of both sexes, in 1986 — the Italians, Portuguese, Greeks, Yugoslavs, Jews, Chinese, South Asians, Indians, and Métis, and Blacks above the means, for each year under consideration.

Table 16.4 presents indexes of net difference in occupational status between each of the ethnic groups and the rest of the labour force. The results for 1971 are consistent with those in Table 16.2. With the exception of the indexes for the British, the Jews, and the South Asians of both sexes, all values for 1971 are negative. As well, in 1971, the Italians, Portuguese,

Table 16.3 Occupational Dissimilarity[a] between Selected Ethnic Groups and the Rest of the Labour Force, by Sex: Canada, 1971, 1981, and 1986

Ethnic group	Male			Female		
	1971	1981	1986	1971	1981	1986
British	15	10	10	16	9	8
French	14	14	14	18	14	14
German	15	15	17	11	9	10
Dutch	16	17	18	15	13	14
Scandinavian	17	18	13	12	12	11
Ukrainian	15	13	14	16	9	11
Polish	15	14	16	14	10	14
Hungarian	21	19	19	20	15	16
Italian	35	26	24	38	25	22
Portuguese	46	42	39	57	48	40
Greek	48	45	42	51	42	37
Yugoslav	33	31	25	35	29	21
Jewish	51	49	49	32	33	34
Chinese	52	44	42	34	30	30
South Asian	46	34	30	31	27	25
Indian and Métis	41	37	38	32	29	30
Black	NI	32	28	NI	30	27
Mean (X)	30	27	26	27	23	21
Std. Dev. (s)	15	13	12	14	12	10
V (s/X)	.50	.48	.46	.52	.52	.48
(Number of occupations)	(498)	(496)	(496)	(464)	(495)	(495)

[a]Each figure in the table indicates the percentage of the ethnic group that would have to have a different occupation in order for there to be no difference between the occupation distribution of that group and the rest of the labour force.
NI: not included.

Source: Special tabulations of census data.

Greeks, Yugoslavs, and Native Indians and Métis have lower overall occupational status than the rest of the groups examined. In 1981 and 1986, the pattern is somewhat different, particularly for males. In addition to British and Jewish males, Scandinavian, Ukrainian, Polish, Hungarian, and South Asian males have positive indexes for both 1981 and 1986. The relative occupational status of Black males is comparable to that of German males in 1981, while the overall rank of Chinese males is similar to that of the Dutch in 1981. Finally, Yugoslav males are positioned between French and Dutch males in 1981 and tied with German males in 1986. Otherwise the basic pattern holds.

Among women, the British and the Jews have positive indexes for both 1981 and 1986, as do the Scandinavians. Overall equality of occupational status vis-à-vis the rest of the labour force in 1981 is indicated for both the French and Ukrainian groups, which are tied at +.01 in 1986. The overall status of Black females falls between that of Polish and Hungarian women in 1981 and is tied with that of both German and Dutch women in 1986. Otherwise, the pattern prevails: Italian, Portuguese, Greek, Yugoslav, Chinese, South Asian, and Indian and Métis women have lower relative occupational status than do women of the other groups under consideration, in both 1981 and 1986. For both sexes, moreover, the Portuguese have the lowest occupational status, and (except for males in 1971) Greeks the second-lowest status, in all three census years. On average, although occupational inequality among ethnic groups appears to have continued to decline between 1971 and 1986, relative variation in occupational status remains very high.

DISCUSSION

The historical comparison of ethnic inequality, as measured by occupational differences, suggests that between 1931 and 1986 a decline in the significance of ethnicity has occurred. The decline has been moderate, however, and ethnic origin continues to influence occupational destination.

Table 16.4 Net Difference in Occupational Status between Selected Ethnic Groups and the Rest of the Labour Force, by Sex: Canada, 1971, 1981, and 1986

Ethnic group	Male			Female		
	1971	1981	1986	1971	1981	1986
British	.13	.06	.05	.14	.06	.04
French	−.06[a]	−.04	−.01	−.02	.00	.01
German	−.08	−.02	−.03	−.09	−.04	−.05
Dutch	−.09	−.06	−.05	−.10	−.06	−.05
Scandinavian	−.08	.01	.01	−.01	.03	.06
Ukrainian	−.09	.01	.02	−.13	.00	.01
Polish	−.08	.03	.05	−.12	−.01	−.02
Hungarian	−.06	.03	.04	−.13	−.03	−.02
Italian	−.22	−.12	−.09	−.35	−.19	−.14
Portuguese	−.38	−.33	−.30	−.62	−.40	−.34
Greek	−.27	−.31	−.28	−.48	−.36	−.31
Yugoslav	−.12	−.05	−.03	−.29	−.18	−.11
Jewish	.36	.30	.34	.24	.27	.29
Chinese	−.04	−.08	−.05	−.20	−.14	−.13
South Asian	.26	.09	.03	.19	−.09	−.11
Indian and Métis	−.35	−.25	−.24	−.23	−.18	−.16
Black	NI	−.02	−.11	NI	−.02	−.05
Mean (|X|)	.17	.11	.10	.21	.12	.11
Std. Dev. (s)	.12	.11	.11	.16	.13	.11
V (s/|X|)	.71	1.00	1.10	.76	1.08	1.00
(Number of occupational ranks)[b]	(498)	(468)	(468)	(464)	(467)	(468)

[a]A negative figure indicates relatively lower overall occupational status, a positive figure relatively higher status. Zero indicates overall equality of occupational status. The greater the absolute size of the index, the greater the inequality.

[b]May not equal the number of occupations in Table 16.3 because of tied ranks.

NI: not included.

Source: Special tabulations of census data.

The trend in occupational dissimilarity indicates a reduction in the ethnic division of labour of roughly 50 per cent in 55 years. Social differentiation based on ethnicity is slowly eroding. The comparable results in ethnic occupational stratification reveal a similar degree of reduction, although over a shorter time span (from 1951 to 1986). These historical comparisons are admittedly crude, and we caution that precise calculations are impossible.

Do these results imply a "collapse" in the vertical mosaic? Using 1971 census data, Porter himself felt that "ethnic stratification" had persisted. For males, Tables 16.3 and 16.4 both reveal very small declines, in differentiation and stratification between 1971 and 1986, affording no firm grounds for repudiating Porter's claim. For females, the 1971 to 1986 changes have been larger, but by 1986 levels of differentiation and stratification among women of various ethnic groups are still similar to those for men.

An alternative method of illustrating how large or how small the reported differences are is to compare the differentiation and stratification among ethnic groups with similar differences between women and men. Using a comparable classification of occupations for the 1981 census, Fox and Fox (1987) report an index of dissimilarity for the occupational distributions of women and men of 61 per cent. This figure is greater than the 1981 averages we report (27 per cent for men; 23 per cent for women) and indeed is greater than the index figure for any single ethnic group. Still, certain ethnic groups, notably the Jewish, Greek, Chinese, and Portuguese among men, and the Portuguese and Greek among women, have dissimilarity scores approaching the figure for gender.

Using socio-economic status as the dimension that best illustrates the issue of vertical mosaic, the ethnic distribution can once more be compared with differences between women and men. In this case, ethnic inequality is greater than is gender inequality (see, e.g., Darroch, 1979: 13). This comparison obscures much of the known inequality between women and men (SES scores combine education and income, and typically women in the labour force are paid less but have higher levels of schooling than men). The index of net difference value for women compared with men is very close to zero in 1986, whereas the average value for ethnicity is .10 among men and .11 among women.

What these two comparisons suggest is that the gendered division of labour is more marked than is the ethnic division of labour. That is, men and women tend to be clustered in "sex-typed" jobs more often than members of specific ethnic groups are concentrated in "ethnic-linked" jobs. However, when the comparison is made on the dimension of socioeconomic status, inequality is more marked among ethnic groups than it is between the genders (granting, however, the limitations of SES comparisons between women and men).

Porter's "vertical mosaic" interpretation of Canadian society rested upon far more than ethnic occupational differentiation. As we noted above, the penetration of ethnic members into elite groups, a key element of the vertical mosaic, has remained limited. Nevertheless, some progress has been made here too, as the new "entrepreneurial" immigration category suggests, and certainly visible minorities have done well in selected occupational niches — among professionals, for example (Lambert, Ledoux, and Pendakur, 1989).

The research design that we have employed prohibits us from investigating which of Porter's two dynamics best explains the continuing level of ethnic inequality: differential immigration or blocked mobility. Our reading of the research literature suggests that immigration continues as the more important factor, especially in terms of visible minorities (McDade, 1988). But even here, the bimodal character of Canadian immigration, to which Porter initially drew attention, continues.

NOTES

The research reported here was supported by an SSHRCC Leave Fellowship and an SSHRCC Research Grant awarded to Hugh Lautard, a Killam Research Fellowship awarded to Neil Guppy, and grants from the University of New Brunswick Research Fund and Faculty of Arts. The authors are grateful for assistance by Dianne Bawn, Nancy Burnham, and Tim MacKinnon.

1. Porter died before this paper was published and it is unclear whether he saw the concluding section, from which this quotation is taken, before his death.

2. For much of Canada's history foreign-born workers have had a higher level of education than have native-born Canadians (see Lagacé, 1968; Boyd, 1985). What this average hides, however, is the tendency for immigrants to be either relatively well or relatively poorly educated.

3. In this particular analysis Porter included the following ethnic groups: English, Irish, Scottish, French, German, Dutch, Italian, Jewish, Polish, Ukrainian, Norwegian, Russian, and a residual ("other") category.

4. Winn's work is the exception here in that he reports on only "selected" ethnic groups and so from the 1981 census neither the British nor the Germans (for example) appear.

5. Prior to 1981 the census question to determine ethnic origin was: "To which ethnic or cultural group did you or your ancestor (on the male side) belong on coming to this continent?" In 1981 the question was: "To which ethnic or cultural group did you or your ancestors belong on first coming to this continent?" Notice, especially, how difficult it is for Native Indians to accurately answer this question. Also in 1981, and for the first time, multiple origins were accepted.

6. Ethnic groups for 1981 and 1986 are based on single responses and exclude those reporting multiple ethnic or cultural origins. In 1981, only 8 per cent of the population reported multiple ethnic origins, but in 1986, 28 per cent did so. The 1986 data used here are more complete than the latter figure would suggest. First, 8 per cent of the population reported two or more British origins (e.g., English and Scottish), and those in the labour force are included in the present study. Similarly, nearly 6,000 persons reported two or more French origins (e.g., French and Québécois), and those in the labour force are included in the present study. As well, our Scandinavian, Yugoslav, South Asian, and Black categories for 1986, although not for 1981, include persons reported multiple origins involving any combination of the respective constituent groups of each of these categories. For example, persons reporting any combination of Danish, Icelandic, Norwegian, Swedish, or simply "Scandinavian" are included as Scandinavians, along with persons who included only one such origin. All other multiple origins are excluded, as are single origins too small for the type of analysis undertaken or too costly to include (e.g., Armenian and Czechoslovakian). In all, the groups included represent 81 per cent of the experienced labour force, as of 1986.

7. The index of dissimilarity may also be obtained by adding all the differences between two percentage distributions, without regard to signs, and dividing the sum by two (Duncan and Duncan, 1955: 494). Each method is subject to rounding, which in the absence of decimals does present a problem for some groups.

8. Specifically, a negative index of net difference indicates the extent to which the probability of a member that the ethnic group in question will have a lower occupational rank than a member of the rest of the labour force exceeds the opposite probability, assuming random pairing. A positive value indicates the opposite

relation, while zero would indicate that the two probabilities are the same (Lieberson, 1975: 279–80).

9. Because there is no occupational ranking for 1931, there are no indexes of occupational inequality for that year.

REFERENCES

Abella, Rosalie. 1984. *Equality in Employment: A Royal Commission Report.* Ottawa: Supply and Services.

Blishen, Bernard R. 1958. "The Construction and Use of an Occupational Class Scale." *Canadian Journal of Economics and Political Science* 24: 519–31.

———. 1967. "A Socio-economic Index for Occupations in Canada." *Canadian Review of Sociology and Anthropology* 4: 41–53.

Blishen, Bernard R., and William K. Carroll. 1978. "Sex Differences in a Socio-economic Index for Occupations in Canada." *Canadian Review of Sociology and Anthropology* 15: 352–71.

Blishen, Bernard R., and Hugh A. McRoberts. 1976. "A Revised Socio-economic Index for Occupations in Canada." *Canadian Review of Sociology and Anthropology* 13: 71–79.

Blishen, Bernard R., William K. Carroll, and Catherine Moore. 1987. "The 1981 Socio-economic Index for Occupations in Canada." *Canadian Review of Sociology and Anthropology* 24: 465–88.

Boyd, Monica. 1985. "Immigration and Occupational Attainment." Pp. 393–446 in M. Boyd et al., eds., *Ascription and Attainment: Studies in Mobility and Status Attainment in Canada.* Ottawa: Carleton University Press.

Boyer, J. Patrick. 1985. *Equality for All.* Report of the Parliamentary Committee on Equal Rights. Ottawa: Supply and Services.

Clement, Wallace. 1975. *The Canadian Corporate Elite.* Toronto: McClelland And Stewart.

Darroch, Gordon. 1979. "Another Look at Ethnicity, Stratification and Social Mobility in Canada." *Canadian Journal of Sociology* 4 (1): 1–28.

Denis, Ann. 1986. "Adaptation to Multiple Subordination? Women in the Vertical Mosaic." *Canadian Ethnic Studies* 18 (3): 61–74.

Duncan, Otis Dudley and Beverly Duncan. 1955. "Residential distribution and occupational stratification." *American Journal of Sociology* 60: 493–503.

Fox, B. and J. Fox. 1987. "Occupational Gender Segregation in the Canadian Labour Force, 1931–1981." *Canadian Review of Sociology and Anthropology* 24 (3): 374–97.

Henry, Frances, and Effie Ginzberg. 1985. *Who Gets the Work?* Toronto: Urban Alliance on Race Relations and the Social Planning Council of Toronto.

Kralt, John. 1980. "Ethnic Origin in the Canadian Census: 1871–1981." In Roman Petryshyn, ed., *Changing Realities: Social Trends Among Ukrainian Canadians.* Edmonton: Canadian Institute of Ukrainian Studies.

Lagacé, Michael D. 1968. "Educational Attainment in Canada." Dominion Bureau of Statistics, Special Labour Force Survey No. 7. Ottawa: Queen's Printer.

Lambert, M., M. Ledoux, and R. Pendakur. 1989. "Visible Minorities in Canada 1986: A Graphic Overview." Policy and Research Unit, Multiculturalism and Citizenship, Ottawa.

Lautard, Hugh, and Donald Loree. 1984. "Ethnic Stratification in Canada, 1931–1971." *Canadian Journal of Sociology* 9 (3): 333–44.

Lieberson, Stanley. 1975. "Rank-sum Comparisons between Groups." Pp. 276–91 in David R. Heise, ed., *Sociological Methodology* 1976. San Francisco: Jossey-Bass.

McDade, Kathryn. 1988. "Barriers to Recognition of the Credentials of Immigrants in Canada." Discussion Paper 88.B.1, Institute for Research on Public Policy, Ottawa.

Pineo, Peter. 1976. "Social Mobility in Canada: The Current Picture." *Sociological Focus* 9 (2): 109–23.

Pineo, Peter, and John Porter. 1985. "Ethnic Origin and Occupational Attachment." Pp. 357–92 in M. Boyd et al., eds., *Ascription and Attainment: Studies and Status Attainment in Canada.* Ottawa: Carleton University Press.

Porter, John. 1965. *The Vertical Mosaic.* Toronto: University of Toronto Press.

———. 1985. "Canada: The Societal Context of Occupational Allocation." Pp. 29–65 in M. Boyd et al., eds., *Ascription and Achievement: Studies in Mobility and Status Attainment in Canada.* Ottawa: Carleton University Press.

Reitz, Jeffrey. 1988. "Less Racial Discrimination in Canada, or Simply Less Racial Conflict? Implications of Comparisons with Britain." *Canadian Public Policy* 14 (4): 424–41.

Robson, Reginald, and Brad Breems. 1986. *Ethnic Conflict in Vancouver.* Vancouver: British Columbia Civil Liberties Association.

Winn, Conrad. 1985. "Affirmative Action and Visible Minorities: Eight Premises in Quest of Evidence." *Canadian Public Policy* 11 (4): 684–700.

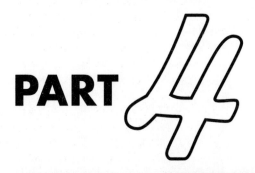

PART 4

SOCIAL INSTITUTIONS

THE SOCIAL STRUCTURES that comprise human societies are nested like Russian dolls or Chinese boxes (see Figure P4.1). There are structures within structures within structures. The smallest are known as microstructures. Microstructures are small, localized sites of face-to-face interaction, such as families. Social relations in **microstructures** tend to be emotionally deep and enduring, which is why people value them for their own sake. **Macrostructures**, in contrast, are larger, less localized, and more impersonal. People participate in macrostructures for specific, instrumental reasons — to earn money, get an education, etc. **Megastructures** are even larger, more remote, and more impersonal. They involve relations between whole societies and between nations.

As Figure P4.1 shows, **institutions** are found at both the micro- and macrostructural levels of society. Institutions are social structures that, to varying degrees, fulfil basic human needs. These needs include:

- the reproduction of the species and the nurturance and primary socialization of small children, a set of functions that is usually performed by the family (see Part 4A);
- the maintenance and renewal of legitimate authority, a set of functions that is performed by the political system (see Part 4B); and
- the production and distribution of material resources, a set of functions that is performed by the economy (see Part 4C).

In keeping with the overall theme of this book, the chapters in this part focus on how powerful social forces, such as the entry of most adult women into the paid labour force, global economic competition, and constitutional reform are reshaping major social institutions. The chapters highlight not just the fact that social institutions fulfil basic human needs, but that basic human needs are flexible and may therefore be fulfilled by a wide variety of institutional forms. The chapters also show that the adaptation of families, political systems, and economies to new conditions is often disorienting for the people who live and work in them. Some people react by organizing resistance to change and attempting to return to the old state of affairs. The very term "institution" may suggest a solid and stable establishment, but in reality social conflict is never far below the surface of any modern institution.

Figure P4.1 The Nested Structures of Society

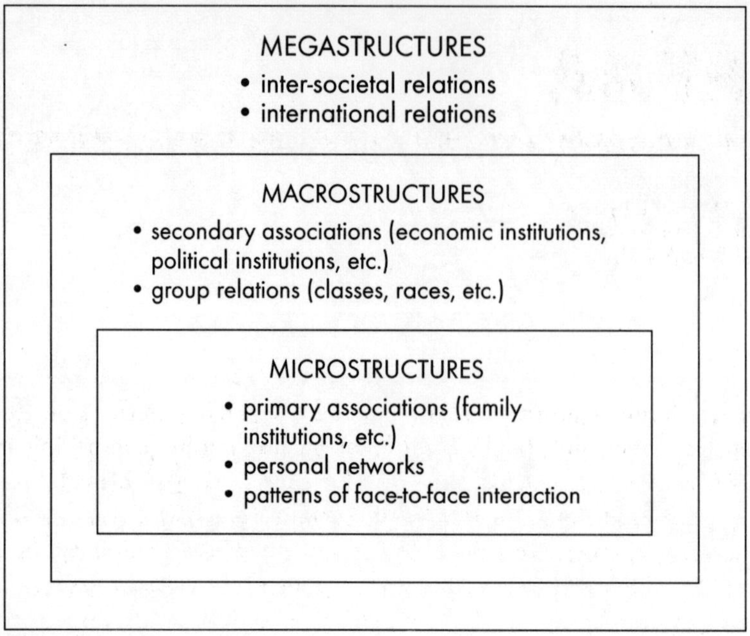

MEGASTRUCTURES
- inter-societal relations
- international relations

MACROSTRUCTURES
- secondary associations (economic institutions, political institutions, etc.)
- group relations (classes, races, etc.)

MICROSTRUCTURES
- primary associations (family institutions, etc.)
- personal networks
- patterns of face-to-face interaction

GLOSSARY

Institutions are micro- and macro-level social structures that address basic human needs, such as reproduction, nurturance and primary socialization (the family), the maintenance and renewal of legitimate authority (the political system), and the production and distribution of material resources (the economy).

Macrostructures are large, non-localized, impersonal sets of social relations. People participate in them for specific, instrumental reasons.

Megastructures are the largest and most impersonal patterns of social relations, sometimes spanning the entire globe, including relations between societies and nations.

Microstructures are small, localized, emotionally intense patterns of social relations. People value such relations for their own sake.

PART 4A

FAMILIES

The **nuclear family** consists of a husband and a wife living in the same household with at least one child. In the **traditional nuclear family** (comprising about 20 percent of Canadian households), only the husband is employed in the paid work force. In the **non-traditional nuclear family** (comprising another roughly 20 percent of Canadian households), both the husband and the wife are employed in the paid work force. In addition, some 35 percent of households are **non-nuclear families**: childless couples, lone parents living with at least one child, and husbands and wives with no children living at home. Finally, about 25 percent of Canadian households are not recognized as families by the Canadian census. These **non-family households** include people living alone and people who are living together but who are neither married nor bound by common law (e.g., gay couples).

As one descends this list of household types, one moves from shrinking to expanding categories. The traditional nuclear family is no longer the predominant family form because so many women have entered the paid work force, especially since the 1960s. Today, both spouses work in the paid work force in about two-thirds of Canadian husband–wife families. Non-nuclear families are increasingly common for several reasons. More women are deciding not to have children so that they can pursue higher education and careers. Others cannot have children with their spouses because they or their spouses are infertile. Infertility affects up to 15 percent of couples and is on the rise, largely, some medical scientists suspect, due to worsening environmental conditions. Non-nuclear families are also more common because the proportion of Canadians who marry is down (from over 90 percent in 1971 to under 85 percent today), the divorce rate is up (by over 700 percent since the early 1950s), and the rate of remarriage after divorce is down (from over 80 percent of divorcees in 1971 to under 70 percent today). Finally, non-family households are more common since more single people (including the elderly) can afford to live on their own and since gay lifestyles are more widely accepted than they used to be, at least in large urban areas.

The facts listed above should not lead one to conclude that the family is in a state of collapse. A countrywide poll taken in 1987 found that over three-quarters of Canadians regard the family as the most important thing in their lives, more important than career and religion. Ninety-two percent of respondents with children at home said that the family is becoming more important to them. The overwhelming majority of adults still want to marry and have children. The family is not a crumbling institution. What is happening, however, is that people are freer than they once were to establish the kinds of family arrangements that best suit them. For instance, because most adult women are now employed in the paid work force, and because changes in divorce laws have made the division of property after divorce more equitable, women now have a measure of economic independence, which gives them greater freedom to end unsatisfying marriages and seek more gratifying relationships. This does not spell the end of the family but the possibility that improved family forms can take shape.

Wife beating was one aspect of many marriages that used to be hushed up but is now increasingly being made public and serving as a precipitant of divorce. Nonetheless, much wife beating still goes unreported and many marriages are still the site of abusive relationships. In Chapter 17, the late Michael D. Smith of York University analyzes the kinds of husbands who are more likely to beat their wives. His survey results show that husbands with relatively low incomes, few years of formal education, and low-status jobs are more likely to beat their wives than higher-status husbands. (This does not mean that higher-status husbands never abuse their wives, just that they are less likely to do so.) Moreover, Smith notes that husbands who beat their wives tend to support **patriarchy**, a social structure in which men have the power to dominate women and an ideology that legitimizes male dominance.

In Chapter 18, C. James Richardson of the University of New Brunswick analyzes major recent changes in Canadian family law and their social consequences. He focusses particularly on divorce. Richardson notes that in the 1960s, 1970s, and early 1980s, the reform of Canadian divorce law was shaped by liberal views on the family. Marriage ceased to be viewed by most Canadians as a sacred institution. Laws were changed to make divorce easier so that presumably more satisfying relationships could be established. Divorcing spouses were encouraged to have their disputes mediated out of court rather than face each other as adversaries in court; the whole question of fault came to be considered legally irrelevant; waiting periods between filing for divorce and actually receiving divorce papers were shortened; joint custody arrangements were encouraged. All these changes were expected to result in less hardship and emotional strain for the divorcing spouses and their children.

By the mid-1980s, however, several parties were criticizing the liberal reform of Canadian divorce law. For example, men's rights groups complained that the new legislation denied them adequate access to their children. Many feminists argued that the reforms failed to deal adequately with the unequal outcomes of separation and divorce for women and men. Frequently, they noted, women who separate and divorce wind up living in poverty, particularly if they have custody of the children. In addition, noted the feminists, because men tend to have more material resources than women, divorce mediation may favour men's interests more than women's. Maybe, said some feminists, it is better for women after all if they get a good lawyer to argue their case instead of relying on divorce mediation.

Richardson's research offers little clear support for any one side in the ongoing debate about Canadian family law reform. For example, he finds that a mere 3 percent of divorcing couples use divorce mediation (far less than what proponents of divorce mediation expected), that women fare better economically in mediation than in a purely legal process (contrary to what many feminists expected), that few men are denied what they consider to be adequate access to their children (contrary to the views of men's rights groups), and that the economic situation of women has neither improved nor worsened as a result of new divorce laws (which supports the feminist view about the unequal outcome of divorce for women and men, but not the more extreme feminist view that mediation renders women worse off economically). Richardson ends by emphasizing the need for more sociological survey research to assess the consequences of family law reform in Canada.

Part of Newton's third law of motion states that the exertion of physical force on an object evokes an opposite reaction from that object. Analogously, every social change evokes a reaction on the part of those who are deeply entrenched in the status quo. In Chapter 19, Lorna Erwin discusses one such case. In the early 1980s, the pro-family movement was organized in Canada in defence of the traditional nuclear family and conservative moral values. Its members spoke out passionately in opposition to feminism, gay rights, abortion, and so forth. Erwin conducted a survey in the late 1980s to determine who the supporters of the pro-family movement are and the likelihood of their developing a broader, **neoconservative** agenda, as they have in the United States. (Neoconservatism is a political ideology that attributes most social problems to too much state involvement in the lives of the citizenry; see the footnote on page 221.) She shows that the supporters of the pro-family movement tend to be relatively well-educated, middle-class, female homemakers over the age of 45 who were raised in traditional nuclear families in small towns or on farms and who practise Catholicism or fundamentalist Protestantantism. Erwin also finds that pro-family movement members are more likely than most Canadians to hold *liberal* views on general political and economic issues. She therefore concludes that Canada is unlikely to follow the American pattern: the chance of a neoconservative movement emerging from the pro-family movement in Canada is small.

GLOSSARY

Neoconservatism is a political ideology that attributes most social problems to too much state involvement in the lives of the citizenry.

Non-family households include people living alone and people who are living together but who are neither married nor bound by a common-law union (e.g., gay couples).

Non-nuclear families include childless couples, lone parents living with at least one child, and husbands and wives with no children living at home.

A **non-traditional nuclear family** is a nuclear family in which both the husband and the wife are employed in the paid work force.

A **nuclear family** consists of a husband and a wife living in the same household with at least one child.

Patriarchy is a social structure in which men have the power to dominate women and an ideology that legitimizes male dominance.

A **traditional nuclear family** is a nuclear family in which only the husband is employed in the paid work force.

Chapter 17

PATRIARCHAL IDEOLOGY AND WIFE BEATING

MICHAEL D. SMITH

The concept of patriarchy has a history within feminist thought that goes back at least to the early part of this century. It first received widespread exposure, however, with the publication of Kate Millett's *Sexual Politics* in 1969. Since then, feminists spanning the entire left-to-right spectrum have used the concept in a variety of ways, most of which boil down to an attempt to understand the system of inequality in society whereby males dominate females. Today, any theoretical work that claims to be feminist probably must sooner or later seriously address the concept of patriarchy (Barrett, 1980).

A patriarchy may be thought of as having two basic components: A structure, in which men have more power and privilege than women, and an ideology that legitimizes this arrangement. This system, which MacKinnon (1983: 638) calls "perhaps the most pervasive and tenacious system of power in history," characterizes most societies, past and present, albeit with significant variations in particular historical epochs, under different modes of production, and across cultures, classes, and other social structures (Barrett, 1980; Beechey, 1979; Burstyn, 1985; Dobash & Dobash, 1979; Edwards, 1987; Eisenstein, 1980; MacKinnon, 1983; Smith, 1983; Ursel, 1986; Yllo, 1984).

Some theorists make a distinction between "social" and "familial" patriarchy. The former term refers to male dominance in society as a whole, the latter term to male dominance in the family (Barrett, 1980; Eisen-stein, 1980; Millett, 1969; Ursel, 1984, 1986). Although ultimately one type of patriarchy cannot be fully understood without reference to the other, this study focused on patriarchy in the familial sphere, which Millett considered to be the most fundamental unit of patriarchy within the patriarchal whole.[1]

The study also focused on the ideological component of familial patriarchy. Millett saw that while the structures of familial patriarchy may have eroded over the past two decades, the ideological basis of the patriarchal family has not eroded at the same pace, if at all (Barrett, 1980; Ferraro, 1988). The literature on familial patriarchy indicates that this ideology centers to a considerable degree on the themes of a wife's obedience, respect, loyalty, dependency, sexual access, and sexual fidelity. A small but growing number of theoretical and empirical studies on the relationship between patriarchy and wife beating suggests that men tend to beat their wives when they violate, or are perceived as violating, these ideals (Dobash & Dobash, 1979).

Although the theory of patriarchy and wife beating is fundamentally concerned with the question of why violence is directed at women as a group, the theory was conceptualized here at the interpersonal level of analysis; ultimately it is individual men who assault their wives and female partners. The main purpose of the study was to test the feminist hypothesis that wife beating results from adherence by battering husbands to an ideology of familial patriarchy.

Source: Excerpted from "Patriarchal Ideology and Wife Beating: A Test of a Feminist Hypothesis," *Violence and Victims* 5, 4 (1990): 257–73. Reprinted by permission of Springer Publishing Company, Inc.

PATRIARCHY AND VIOLENCE AGAINST WOMEN

The Feminist Thesis

In patriarchal societies, men traditionally have had a legal and cultural mandate to control women. This mandate at times has allowed men to rape, batter, and even kill women, both within and outside the family, especially when men perceived that their dominance was threatened. Although the grossest inequalities have now disappeared from most western societies — the law no longer officially sanctions the physical chastisement of wives, for instance — women in general are still subordinate to men, and women are still all too frequently the victims of male violence (Kennedy & Dutton, 1989; Lupri, 1989; Straus & Gelles, 1986; Smith, 1987).

Feminist scholars point increasingly to patriarchy as the main source of violence against women in contemporary society. Although liberal, socialist, radical, Marxist, and other varieties of feminist theorists may disagree on the origins of patriarchy, how it is perpetuated, and what should be done to eliminate it, all would agree that patriarchy provides the structural and ideological underpinnings of male violence against women. This conviction is being expressed more and more explicitly, not only in the literature on wife abuse, but in writings on rape, wife rape, sexual assault, sexual harassment, femicide — on all types of male violence against women (Dobash & Dobash, 1979; Farley, 1978; Kurz, 1989; Russell, 1982, 1984; Schechter, 1982; Schwendinger & Schwendinger, 1983). For most feminists, violence against women on the scale that takes place is only possible in a social context that defines women as subordinate to men.

Feminist contentions notwithstanding, research on the relationship between patriarchy and the physical abuse of women is limited. On the one hand, few systematic attempts have been made to demonstrate quantitatively the existence of such a relationship. On the other hand, most empirical research on the subject is based on qualitative data obtained from small, nonrepresentative samples. Dobash and Dobash (1979), for example, using materials from in-depth interviews with 109 battered women in Scottish shelters, showed that the primary source of the violence was a husband's feelings about his wife's alleged failure to live up to his "ideals" and "expectations" about what it means to be a "good wife." These "ideals" and "expectations" almost always have to do with his jealousy, her domestic duties, and who should control the household money. But what is true for a small number of working-class wives

in Glasgow and Edinburgh is not necessarily true for battered wives in general. Nor does such research tell us how violent men or relationships may differ from nonviolent ones; after all, not all men are batterers. The findings of this sort of work, insightful as they may be, are not generalizable to the population at large. At this point in the development of the theory of patriarchy and wife beating it may be useful to test the theoretical perspectives of the Dobashes and other feminist scholars quantitatively in the general population.[2]

Quantitative Studies Based on Representative Samples of the General Population

Several studies by Yllo, Straus, and their colleagues seem to be the only research of this kind to date. Three of these studies employed wife-beating data from Straus et al.'s (1980) first national survey on family violence and census data on the economic, educational, political, and legal status of women in U.S. states. The measure of "wife beating" was the severe-violence index of the Conflict Tactics Scales (CTS) (Straus, 1979). American states were the unit of analysis.

In the first study, Yllo (1983a, b) found that the rate of violence against wives across states varied curvilinearly according to the status of women in those states. The least egalitarian states had the highest rate of violence; the most egalitarian states had the second highest rate. Yllo suggests that the greater probability of violence in the least egalitarian states may have been a function both of males resorting to force to keep women "in their place" and a lack of alternatives to violent marriage, which kept wives in violent relationships, and, hence, the violence rate high. The greater probability of violence in high-status-of-women states, she speculates, may have resulted from men being frustrated and threatened by the relatively rapid breakdown of traditional sex roles in these states.

In the second study, Yllo (1984) focused on the associations among structural inequality, interpersonal inequality, and wife beating. Interpersonal inequality was measured using an index composed of six items regarding who has "the final say" in marital decision making. She found that the highest rate of wife beating occurred among husband-dominant couples (see also Straus et al., 1980: 192) in high-status-of-women states. The interpretation here is that domination by a husband is perceived by his wife as especially inequitable when it exists in a context of relative gender equality. In such a context, marital inequality becomes a major source of conflict between spouses.

The already dominant husband then resorts to violence to maintain or extend control over his wife.

In the third study, Yllo and Straus (1984) examined the relationships among structural inequality, "patriarchal norms," and wife beating. Patriarchal norms were measured using the same items that made up the interpersonal inequality index, but the index of norms was based on responses to questions about who should have the "final say" in marital decision making. Yllo and Straus found no correlation between structural inequality and patriarchal norms, but they did discover a strong linear relationship between patriarchal norms and wife beating: The more patriarchal the norms, the higher the level of wife beating. This relationship occurred primarily in those states where women's status was highest. In other words, wife beating was most common in a context where the structural status of women was relatively high but where there remained considerable support for patriarchal norms favoring the subordination of women within marriage. Yllo and Straus speculate that this contradiction was a source of conflict among husbands and wives and that such conflict, in some couples, culminated in wife beating.

Indeed, in another analysis of data from the same survey, Coleman and Straus (1986) found that husband-dominant couples had the lowest consensus over the legitimacy of patriarchal norms and the highest rate of conflict about family responsibilities. In turn, as the level of conflict rose, so did the rate of husband-to-wife violence (based on the CTS minor-violence index). These results suggest that it is a lack of consensus between husband and wife as to the legitimacy of patriarchal norms that leads to violence.

Finally, based on a more sophisticated measure of state structural inequality (the Gender Equality Index) and wife-beating data from Straus and Gelles' (1986) second national family violence survey, Straus (1987) confirmed that both structural inequality and wife beating vary considerably across states and that the greater the degree of structural inequality within a given state, the higher the level of wife beating.

These studies provide quantitative support for the feminist theory of patriarchy and violence against women. They also indicate that patriarchal structure and ideology are variables, not constants. None of the studies, however, allows inferences about the relationship between patriarchal ideology and wife beating on an individual level. Discovering that wife beating is most common in states with the highest level of normative support for husband dominance in marital decision making does not demonstrate that patriarchal norms are sources of violence for those individual victims. This would require obtaining some measure of patriarchal norms and some measure of violent victimization from the same individuals and then examining the relationship between these two variables. This should be done in a multivariate analysis, which would show the unique explanatory power of patriarchal norms.

Quantitative Studies Based on Clinical Samples

A second strand of relevant research is made up of quantitative studies that have sought to differentiate mainly clinical samples of physically abusive husbands from comparison groups of nonabusive husbands on the basis of several measures of traditional sex-role expectations. In most of these studies, there is some attempt to link the notion of traditional sex-role expectations theoretically with familial patriarchy; Neidig, Friedman, and Collins (1986: 226), for instance, discuss a conservative orientation on the Spence-Helmreich Attitudes Toward Women Scale in terms of "inequities in the distribution of power within the marital relationship."

Taken together, the results of these studies are inconclusive. Neither Neidig et al. (1986) nor Rosenbaum and O'Leary (1981) were able to distinguish between violent and nonviolent husbands on the basis of abbreviated versions of the Attitudes Toward Women Scale, which assessed subjects' level of agreement with statements about the roles, rights, and privileges of women. Similarly, Dutton (1988: 69–74) failed to find a significant difference between wife assaulters and several control groups on the Burt Attitude Scales, which assessed sex-role stereotyping, adversarial beliefs, and acceptance of interpersonal violence toward women.[3]

On the other hand, Walker (1983) found that battered women perceived their batterers as having more traditional sex-role expectations (based on the Attitudes Toward Women Scale) than nonbattering men with whom the women had had an intimate relationship. Telch and Lindquist (1984) also reported that violent husbands were significantly more likely than nonviolent ones to have traditional sex-role attitudes, as measured by a 22-item scale developed for the study. Saunders, Lynch, Grayson, and Linz (1987), employing a 12-item inventory of beliefs and attitudes specifically about wife beating, found that male batterers were significantly more likely than a sample of advocates for battered women and another sample of male college students to believe that wife beating is justified under certain conditions. (Several items in this scale are similar to items used in the present research, although the two scales were developed independently.) An impressive feature of the Saunders et al. scale is that it is supported by seven tests of validity.

Saunders et al.'s study, together with research on the relationship between attitudes and behavior generally (Fazio, Powell, & Herr, 1983), suggests that an adequate empirical test of the theory of patriarchal ideology and wife beating requires a measure of ideology that closely reflects patriarchal beliefs or attitudes, including those that specifically condone wife beating, as opposed to more general traditional sex-role expectations.[4]

Socioeconomic Characteristics of Wife Beaters

If adherence to the ideology of familial patriarchy indeed varies significantly among males in the general population, what are the socioeconomic characteristics of men who endorse this ideology? The survey literature on woman abuse offers some clues. Most representative sample surveys of the general population reveal that, although abusers are found in every segment of society, they are not evenly distributed throughout society. In particular, they tend to be most common among men with low income, low educational attainment, and low occupational status (Kennedy & Dutton, 1989; Lupri, 1989; Schulman, 1979; Smith, 1987, 1989; Stets & Straus, 1989; Straus, Gelles, & Steinmetz, 1980).

Are such men especially prone to developing an ideology that encourages, supports, or allows wife beating? A number of theoretical perspectives within violent subculture theory, including Bowker's (1983, 1985) speculations about a "patriarchal subculture" of wife beaters and the Dobashs' (1979: 21–22) discussion of the possible "structural and cultural interrelatedness" of violence-doers, suggest this may be the case. Bowker, for instance, theorizes that economic stress makes it difficult for "previolent" blue-collar men to maintain the degree of dominance over their wives to which, according to what they have learned from male peers and others, they are entitled. This perceived deprivation of domination then results in a readiness for violence as a means of reestablishing control.[5] Investigation, however, of what it is about the lives of some men rather than others that may promote the development of an ideology of familial patriarchy was beyond the scope of the present study, which sought

merely to determine the socioeconomic characteristics of men who endorsed such an ideology.

In summary, this study sought answers to two questions: (a) Do men who beat their wives or female partners, compared with men who do not, adhere to an ideology of familial patriarchy? (b) If so, what are the socioeconomic characteristics of these patriarchal wife beaters?

METHOD

Sample and Interviews

The data upon which this analysis is based come from a survey of Toronto women conducted in 1987. Using a method of random digit dialing (Tremblay, 1981) that maximizes the probability of selecting a working residential number, and at the same time produces a simple random sample, a sample of telephone numbers was generated from a list of all telephone exchanges in the Census Metropolitan Area of Toronto. Over 99% of Toronto households have at least one phone.

Female interviewers working for the Institute for Social Research, located at York University, then conducted telephone interviews, averaging 23 minutes, with 604 currently or formerly married or cohabiting women between the ages of 18–50. The interviews took place in January and early February 1987.

The interviewer introduced the study to whoever picked up the phone as a "survey of women in Toronto." She then asked for a list of all women aged 18–50 living in the household and (if any) how many were married or living with a male partner, or had been married or had lived with a male partner within the previous two years. If only one eligible woman resided in the household, she became the respondent; otherwise a respondent was randomly chosen from the list of eligible respondents. The interviewer then introduced the survey more explicitly to the respondent as a study of "how safe women in Toronto feel today." A strongly worded guarantee of confidentiality and anonymity completed the introduction.

The survey response rate, defined as the number of completed interviews divided by the number of estimated eligible respondents, is 56.4% (refusals: 31.2%; noncontacts: 12.4%). This rate is low for several reasons, which have been discussed elsewhere (Smith, 1987), but it is not out of line with rates obtained in other metropolitan area surveys; for example, the urban rate in Straus et al.'s (1980) first national survey on family violence was 60%. A sample and field report provides details regarding the calculation of the response rate and other technical aspects of the present study, including the design and final disposition of the sample, a table of 95% confidence intervals for various sample sizes and percentages, and a copy of the questionnaire (Bates et al., 1987).

A comparison of the characteristics of the sample with 1986 Census data on the population of Metropolitan Toronto indicates that the sample was roughly representative of Toronto women with respect to age, marital status, and ethnicity. Census data on the social, cultural and economic characteristics of Torontonians are not yet available (Smith, 1990).[6]

Definitions and Measurement

Wife Beating

Wife beating was defined as any severe physical assault on a woman by her present or (most recent) former husband or live-in male partner. If an assault caused, or had a high probability of causing, serious (i.e., more than temporary) pain or injury, or was perceived by the victim as designed to cause serious pain or injury, it constituted wife beating. This definition parallels the legal definition of aggravated, as opposed to simple, assault (Straus, 1988). The principal measure of wife beating was the severe-violence index of the 1986 version of the Conflict Tactics Scales (CTS). These scales have been used and refined over the years in dozens of studies dealing wholly or partly with violence against women (see Straus, 1988). The CTS are composed of 19 items describing ways of handling interpersonal conflict. The respondent indicates how often each occurred in the past year, or ever. The first 10 items have to do with reasoning and verbal aggression. The last nine items describe acts of violence, ranging in severity from throwing something at the other person to using a gun or knife. The severe-violence index is made up of the last six of these items (kicked, bit or hit you with his fist; hit or tried to hit you with something; beat you up; choked you; threatened you with a gun or knife; used a gun or knife on you). The rate of severe violence, or what Straus terms "wife beating," is usually calculated as the percentage of women who were victims of one or more of the last six violent acts. (The rates for each individual act are usually very low.) The CTS are internally reliable and have adequate concurrent and construct validity (Straus, 1979, 1990).

In this study, wife beating refers to whether or not a respondent reported having been subject to any of these acts of serious violence ever in the marriage or relationship. Slightly over 7% of the respondents reported having been so victimized. This figure is slightly higher than most of the other CTS-based rates of severe violence obtained in surveys of the general population; it is much lower, of course, than rates that include relatively minor acts of violence (see Smith, 1988). Wife beating was coded 0 = not beaten, 1 = beaten.

The interviewer followed up an affirmative response to any CTS with an invitation to describe the experience or, if more than one, the "worst" experience, probing, as necessary, to establish the severity of the abuse; e.g., was the victim hurt? Did she require medical attention? Were the police informed? Were charges laid? Four disclosures originally labeled minor were recoded as severe violence on the basis of the victim's in-depth account of the incident and its aftermath. No CTS severe-violence report was changed to minor.

Husbands' Patriarchal Ideology

Patriarchal ideology was conceived, after Millett (1969), as a primary component of the patriarchal system and was defined as (a) a set of beliefs that legitimizes male power and authority over women in marriage, or in a marriage-like arrangement, and (b) a set of attitudes or norms supportive of violence against wives who violate, or who are perceived as violating, the ideals of familial patriarchy.

Obedience, respect, loyalty, dependency, sexual access, sexual fidelity — these are prominent themes in the ideology of familial patriarchy. The statements of beliefs shown in Table 17.1 and attitudes shown in Table 17.2 are intended as operational measures of these themes. Some of the statements are versions of items reported in previous research; the rest were constructed for this study. The beliefs items were administered first and the attitudes items second. For each item, the respondent was asked how she thought her husband or partner would respond — that is, for her perception of her husband's beliefs and attitudes.

The use of these perceptual measures can be justified in several ways. First, the importance of attempting to understand and validate women's experiences and perceptions is fundamental to any feminist undertaking (Bograd & Yllo, 1988). Second, because the questions about ideology were derived explicitly from the literature on familial patriarchy and asked in the context of other questions about the respondent's relationship with her husband and about the circumstances, motives, and physical and emotional consequences associated with wife abuse, the ideology variables have some "face" validity (Saunders, 1988). Third, in an examination of the validity of self-reports of "marital violence," Arias and Beach (1987) found

Table 17.1 Husbands' Patriarchal Beliefs

Beliefs*	Strongly Agree	Agree	Disagree	Strongly Disagree
A. A man has the right to decide whether or not his wife/partner should work outside the home.	3%	33%	47%	17%
B. A man has the right to decide whether or not his wife/partner should go out in the evening with her friends.	4	28	54	14
C. Sometimes it is important for a man to show his wife/partner that he is head of the house.	8	45	33	14
D. A man has the right to have sex with his wife/partner when he wants, even though she may not want to.	2	16	60	20

*Coded: 4 = strongly agree
3 = agree
2 = disagree
1 = strongly disagree

Table 17.2 Husbands' Approval of Violence against Wives

Would Your Husband/Partner Approve of a Man Slapping His Wife if...?*	Yes	No	Depends
A. She won't do what he tells her to do	3%	96%	1%
B. She insults him when they are at home alone	4	96	0
C. She insults him in public	6	92	2
D. She comes home drunk	8	90	2
E. She hits him first when they are having an argument	20	76	4
F. He learns she has been having an affair with another man	20	75	5

*Coded: 1 = yes or depends   0 = no

that the need for social approval, as measured by the Marlowe-Crowne Social Desirability Scale, was significantly related to abusive husbands' willingness to report their own use of violence but not to wives' reports of having been victimized; that is to say, wives' accounts of the husbands' behavior were more accurate measures of that behavior than husbands' accounts of their own behavior. Findings of this sort suggest indirectly that the perceptual measures used in the study at hand may be reasonably valid indicators of the degree to which husbands adhere to beliefs and attitudes supportive of familial patriarchy.

The responses to the beliefs statements are relatively normally distributed (Table 17.1). Responses to the attitude items are highly skewed toward non-approval (Table 17.2). The latter distribution is similar to that obtained in other studies of normative support for violence against wives (Greenblatt, 1985).

Respondents' scores were used to form two composite indexes, one for beliefs and one for attitudes. These indexes were labeled Husbands' Patriarchal Beliefs and Husbands' Approval of Violence Against Wives.

Socioeconomic Variables

An earlier analysis of data from this study (Smith, 1990) yielded statistically significant bivariate correlations between wife beating and several socioeconomic variables associated with husbands — namely, low income, low educational attainment, low occupational status, and unemployment. Hotaling and Sugarman (1986) refer to such variables as "risk markers." A risk marker is any attribute of the couple, the victim, or the violence-doer that is associated with an increased probability of violence. A risk marker may or may not imply causality. The risk variables employed in this study were measured as follows:

1. Family Income: total family income from all sources in 1986; if divorced or separated, total income "the last year you were together" (i.e., 1986 or 1985); 1 = less than $10,000, 2 = $10,000–$19,999, 3 = $20,000–$29,999, 4 = $30,000–$39,999, 5 = $40,000–$49,999, 6 = $50,000–$59,999, 7 = $60,000–$69,000, 8 = $70,000–$79,999, 9 = $80,000 or more.

2. Husbands' Educational Attainment: 1 = no schooling, 2 = some elementary school, 3 = completed elementary school, 4 = some high school, 5 = completed high school, 6 = completed community college, 7 = some university, 8 = university degree, 9 = completed postgraduate degree.

3. Husbands' Occupational Status: Blishen and McRoberts' (1976) Socioeconomic Index for Occupations in Canada (continuous variable).

4. Husbands' Employment Status: 0 = unemployed or employed part-time, 1 = employed full-time.

RESULTS

As predicted, the Patriarchal Beliefs Index and the Approval of Violence Index are positively related to Wife Beating and negatively related to the socioeconomic variables, and the socioeconomic variables are negatively related to Wife Beating.

More specifically, feminist theory suggests that men who hold a set of beliefs and attitudes supportive of familial patriarchy are more likely than men who do not hold such beliefs to beat their wives or female partners. The results support this hypothesis. Both Patriarchal Beliefs and Approval of Violence Against Wives were independent, statistically significant predictors of whether or not a woman was ever beaten by her present or former husband or partner; the more patriarchal the husband's beliefs and attitudes, the greater the probability that he beat his wife.

Husbands who adhered to a patriarchal ideology and less-educated husbands were significantly more likely than less patriarchal, more educated husbands to have beaten their wives or partners.

CONCLUSION

Feminist theory suggests that, at the interpersonal level, wife beating results from adherence by battering husbands to an ideology of familial patriarchy. The

research reported here provides quantitative data from a representative sample of women in the general population that supports this thesis. Husbands who, in the eyes of their wives or female partners, espoused a set of beliefs and attitudes supportive of patriarchy in the domestic context were more likely than husbands who did not espouse such beliefs and attitudes to have assaulted their wives at some point in the relationship.

Who are these patriarchal wife beaters? Lower-income husbands, less-educated husbands, and husbands in relatively low-status jobs were significantly more likely than more advantaged husbands to subscribe to an ideology of familial patriarchy. The former were also significantly more likely to have beaten their wives. Investigation of the life conditions of these men that may promote such an orientation was beyond the scope of this study. The results are compatible, however, with several versions of violent subculture theory, including Bowker's (1983, 1985) speculations about a "patriarchal subculture" of wife beaters composed mainly of low-SES males who socialize their peers into the ideology of male dominance and the importance of keeping wives "in line," by force if necessary.

When all the socioeconomic risk markers and indexes of patriarchal ideology were combined in a single model assessing the extent to which these variables predicted wife beating, the combination of husbands' educational attainment, patriarchal beliefs, and patriarchal attitudes parsimoniously explained 20% of the variance in wife beating.

This study has several limitations, the most important of which are as follows. First, as in all such surveys, it is probably safe to assume that a substantial number of victims did not disclose having been beaten. This raises questions about the representativeness of those respondents who did disclose such incidents and, ultimately, about the generalizability of the findings regarding patriarchy and wife beating. Methodological studies designed to determine the extent of underreporting, the presence of reporting biases, and ways to reduce or control for these problems should be a priority in survey research on this sensitive subject. Second, the validity of the indexes of the husbands' patriarchal ideology has not been clearly established. The concurrent validity of these measures should be determined by comparing wives' reports of their husbands' patriarchal beliefs and attitudes with the responses of the husbands themselves. Third, this study did not investigate why low-SES men were more likely than higher-status men to adhere to an ideology of familial patriarchy. Examination of the social forces that explain why some men more than others subscribe to such an ideology would have theoretical significance for the patriarchal subculture thesis and practical significance for social interventions into the lives of patriarchal wife beaters.

What are the policy and treatment implications of the present research? From a policy point of view, the results of this study suggest that educational programs designed to promote understanding of the relationship between familial ideology and wife beating be developed and implemented. The results also point to the importance of finding effective ways to enhance the educational and income-earning opportunities of lower-SES men, men especially likely, apparently, to subscribe to an ideology of familial patriarchy. As for the treatment of wife beaters, the findings support a "profeminist" model, one that challenges the "sexist expectations" that inhibit some violent men from learning and applying new skills for interacting with their partners (Adams, 1988).

NOTES

The author is grateful to the LaMarsh Research Programme on Violence and Conflict Resolution (York University), the Metro Action Committee on Public Violence Against Women and Children, the Ministry of Community and Social Services in cooperation with the Ontario Women's Directorate, and the Social Sciences and Humanities Research Council of Canada for funding this research. He also wishes to thank Desmond Ellis and Michael Hall for their critical comments on an earlier draft of this chapter.

1. Some theorists argue that patriarchal power in late capitalist society is located more in the social sphere, especially the state and its agents, than the familial sphere (e.g., Ursel, 1984. Be that as it may, most would probably agree with Kaufman (1987: 10) that "within itself, to a greater or lesser extent, the family reflects, reproduces, and recreates the hierarchical gender system of society as a whole." Household patriarchy surely should remain a central concern in the study of male violence against female intimates (see also Martin, 1977; Millett, 1969; Smith, 1983).

2. Some feminist scholars (e.g., Breines & Gordon, 1983; Dobash & Dobash, 1979) have contended that quantitative methods are inappropriate in feminist research on wife beating because such methods inevitably miss the complexities, ambiguities, and contradictions that characterize relations between husbands and wives. This point is well taken. On the other hand, the sometimes sweeping indictments of quantitative research made by feminist critics are unwarranted. As Yllo (1984) points out, feminist research on wife beating is not inherently linked to any particular methodology. Saunders' (1988) research is an example of how quantitative methods,

including the use of the CTS, can be integrated effectively with a feminist theoretical analysis.

3. Neither Coleman et al. (1980) nor LaViolette et al. (1984) found a significant difference between abusers' and nonabusers' scores on the Bem Sex-Role Inventory. Rosenbaum (1986) reported that abusive husbands were lower than nonabusive husbands on masculinity, as measured by Spence et al.'s Personal Attributes Questionnaire. Most researchers regard these inventories as measures of a personality trait rather than of attitudes or norms.

4. After reviewing some of the same studies, plus several unpublished ones, Hotaling and Sugarman (1986: 119) concluded that traditional sex-role "expectations" or "orientations" are a "consistent nonrisk marker" among male characteristics hypothesized to be associated with wife beating, possibly because nonviolent men hold "as patriarchal a set of beliefs" as violent men. But sex-role "expectations" and "orientations" are not the same (Note 3). If one deletes the sex-role "orientations" studies and adds Walker's (1983) and Saunders et al.'s (1987) studies, which Hotaling and Sugarman did not review, then the appropriate conclusion is that the results of this body of work are inconclusive.

5. In a test of the theory of "intrafamily" violence as an "ultimate resource," Allen and Straus (1980) found that husband dominance was associated with wife beating only among working-class husbands who lacked other resources (e.g., money, and occupational status) that would have legitimized their dominance.

6. Eight representative sample surveys designed to produce estimates of the extent of woman abuse in the general population have been carried out in North American (Schulman, 1979; Straus et al., 1980; Straus & Gelles, 1986; Smith, 1987; Brinkerhoff & Lupri, 1988; Smith, 1988; Kennedy & Dutton, 1989; Lupri, 1989). The present survey compares most directly to three other metropolitan-area surveys conducted in Canada: one in Calgary (Brinkerhoff & Lupri, 1988), one in Edmonton and Calgary (Kennedy & Dutton, 1989), and an earlier study in Toronto (Smith, 1988).

REFERENCES

Adams, D. (1988). "Treatment models of men who batter: A profeminist analysis." In K. Yllo and M. Bograd, eds., *Feminist Perspectives on Wife Abuse* (pp. 176–99). Newbury Park, CA: Sage.

Allen, C., and M.A. Straus. (1980). "Resources, power, and husband-wife violence." In M.A. Straus & G.T. Hotaling, eds., *The Social Causes of Husband-Wife Violence* (pp. 188–208). Minneapolis, MN: University of Minnesota Press.

Arias, I., and R.H. Beach. (1987). "Validity of self-reports of marital violence." *Journal of Family Violence*, 2, 139–42.

Barrett, M. (1980). *Women's Oppression Today: Problems in Marxist Feminist Analysis*. Thetford, Great Britain: Thetford Press.

Bates, C., T. Chi, and D. Northrup. (1987). *Woman Abuse Pilot Study: Phase Two: Sample and Field Report*. North York, Ontario: York University, Institute for Social Research.

Beechey, V. (1979). "On patriarchy." *Feminist Review*, 3, 66–82.

Blishen, B., and H.A. McRoberts. (1976). "A revised socioeconomic index for occupations in Canada." *Canadian Review of Sociology and Anthropology*, 13, 71–79.

Bograd, M. and K. Yllo, eds. (1988). *Feminist Perspectives on Wife Abuse*. Newbury Park, CA: Sage.

Bowker, L.H. (1983). *Beating Wife-Beating*. Lexington, MA: D.C. Heath.

———. (1985). "The effects of national development on the position of married women in the Third World: The case of wife-beating." *International Journal of Comparative and Applied Criminal Justice*, 9, 1–13.

Breines, W., and L. Gordon. (1983). "The new scholarship on family violence." *Signs: Journal of Women in Culture and Society*, 8, 491–531.

Brinkerhoff, M., and E. Lupri. (1988). "Interspousal violence." *Canadian Journal of Sociology*, 13, 407–434.

Burstyn, V. (1985). "Masculine dominance and the state." In V. Burstyn and D. Smith, eds., *Women, Class and the State* (pp. 45–83). Toronto: Garamond Press.

Coleman, D.H., and M.A. Straus. (1986). "Marital power, conflict, and violence in a nationally representative sample of American couples." *Violence and Victims*, 1, 141–57.

Coleman, K.H., M.L. Weinman, and B.P. Hsi. (1980). "Factors affecting conjugal violence." *Journal of Psychology*, 105, 197–202.

Dobash, R.E., and R. Dobash. (1979). Violence against Wives: A Case against the Patriarchy. New York: Free Press.

Dutton, D.G. (1988). *The Domestic Assault of Women: Psychological and Criminal Justice Perspectives*. Boston: Allyn and Bacon.

Edwards, A. (1987). "Male violence in feminist theory." In J. Hanmer and M. Maynard, eds., *Women, Violence, and Social Control* (13–29). Atlantic Highlands, NJ: Humanities Press International.

Eisenstein, Z. (1980). *Capitalist Patriarchy and the Case for Socialist Feminism*. New York: Monthly Review Press.

Farley, L. (1978). *Sexual Shakedown: The Sexual Harassment of Women on the Job*. New York: McGraw Hill.

Fazio, R.H., M.C. Powell, and P.M. Herr. (1983). "Toward a process model of attitude-behavior relations." *Journal of Personality and Social Psychology*, 44, 723–35.

Ferraro, K.J. (1988). "An existentialist approach to battering." In G.T. Hotaling, D. Finkelhor, J.T. Kirkpatrick, and M.A. Straus, eds., *Family Abuse and Its Consequences: New Directions in Research* (pp. 126–38). Newbury Park, CA: Sage.

Fox, J. (1984) *Linear Statistical Models and Related Methods*. New York: Wiley.

Greenblatt, C.S. (1985). "Don't hit your wife ... unless ...: Preliminary findings on normative support for the use of physical force by husbands." *Victimology: An International Journal*, 10, 221–41.

Harrell, F.E., Jr. (1986). *The LOGIST Procedure. In SUGI Supplemental Library Users' Guide*. Version 5 Edition (pp. 269–92). Cary, NC: SAS Institute Inc.

Hotaling, G.T., and D.B. Sugarman. (1986). "An analysis of risk markers in husband to wife violence: The current state of knowledge." *Violence and Victims*, 1, 101–24.

Kaufman, M. (1987). "The construction of masculinity and the triad of men's violence." In M. Kaufman, ed., *Beyond Patriarchy: Essays by Men on Pleasure, Power and Change* (pp. 1–29). Toronto: Oxford.

Kennedy, L.W., and D.G. Dutton. (1989). "The incidence of wife assault in Alberta." *Canadian Journal of Behavioural Science*, 21, 40–54.

Kurz, D. (1989). "Social science perspectives on wife abuse: current debates and future directions." *Gender and Society*, 3, 489–505.

LaViolette, A.D., O.W. Barnett, and C.L. Miller. (1984). *A Classification of Wife Abuse on the Bem Sex Role Inventory*. Paper presented at the Second National Conference on Research on Domestic Violence, Durham, NH.

Lupri, E. (1989). "Male violence in the home." *Canadian Social Trends*, 14, 19–21.

MacKinnon, C.A. (1983). "Feminism, Marxism, method, and the state: Toward feminist jurisprudence." *Signs: Journal of Women in Culture and Society*, 8, 635–58.

Martin, D. (1977). *Battered Wives*. New York: Pocket Books.

Millett, K. (1969). *Sexual Politics*. New York: Avon.

Neidig, P.H., D.H. Friedman, and B.S. Collins. (1986). "Attitudinal characteristics of males who have engaged in wife abuse." *Journal of Family Violence*, 1, 223–33.

Rosenbaum, A. (1986). "Of men, macho, and marital violence." *Journal of Family Violence*, 1, 121–29.

Rosenbaum, A. and K.D. O'Leary. (1981). "Marital violence: Characteristics of abusive couples." *Journal of Consulting and Clinical Psychology*, 49, 63–71.

Russell, D.E.H. (1982). *Rape in Marriage*. New York: Macmillan.

———. (1984). *Sexual Exploitation*. Beverly Hills: Sage.

Saunders, D.G., A.B. Lynch, M. Grayson, and D. Linz. (1987). "The inventory of beliefs about wife beating: The construction and initial validation of a measure of beliefs and attitudes." *Violence and Victims*, 2, 39–57.

Saunders, D.G. (1988). "Wife abuse, husband abuse, or mutual combat." In K. Yllo and M. Bograd, eds., *Feminist Perspectives on Wife Abuse* (pp. 90–103). Newbury Park, CA: Sage.

Schechter, S. (1982). *Women and Male Violence*. Boston: South End Press.

Schulman, M.A. (1979). *A Survey of Spousal Violence against Women in Kentucky* (Kentucky Commission on

Women, Study No. 792701). Washington, DC: U.S. Government Printing Office.

Schwendinger, J.R., and H. Schwendinger. (1983). *Rape and Inequality.* Beverly Hills: Sage.

Smith, D.E. (1983). "Women, the family, and the productive process." In J.P. Grayson, ed., *Introduction to Society: An Alternate Approach* (pp. 312–44). Toronto: Gage.

Smith, M.D. (1990). "Sociodemographic risk factors in wife abuse: Results from a survey of Toronto women." *Canadian Journal of Sociology*, 15, 39–58.

———. (1987). "The incidence and prevalence of woman abuse in Toronto." *Violence and Victims*, 2, 33–47.

———. (1988). "Women's fear of violent crime: An exploratory test of a feminist hypothesis." *Journal of Family Violence*, 3, 24–38.

———. (1989). "Woman abuse: The case for surveys by telephone." *Journal of Interpersonal Violence*, 4, 308–24.

———. (in press). "Effects of question format on the reporting of women abuse: A telephone survey experiment." *Victimology: An International Journal.*

Stets, J.E., and M.A. Straus. (1989). "The marriage license as a hitting license: A comparison of dating, cohabiting, and married couples." In M.A. Pirog-Good and J.E. Stets, eds., *Violence in Dating Relationships: Emerging Social Issues* (pp. 33–52). New York: Praeger.

Straus, M.A. (1979). "Measuring intrafamily conflict and violence: The conflict tactics (CT) scales." *Journal of Marriage and the Family*, 41, 75–88.

———. (1987). *Social Stratification, Social Bonds, and Wife-Beating in the United States.* Paper presented at the American Society of Criminology Meeting, Montreal.

———. (1988). "How violent are American families? Evidence from the national family violence resurvey and other studies." In G.T. Hotaling, D. Finkelhor, J.T. Kirkpatrick, and M.A. Straus, eds., *Family Abuse and Its Consequences: New Directions in Research* (pp. 14–36). Newbury Park, CA: Sage.

———. (1990). "The conflict tactics scales and its critics: An evaluation and new data on validity and reliability." In M.A. Straus and R.J. Gelles, eds., *Physical Violence in American Families: Risk Factors and Adaptations to Violence in 8,145 Families* (pp. 49–73). New Brunswick, NJ: Transaction.

Straus, M.A., and R.J. Gelles. (1986). "Societal change and change in family violence rates from 1975 to 1985 as revealed by two national surveys." *Journal of Marriage and the Family*, 48, 465–79.

Straus, M.A., R.J. Gelles, and S.F. Steinmetz. (1980). *Behind Closed Doors: Violence in the American Family.* New York: Anchor.

Telch, C.F., and C.U. Lindquist. (1984). "Violent versus non-violent couples: A comparison of patterns." *Psychotherapy*, 21, 242–48.

Tremblay, V. (1981). "Study of telephone sampling techniques." *New Surveys*, 6, 813.

Ursel, E.J. (1986). "The state and the maintenance of patriarchy: A case study of family, labour and welfare legislation in Canada." In J. Dickinson and B. Russell, eds., *Family, Economy and State* (pp. 150–91). Toronto: Garamond.

———. (1984). "Toward a theory of reproduction." *Contemporary Crises*, 8, 265–92.

Walker, L.E. (1983). "The battered woman syndrome study." In D. Finkelhor, R.J. Gelles, G.T. Hotaling, and M.S. Straus, eds., *The Dark Side of Families: Current Family Violence Research* (pp. 31–48). Beverly Hills: Sage.

Yllo, K. (1983a). "Sexual equality and violence against wives in American states." *Journal of Comparative Family Studies*, 14, 67–86.

———. (1983b). "Using a feminist approach in quantitative research: A case study." In D. Finkelhor, R.J. Gelles, G.T. Hotaling, and M.A. Straus, eds., *The Dark Side of Families: Current Family Violence Research* (pp. 277–88). Beverly Hills: Sage.

———. (1984). "The status of women, marital equality, and violence against wives." *Journal of Family Issues*, 5, 307–20.

Yllo, K., and M.A. Straus. (1984). "Patriarchy and violence against wives: The impact of structural and normative factors." *Journal of International and Comparative Social Welfare*, 1, 1–13.

Chapter 18

SOCIOLOGICAL RESEARCH AND FAMILY LAW

C. JAMES RICHARDSON

This chapter first of all draws upon the experience of a decade or more of direct and indirect involvement with research on family law in Canada. For the most part, my role has not been to identify the issues and problems and most certainly not to draft legislation or develop procedural changes. Rather, my task as a sociologist and evaluator has been to observe and to evaluate. I have been asked to develop and conduct research that in the parlance of evaluation has been structured around issues of process, outcome and social impact of legislative and program innovations. In short, is the program or legislative reform performing well, is it reaching its intended objectives and are there unintended or unanticipated consequences?

Second, as a recent contributor to a federal Task Force attempting to predict what are likely to be the family law issues during the 1990s, I was forced to think about the role and impact of family law research over this past decade. This was a period in which, on the one hand, there were substantive and procedural changes in family law and, on the other, new concerns and new issues as various groups — established and emerging — made known their concerns and responded to the demographic changes in marriage, family and divorce.

FAMILY IDEOLOGIES AND FAMILY LAW REFORM

Much of the research undertaken by the Department of Justice in the past decade has, understandably, focused on various aspects of the divorce process in Canada. As I will be describing, the issues seen as pressing at the beginning of the 1980s, particularly with respect to divorce, were ones of process and were largely shaped by liberal and sometimes Utopian views of the family that had their roots in the 1960s and early 1970s. While these issues did not entirely disappear, feminist-based research has had the major impact of directing attention to the outcomes of the divorce process and to the unanticipated and possibly negative consequences of the innovations and changes that it was hoped would make the divorce regime more humane and less adversarial.

Complicating matters is that the 1980s was also a decade in which various fundamentalist groups and movements sought to protect and preserve the sanctity of their version of the family, one clearly at odds with both the liberal views of the 1960s and 1970s and all the versions of feminism. And there were newly formed fathers' rights groups also calling for their version of family law reform. It has, in other words, been a decade of intense debate about family and marriage and the role of law and policy with respect to these institutions (Berger and Berger, 1983). The roots of the debate, of course, go back much further.

As Roderic Beaujot (1988) has recently described, it is in the mid-1960s that we begin to see the kinds of social and cultural changes that gave the decade its particular historical significance. With respect to the family, it was in the years after 1965 that demographers began to observe dramatic structural changes, and sociologists, in turn, began to reformulate their

Source: "Family Law Research in a Decade of Change," in Alexander Himelfarb and C. James Richardson, eds., *Sociology for Canadians: A Reader*, 2nd ed. (Toronto: McGraw-Hill Ryerson, 1992), pp. 253–63. Reprinted by permission of the author.

research questions in light of the ideological changes that accompanied these changes. It was in the mid-1960s that fertility began quite abruptly to decline, that age at marriage began, for the first time in this century to increase, that divorce rather than death of a spouse began to be the major cause of marital dissolution and that the proportion of Canadians ever married began a downward trend. And in the wake of these changes is an aging Canadian population.

Many viewed these demographic changes as a shift in or an erosion of family values. A better sociological explanation is that these behavioral changes were people's (mainly women's) responses to the increasing availability of contraceptive technology, married women's increasing participation in the labour force as we moved into a service economy based on a low-paid and often part-time labour force and the general inability of capitalism to provide a family wage, particularly as expectations rose in the 1960s.

But, of course, the independent role of ideas in shaping and changing society cannot be discounted. Probably, there is a reciprocal relationship between culture and social structure. The cultural transformation that we now associate with the 1960s — the growth of women's liberation and later feminism, a more pervasive sense of individualism (the so-called "me generation") and, more generally, what might best be described as the "de-institutionalization" of the family, were, on the one hand, products of the structural changes but, on the other, producers of these changing social structures. The counter-culture both accelerated and legitimated changes in the individual decisions about nuptiality and fertility, which, when aggregated, become the demographer's statistical data.

By the early 1970s family and marriage — institutions which to the generation before had seemed inviolate, sacred and often "God-given" — were diagnosed as in a state of crisis, as outmoded, as irrelevant and in need of "decent burials." The literature of the time called for "revitalizing," "restructuring," "reconstituting" or "renovating" the very institutions idealized and revered just a decade before.

Monogamous marriage was now seen as out of step with the realities of the sexual revolution and the desire for "self-actualization." The nuclear family was under attack because of the constraints it imposes, the madness it generates and its generally oppressive and patriarchal nature. The catchwords were "swinging," "group marriage," "open marriage," "creative divorce"; and those most committed to the 1960s ideology argued for creation of communal family structures as an alternative to the crisis-ridden nuclear family.

At a less polemical level was the "discovery" that the traditional nuclear family, for a time idealized as the most appropriate family structure, is more stereotype than statistical reality. It is questionable whether even in the 1950s this family form had been the statistical norm, though it most certainly had been the cultural ideal. By the 1970s it was arguably not the prevalent family structure but, rather, one among a number of family forms in contemporary society and may, in fact, have become the minority. It was consistent with the general climate of cultural relativism to argue that family policy should treat all existing familial groups — particularly single parent families — as viable alternatives rather than deviations from the norm or, in any way, problem families.

Given this generally bleak depiction of the nuclear family and family relations, it is hardly surprising that by the 1970s divorce was no longer viewed as a singular and disastrous event but as an integral and normative part of marriage and family life and as often being a creative and liberating solution rather than a problem (Ambert, 1980). As well, emerging concepts such as the "bi-nuclear family," the "blended family" and the "remarriage family" were clearly efforts to capture the notion of a wider and broader definition of family. As was frequently pointed out, where there are children, divorce does not end familial relationships, it changes and complicates them.

From the point of view of the 1990s, the family ideology of the counter-culture strikes most as naive and, in the era of AIDS, its emphasis on sexual liberation, dangerous. Moreover, as was soon to be recognized, the proposed alternatives to conventional family life failed to recognize either biological and psychological constraints or those specifically related to structured social inequality, and are unable to transcend middle-class and sometimes sexist assumptions and biases. Thus the free school movement did not address the needs of disadvantaged groups for whom credentialism is functional for individual upward mobility. Communes, perhaps because they developed in the context of the drug subculture, were generally ill-equipped to deal with the day-to-day realities of child care and socialization, and were seldom premised on sexual equality and an equal division of labour. More open and permissive sexual arrangements seemed primarily to benefit men (Ambert, 1976). Moreover, some family forms, such as the female-headed family, much celebrated in the literature of the time, usually emerge not out of choice but from poverty and the inability of men to find regular and reasonably paid work and are abandoned when economic conditions permit.

Nevertheless, our ways of thinking about marriage, family and divorce were irrevocably changed and, as I have argued elsewhere, criticisms of family law and the resulting proposals for a new philosophy and set of objectives in this area were firmly rooted in and influenced by the family ideology and the new rhetoric of the 1960s and early 1970s (Richardson, 1983). From the point of view of the Department of Justice and, in turn, the newly formed Law Reform Commission, the central and most obvious issue in family law was divorce.

DIVORCE AND FAMILY LAW RESEARCH

That divorce was central to family law is hardly surprising. Canada's first uniform divorce legislation had come into force in 1968, literally in the midst of the counter-culture. The rate of divorce, of course, jumped dramatically; but to the surprise of most continued to climb upward over the 1970s and most of the 1980s. It was generally perceived as having reached epidemic proportions and as a pressing social issue in Canadian society. Augmenting this was the general agreement that the 1968 legislation was a compromise which was not forward looking and which did not reflect the changing realities and conceptions of family life either before or after marital dissolution. Finally, divorce is the one area of family law that quite unambiguously falls under federal jurisdiction and where initiatives could be undertaken.

During the early part of the 1980s, family law research and program initiatives were mainly concerned with addressing the criticisms of the Divorce Act, 1968. The issues were mainly ones of process and centred around the philosophical, legal and administrative shortcomings of the divorce regime as it had developed during the 1970s. These shortcomings had been identified and discussed in a number of working papers commissioned by the Law Reform Commission. These criticisms centred on the inappropriateness of the adversary approach in family law, the irrelevance, generally, of fault grounds, the futility and hardship of long waiting periods to demonstrate marriage breakdown and administrative and structural problems, notably, fragmented jurisdictions and lack of support services such as divorce mediation and enforcement services.

The Law Reform Commission advocated the reform of the divorce legislation and the establishment of unified family courts across Canada. While new divorce legislation was to lie somewhere in the future,

the Department of Justice did, in the late 1970s, decide to test empirically the unified family court conceptual model. Following negotiations with four provinces, demonstration projects were established in St. John's, Fredericton, Hamilton-Wentworth and Saskatoon between 1977 and 1979. All were three-year projects funded jointly by the federal government and the participating provinces; and all were, through separate but collaborative evaluations, designed to generate data to determine whether the model proposed could be implemented more generally.

While the evaluations are generally positive about the unified family court model, and the initial courts are still in operation, it is only in New Brunswick that the concept has been extended province-wide. Still, this particular initiative is a good example of a rational problem-solving model: a set of issues were identified, alternative solutions were proposed, a model was developed, implemented (on an experimental basis), evaluated and the results fed back to those working in these and similar family courts.

As was described in the synthesis report, the evaluations had generally shown the superiority of unified family courts over the existing court system. However, it was also noted that, for both technical and financial reasons, it had not been possible for researchers to do much in the way of outcome evaluation. It had not, for example, been possible to show the long-term impact of the social arm (the conciliation counselling and later divorce mediation service) in reducing the adversary process and in bringing about more amicable and responsible settlements, which would better protect the interests of the children of the marriage and maintain maximum access to both parents.

In the 1983 synthesis report, it was recommended that there was need for further knowledge-building and evaluation research on "conciliation counselling" as it was then called. In 1984, and probably quite independent of this recommendation, the then Minister of Justice announced a sizeable budget, both to encourage and promote divorce mediation (as it was now called) and to undertake research on this intervention. This was announced in conjunction with proposals for divorce reform. While that particular set of proposals died on the order paper, funds for research on divorce mediation remained intact.

The main research initiative consisted of two longitudinal research projects on court-based divorce mediation in Canada. The first project, entitled the *Divorce and Family Mediation Study* (Richardson, 1988; 1989a) examined divorce mediation in St. John's, Montreal and Saskatoon; the second project focused on the Winnipeg court where there was mandatory divorce mediation in contested custody cases (Sloan and Greenaway, 1988).

The two research projects each took as their starting point to test the belief that children in divorce will suffer less if conflict is contained and contact with both parents remains ongoing (Wallerstein and Kelly, 1980; Richardson, 1987). More specifically, the research was an empirical testing of the claim of divorce mediation proponents that the objectives of reducing conflict and maximizing post-divorce parenting are better accomplished through this approach to dispute resolution than through a purely legal process. The research also examined whether, as claimed, settlements reached through divorce mediation are more long lasting and therefore less costly because they involve fewer returns to court for variation or enforcement of support and custody orders. An underlying assumption was that joint legal custody, or, as many prefer, shared parenting, is generally the preferred option and one indicator of a "successful" divorce. Divorce mediation was "the way to go" because, in contrast to the traditional adversary process, it offered promise that these and other goals could be more effectively and more cheaply achieved.

As I have tried to make clear, the major policy and research initiatives of the 1980s were, in their embryo stage, shaped by and driven by the family ideologies of the early 1970s and, to a large extent, were products of the work and research undertaken by the Law Reform Commission of Canada. However, in the early 1980s it was, quite clearly, groups concerned with the status of women in Canadian society who set most of the agenda with respect to the debate about the family and family law; it was their concerns that became quite central to the divorce mediation research and, more generally, virtually all of the federally funded research on family law.

The issues that emerged were two-fold. The first centred on the implications of assumptions in the new family law about sexual equality and gender neutrality (Weitzman, 1985). The result was a much greater emphasis on the unequal outcomes of separation and divorce for women compared with men, particularly where the former have custody of the children and find themselves now living in poverty.

The second, and related, concern has been about the unintended consequences of informal justice or alternative dispute resolution approaches, particularly divorce mediation. There is distrust among feminist scholars that these alternatives, introduced so enthusiastically by earlier critics of the divorce process, may,

because of power imbalances between spouses and larger patterns of sexual inequality, be detrimental to women's interests and contribute to the feminization of poverty following separation and divorce (Bottomley, 1985; Bailey, 1990). Thus, the research also sought to investigate the criticisms of these feminist scholars: that there were negative consequences for women who eschewed a strong lawyer in favour of a mediated settlement of custody, access and financial matters.

These and other criticisms and concerns about the detrimental effects of family law on women were sufficiently focused and so forcibly and persistently articulated as to have had a major impact on the drafting of the provisions of the proposed reform of Canada's divorce legislation in the mid-1980s. To a considerable extent, these overwhelmed the earlier concerns about family law and its administration, which had led to experiments with unified family courts and research on divorce mediation. In short, by the time the legislation had reached the discussion and consultation stage, new issues had emerged and had become more focused in the political agenda of various interest groups.

Indeed, by the time Bill C-47 (the Divorce Act, 1985) reached the Committee stage, many women's groups, religious groups of long-standing existence, and newly formed fathers' rights groups were anxious to make their concerns known and to press for amendments to the proposed legislation. The criticism by religious and fundamentalist groups, what Margrit Eichler (1988) refers to as the "patriarchal family movement," was diffuse. It was ultimately aimed at making divorce more difficult to obtain on the premise that more liberal divorce laws threaten the sanctity of the family. The concern of fathers' rights groups was focused mainly on the inclusion of a presumption of joint legal custody, though this was not very clearly defined.

Women's groups were also focused in their concerns. Much of their effort went to opposing a presumption of joint legal custody, which they felt should be an arrangement entered into voluntarily and never imposed as a means of reaching a settlement. They also wished to broaden the grounds for variation of spousal support orders to soften the economic impact of divorce on older women who had not been in the labour force. Here the concern was that the objective of promoting self-sufficiency, if interpreted too narrowly or taken too literally, would, for such women, simply increase their poverty following divorce. This was opposed by various lawyers' groups who wanted legislation that would allow for finality and greater certainty in advice given to their clients. As well, the recently formed association of Family Mediation Canada wished there to be a provision requiring a mandatory visit to divorce mediation where child custody is being contested. Finally, there were some who urged that the language of "custody" and "access" be abandoned in favour of terms such as "primary caregiver" and "secondary caregiver."

In sum, by the time the new divorce legislation was ready for passage, four major issues had emerged: a presumption of joint custody; mandatory mediation; factors and objectives of spousal support, especially potential abuse of the objective of self-sufficiency; and variations of support orders. The result was that some of the clarity of the objectives set out in the earlier Law Reform Commission recommendations had become muddied by the need to respond to the competing and conflicting demands and interests of feminists, fathers' rights groups and various fundamentalist religious groups.

As in 1968, the legislation was again an attempt by the government to find compromises that would meet these sometimes conflicting demands. An evaluation component was built in and funded prior to the legislation ever going before Parliament. It was therefore possible to join the first phase of the evaluation of the divorce legislation to one of the divorce mediation research projects and collect baseline information in at least a sample of Canadian research sites before the legislation came into force (Richardson, 1987). And the second phase of the evaluation was able to replicate the research design of Phase I about three years later (Richardson, 1990).

THE IMPACT AND POLITICS OF APPLIED RESEARCH

There is inevitably a lag between identification of a problem and a response in the form of law reform. This is partly due to the length of time required to formulate, undertake and disseminate policy-oriented social research and, on the basis of the findings and conclusions, to draft the necessary legislation. However, the larger problem is that politicians are often reluctant to act until there is perceived to be consensus that the legislative reform is overdue and that there is, on balance, political gain from supporting the proposed initiative or legal reform.

New legislation is almost never the independent variable bringing about certain kinds of changes. Rather, new legislation is itself part of the changing objective and subjective realities and is to a large extent a dependent variable. The most obvious example is the

sexual assault legislation, which is generally perceived as having simply brought the Criminal Code of Canada in line with prevailing attitudes, practices and philosophies with respect to how victims of sexual crimes should be treated. Similarly, the provisions in the new divorce legislation do not so much cause change as reflect the already existing shift in attitudes and practices, many of which had already been incorporated into provincial legislation.

In the period between the Law Reform Commission's studies, the federal initiatives and our research, many changes had occurred in family law. All provinces and territories had, by then, enacted legislation concerning division of matrimonial property, child custody and child and spousal support essentially modelled on the seminal Ontario legislation. It is apparent, too, that through less formal means many of the problems identified by the Law Reform Commission were being addressed. In terms of attitudes and practices, family law in the 1980s was no longer the same as the Law Reform Commission had depicted it in the 1970s. For example, alternatives to the adversarial approach, such as divorce mediation, which was seen as novel and controversial in the 1970s, had become institutionalized in at least some parts of Canada by the mid-1980s. And, while there no doubt remained some extremely litigious lawyers in the area of family law, we found that many were coming to believe that when custody and access are at issue, a better settlement results from negotiation rather than from litigation. Moreover, there now seemed to be few family court judges who believed that, in the matter of custody, the adversarial approach will "reveal the truth" of who is the better parent. Many were coming to rely much more — sometimes invariably — on custody assessments or investigations, or they were referring the disputing spouses to mediation (Richardson, 1988).

It is not surprising, then, that neither of the major research projects by the Department of Justice was able to show major differences either between mediated and adversarial settlements or between the period just before and three years after the new divorce legislation. What differences there were between mediated and nonmediated settlements tended to be subtle rather than dramatic and similar to what had been found elsewhere. The reports were, therefore, in general agreement with Kenneth Kressel (1985: 26–27), who, after a careful review and analysis of the American research, concluded that "mediation is a vehicle of social influence which is not inherently superior to any other method of conflict resolution. Like the others, it has its own decided liabilities as well as assets."

It seems that both proponents and opponents of divorce mediation might have overstated their cases. The former dichotomized a world that is not dichotomous. As Sloan and Greenaway (1988: 7), authors of the Winnipeg study on divorce mediation, put it:

> *Researchers falsely conceive of mediation as branching from a "fork in the road." One branch is the "traditional adversarial approach," the other is mediation. One is the side of reason and compromise; the other the side of irrational power plays. This view masks the complexity of dispute resolution and the extent to which modes of resolution are mixed together; it also underestimates the rationality of the court process as well as the irrational aspects of mediation.*

This is further evidenced by the data from the evaluation of the Divorce Act, 1985, which suggests that even with the encouragement built into the legislation for people to mediate their disputes, the demand curve for this intervention — whatever the service delivery model — is quite flat: approximately three percent of divorcing couples use this approach. This figure has not changed in the past five years and is also remarkably similar to what has been reported in the United States, where there has been much greater emphasis on alternative dispute resolution than in Canada (Kressel, 1985). In short, the rhetoric of the early 1980s suggested that divorce mediation was a new but burgeoning field which promised a radically new and growing approach to resolving family law matters. For the divorce mediation community, the reality has been disappointing. But, on the other hand, the feminist case against divorce mediation was not supported empirically. Rather, it was found that even after controlling for level of family income, women generally fared better economically in mediation than through a purely legal process (Richardson, 1988).

Similarly, while there were not great differences found between the divorce processes prior to and following the evaluation of the Divorce Act, 1985, there is evidence that the new provisions had been successful in meeting many of the objectives sought from this legislative reform. This is especially so with respect to the first of the stated objectives, that of reducing the adversarial nature of the divorce process. While it is apparent that many of the changes to a less adversarial approach to marriage breakdown had occurred previous to the legislation, philosophical and procedural changes in the present legislation have served to actualize and, perhaps, hasten these trends (Richardson, 1990).

Concerns expressed about the erosion of women's rights to custody of their children and the contrasting concerns of men who feel denied equality with respect to sole custody or to access to their children were generally not borne out by the data from either the divorce mediation research or the evaluation of the divorce legislation. While there are undoubtedly men who have been denied access to their children, they were not evident in the four-city sample of divorcing families at either of the time periods. Nor does it appear that men are now more likely to be awarded sole custody than they were in the past. Nor, finally, is it evident that the spousal support objectives contained in the new legislation have had the unintended consequence of worsening the situation of women, particularly those coming out of long-term marriages.

At the same time, the evaluation shows quite clearly that the legislation had no measurable impact on reducing the unequal economic consequences for women and children of divorce; and it remains the case that whereas only about 10 percent of divorced men have incomes below the poverty line after paying support, upwards of 60 percent of women with custody of the children have, including the support payments, incomes below the poverty lines for various family sizes. These findings did not take into account that women may have remarried and that men, far from living in one-person households, were quite likely to be remarried or repartnered and to have new dependent children. Nor, to turn it around, did this analysis consider the implications of noncompliance with support orders, that a sizeable proportion of men do not make their support payments or do not do so regularly and predictably.

At the conclusion of the research, the reports on the research findings about divorce mediation and the impact of new divorce legislation were quite widely distributed: there were oral presentations to a number of different audiences and a number of enquiries from journalists. Yet, in the aftermath of the research, it was apparent from questions raised at presentations and subsequent publications that for feminists, for fathers' rights groups and for many members of the divorce mediation community in Canada, the research findings had rather limited impact on prevailing views and wisdoms about divorce mediation particularly or the divorce process more generally. The following contentions or beliefs are illustrative rather than exhaustive.

1. *Custody of the children is one of the more contentious matters in divorce.*

    While contested custody disputes are certainly bitter and emotionally draining on judges, the available research suggests that in the four to five percent of contested divorces, custody is less often at issue than financial matters such as division of property and spousal and child support. And, most Canadian judges faced with a custody dispute will order a custody assessment.

2. *Men generally want more access to the children of the marriage than is granted by the courts or allowed by mothers with sole custody.*

Evidence from the DFMS and Phase II of the evaluation of the Divorce Act, 1985 suggests that the major problem is that men do not live up to the agreed upon access arrangements or do so irregularly and unpredictably. This is further borne out in the follow-up study of DFMS clients. Denial of access by the courts or later by the custodial parent is extremely rare.

3. *There is increasing pressure for joint legal custody from the courts, from mediators and from fathers.*

While the proportion of joint legal custody awards has moved upwards from about nine to 13 percent of all awards since the Divorce Act, 1985 came into force, it is evident that most divorcing individuals do not want or seriously consider this option. For those who do opt for joint legal custody, it is generally the first choice and one which most (men somewhat more than women) would choose again. There is a high degree of satisfaction with these arrangements (Irving et al., 1984; Morris, 1988; Richardson, 1988). There is no evidence, then, that joint custody is being imposed on couples who cannot agree about sole custody.

4. *Gender neutrality approaches in family law have led to Courts being more willing to grant sole custody to fathers than in the past; as a result, women may be forced to barter away their support rights in order to keep their children.*

While analyses of reported case law provides some support for the first part of this assertion (Boyd, 1987), the latter assertion seems to be purely speculative, unsupported even by anecdotal evidence. Statistically the likelihood of men receiving sole custody has not changed in nearly two decades (10 to 11 percent of all cases). When men request sole custody it is granted in about 40 percent of cases, generally when the wife, for a variety of reasons, does not want sole custody. Under these circumstances, joint legal custody and split legal custody are also more common (about 20 percent). It remains the case that when women specifically request sole custody, men are virtually excluded from the likelihood of receiving custody since in 97 percent of such cases custody is awarded to the mother.

5. *The traditional adversary system is still the prevalent mode of settlement of divorce cases and continues to be destructive to divorcing couples and their children.*

This view can still be found in various articles and presentations by proponents of divorce mediation. While it is true that few divorcing people use approaches such as divorce mediation, most are able to work out a settlement on their own or with the assistance of their lawyers, who may sometimes negotiate a settlement. As noted earlier, there is considerable reason to believe that even if earlier depictions of the adversary system were fundamentally correct, the evidence from the divorce mediation and divorce evaluation research indicates that there has been an important shift in both attitudes and practices particularly with respect to custody and access disputes to more humane, socially conscious and less litigious approaches.

6. *There are in most divorces sufficient resources so that more equitable settlements coupled with tougher and more efficient enforcement procedures could substantially reduce economic hardship of women and children following separation and divorce.*

There is considerable research which provides empirical support for this assertion; on *average*, most divorced men could afford to pay more in support than is now generally the case without themselves also ending up with incomes below the poverty line. However, most of the cases cited in policy discussions are based on contested cases where there is an atypically high level of affluence which is not the general picture for the divorcing population particularly in the more impoverished regions of Canada. Moreover, such analyses do not take into account the high rate of remarriage and that many men will have obligations to a second family. It is clearly a policy and value question as to which set of children should be left impoverished.

It is inevitable and hardly surprising that the same objective statistics and research findings will be viewed quite differently by different groups, often with clashing interests and perspectives. Thus, some will see a glass half empty while others see a glass half full. But as I thought over the general reception to the conclusions to the research, it seemed to me that there was another level or dimension to the problem: there is, today, a growing disjuncture in modes of inquiry, discourse and what is considered fact; in other words, groups concerned with improving family law seem to be talking past one another.

At present, the dominant paradigm in most of the social sciences is quite clearly feminism. The long struggle to incorporate feminist perspectives into the social sciences and humanities, the law and social policy has been largely successful. This change has meant more than simply "bringing women in" or reformulating the language. Feminism also challenges the traditional methodologies of the social sciences: quantitative methods; various forms of survey research; use of census data; commitment to the metaphor of the classical experimental design; hypothesis testing, and the like.

Such approaches are rejected by many feminist scholars and replaced by more qualitative approaches, which draw upon women's "lived" experiences and definitions of situation or, in the case of legal scholars, close analysis of reported family law cases. Such cases are viewed as important because they create precedence, which, in turn, guides family law practitioners in advising clients as to the likely outcome were they to contest the matter (cf.: Mnookin and Kornhauser, 1979). And perceptions about trends and problems in various aspects of family law are strongly influenced by this kind of research. It is these approaches that inform many publications in the family law journals and presentations at conferences on women and the law and which are likely to capture the attention of the media and the popular press (e.g.: Crean, 1990).

The difficulty is that reported cases make up a very tiny minority of divorce cases or even of contested cases and are, by definition, the unusual ones. They are unusual in the degree and nature of conflict but probably also in the level of affluence of the disputants. Thus, as Mossman (1986) has observed, there is a middle-class bias in much of the thinking about family law. Certainly what is learned from a random sample of the divorcing population or from analysis of data from the Central Divorce Registry provides a quite different picture of divorce from the one derived from these other methodologies. Such research does not reveal many cases of interest to legal scholars, and it does not interest the media or the popular press. Issues related to dual-career families, business assets, marital property and joint custody seem far removed from the reality of most divorcing people, many of whom have uncertain and poorly paying jobs rather than careers, little in the way of property to divide and custody is not at issue.

There remains, then, a considerable gap between what research has been able to show empirically through sample survey research and Census data on divorce generated from the Central Divorce Registry forms and the prevailing concerns and wisdom about divorce and its outcomes among those writing about family and who draw upon other kinds of sources and methodologies.

It is easy enough to draw up a list of probable family law issues: the persisting economic consequences and inequalities between men and women following divorce; the meaning and practical application of the "best interests of the child" principle; the possible unintended consequences of various modes of informal justice; the issue of marital and family status and what, under law should be defined as a family from the point of view of state benefits and individual rights and obligations; the social and legal implications of the reproductive technologies; and the ongoing problem of family violence. It is much harder to suggest how these can be transformed into family law *research* issues which will have traditional credibility and, at the same time, incorporate the methodological approaches emerging out of feminist scholarship and research, and thereby have credibility among those directly concerned with influencing social policy.

An important contribution of the research funded by the Department of Justice in the 1980s has been the development of knowledge-building about the divorce process and divorce outcomes. At the same time, it will certainly be necessary to develop research designs that incorporate the methodologies emerging out of the feminist perspective. However, these will be no substitute for continuing collection and analysis of basic statistics on divorce, which can be derived from the Central Divorce Registry Data. In the 1980s these were augmented by more detailed studies of the Canadian divorce process in selected jurisdictions. Without necessarily focusing on a specific issue such as divorce mediation, efforts should be made to conduct further detailed studies on the divorce process and the post-divorce situation of families in other, and perhaps more representative, jurisdictions in Canada. It is, for example, quite possible that there is a lag between patterns and trends found in reported contested custody cases and what is occurring in the larger population of uncontested divorce cases. Continuing collection and analysis of national statistics and survey research informed by feminist perspectives has the potential to augment rather than compete with the methodological approaches likely to be more prominent in the 1990s.

REFERENCES

Ambert, Anne-Marie. 1976. "Swinging: A Study of Decision Making in Marriage." In *The Canadian Family in Comparative Perspective*, Lyle Larson, ed. Toronto: Prentice-Hall Canada.

————. 1980. *Divorce in Canada*. Toronto: Academic Press.

Bailey, Martha. 1990. "Unpacking the 'Rational Alternative': A Critical Review of Family Mediation Movement Claims." *Canadian Journal of Family Law* 8: 61–94.

Beaujot, Roderic. 1988. "The Family in Crisis?" *Canadian Journal of Sociology* 13(3).

Berger, Brigitte, and Peter Berger. 1983. *The War Over the Family: The Search for a Middle Ground*. New York: Basic Books.

Bottomley, Ann. 1985. "What is Happening to Family Law? A Feminist Critique of Conciliation." In *Women in Law*, Julia Brophy and Carol Smart, eds. London: Routledge and Kegan Paul.

Boyd, Susan. 1987. "Child Custody and Working Mothers." In *Equality and Judicial Neutrality*, S. Mahoney and K.E. Mahoney, eds. Toronto: Carswell.

Crean, Susan. 1988. *In the Name of the Fathers: The Story Behind Child Custody*, Toronto: Amanita Enterprises.

Eichler, Margrit. 1988. *Families in Canada*. Toronto: Gage.

Irving, Howard, et al. 1984. "Sharing Parenting: An Empirical Study Using a Large Data Base." *Family Process* 23: 561–69.

Kressel, Kenneth. 1985. *The Process of Divorce*. New York: Basic Books.

Mnookin, R., and L. Kornhauser. 1979. "Bargaining in the Shadow of the Law." *Yale Law Journal*.

Morris, Celise. 1988. "The Politics and Experience of Co-Parenting: An Exploratory Study of Shared Custody in Canada." *The Criaw Papers* No. 20.

Mossman, Mary Jane. 1986. "Family Law and Social Welfare in Canada." In *Family Law and Social Welfare Legislation in Canada*, I. Bernier and A. Lajole, eds. Toronto: University of Toronto Press.

Richardson, C. James. 1983. *Attempting to Restructure Family Law: Unified Family Court Experiments in Canada*. Ottawa: Department of Justice, Canada.

————. 1986. *Evaluation of the Divorce Act, 1985: Baseline Study*. Ottawa: Department of Justice, Canada.

————. 1987. "Children of Divorce." In *Family Matters*, K. Anderson et al. Toronto: Methuen.

————. 1988. *Divorce and Family Mediation Research Study in Three Canadian Cities*. Ottawa: Department of Justice, Canada.

————. 1989a. *Court-Based Divorce Mediation in Four Canadian Cities: An Overview of Research Findings*. Ottawa: Ministry of Supply and Services.

————. 1989b. *Research Initiatives in the Area of Divorce Mediation*. Ottawa: Department of Justice, Canada.

————. 1990. *Evaluation of the Divorce Act, 1985: Implementation and Monitoring* Ottawa: Department of Justice, Canada.

Sloan, R., and W. Greenaway. 1988. *Divorce and Family Mediation Study: Winnipeg*. Ottawa: Department of Justice.

Wallerstein, Judith, and Joan Kelly. 1980. *Surviving the Breakup*. New York: Basic Books.

Weitzman, Lenore. 1985. *The Divorce Revolution: The Unexpected Consequences for Women and Children in America*. New York: The Free Press.

Chapter 19

NEOCONSERVATISM AND THE CANADIAN PRO-FAMILY MOVEMENT

LORNA ERWIN

Unlike their American counterparts, Canada's anti-feminist forces — the pro-family movement — were not initially hostile to the welfare state. In the early and mid-'80s when REAL (an acronym standing for Realistic Equal Active for Life) Women and a handful of kindred organizations[1] arose to denounce feminist influences on the schools, the courts, the media, and even the governments of the day, there was little attempt in the pro-family defense of the traditional housewife to tie feminists to the alleged excesses of "runaway" social spending or "confiscatory" taxation. While in the United States, the very emergence of a "New Right" during the Carter and Reagan presidencies was predicated on the fusion of a cultural politics of family, sexuality, and reproduction with a backlash against welfare and government spending,[2] the leaders and publications of Canadian anti-feminism paid little attention to state programs per se. And even when they opposed new initiatives, as they consistently have in the case of a national daycare program, they eschewed neoconservative rhetoric.

For such leaders, no less than for our former prime minister, social programs remained a "sacred trust." There was no New Right during the 1980s to bolster the neoconservative agenda of the Mulroney government, which meant that what the government managed to achieve in cutting back income-maintenance and social-assistance programs, and in other deregulatory and redistributory measures, had to be achieved

mainly by stealth. Nevertheless, since 1987 a notable shift towards neoconservative discourse has occurred in pro-family ideology. Where once it was sexual liberation and women's employment outside the home that were at the centre of movement discourse, now it is the intrusive, feminist-driven state with its confiscatory levels of taxation.

With frequent acknowledgments to the Hoover Institution and the Fraser Institute, pro-family leaders now present the family as a self-sufficient unit needing little help from governments. Social welfare "giveaways" only demoralize the family while fiscally conservative policies strengthen it. That such a shift in rhetoric comes at a time of rapid changes of leadership and a kind of stasis in movement affairs raises inevitable questions about the movement's likely impact on Canada's political life. Are we now, finally, to see a full-blown religious right in English-speaking Canada, just as this phenomenon has suffered a major defeat in the U.S. presidential election? This question is all the more compelling in light of recent reports of the Reform Party's success in appealing to evangelical Protestants (cf. *The Globe and Mail*, December 30, 1992: 1).

This chapter explores the likelihood of the pro-family leadership succeeding in this endeavour. To this end, the origins and the ideological development of the movement are discussed and empirical data on the socio-demographic background and the political beliefs

Source: "Neoconservatism and the Canadian Pro-Family Movement," *Canadian Review of Sociology and Anthropology* 30, 3 (1993): 401–20. Reprinted by permission of the publisher.

of the membership are presented. In light of these data, the movement's potential to generate a consensus among its membership in support of a broad attack on social services and welfare spending is explored.

SOCIAL MOVEMENTS AND CONSENSUS MOBILIZATION

Linked to the question of national impact is a prior question of mobilization. While the literature on social movements is rich in theories concerning how movements get started, there is little to guide explorations of the maintenance and reactivation of membership commitment — especially when leaders of existing movements attempt to redefine the groups and social influences that are to be opposed. Even the more recent theoretical developments in the field, resource mobilization theory and the new social movement approach, shed little light on such matters. While the first concentrates on the mobilization of resources and the costs and benefits of participation, it does not concern itself with the formation of mobilization potentials at all. As for new social movement theory, this paradigm does focus on the mobilization potential of contemporary social movements, but it assumes that mobilization potentials form spontaneously through societal developments. Overlooked is the part that social movements themselves play in defining situations that move individuals to action (Klandermans, 1988). Moreover, both these approaches are chiefly concerned with the emergence of social movements, rather than with how commitment is sustained or redirected.

This lacuna in the literature is curious given that the success of any particular movement campaign is usually dependent upon its staying power — that is, on its ability to affect both consensus and action mobilization (i.e., the activation of commitment by individuals who already belong to the movement). It cannot be taken for granted that rank-and-file members feel that the concrete goals of leaders and movement organizations are related to their dissatisfactions and aspirations; nor can it be assumed that such adherents will consistently believe that participation in the movement's activities is effective (Klandermans, 1988). Even in the case of en bloc engagement, individuals have to decide whether and to what degree they will conform to the collectivity, particularly if the movement is promoting views that differ from those around which it originally mobilized.

In one of the few attempts to illuminate the relationship between ideology and participant mobilization, David A. Snow and Robert D. Benford (1988) develop a series of useful concepts in their cross-cultural analysis of the peace movement. The term *framing*, an extension of Goffman's frame analysis (Goffman, 1974), is used to illuminate the signifying work that social movements do. It focuses, in other words, on the process of mobilizing adherents by assigning meaning to relevant events and conditions. In this view, the mobilization or activation of adherents is contingent upon the linkage of individual and movement interpretive orientations, such that "some sets of individual interests, values, and beliefs and social movement activities, goals, and ideology are congruent and complementary" (Snow et al., 1986: 464). While Snow and Benford identify various sets of factors that affect the "mobilizing potential" of a movement's framing efforts, only one set — what they refer to as *phenomenological constraints* — will be drawn on here.[3]

Phenomenological constraints involve three interrelated but analytically distinct factors: (1) *empirical credibility*; (2) *experiential commensurability*; and (3) *narrative fidelity*. Empirical credibility refers to the fit between the framing and events in the world. Are there events or occurrences that can be pointed to as legitimating evidence for the claims of the movement to its supporters? Experiential commensurability refers to the interpretive lens through which the "evidence" is filtered, especially in light of the personal experiences of individuals, which usually act as an important screening mechanism. Do the framing efforts interpret threatening events and developments in ways that harmonize with the ways in which these events, etc., are currently being experienced? Or are such framing efforts too abstract, too distant from the everyday existence of participants? To illustrate, Snow and Benford (1988: 209) suggest that it was precisely such a lack of experiential commensurability in the peace movement's "doomsday campaign" in the United States that explains the difficulties American peace activists encountered, compared with European and Japanese activists, in concretizing the nuclear threat to their compatriots. Apparently a "doomsday" frame did not resonate among Americans as it did among European and Japanese citizens, and, consequently was a weak prod to action. As for the third of Snow and Benford's phenomenological constraints, narrative fidelity, this refers to the degree to which framings strike a responsive chord with the cultural heritage of movement supporters. In sum, the more credible, experientially commensurable, and culturally resonant, a leaderships' framing efforts are, the more likely action mobilization will occur.

Or as Antonio Gramsci (1971) argues in his discussions of hegemony and revolution, "political education" must begin with and be linked to the nature and structure of the belief system that is the objective of transformation. It follows that when these linkages are effective, new symbols or goals can become the unifying points in the organization of the collective struggle. When they fail, the future of the movement is threatened.

DATA AND METHODS

The primary data for this examination of the pro-family movement were gathered in 1986–87 in a mail-out questionnaire survey of English-speaking supporters from across Canada ($N = 812$). When I undertook this research there was an absence of data on the national membership of the anti-abortion/pro-family forces in both Canada and the United States. Generalizations about movement participants were almost entirely based on small and localized samples of leaders, or "activists" — an unsatisfactory strategy for my purposes, since it was precisely the differences that usually divided leaders and followers, and the tensions that marked their relations, that I found problematic. These differences and tensions would be especially crucial, I felt, in any assessment of the likely impact of the movement on Canadian politics generally. But this entailed the problem of establishing the outer boundary of the movement. I needed some way of distinguishing between individuals who did identify with and contribute to the movement, however minimally, and those who were simply passive well-wishers.

It was, in any case, with these considerations in mind that I sought to make use of the subscription list of *The Interim*. This is a non-sectarian monthly publication, begun in 1983 and edited in Toronto, which bills itself as "Canada's Pro-Life, Pro-Family Newspaper." Without a rival in the field, *The Interim* already had a readership that numbered in the tens of thousands by 1986. It circulated in all parts of English-speaking Canada, and was not tied to any particular organization or subsection of the pro-family universe. Its claim of being the national voice of the movement was thus a reasonable one. Hence my assumption that its subscribers (almost all of whom had paid $9.00 for an annual subscription) were supporters of the cause it served — an expectation that was well borne out by the data that the survey yielded on pro-family activities.

To obtain a random sample of names and addresses from *The Interim*'s computerized list of subscribers ($N = 46,683$) every 39th name was selected,

producing a total of 1,197 names and addresses. Questionnaires were sent to each of these, as were reminder cards. Deaths, vacated dwellings, and inaccurate addresses eliminated 118 of these selections, reducing the base to 1,079. From this base, 812 questionnaires were returned, a response rate of 75 per cent.

The questionnaire was divided into four sections: (1) participation in the movement; (2) social and moral attitudes; (3) political attitudes and behaviour; and (4) socio-economic information. Where feasible, the survey included questions that allow comparisons between pro-family adherents and the Canadian public. These questions were taken from various attitudinal and behavioural studies, such as the National Election Survey (1984), the Quality of Life Survey (1981), the Canadian Census (1985), and various years of the Gallup Poll.[4]

In addition to the survey, the analysis that follows is informed by interviews carried out with 28 movement leaders from across Canada and with 40 ordinary members mostly from Southern Ontario; and by my own observation of pro-family conferences, rallies, and workshops.

ORIGINS AND FRAMING STRATEGY

Although it is often the case that the inconspicuous protests and refusals that characterize the behaviour of future activists make it difficult to determine just when a movement begins (cf. Freeman, 1983: 8–10), this is hardly true of the pro-family movement in Canada. In fact, the movement was organized by a number of key anti-abortion activists, whose initial idea was to broaden the base of their cause, chiefly by targeting feminists and their handmaidens in the schools, the government, and the media. That these activists were drawn from the hardline, no-compromise sector of the anti-abortion movement is significant, especially in light of a conventional association of intransigence on moral issues with religious fundamentalism.

In fact, the hardliners set out to deemphasize the movement's ethical and religious vocabulary, though not to eliminate it altogether. The point was to frame the issue of abortion as a manifest symptom of social decay and elite irresponsibility. The rising toll of abortions, in this view, was the most visible evidence of a widespread rejection of the values associated with the breadwinner ethic and the traditional family — a rejection that was rooted in the movement of women into paid employment, in the social derogation of housewives, and especially in the increasing legitimacy of feminism and feminists. This latter focus became increasingly salient from the late '70s on, as the hard-liners split from the more moderate anti-abortionists in order to become more actively involved in politics. In Ontario, this was reflected in efforts, undertaken in the early '80s, to oppose Bill 7, the Homosexual Rights bill. It was also reflected in attempts throughout the decade to elect anti-abortion and pro-family candidates in provincial and federal elections.

It was in 1983, however, that the dissident anti-abortionists were presented with the opportunity they needed when a proposal to scrap the tax exemption for dependent spouses was put forward by federal cabinet minister Judy Erola. The upshot was REAL Women. "I felt tremendous indignation," one of REAL Women's founders told me about Erola's proposal.

> What feminists had always implied, that a woman who stays home is a second-class citizen, was now being translated into public policy. I called some of my pro-life friends and got in touch with some of the local groups and they were just fuming too.... So they called other pro-lifers, and it just kind of snowballed. We decided to form our own group, one that would speak for the silent majority, the real women of Canada.

Equally shocking to REAL Women's founders were the constitutional developments of a year or so earlier, when feminists dramatically succeeded in writing gender-equality provisions into the new Canadian Charter of Rights and Freedoms. Society, it was claimed by the new organization, was now embroiled in an "undeclared civil war," one which pitted an "anti-family," materialistic "vocal minority" against an anti-materialistic "silent majority." Led by elite feminists and gay rights activists, "anti-family" groups had seized control of mainstream institutions and were launching a "wholesale, frontal attack" on traditional values. As for the policy goals of the new movement, these were largely restricted to measures aimed at shoring up the position of full-time homemakers (by improving their tax exemptions and pension benefits, increasing family allowances, and the like — proposals that for the most part were deemphasized after the movement entered its neoconservative phase). But apart from insistent demands that the federal and provincial grants sustaining women's organizations be ended, which was the centrepiece of its campaign to delegitimize feminism, the pro-family founders weren't all that interested in policy. Rather, their analyses of Canada's deteriorating social fabric seemed designed to lend rhetorical encouragement to the idea that sacrifice to family was still a woman's surest path to happiness and fulfilment.

Finally, it is important to point out that appeals to potential recruits continued to be framed in religious terms, even if the main emphasis was a kind of secularized patriotism. It was still the Christian duty of those who believed in "the family" to fight for its survival. By the same token, if the "anti-family" forces were not successfully challenged, then both "the nation and the foundation of individual well-being" would be lost.

PROFILE OF THE PRO-FAMILY MEMBERSHIP

So much for the initial framing efforts of the pro-family leadership. Let us now address Snow and Benford's questions about the phenomenological fit between these framing efforts and the interests, experiences, and cultural-political heritage of the movement's early recruits.

Among the most striking findings to emerge from the survey data collected for this study are those that underscore the homogeneity of pro-family supporters, especially in terms of their generational experiences and religious commitments.[5] A solid majority of this predominantly female constituency is middle-aged (58% are women and 62% of all respondents, women and men, are 45 years or older). Equally significant, 69 per cent of them were raised in small towns or on farms, and 71 per cent grew up in families whose mothers did not work outside the home.

And despite these Depression-era, rural, small-town beginnings (or perhaps because of them), they are relatively middle-class and well-educated. Thus 35 per cent of pro-family individuals have a university degree (46% of the men and 27% of the women), compared with only 10 per cent of Canadians generally, according to Quality of Life (QOL) data. (Unless otherwise specified, all comparisons of this kind are based on QOL surveys.) Likewise, 27 per cent are professionals or semiprofessionals, compared with only 14 per cent of Canadians generally. Indeed, of the 50 per cent of pro-family respondents who are employed, some 54 per cent are professionals or semiprofessionals, compared with 23 per cent of all Canadians.

Regarding both individual and family income, here comparisons are less revealing — chiefly, I would speculate, because so many of this relatively aged group are either retired or full-time homemakers. Thus 41 per cent of the male respondents earned at least $40,000 annually (again in 1986–87 dollars), compared with only 8 per cent for all Canadian men (Census of Canada, 1986: 93–114). Yet median family income for all pro-family respondents was only $250 higher than the 1986 Canadian average: $35,000 versus $34,750 (Census of Canada, 1986: 93). Such modest family incomes would seem to validate the movement's claim that its members espouse antimaterialist values. They, at any rate, reflect the fact that 51 per cent of women respondents are full-time homemakers, with 25 per cent indicating they are "satisfied" and 75 per cent saying they are "very satisfied" in this role. By the same token, very few indicate a desire for employment on either a full-time or part-time basis (.2% want a full-time job versus 8% of all Canadian homemakers; and 6% a part-time job versus 29% of all Canadian homemakers). Not surprisingly, pro-family members have large families and stable marriages: 74 per cent are currently married, only 3 per cent have ever experienced divorce or separation, and 57 per cent have three children or more.[6]

Turning now to religion, the mainstream Protestant denominations (United and Anglican) are very poorly represented among pro-family supporters, with 95 per cent being either Catholic or fundamentalist. Ninety-three per cent say that their religious beliefs are important to them, while 96 per cent report church attendance of at least once a week. Given this exceptional level of commitment, it is hardly surprising that a majority of them (56%) got involved in the movement through their church. Significantly enough, 72 per cent had never been politically active prior to their involvement in one of the anti-abortion/pro-family organizations.

Indeed, the beliefs and motivations underlying their participation in the movement are remarkably similar — and also highly congruent with the initial framing efforts of the movement (see Table 19.1). Thus a common belief — expressed in both the questionnaires and in the 68 interviews undertaken for this study — is that pro-family supporters are engaged in a righteous crusade against adversaries variously depicted as "wealthy," "well-educated," "anti-family," "materialistic," and "sexually promiscuous." They are likewise described as "atheists," or "secular humanists" and "radical feminists who hate men." Associated with the anti-family forces are a number of prominent organizations: the United Church, the New Democratic Party, the National Action Committee, and Planned Parenthood, as well as all feminist, pro-choice, and gay rights groups.

As for the extent of this constituency's participation in the movement, here too there is evidence that the framing efforts of the leadership were highly successful. Forty-four per cent of the survey respondents report giving their time on a regular basis; 76 per cent say they have gone to the trouble of contacting a politician, and 48 per cent have protested at a clinic or hospital where abortions are being performed. Ninety per cent also report making financial contributions beyond the membership fees charged by REAL Women and most of the other groups. (The average donation was $75, with 31% donating $100 or more.) Finally, while 31 per cent voiced disapproval of movement actions, only 8 per cent had Canadian activities in mind. The rest exclusively cited tactics used in the United States, particularly the fire-bombing of abortion clinics.

THE TURN TOWARDS NEOCONSERVATISM

By 1987, after four years of existence, REAL Women could plausibly claim a groundswell of national support. Affiliates had been established in every province and region of the country, and — to judge by the circulation figures of *The Interim* — a national membership of roughly 100,000 had been recruited to the various

Table 19.1 Responses of Pro-Family Respondents to the Question: "Please indicate how important the following concerns were to you in your decision to become involved in the pro-family movement."

	Very Important	Fairly Important	Not Important	Total %	Number of Cases
Opposition to abortion	99	.3	.2	100	810
Support for traditional values	67	22	11	100	806
Opposition to pornography	62	23	15	100	802
Opposition to secular humanism	55	28	17	100	803
Opposition to the gay rights movement	52	26	22	100	800
Opposition to the feminist movement	48	33	19	100	802
Opposition to sex education in schools	46	34	20	100	796

pro-family groups. Clearly, the leaders' framing strategy, which had linked a decline of support for the traditional family to an elitist feminist ascendancy, had struck a responsive chord. Indeed, despite a partial downplaying of religion, there is every indication, to judge by the data presented above, that the leadership succeeded very well in evoking and projecting themes that accorded with the marked religiosity and the unusual "life worlds" of the membership. In Snow and Benford's terms, these ideological frames acted as effective prods to mobilization because of the large extent to which they were commensurate with both the lived realities and "inherent ideology" of a large constituency of Canadians.

In December, 1987, however, this framing strategy was altered. A statement entitled "Towards a Pro-Family Economy," appearing in the newsletter of REAL Women, marked the change: In the past, it began,

> the pro-family movement has emerged in Canada to battle the "social issues," i.e., abortion, pornography ... radical feminism, etc. With but few exceptions, we have given little attention to the monetary issues affecting Canadian families — the government tax and spend machine. Among economists, Canadians are defined as a people whose attitudes display little sympathy towards reducing government spending programs and reducing individual tax rates. The Department of Finance holds the idea that the "Canadian psyche" is such that we are willing to pay substantially higher rates to maintain the government programs and giveaways we have come to expect. Hasn't the time come to tell the Department of Finance they are reading the Canadian public wrong? (REALity, VI(1): 1).

This statement went on to comment on a White Paper on tax reform issued by the Conservative government in Ottawa, praising its proposals for lowering corporate taxes, while suggesting that its projected reduction of personal income taxes didn't go far enough.

Then, a few months later, another change was registered, when the organization's newsletter dropped the scriptural passages that framed its masthead. We have gone through "a year of difficulties over changing our original directions," a May, 1988, REALity Update stated, cryptically, in an announcement that the organization was moving its national office to Ottawa. The difficulties, which had come to a head at a February, 1988, conference, involved infighting between old and new board members over the role that "Christian" and "family" values would play in the organization's campaign to become more policy-oriented (read

neoconservative). After the ousting of REAL Women's president and several board members, The Interim published a highly negative account of the recent takeover, and it and other anti-abortion groups began distancing themselves from the Ottawa-based board. This didn't seem to phase the new board members, however, as notes and articles in the newsletter became peppered with references to entrepreneurial freedom, the free market economy, high taxes, and government intrusions. Pay equity and affirmative action, the Spring, 1987, issue of REALity states,

> are a blueprint for the radical restructuring of our society.... The philosophy underlying this proposed legislation is just another factor introduced to undermine our free market.... It is an attempt at the wholesale redistribution of income implemented and watched over by a vast unprecedented bureaucracy with great power and little accountability (REALity, V(1): 1–2).

Regarding daycare, a similar note was being struck:

> Free universally available daycare ... will direct national finances straight towards a catastrophe of appalling dimensions with unimagined repercussions. National bankruptcy is the hillside to which the aircraft is headed.... The debt picture of Canada is such that ... the burden of a daycare tax would shock and oppress the nation (REALity, VI(1): 8).

Underlying this new emphasis on state intrusiveness and fiscal calamity was the notion that the family worked best as a self-sufficient unit. Social welfare "give-aways" only weakened the family, while fiscally conservative policies tended to strengthen it. Was this new framing venture, as it were, one that played well with the membership? Did it lend itself to the tasks of building consensus and action mobilization? Unfortunately, there exist no longitudinal survey data that might answer this question definitively. There is however, considerable evidence from the 1986–87 survey to suggest why the movement has lost its momentum.

POLITICAL ATTITUDES OF THE PRO-FAMILY MEMBERSHIP

While the causal link between feminist influences and the incidence of family pathology and breakdown is widely believed, pro-family adherents are much more accepting of what they perceive to be the impact of feminism in the public realm. Thus, as Table 19.2 indicates, over 90 per cent of respondents "agree" or

Table 19.2 Responses of Pro-Family Respondents to the Question: "Here are some opinions that you hear different people giving about the feminist movement. Please indicate whether you strongly agree, agree, disagree, or strongly disagree with the following statements."

	Strongly Agree	Agree	Strongly Disagree	Disagree	Total %	Number of Cases
		(Percentages)				
Feminism has led to a devaluation of motherhood	61	31	2	6	100	782
Feminism has undermined traditional family values	53	38	2	7	100	762
Feminists don't understand the needs of homemakers	28	50	3	19	100	701
The majority of Cnd. women don't support the goals of the feminist movement	41	50	2	7	100	649
Feminism has helped women in the work force	9	65	5	21	100	683
Feminism has contributed to an improvement in the status of women	7	42	16	35	100	709

"strongly agree" that feminism has "devalued motherhood" and "undermined traditional family values"; some 78 per cent agree that "feminists do not understand the needs of homemakers"; and 91 per cent either "agree" or "strongly agree" that "most Canadians do not support feminist goals." Yet there is also a perception among 74 per cent of pro-family respondents that "feminism has helped women in the work force"; and almost half (49%) say that it has "contributed to an improvement in the status of women."

The membership's feelings about government involvement in daycare, a policy the movement is vehemently opposed to, are also mixed. While there is almost no support for the idea of a state-funded national scheme, subsidies for families that require daycare and live below the poverty line are acceptable to 42 per cent of the membership — a view that is seemingly at odds with the movement's concern for eliminating all daycare funding. At the very least, such attitudes suggest that the movement's inflexible views in this area are not widely shared by the membership.

And as with daycare, so too with attitudes towards government generally. Consider the findings of Table 19.3, in which there is little to suggest the complex of pro-business/anti-government attitudes that has been prevalent among the religious right in the United States. Thus pro-family respondents are somewhat more distrustful of unions than their QOL counterparts (81% versus 70%); they are more distrustful of big business, too (84% versus 74%). Both groups are roughly equal in their feelings about the federal government (47% versus 50%). But this last finding is not a distrust of govern-

ment per se, to judge by the much lower figures for provincial governments (29% versus 28% for QOL respondents). Significantly enough, only religious leaders are felt — by 62 per cent of pro-family respondents — to have "much too little" or "too little" power.

In Table 19.4 there is also little evidence of neoconservative tendencies among the pro-family supporters. Indeed, on some indicators they appear to be equally or even more liberal than Canadians generally. Thus pro-family respondents want more government commitment to help the poor (77% versus 64% for QOL respondents); less to fight crime (66% versus 74%); and about the same for assisting the unemployed (37% versus 36%). Only when an issue identified with feminism is raised, does the pro-family group digress sharply from the Canadian norm, with only 19 per cent (versus 56%) wanting more government effort to eliminate discrimination against women.

Finally, consider the responses to the statements featured in Table 19.5. On 2 out of 3 questions, the pro-family respondents are stronger on what might be called the egalitarian position; and on the third — concerning the desirability of the gap between the rich and the poor — there is little to choose between them and Canadians generally (63% versus 67% for QOL respondents).

DISCUSSION

All told, these data on political attitudes suggest that if the pro-family constituency is not all that enthusiastic about extending income supports and social services, neither are they about to be mobilized for a campaign

Table 19.3 Responses of Pro-Family and Quality of Life Respondents to the Question: "Some groups in Canada have more power than others to get the things they want. Please indicate if you think each of the groups listed below has too much power for the good of the country, too little power, or about the right amount of power."

	Too Much Power	About Right Amt. of Power	Too Little Power	Total %	Number of Cases
		(Percentages)			
THE MEDIA					
Pro-family	85	13	2	100	770
LARGE CORPORATIONS					
Pro-family	84	15	1	100	752
Quality of Life	74	23	3	100	2948
LABOUR UNIONS					
Pro-family	81	17	2	100	770
Quality of Life	70	22	8	100	2948
FEDERAL GOVERNMENT					
Pro-family	47	47	6	100	725
Quality of Life	50	39	11	100	2948
PROVINCIAL GOVERNMENT					
Pro-family	29	61	10	100	727
Quality of Life	28	52	20	100	2948
RELIGIOUS LEADERS					
Pro-family	.05	36	62	100	721

Note: The "much, too much power" and "too much power" and the "much, much too little" and "much too little" categories are combined.

against the "government tax and spend machine." Except where sexual, reproductive, and family issues are concerned, their economic and political attitudes would seem to be somewhat more liberal than those of Canadians generally. "We live in a very prosperous country," I was told by one of the ordinary members I interviewed,

> one in which no child should ever go hungry. I'd like to see the government revise the tax system: tax low income families much, much less and increase the taxes on the wealthy, particularly if they're single. And what about charity — people are so materialistic today, they have garage sales instead of giving stuff to the poor. It just makes me sick. We were poor during the Depression. My dad had died, but we never went hungry. The church and our neighbours helped us out until we got on our feet again.

Genuine as they are, such sentiments are still likely to be overwhelmed by the exceptional sexual, reproductive, and family concerns mentioned above. We see this especially in the fact that, despite the centrality of

so much of their political thinking, pro-family individuals are deeply distrustful of the mainstream parties, including the federal Conservatives, whom they might be expected to support.

Thus, in response to a question on federal voting intentions (as of 1986–87), only 23 per cent were prepared to vote for one of the three main parties, with the Conservatives (11%) and Liberals (10%) roughly splitting this vote equally. This would seem to auger well for the Reform Party (which hadn't been launched at the time the survey was completed). And this indeed is what some of the movement's leaders devoutly wish. "I'm very enthusiastic about the Reform Party," the current president of REAL Women stated in a recent interview.

> We don't tell our members how to vote but ... [w]e're both against equal pay for work of equal value, we're against so much government intervention into family and private life, which is what the radical feminists want. If they got their way, there'd be no private life left. The Reform Party seems to support many of the philosophical ideas that we have (Sharpe and Braid, 1992: 145–46).

Table 19.4 Responses of Pro-Family and Quality of Life Respondents to the Question: "How much effort do you think the government should put into the activities listed below?"

	More Effort	Same Amount of Effort	Less Effort	Total %	Number of Cases
		(Percentages)			
FIGHTING PORNOGRAPHY					
Pro-family	89	9	2	100	787
HELPING THE POOR					
Pro-family	77	21	2	100	781
Quality of Life	64	32	4	100	2840
CRIME PREVENTION					
Pro-family	66	33	1	100	772
Quality of Life	74	24	2	100	2887
EDUCAÏTION					
Pro-family	40	33	8	100	765
Quality of Life	55	42	3	100	2880
ASSISTING THE UNEMPLOYED					
Pro-family	37	44	18	100	768
Quality of Life	36	40	24	100	2808
PROTECTING THE RIGHTS OF THE DISABLED					
Pro-family	60	39	1	100	753
PROTECTING THE RIGHTS OF NATIVE PEOPLE					
Pro-family	43	42	13	100	742
Quality of Life	48	41	11	100	2791
ESTABLISHING EQUAL PAY FOR WORK OF EQUAL VALUE PROGRAMS					
Pro-family	33	33	32	100	759
ELIMINATING DISCRIMINATION AGAINST WOMEN					
Pro-family	19	33	42	100	722
Quality of Life	56	35	9	100	2836
PROTECTING HOMOSEXUALS FROM DISCRIMINATION IN EMPLOYMENT					
Pro-family	5	24	63	100	721

Note: The "much more effort" and "more effort" and the "much less effort" and "less effort" categories are combined.

Leaders of the Alberta Federation of Women United for Families have also publicly endorsed Preston Manning, whose fundamentalist background and anti-abortion/pro-family views are well-known in Alberta and perhaps elsewhere in the West. So far, however, the Reform Party has accented its neoconservative orthodoxy over its pro-family appeals. And Manning's promise of dealing with "moral" issues (like abortion) by referenda (Manning, 1992: 108) is a compromise which may not win that many votes from the pro-family constituency, especially in light of the recent work done by the federal Conservatives' Family Caucus to shore up the party's appeal to the religious right.

Consisting of some 32 backbench MPs, the Family Caucus, like the Reform Party, was launched since the survey data for this study were collected. (In fact, some 86% of pro-family respondents were of the opinion that, since their electoral sweep in 1984, the Tories had done little or nothing about pro-family concerns.) Caucus members meet with pro-family leaders, and some of its members have addressed pro-family

Table 19.5 Responses of Pro-Family and Quality of Life Respondents to the Question: "Here are a series of statements about social economic issues. Choose the answer that comes closest to your own opinion."

	Agree	Neither Agree nor Disagree	Disagree	Total %	Number of Cases
		(Percentages)			
PEOPLE WITH HIGH INCOMES SHOULD PAY MORE TAXES					
Pro-family	77	8	14	100	760
Quality of Life	57	13	30	100	2836
TOO MUCH DIFFERENCE BETWEEN RICH & POOR					
Pro-family	63	23	13	100	767
Quality of Life	67	15	17	100	2841
UNEMPLOYMENT IS HIGH BECAUSE WELFARE IS TOO EASY TO GET					
Pro-family	50	16	32	100	772
Quality of Life	67	11	22	100	2860

Note: The "strongly agree" and "agree" and the "strongly disagree" and "disagree" categories are combined.

functions. (The Caucus quietly bills itself as a "defender of Christian values.") Moreover, it supports various pro-family positions, including the recriminalization of abortion, the elimination of tax breaks for common-law couples, and the development of a child tax benefit program weighted in favour of the working poor rather than welfare recipients. It has also been credited with preventing amendments to the *Human Rights Act* that would recognize same-sex marriages, and with killing the Tory's national daycare scheme (*The Ottawa Citizen*, March 2, 1993: A3). Given all this, the Family Caucus might well outbid the Reform Party and draw pro-family voters to the Tories — though this isn't likely to happen if "feminist" Kim Campbell becomes the next Conservative leader. (Campbell's two divorces and her resignation from William Vander Zalm's cabinet over the abortion issue are not likely to endear her to pro-family supporters.)

Clearly, it is the Reform Party that has the best chance of corralling the pro-family vote (in the sense that President Reagan was able to corral the religious right in the United States). Nevertheless, if the survey data of this study are any guide, it won't happen. Essentially, we are dealing with a constituency of militant single-issue (or cluster-issue) voters, whose sympathy for the economic program of Manning's neoconservatism is too weak to induce them to abandon their normal practice of voting for pro-family candidates — Tory, Liberal, Reform, or independent — wherever such candidates may present themselves. As a political force, they may help to defeat feminist-backed measures — like the national daycare scheme promised by the Tories in 1988. That in itself is no small achievement, but it is not a sign that an American-style new right is in the offing.

CONCLUSION

The outlook of pro-family supporters is clearly reflective of their material and social interests; more specifically, both their world view and lifestyles are characterized by a deep-seated traditionalism that rests on the economic privileges of the middle-class and strict adherence to a conservative, religiously-based moral code. The ideology of familialism, in Michele Barrett and Mary McIntosh's term (1982), that largely defines their world view is also embedded in their traditional family and gender arrangements. Indeed, it presents these relations as normal and right. In this light, their consciousness of the cultural and moral differences that separate them from mainstream society is not false. Indeed, the issues that concern pro-family adherents most deeply — i.e., women's abandonment of full-time homemaking, easier divorce legislation, the increasing secularization of society, and changing sexual mores and practices — do represent a threat to their way of life. Hence their sense of disquiet and righteous anger as the schools, courts, media, and other institutions that once upheld their values have become more tolerant of unconventional living arrangements and non-conforming groups.

The structural and cultural location of pro-family supporters, their experiences, and their religious and moral outlook, therefore predisposed them to the initial framing efforts of the movement. Yet, co-existing with the moral traditionalism and religious populism of movement supporters is a kind of political conservatism which, paradoxically enough, is supportive of Canada's long-standing public-enterprise traditions, especially as these traditions mandate collective provision for basic needs. Hence, for example, their opposition to universal daycare, on the one hand, and their acceptance of some public subsidization in this area, on the other. By the same token, it is not the government or the state per se that is distrusted or reviled, as it is metropolitan elites and institutions: feminists above all, but also media and large corporations.

Given that the majority of the membership were political neophytes, the movement was clearly successful in its initial mobilization efforts. The likelihood, however, of its sustaining that commitment is now less certain. To revisit Snow and Benford's categories, the data reported here suggest that the movement's turn towards neoconservatism will not have empirical credibility, experiential commensurability, or narrative fidelity with the rank and file. The membership's lack of support for cutbacks in social services coupled with their acknowledgement of the structural factors, particularly economic hardship, that influence contemporary family relations, may lead them to view the leadership's demand for social welfare cutbacks as misplaced and unduly harsh. Again in Snow and Benford's term, the pro-family movement may well be confronted with the problem of "frame over-extension"; that is, an expansion of the boundaries of their primary framework to incorporate positions that have little resonance with the membership and may indeed run counter to the "inherent ideology" of many of them (1988: 206).

One theoretical implication of this analysis is the support it lends to Snow and Benford (1988) and Klandermans (1988) to the effect that the process of sustaining consensus or redirecting a movement's participants may be a more interactive, multi-dimensional, and ultimately hazardous undertaking than is generally appreciated. Finally, apropos of the future of the pro-family movement, the data suggest that its neoconservative prospects are limited. Despite the leadership's current flirtation with the Reform Party, a full-blown new right on the American model, with its fusion of a cultural and economic offensive, is unlikely. Our neoconservatives will have to continue to use stealth and indirection (as in the free trade agreements) if the dismantling of the Canadian welfare state is to proceed apace.

NOTES

Funding for the research reported herein was provided by the Faculty of Arts Research Grant (York University). I'm also grateful for the comments on earlier versions of this chapter provided by S.A. Longstaff, Michael D. Ornstein, Gordon Darroch, and three anonymous reviewers.

1. REAL Women is the most visible and active pro-family group in Canada. It is a national organization, which began in Toronto and quickly established affiliates in each of the provinces. Later, in 1988, it moved its headquarters to Ottawa. Other pro-family organizations include: the Coalition for Family Values, Renaissance Canada, the Alberta Federation of Women United for Families (AFWUF), Positive Parents, and various anti-abortion and religiously based groups.

2. See Eisenstein, 1989; Whitaker, 1987; Gordon and Hunter, 1977–78; and Petchesky, 1985 for discussions of the New Right's successful fusionist strategy in the United States.

3. The other sets of constraints discussed by Snow and Benford include: (1) the robustness, completeness, and thoroughness of the framing effort; (2) the internal structure of the larger belief system with which the movement seeks to affect some kind of cognitive ideational alignment; and (3) cycles of protest.

4. The 1981 Quality of Life (QOL) study was conducted by the Institute for Social Research at York University. The 1984 National Election Survey was conducted by Canadian Facts, a private survey and marketing firm. The Canadian Gallup Polls are national polls conducted by the Canadian Institute of Public Opinion and Census of Canada data are published by Statistics Canada. Respondents in each of these surveys are selected randomly and the target population includes all Canadian residents 18 years or older.

5. For a more detailed discussion of the class backgrounds of the pro-family leadership and rank and file see, Erwin (1988; forthcoming).

6. The respondents in this sample tend to fit the demographic profile and lifestyle pattern characteristic of participants in anti-abortion, anti-ERA, and anti-pornography organizations. Studies of these groups have found that growing up in a smaller-sized community, having a large family, being in stable marriages, and being a Catholic or Protestant fundamentalist with a high level of religiosity correlates with support for moral reform movements (Page and Clelland, 1978; Zurcher and Kirkpatrick, 1976; Wood and Hughes, 1984; Brady and Tedin, 1976; Leahy, Snow and Worden, 1983; Petersen and Mauss, 1976; Singh and Leahy, 1978; and Luker, 1984).

REFERENCES

Barrett, Michele, and Mary McIntosh. 1982. *The Anti-Social Family*. London: Verso.

Brady, David W., and Kent L. Tedin. 1976. "Ladies in Pink: Religion and Political Ideology in the Anti-ERA Movement." *Social Science Quarterly* 59 (March): 198–205.

Census of Canada. 1986. *Estimates of Families in Canada*, Catalogue No. 99-526.

Eisenstein, Zillah. 1989. "Liberalism, Feminism and the Reagan State: The Neo-Conservative Assault on (Sexual) Equality." Pp. 236–62 in Ralph Milliband, Leo Panitc, and John Seville, eds., *The Socialist Register*. London: The Merlin Press.

Erwin, Lorna. 1988. "The Pro-Family Movement in Canada." Pp. 266–78 in Peta Sheriff, ed., *Feminist Research: Retrospect and Prospects*. Toronto: McGill-Queens University Press.

———. Forthcoming. *The Politics of Anti-feminism: The Pro-Family Movement in Canada*. Toronto: University of Toronto Press.

Freeman, Jo, ed. 1983. *Social Movements of the Sixties and Seventies*. New York: Longman.

Goffman, Erving. 1974. *Frame Analysis*. New York: Harper Colophon.

Gordon, Linda, and Allen Hunter. 1977–78. "Sex, Family, and the New Right: Anti-feminism as a Political Force." *Socialist Review*, 12 (November–February): 9–25.

Gramsci, Antonio. 1971. *Selections from the Prison Notebooks*. Translated by Q. Hoare and G. Nowell-Smith. London: Lawrence and Wishart.

Klandermans, Bert. 1988. "The Formation and Mobilization of Consensus." Pp. 173–96 in Bert Klandermans, Hanspeter Kriesi and Sidney Tarrow, eds., *International Social Movement Research*. London: JAI Press Inc.

Leahy, Peter J., David A. Snow, and Steven Worden. 1983. "The Anti-abortion Movement and Symbolic Crusades: Reappraisal of a Popular Theory." *Alternative Lifestyles*, 6 (Fall): 27–47.

Luker, Kristin. 1984. *Abortion and the Politics of Motherhood*. Berkeley: University of California Press.

Manning, Preston. 1992. *The New Canada*. Toronto: Macmillan.

Page, Ann L., and Donald A. Clelland. 1978. "The Kanawha County Textbook Controversy: A Study of the Politics of Lifestyle Concern." *Social Forces* 57: 265–81.

Petchesky, Rosalind. 1985. *Abortion and Woman's Choice: The State, Sexuality, and Reproductive Freedom*. Boston: Northeastern University Press.

Petersen, Larry R., and Armand L. Mauss. 1976. "Religion and the 'Right to Life': Correlates of Opposition to Abortion." *Sociological Analysis* 37: 243–54.

REALity 1984. II, No. 2 (Fall).

———. 1985. III, No. 3.

———. 1986. IV, No. 4 (Summer).

———. 1987. V, No. 1 (Spring).

———. 1987. VI, No. 1 (Christmas).

———. 1988. VI, No. 1 (Fall).

REALity Update. 1986. January (no volume indicated).

———. 1988. May (no volume indicated).

Sharpe, Sydney, and Don Braid. 1992. *Storming Babylon: Preston Manning and the Rise of the Reform Party*. Toronto: Key Porter Books.

Singh, Khrisna B., and Peter J. Leahy. 1978. "Contextual and Ideological Dimensions of Attitudes Toward Discretionary Abortion." *Demography* 15 (August): 381–88.

Snow, David A., and Robert D. Benford. 1988. "Ideology, Frame Resonance, and Participant Mobilization." Pp. 197–217 in Bert Klandermans, Hanspeter Kriesi and Sidney Tarrow, eds., *International Social Movement Research*. London: JAI Press Inc.

Snow, David A., Louis A. Zurcher, and Sheldon Ekland-Olson. 1986. "Social Networks and Social Movements: A Microstructural Approach to Differential Recruitment." *American Sociological Review* 45: 787–801.

Whitaker, Reg. 1987. "Neo-conservatism and the State." Pp. 1–31 in Ralph Milliband, Leo Panitch, and John Saville, eds., *The Socialist Register*. London: The Merlin Press.

Wood, Michael, and Michael Hughes. 1984. "The Moral Basis of Moral Reform: Status Discontent vs. Culture and Socialization as Explanations of Anti-Pornography Social Movement Adherence." *American Sociological Review* 49: 86–99.

Zurcher, Louis A., and George R. Kirkpatrick. 1976. *Citizens for Decency: Antipornography Crusades as Status Defense*. Austin: University of Texas Press.

PART 4B

POLITICS

In Chapter 20, American political scientist Benjamin R. Barber argues provocatively that the planet is falling apart and coming together at the same time. What Barber means is that in the former Yugoslavia, the former Soviet Union, and many other parts of the world, old hatreds based on nation, ethnicity, race, and religion are intensifying and seeking to re-establish ancient borders. At the same time, however, existing national borders are breaking down because of flourishing worldwide markets for standardized goods, the growing interdependency of countries on each others' resources, instant and widely accessible international communication, and the growing recognition that ecological problems are global in character. According to Barber, democracy is promoted neither by narrow parochialism ("Jihad": Arabic for holy struggle) nor by the push to global homogenization ("McWorld"). Quite the contrary. Jihad is grounded in exclusion and, in extreme cases, fanaticism and authoritarianism. McWorld requires orderly markets rather than social justice and equality, and it erodes community, identity, and independence.

The growth of McWorld is certainly evident in the 1989 free trade deal between Canada and the United States, which promotes the untaxed movement of goods, services, capital, and labour between the two countries. As the Canadian and US economies become more highly integrated, Canada is becoming more like the United States. For example, the removal of trade barriers between the two countries means that Canadian workers have to compete with American workers for jobs. If Canadians demand higher wages and superior social services, then jobs will drift southward, where wages and taxes are lower. It is therefore no coincidence that fewer Canadian workers are unionized now than in the mid-1980s, wage levels are dropping in real terms, and social services are being cut. All this promotes the decline of Canada as an independent political community: with less money available for national rail services, public broadcasting, and a social safety net, many of the institutions that tie Canada's regions together are getting weaker.

In Chapter 21, R. Jack Richardson, formerly of McMaster University, analyzes some of the important class forces underlying the decoupling of the Canadian nation-state. He shows that Canadian business ownership is becoming increasingly **concentrated**, which is to say that a handful of giant corporations and **enterprises** control more and more of the Canadian economy. (An enterprise is a group of corporations with the same owner.) Just five banks controlled over 90 percent of Canadian bank assets in 1981. In 1987, the seventeen largest Canadian non-financial enterprises controlled nearly 75 percent of all corporate assets in the country. Richardson argues that large businesses such as these are the major forces behind Canada's free trade movement. They are keen to expand into the American market, especially now that they own most of the Canadian assets worth controlling, and they have managed to shape Canadian government policy to match their shared interest in free trade.

The promotion of free trade by big business is not the only force underlying the disintegration of Canada. In fact, Canada was a loosely structured entity from the start. The country was not created out of some unifying and widespread sense of nationhood but because, in the 1860s, its business and political leaders faced the loss of British and American export markets, the burden of a crippling debt load, and the threat of American expansionism. They regarded Confederation as a means of creating a new market and an expanded tax base by encouraging mass immigration and promoting economic growth. In order to forge a union, the Fathers of Confederation were careful to avoid consulting ordinary citizens for fear of having their plan rejected. And they drafted a founding document, the British North America Act, that played down the deep conflicts of interest and culture that distinguished the British North American colonies, even leaving ambiguous the question of how power would be distributed between federal and provincial governments. This pragmatic vagueness left the door open to the bickering and bargaining that has characterized federal–provincial relations ever since. Quebec has led the fight to gain more control over taxation, resource revenues, immigration policy, language use, etc., from the federal government, but other provinces have not been far behind. In Chapter 22, I outline how and why Quebec has led the movement to decentralize federal authority, and why, since the early 1970s, outright separation from Canada has become a more popular idea in that province. Separatism has encouraged a certain degree of intolerance in Quebec against residents who are not "pure wool" Québécois. Quebec nationalism is the moderate Canadian version of Jihad.

A third force leading to the decoupling of the Canadian community and the erosion of democracy in this country is the constitution adopted in 1982 by all the provinces aside from Quebec. The Charter of Rights and Freedoms contained in the constitution entrenches the rights of individuals and gives the judiciary substantial new powers. The courts may now review legislation and deny government's right to pass laws and engage in activities deemed questionable. The courts, however, consist of judges who are appointed, not elected, to office. Does this mean that Canadian democracy is weakened by the Charter, and that group rights will suffer as a result? In Chapter 23, W.A. Bogart of the University of Windsor makes just that case. He points out that courts have traditionally acted to protect vested interests rather than the interests of disadvantaged and ordinary citizens; that courts can sap democracy by removing important decision-making power from elected officials; and that resolving disputes by litigation is so expensive that most ordinary citizens are unable to afford it. Bogart illustrates the political dangers inherent in the Charter by examining how it is likely to fail to deal with pressing aboriginal issues.

The Charter, the devolution of powers to the provinces, and free trade are turning Canada into a new political entity, the outlines of which are still obscure — but not necessarily bleak. Barber proposes global confederacy as an antidote to the twin ills of Jihad and McWorld. He hopes that throughout the world there will emerge a series of loose, decentralized regions, smaller than today's countries, that would protect minority rights and cultures and that would be tied together in economic associations that are larger than today's countries. From the point of view of Barber's ideal, is Canada one of the most advanced countries in the world?

GLOSSARY

Concentration of ownership refers to the degree to which business assets are controlled by a small number of owners.

An **enterprise** is a group of corporations controlled by the same owner.

Chapter 20

JIHAD vs. McWORLD

BENJAMIN R. BARBER

Just beyond the horizon of current events lie two possible political futures — both bleak, neither democratic. The first is a retribalization of large swaths of humankind by war and bloodshed: a threatened Lebanonization of national states in which culture is pitted against culture, people against people, tribe against tribe — a Jihad in the name of a hundred narrowly conceived faiths against every kind of interdependence, every kind of artificial social cooperation and civic mutuality. The second is being borne in on us by the onrush of economic and ecological forces that demand integration and uniformity and that mesmerize the world with fast music, fast computers, and fast food — with MTV, Macintosh, and McDonald's, pressing nations into one commercially homogenous global network: one McWorld tied together by technology, ecology, communications, and commerce. The planet is falling precipitantly apart *and* coming reluctantly together at the very same moment.

These two tendencies are sometimes visible in the same countries at the same instant: thus Yugoslavia, clamoring just recently to join the New Europe, is exploding into fragments; India is trying to live up to its reputation as the world's largest integral democracy while powerful new fundamentalist parties like the Hindu nationalist Bharatiya Janata Party, along with nationalist assassins, are imperiling its hard-won unity. States are breaking up or joining up: the Soviet Union has disappeared almost overnight, its parts forming new unions with one another or with like-minded nationalities in neighboring states. The old interwar national state based on territory and political sovereignty looks to be a mere transitional development.

The tendencies of what I am here calling the forces of Jihad and the forces of McWorld operate with equal strength in opposite directions, the one driven by parochial hatreds, the other by universalizing markets, the one recreating ancient subnational and ethnic borders from within, the other making national borders porous from without. They have one thing in common: neither offers much hope to citizens looking for practical ways to govern themselves democratically. If the global future is to pit Jihad's centrifugal whirlwind against McWorld's centripetal black hole, the outcome is unlikely to be democratic — or so I will argue.

McWORLD, OR THE GLOBALIZATION OF POLITICS

Four imperatives make up the dynamic of McWorld: a market imperative, a resource imperative, an information-technology imperative, and an ecological imperative. By shrinking the world and diminishing the salience of national borders, these imperatives have in combination achieved a considerable victory over factiousness and particularism, and not least of all over their most virulent traditional form — nationalism. It is the realists who are now Europeans, the utopians who dream nostalgically of a resurgent England or Germany, perhaps even a resurgent Wales or Saxony. Yesterday's wishful cry for one world has yielded to the reality of McWorld.

Source: Originally published in *The Atlantic Monthly*, March 1992, pp. 53–65. Revised as the introduction to *Jihad Versus McWorld* (Times Books, 1995), a volume that discusses and extends themes of the original article. Reprinted by permission of the author.

The Market Imperative

Marxist and Leninist theories of imperialism assumed that the quest for ever-expanding markets would in time compel nation-based capitalist economies to push against national boundaries in search of an international economic imperium. Whatever else has happened to the scientistic predictions of Marxism, in this domain they have proved farsighted. All national economies are now vulnerable to the inroads of larger, transnational markets within which trade is free, currencies are convertible, access to banking is open, and contracts are enforceable under law. In Europe, Asia, Africa, the South Pacific, and the Americas such markets are eroding national sovereignty and giving rise to entities — international banks, trade associations, transnational lobbies like OPEC and Greenpeace, world news services like CNN and the BBC, and multinational corporations than increasingly lack a meaningful national identity — that neither reflect nor respect nationhood as an organizing or regulative principle.

The market imperative has also reinforced the quest for international peace and stability, requisites of an efficient international economy. Markets are enemies of parochialism, isolation, fractiousness, war. Market psychology attenuates the psychology of ideological and religious cleavages and assumes a concord among producers and consumers — categories that ill fit narrowly conceived national or religious cultures. Shopping has little tolerance for blue laws, whether dictated by pub-closing British paternalism, Sabbath-observing Jewish Orthodox fundamentalism, or no-Sunday-liquor-sales Massachusetts Puritanism. In the context of common markets, international law ceases to be a vision of justice and becomes a workaday framework for getting things done — enforcing contracts, ensuring that governments abide by deals, regulating trade and currency relations, and so forth.

Common markets demand a common language, as well as a common currency, and they produce common behaviors of the kind bred by cosmopolitan city life everywhere. Commercial pilots, computer programmers, international bankers, media specialists, oil riggers, entertainment celebrities, ecology experts, demographers, accountants, professors, athletes — these compose a new breed of men and women for whom religion, culture, and nationality can seem only marginal elements in a working identity. Although sociologists of everyday life will no doubt continue to distinguish a Japanese from an American mode, shopping has a common signature throughout the world. Cynics might even say that some of the recent revolutions in Eastern Europe have had as their true goal not liberty and the right to vote but well-paying jobs and the right to shop (although the vote is proving easier to acquire than consumer goods). The market imperative is, then, plenty powerful; but, notwithstanding some of the claims made for "democratic capitalism," it is not identical with the democratic imperative.

The Resource Imperative

Democrats once dreamed of societies whose political autonomy rested firmly on economic independence. The Athenians idealized what they called autarky, and tried for a while to create a way of life simple and austere enough to make the polis genuinely self-sufficient. To be free meant to be independent of any other community or polis. Not even the Athenians were able to achieve autarky, however: human nature, it turns out, is dependency. By the time of Pericles, Athenian politics was inextricably bound up with a flowering empire held together by naval power and commerce — an empire that, even as it appeared to enhance Athenian might, ate away at Athenian independence and autarky. Master and slave, it turned out, were bound together by mutual insufficiency.

The dream of autarky briefly engrossed nineteenth-century America as well, for the underpopulated, endlessly bountiful land, the cornucopia of natural resources, and the natural barriers of a continent walled in by two great seas led many to believe that America could be a world unto itself. Given this past, it has been harder for Americans than for most to accept the inevitability of interdependence. But the rapid depletion of resources even in a country like ours, where they once seemed inexhaustible, and the maldistribution of arable soil and mineral resources on the planet, leave even the wealthiest societies ever more resource-dependent and many other nations in permanently desperate straits.

Every nation, it turns out, needs something another nation has; some nations have almost nothing they need.

The Information-Technology Imperative

Enlightenment science and the technologies derived from it are inherently universalizing. They entail a quest for descriptive principles of general application, a search for universal solutions to particular problems, and an unswerving embrace of objectivity and impartiality.

Scientific progress embodies and depends on open communication, a common discourse rooted in rationality, collaboration, and an easy and regular flow and exchange of information. Such ideals can be hypocritical covers for power-mongering by elites, and they may be shown to be wanting in many other ways, but they are entailed by the very idea of science and they make science and globalization practical allies.

Business, banking, and commerce all depend on information flow and are facilitated by new communication technologies. The hardware of these technologies tends to be systemic and integrated — computer, television, cable, satellite, laser, fiber-optic, and microchip technologies combining to create a vast interactive communications and information network that can potentially give every person on earth access to every other person, and make every datum, every byte, available to every set of eyes. If the automobile was, as George Ball once said (when he gave his blessing to a Fiat factory in the Soviet Union during the Cold War), "an ideology on four wheels," then electronic telecommunication and information systems are an ideology at 186,000 miles per second — which makes for a very small planet in a very big hurry. Individual cultures speak particular languages; commerce and science increasingly speak English; the whole world speaks logarithms and binary mathematics.

Moreover, the pursuit of science and technology asks for, even compels, open societies. Satellite footprints do not respect national borders; telephone wires penetrate the most closed societies. With photocopying and then fax machines having infiltrated Soviet universities and *samizdat* literary circles in the eighties, and computer modems having multiplied like rabbits in communism's bureaucratic warrens thereafter, *glasnost* could not be far behind. In their social requisites, secrecy and science are enemies.

The new technology's software is perhaps even more globalizing than its hardware. The information arm of international commerce's sprawling body reaches out and touches distinct nations and parochial cultures, and gives them a common face chiseled in Hollywood, on Madison Avenue, and in Silicon Valley. Throughout the 1980s one of the most-watched television programs in South Africa was *The Cosby Show*. The demise of apartheid was already in production. Exhibitors at the 1991 Cannes film festival expressed growing anxiety over the "homogenization" and "Americanization" of the global film industry when, for the third year running, American films dominated the awards ceremonies. America has dominated the world's popular culture for much longer, and much more decisively. In November of 1991 Switzerland's once insular culture boasted best-seller lists featuring *Terminator 2* as the No. 1 movie, *Scarlett* as the No. 1

book, and Prince's *Diamonds and Pearls* as the No. 1 record album. No wonder the Japanese are buying Hollywood film studios even faster than Americans are buying Japanese television sets. This kind of software supremacy may in the long term be far more important than hardware superiority, because culture has become more potent than armaments. What is the power of the Pentagon compared with Disneyland? Can the Sixth Fleet keep up with CNN? McDonald's in Moscow and Coke in China will do more to create a global culture than military colonization ever could. It is less the goods than the brand names that do the work, for they convey life-style images that alter perception and challenge behavior. They make up the seductive software of McWorld's common (at times much too common) soul.

Yet in all this high-tech commercial world there is nothing that looks particularly democratic. It lends itself to surveillance as well as liberty, to new forms of manipulation and covert control as well as new kinds of participation, to skewed, unjust market outcomes as well as greater productivity. The consumer society and the open society are not quite synonymous. Capitalism and democracy have a relationship, but it is something less than a marriage. An efficient free market after all requires that consumers be free to vote their dollars on competing goods, not that citizens be free to vote their values and beliefs on competing political candidates and programs. The free market flourished in junta-run Chile, in military-governed Taiwan and Korea, and, earlier, in a variety of autocratic European empires as well as their colonial possessions.

The Ecological Imperative

The impact of globalization on ecology is a cliché even to world leaders who ignore it. We know well enough that the German forests can be destroyed by Swiss and Italians driving gas-guzzlers fueled by leaded gas. We also know that the planet can be asphyxiated by greenhouse gases because Brazilian farmers want to be part of the twentieth century and are burning down tropical rain forests to clear a little land to plough, and because Indonesians make a living out of converting their lush jungle into toothpicks for fastidious Japanese diners, upsetting the delicate oxygen balance and in effect puncturing our global lungs. Yet this ecological consciousness has meant not only greater awareness but also greater inequality, as modernized nations try to slam the door behind them, saying to developing nations, "The world cannot afford your modernization; ours has wrung it dry!"

Each of the four imperatives just cited is transnational, transideological, and transcultural. Each applies impartially to Catholics, Jews, Muslims, Hindus, and Buddhists; to democrats and totalitarians; to capitalists and socialists. The Enlightenment dream of a universal rational society has to a remarkable degree been realized — but in a form that is commercialized, homogenized, depoliticized, bureaucratized, and, of course, radically incomplete, for the movement toward McWorld is in competition with forces of global breakdown, national dissolution, and centrifugal corruption. These forces, working in the opposite direction, are the essence of what I call Jihad.

JIHAD, OR THE LEBANONIZATION OF THE WORLD

OPEC, the World Bank, the United Nations, the International Red Cross, the multinational corporation ... there are scores of institutions that reflect globalization. But they often appear as ineffective reactors to the world's real actors: national states and, to an ever greater degree, subnational factions in permanent rebellion against uniformity and integration — even the kind represented by universal law and justice. The headlines feature these players regularly: they are cultures, not countries; parts, not wholes; sects, not religions; rebellious factions and dissenting minorities at war not just with globalism but with the traditional nation-state. Kurds, Basques, Puerto Ricans, Ossetians, East Timoreans, Québécois, the Catholics of Northern Ireland, Abkhasians, Kurile Islander Japanese, the Zulus of Inkatha, Catalonians, Tamils, and, of course, Palestinians — people without countries, inhabiting nations not their own, seeking smaller worlds within borders that will seal them off from modernity.

A powerful irony is at work here. Nationalism was once a force of integration and unification, a movement aimed at bringing together disparate clans, tribes, and cultural fragments under new, assimilationist flags. But as Ortega y Gasset noted more than sixty years ago, having won its victories, nationalism changed its strategy. In the 1920s, and again today, it is more often a reactionary and divisive force, pulverizing the very nations it once helped cement together. The force that creates nations is "inclusive," Ortega wrote in *The Revolt of the Masses*. "In periods of consolidation, nationalism has a positive value, and is a lofty standard. But in Europe everything is more than consolidated, and nationalism is nothing but a mania...."

This mania has left the post-Cold War world smoldering with hot wars; the international scene is little more unified than it was at the end of the Great War, in Ortega's own time. There were more than thirty wars in progress last year, most of them ethnic, racial, tribal, or religious in character, and the list of unsafe regions doesn't seem to be getting any shorter. Some new world order!

The aim of many of these small-scale wars is to redraw boundaries, to implode states and resecure parochial identities: to escape McWorld's dully insistent imperatives. The mood is that of Jihad: war not as an instrument of policy but as an emblem of identity, an expression or community, an end in itself. Even where there is no shooting war, there is fractiousness, secession, and the quest for ever smaller communities. Add to the list of dangerous countries those at risk: In Switzerland and Spain, Jurassian and Basque separatists still argue the virtues of ancient identities, sometimes in the language of bombs. Hyperdisintegration in the former Soviet Union may well continue unabated — not just a Ukraine independent from the Soviet Union but a Bessarabian Ukraine independent from the Ukrainian republic; not just Russia severed from the defunct union but Tatarstan severed from Russia. Yugoslavia makes even the disunited, ex-Soviet, nonsocialist republics that were once the Soviet Union look integrated, its sectarian fatherlands springing up within factional motherlands like weeds within weeds within weeds. Kurdish independence would threaten the territorial integrity of four Middle Eastern nations. Well before the current cataclysm Soviet Georgia made a claim for autonomy from the Soviet Union, only to be faced with its Ossetians (164,000 in a republic of 5.5 million) demanding their own self-determination within Georgia. The Abkhasian minority in Georgia has followed suit. Even the good will established by Canada's once promising Meech Lake protocols is in danger, with Francophone Quebec again threatening the dissolution of the federation. In South Africa the emergence from apartheid was hardly achieved when friction between Inkatha's Zulus and the African National Congress's tribally identified members threatened to replace Europeans' racism with an indigenous tribal war. After thirty years of attempted integration using the colonial language (English) as a unifier, Nigeria is now playing with the idea of linguistic multiculturalism — which could mean the cultural breakup of the nation into hundreds of tribal fragments. Even Saddam Hussein has benefited from the threat of internal Jihad, having used renewed tribal and religious warfare to turn last season's mortal enemies into reluctant allies of an Iraqi nationhood that he nearly destroyed.

The passing of communism has torn away the thin veneer of internationalism (workers of the world unite!) to reveal ethnic prejudices that are not only ugly and deep-seated but increasingly murderous. Europe's old scourge, anti-Semitism, is back with a vengeance, but it is only one of many antagonisms. It appears all too easy to throw the historical gears into reverse and pass from a Communist dictatorship back into a tribal state.

Among the tribes, religion is also a battlefield. ("Jihad" is a word whose genetic meaning is "struggle" — usually the struggle of the soul to avert evil. Strictly applied to religious war, it is used only in reference to battles where the faith is under assault, or battles against a government that denies the practice of Islam. My use here is rhetorical, but does follow both journalistic practice and history.) Remember the Thirty Years War? Whatever forms of Enlightenment universalism might once have come to grace such historically related forms of monotheism as Judaism, Christianity, and Islam, in many of their modern incarnations they are parochial rather than cosmopolitan, angry rather than loving, proselytizing rather than ecumenical, zealous rather than rationalist, sectarian rather than deistic, ethnocentric rather than universalizing. As a result, like the new forms of hypernationalism, the new expressions of religious fundamentalism are fractious and pulverizing, never integrating. This is religion as the Crusaders knew it: a battle to the death for souls that if not saved will be forever lost.

The atmospherics of Jihad have resulted in a breakdown of civility in the name of identity, of comity in the name of community. International relations have sometimes taken on the aspect of gang war — cultural turf battles featuring tribal factions that were supposed to be sublimated as integral parts of large national, economic, postcolonial, and constitutional entities.

THE DARKENING FUTURE OF DEMOCRACY

These rather melodramatic tableaux vivants do not tell the whole story, however. For all their defects, Jihad and McWorld have their attractions. Yet, to repeat and insist, the attractions are unrelated to democracy. Neither McWorld nor Jihad is remotely democratic in impulse. Neither needs democracy; neither promotes democracy.

McWorld does manage to look pretty seductive in a world obsessed with Jihad. It delivers peace, prosperity, and relative unity — if at the cost of independence, community, and identity (which is generally based on

difference). The primary political values required by the global market are order and tranquillity, and freedom — as in the phrases "free trade," "free press," and "free love." Human rights are needed to a degree, but not citizenship or participation — and no more social justice and equality than are necessary to promote efficient economic production and consumption. Multinational corporations sometimes seem to prefer doing business with local oligarchs, inasmuch as they can take confidence from dealing with the boss on all crucial matters. Despots who slaughter their own populations are no problem, so long as they leave markets in place and refrain from making war on their neighbors (Saddam Hussein's fatal mistake). In trading partners, predictability is of more value than justice.

The Eastern European revolutions that seemed to arise out of concern for global democratic values quickly deteriorated into a stampede in the general direction of free markets and their ubiquitous, television-promoted shopping malls. East Germany's Neues Forum, that courageous gathering of intellectuals, students, and workers which overturned the Stalinist regime in Berlin in 1989, lasted only six months in Germany's mini-version of McWorld. Then it gave way to money and markets and monopolies from the West. By the time of the first all-German elections, it could scarcely manage to secure three percent of the vote. Elsewhere there is growing evidence that *glasnost* will go and *perestroika* — defined as privatization and an opening of markets to Western bidders — will stay. So understandably anxious are the new rulers of Eastern Europe and whatever entities are forged from the residues of the Soviet Union to gain access to credit and markets and technology — McWorld's flourishing new currencies — that they have shown themselves willing to trade away democratic prospects in pursuit of them: not just old totalitarian ideologies and command-economy production models, but some possible indigenous experiments with a third way between capitalism and socialism, such as economic cooperatives and employee stock-ownership plans, both of which have their ardent supporters in the East.

Jihad delivers a different set of virtues: a vibrant local identity, a sense of community, solidarity among kinsmen, neighbors, and countrymen, narrowly conceived. But it also guarantees parochialism and is grounded in exclusion. Solidarity is secured through war against outsiders. And solidarity often means obedience to a hierarchy in governance, fanaticism in beliefs, and the obliteration of individual selves in the name of the group. Deference to leaders and intolerance toward outsiders (and toward "enemies within") are hallmarks of tribalism — hardly the attitudes required for the cultivation of new democratic women and men capable of governing themselves. Where new democratic experiments have been conducted in retribalizing societies, in both Europe and the Third World, the result has often been anarchy, repression, persecution, and the coming of new, noncommunist forms of very old kinds of despotism. During the past year, Havel's velvet revolution in Czechoslovakia was imperiled by partisans of "Czechland" and of Slovakia as independent entities. India seemed little less rent by Sikh, Hindu, Muslim, and Tamil infighting than it was immediately after the British pulled out, more than forty years ago.

To the extent that either McWorld or Jihad has a *natural* politics, it has turned out to be more of an antipolitics. For McWorld, it is the antipolitics of globalism: bureaucratic, technocratic, and meritocratic, focused (as Marx predicted it would be) on the administration of things — with people, however, among the chief things to be administered. In its politico-economic imperatives McWorld has been guided by laissez-faire market principles that privilege efficiency, productivity, and beneficence at the expense of civic liberty and self-government.

For Jihad, the antipolitics of tribalization has been explicitly antidemocratic: one-party dictatorship, government by military junta, theocratic fundamentalism — often associated with a version of the *Führerprinzip* that empowers an individual to rule on behalf of a people. Even the government of India, struggling for decades to model democracy for a people who will soon number a billion, longs for great leaders; and for every Mahatma Gandhi, Indira Gandhi, or Rajiv Gandhi taken from them by zealous assassins, the Indians appear to seek a replacement who will deliver them from the lengthy travail of their freedom.

THE CONFEDERAL OPTION

How can democracy be secured and spread in a world whose primary tendencies are at best indifferent to it (McWorld) and at worst deeply antithetical to it (Jihad)? My guess is that globalization will eventually vanquish retribalization. The ethos of material "civilization" has not yet encountered an obstacle it has been unable to thrust aside. Ortega may have grasped in the 1920s a clue to our own future in the coming millennium.

Everyone sees the need of a new principle of life. But as always happens in similar crises — some people attempt to save the situation by an artificial intensification of the very principle which

has led to decay. This is the meaning of the "nationalist" outburst of recent years ... things have always gone that way. The last flare, the longest; the last sigh, the deepest. On the very eve of their disappearance there is an intensification of frontiers — military and economic.

Jihad may be a last deep sigh before the eternal yawn of McWorld. On the other hand, Ortega was not exactly prescient; his prophecy of peace and internationalism came just before blitzkrieg, world war, and the Holocaust tore the old order to bits. Yet democracy is how we remonstrate with reality, the rebuke our aspirations offer to history. And if retribalization is inhospitable to democracy, there is nonetheless a form of democratic government that can accommodate parochialism and communitarianism, one that can even save them from their defects and make them more tolerant and participatory: decentralized participatory democracy. And if McWorld is indifferent to democracy, there is nonetheless a form of democratic government that suits global markets passably well — representative government in its federal or, better still, confederal variation.

With its concern for accountability, the protection of minorities, and the universal rule of law, a confederalized representative system would serve the political needs of McWorld as well as oligarchic bureaucratism or meritocratic elitism is currently doing. As we are already beginning to see, many nations may survive in the long term only as confederations that afford local regions smaller than "nations" extensive jurisdiction. Recommended reading for democrats of the twenty-first century is not the U.S. Constitution or the French Declaration of Rights of Man and Citizen but the Articles of Confederation, that suddenly pertinent document that stitched together the thirteen American colonies into what then seemed a too loose confederation of independent states but now appears a new form of political realism, as veterans of Yeltsin's new Russia and the new Europe created at Maastricht will attest.

By the same token, the participatory and direct form of democracy that engages citizens in civic activity and civic judgment and goes well beyond just voting and accountability — the system I have called "strong democracy" — suits the political needs of decentralized communities as well as theocratic and nationalist party dictatorships have done. Local neighborhoods need not be democratic, but they can be. Real democracy has flourished in diminutive settings: the spirit of liberty, Tocqueville said, is local. Participatory democracy, if not naturally apposite to tribalism, has an undeniable attractiveness under conditions of parochialism.

Democracy in any of these variations will, however, continue to be obstructed by the undemocratic and antidemocratic trends toward uniformitarian globalism and intolerant retribalization which I have portrayed here. For democracy to persist in our brave new McWorld, we will have to commit acts of conscious political will — a possibility, but hardly a probability, under these conditions. Political will requires much more than the quick fix of the transfer of institutions. Like technology transfer, institution transfer rests on foolish assumptions about a uniform world of the kind that once fired the imagination of colonial administrators. Spread English justice to the colonies by exporting wigs. Let an East Indian trading company act as the vanguard to Britain's free parliamentary institutions. Today's well-intentioned quick-fixers in the National Endowment for Democracy and the Kennedy School of Government, in the unions and foundations and universities zealously nurturing contacts in Eastern Europe and the Third World, are hoping to democratize by long distance. Post Bulgaria a parliament by first-class mail. Fed Ex the Bill of Rights to Sri Lanka. Cable Cambodia some common law.

Yet Eastern Europe has already demonstrated that importing free political parties, parliaments, and presses cannot establish a democratic civil society; imposing a free market may even have the opposite effect. Democracy grows from the bottom up and cannot be imposed from the top down. Civil society has to be built from the inside out. The institutional superstructure comes last. Poland may become democratic, but then again it may heed the Pope, and prefer to found its politics on its Catholicism, with uncertain consequences for democracy. Bulgaria may become democratic, but it

may prefer tribal war. The former Soviet Union may become a democratic confederation, or it may just grow into an anarchic and weak conglomeration of markets for other nations' goods and services.

Democrats need to seek out indigenous democratic impulses. There is always a desire for self-government, always some expression of participation, accountability, consent, and representation, even in traditional hierarchical societies. These need to be identified, tapped, modified, and incorporated into new democratic practices with an indigenous flavor. The tortoises among the democratizers may ultimately outlive or outpace the hares, for they will have the time and patience to explore conditions along the way, and to adapt their gait to changing circumstances. Tragically, democracy in a hurry often looks something like France in 1794 or China in 1989.

It certainly seems possible that the most attractive democratic ideal in the face of the brutal realities of Jihad and the dull realities of McWorld will be a non-federal union of semi-autonomous communities smaller than nation-states, tied together into regional economic associations and markets larger than nation-states — participatory and self-determining in local matters at the bottom, representative and accountable at the top. The nation-state would play a diminished role, and sovereignty would lose some of its political potency. The Green movement adage "Think globally, act locally" would actually come to describe the conduct of politics.

This vision reflects only an ideal, however — one that is not terribly likely to be realized. Freedom, Jean-Jacques Rousseau once wrote, is a food easy to eat but hard to digest. Still, democracy has always played itself out against the odds. And democracy remains both a form of coherence as binding as McWorld and a secular faith potentially as inspiriting as Jihad.

Chapter 21

CANADA AND FREE TRADE: WHY DID IT HAPPEN?

R. JACK RICHARDSON

INTRODUCTION

On January 1, 1989 the Canada–USA Trade Agreement, otherwise known as "Free Trade," was implemented. Over the past four years there have been countless debates about the costs and benefits of this deal. These debates began when the idea was first conceived, continued throughout the negotiations, and persist even now. The purpose of this paper is *not* to add to this ongoing discussion. Instead, the purpose is to attempt to explain *why* this agreement was pursued so doggedly and ultimately consummated by the Government of Canada.

When campaigning for the leadership of the Progressive Conservative Party in 1983, Brian Mulroney declared that Free Trade was not for Canada.

> *This country could not survive with a policy of unfettered free trade.... We'd be swamped. We have in many ways a branch-plant economy.... All that would happen with that kind of concept would be the boys cranking up their plants throughout the United States in bad times and shutting their entire branch plants in Canada.... Free Trade with the United States is like sleeping with an elephant. It's terrific until the elephant twitches, and if it ever rolls over, you're a dead man. That's why free trade was decided in an election in 1911. It affects Canadian sovereignty and we will have none of it, not during the leadership campaign or at any other time (Mulroney, 1983).*

When campaigning in the 1984 election, he never once supported the Free Trade idea. Yet, six months later, he and President Reagan proclaimed mutual support for a Free Trade deal at the "Shamrock Summit." During this term of office, he persevered with a very difficult process to conclude the Free Trade negotiations and to obtain passage of the enabling legislation through the House of Commons.

The present government is notable for tailoring election issues to the polls. Yet, throughout the evolution of the Free Trade negotiations, and certainly going into the last election, more Canadians opposed the agreement than supported it. Nevertheless, the Progressive Conservatives called an election in which this became the dominant issue.

Thus, despite all these contradictions, the Mulroney Government steadfastly pursued a difficult process to conclude the Free Trade negotiations and ultimately to pass the enabling legislation. How do we explain this paradox?

The explanation that I will propose is based on two basic concepts. The first could be termed the "Power Balance Model" — i.e., the stronger and more organized the dominant class and the weaker and less organized the subordinate class(es), the greater the degree to which the state will reflect the interests of the dominant class and hence the lesser the degree of state autonomy.

The second concept, of Finance Capital, will be used to analyse the degree of strength and organization of the dominant (capitalist) class. We will begin with this element of the analysis.

Source: Excerpted from "Free Trade: Why Did It Happen?" *Canadian Review of Sociology and Anthropology* 29, 3 (1992): 307–28. Reprinted by permission of the publisher.

THE THEORY OF FINANCE CAPITAL

The concept of finance capital refers to two parallel processes. One is the growth and concentration of financial and non-financial corporations. The other is the development of market and non-market ties, such as shareholdings and directorship interlocks, between and among these two sets of corporations (Hilferding, 1970). The theory proposes that the largest and most profitable financial and non-financial corporations that dominate the economy are interconnected by these relationships into a cohesive network that provides the social cement for this dominant group.

Harvey (1982) proposes that the modern state rests on the foundation of finance capital with its economic domination by a few huge financial-industrial complexes. These tend to set the pace of economic growth of a society. Thus, it is to the advantage of the state to act in the best interests of finance capital to achieve the political benefits of economic growth (Hilferding, 1970; Harvey, 1982).

In turn, the interlocked spheres of interest of finance capitalists provide the social cement which unites this "inner circle" and permits it to establish not only economic hegemony but also political leadership (Useem, 1984; Ornstein, 1984; Carroll, 1986; Richardson, 1990). Indeed, Useem (1984) shows that the "inner circle" has been very effective in imposing the views of finance capital on governments.

The Canadian economy has historically been notable for the development of huge, centralized economic institutions (Innis, 1971) and a high degree of economic concentration — e.g.:

> Already [i.e., pre-World War I] it is estimated, less than fifty men control $4,000,000,000, or more than one-third of Canada's material wealth as expressed in railways, banks, factories, mines, land and other properties and resources (Myers, 1972: xxxi).

The concentration of the Canadian economy continues to-day, and, indeed, has been increasing recently (Grabb, 1990). For example, the top 100 enterprises account for 66.9 per cent of corporate assets controlled by the 400,000 Canadian companies (Khemani, 1988). Thus, the remaining 399,900 enterprises account for less than one-third of Canadian corporate assets. To put these data in perspective, this degree of corporate concentration is more than twice the level found in the economies of Canada's largest trading partners — the United States, Germany and Japan (Marfels, 1988). Thus, it seems reasonable to

conclude, in concordance with finance capital theory, that a few huge enterprises can wield market power over the nearly 400,000 smaller firms who fight for survival in the competitive marketplace.

Traditionally, the big banks have dominated the Canadian financial realm. The banks' recent takeover of virtually all the large Canadian-controlled investment dealers has increased the strength and operational diversity of these institutions. On the other hand, there has been a dramatic rise in the strength of the Canadian trust industry. By 1984 the assets which the trusts control and administer amounted to more than 80 per cent of the Canadian assets of the banks. This trust industry is also highly concentrated, as the four largest trust companies now control over three-quarters of all trust company assets (Richardson, 1988). In Quebec, two huge new financial institutions have emerged as important actors in the emergence of a domestically-controlled economy. The government-controlled Caisse de dépôt et placement du Québec has rapidly become Canada's largest pension fund and controls $37 billion in assets. Close behind is the credit union network Confédération des Caisses Populaires et d'Économie Desjardins du Quebec, with $30 billion in assets (*The Globe and Mail*, March 16, 1990; March 20, 1990). These two institutions now rank right behind the big five banks in size. Thus, although the banks' domination of the Canadian financial realm is now diminished, the whole financial industry remains highly concentrated and dominated by about 11 huge financial enterprises.

On the other side of the financial–non-financial interface, there has recently been growing concentration and conglomeration among non-financial enterprises. After a decline between 1969 and 1978, the conglomerate part of the Canadian economy has grown rapidly. In fact, Niosi concludes:

> The rise of conglomerate concentration, if it proceeds at the same swift pace of the latest period, will produce a new type of economy and society. Far from the mythical model of pure and perfect competition, and rather different also from the more realistic imperfect or oligopolistic schemes, new types of enterprises and markets are emerging that challenge our present understanding of Canadian society (1978: 16).

Looking specifically at non-financial enterprises, I studied the *Financial Post*'s data for the 397 largest non-financial corporations for the years 1978 and 1987 to analyse the process of corporate concentration.[1] We find that, during this period, Canadian-controlled corporate assets of *Financial Post*'s largest corporations increased from 43 to 50 per cent, while the foreign-controlled proportion declined from 29 to 25 per cent and there was a decrease from 27 to 24 per cent in the government sector.

However, these data were compiled on the basis of individual corporations. Analysis of corporate concentration is more appropriately conducted when the unit of analysis is the enterprise (which may include several corporations under common control). Consequently, I collapsed the Canadian corporate sector into enterprises. In 1987, there were 17 enterprises with assets over $3 billion. This seemed a reasonable number and size of enterprises that could collectively dominate the Canadian corporate economy.

In 1978 the 17 largest enterprises controlled 63.6 per cent of the assets of *Financial Post*'s largest Canadian corporations. By 1987, 74.5 per cent of the assets of the 186 largest Canadian non-financial corporations were controlled by just 17 dominant enterprises. More detailed analysis indicates that much of this increase in the share of the economy controlled by these powerful corporations resulted from acquisitions — i.e., ten of the 30 largest enterprises in 1978 disappeared as they were taken over by four giant conglomerates.

In 1987, 25 per cent of the assets of the *Financial Post* 500 companies were foreign-controlled. This segment, too, is becoming more concentrated. Just two years ago, for example the giant Imperial Oil Limited acquired Texaco Canada and Amoco acquired Dome Petroleum. From all of this, we can conclude that corporate concentration, a fundamental defining characteristic of finance capital, is increasingly present to a remarkable degree in the Canadian economy.

The concept of finance capital rests on integration as well as corporate concentration. Directorship interlocks among the dominant corporations are one means of achieving a degree of integration. The most extensive studies of Canadian directorship interlocks were derived from a data base comprising all the interlocks between the 200 largest financial and non-financial firms over the period from 1946 to 1976 (Carroll, Fox and Ornstein, 1982). They found that nearly all these firms were tightly linked in a single dense network. Within this network, the five big Canadian banks served as the principle nodes integrating both the different economic sectors and the Canadian- and foreign-controlled firms. The structure of this network was found to predominantly fulfil an integrative function, rather than one of planned liaisons between individual firms (Ornstein, 1984; Carroll, 1986; Richardson, 1987).

Recent analysis has shown that, as the banks' domination of the financial realm declined in the 1980s, their predominant position in the network of directorship interlocks also diminished. Nevertheless, they continue to provide bridges which link the various cliques in the Canadian inter-corporate network (Carroll, 1989).

While the structure of directorship interlock networks can be proposed as evidence of economic integration, evidence of inter-corporate ownership is even more compelling. Since profit is the ultimate objective of capitalist enterprise, joint ownership among the dominant enterprises would tie them inexorably together in pursuit of common goals. Indeed, a dense network of inter-enterprise ownership would clearly provide the structural foundation for the ascendancy of common interests over narrow and parochial ones.

We find that 15 of the 17 dominant Canadian-controlled enterprises participate with others in this hegemonic group in joint ownership. That is, they hold significant minority shareholdings in each other and/or jointly hold with other dominant enterprises significant shareholdings in enterprises which are not among the top 17. This is a very dense network of inter-enterprise ownership. In fact, over 44 per cent of all possible connections between enterprises have been made. This pervasive inter-corporate ownership among the dominant Canadian non-financial enterprises provides further and more compelling evidence that the concept of finance capital applies to contemporary Canada. It also clearly demonstrates the structural integration that has taken place among the enterprises that account for three-quarters of the activity of large Canadian corporations.

Beyond economic integration in general terms, the integration of financial and non-financial capital pools is a key element of the concept of finance capital. A chain of developments began in the 1970s which transformed the relationships between Canadian financial and non-financial realms. One such development is associated with the emergence of the large, powerful and highly concentrated trust industry. Within the last decade every one of the ten largest Canadian trust companies (which collectively control over 90% of the trust company assets) has been acquired by nine rapidly-growing non-financial conglomerates — most of which are among the 17 dominant enterprises in Canada.

The Canadian insurance industry is another important source of long-term capital for industrials — historically a far greater one than the trusts. In the past decade, this industry (with the exception of mutual companies which are owned by their policy holders) has largely been acquired by several of the huge non-financial conglomerates. These same dominant non-financials have also acquired the three largest Canadian merchant banks. Thus, the dominant Canadian non-financials make huge inroads into the financial sector through their control of the trust industry, insurance and merchant banking.

This analysis of recent developments in the proliferation of ownership ties between financials and non-financials extends Carroll's (1989) conclusions concerning the recomposition of Canadian finance capital derived from his analysis of directorship interlock networks. It also indicates a significant recent increase in both corporate concentration and financial–non-financial integration. These latter developments inevitably produce a new and higher degree of cohesion, unity and strength for the hegemonic group of enterprises which comprises Canadian finance capital.

The recent transformation of Canadian finance capital has both economic and social consequences. The concentration and integration of economic institutions is replacing the decisions of hundreds of thousands of independent actors in the Canadian market with decision-making by the small group of 17 dominant enterprises, backed up by access to huge financial resources, and a similarly small group of foreign-controlled multinationals. Traditional fiscal and monetary devices to affect economic activity have relied on their effect on a myriad of independent corporate decisions. Now, instead, if economic policy is to be effective, it must be negotiated with a very small group of economic actors. This places these economic actors in a position where they can exercise veto power on many governmental initiatives. Ultimately, the state tends to follow the priorities of the powerful group of finance capitalists in order to obtain the advantages of economic growth (Harvey, 1982). Because of the dense interconnections among the dominant enterprises in the economy, it also becomes easier for this group to perceive their collective interests and to articulate them.

In this section I have demonstrated the transformation and strength of Canadian finance capital. However, there are other classes in Canada and other actors in Canadian political economy. To analyse more fully why the interests of finance capital won the day, we turn now to the Power Balance Model.

THE POWER BALANCE MODEL

According to the Power Balance Model, the degree of state autonomy is a function of the balance of power and resources between the dominant and subordinate class(es) (Brym, 1985; 1989). That is, the greater the relative strength of subordinate classes, the greater the degree to which the state can respond to subordinate class demands (Cuneo, 1979; Korpi, 1983; Gourevitch, 1977; Kurth, 1979; Skocpol, 1980). Indeed, given the constraint that their actions sustain the capitalist system, the greater is the need for politicians and state officials to respond to these demands in order to keep their jobs (Brym, 1985).

Historically, the Canadian capitalist class has been relatively strong, oligopolistic and densely interlocked (Brym, 1989; Ornstein, 1989). In fact, the current Canadian network of directorship interlocks is among the most centralized and dense of any of the advanced capitalist economies (Ornstein, 1989). The Canadian working class, on the other hand, has been comparatively weak. By international standards (with the significant exception of the United States), the degree of unionization is low. A Canadian working class party has never been represented in a federal cabinet, let alone formed a federal government (Brym, 1989). The agricultural classes have also been historically weak in Canada. Laxer (1989) persuasively documents the elements of this historical weakness and their consequences on the balance of power. The result of this historical relative strength of the Canadian capitalist class, combined with the relative weakness of subordinate classes, has been a comparatively weak, non-intrusionist state (Atkinson and Coleman, 1989; Brym, 1989).

There have, of course, been variations in this power balance, and consequently in the autonomy of the Canadian state, over time. The period from World War II to the 1981–82 recession was one of comparatively high labour strength. For example, the state finally responded favourably to working class demands for Unemployment Insurance (Cuneo, 1979). The 1960s and 1970s may be recalled as the golden years of organized labour in Canada. In these two decades, unions went from strength to strength. Total union membership more than doubled and union density increased significantly, as well. At the same time, business concentration and integration had not yet reached the degree that the foregoing analysis demonstrates that it achieved in the 1980s. Atkinson and Coleman also conclude that business's associational system lacked "the integrational and organizational capacity to aggregate business interests in a manner that transcends narrow, short-term concerns" (1989: 47). The result was the rise of the *comparatively* autonomous and interventionist state of the Trudeau era (Brym, 1989).

Things have changed since the 1981–82 recession. We have seen that there has been a significant increase in corporate concentration in the last decade. There has also been an integration of financial and non-financial capital, which ties it into a tightly-knit network of common interests. This new structure provides the conditions under which general class interests can override the narrow concerns of individual firms. The cohesiveness also provides a source of strength which business can use to press its interests on government.

One of these collective interests is Free Trade. The large conglomerates which form the heart of Canadian finance capital have been growing so quickly and have such major sources of capital at their disposal that their major challenge has been to find opportunities for further expansion (Francis, 1986). These opportunities are limited in Canada because the large conglomerates already control three-quarters of the assets that are worth acquiring. Therefore, expansion to the United States is the logical next step. Indeed, several of these dominant enterprises have already made some very large American acquisitions (Carroll, 1989; Richardson, 1990). Secure access to American corporate assets via a Free Trade Agreement is thus of the utmost importance to the perceived interest of these burgeoning giants.

This economic structure produced the ideal conditions under which its institutional counterpart — the Business Council on National Issues (BCNI) could emerge. Formed in 1976 as a reaction to the Trudeau era, its membership consists of the chief executive officers of 150 leading Canadian corporations (Langille, 1987). Important among this membership are the 17 dominant Canadian non-financial enterprises, which provide 27 of these members. The BCNI fulfils the important function of linking these with other large Canadian and foreign-controlled non-financials and the big banks (Table 21.1). Thus, its membership integrates all of the key sectors of the Canadian economy — the resource/staples sector, the financial sector, the domestic manufacturing sector processing staples and the foreign manufacturing sector producing consumer goods (Atkinson and Coleman, 1989). Langille concludes that this institution has performed very effectively as a business lobby group:

The current harmonious relationship between capital and the Canadian state is the product of a successful capitalist offensive to reduce the autonomy of a state which appeared to be growing beyond their control (1987: 70).

Table 21.1 BCNI Membership

17 Dominant enterprises	27
Other Canadian non-financials	40
Foreign-controlled non-financials	41
Government-controlled non-financials	2
Total non-financial	110
Big banks and their subsidiaries	11
Other Canadian financials	11
Foreign-controlled financials	8
Total financial	30
Law, Accounting and Consulting firms	7
Trade associations	3
Total BCNI membership	150

Source: Business Council on National Issues (1989).

There are many areas in which the interests of finance capital and its institutional manifestation the BCNI converge. Reductions in the deficit, the welfare state and the size of government are important among these. Free Trade is also important.

Multinationals, by definition, favour the free flow of capital, goods and services (Milner, 1987). The multinational segment of the Canadian economy includes not only foreign-controlled firms, but also Canadian-controlled multinationals. In fact, direct investment by Canadian multinationals in the United States is growing so rapidly that by 1985 it amounted to 60 per cent of American direct investment in Canada. At current growth rates it could be equal by 1991 (Niosi, 1982; 1985; *The Globe and Mail,* Feb. 26, 1988).

The resources/staples sector of the Canadian economy exists, primarily, to supply the American market. Although their products, by and large, are not subject to American tariffs, they *have* been harassed by formal and informal import quotas, and other protectionist trade measures. Consequently, this sector would strongly favour any trade agreement that would help provide secure access to the American market. The Canada–United States Trade Agreement, allegedly, will help provide them with this security.

At the time of the National Policy and to a lesser degree in 1911, Canadian manufacturing industry was protectionist. Since that time, much of this industry has come under foreign control. Other large Canadian-controlled manufacturers have become multinationals. Both of these groups would logically favour Free Trade, as noted above. So would the segment that produces semi-finished goods for export. Thus, we see that the general interest of the manufacturing segment of the economy is served by Free Trade.

The interests of the financial sector are more ambivalent. To the extent that Free Trade improves the profitability and enhances expansion of the above sectors, financial institutions gain profitable outlets for capital. Canadian banks would gain national treatment in the United States, which facilitates their expansion activity south of the border. However, the banks would face significantly increased competition from the proposed national treatment of American financial institutions in Canada. (In fact, American Express, which gained a banking licence on July 1, 1990, is getting *better than* national treatment — allegedly in return for their support of Free Trade in the United States). However, by far the most dynamic segment of the Canadian financial industry is that which has been acquired by the dominant non-financial enterprises. For this key segment of the Canadian economy, the overriding objective is access to national treatment to expand and operate in the United States.

All of these developments have been taking place within the current internationalization of the global economy. In part, they are a result of the profound changes that this wider development has promoted. The implication of these changes is that capital, more than ever before, knows no boundaries (Fennema and van der Pijl, 1987; Carroll, 1989). It is flowing ever more freely from jurisdiction to jurisdiction. This mobility of capital, along with the continuing immobility of labour, increases the relative power of capital vis-à-vis labour on the global scene. Closer to home, Marchak argues:

> The Agreement, like the ideology of "free markets" and like the whole of the "new right" economics, is profoundly attached to individualism, and specifically to the rights of individual investors to move their capital around as they please (1989: 223).

We have seen that Canadian big business has been vastly strengthened by the recent developments in concentration and integration, that the interests of finance capital converged in favour of Free Trade and that it has developed a powerful institutional voice — the BCNI. But the Power Balance Model requires that we show more than this. What about the strength of subordinate classes?

Organized labour has been substantially weakened over the past decade. Canadian union density has fallen from a peak of 40 per cent in 1983 to 36.2 per cent in 1989 — the lowest percentage since 1974.

Even with this decline, however, Canadian union density remains more than double the percentage in the United States (Coates, Arrowsmith and Courchene, 1989). Thus, Free Trade would weaken Canadian labour even further as it puts it into more direct competition with non-unionized and low-waged American workers.

Equally important is increasing heterogeneity as a factor which weakens the strength and organizational unity of labour. Lash and Urry (1987) extensively document the increasing heterogeneity of the labour force in Western Europe and the resultant weakening of labour's power and influence in the political arena. In Canada, this fragmentation can be seen in many related developments. In 1977 the Canadian Labour Congress (CLC) contained over 70 per cent of organized workers, whereas by 1989 this proportion within the CLC had declined to only 57.8 per cent (Kumar and Coates, 1989). Furthermore, almost all the jobs created since 1982 have been in the service sector (which now employs seven out of ten workers, versus less than half in the 1950s). In this sector, "a vast and increasing majority of jobs are low-paying, low-skill, less secure and largely non-unionized" (Kumar and Coates, 1989: 6). In fact, between 1981 and 1988, the average annual increase in part-time employment was 3.4 per cent, while it was only 1.2 per cent for full-time employment (McKitrick, 1989). Part-time jobs are, of course, much less likely than full-time jobs to be unionized.

This decline in union density, fragmentation of the labour force and downgrading of jobs has had its effects on labour's political power and influence. When the Progressive Conservative government first entered office it spent a total of $1.7 billion (in constant 1981 dollars) on labour market programs such as direct job creation, national job training, the Canada Mobility Programme, etc. By 1987–88, these expenditures had declined to $1.1 billion (McKitrick, 1989). Since then, the Unemployment Insurance Programme has been gutted, reducing federal funding on labour programs even further. All this seems a good indicator of the waning influence of labour and the increasing influence of capital on the Canadian federal government.

One observer notes the weakness of organized labour by contrasting:

> the floundering CLC response to free trade with the strong and effective campaign by senior citizens against the de-indexing of Old Age Security in the mid-1980s. The seniors, with virtually no

*resources and infrastructure, forced the govern-
ment to retract its legislation. The CLC, with
more than two million members and an integrated national and provincial network at its
disposal, provided neither the organizing skills
nor the leadership needed for an effective campaign against free trade (Werlin, 1990).*

While this does indicate the results of the increasing fragmentation and reduced union density of
labour, it speaks more to the *balance* of power between
the dominant and subordinate class. Grey power was
effective in the mid-1980s partly because its objectives
were not explicitly opposed to the central thrust of
finance capital. Not only did the interests of labour
and finance capital directly clash over Free Trade, but
finance capital's increasing strength and unity had
given it increased power — and thus reduced the state's
autonomy in the interim.

With respect to the agricultural classes, Laxer
(1989) extensively documented their historical weakness and fragmentation along ethnic lines. This weakness has been exacerbated by the long term movement
of people off the farm,[2] and the dramatic decline in
world wheat prices over the past decade. Currently the
French-English ethnic division remains and a regional
division over Free Trade has weakened the agricultural
class even further. The export farm sector is concentrated in Western Canada. The Canadian Cattlemen's
Association has mobilized much of this sector to push
for liberalized international trade. On the other hand,
the supply-managed sector is concentrated in Ontario
and Quebec. It is fearful of the impact of trade liberalization in general and of CUSTA in particular on the
viability of their farm economy. In sum, the declining
and badly weakened agricultural classes can wield little
power against the might of finance capital.

We have seen, then, that the consolidation of finance
capital has significantly strengthened the Canadian capitalist class. Conversely, the strength of labour and agriculture — the subordinate classes — has declined. The
result, according to the Power Balance Model, is a significant reduction in the autonomy of the state.

Evidence of this reduced autonomy can be seen in
its starkest form by contrasting the interventionist
Trudeau era of the mid-1970s with the actions of the
present government. During the former era, state policy centred on the Foreign Investment Review Agency
(FIRA), Canadianization, the NEP, the Anti-Inflation
Board, crown corporations and regulation. A decade
later, FIRA and the NEP have been scrapped, the
monetary policy of the "free market" and high interest

rates has replaced legislated wage and price controls,
virtually all regulated industries have been deregulated,
crown corporations are being privatized and government policy focuses on internationalization rather than
Canadianization.

We can also see the reduced autonomy of the state
by contrasting the strong federal state of the 1970s
with its dramatically weaker counterpart a decade later.
Meech Lake was the constitutional manifestation of
this development because it emasculated the federal
government's power to set the Canadian socio-
economic agenda. For example, McNaught writes:

*Already the federal power, the power that could
still speak and act for a dangerously diminished
Canada, is menaced by the midnight madness of
Meech Lake (McNaught, 1990).*

The present government did not rely solely on
Meech Lake, however, to begin this devolution of
power. It is intentionally diminishing its influence in
the key policy area of Health, Education and Welfare.
In the brief period between 1984–85 (the year the Progressive Conservatives took office) and 1988–89, federal transfer payments to the provinces within this
envelope have declined from 4.4 per cent to 3.9 per
cent of GDP, and from 28.1 per cent to 22.9 per cent
of provincial spending on Health, Education and Welfare (Donner, 1990). The subsequent 1990 and 1991
federal budgets make a substantial further reduction in
federal contributions and influence in this area.

We see that the power and influence of the Canadian state has declined very significantly over the past
few years. It declines even further with the implementation of CUSTA because this agreement significantly
restricts the government's ability to act in the economic realm (and many propose in the social realm as
well). Since Free Trade is seen to be in the interest of
finance capital, it should be no surprise that it became
the policy of the present government: according to the
Power Balance Model, the state's autonomy had significantly declined.

STRUCTURE VERSUS AGENCY[3]

To this point, the argument has been exclusively structural. Structural changes, which strengthened the dominant class and weakened the subordinate classes, have
been shown to produce the conditions which should
reduce the degree of autonomy of the state. But what
about agency? How were these favourable structural
conditions *utilized* by the dominant class to produce
their potential result? The massive intervention to

achieve Free Trade (which we have shown to be in the interests of finance capital) provides an ideal example of such agency.

The voice of finance capital, the BCNI began to lobby for Free Trade as early as 1981 (Salutin, 1989). It later used its clout to convince the Macdonald Commission of the importance of a free trade deal with the United States. In fact, Donald Macdonald took the unprecedented step of promoting such a deal *before* the Commission had concluded its deliberations (Drache and Cameron, 1985; Langille, 1987). By 1984, their efforts to persuade the new federal government began to pay off. The Minister for International Trade, James Kelleher, incorporated the BCNI position at a forum for lowering tariffs, removing non-trade barriers and solving disputes in his discussion paper on "How to Secure and Enhance Canadian Access to Export Markets." Then the BCNI urged Prime Minister Mulroney to begin discussions with the United States and travelled to the United States to meet with business leaders and cabinet leaders for the same reason (Langille, 1987: 68). By this time, Langille concludes, the BCNI "has become the most powerful and effective interest group in Canada — to the point where it can now exercise hegemony over both the private sector and the state" (1987: 70).[4] Thomas D'Aquino, President of the BCNI, illustrated his own conception of its power as the voice of finance capital vis-à-vis other institutions by claiming "no one tells us what to do — no one. We do what we want to when we want to do it" (quoted in the *The Toronto Star*, Nov. 17, 1988).

By 1987, the BCNI added a new dimension to its efforts to promote the Canada-United States Trade Agreement by forming a single-issue lobby group, the Canadian Alliance for Trade and Job Opportunities (CATJO) (Langille, 1987; Salutin, 1989). CATJO then began to crank up a massive promotional campaign. Nick Filmore concludes that business spent over $18 million in the two years leading up to the 1988 election promoting Free Trade (Salutin, 1989: 269).

Specifically, during this Free Trade election, CATJO spent $4.2 million on political advertising alone. Never before has the Canadian electorate been exposed to such a massive campaign. In fact, the funds CATJO pumped into the campaign exceeded the combined total spending of the two opposition parties (*The Toronto Star*, Nov. 22, 1988; *Time*, Dec. 5, 1988). In the end, this massive spending simply overwhelmed the opposing Pro-Canada Network's highly effective cartoon booklet, "What's the Big Deal?", which cost a mere $700,000 (Salutin, 1989: 260). CATJO's four-page spread

appeared four times in the last three weeks of the election campaign in all the major Canadian newspapers, and in other media as well (Salutin, 1989: 171, 179, 188). Two weeks before the election, two members of the BCNI took further action. The Canadian Chamber of Commerce urged its 170,000 members to hold workplace meetings with employees to pressure them to support Free Trade, and the Canadian Manufacturers' Association did the same (Salutin, 1989: 172).

This "unprecedented media campaign of the business community" (Brodie, 1989: 180) had its effect. Just before the media blitz, the Gallup and Angus Reid polls showed Canadian opinion was strongly against Free Trade — by 42 per cent to 34 per cent and 54 per cent to 35 per cent, respectively (Salutin, 1989: 142, 154). The Gallup poll published November 17 (but taken prior to CATJO's blitz) showed the Liberals with a strong lead, with 43 per cent of the electorate, compared to the PC's 31 per cent and NDP's 22 per cent support (Salutin, 1989: 193). However, by the time of the November 21st election, opinion had (temporarily) swung in favour of Free Trade and the Tories won the election with a plurality of 43 per cent of the votes. Brodie captures the essence of this fusion of structure and agency, as she concludes: "The most unique aspect of the 1988 campaign was the unprecedented unity and overt involvement of the capitalist class" (1989: 181).

It would be foolish to conclude that the actions of finance capital and its instruments, the BCNI and CATJO, were the *only* influences on the outcome of the Free Trade election. There were, of course, others. Perhaps the most noteworthy of these was the ineptitude of the opposition parties. The Liberals suffered an unpopular leader and even endured an aborted "Palace Revolt" during the campaign. The NDP virtually ignored Free Trade — *the* issue of the election — and campaigned harder and more effectively against the Liberals than against the Tories during the crucial final two weeks. Nevertheless, the above account clearly demonstrates finance capital's effectiveness in promoting Free Trade to the Mulroney government, and then in intervening in the ensuing election.

NOTES

The author gratefully acknowledges the perceptive comments of Robert Brym, Carl Cuneo, Claude Denis, Harvey Krahn, Gordon Laxer, Michael Smith and the Sociology Editor and anonymous reviewers of the *CRSA*, as well as the research assistance of Sandra Badin. This is a revised version of a paper presented at the Annual Meetings of the Canadian Sociology and Anthropology Association, Victoria, May, 1990.

1. These data were derived from the *Financial Post* (1979; 1988). Both issues reported the 500 largest non-financial corporations. However, their method of compilation changed during this period. To achieve consistency, I had to eliminate some of the smallest firms in a few industries for the year 1978. The largest 397 firms survived and are compared with the 397 largest firms reported for 1987.

2. In the 1890s, farmers and farm workers comprised nearly half the Canadian workforce. This proportion declined to one-quarter by the 1940s and one-tenth by the 1960s (Leacy, 1983: Table D86–106). See also the discussions in Cuneo (1984); Darroch (1991) and Hunter (1986).

3. The author is indebted to Gordon Laxer and two anonymous CRSA reviewers for pointing out the lack of attention to agency and historiography in a previous draft.

4. Others, however, are not so sanguine about the power of the BCNI. Although not contesting its influence on Free Trade, some point to its *lack* of success in other policy areas (Coleman, 1986; 1988; Ornstein, 1989).

REFERENCES

Atkinson, Michael M., and William D. Coleman. 1989. *The State, Business and Industrial Change in Canada.* Toronto: University of Toronto Press.

Brodie, Janine. 1989. "The 'Free Trade' election." *Studies in Political Economy* 28 (Spring): 175–82.

Brym, Robert J. 1985. "The Canadian capitalist class, 1965–1985." Pp. 1–20 in Robert J. Brym, ed., *The Structure of the Canadian Capitalist Class.* Toronto: Garamond.

———. 1989. "Canada." Pp. 177–206 in Tom Bottomore and Robert J. Brym, eds., *The Capitalist Class: An International Study.* New York: New York University Press.

Business Council on National Issues. 1989. *Membership.* Ottawa: Business Council on National Issues.

Campbell, R.M. 1989. "Post mortem on the Free Trade election." *Journal of Canadian Studies* 24(1): 3, 4, 163–65.

Carroll, William K. 1986. *Corporate Power and Canadian Capitalism.* Vancouver: University of Vancouver Press.

———. 1989. "Neoliberalism and the recomposition of finance capital in Canada." *Capital and Class* 38: 81–112.

Carroll, William K., John Fox, and Michael D. Ornstein. 1982. "The network of directorship interlocks among the largest Canadian firms." *The Canadian Review of Sociology and Anthropology* 19(1): 44–69.

Coates, Mary Lou, David Arrowsmith, and Melanie Courchene. 1989. *The Labour Movement and Trade Unionism.* Kingston: Industrial Relations Centre, Queen's University.

Coleman, William D. 1986. "Canadian business and the state." Pp. 243–90 in Keith Banting, ed., *The State and Economic Interests.* Toronto: University of Toronto Press.

———. 1988. *Business and Politics: A Study of Collective Action.* Toronto: University of Toronto Press.

Cuneo, Carl J. 1979. "State, class and reserve labour: the case of the 1941 Canadian Unemployment Insurance Act." *The Canadian Review of Sociology and Anthropology* 16(2): 147–70.

———. 1984. "Has the traditional petite bourgeoisie persisted?" *Canadian Journal of Sociology* 9: 269–301.

Darroch, Gordon. 1991. "Class and Stratification." Pp. 225–56 in Lorne Tepperman and R. Jack Richardson, eds., *The Social Bond* (2nd ed.). Toronto: McGraw-Hill Ryerson.

Donner, Arthur. 1990. "Ottawa shedding economic control." *The Toronto Star.* Toronto, March 12.

Drache, Daniel, and Duncan Cameron. 1985. "Introduction." Pp. ix–xxxix in Daniel Drache and Duncan Cameron, eds., *The OTHER Macdonald Report.* Toronto: Lorimer.

Fennema, Meindert. 1982. *International Networks of Banks and Industry.* The Hague: Martinus Nijhoff.

Fennema, Meindert, and Kees van der Pijl. 1987. "International bank capital and the new liberalism." Pp. 298–319 in Mark S. Mizruchi and Michael Schwartz, eds., *Intercorporate Relations: The Structural Analysis of Business.* Cambridge: Cambridge University Press.

Financial Post. 1979. *Survey of Industrials: The Financial Post Industry's 500.* Toronto: Financial Post.

———. 1988. *Survey of Industrials: The Financial Post Industry's 500.* Toronto: Financial Post.

Francis, Diane. 1986. *Controlling Interest.* Toronto: Macmillan.

Gold, David, Clarence Lo, and E.O. Wright. 1975. "Recent developments in Marxist theories of the capitalist state." *Monthly Review* 27(5): 29–43.

Gourevitch, P.A. 1977. "International trade, domestic coalitions, and liberty: Comparative responses to the crisis of 1873–1896." *Journal of Interdisciplinary History* VIII(2): 281–313.

Grabb, Edward G. 1990. "Who owns Canada? Concentration of ownership and the distribution of economic assets, 1975–1985." *Journal of Canadian Studies* 25(2): 72–93.

Hamilton, Nora. 1981. "State autonomy and dependent capitalism in Latin America." *British Journal of Sociology* 32(3): 305–29.

Harvey, David. 1982. *The Limits to Capital.* Oxford: Basil Blackwell.

Hilferding, Rudolf. 1970. *Le Capital Financier.* Paris: Editions de Minuit [1910].

Hunter, Alfred. 1986. *Class Tells*, 2nd ed. Toronto: Butterworths.

Innis, Harold A. 1971. *A History of the Canadian Pacific Railway.* Toronto: University of Toronto Press [1923].

Khemani, R.S. 1988. "The dimensions of corporate concentration in Canada." Pp. 17–38 in R.S. Khemani, D.M. Shapiro, and W.T. Stanbury, eds., *Mergers, Corporate*

Concentration and Power in Canada. Halifax: The Institute for Research on Public Policy.

Korpi, Walter. 1983. *The Democratic Class Struggle*. London: Routledge and Kegan Paul.

Kumar, Pradeep, and Mary Lou Coates. 1989. *Industrial Relations in 1989: Trends and Emerging Issues*. Kingston: Industrial Relations Centre, Queen's University.

Kurth, James R. 1979. "The political consequences of the product cycle: Industrial history and political outcomes." *International Organization* 33(1): 1–34.

Kuttner, Robert. 1989. "Bloc that Trade: The second marriage of Keynes and Adam Smith." *New Republic* April 17: 18.

Langille, David. 1987. "The Business Council on National Issues and the Canadian State." *Studies in Political Economy* 24: 41–85.

Lash, Scott, and John Urry. 1987. *The End of Organized Capitalism*. Madison: University of Wisconsin Press.

Laxer, Gordon. 1989. *Open for Business: The Roots of Foreign Ownership in Canada*. Toronto: Oxford University Press.

Leacy, F.H., ed. 1983. *Historical Statistics of Canada*. Ottawa: Statistics Canada.

Marchak, M.P. 1989. "The Ideology of Free Trade: A Response to Smith." *Canadian Public Policy — Analyse de Politiques* XV(2): 220–25.

Marfels, Christian. 1988. "Aggregate concentration in international perspective." Pp. 53–88 in R.S. Khemani, D.M. Shapiro, and W.T. Stanbury, eds., *Mergers, Corporate Concentration and Power in Canada*. Halifax: Institute for Research on Public Policy.

Marx, Karl. 1963. *The Eighteenth Brumaire of Louis Bonaparte*. New York: International Publishers.

McKitrick, Ross. 1989. *The Economy and Labour Markets*. Kingston: Industrial Relations Centre, Queen's University.

McNaught, Kenneth. 1990. "Canada's heritage squandered." *The Globe and Mail*, January 16.

Milibrand, Ralph. 1977. *Marxism and Politics*. London: Oxford University Press.

Milner, H. 1987. "Resisting the protectionist temptation: Industry and the making of trade policy in France and the United States during the 1970s." *International Organization* 41(4): 639–65.

Mintz, Beth, and Michael Schwartz. 1985. *The Power Structure of American Business*. Chicago: University of Chicago Press.

Mulroney, Brian. 1983. Address to the National Leadership Convention of the Progressive Conservative Party, June (Quoted in *The Toronto Star,* July 22, 1988).

Myers, Gustavus. 1972. *A History of Canadian Wealth*. Toronto: Lorimer [1914].

Niosi, Jorge. 1978. *The Economy of Canada*. Montreal: Black Rose.

———. 1982. *Les Multinationales Canadiennes*. Montreal: Boreal.

———. 1985. "Continental Nationalism: The strategy of the Canadian bourgeoisie." Pp. 53–66 in Robert J. Brym, ed., *The Structure of the Canadian Capitalist Class*. Toronto: Garamond.

Ornstein, Michael D. 1984. "Interlocking directorates in Canada: Intercorporate or class alliance." *Administrative Science Quarterly* 29: 210–31.

———. 1989. "The social organization of the Canadian capitalist class in comparative perspective." *The Canadian Review of Sociology and Anthropology* 26(1): 151–77.

Pfeffer, Jeffrey, and Gerald R. Salancik. 1978. *The External Control of Organizations*. New York: Harper and Row.

Richardson, R. Jack. 1987. "Directorship interlocks and corporate profitability." *Administrative Science Quarterly* 32: 367–86.

———. 1988. " 'A sacred trust': The trust industry and Canadian economic structure." *The Canadian Review of Sociology and Anthropology* 25(1): 1–22.

———. 1990. "Economic concentration and social power in contemporary Canada." Pp. 341–51 in James Curtis and Lorne Tepperman, eds., *Images of Canada: The Sociological Tradition*. Scarborough: Prentice-Hall.

Salutin, Rick. 1989. *Waiting for Democracy*. Markham: Viking.

Scott, John. 1985. *Corporations, Classes and Capitalism*, 2nd ed. London: Hutchinson.

Skocpol, Theda. 1980. "Political response to capitalist crisis: Neo-Marxist theories of the state." *Politics and Society* 10: 155–201.

Statistics Canada. 1988. *Intercorporate Ownership*. Ottawa: Supply and Services Canada.

Useem, Michael. 1984. *The Inner Circle*. New York: Oxford University Press.

Werlin, Dave. 1990. "New leadership needed." *The Globe and Mail*, February 7.

Wright, Eric Olin. 1978. *Classes, Crises and the State*. London: New Left Books.

Chapter 22

THE QUEBEC QUESTION

ROBERT J. BRYM

After the English conquest in 1760 New France changed dramatically.[1] However, a policy of strict domination and assimilation, such as would be applied to the aboriginal peoples, was unworkable in New France. The *Canadiens* were nearly as numerous as the aboriginal peoples in the northern half of the continent, but much more densely settled and technologically advanced. The British recognized that any attempt to impose the Church of England, the English language, and English civil law in the former French colony could result in unacceptably high levels of conflict. They therefore sought to accommodate two *Canadien* elite groups, the agricultural landowners and the Catholic establishment, in the belief that these elites would build up loyalty to Britain among the population as a whole. But while the rights and privileges of the landowners and the clergy were reinforced, the position of a third elite, the merchants engaged mainly in the fur trade, was undermined. Commerce was taken over by the British. The wealthier *Canadien* merchants consequently returned to France; their less prosperous colleagues stayed, but were allowed neither to take delivery of goods from France nor to establish ties with British trading firms. As a result, most of the remaining *Canadien* merchants became farmers.

In this manner, business became a British domain, agriculture, religion, and politics the province of the French. This pattern of ethnic stratification remained more or less intact for two hundred years. True, by 1950 most farmers had been transformed into urban, industrial workers. A modest contingent of *Québécois* had become physicians, lawyers, and members of the "new middle class" of administrators, technicians, sci-

entists, and intellectuals. But the upper reaches of the stratification system remained overwhelmingly British-controlled. Thus, in 1961, British-origin men in Montreal earned on average 49 percent more than French-origin men; in the province of Quebec, people of English origin were 57 percent more likely than those of French origin to be professionals and managers, and 45 percent less likely to be blue-collar workers; in Canada as a whole, there was only a handful of French-origin captains of industry.[2]

Apart from its quite rigid system of ethnic stratification, Quebec in mid-century was remarkable because of its undeveloped government services. Health, education, and welfare were largely controlled by the Catholic church. Intervention of the government in economic matters was almost unknown. As a result of this political backwardness, members of Quebec's new middle class, together with unionized workers, began campaigning to modernize the provincial political system in the late 1940s. They pressed for more liberal labor laws that would recognize the right of all workers to strike. They wanted state control over education and a new curriculum that stressed the natural and social sciences rather than classical languages and catechism. They desired a government that would supply a wide range of social services to the population. They demanded that the state provide better infrastructure for economic development and assist francophone entrepreneurs expand their businesses. The partial realization of these aims in the course of the 1960s came to be known as the "Quiet Revolution." Because of the Quiet Revolution, Quebec could by the early 1970s boast a political system as advanced as that of any other Canadian province.

Source: "Race and Ethnicity," in Irving M. Zeitlin with Robert J. Brym, *The Social Condition of Humanity*, Canadian ed. (Toronto: Oxford University Press, 1991), pp. 166–69. © Oxford University Press Canada 1991. Reprinted by permission of the publisher.

Nonetheless, the modernization of the Quebec state failed to resolve a set of interrelated issues: the potential demographic decline of the *Québécois*, the assimilation of immigrants into English culture, the persistent ethnic stratification of Quebec society, and the continued use of English as the language of private industry.

In 1956 *Québécois* women were giving birth to more children on average than women in any other province. But by 1981 they were giving birth to fewer children on average than women in any other province — indeed, considerably fewer than the 2.1 children that women must on average bear in order to ensure that the size of the population does not decline.[3] Reviewing this trend in the 1970s, many *Québécois* began to feel that they were fast becoming an endangered species. Such fears were reinforced by the preference of most new immigrants in Quebec to send their children to English-language schools. Together, these basic demographic processes threatened to diminish the size — and therefore, potentially, the power — of Quebec's francophone population.

It also became apparent during the 1970s that upper management positions in the private sector remained the preserve of English-origin Canadians. The Quiet Revolution helped create many thousands of jobs for highly educated francophones in the government bureaucracy, the educational system, and in new Crown corporations such as Hydro-Québec. But English remained the language of choice in the private sector because the largest and technologically most advanced businesses were controlled by English Canadians and Americans. This situation was felt particularly keenly when the expansion of the state sector slowed down in the early 1970s and the francophone new middle class therefore reached the limits of its upward mobility. Figures on the Canada-wide ethnic distribution of income illustrate the problem. In 1961 Canadians of English origin earned on average 28 percent more than Canadians of French origin. By 1971 the occupational effects of the Quiet Revolution had reduced the English advantage to 10 percent. But fifteen years later, in 1986, improvement in the French position had halted and even reversed: Canadians of English origin were earning 11 percent more than Canadians of French origin. The English advantage was greater in Quebec considered alone and greater still in Montreal considered alone.[4]

In the 1960s the Quebec state had intervened energetically in the life of the francophone community in order to ensure its survival and improve its status. But because of the problems just listed it became clear to many *Québécois* in the course of the 1970s and 1980s that the survival and prosperity of their community also required active state intervention in non-francophone institutions. Many *Québécois* came to believe that most shares of banks, trust companies, and insurance firms should be held in Quebec and these financial institutions should be obliged to reinvest their profits in the province. It was also commonly argued that the state should increase its role as economic planner and initiator of development and should forbid foreign ownership in cultural enterprises. Finally, the *Québécois* increasingly demanded compulsory French-language education for the children of most immigrants; obligatory use of French in private sector upper management; and the mandatory use of French-only signs in public places.

The great majority of English Quebeckers viewed all these proposed changes as a danger to their economic well-being and an infringement on their minority rights. But most *Québécois* regarded them as the only means by which their community could survive and attain equality with the anglophones. Moreover, since the Quebec state did not have the legal authority to enact some of the proposed changes, most *Québécois* felt that the province ought to negotiate broader constitutional powers. A substantial minority of *Québécois* went a step further: they were convinced that Quebec ought to become a politically sovereign nation, albeit economically associated with Canada.

In 1976 the pro-independence *Parti québécois* won the provincial election. In 1980 it held a referendum to see whether Quebeckers favored "sovereignty-association." On the whole, they did not: 59.6 percent of the population voted against the government's proposition, 40.4 percent for it. Even among francophones the "yes" vote reached only 48 percent. The francophones most likely to vote "yes" were between 21 and 35 years of age. Voting "yes" was also associated with having a higher education, with being a union member, with working in the public sector, and with not practicing Catholicism.[5]

Quebec nationalism was markedly weakened by the referendum defeat. Partly for that reason, the *Parti québécois* lost the 1985 provincial election.

And shortly thereafter the new Liberal government of the province demonstrated that it was willing to soften Quebec's constitutional demands. In 1982 all the provinces except Quebec had signed the Canadian Constitution. The Quebec Liberals now agreed to endorse that document, thereby giving up the decades-long struggle to increase Quebec's constitutional powers.

Before signing, Quebec asked only that a few modest demands be endorsed by the federal government and the other provinces. These demands were set out in the 1987 Meech Lake Accord. Among the most important provisions of the Accord was a declaration that Quebec is a "distinct society" that has the right to preserve and promote its identity. But the Accord recognized minority language rights. And it stressed that acknowledgment of Quebec's unique status would in no way diminish either provincial or federal powers. Most of the other provisions merely entrenched established practices. In short, compared with Quebec's demands in the 1960s and 1970s for more constitutional authority, the Meech Lake Accord was pretty weak broth.

Nonetheless, two provinces, Manitoba and Newfoundland, refused to sign the Accord. And as the June 1990 ratification deadline approached, it became clear that various segments of Canadian society were in fact deeply opposed to granting Quebec special status within Confederation. In particular, women's groups, aboriginal groups, members of some other minority ethnic groups, and many Canadians in Newfoundland and the Prairies argued that ratifying the Meech Lake Accord would amount to sacrificing their rights and special interests for the sake of Quebec. As a result, the Accord was not ratified.

The *Québécois*, for their part, felt rejected, insulted, and enraged. Having asked for so little, and received nothing, they began to sense that there might not be a place for them in Confederation after all. Thus, in July 1990, a public opinion poll conducted in Quebec showed that 62.2 percent of the province's population favored sovereignty — far more than at any other time in Quebec history. In the 1994 Quebec provincial election, the *Parti québécois* was re-elected and immediately began planning a second referendum on sovereignty-association. In 1995, a second referendum on sovereignty was held in Quebec and the forces opposed to separation won by the narrowest of margins — about 1 percent. Subsequently, the charismatic Lucien Bouchard became head of the *Parti québécois*, promising a third referendum by 1998. Canada's future was again uncertain as the full legacy of the Conquest became clear.

NOTES

1. Kenneth McRoberts, *Quebec: Social Change and Political Crisis*, 3rd ed. (Toronto: McClelland and Stewart, 1988 [1976]).

2. Robert J. Brym with Bonnie J. Fox, *From Culture to Power: The Sociology of English Canada* (Toronto: Oxford University Press, 1989), 108.

3. A. Romaniuc, "Fertility in Canada: From Baby-boom to Baby-bust," *Current Demographic Analysis* (Ottawa: Statistics Canada, 1984), 14–18. This figure assumes a stable population in which the number of emigrants equals the number of immigrants.

4. Brym with Fox, *Culture to Power*, 108; *Dimensions: Profile of Ethnic Groups: Census Canada 1986* (Ottawa: Statistics Canada, 1989), 1–7, 1–8; 1971 *Census of Canada: Profile Studies: Ethnic Origins of Canadians*, Vol. 5, Part 1 (Ottawa: Statistics Canada, 1977), 68, 76; *Royal Commission on Bilingualism and Biculturalism Report: The Work World*, Book 3A, Parts 1 and 2 (Ottawa: Queen's Printer, 1969), 16. Income data for 1961 are for males only. Canada-wide figures are given because 1986 Quebec and Montreal breakdowns have not been published.

5. McRoberts, *Quebec*, 327–29.

Chapter 23

CANADIAN COURTS, DEMOCRACY, AND ABORIGINAL ISSUES

W.A. Bogart

What is the basis for scepticism about the value of the Charter? Though presented in different forms, the arguments can be summarized in three points. The first concerns substantive outcomes and claims that the elected members of government and their agencies have been the more effective vehicle for improving the lives of most Canadians in many circumstances. The second relates to process and asserts that the best chance for a vigorous, responsive, and respected democracy comes from elected representatives. The third is about the costs of access to the courts which privilege the powerful and organized and thus allow them disproportionate use of judicial review, either to dismantle legislation and programs or to shield themselves from attack by government or other groups. These three points are comparative. This is not to deny that courts have sometimes acted in admirable ways[1] or that there have been some progressive — even visionary — judges: on the Supreme Court alone names such as Rand, Laskin, Dickson, and Wilson easily come to mind. Nor is it to claim that legislatures and their agents have always reached just outcomes by adequate processes. What is contended is that, relatively, the chance for greatest justice will come from legislatures.

The first argument claims that assistance of the disadvantaged and the poor, as well as ordinary citizens, has more often happened because of legislative action.[2] Whether in health, occupational safety, workers' rights,

housing, peace and order in the streets, or other aspects of life, the advancement has come because of the popular support of political will. In this view, government, while open to searing criticisms about waste and inefficiency, has also been the agent of civilizing and progressive change. It has mediated between those who wish *laissez-faire* and the enrichment of the few (regardless of the consequences) and those who insist upon a basic claim to entitlement for all. Conversely, this argument contends that the historical record reveals that courts, rather than achieving conditions to nurture and protect ordinary people in their everyday lives, have instead been uncaring or actively hostile. The explanation for this lies in an embrace of liberal ideology and an active suspicion of the political process as intrusion upon the purity of the judge-made common law that did not develop to meet these ends. State regulation and programs, designed to be responsive to the concerns of such people, have often been cut back under the guise of interpretation of statutes when in reality it was to allow the ideas of the judiciary to hold sway.

History prompts many sceptics to be wary of judges and to prefer the hazards of the legislative processes to handle the complex social and economic problems of Canadian society. In discussing the intrusiveness of the courts in reviewing administrative action, Arthurs observed: "[T]o the extent that contemporary claims for judicial pre-eminence are based

Source: Excerpted from *Courts and Country: The Limits of Litigation and the Social and Political Life of Canada* (Toronto: Oxford University Press, 1994), pp. 267–77. © Oxford University Press Canada 1994. Reprinted by permission of the publisher.

upon the perceived superior performance of the courts, it is necessary to remind ourselves, by an examination of the historical evidence, that the courts utterly failed to deal with most significant legal repercussions of the Industrial Revolution in the nineteenth century and with the revolutions of rising expectations in the twentieth."[3] And even commentators, much more accepting of the judicial role in review of administrative action, point out the judicial indifference and awkwardness in responding to the complexities of twentieth-century society.[4]

What of civil liberties, as traditionally conceived, and the protection of minorities? There were a few valiant attempts by some judges in the implied Bill of Rights cases.[5] But we know all too well the list of cases under the actual Bill of Rights, which displayed the Supreme Court's lack of enthusiasm[6] even though it initially manifested some promise of vigour. Alan Borovoy is instructive:

> *Historically at least, Canadian judges have shown something less than enthusiasm for the principles of civil liberties. Since 1960 there has been a statutory Bill of Rights operating at least at the federal level. The language of the bill could have sustained some far-reaching protections for human rights and civil liberties. Regrettably, that same language could also support a more feeble construction. With few exceptions the senior Canadian courts chose the latter approach.*[7]

So any initial flourishes under the Charter, admirable though they might be — former Chief Justice Brian Dickson's warning that the Charter must not be a club against the disadvantaged[8] — have to be put in the balance against that record.

The second argument urges that for democracy not to be sapped but invigorated, basic decisions affecting the people must be made by elected representatives. This point does not suggest that such a process has not led to mistakes, sometimes horrible ones, such as our failure to save as many Jews as we could have in the Second World War.[9] The tragedies that beset our Amerindians is surely another. Nor does it suggest that there are not major impediments to popular participation.[10] What it argues is that concerted efforts should be exerted to eliminate them and that we should not rely upon a small unelected corps. Unlike the first argument, the concern here is not so much that judges will impose their views on a democratic majority. Rather, the worry is that critical, social, and political questions will be translated into legal issues that will be left to judges and lawyers instead of the citizenry working out acceptable and supportable solutions.[11]

In this view, even a cycle of progressive and enlightened decisions entails costs, although the results may be desirable. There may be benefits, but they come from a small group of judges and lawyers who are bound together by a limited set of ideas and attitudes and who impose conclusions rather than persuade and build consensus among the electorate. The danger is that the basis for having citizens make their own decisions and face future issues will be eroded, and that the resentment felt by having solutions handed down will make future progress even more difficult and may even contribute to regressive backlash.

The third point focuses upon the costs of any court response. The contention is that whatever meaning is possible in interpreting the Charter, it will inevitably come to be slanted towards the rich and the organized. Obviously, access to the political and bureaucratic processes is imperfect, but it is not as expensive and complicated and is available without necessarily being mediated through the language of the law, a discourse largely available only to lawyers.[12] A number of isolated figures for the costs of litigation illustrates how expensive it can be[13] and the problems this engenders has been recognized by some judges.[14] The successful argument by Southam Newspapers that a search of its offices by anticombine officials should be struck down took over two and a half years and cost about $200,000. The unsuccessful suit by Operation Dismantle to have cruise missile testing declared unconstitutional cost about $50,000, despite the fact that its lawyers charged reduced fees and the action was determined at a preliminary stage.[15]

We can further illustrate the benefits and pitfalls around Charter litigation by focusing on one of the most critical issues now facing us: Amerindians and their relationship to the rest of Canada. One can scarcely argue that historically politics and governments have done well by the First Peoples. The critical question is: will litigation move us to constructive resolution or will it deflect us further?

Their tale of hopelessness and squalor lies across our conscience. In a country with one of the highest standards of living in the world and proclaimed for its tolerance, the plight of Aboriginals is a searing exception. Yet Amerindians are no longer complacent. As with any movement for change, the law becomes a flashpoint, simultaneously reflecting inequities as well as possibilities for change. Land claims, international law, the criminal justice system and constitutional reform are prominent areas where the law and, for our purposes, the law of the judges have been closely examined. Such pressure for and expectation of change provides an excellent opportunity to examine how the ideas about the Charter and, generally, ideas about the effect of litigation are reflected in issues that make insistent claims upon our attention. Some of the sharply conflicting ideas about Charter litigation are thrown into relief by the oppressive circumstances that beset Aboriginals.

There is no serious challenge to the tale of misery. Death for Aboriginals comes mostly because of poisoning, accidents, and violence with an incidence for these three times that of Canadians as a whole. It is small wonder that there is such discrepancy in life expectancy: males, 72; native males, 60–62; females, 79; native females, 63–69. The number of Aboriginals in federal prisons doubled between 1977 and 1987; while they are only about 3 per cent of the population, they constitute 10 per cent of inmates in federal prisons. A 1985 study by the Department of Indian and Northern Affairs revealed that 38 per cent of reserve housing did not have running water, indoor toilets, and/or a bath or shower and 47 per cent failed to comply with basic standards of physical conditions. The official unemployment level has been two and a half times the overall rate. In 1981, 36 per cent of the Canadian population had some form of postsecondary education with only 19 per cent of Amerindians achieving this level, and a decade latter there is no indication that relative conditions have altered significantly.[16]

Behind these bare statistics lie tales of degradation that are scarcely describable. The media now confronts us with a continual documentation of broken communities and broken lives. Aboriginals have been relocated to accommodate mining, logging, hydroelectric dams, and for any number of other reasons, including the administrative convenience of the Department of Indian Affairs. Merely one example of this destruction through dislocation is provided by the fate of the Osnaburgh band of Ojibwa. In 1959, a small plot of land in northwestern Ontario was chosen for this band by the department because the highway made it easier to provide services. It was also the case that the nearest lake was too shallow and swampy to support the traditional fishing, housing was substandard, and the water undrinkable: "Thirty years after the relocation, the Ojibwas were suffering a 97 per cent unemployment rate, and 80 per cent had serious alcohol problems. Children as young as 10 were drinking liquor and sniffing gasoline."[17]

Yet documenting the suffering and the wrongs is one thing and redressing the tragedies is another.

Substantial differences emerge in how to address this misery, particularly concerning the role of the judges. In fairness, thoughtful commentators, regardless of their views of litigation, at least make some attempt to place law in a larger context and acknowledge that undue emphasis on litigation may actually frustrate change by obscuring the circumstances that trap Amerindians in such fundamental inequality. There are, therefore, calls for reforms to specific institutional arrangements such as fiscal policy, education policy, health care, child welfare, policing, criminal justice, resource management, and economic development and changes in political responsibilities towards the First Peoples and the dominant culture's perception of responsibility.[18] Nevertheless, these more encompassing prescriptions are generally short on how this integration of law and such channels of reform could take place. For most, the emphasis sooner or later is on the judges' role.

This literature has a number of contributors who are undoubtedly well-intentioned and make genuine attempts to be sensitive, but who nevertheless create substantial pressure to assimilate the claims of the First Peoples. The difficulties are seen as redressable through more engaged and rigorous analysis, which will guide us in our use of litigation, particularly under the Charter, and obviate angst about cultural hegemony, even while acknowledging that anxiety.[19] Once better tests are formulated, particularly to balance individual and collective aspirations and to define Aboriginal claims more precisely, the First Peoples can shelter in the warm embrace of human rights dispensed by the judiciary. One such proponent asserts:

> [The Charter] is an interpretive prism, and the refraction which it provides will protect the rights and freedoms of the aboriginal peoples of Canada.[20]
>
> ... The key challenge that remains is to translate the theoretical generalities presented here into arguments in concrete cases, for it is only by this process that ... the Constitution Act, 1982 can serve to enhance the rights of the aboriginal peoples of Canada.[21]

Such attitudes have evoked strong responses charging that "better" arguments and tests can actually disguise fundamental differences between Aboriginals and the dominant society. "Solutions" from those outside the culture can actually add to the subjugation; human rights "progress" that assimilates Amerindians' issues to those in the rest of society may itself be a form of oppression. One such reaction comes from Patricia

Monture, legal academic and Aboriginal, when re-evaluating her experiences at a conference where these issues were treated with detached and clinical analysis:

> *I do not have any control over the pain and brutality of living the life of a dispossessed person. I cannot control when that pain is going to enter my life. I had gone away for this conference quite settled with having to deal with racism, pure and simple. But, I was not ready to have my pain appropriated. I am pretty possessive about my pain. It is my pain. I worked hard for it. Some days it is all I have. Some days it is the only thing I can feel. Do not try to take that away from me too. That was what was happening to me in that discussion. My pain was being taken away from me and put on the table and poked and prodded with these sticks, these hypothetical 'Let's see what happened next.' I felt very very much under a microscope, even if it was not my own personal experience that was being examined.*[22]

The extraordinary complexities of responding to the plight of the Amerindians without doing further harm can be illustrated by looking at the work of Patrick Macklem and Mary Ellen Turpel. Both are eloquent young legal academics. Macklem is a white male, and Turpel is a woman of Aboriginal origins. Macklem represents faith in post-Charter litigation and its capacity to respond to almost any problem. Turpel is the voice of scepticism about how oppression can parade as enlightenment.

Macklem's work begins with a fine documentation of the Aboriginals' insurgency against the squalor of their lives. He then analyses at length a number of areas of law, all with judicial amplification — Aboriginal title, treaty rights and interpretation, distribution of legislative authority over First Peoples, the Aboriginal section (s. 35[6]) of the Constitution — demonstrating clearly how First Peoples' aspirations for greater control over their lives has been and is being systematically denied: "[T]he law governing native people in Canada is resistant to claims to self-government because of the unquestioned adherence to basic categories of the Anglo-Canadian legal imagination effected by the denial and acceptance of native difference. The result is a set of principles which work to establish and maintain a hierarchical relationship between native peoples and the Canadian state."[23] At this point, he invokes the ethereal to suggest that the law, particularly litigation, can be turned upon itself to redress the very problems it has created or at least

ratified ("moments of transformative possibility").[24] There are two essential building blocks to all of this. First is his citing of the insights of "post-realist scholarship" that the law is "a set of practices that constitutes economic, social and political relations among individuals and groups in society which is itself open to transformation."[25] Second, he asserts that the First Peoples have an abiding confidence in the Supreme Court: "an institution which native people trust."[26] He then goes on in some detail to show that in each of the categories discussed earlier, there are ways to reshape the existing law, which is mostly made and remade by the judges:

> *... [T]he common law of aboriginal title contains the seeds of a doctrinal approach to the nature and scope of native proprietary interests in ancestral and reserve lands which respects the fact of original occupation. The law governing the distribution of authority contains an interpretive approach with respect to the applicability of provincial laws of general application that could be extended to all forms of state regulation so as to carve out a sphere of activity immune from legislative intervention in which forms of native self-government could take root and flourish. Treaty jurisprudence ought to be refashioned so as to reconceptualize the purpose of treaties to be the protection of particular forms of self-government, and the broad and purposive method of interpretation currently accepted by the judiciary ought to be redirected so as to conform to such a purpose. Constitutional jurisprudence ought to deepen the requirement that native people be consulted in the formation of laws that affect their individual and collective identities so that native consultation and consent become preconditions of the constitutionality of laws that regulate native forms of life.*[27]

Such invocation of the courts to not only change but be transformed into our standard-bearers is a regular characteristic of post-Charter scholarship. So too is the absence of an inquiry into a central question: if Aboriginal claims (as well as those of women, visible minorities, lesbians and gays, etc.) were systematically thwarted in courts before the Charter, should we not consider that the Charter with its enhanced powers for the judges will exacerbate their plight? To talk in terms of the judges' law as "a powerful source of potential social transformation"[28] is to assume that which is highly questionable. To flatly assert that the Supreme Court is "an institution which native people trust" is to deny evidence to the contrary. Consider just one reaction, that of an elder of the Teslin Tlingit band of the Yukon: "The [C]harter puts the rights of the individual ahead of the group ... [i]n our culture, the rights of the group must come ahead of the individual."[29]

Even if there are progressive decisions from the courts — and there is some evidence of this[30] — do we not have to be fundamentally concerned that they would not "transform" but rather convert and corral what little is left of a culture that is so very different from the dominant one, including substantial diversity within itself?

In contrast to Macklem, a deeply sceptical reaction comes from Mary Ellen Turpel.[31] One of the greatest sources of this wariness is the rights paradigm, particularly as manifested in the Charter. She begins by reminding us that good intentions are not enough, that it is possible to be killed by kindness: "assistance aimed at human rights progress may actually be part of the oppression Aboriginal peoples experience."[32] But in turn the very paradigm of rights through the adjudicative model is called into question. The courts as agents for this model animated by concerns for proprietary entitlement are argued to be alien to the Amerindians:

> A traditional concern with respect to the conceptual and institutional framework for judging rights claims is the elitist and culturally-specific (European) character of the court. This concern involves both the issue of the cultural difference which arises because such a formalized adversarial and impersonal institution is unknown amongst Aboriginal peoples, and the political problem of cultural hegemony raised by the fact that the representatives of the dominant (settler) communities write and "interpret" the law for all Canadians, and do so within a conceptual framework of rights derived from the theory of a natural right to private property.[33]

As Turpel asserts, such a world view is antithetical to Aboriginals. She explains that Amerindians structure their societies around the Four Directions: trust, kindness, sharing and strength, responsibilities that each person owes to others in terms of social life. In such a context, it is difficult to even talk in terms of "rights" since there is no ownership of private property and no exclusionary spheres of social life.[34] She ends on a depressed note, starkly different from Macklem:

> It is difficult for me to see any potential for sensitivity to the cultural differences of Aboriginal peoples in the constitutional rights paradigm.... I find it impossible to be reconstructive or instrumental in my analysis.... The rights paradigm and interpretive context of Canadian constitutional law is so unreceptive to cultural differences that, as a result, it is oppressively hegemonic in its perception of its own cultural authority.[35]

A drift to the judicialization of rights to deal with fundamental problems that beset us was vividly illustrated by the ill-fated Charlottetown Accord and how it would have treated Aboriginal issues by dealing in the courts at a fundamental level. The First Peoples pushed very hard in that round for recognition of the "inherent right of self-government." As part of a many-faceted deal, such a right — undefined and only briefly described — was incorporated.[36] All the while we heard much about empowerment and autonomy and control. These are noble, essential aspirations for people who have been so marginalized and ill-treated. But at the same time we heard little about illiteracy, life expectancy, infant mortality rates, substance abuse, and the other blights that plague Aboriginals. The hope was that self-government would untap and harness the wills and abilities of the people themselves to expel these demons.[37] The fear — largely unspoken — was that self-government would be a black hole that endlessly absorbs fractious debates about forms and procedures — perhaps mostly among the people themselves — while the list of woes would advance, conscribing ever more victims for its miserable cause.

At critical points courts would have been plunged into this. The agreement stipulated that there would be a five-year period during which the respective parties were to negotiate over the meaning and implementation of self-government.[38] In addition, there appeared to be some contemplation that a specialized tribunal would make some of these decisions. What is clear is that after five years, courts would have been called upon to make a myriad of judgements at a fundamental and structural level concerning Aboriginal governments "as one of three orders,"[39] to which the Charter applied,[40] even while there were charges (some made through lawsuits) from some Amerindian women that their Charter entitlements were not sufficiently protected.[41] With virtually no guidance, the judges would have made decisions about "languages, cultures, economics, identities, institutions and traditions"[42] and, subject to any framework to be found in a subsequently negotiated accord, about "federal and provincial governments ... providing ... Aboriginal peoples with fiscal or other resources, such as land, to assist those governments to govern their own affairs...."[43]

Such wrenching decisions with unforeseen long-term consequences would have been handed over to courts with their lack of accountability and lack of involvement in the ongoing negotiation and compromise that would have been absolutely essential if this arrangement was to work. In the face of increased judicial power, politicians may recede and allow courts to grapple with issues regardless of the courts' capacity, no matter how untoward the consequences.

Yet the Charlottetown Accord failed. It was rejected for many possible reasons, some of which have had little to do with the arrangements for self-government. Nevertheless, there is substantial evidence that the Amerindians themselves were divided along several lines, including gender, and, in the end, a substantial proportion did not support the Accord.[44] One thing is certain: the rejection of the Accord was accompanied by deep dissatisfaction with popular politics. In the wake of such a mess, it would hardly be surprising if people turn increasingly to the courts, if only by default. In all of this, blaming the courts is beside the point. The critical question is whether we will have the patience and fortitude to see that judicialization of rights is no substitute for the rehabilitation of politics.

Such politics could confront the plight of our Aboriginals on a variety of fronts, including experiments with self-government that would be bold in concept and careful in execution.[45]

NOTES

1. For instance, see Russell's brief but spirited defence of the judiciary and its protection of some civil liberties based on the "pragmatic and empirical": P. Russell, "The Political Role of the Supreme Court of Canada in Its first Century" (1975), 53 *Canadian Bar Review* 576, at 592–93: "Our judges have been at their best in the field of civil liberties when, instead of being asked to theorise about such abstractions as 'equality before the law' or 'due process of law,' they have been called upon to identify the rights implicit in the working of our basic institutions of government...." Another instance of courts attempting to protect minorities occurred in the treatment of Franco-Manitobans: see K. Roach, "The Role of Litigation and the Charter in Interest Advocacy," in F. Seidle, ed., *Communities, the Charter and Interest Advocacy* (Montreal: Institute for Research on Public Policy, forthcoming).

2. P. Monahan, *Politics and the Constitution: The Charter, Federalism and the Supreme Court of Canada* (Toronto: Carswell, 1987), at 42–43.

3. H.W. Arthurs, "Jonah and the Whale: The Appearance, Disappearance and Reappearance of Administrative Law" (1980), 30 *University of Toronto Law Journal* 225, at 225–26.

4. J.M. Evans et al., eds., *Administrative Law Cases, Text and Materials*, 3rd ed. (Toronto: Emond Montgomery, 1989), 12–14.

5. For example, *Re Alberta Statutes*, [1938] Supreme Court Reports 100 and *Switzman v. Elbling*, [1957] Supreme Court Reports 285.

6. R. Cheffins and P. Johnson, *The Revised Canadian Constitution: Politics as Law* (Toronto: McGraw-Hill Ryerson, 1986), at 133, observe: "It is absolutely clear that no Canadian court has ever based a decision on the implied bill of rights."

7. A. Borovoy, *When Freedoms Collide: The Case for Our Civil Liberties* (Toronto: Lester & Orpen Dennys, 1988), at 208.

8. *Edwards Books and Arts Ltd. v. R.*, [1986] 2 Supreme Court Reports 713, at 779: "In interpreting and applying the Charter I believe that the courts must be cautious to ensure that it does not simply become an instrument of better situated individuals to roll back legislation which has as its object the improvement of the condition of less advantaged persons."

9. I. Abella and H. Troper, *None Is Too Many: Canada and the Jews of Europe, 1933–1948* (Toronto: Lester & Orpen Dennys, 1982).

10. Monahan, *Politics and the Constitution*, at 120, discussing some of the foibles.

11. P. Russell, "The Political Purposes of the Canadian Charter of Rights and Freedoms" (1983), 61 *Canadian Bar Review* 30, at 52.

12. M. Valiante and W.A. Bogart, "Helping 'Concerned Volunteers Working Out of Their Kitchens': Funding Citizen Participation in Administrative Decision Making" (1992), 31 *Osgoode Hall Law Journal* 1.

13. A. Petter, "The Politics of the Charter" (1986), 8 *Supreme Court Law Review*, at 479 et seq.

14. Ibid., 483, citing remarks made by Chief Justice Dickson to the mid-winter meeting of the Canadian Bar Association in Edmonton, 2 February 1985.

15. A point in response might be that the problem of access is not as acute as it first appears because most Charter cases involve criminal matters where there is provision for legal aid. Assuming that the amount and scope of coverage in legal aid is otherwise adequate, there are still many problems with access. First, the preponderance of criminal cases under the Charter simply invites the question of what the statistical profile would look like if there were adequate access for other kinds of issues. Second, there can be many other interests implicated in criminal cases such that any number of groups and organizations may wish to participate through intervention. Here, again, problems of resources and access arise.

16. These various statistics are taken from P. Macklem, "First Nations Self-Government and the Borders of the

Canadian Legal Imagination" (1991), 36 *McGill Law Journal* 383, at 386, and A.J. Piggner, "The Socio-Demographic Conditions of Registered Indians," in J.R. Ponting, ed., *Arduous Journey: Canadian Indians and Decolonization* (Toronto: McClelland & Stewart, 1986).

17. G. York, "Children Without a Life Seek Euphoria in Despair," *The Globe and Mail*, 6 February 1993, A3.

18. P. Macklem, "First Nations Self-Government and the Borders of the Canadian Legal Imagination" (1991), 36 *McGill Law Journal*, at 454–55.

19. W. Pentney, "The Rights of the Aboriginal Peoples of Canada in the Constitution Act, 1982: Part I — The Interpretive Prison of Section 25" (1988), 22 *University of British Columbia Law Review* 21, at 22:

    [T]his article is founded on the supposition that it is legitimate and appropriate to articulate and interpret the rights of the aboriginal peoples of Canada in a language and in the context of an institutional structure that is non-aboriginal. Many aboriginal peoples reject this approach because they do not recognize the legal and political structure as legitimate. I do not seek to dispute that view. The modest assumption....

20. Ibid., 59.

21. W. Pentney, "Part II — Section 35: The Substantive Guarantee" (1988), 22 *University of British Columbia Law Review* 207, at 278.

22. P. Monture, "Ka-Nin-Geh-Heh-Gah-E-Sa-Nonh-Yah-Gah" (1986), 2 *Canadian Journal of Women and the Law* 159, at 163–64.

23. Macklem, "First Nations Self-Government," at 394–95; see also P. Macklem and R. Townshend, "Resorting to Court: Can the Judiciary Deliver Justice for First Nations?" in D. Engelstad and J. Bird, eds., *Nation to Nation — Aboriginal Sovereignty and the Future of Canada* (Toronto: Anansi, 1992).

24. Macklem, "First Nations Self-Government," at 387.

25. Ibid., 394.

26. Ibid., 393.

27. Ibid., 455.

28. Ibid., 394.

29. D. Shoalts, "Natives Value Justice Differently," *The Globe and Mail*, 9 September 1991, A1. See also O. Dickason, *Canada's First Nations: A History of Founding Peoples from Earliest Times* (Toronto: McClelland &

Stewart, 1992), especially chapter XXIII, "Canadian Courts and Aboriginal Rights."

30. For example, the recent British Columbia Court of Appeal's judgement in *Delgamuukw v. The Queen:* see F. Cassidy, "On the Road to Recognition of Canadian Native Rights," *The Globe and Mail*, 9 July 1993, A21.

31. M.E. Turpel, "Aboriginal Peoples and the Canadian Charter: Interpretive Monopolies' Cultural Differences" (1989–90), 6 *Canadian Human Rights Yearbook* 3.

32. Ibid., 13.

33. Ibid., 23.

34. Ibid., 29.

35. Ibid., 44.

36. This analysis is based on the "Text of the Charlottetown Agreement: Revised Draft: 2:30 p.m., 28 August 1992," *The Globe and Mail*, 1 September 1992, A1, A8–9.

37. M. Cernetig, "Natives Envision Breaking Vicious Cycle," *The Globe and Mail*, 14 July 1992, A1.

38. Charlottetown text, supra, note 36, at s. IV, A42.

39. Ibid., s. IV, A41.

40. Ibid., s. IV, A43.

41. S. Delacourt, "Text Being Altered Native Women Say," *The Globe and Mail*, 19 September 1992, A4; M. Landsberg, "Unity Deal Will Rob Native Women of Key Rights," *The Toronto Star*, 22 September 1992, B1; S. Fine, "Native Women Aim to Block National Referendum in Court," *The Globe and Mail*, 13 October 1992, A10. For a discussion of these issues in a larger context, see S. Wesner, "First Nations Women and Government Policy, 1970–92: Discrimination and Conflict," in S. Burt et al., *Changing Patterns — Women in Canada*, 2d ed. (Toronto: McClelland & Stewart, 1993), 92.

42. Supra, note 36, s. IV, A41(a).

43. Ibid., s. IV, C50.

44. S. Venne, "Treaty Indigenous Peoples and the Charlottetown Accord: The Message in the Breeze" (1993), 4 *Constitutional Studies* 43.

45. J. Simpson, "Paying for Native Self-Government: If Nunavat's the Model, It's a Big Tab," *The Globe and Mail*, 4 February 1993, A20; T. Siddon, "Nunavat: A Price Worth Paying," *The Globe and Mail*, 3 March 1993, A19.

PART 4C

THE ECONOMY AND WORK

Public opinion polls periodically ask Canadians to list the most important problems that worry them. Invariably, economic issues head the list. That should not be surprising. People must eat before they can engage in politics, art, and all other human activities. Besides, in most societies, wealth is culturally defined as the single criterion that best defines a person's worth. Our preoccupation with economic issues rests on these two facts: economic production fulfils one of the most basic human needs, and wealth is highly valued as a symbol of merit.

Today, unemployment and the national debt are Canadians' chief economic concerns. Since World War II, both have skyrocketed.

When successive post-World War II governments constructed the Canadian welfare state, instituting a national health service, unemployment insurance, old age pensions, a larger and more accessible system of higher education, and so forth, they often borrowed money to finance those programs. They counted on rapid economic growth to generate the tax revenue to pay off the debt. Until 1973, the plan worked. Thereafter, growth lagged. Soon, governments were so strapped for funds to pay for social programs that they not only had to borrow enormous sums of money to maintain them, they even had to borrow money to pay interest on the existing debt. Today, Canadian governments owe well over half a trillion dollars, and interest payment on the debt is the biggest single expense in the annual budget of the federal government.

The unemployment rate fluctuates with the phase of the business cycle. During "boom" periods the rate falls. During "slack" periods the rate rises. Ignoring short-term fluctuations, however, the long-term trend is upward. While a 5 percent rate of unemployment was considered scandalous in the 1960s, a rate approaching 10 percent now seems normal — and that during boom periods.

Most Canadian sociologists attribute the long-term rise in unemployment and the growing debt to a structural weakness of the Canadian economy. Since World War I, and especially since the 1950s, both the manufacturing and the resource sectors have been substantially foreign-owned, mainly by corporations with head offices in the United States. This has constrained job growth in three ways. First, much of the capital that could be reinvested in Canada to create jobs has wound up in the coffers of US-based multinational corporations in the form of profits, management fees, royalties, and the like. Second, much of the manufacturing that takes place in Canadian branch plants has involved merely the assembly of parts made elsewhere. Third, the mandate of branch plants involved in manufacturing has usually been just to service the Canadian market, not to expand internationally. For all these reasons, Canada has comparatively few of the kinds of factory jobs that generate secure, well-paying employment in Germany, Sweden, Japan, South Korea, and elsewhere. Chronically high unemployment results in less taxes being collected to pay for social programs and more demands being made on those programs. Consequently, the debt soars.*

In Chapter 24, Gordon Laxer of the University of Alberta offers an innovative explanation for Canada's high level of foreign ownership. Conventional explanations emphasize Canada's proximity to the United States, the world's most powerful economic machine, as the main cause of American domination. Laxer tries instead to solve the riddle of foreign ownership by analyzing how Canada and other **late-industrializing countries** managed to raise the capital needed to industrialize. (The late-industrializing countries are those whose manufacturing "take-offs" date from the 1880s and 1890s. Canada, Japan, and Sweden are among the chief examples.) Laxer discovers two patterns of capital mobilization: the European model, followed also by Japan, which involved the mobilization of domestic capital, and the Canadian model, which involved the mobilization of foreign capital.

The countries that raised capital domestically, such as Sweden and Japan, established robust, independent manufacturing sectors. Laxer discovers the social roots of the European model in the strong and united agrarian classes of the successful late-industrializing countries. At the turn of the century, farmers and large landowners in the late-industrializing countries wanted three things: easy access to capital so that they could purchase more land; military protection of land, including, in some cases, territorial expansion by military means; and cheap government. Where they were powerful and united, agrarian classes forced governments to give them what they wanted, and in the process they inadvertently helped to mobilize domestic capital for industrialization. Accordingly, by running government cheaply, less money was squandered and more capital was made available for investment. The demand for military protection and expansion encouraged the state to sponsor a domestically owned and technologically independent military manufacturing sector, thereby laying the foundation for later technological innovation and government involvement in economic planning. The call for easy access to capital involved the breakup of old commercial banking systems, oriented toward short-term loans, and the creation of investment banks, oriented toward long-term loans. This made capital available for industrial investment too.

Well-to-do French-Canadian and English-Canadian businessmen and their political representatives had established a solid working relationship in the years leading up to and following Confederation. Canadian farmers, however, unlike their counterparts in Sweden and Japan, were politically weak and disunited because of the French-English conflict. They therefore had relatively little influence on public policy. As a result, Canadian farmers did not have the unintended but beneficial effects on the growth of manufacturing that rural classes had in Sweden and Japan. Canada remained dependent on Britain for military protection rather than developing a military manufacturing base of its own. The state squandered enormous sums of money on the construction of unnecessary transcontinental railway lines, gilding the pockets of rich bondholders and making investment capital scarcer. Investment banking developed late. Consequently, there was a shortage of domestic capital for investment

---

*Neoconservatives explain things differently. They regard burgeoning social programs as the main cause of high unemployment and the huge debt. In their view, a large and growing number of Canadians do not want to work because they can easily collect government benefits. Cut benefits, they say, and both the unemployment rate and the debt will fall.

A small minority of Canadians undoubtedly abuse the system of state benefits. However, the neoconservative argument is flawed. The great majority of people who do not work are either trying to find jobs but cannot because they do not exist; or unable to work because they have disabilities or are poor female heads of single-parent households and must take care of their children full-time due to the lack of a state-funded day-care system. Cutting the benefits of the welfare state thus does little to alleviate the structural problems of the Canadian economy.

in manufacturing. Canadian plans to encourage industrialization centred on the National Policy, implemented in 1879. Tariffs were placed on foreign-manufactured goods in order to foster Canadian industrial growth. As a result, American companies simply set up branch plants in Canada in order to jump the tariff wall. Foreign investment flowed in to compensate for the shortage of domestic capital.

An important implication of Laxer's analysis is that foreign control of the Canadian economy is not inevitable. But it is also obvious that solving the problem would require some massive policy changes. The persistent and virtually all-consuming conflict between Quebec and the rest of the country and, more generally, between the federal and provincial governments, would have to be resolved (see the "Introduction" to Part 4 and Chapter 22). That would allow Canadians to mount a concerted effort to develop and implement an industrial policy aimed at greater independence and manufacturing growth. Canadians could then begin to learn from the successful late industrializers (including, most recently, South Korea, Taiwan, Singapore, and Hong Kong) what it will take to be an economic "winner" in the 21st century: high levels of domestic saving to create a large pool of domestic investment capital, increased emphasis on technical education and research with industrial applications, greater stress on producing manufactured goods for the export market, and government coordination of industrial policy (see Chapter 32).

Successful late industrializers differ from Canada not just at the level of state policy but also at the level of the social organization of work. In Chapter 25, Harvey Krahn and Graham Lowe of the University of Alberta discuss Swedish- and Japanese-inspired programs to improve the quality of working life and their limited implementation and success in Canada since the mid-1970s.

Eighty years ago, the celebrated German sociologist Max Weber wrote admiringly of the "technical superiority" of bureaucracies "over any other form of organization." **Bureaucracies**, wrote Weber, are more precise, faster, less ambiguous, more discrete, and cheaper than all other ways of organizing business, education, law, the military, and so forth. They achieve their efficiency because they embody a specialized division of labour, a strict hierarchy of authority, clear regulations, impersonality, and a staff that is technically qualified to do its job. Note, however, that Weber was comparing bureaucratic efficiency only with decision-making by (1) charismatic and capricious rulers, and (2) the unquestioned, unchanging, and often irrational routines of tradition. Note also that he did not witness the more recent experience of bureaucracies that are slow, inflexible, and dehumanizing.

Quality of working life (QWL) programs are based on the idea that Weber's analysis of bureaucratic efficiency was too rosy. Heavily bureaucratized industrial organizations, assembly line-production, and a highly fragmented division of labour often create alienated workers, high absenteeism and turnover, slow adaptation to changing market conditions, and low productivity. In contrast, QWL programs recommend eliminating various levels of middle management (the establishment of "flattened" organizational structures), allowing worker participation in a variety of tasks and jobs related to their main functions, the creation of teams of a dozen or so workers who are delegated authority to make a variety of work-related decisions themselves, and the formation of "quality circles" of workers to monitor and correct defects in products and services. Krahn and Lowe point out that the implementation of such ideas in Canada has been limited and has met with mixed results. But they also make it apparent that many valuable lessons can be learned from these new forms of work organization that can help to improve the quality of working life and make the Canadian economy more productive.

GLOSSARY

Bureaucracies are secondary associations that operate more precisely, faster, less ambiguously, more discretely, and cheaper than traditional and charismatic forms of decision-making. They achieve their efficiency because they embody a specialized division of labour, a strict hierarchy of authority, clear regulations, impersonality, and a staff that is technically qualified to do its job.

The **late-industrializing countries** are those whose manufacturing "take-offs" date from the 1880s and 1890s, about a century after the Industrial Revolution began in England. Canada, Japan, and Sweden are among the chief examples.

The **quality of working life** movement recommends eliminating various levels of middle management, allowing worker participation in a variety of tasks and jobs related to their main functions, the creation of teams of a dozen or so workers who are delegated authority to make a variety of work-related decisions themselves, and the formation of "quality circles" of workers to monitor and correct defects in products and services.

Chapter 24

THE ROOTS OF CANADIAN DEPENDENCE

GORDON LAXER

In 1983 a United Nations survey found that the value of foreign direct investment was higher in Canada than in any other country in the world. There was more such investment in Canada in absolute, quantitative terms than there was in the United States, making Canada's level of foreign ownership more than ten times as great on a per capita basis.[1] With 0.5 per cent of the world's people, Canada was the recipient of 17 per cent of all global foreign direct investment.[2] In this regard Canada was clearly different from the other advanced countries.

How can we account for this difference? This question has been the subject of academic inquiry since the 1930s. Standard theories have been developed, all resting on one essential fact: Canada's location in North America.

With the rise of anti-colonial struggles in the early 1960s, a favourite explanation for Canada's curious economic position was derived from Third World dependency theories. Based on the theme of external domination, this theory has several variations. One has to do with the modern corporation — an American invention. The new corporate structure allowed for better administration of geographically dispersed units of production and sales; its flexibility and decentralization enabled businesses to expand abroad as well as into different economic sectors. Thus, according to the theory, it was only natural that Canada, sitting next to the United States, would be subject to early and massive intrusion of American subsidiaries. Other variations on the theme of external domination focus on

pressure exerted by the US state and the alliances between local elites and imperial powers that are a standard element in dependency theories: in this case, corporate alliances formed with Canadian elites. In the dependency view, however, the latter — the only domestic contribution to the scenario — have involved so few Canadians that they cannot be considered evidence of self-determination on Canada's part.

Geographic proximity to a greater power provided an older explanation. In the 1920s Canadian academics discovered the importance of geography, climate, and economics in the determination of history. These factors were added to the narrow and stuffy early interpretations of Canadian history, which had been confined to laws, constitutions, political institutions, and great leaders. Linked to the American-frontier thesis, these new factors crowded out competing explanations.

Cultural similarity, an argument put forward by Goldwin Smith in the 1890s, is the oldest theory of Canadian dependence. According to this line of reasoning, it was because Canadians did not view Americans as foreign that they did not resist US economic control. With the relatively free movement of peoples across the border and the spillover of American culture into Canada through periodicals and, later, radio, movies, and television, Canadians failed to develop a very distinct consciousness.

All these theories accept what has become the dominant theme in Canadian culture: that Canada has been a passive entity moulded by overwhelming natural forces and by equally overwhelming external human forces. They are inadequate because the Canadian people themselves barely enter their purview. During the years when Canada went through its own industrial revolution, between Confederation and the First World War, the government had the capacity to take action on many issues, including the extent and type of foreign investment. The effectiveness of restrictions on foreign control of banks was testimony to the country's ability to choose its own economic destiny. Canada's recent difficulties in extricating itself from foreign ownership, notably in the oil and gas sector, do not prove that, from the beginning, Canada never had a choice. It is much easier for a country to avoid massive levels of foreign ownership and control at an early point in its development, as did Japan, or to reverse the process at an early stage, as did Norway, than to remove vested foreign interests once they have become well entrenched.

Another flaw in the external-domination theme is that American business did not even begin to undergo the changes that gave birth to the modern corporation until the 1920s — that is, not until American subsidiaries had already gained a decisive grip on Canadian manufacturing and resource sectors. Thus the development of the modern corporation was not a necessary condition for the establishment of transnational corporations.

Proximity to the United States does not in itself explain investment penetration either. Mexico received a large amount of early American attention, but it was able to reverse the situation in the 1911 revolution and later in the 1930s, with the creation of Pemex, the state-owned oil company. If Mexico had sufficient autonomy to decide whether or not it wanted American investment, can it be argued seriously that Canada did not? Nor was the United States the only technologically dynamic society to control production in adjacent countries (the heart of the argument about Canada's unique geographic position); Germany, too, set up branch plants in neighbouring countries in the several decades before the First World War, but it did not go on to dominate them economically.

This leads us to the oldest argument: cultural and linguistic similarities. Perhaps Canadians so identified with their neighbours to the south that they did not care to be economically independent. Canadians have often seemed to favour close economic ties with the American giant, and English, if not French, Canadians have been uncertain about their cultural distinctiveness. There is little doubt that Canada would have enacted tougher investment restrictions if the Japanese had bought as much of Canadian industry as the Americans did. But this argument gets us only so far. Canadian political leaders generally resisted the overwhelming pull of the United States during the National Policy period, from 1879 to the 1930s, and Canadians — though at times only a bare majority — supported them. If national autonomy had been of little importance, would Canada have gone to the trouble of building the Canadian Pacific Railway entirely through Canadian territory? Would voters have rejected reciprocity with the United States in 1891 and again in 1911? Would farmers have broken from the American Grangers in the 1870s or from the American Patrons of Industry in the 1890s? These episodes and others demonstrate that English-speaking Canadians valued their distinctive nationality even though they spoke the same language as Americans.

The whole question of nationality and cultural similarity poses other questions, questions that lead away from the standard explanations to the effect that Canada was not the master of its own destiny. If it is accepted that ideas and culture can have a determining influence on history, resistance to US economic penetration must have been possible; Canadians must have been able to determine their own fate. Why, then, did Canada not restrict American direct investment in Canadian resources and manufacturing industries during the National Policy era? This question moves us to the heart of the matter — to the internal politics that underlay state policy formation.

To gain perspective, I have used a comparative framework. The standard explanations for Canada's unusual degree of foreign ownership rely too heavily on the Canadian data and Canadian perspectives to shed light on why domestic policies diverged from those of other countries in similar economic circumstances. The archives, the statistics, the events, and the personalities of Canadian history are the invaluable tools of Canadian historians. They explain the choices, the influences, and the context within which state policies were made. But, as crucial and insightful as these forms of inquiry are, they cannot explain why Canadians apparently never considered, let alone implemented, policies adopted by other countries in similar dilemmas.

Students of Canadian history have generally held the same narrow assumptions about the Anglo-American world as did the leaders, the classes, and the communities they studied. The examples of development in other advanced capitalist societies have usually been assumed to be inapplicable to Canada. Even the American experience has not been fully assimilated by Canadian historians. The myriad ways in which American society has influenced Canada have been explored in depth, but the ways in which the US broke out of a staple-exporting relationship with industrial Britain have barely been acknowledged. Largely absent, too, has been any examination of the political controversies surrounding American banking, land, and railway policies. Whereas in the US such policies have given rise to high political drama, in Canada they have usually been treated as nothing more than tiresome technical matters in which ordinary Canadians could have no influence. Finally, Canadian scholars have largely neglected the American populist movements of the 1800s: it was populist nationalism that put the issues of foreign ownership of banks, western lands, and mines on the US political agenda in the nineteenth century.

Moreover, if important elements of American history have been neglected in explaining Canadian economic dependence, the experiences of European countries and of Japan have been ignored almost entirely. I break with the tradition by analyzing Canadian industrial development from the perspective of European experience.

We know that Canada adopted the National Policy as the means to achieve economic and political independence within North America. And we know that in part it failed. The failure was greatest in the area of foreign investment, which acted as a bridgehead for later threats to Canadian economic, political, and cultural sovereignty. The National Policy was a carbon copy of the original "American system" of Henry Clay, created sixty years earlier. I have argued that, in the altered conditions of development in the late nineteenth century, the "European system" was more appropriate for Canada.

The European system of late-follower development evolved in particular international circumstances and in response to internal pressures. By the late nineteenth century there were already several advanced industrial countries competing for the markets and even the real estate of the world. Industrial progress had improved transportation and communications so dramatically that the world was becoming a single economic and political system. Less-developed countries either created independent industrial economies of their own or fell into economic dependence on the already-developed powers. Leaders of the late-follower countries saw the risk clearly enough and determined to maintain their sovereignty. Canadians' desire not to continue as "hewers of wood and drawers of water" for the industrial nations was felt as strongly as similar sentiments elsewhere.

Several institutional modifications of England's laissez-faire model were at the heart of the European system (and its Japanese variant). Banks now engaged in long-term lending, and domestic capital was gathered in new ways to finance risky new industries. There was no basic conflict of the type R.T. Naylor has outlined between commercial and industrial capitalists. The state generally refrained from encouraging the wasteful use of scarce domestic capital on unneeded infrastructure, and some degree of technological independence was achieved through native invention or the imitation of foreign technologies in domestically controlled businesses. The desire to keep armed forces independent of foreign, possibly enemy, supplies underlay much of the late-follower state's drive to industrial independence.

Canada followed none of these patterns, and it was the only late follower to rely so heavily on foreign-controlled inputs in its development. Foreign direct investment, management, and technology, and reliance on big power military protection, became substitutes for the European system.

Could Canada have succeeded in fully breaking free from its hewer-of-wood role had it adopted the European system? Here we run up against two enduring myths that have been used to explain Canada's continued economic dependence. The first contends that Canadians were too conservative or unenterprising to develop industry by themselves. The second holds that the population was too small and scattered for the creation of a market suitable for efficient development.

The image of nineteenth-century Canada as a land of rustic backwardness is as false as the myth it supports. Before the American branch plants arrived in significant numbers (between 1900 and 1914), Canada was already the eighth largest manufacturing country in the world, no mean feat for a nation with a small population. American capital and know-how did not make Canada an advanced country — it was the other way round. The developed nature of Canada's industry, labour force, and standard of living attracted American subsidiaries northward. At the turn of the century — *before* Canada became a branch-plant economy — Canadians were enterprising enough to export sophisticated industrial goods, developed and made in domestically owned businesses, to such markets as Germany, Britain, and France.

The second myth, that the small size of the domestic market was an obstacle to independent development, is an excuse for failure. The examples of the small industrial countries of Western Europe are relevant. Sweden was chosen here for intensive study because it provides the ideal model for comparison with Canada. Other small European countries, such as Switzerland, Belgium, and the Netherlands, were more developed at an earlier point than Canada and so had advantages for independent development that Canada did not share; Austria was the centre of an important empire in the late nineteenth century, hardly a comparable situation to Canada's. Sweden, however, began industrial development as late as Canada and with a domestic market as small or smaller (even if Norway is included); in fact, it was the only other late-follower country with a small population. Finally, Sweden's northern character, its resource-exporting relationship with Britain in the 1800s, and its social and cultural similarities to Canada add to the power of the comparison.

Sweden broke out of its dependence on exporting staple products to metropolitan countries and became an important centre of manufactured exports itself. It made this transition in the same period in which the National Policy was in effect in Canada and without recourse to much foreign direct investment. During these years Sweden adopted a variant of the European system. Investment banks contributed to Swedish development by making long-term investments in domestic industry and technology. In addition, both the education system and the risk-taking banks encouraged invention. Frugality in state expenditures, especially in railway building, helped Sweden to contain its voracious appetite for foreign capital, which came almost entirely in the form of loans. Foreign ownership was discouraged by strong Swedish opposition as well as by the vigour of internal development.

The state was central to Sweden's success in the European system, but the country's development was not an automatic or even a very deliberate process. The interplay of class forces in the context of a well-developed and relatively homogeneous national consciousness led to the adoption of various components of Sweden's economic policies. Rural classes had an important political influence on the shape of industrial policies. The nobility had been in transition for some time from a rural base to leadership in commerce, industry, and, of course, the state. Early industrialization also saw the rise in importance of independent farmers — both large and small — in the political system. All these rural classes helped to push state policies in the direction of the European system. Such influence was most notable in the areas of government expenditures and economic nationalism, but it was also evident in the evolution of investment banking and in Sweden's emphasis on military preparedness.

The Swedish case tells us several important things about Canada's possibilities at the time of the National Policy. First, a late-follower country with a small market and population could make a successful transition to independent industrial development. Second, dependence on staple exports need not have inhibited such a course. Internal politics and national consciousness, however, did affect the outcome, and classes outside commerce and industry played decisive roles in determining state economic policies.

If the European system, adopted in some form by all other late-follower countries, could have helped it achieve the goals of independent development, why did Canada not adopt it? This question leads to consideration of the politics of Canadian development at the time of the National Policy, a line of inquiry treated as unimportant in the standard explanations of Canadian economic dependence.

Canada's failure to adopt a variant of the European system was in large part the result of the weakness of agrarian influence in early development. Although the industrial revolution eventually relegated agriculture to a minor place in the economic scheme of things, agrarian classes usually had a major impact on the direction of early industrialization before their influence ebbed away. The implications of the peculiar weakness of agrarians in Canada during this early period lies at the heart of the new perspective presented here.

Farmers did have considerable impact on politics in Canada, as in all new settler societies, but their influence was at its strongest before and after initial industrialization. During the period when industry began to transform Canadian society — roughly from just before Confederation to the First World War — independent and organized agrarian voices were strangely quiet. It was in the latter part of this period that American direct investment established a solid hold on the Canadian economy. This was also the time in which the Canadian state was formed. The lack of independent agrarian input affected the nature of both processes. Agrarian weakness was the political peculiarity that, I have argued, accompanied the economic peculiarity of Canada's heavy reliance on foreign ownership for development.

It is impossible to know the exact impact of the political weakness of organized farmers on the course of Canadian industrialization. The best we can do is attempt to recognize the directions in which effective pressure by independent farmers' movements might have led. The politics of farmers before the 1837 rebellions, when their voice was strong in central Canada, and the re-emergence of agrarian populism immediately after the First World War, in Western Canada and Ontario, give us a lot to go on. So too do the sporadic agrarian movements in the 1850s, 1870s, and 1890s, during initial industrialization. The political impact of agrarians in the same economic phase in the United States and other countries also indicate the general nature of farmer politics in that economic phase.

All of these sources indicate that the effect of organized agrarian movements was to push politics in the direction of the European system. Two elements in particular stand out in the program of agrarian movements in nineteenth- and early twentieth-century Canada: the repeated attempts to free up banking and credit and to promote economy in government. These demands ran consistently through farmers' movements as the locus of organization shifted from east to west and the economy was transformed from pre-industrial to industrial. They were also characteristic of agrarians in other countries during initial industrialization.

Further elements of agrarian impact were evident in other societies where agrarians held or shared power, but were either absent or barely noticeable in Canada. These were opposition to foreign economic penetration and an emphasis on military defence of the homeland. Both emanated from agrarians' attachment to the land, which went beyond mere economic rationality. Agrarian reaction was generally strong both to threats to the land from invasion and to the exploitation and control of natural resources by foreign capitalists. Perhaps holding power or being able to influence the political agenda led agrarians outside Canada to these statist tendencies. The only counterparts to the latter in Canada have been a general concern with threats to the territorial sovereignty of Canada and a greater opposition to foreign ownership of resources than to other types of foreign ownership, and these reactions have not been confined to farmers. The fact that Canadian farmers — indeed, all ordinary citizens — had little to do with the formation of the state probably accounted for the weakness of populist nationalism. The contrast with the United States in this respect is striking.

If farmers' influence would have pushed the National Policy in the direction of the European system, why then were Canadian farmers so weak? This was the period in which their influence should have been at its peak. By the late nineteenth century farmers in central and eastern Canada had gone beyond the pioneering phase and made up almost half the population. A wide franchise and the achievement of self-government in the late 1840s also created favourable conditions for strong populist influence. One of the curious aspects of Canadian history was the blossoming of agrarian strength after the First World War, when the number of farmers had already declined in relative terms as a result of industrialization and urbanization.

Farmer influence was weak during the formative period of early industrial development for two reasons. The British connection and fear of US manifest destiny cast populist influences in Canada as disloyal. More important, the intensity of sectional tensions between English and French, Protestant and Catholic, relegated class conflicts and class movements to a secondary level of importance. Ethno-national tensions occurred not only in central Canada but also in the west with the Riel rebellions and the Manitoba schools question; they were in evidence in New Brunswick as well. These tensions hurt several farmers' movements in English Canada, most notably in the 1850s and 1890s. Victory seemed at hand in the 1921 federal election — the farmers' Progressive Party won the largest number of seats of any party in English Canada — but in failing, as always, to make a significant bridge across ethno-national lines to Quebec, the agrarians lost the election. Sectional conflict between English and French diverted Canadian politics away from class-based issues and divisions.

The weakness of farmers' movements affected a number of policies, all contributing to the victory of a branch-plant economy. The banks successfully resisted a century of agrarian assaults and failed to change their conservative approach to financing industry, while the state either encouraged the most foolish schemes or supported sensible projects but at the highest costs. In both cases the need for foreign capital was accentuated. Second, because farmer opposition to unfavourable land and railway policies had little effect, settlement of the prairies was delayed for about twenty years — which in turn slowed the pace and scale of Canadian industrial progress in the decades immediately preceding the first major invasion of American branch plants. Finally, the weakness of populist nationalism set the stage for open-door policies in regard to foreign investment.

One might ask whether the history of the social origins of foreign ownership has any relevance for Canada as it nears the twenty-first century. It does. If Canada is to plan successfully for the new economy in the years ahead, an understanding of how it got to its present situation is essential. In this chapter I have challenged several enduring myths that have confused Canadians. The idea that Canada would have remained an economic backwater if not for the massive intrusion of American capital and know-how is false. So too is the deeply held notion that Canada's fate lies in the hands of external human powers and overwhelming natural forces. Lastly, the belief that Canada has too small a population to make an important and independent contribution to the new international economy is also false.

Above all, we can learn from Canadian history that economics cannot be understood without reference to the social life of the people. Internal problems arising from tensions among Canadians along anglophone/francophone and regional or other lines must be settled on an equitable basis of mutual respect, so that Canadians do not stand divided on questions of economic development and the penetration of foreign corporations.

If internal inequities continue to plague Canada, domestic elites will be free to look after their own interests — even though these usually conflict with the best interests of Canada and its people.

NOTES

1. The Americans considered a corporation foreign-controlled when foreign assets reached 10 per cent, whereas Canada waited until foreign ownership reached 50 per cent before designating the company foreign-controlled.
2. United Nations Centre on Transnational Corporations, *Salient Features and Trends in Foreign Direct Investment* (New York: United Nations, 1983), 34.

Chapter 25

NEW FORMS OF MANAGEMENT AND WORK

Harvey Krahn and Graham Lowe

WORK HUMANIZATION THROUGH JOB REDESIGN

Quality of Working Life Programs

Human relations theory has strongly influenced *quality of working life (QWL)* programs. A common ideological thread unites these approaches. Employees are supposed to be treated humanely and provided with good working conditions. Beyond a few concessions in the realm of decision making, most of the authority remains with management. However, some reforms in Canada and elsewhere, particularly Scandinavia, achieve the dual goals of significantly redistributing power and enhancing the quality of working life. In such instances everyone in the organization stands to benefit, particularly because productivity gains often result.

QWL became a buzzword among managers, public policy makers, academics, and consultants during the 1970s. QWL is an umbrella term covering many different strategies for humanizing work, improving employee–employer cooperation, redesigning jobs, and giving employees greater participation in management. In North America, management has usually initiated these programs. The underlying goal has been to improve employee satisfaction, motivation, and commitment. The expected payoffs are higher productivity, better quality products, and bigger profits. Its proponents have stressed that, ideally, employers and

employees will all benefit: "With QWL there are no losers — everyone wins."[1]

The spread of the work reform movement is due to a convergence of factors. Managers are struggling to adapt to growing international competition, shifting product markets, and automation. While these challenges open the door for more creative and flexible means of organizing work, they are not the only pressures for change. At the same time, demands from workers and unions for more satisfying, healthier, and less authoritarian workplaces are increasing. Theoretically, QWL claims to combine both humanistic and economic objectives: challenging, involving, and rewarding work experiences for employees and, for the employer, more productive utilization of the firm's human resources. Yet the lofty rhetoric of QWL advocates often fails to translate into successful applications.

A quick overview of some of the major QWL techniques would be useful. *Job enlargement* is meant to expand a job horizontally, adding related tasks to put more variety into the work done by an individual worker. *Job enrichment* goes further by combining operations before and after a task to make for a more complex and unified job. For example, in the case of a machine operator in a clothing factory, job enrichment might mean that the operator would now be responsible for obtaining necessary materials, doing the administrative paperwork associated with different

Source: Work, Industry, and Canadian Society, 2nd ed. (Toronto: Nelson Canada, 1993), pp. 214–24. Reprinted by permission of the publisher.

production runs, and maintaining the machines. This might not be an enormous change, but it would lead to a more varied, demanding, and responsible job. *Job rotation* has workers moving through a series of work stations, usually at levels of skill and responsibility similar to their original task. This tactic is frequently used to inject variety into highly repetitive, monotonous tasks. When job rotation is combined with more fundamental redesign strategies (especially the use of work teams), an employee can develop a considerable range of new skills.

An *autonomous work team* consists of roughly a dozen employees who are delegated collective authority to decide on work methods, scheduling, inventory, and quality control. They might also perform what previously would have been supervisory tasks, such as administration, discipline, and even hiring. *Quality circles*, with a narrower mandate of having workers monitor and correct defects in products or services, are perhaps the best known application of the team concept. But, as we shall see below, quality circles often fall short of redistributing authority to rank and file workers.

QWL Assessed

The smorgasbord of QWL programs implemented by Canadian employers has resulted in both successes and failures. Attempts at work reform have generated heated debate between advocates, usually managers and QWL "experts," and critics who are often trade unionists. What does the evidence tell us about the costs and benefits of QWL? We are beginning to get a clearer picture through recent research of the extent and impact of QWL-type work reorganization in Canada. Richard Long's survey of 946 private sector firms reveals that what he terms "workplace innovation" in Canada is somewhat behind that in the United States.[2] About 10 percent of the firms Long surveyed had semiautonomous work groups, and about 8 percent had some form of gain (profit) sharing. This may seem low, but it nonetheless represented a major new trend in the 1980s.

Some of the most significant advances have been in the auto industry. North American auto and auto parts manufacturers appear to have combined new automated technologies and QWL schemes in a strategy to regain their competitive position against the "imports." Chrysler Corporation president, Robert Lutz, heralded the firm's new line of C cars as "really a story about teamwork."[3] A survey by the Canadian Auto Workers Union (CAW) revealed that one-third of Canadian auto industry plants have some kind of QWL or "employee involvement" scheme.[4] A study of quality control circles at a General Motors plant concluded that the scheme was intended to raise productivity and trim costs by co-opting production workers to solve management's quality problems. Little work humanization resulted.[5] The CAW admits that it faces a dilemma in responding to industry initiatives: while QWL can lead to improvements in working conditions and often has workers' support, the longer-run impact may be to weaken the union's ability to fight concessions.

Donald Nightingale's research, which was one of the earliest evaluations of QWL in Canada, compared ten firms with varying degrees of participative management with a matched sample of ten traditionally managed firms. The essence of workplace democracy, Nightingale asserts, is "that labour as a legitimate stakeholder in the enterprise has a moral right to play a role in the management of the enterprise."[6] A further assumption is that an individual's potential can be best developed in nonauthoritarian work structures with meaningful and interesting tasks. Equally important is the premise that bureaucratic organizations and Taylorist work-design principles stifle personal development.

Nightingale compared the traditional and democratic firms in several ways. The value systems in democratic firms reflected a human relations approach. However, the quality-of-working-life benefits of participative management were modest at best. For instance, no significant differences were observed between the two types of organizations in their rates of employee stress symptoms. Workers in democratic organizations, especially the rank and file, experienced slightly higher job satisfaction. They also expected more from their jobs, especially in the realm of decision making. In addition, their mental health was slightly better than that of the comparison group in traditional firms. Interestingly, Nightingale did not examine productivity differences, on the grounds that this could not be accurately measured across twenty firms.

Other evaluations of Canadian QWL initiatives document positive effects, ranging from higher employee satisfaction, morale, commitment, and concern with economic performance to better earnings, improved supervision and labour relations, and productivity gains. On the negative side, QWL initiatives have also resulted in declining work performance, heightened union–management tensions, employee dissatisfaction, and a breakdown in communications.[7] One electronics firm that introduced an employee stock ownership plan, employee representation on the board of directors, and an elected employee council found the overall impact on nonmanagerial employees to be negative.[8] Don Wells's two case studies of QWL found that implementation had been imposed by top management, and brought few improvements in job content. Subsequently, more authority was delegated to a handful of workers and workplace relationships improved, although in one plant these changes came during massive layoffs.[9]

A series of case studies by the Economic Council of Canada, part of its survey of workplace automation in Canada, showed that successful technological change included work reorganization and better human resource development. Some of the firms studied applied a sociotechnical approach to ensure that jobs were redesigned to use technology in ways that increased worker skills, discretion, and responsibility. Moreover, workers directly participated in the innovation process and received adequate training to equip them for the new work environment.[10]

Shell's Sarnia Chemical Plant

The flagship of the North American QWL movement is Shell's chemical plant in Sarnia, Ontario.[11] It is unique because union and management actively collaborated in the sociotechnical design of the plant right from the planning stage in 1975. In comparison with existing organizations, such new, or *greenfield*, sites offer greater scope for innovative work arrangements. Shell's goal was a "post-bureaucratic" organization suitable for the kind of continuous-process technology found in the petro-chemical industry, which would also facilitate employee control, learning, and participation.

Six teams of twenty workers run the plant around the clock, 365 days of the year. Along with two coordinators, a single team operates the entire plant during a shift, and is even responsible for hiring new team members when vacancies occur. Teams are supported by technical, engineering, and managerial personnel, along with a group of maintenance workers, who also teach team members craft skills. The organizational structure is quite flat, having only three authority levels from top to bottom. Team members have no job titles and rotate tasks regularly. Pay is based on knowledge and skills obtained through job training. It takes about six years of training for an operator to reach the maximum pay level.

This design, in short, empowers workers and allows them to utilize and develop their skills. Continuous-process technology may lend itself more readily to this approach, mainly because of the huge capital investment per worker and the enormous losses to the firm should the system malfunction. There is, therefore, a clear economic incentive for management to go to considerable lengths to obtain employee commitment. By tapping the talents of its employees, Shell is creating a safer and more productive operation. The restrictive work environment that Shell and the Energy and Chemical Workers' Union sought to erase is captured in one employee's dissatisfaction with former conditions:

> *The foreman handed out orders and everyone got away with as much as possible. Here you have freedom, but you have to be responsible. I figure that's a lot better way to operate than having a foreman hovering over me, double-checking every 15 minutes. I'm a responsible person and I don't need that kind of hassle.*[12]

According to the director of the union, the Shell plant eliminated authoritarian bureaucracy and provided members with opportunities to improve the quality of their work life.[13] In this application, the sociotechnical design seems to have achieved its objectives: a high level of production efficiency, smoothly functioning teams, and mutually beneficial collaboration between union and management.[14]

On the whole, autonomous work teams appear to have the greatest potential for significantly reallocating decision-making power, as well as for creating more interesting, challenging, socially integrated, and skilled work.[15] Why, then, has the Canadian labour movement been a vocal critic of QWL? The drawback for unions is that management has frequently used QWL to circumvent collective agreements, rationalize work processes, and co-opt workers into solving problems of quality and productivity.[16] QWL has often been used to undermine union bargaining power and frequently spearheads labour relations schemes intended to keep firms union-free. From the labour movement's perspective, gains in the quality of work life are therefore best achieved via collective bargaining. Thus, after considerable internal debate, the CAW adopted a policy on work reorganization. Essentially, it supports the involvement and empowerment of workers provided there is a true partnership and union objectives are not undermined. Rarely does this happen, though. But as former CAW president Bob White points out: "Workers should not be misled into believing that with these so-called new programs [QWL], management is offering us a partnership. None of the examples of the new work organization promoted by management includes workers or their union in any meaningful way in the decision-making process."[17]

In the Shell chemical plant, the union's involvement came only after guarantees that it would be a full partner in the QWL process, and that its ability to represent the interests of employees would not be undermined. It is noteworthy that members of the same union at an adjacent older refinery wanted nothing at all to do with QWL. But the Shell experience appears to be atypical. More common is the stance of the auto workers' union: "We do not oppose QWL experiments. Contrary to popular conceptions, unions don't spend most of their daily lives dealing with monetary problems; dealing with the 'quality of work life' of our members is already a dominant concern."[18] The union then lays out three preconditions (which rarely are met) for its involvement in QWL: management's main goal must be to improve the quality of working life of employees; productivity gains must be a byproduct of this, not the overriding concern; and changes must in no way weaken the position of the union.

SWEDISH WORK REFORMS

The promise of work humanization has been more fully realized in Sweden, which has been a pioneer in work reform. Decades of social democratic government, a strong labour movement representing over 90 percent of the labour force, and legislation giving individuals the right to meaningful jobs provide fertile grounds for the humanistic work reforms that have taken place in Sweden. The widely publicized Volvo Kalmar plant, which opened in the early 1970s, is based on a sociotechnical work design. The assembly line was replaced by battery-powered robot carriers, which automatically move car bodies to different work teams, each of which is responsible for a phase of assembly. Productivity and quality improved, but the new factory's potential, especially as embodied in the robot carriers, has not been fully tapped. One of the limitations of the Kalmar plant's sociotechnical design is that a computer — not the work teams — controls the movement of the carriers. Task cycles are still fairly short and are largely restricted to direct production. Despite Kalmar's team approach, the elimination of conventional assembly-line production methods, and the plant's pleasant physical environment, the jobs in the plant provide little scope for personal development or for the use of skills and initiative. Workers still complain that their jobs are boring.

A more effective solution to the alienating monotony of assembly-line work can be found in Saab's main auto plant at Trollhattan. The body assembly shop faced problems typical in mass production: high turnover and absenteeism, low quality, widespread dissatisfaction, and a numbingly fast work pace. Reforms initiated in the early 1970s sought to improve the work environment, make jobs intrinsically more satisfying, and boost productivity. As at Volvo, the local union played an active role.

Some remarkable changes have resulted. The assembly line has been eliminated. Autonomous teams of workers, or *matrix groups*, devote about forty-five minutes at a time to completing an integrated cycle of tasks. In one section of the shop, eighty-five robots have taken over arduous, repetitive welding jobs. Groups of twelve workers control the entire production process in their area. This involves programming the computers and maintaining the robots, ensuring quality control, performing related administrative work, and cleaning up their work space. *Buffer zones* allow teams to build up an inventory of completed bodies, giving them greater flexibility over how they use their time. (These buffers, incidentally, were an original feature of the Volvo plant but were later removed.) Skill development, new learning opportunities, and a broader approach to job design provide the teams with what Saab calls "control and ownership" of their contribution to the production process. Far from being victims of work degradation and deskilling through robotics, these Saab employees have reaped the benefits of upgraded job content and decision-making autonomy.[19]

JAPANESE MANAGEMENT AND INDUSTRIAL ORGANIZATION

While there are relevant lessons Canadians can learn from the Swedish experience of industrial democracy and work humanization, it has been the Japanese approach to work that has captured most of the attention recently. The phenomenal success of Japanese corporations in world markets has led many people to conclude that their management systems, industrial organization, and technology are superior. There is now a voluminous amount of literature on Japanese industry that tries to cast light on what is distinctive about the Japanese approach, why it is so successful, and to what extent it can work in North America. Sociologically, the important issue is whether the Japanese industrial system can be translated into theories of social and economic organization (which would mean its features could be adopted elsewhere) or if Japan's distinctiveness in these respects owes more to its culture and history (making application outside Japan very difficult).[20]

The Japanese Employment System

The four basic elements of the Japanese approach, which typically are found in only the major corporations, include: (1) highly evolved internal labour markets, with features such as life-time employment (*Nenko*), seniority-based wages and promotions, and extensive training; (2) a division of labour built around work groups rather than specific positions, a feature that is the basis for the well-known *quality circles*; (3) a consensual, participative style of decision making involving all organizational levels (*Ringi*); and (4) high levels of employee commitment and loyalty. A closer analysis of these aspects of Japanese firms leads to some interesting conclusions. In particular, from a comparative perspective the differences between North American and Japanese firms and management styles are probably overstated. Moreover, the Japanese system of employment owes more to principles of industrial organization than to any uniqueness in Japan's history or culture.[21] Increasingly, Japan seems to be at the cutting edge of the new approaches to management and work organization.

To elaborate briefly, perhaps the core of the Japanese work organization is the internal labour market. As James R. Lincoln and Kerry McBride observe, Japanese employers strive to maintain a well-functioning internal labour market and to obtain a high level of employee commitment to the firm over the long term.[22] Teams share responsibility and accountability. When this is coupled with the consensus-building networking process used to make decisions, it is easy to see how individual workers are well integrated in their workplace. How bottom-up is Japanese corporate decision making? Actually, it is a hybrid system, combining both centralized authority in the hands of executives, who bear responsibility for decisions, with consultations that ensure everyone has some input. *Ringi* refers to lower- or middle-level managers making petitions, which circulate and slowly build consensus, thereby gaining a high probability of adoption.

On the shop floor, participation commonly takes the form of quality circles (QCs). Made famous by Toyota, QCs are now well institutionalized in Japanese industry. Some, such as those at Toyota, are essential to maintaining and improving high levels of quality. Yet, as Lincoln and McBride observe, others "may be little more than collective suggestion-making exercises, imposed by management, for which workers receive little training."[23] While the contribution of QCs to Japan's industrial success remains a moot point, sociologist Stephen Wood offers an insightful analysis of how they represent a potentially pathbreaking approach to worker participation.[24]

Wood notes that the issue of workers' *tacit skills*, or intuitive expertise about how to do their job, figures prominently in debates about the introduction of new technology, deskilling, and management control. For example, without the aid of workers' informal expertise, the bugs in many new automated systems simply would not be overcome. What is especially innovative about Japanese organization, then, is how it harnesses the "tacit skills and latent talents" of workers. Wood dismisses arguments that this may just be another power grab by management — Taylorism Japanese-style. Instead, what Japanese industry has shown is that production systems can always be improved and that industrial engineers and other technical experts do not have the final word on these matters. QCs and other forms of participation enlarge workers' overall knowledge of the business and sharpen their analytical and diagnostic skills.

The Japanese Approach in North America

How far have these Japanese management and organizational innovations infiltrated North America? Quality, teams, and participative management are the new management buzz words. Some industrial design concepts, particularly Toyota's *just-in-time* (JIT) system of parts delivery, have been more readily adapted for use outside Japan than have aspects of Japanese management or work organization.[25] JIT reduces inventory overhead costs, forges a stronger alliance between a firm and its suppliers, makes it easier to change production specifications, but does not require major changes in job design.

QCs also have become popular among North American firms browbeaten by Japanese and other foreign competitors. However, they do not go as far in the delegation of authority to autonomous work teams, as are in place at the Shell chemical plant mentioned above. QCs seem to place responsibility for monitoring quality and troubleshooting problems on production workers without a commensurate expansion of their authority or increased rewards.[26] As Lincoln and McBride conclude, QCs are often seen by North American workers as just one more chore imposed on them by management.[27]

The obvious place to look for the successful adaptation of Japanese employment techniques is in Japanese transplants (local plants owned and operated by Japanese firms) or in their joint ventures with North

American firms. Even here we find very mixed results. At one end of the continuum is the NUMMI plant in California, a joint venture between Toyota and General Motors that has the active cooperation of the United Auto Workers union. Using methods imported by Toyota, employees work in teams and contribute ideas, but the daily management style is distinctly American.[28] However, the norm in transplants or joint ventures may be much closer to the other end of the continuum. As Ruth Milkman's investigation of employment conditions in Japanese transplants in California found, these firms closely resembled American firms employing nonunion labour, few had introduced QCs, and many local managers were unfamiliar with the principles of Japanese work organization or management approaches.[29] These firms' employment strategies emphasized cost reduction, leading them to take full advantage of low-wage immigrant labour.

In Canada there are 530 Japanese-owned plants.[30] The most prominent are the Ontario plants of Honda, Toyota, and CAMI (a Suzuki–GM joint venture). The Japanese managers at these three plants have had to develop a hybrid system, modifying aspects of the Japanese approach in a way that is acceptable to Canadian workers. For example, one key to Japanese management's success is "fastidious housekeeping," which emphasizes cleanliness, reduced clutter, keeping things orderly, as well as consistency in maintaining these goals and mutual respect. Canadian workers at Honda replaced this with their own version of good housekeeping, but dropped the principles of mutual respect and consistency. The major success story among Japanese transplants is Toyota's Cambridge, Ontario, plant, whose Corollas won the coveted J.D. Power and Associates award for the highest quality car in North America (based on surveys of car owners). From the Toyota workers' point of view, benefits include job flexibility, free uniforms, consensus decision making, team work, good pay, and job security. However, there are drawbacks, including regular overtime, open offices for managers, no replacement workers for absent team members, ergonomic problems, close scrutiny of absenteeism and lateness, and only selective implementation of employee suggestions.

To wrap up this discussion of Japanese management, we will return to the theme of change. Just like its competitors, Japanese industry faced a barrage of new challenges in the 1980s that altered its employment system.[31] Probably the peak performance of the Japanese model described above was in the 1970s. Even then it faced criticism, such as: the stifling of individual creativity through Nenko and "groupism"; discrimination against nonlifetime employees, particularly women; labour market rigidities that made the horizontal movement of workers among firms difficult; and long hours of work often at an intense pace.[32]

The system has been continually evolving, but a major transformation was sparked in the 1980s by the pressures of new technologies, globalization, the shift to services, and a strong yen, which drove up the cost of Japanese exports. Additional stimuli for change were an aging workforce, the different attitudes of young workers, and the growing number of women workers. Firms have struggled to cut jobs without laying off workers. The pure seniority principle has given way to other means of rewarding and motivating workers. And the mobility of workers across firms and during the course of their working lives is increasing. This restructuring of the Japanese employment system reflects principles similar to those advocated by new-style North American management. It will be interesting to see if this signals the start of a growing convergence of Japanese and North American approaches to organizing and managing work.

NOTES

1. For a critical assessment, see James Rinehart, "Improving the quality of working life through job redesign: work humanization or work rationalization?" *Canadian Review of Sociology and Anthropology* 23 (1986): 507–30, at 508. For definitions of QWL, see Ted Mills, *What Is Quality of Working Life?* (Ottawa: Labour Canada, 1981); Rayald Dorian, ed., *Adapting to a Changing World: A Reader on Quality of Working Life* (Ottawa: Labour Canada, 1981); J.B. Cunningham and T.H. White, eds., *Quality of Working Life: Contemporary Cases* (Ottawa: Labour Canada, 1984); and Kolodny and Stjernberg (1986). Keith Newton, "Quality of Working Life in Canada: A Survey," in W. Craig Riddell, ed., *Labour–Management Cooperation in Canada* (Toronto: University of Toronto Press, 1986: 74) broadly defines QWL as encompassing "the total ecology of work, including the linkages uniting individuals and their social relations, their work organizations and the larger society in which they live."

2. Richard J. Long, "Introducing employee participation in ownership and decision making," in Cunningham and White, eds., *Quality of Working Life: Contemporary Cases*. Also see Hem C. Jain, "Worker participation in Canada: current developments and challenges," *Economic and Industrial Democracy* 11 (1990): 279–90; Jacquie Mansell, *Workplace Innovation in Canada* (Ottawa: Economic Council of Canada, 1987).

3. *The Globe and Mail*, February 3, 1992, B4.

4. David Robertson and Jeff Wareham, *Technological Change in the Auto Industry* (Willowdale, ON: Canadian Auto Workers (CAW), 1987), 42.

5. James Rinehart, "Appropriating workers' knowledge: quality control circles at a General Motors plant," *Studies in Political Economy* 14 (1984): 75–97.

6. Donald Nightingale, *Workplace Democracy: An Enquiry into Employee Participation in Canadian Work Organizations* (Toronto: University of Toronto Press, 1982), 49–50.

7. Cunningham and White, eds., *Quality of Working Life: Contemporary Cases*.

8. Long, "Introducing employee participation in ownership and decision making."

9. Don Wells, *Soft Sell: "Quality of Working Life" Programs and the Productivity Race* (Ottawa: Canadian Centre for Policy Alternatives, 1986).

10. Gordon Betcherman, Keith Newton, and Joanne Godin, eds., *Two Steps Forward: Human Resource Management in a High-Technology World* (Ottawa: Economic Council of Canada, 1990).

11. This plant is described and evaluated in Tom Rankin, *New Forms of Work Organization: The Challenge for North American Unions* (Toronto: University of Toronto Press, 1990); Louis E. Davis and Charles Sullivan, "A labour management contract and quality of working life," *Journal of Occupational Behavior* 1 (1980): 29–41; Norman Halpern, "Sociotechnical systems design: the Shell Sarnia experience," in Cunningham and White, eds., *Quality of Working Life: Contemporary Cases*; and Neil Reimer, "Oil, chemical and atomic workers international union and the quality of working life — a union perspective," *Quality of Working Life: The Canadian Scene* (Winter 1979): 5–7.

12. *The Globe and Mail*, February 11, 1985.

13. Reimer, "Oil, chemical and atomic workers international union and the quality of working life — a union perspective," 5.

14. See Halpern, "Sociotechnical systems design: the Shell Sarnia experience," 58–59.

15. Rinehart, "Improving the quality of working life through job redesign: work humanization or work rationalization?" 519; B. Gardell and B. Gustavsen, "Work environment research and social change: current developments in Scandinavia," *Journal of Occupational Behavior* 1 (1980): 3–17, at 9.

16. For critiques of QWL, see Robertson and Wareham, *Technological Change in the Auto Industry*; John F. Stinson Jr., "Multiple jobholding up sharply in the 1980's," *Monthly Labor Review* (July 1990): 3–10; Jean Claude Parrot, "Why we continue to struggle," in G.S. Lowe and H.J. Krahn, eds., *Working Canadians* (Toronto: Methuen, 1984); Wells, *Soft Sell: "Quality of Working Life" Programs and the Productivity Race*; Gilbert Levine, "Industrial democracy is workers' control," in Lowe and Krahn, eds., *Working Canadians*;

Gerry Hunnius, "Co-determination — a capitalist innovation," in Lowe and Krahn, eds., *Working Canadians*; Donald Swartz, "New forms of worker participation: a critique of quality of working life," *Studies in Political Economy* 5 (1981): 55–78; Rinehart, "Appropriating workers' knowledge: quality control circles at a General Motors plant"; and Rinehart, "Improving the quality of working life through job redesign: work humanization or work rationalization?"

17. CAW-Canada (National Automobile, Aerospace and Agricultural Implements Workers Union of Canada), *CAW Statement on the Reorganization of Work* (North York, ON: CAW, 1988).

18. United Auto Workers, "Can capital and labour cooperate?" in Daniel Drache and Duncan Cameron, eds., *The Other Macdonald Report* (Toronto: James Lorimer, 1985), 152.

19. On Volvo Kalmar, see Berth Jonsson, "The Volvo experiences of new job design and new production technology," *Working Life in Sweden* 18 (September 1980), and Stefan Aguren, Christer Bredbacka, Reine Hansson, Kurt Ihregren, and K.C. Karlson, *Volvo Kalmar Revisited: Ten Years of Experience* (Stockholm: Efficiency and Participation Development Council, 1985). On Saab's work reorganization, see John Logue, "Saab/Trollhattan: reforming work life on the shop floor," *Working Life in Sweden* 23 (June 1981), and Jan Helling, "Innovations in work practices at Saab-Scania (Saab-Scania Personnel Division)," paper delivered at the U.S.–Japan Automotive Industry Conference, Ann Arbor, Mich., March 5–6, 1985. These accounts of the Volvo and Saab factories are also based on Graham S. Lowe's personal observations and discussions with union officials, management, and shop-floor workers during visits to both plants, in September 1985, as a guest researcher at the Swedish Centre for Working Life, Stockholm. For a more critical view, see Donald R. Van Houten, "The political economy and technical control of work humanization in Sweden during the 1970s and 1980s," *Work and Occupations* 14 (1990): 483–513.

20. James R. Lincoln and Kerry McBride, "Japanese industrial organization in comparative perspective," *Annual Review of Sociology* 13 (1987): 289–312.

21. Ibid.; James R. Lincoln, "Japanese organization and organization theory," *Research in Organizational Behavior* 12 (1990): 255–94; Gary G. Hamilton and Nicole Woolsey Biggart, "Market, culture, and authority: a comparative analysis of management and organization in the Far East," *American Journal of Sociology* 94 (1988): S52–S94.

22. Lincoln and McBride, "Japanese industrial organization in comparative perspective," 297. This paragraph draws mainly on this source (299–301).

23. Ibid., 300. On Toyota's QCs, see Robert E. Cole, *Work, Mobility, and Participation* (Berkeley: University of California Press, 1979).

24. Stephen Wood, "The Japanese management model," *Work and Occupations* 16 (1989): 446–60.

25. Stephen Wood, "The transformation of work?" in Stephen Wood, ed., *The Transformation of Work? Skill, Flexibility and Labour Process* (London: Unwin Hyman, 1989). Robertson and Wareham, *Technological Change in the Auto Industry*, 12–15.

26. These concepts are discussed in David Knights, Hugh Willmott, and David Collison, eds., *Job Redesign: Critical Perspectives on the Labour Process* (Aldershot, England: Gower, 1985). On quality circles, see Keith Bradley and Stephen Hill, "After Japan: the quality circle transplant and productive efficiency," *British Journal of Industrial Relations* 21 (1983): 291–311, and the Canadian case study of Rinehart, "Appropriating workers' knowledge: quality control circles at a General Motors plant."

27. Lincoln and McBride, "Japanese industrial organization in comparative perspective," 301.

28. Rosabeth Moss Kanter, *When Giants Learn to Dance: Mastering the Challenges of Strategy, Management, and Careers in the 1990s* (New York: Simon and Shuster, 1989), 274.

29. Ruth Milkman, *Japan's California Factories: Labor Relations and Economic Globalization* (Los Angeles: Institute of Industrial Relations, University of California, Los Angeles, 1991).

30. This account of Japanese firms in Canada draws on Ann Walmsley, "Trading places," *Report on Business Magazine* (March 1992): 17–27.

31. This paragraph is mainly based on D.H. Whittaker, "The end of Japanese style employment?" *Work, Employment & Society* 4 (1990): 321–47, and Tomasz Mroczkowski and Masao Hanaoka, "Continuity and change in Japanese management," *California Management Review* 31 (1989): 39–53.

32. See the highly critical personal account of life in a Toyota factory in Satoshi Kamata, *Japan in the Passing Lane: An Insider's Account of Life in a Japanese Factory* (New York: Pantheon, 1983).

PART 5

CRIME AND DEVIANCE

DEVIANCE IS BEHAVIOUR THAT departs from a norm. It ranges from harmless fads to the most violent crimes. In a sense, all deviance is anti-institutional because it seeks to achieve acceptable goals, such as getting rich or happy, by means that are generally disapproved of, and often illegal. But deviance is also institutionalized behaviour because it is socially learned, organized, and persistent. Accordingly, an individual is more likely to become a deviant if he or she is exposed to more deviant than non-deviant role models. Moreover, the deviant role is learned by means of socialization; just as medical students are socialized into the role of doctor, so professional robbers must learn the moral code of thieves. And deviants, including criminals, establish counter-institutions — cliques, gangs, mafias, and so forth — with their own rules of behaviour and their own subcultural norms.

In Chapter 26, Carl B. Klockars underlines the normality of deviance by analyzing how a fence (a person who disposes of stolen goods) views his own behaviour. Vincent, the fence interviewed in depth by Klockars, regards his actions as no better and no worse than those of people engaged in legitimate professions, and he develops an elaborate set of rationalizations to justify his work. "What I did harmed nobody." "I'm no worse than others." "He had it coming it to him." "I did it out of loyalty to my friends." "I'm not to blame; it's the fault of the terrible conditions in which I was raised." These are just some of the rationalizations that deviants use to render their actions morally acceptable to themselves and others. They are not the rantings of madmen. They are the musings of people who are embedded in subcultures with norms that differ from those of legitimate society.

Criminal behaviour worries the Canadian public more today than it did even five years ago, and much more than it did ten or twenty years ago. There is much talk about crime waves and mounting random violence. Many people are afraid to walk alone outside at night. In big cities, many people have equipped their homes with burglar alarms and installed steel bars on their basement windows.

There is no doubt that crime rates have risen since the 1960s, but are current fears exaggerated? Most people rely on the mass media for information about crime trends. The police rely on information they collect in the course of doing their work. Reported criminal incidents, apprehensions, convictions, and incarcerations are all recorded in order to determine, among other things, whether crimes of various types are on the rise. Both public and police sources of information are, however, subject to bias. The mass media are often inclined to exaggerate the extent of criminal behaviour because doing so increases audience size and therefore the amount of money that businesses are willing to pay for advertisements. The police may record more crime not just because there is more, but also because more officers are looking harder for criminals and because the public is more willing to report certain types of crimes.

Because of these biases, sociologists prefer to supplement official police statistics with **victimization surveys**, polls of representative samples of citizens that seek to determine whether and under what circumstances people are victims of crime. Victimization surveys often yield results that differ from official statistics. In Chapter 27, Rosemary Gartner and Anthony N. Doob of the University of Toronto compare the results of government-sponsored victimization surveys conducted in Canada in 1988 and 1993. Their findings lead us to conclusions that differ from recent public and police perceptions of crime. They found that in both 1988 and 1993, just under a quarter of Canadians were victims of at least one crime in the preceding year. Overall, victimization rates remained steady or *decreased* during the five-year period, depending on the type of crime examined. It was also discovered that while Canadians think that crime rates are rising, they believe that the rise is occurring some place other than their own neighbourhood. Thus it is not personal experience that accounts for recent perceptions of rising crime rates. Rather, Gartner and Doob conclude that such perceptions result partly from mass media "hype" and partly from the fact that robberies and assaults occur more frequently in public settings than they used to. They conclude by arguing that discrepancies between police statistics and victimization surveys are partly due to the fact that the victims of some crimes, such as spousal assault and school violence, are more willing to report events to the authorities than they used to be. Increased reporting does not, however, necessarily mean increased crime.

If most people believe that crime is on the rise, many also believe that the alleged crime wave is in part a racial phenomenon. Canadian blacks in particular rank high in the public's perception of criminal villains. Some people — including a handful of academics, such as University of Western Ontario psychology professor Philippe Rushton — go so far as to claim that there is a *genetic* link between race and crime. He contends that Negroids (blacks) are genetically predisposed to commit more criminal acts than Caucasoids (whites), while whites are genetically predisposed to commit more criminal acts than Mongoloids (orientals). He cites crime statistics from the United States, the United Kingdom, and other countries showing that crime rates do indeed vary along racial lines, as he predicts.

In Chapter 28, Julian V. Roberts and Thomas Gabor of the University of Ottawa criticize Rushton's views. They show, among other things, that crime rates vary *within* racial groups, depending on historical period and society. Homicide rates are very low among blacks in Africa and Chinese in Hong Kong, but very high among blacks in the Bahamas and even higher among Filipinos in the Philippines. Yet if Rushton's genetic theory were correct, blacks would have universally higher crime rates than orientals. Roberts and Gabor also show that race-specific crime rates vary by type of crime. For instance, in the United States, whites have much higher rates of white-collar crime (fraud, embezzlement, etc.) than do blacks. These and other facts analyzed by Roberts and Gabor demonstrate that genetic factors peculiar to each race do not cause crime. Roberts and Gabor instead attribute high rates of "street crime" among blacks in the United States and the United Kingdom exclusively to social factors: where they face high levels of discrimination, widespread poverty, and differential treatment by the criminal justice system, blacks are convicted of more street crime.

Crime statistics by race are not widely available in Canada, but those that are available often contradict Rushton's argument. For example, the homicide rate among aboriginal Canadians is more than ten times higher than that among whites, but Rushton's theory predicts the opposite since aboriginal Canadians are of Mongoloid descent. Canadian aboriginals do, however, resemble American blacks in terms of the social conditions in which they live, a fact that is consistent with Roberts's and Gabor's theory.

In Chapter 29, Rhonda L. Lenton of McMaster University tackles yet another commonly held belief about crime in her comparative analysis of homicide rates in Canada and the United States. Crime rates in the United States — especially rates of violent crime — are higher than those in Canada. This difference is sometimes attributed to the greater anti-authoritarianism and lawlessness of American culture, which supposedly derives from the early frontier experience of the United States. In contrast, it is sometimes held that Canadians' greater respect for law and order keeps crime rates lower here. Our enduring ties to England, and the predominance of the relatively authoritarian Roman Catholic and Anglican churches in Canada, presumably reinforce that respect. Lenton, however, shows otherwise. Homicide rates in Canada are not highest in areas with relatively few people of British origin and few Roman Catholics and Anglicans. Rather, they are highest in areas with the highest proportion of aboriginal Canadians, percentage of families reporting no income, and levels of infant mortality. This leads her to suggest that, in general, homicide rates vary with social-structural, not cultural, differences: high levels of racial discrimination and income inequality result in high homicide rates. In that light, it is not surprising that Canada has a lower homicide rate than the United States since a smaller proportion of people suffer from racial discrimination in Canada and the level of income inequality is lower.

GLOSSARY

Deviance is behaviour that departs from a norm.

Victimization surveys are polls of representative samples of citizens that seek to determine whether and under what circumstances people are victims of crime.

Chapter 26

THE PHILOSOPHY OF A PROFESSIONAL FENCE

Carl B. Klockars

The more weakened the groups to which [an individual] belongs, the less he depends on them, the more he consequently depends only on himself and recognizes no other rules of conduct than what are founded on his private interests.

— *Émile Durkheim*, Suicide: A Study in Sociology, 1897

It is not my contention that all fences see or justify their behavior as Vincent does, any more than I maintain that they all do business exactly as he does. I do contend, however, that Vincent's explanations are something more than the rationalizations of one particular man with a particular life history. Vincent is neither neurotic nor psychotic. His apologia is persuasive, successfully mitigating the seriousness of his criminality not only to himself but to some others as well. To discard his explanations as simply fragments of illogic, defense mechanisms, or rationalizations would seem at minimum a wasteful use of rather precious testimony.

Vincent is an especially good source for an elaborate apologia. On the one hand he loves his work, knows no other business, and has worked at criminal receiving for more than thirty years. He also has a substantial stake in his identity in this document. On the other hand, he is getting old, has seen a number of his peers die, and is wealthy enough to pack in the business immediately and never want for anything. He is still an Italian Catholic who once took the good sisters' warnings seriously. He has been extraordinarily successful all through his life in persuading people to do what they ought not to do.

One of the problems involved in securing a professional criminal's account for his life is that the only time he need offer it is when he comes into contact with curious or critical members of legitimate society who know he is a criminal. Consequently, one can probably not credit the apologetics of most professional criminals as authentic "working philosophies." But I think the situation with Vincent is different. He is a *public*, professional criminal; almost everyone he knows is aware that he is a fence. His friends and acquaintances include both upperworld and underworld types. In addition, part of his business includes giving off the impression that what he is doing is not "really bad" even though everybody knows it is illegal. The "public" fence always straddles the boundary between the insiders and outsiders in society. His success depends upon getting insiders to cooperate with outsiders through him. I do not believe that the apologia I present was constructed just for me. I know that Vincent has explained his mode of life to many others in the same way, and I am further convinced that this is in fact the way he sees what he does.

Although there are no hard data on the subject, it is clear that there is a substantial trade in stolen property.[1] This trade requires, at least in part, the knowing participation of otherwise law-abiding citizens. I venture to suggest that a good many of those who would buy stolen property would be outraged at the thought of committing robbery, burglary, or larceny them-

Source: The Professional Fence (New York: The Free Press, 1974), pp. 135–61. Copyright © 1974 by Carl B. Klockars. Reprinted with the permission of The Free Press, a Division of Simon & Schuster, Inc.

selves. Vincent's apologia inevitably plays on themes which support trade in stolen property in the society at large. His explanations are thus cultural artifacts, configurations of sentiment, reason, and perspective which are frequently effective in the rhetoric of our culture in defining the buying of stolen property as acceptable or excusable behavior. This view of Vincent's testimony suggests that the criminologist seeking to understand the role of the fence in society and the sociology of the trade in stolen goods may begin to do so by considering not only the truth of Vincent's apologia (that is, the extent to which it approximates his actual behavior and its effects), but also its capacity to assuage the norms which prohibit buying stolen property (and thus free men to do so if the situation presents itself).[2]

VINCENT SWAGGI: *APOLOGIA PRO VITA SUA*, PART I — "I DON'T DO NOTHING WRONG"

Legally, Vincent's acts constitute criminal receiving of stolen property. In the state in which Vincent works, a conviction carries the penalty of imprisonment for up to five years plus a fine of as much as $1,000. With the state's indeterminate-sentence law operating so as to perfunctorily reduce all sentences to one-half the maximum penalty, the maximum time Vincent would serve would be two and one-half years. Vincent correctly considers his conviction exceedingly unlikely and his serving a maximum sentence impossible. In more than thirty years of criminal receiving, Vincent has spent only eight months in jail; his only conviction for receiving was more than twenty years ago. The judgment of the law, except insofar as it codifies certain normative evaluations, is irrelevant to Vincent.

Only Vincent's buying and selling of stolen property threatens his respectability. At first glance, such a statement seems a truism; certainly the reason Vincent is of interest to criminology is that he is a fence. Yet, the context in which otherwise deviant or criminal behavior occurs enormously affects society's evaluation of that behavior. Consider the words with which our language reflects a social evaluation of those who violate an identical law in the case of prostitution. Is a "kept woman" a "slut"? Is an "escort" a "whore"? Is a "lady of the evening" a "hooker"? Certainly no poet, specialist in meaning and impression, would use such words interchangeably. Homosexuality, generally regarded as deviant, seems infinitely more acceptable to society when it is packaged in respectable speech and attire than when it appears in lisping drag. Likewise, it seems easier for society to regard the addiction of the physician or the alcoholism of the housewife as a "disease" than to accept the same affliction in the street addict or skid-row bum. Although other factors are also effective in shielding the white collar criminal from the social and legal definition of his acts as crime rather than as civil or administrative violations, it would seem that his face of respectability saps our enthusiasm to class and house him with "real" convicts.[3]

The apparatus and behavior of the fence are not especially different from that of the legitimate businessman. They exist as synecdochical evidence of respectability and affirm that, with the exception of the fact that the fence buys and sells property which is stolen, he is no different from his legitimate-businessman counterparts. For Vincent, his store, his customers, and his legitimate associates simplify his *apologia pro vita sua.* He need not contend with offensive side effects of his deviance on his presentation of self for they are absent or minor. Instead, he can get right on to the business of showing why his buying and selling stolen goods ain't really that bad after all.

Denial of Responsibility

> *The way I look at it, I'm a businessman. Sure I buy hot stuff, but I never stole nothing in my life. Some driver brings me a couple a cartons, though, I ain't gonna turn him away. If I don't buy it, somebody else will. So what's the difference? I might as well make money with him instead of somebody else.*

In the above statement Vincent (1) denies that he ever stole anything in his life. He then asserts either directly or by implication (2) that there is an important distinction between stealing and receiving stolen goods; (3) that the criminal act of receiving would take place even if he were not the one to do it; and (4) that he does not cause the goods to be stolen. Let us consider each of these defenses separately.

He Never Stole Anything in His Life

In two rigorous senses Vincent has stolen. First, in a number of anecdotes about his childhood, Vincent has described his juvenile industry at theft. He dismisses those events as irrelevant to the above statement, explaining that although he says "never in my life," his childhood does not count. This is illogical in a strict sense of the words used. However, biographical claims are often intended more as moral advertisements than historical descriptions. When such is the intention, it is quite acceptable social form to exclude from public reflections on "true character" those moments of one's life when one was not in full control of one's self. Consider such statements as, "All my life I've followed the Golden Rule." (From age 2? 7? 19? 21?) Or, "He really is a gentle man, but watch out when he's drunk."

Second, according to a strict legal interpretation of his adult behavior, Vincent does steal. He does, as the common-law definition of theft provides, "take the goods of another, without permission, with the intent to permanently deprive that person of his rightful property." However, the law makes distinctions between theft and receiving (often attaching a lower penalty to receiving), and I suspect that few readers are troubled by Vincent's simultaneous claim both that he has never stolen anything and that he does buy stolen property. It is, for most of us, an understandable social distinction. What Vincent means is that he is not a thief.

There Is an Important Distinction Between Stealing and Receiving

Vincent claims not to be a thief, and we understand what he means. For Vincent himself, there are differences not only between thieves and receivers, but also between thieves and drivers.

> See, Carl, what you gotta understand is when I say "driver" I don't mean "thief." I don't consider a driver a thief. To me, a thief is somebody who goes into a house an' takes a TV set and the wife's jewelry an' maybe ends up killin' somebody before he's through. An' for what? So some nothin' fence will steal the second-hand shit he takes? To me that kind a guy is the scum of the earth.
>
> Now a driver, he's different. A driver's a workin' man. He gets an overload now an' then or maybe he clips a carton or two. He brings it to me. He makes a few bucks so he can go out on a Friday night or maybe buy his wife a new coat. To me, a thief an' a driver is two entirely different things.

Those things which distinguish the driver and the thief in Vincent's estimation may point to distinctions that the larger society makes between receiving stolen goods and actually stealing them. The fence, like the driver, does not enter homes or stores to remove property; there is no danger of violence in his presence. A thief, on the other hand, could do anything: he may

well be a drug addict, rapist, robber, burglar, or assaulter, or, if the situation arose, a murderer. Society has no clear expectations about the limits of criminality involved.

On the other hand, a fence, Vincent claims, is a businessman who buys and sells stolen property. Like the driver, the fence commits his crime in the course of behavior which differs only minutely from that of legitimate members of his trade. And like the driver, the fence has a relatively stable social identity: the driver will presumably be at work again tomorrow; Vincent is in his store every day of the week. Vincent buys and sells things, waits on customers, and walks public streets openly. Truck drivers perform public tasks as well. Thieves are shadowy figures, sneaking around behind the scenes and even hiding their right names behind aliases.[4]

In sum, when Vincent begins his apologia by saying "I never stole nothin' in my life," he magnifies a common distinction between a receiver and a thief. He means, first, that he does not actually take merchandise from its owners. But second, and more importantly, he means that the fear, disgust, and distaste which "thief" connotes to some people should not and do not properly apply to him. The law, his customers, his friends, and his neighbors know there are differences between thieves and receivers, and so does Vincent.

Receiving Would Take Place Even Without Him

By saying "If I don't buy it, somebody else will," Vincent attempts to minimize his responsibility by pointing to the presumed consequences of the private refusal to buy. They are, he asserts, nil; therefore his responsibility is nil. This is a patently attractive moral position, and one which is echoed frequently. Let us first examine the accuracy of the assertion before evaluating the moral position which Vincent derives from it.

Would someone else buy the merchandise if Vincent refused? I think they probably would. Although Vincent is able to dispose of some merchandise which other fences might have great difficulty selling (e.g., dental supplies), the vast majority of merchandise in which Vincent trades could be handled by many other fences. The related question, of course, is whether or not the particular thief or driver who approached Vincent with stolen property would be able to locate another fence to sell to if Vincent refused. This is problematic. In my estimation, many would find another outlet almost immediately, some would find one after a bit of looking and asking, and a very few might not be able to find another buyer.

Depending on the character both of the merchandise and of his friends and neighbors, the thief or driver might well be able to sell stolen merchandise to them at a better price than he could get from Vincent.

If the accuracy of Vincent's statement is conceded, its moral implications remain to be considered. Certainly one can find examples of the same form of rationalization being offered in quite disparate social situations. The physician on trial for performing a criminal abortion claims that he performed the requested operation rather than have the woman find another, possibly less competent, conspirator. The arms manufacturer claims that he cannot be held responsible for a war because if he had not sold weapons to the participants they would have bought them elsewhere. Likewise, the conscripted soldier who opposes war but fights anyway may take comfort in the knowledge that his participation will not affect the waging of a given war or its outcome.

The moral position upon which such arguments rest is that a person's culpability for participation in an immoral or illegal act disappears or is mitigated if the act is likely to occur even if he does not participate in it. Such a position can be extended to cover situations even less pleasant that those listed above. For example, it removes responsibility in almost all incidents of mob violence. Is no one in a lynch mob responsible because others are also willing to string the victim up? Is looting at a riot scene excusable because others are looting too? Is vandalism blameless when it is a group affair? To push the position harder still, one could envision a small team of paid professional killers who always shoot their victims simultaneously so that no one gunman feels guilty. Even firing squads, so legend has it, reject such nonsense by actually loading one gun with blanks.

Responsibility for action is responsibility for action. Whether or not an act is likely to occur without one is simply irrelevant to the evaluation of one's own conduct. To surrender that elementary premise of simple moral philosophy is to abandon the responsibility to refuse to participate when one believes that others are doing wrong. Middle-class mothers everywhere, sensitive always to the seductions of the world, have correctly admonished their children who "went along with the crowd": "Just because everybody else jumps off a cliff doesn't mean you have to." It is an admonition of considerable rhetorical sophistication which has absolutely nothing to do with jumping off of cliffs, but gets instantly to the heart of patently attractive denials of responsibility like "If I don't buy it somebody else will."

He Does Not Cause the Goods to Be Stolen

With this statement Vincent suggests his relationship to drivers (and, by extension, thieves) who supply him with stolen merchandise. In Vincent's consideration he is merely commercial respondent to theft whereas it is thieves and drivers who must bear responsibility for it.

For Vincent, the etiology of theft is a considerably less difficult problem than it is for criminologists: people steal because they want money. Why else should anyone steal? In general, why they want money is their own business, but Vincent, like most small businessmen, is close enough to those he works with to reflect on their motives. For most thieves, Vincent finds that drugs, gambling, and "high living" (Cadillacs for blacks is Vincent's most frequent example) are the main incentives for illegal earnings. Drivers, on the other hand, often use the proceeds from what they sell to add "a little extra" to the family income. To Vincent, it is preposterous to suggest that it is he, rather than the factors which thieves and drivers themselves cite, that is responsible for theft.

Some recent criminology, at least, claims otherwise:

> This coaching (in methods of theft) by the fence in rational criminal techniques may lead to a reevaluation of the risks involved in criminal activity, which can be an important escalating career contingency.... Additionally, this same effect is achieved merely by meeting the fence and concluding a successful transaction with him.
>
> If we can argue ... that we will always "produce" deviants so long as we have an established machinery for processing them, then it might also be legitimate to suggest that the same can be said about the impact of supporting elements. Thus the continued existence of fences, tipsters, and similar types will tend to assure that we will always produce new deviants.[5]

Thus, Shover contends that fences encourage thieves and drivers by approving of their stealing and advising them how to steal successfully. In addition, fences may, simply by their continued existence and availability as fences, tend to assure the continuing existence of a population of drivers and thieves.

Shover's argument is compelling, and with a few technical reservations Vincent is inclined to agree with this sophisticated sociological rendition of the old adage "If there were no receivers, there would be no thieves." However, Vincent's sense of his own personal responsibility for the stealing by thieves and drivers is quite a different matter. It is at this individual level that the norms of Vincent's world and Shover's sociology part company.

In the same way that Shover's argument suggests that the continued existence of public bars assures the continued existence of a population of alcoholics, or the manufacture of high-powered cars "produces" highway speeders, or the existence of gambling casinos "escalates the career contingencies" of compulsive or intemperate gamblers, Vincent concedes that fences are a part of the machinery that sustains and encourages theft. But with a logic that I suspect is familiar to, at least, bartenders, high-powered car manufacturers, and casino owners, he argues that "I don't force anybody to do business with me who doesn't want to." Vincent further insists that adults are adults and "should know what they are doing."

Vincent views his own life history with a similar sense of individual responsibility. He can see how some of his early experiences — street hustling, his orphanage term, his association with his Uncle Hoppo — may have encouraged his becoming a fence. ("I guess I picked up a lot of my ideas from hangin' around with Hoppo and those guys.") But there is no sense in which Vincent would blame anyone else for where he is and what he does today. To do so would strike Vincent as unmasculine, the mark of a weak person or cry baby.[6]

In denying his responsibility for theft in this way, Vincent takes the question of his responsibility to an area with which he is most familiar — one in which moral and legal grounds for establishing responsibility are constantly shifting. Consider the case of the vendor of alcoholic beverages. One can state categorically that if there were no alcohol there would be no abuse of alcohol, no alcoholics, no drunken driving, no public drunkenness. Nevertheless, it is generally conceded that vendors of alcohol ought not to be held responsible for their customers' abuse of it. Normally, the consumer bears the total responsibility for his use or misuse of what he buys. However, in particular circumstances, the vendor may acquire both legal and moral responsibilities for his customers. He cannot, for example, sell liquor to minors, nor, according to the law in many states, can he sell it to an obviously intoxicated person. In still other states, the law requires that he provide transportation home for a patron who is unfit to drive. In each of these special cases the loss or absence of the consumer's adult capacities may legally if not morally oblige the vendor to assume them. There is some point beyond which legal responsibility cannot be extended for practical reasons, but how far ought one to extend moral responsibility? Should a bartender serve a customer who has cirrhosis? Or, are even the above laws too morally and legally paternalistic, denying one's right to get drunk in public if he wants to?[7] There are no certain grounds, legal or moral, upon which to settle such questions.

Similar problems, both moral and legal, are involved in many transactions between buyers and sellers. The question is always "Who is responsible?" and, ultimately, it must be resolved in favor of one party or the other. The bartender must know if he is obliged to serve the intoxicated person who demands another drink or if he is obliged to refuse him and call a taxi to take him home. When Vincent argues that it is the thief or driver and not he who is responsible for theft, he employs a notion of responsibility which is derived from and is peculiar to business transactions. For Vincent, responsibility is an either/or proposition, as it must be in relations between buyers and sellers. It works on the principle of subtraction: if the thief is responsible for his stealing then Vincent is not.

The highly peculiar quality of Vincent's subtractive sense of responsibility becomes apparent when one takes it out of the context of business transactions. Elsewhere, the notion of responsibility is governed not by a principle of subtraction but by a principle of addition. It is perfectly normal to refer to two, three, ten, or even hundreds of people as being responsible for a given act or event. And it is, of course, with this additive concept of responsibility that the law prohibiting criminal receiving is justified and the moral responsibility of the criminal receiver established. Simply stated, the thief is responsible for his stealing and the criminal receiver is responsible for encouraging that theft.

Denial of Victims

The first line of defense in Vincent's apologia is his denial of responsibility for theft and his argument that for him to refrain from buying stolen goods would be inconsequential. His second line of argument is to deny that his activities have any meaningful victims or inflict any significant injury. To appreciate Vincent's second defense one must consider some of the experiences from which he reasons.

More than most people, Vincent witnesses extensive violations of the law against receiving. He sees respectable society, including police and judicial officials, coming to him for bargains that they know are suspect. Because of his reputation, he is often solicited by otherwise legitimate businessmen interested in buying something that they deal in should he come across it. He also encounters respectable types who find something romantic about his being a fence. For example:

> I got to know my doctor real good when I was in for my last operation. Somebody told him about me, I guess. Well, I started telling him about stuff, you know, buyin', sellin', thieves, boosters. He just couldn't get over it. He wanted me to get him some hot suits. You know, have him pick out the suits and send some boosters in to get 'em. He really wanted to do it. You shoulda seen how excited he was talkin' about swag. Imagine a guy like that, a big doctor an' all, getting so excited about hot stuff.

This widespread trafficking with him, and occasional fascination for his work, have consequences for the way Vincent sees his own behavior. First of all, he is conscious of a certain hypocrisy in society's attitude toward dealing in stolen property. He is aware of the legal prohibition against receiving, yet sees frequent evidence of willful, guilt-free violation of it by those who ought to know better. Vincent's recall of occasions when highly respectable citizens bought stolen goods or what they thought were stolen goods is extremely acute. Legitimate citizens of high status are truly "significant others" for Vincent.

Indeed, Vincent sees the patronage of such legitimate citizens as a reflection of his own worth. Their buying from him and maintaining friendly relations with him are considered by Vincent to constitute an important vindication of the possibly shady character of what he does. It is true that Vincent is an attractive and enjoyable person; but even if his friendly acquaintances seek him out only for this social aspect of his personality, Vincent finds it easy to perceive that they are not sufficiently offended by his receiving to limit their association with him.[8]

Given the highly supportive character of Vincent's immediate environment, he is able to think of his victim and the injury he receives as someone or something "out there," removed from him physically and normatively, and separated by the intervening actions and responsibility of the thief or driver. Only very rarely does Vincent ever confront the victim of a theft. The latter is likely to direct his rage at the thief, his employee's carelessness, or his faulty security system rather than at the fence who eventually buys what was stolen from him.

From this detached perspective, Vincent contemplates the extent of his victims' losses:

> Did you see the paper yesterday? You figure it out. Last year I musta had $25,000 worth a merchandise from Sears. In this city last year they could'a called it Sears, Roebuck, and Swaggi. Just yesterday in the paper I read where Sears just had the biggest year in history, made more money than ever before. Now if I had that much of Sears's stuff can you imagine how much they musta lost all told? Millions, must be millions. And they still had their biggest year ever.

Vincent reads Sears's declaration of success as evidence of the inconsequential character of his receiving their stolen merchandise. Hence he considers any possible claim on their part that he or hundreds of others like him are substantially harming business as at least greedy if not absurd. The logic of such an analysis is the same, on a larger scale, as the "Ma Bell can afford it" reasoning invoked by the pay-phone patron who receives a windfall from a malfunctioning unit. Vincent does not stop there in his consideration of Sears's success, however.

> You think they end up losing when they get clipped? Don't you believe it. They're no different from anybody else. If they don't get it back by takin' it off their taxes, they get it back from insurance. Who knows, maybe they do both.
>
> Carl, if I told you how many businessmen I know have a robbery every now an' then to cover expenses you wouldn't believe it. What does it take? You get some trusted employee, and you send him out with an empty truck. He parks it somewhere an' calls in an' says he was robbed. That's it. The insurance company's gotta pay up. The driver makes a couple a hundred bucks and it's an open-an'-shut case. You can't do it every year but once in a while it's a sure thing.
>
> Oh, there's millions a ways to do it. You come in in the mornin' an' break your window. Call the cops, mess some stuff up. Bang! You got a few thousand from the insurance company. I'm tellin' ya, it happens all the time.

Thus Vincent denies significant injury to Sears not only because of their net profits but because they can be seen as recovering most of their loss from insurance payment or through tax write-offs.[9] The reality for Vincent, in sum, is the comparatively trivial effect of theft on the insured victim. Inconvenient, perhaps; devastating, no! Hence, no real injury, no real victim.

The problem remaining is the general effect on pricing that theft produces. As a businessman, Vincent is in agreement with his counterparts that theft and shrinkage result in higher mark-ups and higher prices. But Vincent again falls back on the question of the ultimate consequences of his particular refusal to buy. Assuming his thieves and drivers could not find anyone else to sell to, the entire result of Vincent's private refusal to buy might amount to a penny a person for the entire year, if it were distributed over the total population of the city. And on the other side of the ledger, Vincent reckons that some of his other services to the general welfare of the community more than balance what he takes out.

The questions of the moral responsibility involved in buying stolen goods, and of the consequences of such an act for any putative victims, would be even less problematic for Vincent's customers than for Vincent were they to confront them. Given that a particular item is on Vincent's shelf and is known to be stolen, a particular purchase will not affect Vincent's survival as a fence. I do not believe that a rational economic argument can be made against an individual decision to buy stolen goods. The claim that theft costs everyone as reflected in higher costs and insurance rates is inadequate. It costs everyone surely, but those who buy stolen goods manage to offset these higher costs and rates. In fact, were it simply a question of a personal economic strategy, one might argue that the only way to beat the consequences of the thieves' market is to patronize it. The only argument left seems to be to appeal to a responsibility to the general welfare of others.

To legalize receiving stolen goods would legitimize an institution which is intolerable. It would encourage theft and have a pernicious effect on society. Clearly it is an absurd suggestion. But the conflict is still real. The department-store sweater costs $15.99. Vincent is selling it for $10.00. In this particular case it is a question of saving $5.99 or making an economic gesture to the general welfare. All day long Vincent sees the general welfare lose out to bargains.

VINCENT SWAGGI: *APOLOGIA PRO VITA SUA*, PART II — "I THINK I'M A PRETTY DECENT GUY"

To this point Vincent's apologia has focused on what he considers to be the particularly benign features of his occupation. He finds no victims and no real injury. He denies responsibility for theft and its encouragement. He maintains that his private refusal to buy stolen property would be inconsequential. Vincent reaches these conclusions about the character of what he does by interpreting his day-to-day behavior in the most favorable possible way. I have been able to point to these errors in Vincent's analysis because this portion of his apologia was an analysis of concrete events. In short, I could compare Vincent's evaluation of what he does and has done with descriptions of the events themselves.

In this second portion of his apologia Vincent changes the character of his account from a professional, offense-specific defense of his criminal career to a more general evaluation of his character. The assertion Vincent made in Part I of his *Apologia Pro Vita Sua* was that he didn't do anything wrong; the assertion he makes in Part II is that he is, all things considered, a nice guy.

Because the terms of Vincent's argument change in this second portion of his apologia, it is difficult to criticize what he says. Specific acts, their consequences and interpretation, are not at issue. Hence the critic of Vincent is disarmed, because no particular act of Vincent's will disprove his claims. Contrariwise, the nature of the way Vincent makes his argument ensures that a complete display of evidence in favor of his claim (viz., in spite of everything he has done, he is a decent fellow) need not — indeed cannot — be made. I have called the sensibility within which Vincent comprehends his good character "the metaphor of the ledger."

The Metaphor of the Ledger

Sure I've done some bad things in my life. Who hasn't? Everybody's got a skeleton in his closet somewhere. But you gotta take into account all the good things I done too. You take all the things I done in my life and put 'em together, no doubt about it, I gotta come out on the good side.

As a businessman, Vincent is familiar with the use of a ledger for evaluating the success or failure of enterprise. He knows that there are different ways of setting up and managing accounts. Some entries are puffed a bit more than they deserve; other profits don't show up in the counting. Occasionally, one shows a loss so as to make things look normal or to prevent having to pay too much in the end. Business accounts, properly managed by able accountants, set things in order for the businessman and those who are interested in judging what he has accomplished. When all is said and done, the ledger tells whether or not one comes up in the red or in the black.

A metaphorical ledger is equally useful in evaluating life histories: good in the credit column is balanced against evil in the debit column. Thus, acts of charity and benevolence offset entries of greed or selfishness. It is an attractive metaphor. From the scales of justice to the Great Book of St. Peter, the notion of a balancing between good and evil has proven to be a persuasive one for the common comprehension and consideration of penance, indulgence, grace, judgment, atonement, salvation, and contrition.[10]

To Vincent, a businessman all his life, the metaphor of the ledger comes easily. In accounting for his conduct, Vincent considers his criminality and his exemplary behavior on the same balance sheet.

When it comes to fences I consider myself in a class by myself. I don't consider your street-corner fences, buyin' an' sellin' secondhand stuff, to be anything like me at all. For one thing they're all no good. They're all cheap, greedy bastards who'd sell their mother if they had a chance. I figure I have a certain class, ya know, a certain way of doin' things. To me them guys are nothin'. They're stupid, ignorant people. I can't even stand bein' around 'em.

Thieves and Drivers

In reckoning credits for his self-evaluation, Vincent points to those good things he has done for people which his role did not require him to do. For example:

Take what I done for Artie, for instance. Now there's a guy, he's been a thief for years, an' nothin' to show for it. That year alone I musta given him $25,000. One day I'd give 'em a hundred bucks, the next day he'd be back askin' for a loan. So I had a talk with him. I told him, "Look, you're makin' good money. Why don't you put it toward a house?" So we set up a little deal where I'd keep a little each time we had a deal; then when he had enough we'd put it toward a house.

Well it took about three months an' he had about $1,500 with me. So I got a real-estate agent I knew to get him a place, nothin' fancy but a pretty good neighborhood. It was colored but clean. Well, you know what happened? His wife came down with his kids an' she couldn't thank me enough. They had been livin' in one of those welfare high rises and she hated it. Every now an' then she comes by to tell me how things are goin'.

Don't get me wrong. I made a lot of money off of Artie, but I set him straight too.

What places Vincent's efforts in Artie's behalf on the credit side of the ledger is the fact that Artie and his wife appreciated Vincent's assistance and that Vincent did not have to give it. Vincent has repeated similar anecdotes to me frequently.

I am good to children. You know "Eyeball," right? All the trouble I had with him? His wife came in at Christmastime last year. When she left she had at least a hundred dollars worth of clothes and toys for her kids. I knew Eyeball was in jail an' she didn't have nothin'. Carl, if you knew how much stuff I gave to people, outright gifts, you wouldn't believe it.

Would you believe it if I told you that I got a thief who calls me "his white father"? It's true. I been good to him. Posted bail for him a couple of times. He tells everybody, "Vincent Swaggi, he's my white father."

The matter of the posted bail in the second anecdote raises a number of complications in the matter of crediting Vincent's generosity. One could interpret Vincent's bailing out the thief as self-serving, since Vincent knew that once back on the street, the thief would resume bringing him merchandise. The extent to which such actions should be seen as impelled by generosity becomes even more problematic in those cases where Vincent benefits more than does the recipient. Many people turn to Vincent for "help" when they are in a jam and don't know what to do. Providing alibis, referrals to persuasive lawyers, loans at high interest, and the kind of encouragement a man occasionally needs to get back to his work are all well appreciated. Just a little bit of help sometimes pays off handsomely.

I had this guy bringin' me radios. Nice little clock radios, sold for $34.95. He worked in the warehouse. Two a day he'd bring me, an' I'd give him fifteen for the both of 'em. Well, after a while he told me his boss was gettin' suspicious 'cause inventory showed a big shortage. So I asked him how he was gettin' the radios out. He says he puts 'em in his locker at lunch an' takes 'em to me after work. So I ask him if anybody else is takin' much stuff. He says a couple of guys do. I tell him to lay off for a while an' the next time he sees one of the other guys take somethin' to tip off the boss. They'll fire the guy an' clear up the shortage. Well he did it an' you know what happened? They made my man assistant shipper. Now once a month I get a carton delivered right

*to my store with my name on it. Clock radios,
percolators, waffle irons, anything I want, fifty
off wholesale.*

Though Vincent is reluctant to place such profitable assistance in his credit column, one must consider the matter from the perspective of the newly appointed shipper: Vincent advised him well. He saved him from his suspicious boss, cleared his reputation, got him promoted, probably with a raise, and made it possible for him not only to increase his earnings from theft but to steal with greater security as well. For Vincent, on the other hand, such an incident cancels itself out; it was good advice which paid off. Yet, although such events cannot, because they paid off so well, be offered individually as evidences of virtue, in the aggregate they enhance Vincent's professional self-conception. However, they leave a residual magnanimity which surfaces in statements such as the following:

*I treat the people I deal with right. If they're in a
jam an' I can help 'em out, I'll do it. And I don't
mean just your high class types either. I mean
thieves, drivers, police, customers, anybody. I'm
known for helpin' people out when I can.*

*You don't have to be a bastard to be in this business, you know. You can treat people decent.
Some guys, like my brother, never learn that.
They think a black man comes into the store, you
can push 'm around, call him "colored" or "boy";
you just can't do that no more. Times have
changed.*

*I am liked by the people I do business with. No
doubt about it. They know I treat 'em right.
Look at my window. You see any grate over it?
How long have you known me? More than a
year now, right? Did you ever see that window
broken? With all the characters I do business
with, how long do you think it would be before
somebody threw a brick through it if they didn't
like me? I am known for bein' good to people.
That window's been there ever since I had this
store. Nobody ever touched it.*

Vincent is sensitive to the opinions people have of him, even if those people are only thieves and drivers. When his daughter's home was robbed, he explained, "You know, Carl, if it's somebody I know, I'm hurt. If not, God bless 'em." This remark, although a bit more sentimental than usual for Vincent, is interesting. It reveals both an expectation of occupational loyalty and a kind of professional respect. "God bless 'em"

ought not to be interpreted as implying a passive response, however. Vincent worked very hard at locating the culprits.

The difficulty in finding unambiguously creditable behavior for the positive side of the ledger is that in relations with thieves and drivers the roles of "good fence" and "decent guy" are in part congruent. Self-interest becomes visible in generosity, and profits make altruism suspect. Such an opinion is possible, though, only to those permitted a full account of the fence's operations. While Vincent is aware of the payoffs for him in acts of apparent generosity and assistance, his thieves are not. If Vincent is liked, appreciated, and thanked, he does not advertise his altruism; in fact, he is likely to minimize the importance of his own acts. ("It was the least I could do. Don't get me wrong, I made a lot of money off of him.") By doing so he is thus freed to accept the gratitude and appreciation of those he helped. These responses Vincent remembers, reminds me of, and credits to the good side of the ledger.

Customers

Vincent's customers provide him with frequent opportunities for creditable behavior, but just as with thieves and drivers, questions of self-interest plague Vincent's accounting. "Bargains," "just-for-you" prices, and doing people "favors" by selling them merchandise at 30% below wholesale evoke favorable attitudes, but just don't qualify as hard evidence of goodness, because they are too much a part of what is required in a fence's business. The following incident is clearly creditable to the good side of the ledger, but it also suggests how difficult it is to be good when self-interest is suspected.

*The other day this old lady comes in my store.
She's Irish, got a brogue so thick you could cut it
with a knife. I can tell she ain't got much. I
mean her clothes were cheap an' she's got this real
thin cloth coat on. You remember how cold it
was last Wednesday? Well, she's real old-country,
kerchief on the back of her head an' all.*

*She says she's lookin' for a sweater 'cause it's
so cold out. I tell her she don't need a sweater,
what she really needs is a good heavy coat. She
says she ain't got enough money for a coat now.
So I ask her how much she got an' she says six
dollars. "Six dollars," I say. "Are you in luck,
Mother. I have a special sale on coats today, but
you can only get one if you're Irish."*

*"I'm Irish," she says. "No," I say, "really?"
I'm givin' her the whole bullshit, you know.*

Anyway, I show her three coats I got in the back. They were samples, retail maybe $45 or $50. "Are you selling these for only six dollars?" she says. "Ya," I say, "but only today and only if you're Irish. Are you sure you're Irish?" "Aye," she says, "I sure am." Then you know what she says to me? She says, "What's wrong with these coats?" Fifty dollar coats for six dollars and she asks me what's wrong. "The buttons are the wrong color. They're black an' they should be brown." I gotta tell her somethin' or she wouldn't buy it. So I take her six bucks so she won't think it's charity.

You know, she comes back to shop every so often. Do you know she still doesn't understand I gave her that coat. She thinks I had to sell that coat for six bucks 'cause the buttons were black instead of brown.

It is important to remember that within a few minutes after this incident of generosity Vincent was probably back at his characteristically very sharp trading. There is no illogic in bargaining extremely hard at one moment and virtually giving away goods at the next. The former confirms a professional, businesslike self-conception; the latter demonstrates that one is a good man.

Generosity and creditable behavior are possible only when the motives of Vincent's customers are innocent. To be generous when the recipient of your generosity is an able and aggressive economic foe not only is unprofessional but also leaves one open for being seen as a sucker.

I got this guy who comes in every so often, he's an insurance agent. He walks all over my store — behind the counter, in the back room, everywhere. He's a real tight bastard, a Jew. I can't stand him, you know. One day I got a store full of customers. I'm sellin' like mad. He's pullin' stuff off my shelves an' he comes over with a couple of sweaters. "How much for me, Vince?" he says. I say, "Whaddaya mean, 'how much for me?'" So he says, "You know, what's my price on this stuff?" So I really let him have it. I start yellin', "What the hell makes you think you get a special price? What makes you think you're better than anybody else? Take this old lady here. You think you're better than her? She's the one who really deserves a special price." Well, the whole store gets upset. The guy don't know what to do. "OK, OK, Vince," he says. "Take it easy. I didn't mean nothin'. Take it easy. Tell me what the price is, I'll pay it." "No," I says. "To you it's not for

sale; you ain't buyin' nothin' in here today." I told him that. Threw him right outta the store. I'll tell you, sometimes I just can't stand that kind a guy.

With those who by definition do not act out of self-interest, on the other hand, charity and generosity are easy to establish.

You know how much I do for children, right? The other day this nun comes in from the House of the Good Shepherd. Oh, I known her for years. If you knew the stuff I gave her — shoes, clothes, toys, everything. Well, she comes in and my brother and Kelly, Happy, an' another hood are all in the store too. Well, I give her a pile of girls' dresses I was savin' up. Then I says, "Wait a minute, Sister, I think we can do a little more for you." So then I turn to everybody in the store an' I say, "When was the last time you gangsters did anything for the little children of this world?" I said, "I'm gonna give Sister here twenty dollars an' I'm gonna put four tens out on the counter. Each one of you guys puts up a ten, the Sister here gets another ten too." Well, my brother, he runs in the back room, and that fatso, Happy, runs out the door. Both of 'em have more money than they know what to do with, but they're just cheap bastards. So Kelly and the other hood are stuck. They gotta put up the dough or they look bad. Well, I gave the Sister the other twenty, too. On the way out, she says to me, "Are those men really gangsters?" I said, "Ya, they been in rackets all their lives." Then she says to me, "Hmmm, they did look a little shady."

The Police

Sometimes Vincent claims credit for his actions for reasons more subtle than outright charitableness or benevolence. This is particularly so with respect to his acts of cooperation with the police.

I had a computer once, you know. [I respond, "A computer?"] Ya, a computer. Two guys drove up to my store in a truck. They said they had a machine in the truck they wanted me to look at. It was a computer right out of the University. I don't know how they got it out, but it was about as big as that chair [a large recliner]. I said, "Look, there ain't nobody nowhere gonna touch that. It must have a million numbers on it." Well, we talked about it for a while an' they took my advice. I gave 'em fifty bucks an' told 'em to unload it on my platform. Then I called this Inspector I know an' told him what I had. Do you know he got the report it was missin' right while I was talkin' to him on the phone? That machine was worth twenty or thirty thousand dollars. If I didn't take it off those shines, they would'a dumped it in the river. See, the police department knows that I'll help 'em out when I can. An' I never took no reward for doin' that, either.[11]

Vincent's assistance here qualifies as creditable behavior not so much because it was virtuous in itself (the computer was returned rather than destroyed), but because no special claim for its goodness was made (no reward was taken).

And sometimes Vincent's motives for what would be considered creditable behavior are more subtle than those of either simple benevolence or simple self-interest or a mixture of both:

I had two guys, black guys, drive up one day. They had rifles. I could tell just by lookin' at 'em they were Army rifles. So I told 'em I'd take all they could get, an' they said they had thousands of 'em. They left, and right away I got on the phone to a guy I knew from the FBI. I told him I didn't want the guys arrested, but I didn't want all these guns gettin' into the hands of Black Power, either. So I got the OK to buy. They found out they were comin' out of a boxcar an' stopped it. I figure I done a good thing there, don't you?

I agreed, as Vincent knew I would. And so did the FBI. Vincent demonstrated not only civic responsibility but also self-sacrifice. He could have made a great deal of money. He also evidenced certain limits on what he will do, apparently owing in this case to his harboring certain fears and attitudes regarding potential recipients of the weapons. But self-interest is always in dogged pursuit of Vincent. The reader is invited to consider the above anecdotes in light of Simmels classic understanding of gratitude:

This irredeemable nature of gratitude shows it as a bond between men which is as subtle as it is firm. Every human relationship of any duration produces a thousand occasions for it, and even the most ephemeral ones do not allow their increment to the reciprocal obligation to be lost. In fortunate cases, but sometimes even in cases abundantly provided with counter-instances, the sum of these increments produces an atmosphere of generalized obligation (the saying that one is "obliged" ["verbunden"] to somebody who has earned our thanks is quite apt), which can be redeemed by no accomplishments whatever. This atmosphere of obligation belongs among those "microscopic," but infinitely tough, threads which tie one element of society to another, and thus eventually all of them together in a stable collective life.[12]

Deviant Behavior and the Metaphor of the Ledger

No one has ever seen a real "ledger" for life. Yet it is an old theme, and one which has caused no small amount of controversy. The theological grounds of the debate between Luther and the Roman Catholic Church were not simply the abuses of the Roman Church in selling indulgences, but whether or not good works (like giving money to the church) could, in the heavenly ledger, balance out sins.[13] However, in no way does the metaphor of the ledger disappear with the Reformation. One finds it equally reflected in the values weighed and balanced under the calculus of price in utilitarian ethics.[14]

But Vincent's sense of the metaphor of the ledger is neither careful Catholic theology nor a neo-Benthamite utilitarianism. It is, rather, a common-sense perception of the vague standard by which most of us evaluate men — one that is metaphorically embedded in our language almost everywhere we speak of evaluation. Consider "pay off," "dividend," "cost," "value," "price," "good" and "goods," "waste," "profit," and "debt." The words of business come easily to us in our reflections on morality. The judge declaring that the prisoner has "paid his debt to society" speaks in the moral metaphor society is willing to hear. Vincent — a businessman, Catholic, and self-made man — takes to the metaphor of the ledger naturally. It does not emerge as his instrument for moral evaluation in concrete references to a real book of life or a real ledger kept in heaven. Vincent does not believe in such a real book in any way. Rather, the mechanism of the metaphor of the ledger is hidden in the way he organizes his apologia and the impression he intends from offering his positive anecdotes.

When Vincent says, "You gotta take into consideration all the good things I done, too," the question in response might well be "Why?" To ask it would be to challenge the metaphor of the ledger hidden within it.

But Vincent would not understand the question, any more than most of us would think to ask it. The metaphor of the ledger is driven deeply enough in our consciousness that the question would be dismissed as annoying "philosophical meddling" with what everybody knows is "just common sense."

But, as we have seen, Vincent's eye for the loophole works as well with the metaphor of the ledger as it does with the morality (and law) of criminal receiving. His sense for the balance between good acts and bad, for the credit he earns for his charity, and for the existence of a debit column in every man's ledger allows him to make a favorable accounting of his life. In so doing, he manages to preserve his faith in a moral order not notably different from that which most of us accept. However, his sense of the metaphor of the ledger allows him to loosen the restraints of that moral order just enough to emerge from a thirty-year criminal career with a positive, moral, decent self-image.

NOTES

1. There is no way to make a reliable estimate of the total value of goods passing through the hands of fences like Vincent each year. Since 99% of Vincent's merchandise is new, it is certain that most of it comes from wholesale and retail businesses, including manufacturers, distributors, shippers, and warehouses. Business losses are uniformly entered under the category of "shrinkage," which includes employee theft, shoplifting, bookkeeping errors, and some forms of embezzlement. In 1963 the "shrinkage" total for retail stores, estimated at retail prices, was $1,757,000,000. Of this figure, it was further estimated that $1,318,000,000 was due to some form of dishonesty. There is no way of estimating what percentage of this figure represents merchandise that was eventually fenced. One must remember also that this figure applies only to retail businesses and does not include burglary, hijacking, or theft from the cargo industry, including trucking, shipping, or air freight. President's Commission on Law Enforcement and the Administration of Justice, Task Force on *Assessment, Crime and Its Impact — An Assessment* (Washington, D.C.: Government Printing Office, l967), pp. 48–49.

2. Essays in the theoretical tradition that this chapter follows include the following: C. Wright Mills, "Situated Actions and Vocabularies of Motive," *American Sociological Review* 5 (1940): 904–13; Marvin B. Scott and Stanford M. Lyman, "Accounts," *American Sociological Review* 33 (1968): 46–62; Gresham Sykes and David Matza, "Techniques of Neutralization," *American Sociological Review* 22 (1957): 967–69; and especially David Matza, *Delinquency and Drift* (New York: John Wiley and Sons, 1964). The full theoretical grounds of this

perspective on the social order as I understand it are best set forth by Kenneth Burke in *A Grammar of Motives* (New York: Prentice-Hall, 1945) and *Permanence and Change* (New York: Bobbs-Merrill Co., 1965).

3. Cf.: "Legislators admire and respect businessmen and cannot conceive of them as criminals; that is, businessmen do not conform to the popular stereotype of 'the criminal.'" Edwin H. Sutherland, "Is White Collar Crime Crime?" in *White Collar Criminal*, ed. Gilbert Geis (New York: Atherton Press, 1968), p. 360. See also Richard Austin Smith, "The Incredible Electrical Conspiracy," *Fortune* (April 1961), pp. 132–80, for an application of Sutherland's observation.

4. The matter of "potential for deviance," by which I mean people's estimations of the probability that one type of deviance implies the capacity for other types, merits systematic criminological examination. As an example, our treatment of the insane by incarceration seems to presume that relatively mild violations of social propriety suggests a capacity for more serious and perhaps violent deviance. Similarly, before the time when long hair was co-opted by an economic establishment willing to capitalize on it, long hair seemed to be regarded by many as a certain sign of the willingness of the wearer to engage in other, non-tonsorial, forms of deviance. Likewise, society may well assume that, all other things being equal, a thief has a greater "potential for deviance" than a fence.

5. Neal Shover, "Structures and Careers in Burglary," *Journal of Criminal Law, Criminology, and Police Science* 63 (1972), pp. 545–49.

6. Or, occasionally, the ploy of criminals hustling those with social-worker mentalities (Robert Earl Barnes, "The Fence: Crime's Real Profiteer," *Reader's Digest* [September, 1973], p. 155):

   My criminal career began when I was ten years old and I stole a bundle of comic books from a drugstore doorstep. When I tried to trade them to the local barber for some in his shop I hadn't read, he wouldn't barter — but he did offer to buy all the comics I could provide for two cents each. He never asked, but I'm sure he knew they were stolen. From that first transaction, I learned what every professional thief must know there's no use stealing unless you know someone willing to pay for the goods you steal....

7. A case in point: an article in the London *Times*, for Friday, March 8, 1974, entitled "Publican Criticized over Death of Customer."

   A publican served two double measures of Chartreuse and five double Pernods to a customer who had already drunk 11 or 12 pints of beer an inquest heard today. The customer fell off his bar stool and died.... The coroner said both Mr. Moseley [the publican] and Mr. Lewis [the man with whom the

*customer was engaged in a drinking competition]
were both stupid and irresponsible in their actions.
Mr. Ross's [the dead customer's] drinking was
incredible and abnormal and Mr. Moseley in particular ought to have realized it was reaching the
danger level. Irresponsibility did not amount to
manslaughter.*

8. The idea of *innocence by association* raises important
questions for researchers in the sociology of deviance.
Simply by associating with deviants the field researcher
gives tacit reinforcement to them. My association with
Vincent was interpreted by him as quite complimen-
tary, and the vast majority of thieves I have interviewed
have felt similarly flattered. My generally nonjudgmen-
tal attitude was uniformly construed as approval. Likewise, I find that a text like my own is easy to interpret as
being supportive of deviant careers in spite of my
protestations that it is primarily descriptive and analytical, in the way sociology must be. A similar case can be
made regarding the degree of attention paid to militant
blacks in the liberal press. (See Nathan Glazer and
Daniel P. Moynihan, *Beyond the Melting Pot*, 2nd ed.,
rev. [Cambridge: M.I.T. Press, 1970], p. lxxxvii.)

9. Months after Vincent told me about his views on Sears's
profits in spite of their losses from theft, I ran across the
following obscure news item (John Manning, ed., "No
Money Down" [Philadelphia: Publication of the Model
Cities Consumer Protection Program, vol. 1, no. 3], p.
3). It is rather perverse to print it here but I cannot
resist the irony.

*SEARS FASTBUCK: Second Income News relates
how Richard W. Sears, founder of Sears, Roebuck,
got started in business. Sears was a railroad telegra-
pher with a sideline business of selling watches. His
gimmick was to buy watches at $2 apiece, affix $20
price-tags, and mail them to fictitious locations
across the country. When the packages came back
"undeliverable," Sears would open them in presence
of fellow employees and palm the watches off as
"bargains" — at $10 apiece.*

10. Reference to a Book of Life wherein all of man's deeds
are recorded is found throughout Scripture. For example, Rev. 20: 11–15 states:

*[11] Then I saw a great white throne and him who
sat upon it; from his presence earth and sky fled away,
and no place was found for them. [12] And I saw the
dead, great and small, standing before the throne,
and books were opened. Also another book was
opened which is the book of life. And the dead were
judged by what was written in the books, by what
they had done. [13] And the sea gave up the dead in
it, Death and Hades gave up the dead in them, and
all were judged by what they had done. [14] Then
Death and Hades were thrown into the fire; [15]
And if any one's name was not found written in the
book of life, he was thrown into the lake of fire.*

11. Maurer notes that pickpockets occasionally return wal-
lets containing valuable papers to their owners after the
money has been removed. Usually this is done by disposing of the empty wallet in a post office box. "This is
not done," says Maurer, "for reasons of sentiment, or
fair play, or consideration for the sucker. It is done for
reasons of public relations...." David W. Maurer, *Whiz
Mob* (Gainsville, Fla.: Publication of the American
Dialect Society, 1955), p. 119. "Public relations" are far
more essential to the fence than to the pickpocket, and
the similarity in public relations technique is notable.

12. George Simmel, "Faithfulness and Gratitude," in *The
Sociology of George Simmel*, ed. and trans. Kurt Wolff
(New York: The Free Press, 1964), p. 395.

13. In 1517 Luther posted his Ninety-Five Theses on the
side door of the Castle Church at Wittenberg. Theses
no. 40 and no. 44 (quoted in John Dillenberger, ed.,
Martin Luther [New York: Doubleday and Co., 1961],
p. 494) are particularly relevant:

*no. 40 A truly contrite sinner seeks out, and loves to
pay, the penalty of his sins, whereas the very multitude of indulgences dulls men's consciences, and
tends to make them hate the penalties.
no. 44 Because, by works of love, love grows and a
man becomes a better man; whereas, by indulgences,
he does not become a better man, but only escapes
certain penalties.*

14. See "Secular Mysticism in Bentham" in Burke, *Permanence and Change*, pp. 188–94, for Burke's study of the
metaphors which seduced Bentham.

Chapter 27

CRIMINAL VICTIMIZATION IN CANADA, 1988–1993

ROSEMARY GARTNER AND ANTHONY N. DOOB

In 1988, a survey on personal risk related to criminal victimization was initiated as part of the General Social Survey program. It examined the prevalence and the social and demographic distribution of eight specific types of criminal victimization experiences: sexual assault, robbery, assault, break and enter, motor vehicle theft, theft of personal property, theft of household property and vandalism. Sexual assault, robbery and assault were combined with theft of personal property to produce the cumulative category "personal victimization." The remaining specified types of victimization were collapsed in the aggregate category "Household victimization." This survey also examined the victim's experience of crime, the reason victims decide to report offenses to the police, and Canadians' perceptions of the level of crime around them. This survey was replicated in 1993.

The purpose of this report is to explore the changes which have or have not occurred since 1988, rather than to look in detail at the nature and consequences of victimizations that were reported in the most recent survey.

METHODOLOGY

Early in 1988 and throughout 1993, the General Social Survey conducted telephone interviews with approximately 10,000 Canadian adults aged 15 years or older. Respondents were asked about their experiences with crime and the criminal justice system over a previous 12-month period.[1] The sample in both cases covered the non-institutionalized population throughout the ten provinces. On the basis of these interviews, statistical estimates were made of the incidence of certain crimes in the general adult population and on Canadians' perceptions of risk and attitudes to various components of the justice system.

Repeating a survey allows for the examination of changes over time. However, the types of questions and the context in which they are asked are important variables in interpreting results. In replicating surveys there is always a dilemma between whether to use the identical questions used in the previous cycle in order to compare survey results or to make improvements in the manner in which the questions are framed, based on knowledge gained from the previous survey.

For example, in the 1988 survey, respondents were asked about being "attacked." They were told that "an attack can be anything from being hit, slapped, pushed or grabbed, to being shot, raped or beaten." In 1993, a similar question was asked but the word "raped" was omitted from the list of examples of an "attack." However, in addition, two further questions were asked: "... has anyone forced you or attempted to force you into any sexual activity when you did not want to, by threatening you, holding you down or hurting you in some way ..." and "... has anyone ever touched you against your will in any sexual way. By this I mean anything from unwanted touching or

Source: "Trends in Criminal Victimization: 1988–1993," Statistics Canada, *Juristat*, Catalogue No. 85-002, Vol. 14, No. 13 (Ottawa: Canadian Centre for Justice Statistics, June 1994), pp. 1–19. Reproduced by authority of the Minister of Industry, 1995. The data in all tables and figures are taken from surveys published by the Service Bulletin of the Canadian Centre for Justice Statistics, Statistics Canada. Reproduced by authority of the Minister of Industry, 1995.

grabbing to kissing or fondling." Not surprisingly, the number of sexual assaults reported in 1993 was considerably higher than the number reported in 1988. Different questions were asked and, as one would expect, different results were obtained.

Clearly the 1993 questions on sexual assault are an improvement over the previous questions. Similarly, some of the other questions were changed so as to obtain a more thorough picture of respondents' views of crime and the criminal justice system.

It is felt, however, that the differences in the two survey instruments — other than for sexual assault — should have no significant impact on the levels of crime reported in the 1988 as compared with the 1993 survey. There is confidence, therefore, about the comparisons across time contained in this report.

RISK OF PERSONAL VICTIMIZATION

The data from the recent General Social Survey (GSS) describe the criminal victimization experiences of Canadians aged 15 and over. By comparing the victimization rates obtained from this survey with those from 1988, it can be determined whether Canadians experience more crime now than five years ago.

As shown in Table 27.1, the results of the 1993 survey indicate that overall victimization rates have not changed substantially since 1988 — that is, essentially the same proportion of the population (24%) experienced at least one instance of criminal victimization in 1993 as compared with 1988.[2]

The 1988 and 1993 data are reasonably consistent across crime categories (see Table 27.2). GSS assault

Table 27.1 Proportion of Population Victimized One or More Times, by Victim Characteristics, Age 15+, Canada, 1988 and 1993

| | Victimized by frequency (%) | | | | | |
| | Once | | Twice or More | | Total | |
Victim Characteristics	1988	1993	1988	1993	1988	1993
Canada	15	16	8	7	24	24
Males	16	17	9	7	25	24
Females	14	15	8	7	22	23
Urban	17	18	10	8	27	27
Rural	12	12	6	5	18	17

Source: General Social Survey, 1988 and 1993.

Table 27.2 Personal Victimization Rates per 1,000 Population, by Type of Incident and Victim Characteristics, Age 15+, Canada, 1988 and 1993

| | Type of Incident | | | | | | | |
| | Theft Personal Property | | Sexual Assault | | Robbery | | Assault | |
Victim Characteristics	1988	1993	1988[1]	1993	1988	1993	1988	1993
Canada	59	51	—	17	13	9	68	67
Urban	70	57	—	18	14	9	72	72
Rural	46	36	—	14	—	—	56	53
Age — 15–24	123	93	—	48	39	23	145	155
25–44	65	61	—	17	10	9	80	69
45–64	22	29	—	—	—	—	19	38
65+	—	—	—	—	—	—	—	—
Male	58	51	—	—	17	12	74	68
Female	61	51	—	29	10	6	63	66

[1]There were too few cases reported in 1988 to make statistically reliable estimates. New questions concerning sexual assault were added to the 1993 survey.

— amount too small to be meaningful.

Source: General Social Survey, 1988 and 1993.

Figure 27.1 Personal Victimization Rates per 1,000 Population, by Type of Incident, Age 15+, Canada, 1988 and 1993

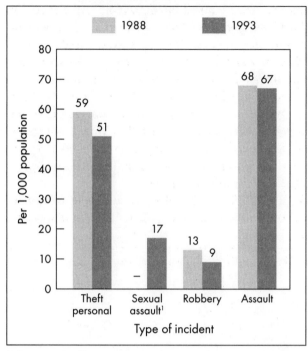

[1]There were too few cases reported in 1988 to make statistically reliable estimates. New questions concerning sexual assault were added to the 1993 survey.

Source: General Social Survey, 1988 and 1993.

rates show little change over time; from 68 per 1,000 population in 1988 to 67 per 1,000 population in 1993. GSS robbery rates decreased by 31%, from 13 to 9 per 1,000 population during this same time period. Personal theft rates also decreased by 14% from 59 per 1,000 in 1988 to 51 per 1,000 in 1993.

Characteristics of Personal Victimizations

In 1993, as seen in Table 27.3, violent victimizations were more likely to have been committed by strangers and were more likely to have been committed in public places than in 1988. The proportion of robberies committed by strangers increased from 45% to 67%. When interpreted in the context of the overall decrease in robbery victimizations, it would appear that the overall risk of being robbed by a stranger in Canada did not substantially change in the five-year period between the two surveys.[3] The proportion of assaults committed by strangers increased from 27% to 38%. Nevertheless, the majority of sexual assaults and assaults were committed by offenders known to the victim in 1993, as in 1988. Only in the case of robberies did strangers make up a majority of offenders.

The locations of victimizations reflect these patterns of victim–offender relationships and the shift toward more public victimizations. The majority of

Table 27.3 Violent Victimizations by Type of Incident and Incident Characteristics, Age 15+, Canada, 1988 and 1993

| | Incident Type | | | | | |
| | % of Sexual Assaults | | % of Robberies/Attempts | | % of Assaults | |
Incident Characteristics	1988	1993	1988	1993	1988	1993
COMMITTED						
– by stranger	—	22	45	67	27	38
– by acquaintance	—	58	33	—	43	38
– by relative	—	—	—	—	22	19
– unknown/not applicable	—	—	—	—	8	5
– by single offender	—	81	68	54	73	81
– by multiple offenders	—	—	29	44	20	15
– unknown	—	—	—	—	7	4
– with weapon	—	—	28	—	19	14
LOCATION						
– victim's home	—	30	32	—	41	31
– other residence	—	17	—	—	9	5
– restaurant/bar	—	17	—	—	9	10
– commercial	—	24	—	—	18	24
– public place/other	—	—	42	57	21	27
– not stated	—	—	—	—	—	—

Source: General Social Survey, 1988 and 1993.

robberies and assaults occurred outside of a residence and this proportion increased over time.

Only sexual assaults were about as likely to take place in a residence as elsewhere.

In most victimizations recorded in 1988 and 1993, offenders acted alone and without weapons. However, according to the 1993 survey, the percentage of robberies committed by multiple offenders increased from 29% to 44%. Furthermore, weapon use decreased over time for violent victimizations in total and individually for assaults and remained too negligible to estimate for robberies and sexual assaults (see Table 27.3).

Personal Victimization Risk Factors — The 1993 Survey

As with levels of crime, the social and demographic characteristics associated with overall personal victimization changed little between 1988 and 1993[4] (see Table 27.4). For example, urban dwellers and young Canadians continued to report higher rates of victimization than rural dwellers and older Canadians. Urban dwellers reported a total personal victimization rate almost 44% higher than rural dwellers (155 vs 108 per 1,000). Those aged 15–24 reported a personal victimization rate three times that of those over the age of 24 (318 vs 106 per 1,000).

In the 1993 survey, the total personal victimization rate for women was 11% higher than for men (151 vs 136 per 1,000), largely because of the fact that sexual assaults are rarely perpetrated against males (Table 27.2). For the other personal crimes, women reported similar rates to men in the 1993 survey: personal theft rates were the same for women and men

Table 27.4 Personal Victimization Rates per 1,000 Population, by Victim Characteristics, Age 15+, Canada, 1993

Victim Characteristics	Male	Female	Total
Total	136	151	143
Urban	141	168	155
Rural	105	110	108
Age 15–24	304	333	318
25–44	135	178	156
45–64	73	74	74
65+	—	—	—
Married/Common-Law	85	85	85
Single	245	311	274
Separated or Divorced	187	374	301

Source: General Social Survey, 1993.

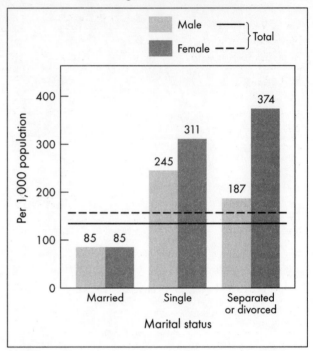

Figure 27.2 Personal Victimization Rates per 1,000 Population, by Sex of Victim, Marital Status, Age 15+, Canada, 1993

Source: General Social Survey, 1993.

(51 per 1,000) and assault rates were nearly the same (66 per 1,000 for women; 68 per 1,000 for men). The robbery rate for men, however, was double that for women (12 per 1,000 for men; 6 per 1,000 for women).

Women's higher rates were especially apparent in urban areas where their rates exceeded men's for each type of personal victimization, with the exception of robberies, and their total victimization rate was almost 20% higher than men's (168 vs 141 per 1,000). Rural women reported a total victimization rate only marginally greater than rural men (110 vs 105 per 1,000).

Gender differences in rates were also greater for certain marital statuses. While married women and men had the same total victimization rates (85 per 1,000), the single women's rate was 27% higher than the single men's rate (311 vs 245 per 1,000), and the rate for separated and divorced women was twice as high as the separated and divorced men's rate (374 vs 187 per 1,000). In fact, separated or divorced women had the highest rate of personal victimization.

As indicated in Table 27.5, victimization rates also differ depending on people's lifestyles and activity patterns. In both the 1988 and 1993 surveys, those who frequently engaged in evening activities away from home reported higher rates of personal victimization. Total personal victimization rates for those who were

Table 27.5 Victimization Rates per 1,000 Population, by Type of Incident, Sex and Number of Evening Activities, Age 15+, Canada, 1993

Sex of Victim and Number of Evening Activities (per month)	Type of Incident		
	Theft Personal Property	Assault	Total Personal
BOTH SEXES	51	67	143
<10 activities	20	34	66
10–19 activities	45	58	130
20–29 activities	48	59	129
30+ activities	89	113	243
MALE	51	68	136
< 10 activities	—	—	37
10–19 activities	42	55	116
20–29 activities	40	54	102
30+ activities	85	120	232
FEMALE	51	66	151
< 10 activities	19	46	84
10–19 activities	47	61	142
20–29 activities	56	64	156
30+ activities	94	104	258

Source: General Social Survey, 1993.

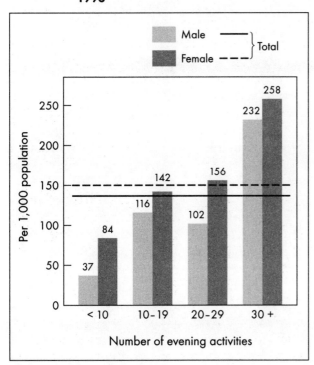

Figure 27.3 Personal Victimization Rates per 1,000 Population, by Sex of Victim and Number of Evening Activities, Age 15+, Canada, 1993

Source: General Social Survey, 1993.

involved in 30 or more evening activities a month were over three times the rates of those who participated in fewer than 10 evening activities a month (243 vs 66 per 1,000), according to the 1993 survey. Personal theft and assault rates for both males and females increase with the number of evening activities.

RISK OF HOUSEHOLD VICTIMIZATION

Respondents were asked about four crimes that might have occurred to their household: break and enters, theft of household property, motor vehicle theft or attempts, and vandalism. The 1993 GSS data on household victimization (Table 27.6) show rates similar to or lower than those found in 1988. Reported rates of break and enters, motor vehicle theft or attempts, and vandalism were lower in 1993 than in 1988. The rate of break and enters decreased by 7%, from 54 to 50 per 1,000 households; the rate of motor vehicle theft or attempts decreased by 27%, from 51 to 37 per 1,000 households; and the vandalism rate decreased by 13%, from 63 to 55 per 1,000.

Household Victimization Risk Factors

Household victimization rates vary according to location and economic status, according to both the 1988 and 1993 surveys (Table 27.6). For all types of household victimizations, rates for households in urban areas are higher than for households in rural areas. The total household victimization rate for urban households was 67% higher than the rate for rural households, according to the 1993 survey (222 vs 133 per 1,000).

Household income is also linked to household victimization rates. While the pattern varies somewhat across different types of victimizations, the total household victimization rate rose steadily with household income in the 1993 survey. At the extremes, households with incomes of $60,000 or more had victimization rates 65% higher than households with incomes of less than $15,000 (254 vs 154 per 1,000).

THE DECISION TO REPORT VICTIMIZATIONS TO THE POLICE

Police statistics and victimization surveys often give different pictures of crime. This is not surprising since the process by which an event gets recorded as a "crime" by police can be seen as a series of discretionary decisions, starting with the citizen identifying the event as a crime and ending with the police officer

Table 27.6 Household Victimization Rates per 1,000 Households, by Type of Incident, Urban/Rural Residence and Household Income, Canada, 1988 and 1993

Households Characteristics	Break and Enter/Attempt		Motor Vehicle Theft/Attempt		Theft Household Property/Attempt		Vandalism		Total Household	
	1988	1993	1988	1993	1988	1993	1988	1993	1988	1993
CANADA	54	50	51	37	48	48	63	55	216	190
Urban	64	56	59	45	54	56	76	64	252	222
Rural	32	40	36	—	35	38	42	38	146	133
INCOME GROUPS										
< $15,000	55	57	—	—	36	—	38	43	163	154
15,000–29,999	58	46	52	—	52	44	59	51	221	172
30,000–39,999	59	77	60	54	75	—	64	58	258	239
40,000–59,999	64	56	80	51	49	58	102	75	296	240
60,000+	63	56	—	42	—	75	101	81	277	254

Source: General Social Survey, 1988 and 1993.

recording the event as a particular "founded" crime. At any stage in the process, a decision can be made which has the effect of ensuring that the event never gets recorded as a crime.

Citizens do not automatically report all crimes to the police — the decision is a complex one based on a number of considerations. Reporting takes time, it may subject the victim to additional stress and it may not be seen as sensible to report for a range of different reasons.

The likelihood of reporting a crime varies enormously from crime to crime. In 1993, of those crimes covered by the GSS, household break and enters were the most likely crimes to be reported to the police and sexual assaults were the most likely to remain

Figure 27.4 Household Victimization Rates per 1,000 Households, by Type of Incident, Canada, 1988 and 1993

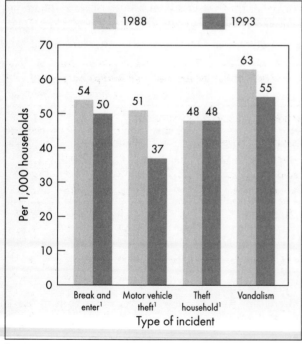

[1]Includes attempts.

Source: General Social Survey, 1988 and 1993.

Figure 27.5 Household Victimization Rates per 1,000 Households, by Household Income, Canada, 1988 and 1993

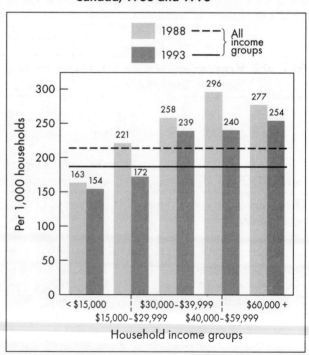

Source: General Social Survey, 1988 and 1993.

Table 27.7 Victimizations Not Reported to the Police, by Type of Incident, Age 15+, Canada, 1988 and 1993

	% Not Reported	
Type of Incident	1988	1993
PERSONAL[1]		
Sexual assault	—	90
Robbery	68	53
Assault	65	68
Theft personal property/attempt	63	56
HOUSEHOLD		
B&E/attempt	28	32
Motor vehicle theft/attempt	42	48
Theft household property/attempt	56	57
Vandalism	54	54
Total Household	45	48

[1]Total "Personal" figures are not presented due to the non-comparability of sexual assault data.

Source: General Social Survey, 1988 and 1993.

unreported (Table 27.7). It is clear from these data that the police are informed about only a small fraction of these personal and household crimes.

Reporting rates for assaults, break and enters, motor vehicle thefts, household thefts, thefts of personal property, and vandalism did not differ much between the two surveys. Robbery was the only crime which showed evidence of substantial change: a higher proportion of robberies were reported to the police in 1993 (47%) than were reported in 1988 (32%).

The reasons for not reporting criminal victimizations to the police are shown in Table 27.8 for the 1993 survey. Because fewer reasons for not reporting were offered to the respondent in 1988 than in 1993, comparisons were rendered impossible. The important finding in this table is that, for the most part, the reasons for non-reporting appear to relate to the perceived usefulness of reporting. Generally speaking, victims who did not report the incident to the police saw the event as one that was best dealt with another way, that was too minor to report, or that they thought the police could not do anything about. However, in about three of ten sexual assaults and in about a fifth of the assaults, one of the reasons that victims gave for not reporting was fear of revenge.

PERCEPTIONS OF CRIME

Statistics about crime — almost always relating to crimes reported to the police — are quite often reported in the mass media. Increases in crime make news. Decreases or no changes in crime rates appear to get somewhat less press coverage. An ordinary Canadian consumer of the mass media, therefore, would likely have encountered a number of stories in the past five years suggesting that crime has increased. The source and meaning of these statistics may not always be considered carefully.

It is not surprising, therefore, that a large proportion of Canadians think that the level of crime in their neighbourhoods has increased (46%) (see Table

Table 27.8 Victimizations Not Reported to the Police by Reason for Not Reporting, by Type of Incident, Age 15+, Canada, 1993

	Reason for not reporting to police (%)[1]								
Incident Type	Dealt with another way	Too minor	Fear of revenge	Insur-ance wouldn't cover	Police couldn't do any-thing	Police wouldn't help	Didn't want to get involved with police	Noth-ing taken	Personal matter
Theft personal property/attempt	43	54	—	26	47	21	34	—	32
Sexual assault	65	30	29	—	28	20	50	21	67
Robbery	70	—	—	—	—	—	—	—	—
Assault	64	48	19	7	27	13	47	22	49
Break & enter/attempt	46	48	—	—	42	—	—	36	—
Motor vehicle theft/attempt	33	65	—	—	52	—	—	—	—
Theft household property/attempt	36	58	—	—	38	—	27	—	29
Vandalism	45	60	—	—	47	—	37	20	33

[1]Proportions do not add to 100 as these are separate variables. Only proportion of affirmative responses shown.

Source: General Social Survey, 1993.

Table 27.9 Perceived Change in the Level of Crime in Neighbourhood, During the Last 5 Years by Urban/Rural Residence, Age 15+, Canada, 1993

	Perceived change in the level of crime in neighbourhood in the last 5 years (%)				
Area	Increased	Decreased	Same	Don't know	Total
All	46	4	43	8	100
Urban	48	4	41	8	100
Rural	40	4	52	4	100

Source: General Social Survey, 1993.

27.9). Those who live in rural areas are somewhat more likely to think that crime in their neighbourhoods has not changed and are somewhat less likely to think that it has increased than are people who live in urban areas.

Generally speaking, it appears that Canadians believe that their own neighbourhoods have about the same amount of crime or less crime than other areas of Canada (Table 27.10). Very few people — about 10% in 1993 — indicate that they think their neighbourhoods have more crime than other places in Canada. Crime may be perceived to be a problem — but, for the most part, most of us see it as being located somewhere else. Canadians view their own neighbourhoods, in comparison to other parts of Canada, in much the same way as they did five years earlier.

Even though most Canadians view their own neighbourhoods as less dangerous than other parts of Canada, a substantial portion — 27% overall, in 1993 — indicated that they felt unsafe walking alone at night in their own neighbourhoods (Table 27.11). This is a slightly higher proportion of Canadians indicating that they feel "unsafe" than five years earlier.

Table 27.10 Perceived Level of Crime in Neighourhood Compared with Other Areas by Urban/Rural Residence, Age 15+, Canada, 1988 and 1993

	Perceived level of crime in neighourhood compared with other areas (%)									
	Higher		About Same		Lower		Don't know/ Not stated		Total	
Area	1988	1993	1988	1993	1988	1993	1988	1993	1988	1993
All	8	10	29	29	57	57	6	4	100	100
Urban	10	11	32	31	53	54	5	4	100	100
Rural	4	5	22	19	71	74	4	2	100	100

Source: General Social Survey, 1988 and 1993.

Table 27.11 Feelings of Safety Walking Alone in Neighbourhood after Dark, by Urban/Rural Residence and Sex, Age 15+, Canada, 1988 and 1993

	Feelings of safety walking alone in neighbourhood after dark (%)														
					Unsafe										
Victim Characteristics	Very Safe		Reasonably Safe		Total Unsafe		Somewhat Unsafe		Very Unsafe		Don't Know		Total	
	1988	1993	1988	1993	1988	1993	1988	1993	1988	1993	1988	1993	1988	1993
TOTAL	40	32	33	40	25	27	17	15	9	12	2	2	100	100
Male	58	48	29	41	11	10	9	6	3	4	1	1	100	100
Female	23	16	36	40	39	42	24	23	14	19	3	2	100	100
URBAN TOTAL	36	27	35	43	28	29	18	17	9	12	1	1	100	100
Male	55	43	32	45	12	11	9	7	3	3	1	1	100	100
Female	18	12	38	41	42	45	27	25	15	20	2	2	100	100
RURAL TOTAL	53	48	28	36	18	15	12	10	6	5	1	1	100	100
Male	70	63	22	30	8	6	6	3	2	2	—	—	100	100
Female	37	31	33	43	28	25	19	16	9	8	2	1	100	100

Source: General Social Survey, 1988 and 1993.

The important change occurring in the past five years was that fewer people indicated they felt "very safe" walking alone at night than was the case five years ago. In 1988, 40% indicated they felt very safe. In 1993, this proportion dropped to 32%.

As in the past, there is a dramatic difference; between males and females with regard to perceptions of safety. Only 10% of males indicated that they felt unsafe walking alone at night in their own neighbourhoods whereas 42% of females felt unsafe. Those living in urban areas — both male and female are more likely to feel unsafe than are those living in rural areas. As with other findings, the pattern is identical to that of five years ago.

As can be seen in Table 27.12, males and females over 65 years of age were more likely than those who were younger to indicate that they felt unsafe walking alone in their neighbourhoods. Between 1988 and 1993 the proportion of those over 65 who indicated that they felt "very unsafe" walking alone at night in their neighbourhoods increased substantially, particularly for females. In 1993, 38% of females over 65 indicated that they felt very unsafe walking alone at night as compared with 24% in 1988.

The variation among different groups in the population is large. For example, in 1993, almost two-thirds of rural males (63%) indicated that they felt very safe walking alone in their neighbourhoods at night in comparison to 12% of urban females.

COMPARING THE GSS AND THE UNIFORM CRIME REPORTING (UCR) SURVEYS: DIFFERENT PERSPECTIVES RESULT IN DIFFERENT PICTURES

Victimization surveys were developed to provide an estimate of the likelihood of personal and household victimizations. They are designed to provide a way of looking at crime from the perspective of individual victims. They describe what has happened to individual Canadians and they describe the way in which people have responded to their victimization experiences. As pointed out earlier, many crimes are not reported to the police. Hence police-reported crimes cannot capture the full experience that people have with crime.

There are, however, some limitations on the data that can be obtained from victimization surveys. They do not, for example, describe crimes (e.g., thefts or vandalism) in which organizations such as schools or corporations are the victims. In addition they do not describe crimes such as impaired driving or drug offenses. The GSS has two other limitations: it samples only those people who were 15 years old and over and who are residents of Canada.

The most commonly cited crime statistics in Canada — those from the UCR survey — give a picture of crime through a different process. These are the reports of crimes that are recorded by the police. Typically, though not always, these crimes come to the

Table 27.12 Feelings of Safety Walking Alone in Neighborhood after Dark, by Sex and Age Group, Age 15+, Canada, 1988 and 1993

| Sex and Age Group | Feelings of safety walking alone in neighbourhood after dark (%) | | | | | | | | | | | | | |
| | Very Safe | | Reasonably Safe | | Total Unsafe | | Somewhat Unsafe | | Very Unsafe | | Don't Know | | Total population 15+ | |
	1988	1993	1988	1993	1988	1993	1988	1993	1988	1993	1988	1993	1988	1993
MALE														
15–24 years	61	50	29	43	9	7	6	5	3	1	—	—	100	100
25–44	61	51	29	40	9	9	7	6	2	3	—	—	100	100
45–64	57	47	28	42	13	11	10	7	3	4	1	—	100	100
65+	41	38	32	37	22	19	15	9	6	10	6	6	100	100
FEMALE														
15–24 years	19	14	37	45	43	40	30	26	14	14	—	—	100	100
25–44	25	17	40	44	34	38	23	25	12	14	1	1	100	100
45–64	26	17	35	40	37	41	23	21	14	20	2	2	100	100
65+	15	13	25	22	49	57	25	19	24	38	11	7	100	100

Source: General Social Survey, 1988 and 1993.

attention of the police as a result of a call from a victim. Police departments respond to these calls and produce crime statistics. There is evidence to suggest that the type and frequency of calls for service to the police may change over time and to vary according to location. For example, as society becomes more concerned about school violence, people may be more likely to report fights to the police rather than dealing with them informally. Similarly, as the police and other justice authorities are seen to be more sympathetic to victims of family violence and sexual assault, those victims may be more willing to report these incidents, and authorities will be more likely to treat them as crimes.

The repetition in 1993 of the victimization component of the GSS survey, which was conducted by Statistics Canada in 1988, provides the opportunity to examine changes in victimization rates as reported by the victims themselves from one point in time to another. It also encourages one to compare these with the figures reported to the police over a similar time period. Notwithstanding other limitations in comparability as described above, 1993 UCR data are not presently available. That is, it is not known at this time whether police-reported crime increased or decreased in 1993 as compared with 1988, which is all that is presently known from the GSS data. However, UCR data from 1988 to 1992 suggest the existence of increases in violent crime (Table 27.13). These trends are not substantiated by the data from the GSS, but a direct comparison of these results is not possible.

Comparisons between UCR and GSS household victimization data are more problematic than personal victimizations due to the fact that UCR property offenses generally include crimes against commercial establishments.[5] Once again, however, UCR reported increases in the rate of many property crimes from 1988 to 1992 (break and enters, theft of motor vehicles and mischief (vandalism)) are not reflected in GSS survey data.

These divergent trends support the contention that the extent and nature of criminal victimizations tapped by police-reported statistics differ from that tapped by victimization surveys. The results of these two surveys should be seen as complementary — they both measure crime but from different perspectives.

CONCLUSION

The clear conclusion from the 1993 General Social Survey data is that individual and household victimization rates did not change appreciably in the five-year period between 1988 and 1993. A substantial portion of Canadians — about 24% — were touched by one or more of the crimes covered by the GSS in the 1993 survey. However, there is no indication that this proportion has changed since 1988.

In the areas that Canadians understandably show most concern — violent victimizations — the data are very clear. Canadians are not at a higher risk than they were five years earlier, overall. There is almost no evidence to support the view that Canadians 15 years and older were more at risk of being victims of any of the crimes examined in the survey in 1993 than they were in 1988. The likelihood of a person being the victim of an assault, robbery, personal theft, and the likelihood of a household being victimized by way of a break and enter, motor vehicle theft, theft of household property, or vandalism, have either decreased or not changed.

NOTES

Published by authority of the Minister responsible for Statistics Canada. © Minister of Industry, Science and Technology, 1994. All rights reserved. No part of this publication may be reproduced, stored in a retrieval system or transmitted in any form or by any means, electronic, mechanical, photocopying, recording or otherwise without prior written permission from Licence Services, Marketing Division, Statistics Canada, Ottawa, Ontario, Canada K1A 0T6.

1. For ease of presentation, the two surveys will be referred to as if they solely related to 1988 and 1993 — the years in which they were carried out. Technically speaking, it is not quite that simple. The 1988 survey, carried out in the first few months of 1988 asked about victimizations that took place in the previous calendar year — 1987. The 1993 survey carried out over the 12 months of 1993 asked about victimizations which occurred in the previous 12 months — in this case, the one-year period often spanned two calendar years, 1992 and

Table 27.13 Police Reported Crime (Uniform Crime Reporting Survey), by Type of Incident per 1,000 Population, Canada, 1988–1992

Type of Incident	1988	1989	1990	1991	1992
Sexual assault	1.0	1.0	1.0	1.1	1.2
Assault	6.4	6.7	7.2	7.8	7.9
Robbery	0.9	1.0	1.1	1.2	1.2
Break & enter residence	8.2	7.6	8.1	9.1	8.9
Theft motor vehicle	3.4	3.8	4.3	5.1	5.3
Mischief	13.9	14.2	15.7	17.0	16.4
Theft (other than shoplifting)	28.9	28.1	29.6	31.8	30.2

Source: Uniform Crime Reporting Survey (UCR), 1988–1992.

1993. The "fear" questions related to their feelings at the time of the survey, 1988 and 1993.

2. It should be remembered that the 1993 survey included additional questions concerning sexual assault that were not included in the 1988 survey. Since the 1993 questions elicited victimizations that would not have been elicited from the questions used in 1988, the overall victimization rates are not strictly comparable.

3. In 1988, 45% of the 13 per 1,000 robberies, or about 6 per 1,000 were committed by strangers. In 1993, 67% of the 9 per 1,000 robberies, or about 6 per 1,000, were committed by strangers.

4. Overall personal victimization rates in 1988 and 1993 are not strictly comparable because of the change in the measurement of the incidence of sexual assaults.

5. The household victimization rates are expressed in terms of the rates per 1,000 households (not total population as is normally the case with UCR). Hence the actual numbers are not comparable.

Chapter 28

RACE AND CRIME: A CRITIQUE

JULIAN V. ROBERTS AND THOMAS GABOR

Canadian criminologists have been challenged recently by the work of a professor of psychology, Philippe Rushton, who claims to have uncovered evidence of significant inter-racial differences in many areas of human behaviour, including criminality (Rushton 1987; 1988; 1989). In January 1987, Professor Rushton delivered a paper at the American Association for the Advancement of Science conference in San Francisco (Rushton 1987). Rushton proposed a genetically-based hierarchy in which blacks (who supposedly evolved earlier than whites or orientals) were, *inter alia*, less intelligent and law-abiding than whites and orientals. Rushton asserts that there are substantial inter-racial differences in crime rates, and that these are accounted for by genetic factors. We shall examine later the credibility of genetic explanations of variations in crime rates. First, it is important to address the context of these assertions, and their likely impact upon society.

Rushton's speculations about race and crime have achieved national coverage exceeding that accorded any research project undertaken by criminologists (*The Globe and Mail* 1989). Part of the reason for this is the aggressive posture adopted by Rushton: he has been interviewed in several newspapers and has appeared on several television programmes with national audiences. In contrast, the reaction from criminologists, but not other professional groups (*The Globe and Mail*, 1989), has been muted. His monopolization of media coverage may, we believe, have had a detrimental impact upon public opinion. It is important, therefore, that

criminologists in Canada respond to his statements. While Rushton's claims about racial influences upon intelligence have been challenged, his assertions about crime have not.

THE EFFECT OF RUSHTON'S VIEWS ON PUBLIC THEORIES OF CRIME CAUSATION

The race/crime controversy has important consequences for public opinion in the area of criminal justice. Many of the important questions in the field of criminology — such as the relative deterrent effect of capital punishment — cannot be addressed by experiments. Accordingly, criminologists have used sophisticated correlational procedures to untangle the relative effects on crime of correlated variables such as genetic and environmental factors. The existence of a simple statistic, then, such as the over-representation in some crime statistics of certain racial minorities, will by itself convince few scholars. Criminologists have become sensitized to the possibility of alternative explanations for apparently straightforward relationships. Members of the public, however, are not so sophisticated in drawing inferences from statistical information. In fact, a great deal of recent research in social psychology has documented numerous ways in which the layperson is led into making unjustified inferences from material such as that which appears in newspapers (Fiske and Taylor 1984; Nisbett and Ross 1980).

Source: "Lombrosian Wine in a New Bottle: Research on Crime and Race," *Canadian Journal of Criminology* 32, 2 (April 1990): 291–305 and 309–13. Copyright by the Canadian Criminal Justice Association. Reprinted by permission of the *Canadian Journal of Criminology*.

Rushton's theories may affect public opinion in this area for several reasons. First, as already noted, the average layperson may not readily seek alternative (i.e., non-genetic) explanations for the over-representation of blacks in certain types of crime. Second, laypersons are less likely to realize that studies on race and crime are essentially correlational, rather than causal in nature. Third, the race/crime hypothesis comes from a highly-credible source, namely a well-published and tenured university professor. Fourth, it is vital to remember that, to the average member of the public, crime is a relatively unidimensional phenomenon: it usually involves violence, loss of property, and is a consequence of a "criminal disposition." Members of the public tend to regard offenders as a relatively homogeneous group (Roberts and White 1986) varying somewhat in their actions but not their motivations. Criminologists have long been aware of the deficiencies of this perception of crime; the multi-dimensional nature of crime and the complexity of motivation render sweeping statements about the etiology of crime invalid. Finally, but not last in importance, some people may be particularly receptive to racial explanations of crime. Thus, views such as those expressed by Professor Rushton may have the unintended effect of inflaming racism in Canada.

Furthermore, Rushton's views received what many laypersons might interpret as substantial support within days of the news media's coverage of his San Francisco address. On February 16, a representative of the Toronto Police Force released statistics showing that blacks were over-represented in the crime statistics in the Jane–Finch area of Toronto (*The Toronto Star* 1989). These data are likely to be misinterpreted by members of the public to constitute evidence supporting a genetic explanation of crime.

For the vast majority of the public, the mass media constitute their primary source of information about crime and criminal justice. Public conceptions of deviance are a consequence of what people read, hear, and see in the media. An abundance of research has demonstrated a direct correspondence between public misperceptions of crime and distorted media coverage of criminal justice issues (Doob and Roberts 1982). Since criminologists have failed to refute Rushton in the news media, we have also relinquished access to the one means of influencing public opinion on this issue. Criminologists may be highly skeptical of Rushton's opinions in the area of crime, but the only way that this skepticism can affect the public is through coverage in the news media. Once again, we note that while Rushton has been criticized by various behavioural geneticists (such as David Suzuki), his assertions regarding race and crime have remained uncontested.

We believe, therefore, that it is important to address the hypothesis that inherited racial traits affect crime rates. We shall examine some methodological issues relating criminality to race. A comprehensive survey of the literature on this topic would occupy a whole issue of a journal; we can only highlight the research findings and point out what we perceive to be the principal flaws in Rushton's argument. We shall draw upon data from Canada, the United States, and the United Kingdom. Finally, it should be made clear from the outset that we are addressing Rushton's theory as it pertains to the phenomenon of crime. We are not behavioural geneticists, to whom we cede the question of whether the general theory of racial differences withstands scientific scrutiny.

THE SCIENTIFIC ARGUMENT: EMPIRICAL RESEARCH ON RACE AND CRIME

1. Problems with the Definition of Race

Rushton relates an independent variable (race) to a dependent variable (crime). The inter-racial comparisons cited by Rushton are predicated on the assumption that people are racially pure. Each racial "category" is held to be homogeneous, but this is now accepted by contemporary anthropologists and biologists to be an antiquated and dangerous myth. Centuries of inter-breeding reduce Rushton's rather crude tripartite classification (black, white, oriental) to the level of caricature. For example, Radzinowicz and King (1977) note that in the United States, close to 50% of those classified as black are over half white by lineage (see also Herskovits 1930; and, for a study of the offenders, Hooton 1939). Many American whites, as well, have some black ancestry; Haskell and Yablonsky (1983: 95) note that:

> *Estimates of the number of blacks who have "passed" into the white society run as high as 7 million. In addition to those millions who have introduced an African mixture into the "white" population of the United States in the relatively recent past, there must have been millions of Africans who were assimilated into the population of Spain, Portugal, Italy, Greece, and other Mediterranean countries. Descendants of those people are now part of the "white" population of the United States.*

Wolfgang and Cohen (1970) cite data showing that no more than 22% of all persons designated as black, in the United States, were of unmixed ancestry. Fully 15% of persons classified as black were more white than black (Wolfgang and Cohen 1970: 7). The pervasiveness of such racial overlap calls genetically-based racial theories of crime into question. (For the rest of this article, for convenience only, we shall continue to refer to inter-racial differences. This does not mean we endorse the racial trichotomy of blacks, orientals and whites advanced by Professor Rushton.) Finally, it is important to bear in mind that crime statistics deal with race as a sociological and not a biological category. In short, the independent variable, as it were, is highly problematic. Now we turn to the dependent measure, official and unofficial measures of crime.

2. The Issue of Over-Representation in Official Crime Statistics

Rushton's evidence for a genetic influence consists of the over-representation of blacks in official statistics of crime in the United States, the United Kingdom, and elsewhere. Specifically he asserts that:

> African descended people, for example, while constituting less than one-eighth of the population of the United States or of London, England, currently account for over 50% of the crimes in both places. Since about the same proportion of victims say their assailant was black, the arrest statistics cannot really be blamed on police prejudice (Rushton 1987: 3).

There are at least two factually incorrect elements here, but first we offer a general comment regarding the issue of over-representation.

A simple correlation between two variables does not constitute evidence of a *causal* relationship. A multitude of other confounding factors must be ruled out before one can contemplate a causal relationship. Even if the relationship between race and crime holds up after careful secondary analyses, this is hardly convincing evidence of genetic influences. The fact that parental alcoholism is correlated with alcoholism in the offspring does not prove a genetic component to alcoholism. Alcohol abuse can be a learned behaviour as well. The same argument applies to the race/crime relationship.

Another point is relevant to the issue of a disproportionate involvement in crime. Virtually every society contains racial and ethnic groups, usually minorities, who are more criminally active in certain crimes than the rest of the population. According to Rushton's theory of criminal behaviour, native Canadians should display lower, not higher, crime rates than non-natives. Unfortunately for the theory, this is not true. The over-representation of native offenders in the criminal justice statistics has been apparent for some time (Griffiths and Verdun-Jones 1989; LaPrairie 1989). Explanations in terms of the social strata in our society occupied by indigenous peoples can easily explain these findings; Rushton's racial theory cannot. According to Rushton's typology this group, being oriental or mongoloid, should display lower, not higher rates of criminality.

According to Rushton's genetic explanation of crime, the crime rates for blacks should be higher than the white crime rates, *and* the rates for native Canadians should be *lower* than the non-native population. The two categories (blacks; natives) are genetically dissimilar; their rates of criminality should reflect this difference (relative to the white population). The fact is that both black Americans and native Canadians share an elevated risk of certain kinds of criminality (relative to the comparable white populations in their respective countries). Such an outcome is, of course, perfectly consistent with a sociological explanation: both minority groups share a protracted history of constrained social opportunity, as well as overt discrimination.

Also in Canada, French Canadians are the most active in the crime of robbery (Gabor, Baril, Cusson, Elie, LeBlanc and Normandeau 1987). In England, Irish immigrants have been over-represented in crimes of assault for years (Radzinowicz and King 1977). In Israel, the Arab population and non-European Jews are more criminally active in conventional crimes than the European Jews (Fishman, Rattner and Weimann 1987). Such over-representation, then, is the rule rather than the exception across different societies.

To return to Rushton's suggestion, two errors can be identified. First, he cites data published in the *Daily Telegraph* (a British newspaper) showing that blacks account for over 50% of the crimes in the United States and the United Kingdom (Rushton 1988). By any measure, this is a considerable exaggeration. If he refers to all reported crimes and not merely index crimes, blacks account for about 29% of all persons charged in the United States (United States Department of Justice 1989).

As well, aggregate statistics based on index crimes alone misrepresent the true picture. Crime is not, as suggested by Rushton's publications, a homogeneous category of behaviours. While blacks in the United

States account for over 60% of arrests for robbery and almost 50% of arrests for murder, they account for about 30% of arrests for burglary and theft, less than 24% of those arrested for arson and about 20% of those arrested for vandalism (United States Department of Justice 1987). Using Rushton's own data, blacks are under-represented in crimes like tax fraud and securities violations. In fact, arrest statistics for white-collar crimes such as fraud and embezzlement are significantly higher for whites. Treating crime as a unitary phenomenon obscures this diversity. These variations reflect differential opportunities for offending, and not, we submit, offence-specific genetic programming.

Differential Treatment of Blacks by the Criminal Justice System

Finally, arrest statistics reflect, to a degree, the more rigorous surveillance by police to which minorities are subject. Data on this point are hard to obtain; the magnitude of the problem is hard to quantify. Nevertheless, the recent release of the "Guildford Four" in England, after 15 years of imprisonment following a wrongful conviction based upon fabricated police evidence, reveals the dangers posed to minorities by an over-zealous police force.

Research in the United States sustains the view that the police are more likely to arrest and charge blacks (Black and Reiss 1967; Lundman, Sykes and Clark 1978). Wolfgang and Cohen (1970: 71) summarize some of this research:

> In comparing arrest statistics for blacks and whites, it is important to remember, then, that one reason for the high arrest rates among blacks is that they are more likely to be stopped, picked up on suspicion and subsequently arrested.

Furthermore, the bias does not remain at the police station: British data (Landau 1981; Landau and Nathan 1983) show that prosecution is more likely for persons of Afro-Caribbean origin. Bias persists at most critical stages of the criminal justice process. As Paul Gordon (1988: 309) noted, summarizing data on the issue:

> Black peoples' experience of the British criminal justice system shows clearly that the rhetoric of the law does not accord with the reality of its practice. The law is not colour-blind, but a means by which black people have been subject to a process of criminalization.

Most recently, Albonetti and her colleagues (1989) have demonstrated that while the influence of race upon pre-trial decisions is complicated, white suspects have the edge over black suspects.

To summarize the data on contact with the criminal justice process, American blacks are clearly over-represented in violent crime statistics, slightly over-represented in property crimes, and under-represented in white-collar crimes. In order to explain this diverse pattern, one has to strain the genetic explanation beyond the breaking point. Are blacks genetically pre-disposed towards street crimes while whites are programmed to commit white-collar crimes? A far more plausible explanation exists: social groups commit crimes as a consequence of their social situations and in response to prevailing criminal opportunities. This environmental perspective explains more findings and requires fewer assumptions. The law of parsimony, then, clearly favours environmental over genetic theories of crime. In short, Rushton's explanation of crime by reference to genetic influences requires acceptance of the position that specific antisocial behaviours are directly related to genetic structure. Modern behavioural geneticists would undoubtedly reject this view.

3. Over-Representation and Alternative Source of Crime Statistics: Victimization Surveys and Self-Reported Criminality

There is convincing evidence that arrest data exaggerate the true incidence of black criminality. Two alternative sources of information on crime make this clear. Overall, FBI data indicate that 46.5% of all violent crimes reported to the police are committed by blacks. However, the victimization survey conducted by the U.S. Department of Justice found that blacks account for only about 24% of violent crimes (United States Department of Justice 1986). Which source presents a more accurate picture of crimes actually committed? With regard to crimes of violence, data derived from victims would appear to be more accurate than arrest data. But it is not just victimization surveys that cast doubt upon the official statistics. A third source of information on crime patterns also shows discrepancies. Rojek (1983) compared police reports with self-reports of delinquency. In the police data-base, race was a significant factor in several offence categories, but this was not true for the self-reports. Other studies using the self-report approach (Williams and Gold 1972) have found a similar pattern: no difference between black and white respondents (Pope 1979) or only slight differences (Hirschi 1969).

Unreported versus Reported Crime

Another explanation for the elevated incidence of black offenders in official crime statistics concerns the issue of unreported crimes. As we have noted, official crime data indicate that blacks are more likely than whites to commit certain crimes (personal injury offences) and less likely than whites to commit other types of crimes. The problem with crime statistics is that the reporting rate is highly variable, depending upon the offence. The types of offences committed by blacks are more likely to be reported than the offences committed by whites. Any examination of aggregate crime statistics is going to over-estimate the true incidence of crime committed by blacks relative to the amount of crime committed by whites.

To conclude, the extent of over-representation of blacks, even in those offences where it occurs, has been exaggerated. In perhaps the most comprehensive study to date which relates crime to race, Michael Hindelang (1982) tested various theories which attempted to explain inter-racial differences. He concluded that the theories of delinquency that best explain the patterns of data were sociological rather than biological. These included Merton's re-formulation of anomie theory (Merton 1968), Cloward and Ohlin's opportunity theory (Cloward and Ohlin 1960), and Wolfgang's sub-culture of violence theory (Wolfgang and Ferracuti 1982).

A final word on the crime statistics utilized by Rushton consists of a caveat: recorded crime is exactly that; it is only a small fraction of all reported and unreported crime. A recent article by Tony Jefferson (1988: 535) makes the point succinctly:

> We do not know *what the real rate of black crime is, nor whether it is on the increase. Take robbery for instance. The British Crime Survey reveals that only 8% of robberies were recorded. If those figures applied to London this would mean that there is a suspect for only 1 in 100 robberies. The comparable figure for burglaries would be 5 in 100. This means that* whatever *the arrest figures, and whatever the victim identifications, the "unknown" element is so great, especially for those crimes where black "over-representation" is seen as greatest, as to make all estimates of black offending strictly conjectural.*

When there is sound reason to suppose that the police are more vigilant with regard to black suspects and offenders, it is clear that if we were able to replace reported with unreported crime rates, the inter-racial differences would diminish still further.

Self-report studies provide insight in another area as well. While Professor Rushton associates "lawlessness" with being black, there is overwhelming evidence indicating that most people, at one point or another, commit acts for which they could be prosecuted. As an example, in a now classic study, Wallerstein and Wyle (1947) surveyed 1700 New York City residents without a criminal record. Fully 99% admitted to involvement in at least one of 49 offences. This evidence suggests that rule-breaking is normal activity on the part of most citizens in Western societies. The selection of norm violators to be prosecuted therefore is critical to an understanding of who becomes officially classified as a criminal. Many observers of the criminal justice system believe that race may be a key factor affecting that selection process. Another classic study, Hartshorne and May's (1928) investigation of children, also showed that dishonesty was both pervasive and situation-specific. There was little cross-situational consistency: children that were dishonest in one situation were honest in others. This emphasis on the social situation as the determinant of behaviour is consistent with an environmental view of crime, and inconsistent with Rushton's genetic theory. (A large body of evidence, drawn from longitudinal, self-report, experimental, and observational research, suggests that law-breaking is widespread in North American society. For a comprehensive review of this literature see Gabor, forthcoming).

4. Within Race Comparisons

(a) Comparisons over Time

In the next two sections, we examine variation in crime rates within race, but across time and cultures. If genetic factors have an important impact upon crime, rates should be relatively stable within race, across both time and cultures. This, however, is not the case. Further undermining Rushton's thesis are the temporal and cross-cultural variations in crime patterns for the black population. Street crime by blacks in the United Kingdom has only recently increased significantly. Just over a decade ago Radzinowicz and King (1977) were able to write that, with the exception of prostitution and other victimless crimes, the black community was as law-abiding as other Britons. Any increase in crime rates within a generation obviously cannot be attributed to genetic factors. This point was made recently by Anthony Mawson (1989) in the context of explanations of homicide in terms of Darwinian selection (Daly and Wilson 1988). Mawson (1989: 239) notes the inability of biological explanations of homicide to account for fluctuations in homicide rates over a short period of time:

> *Thus, it seems doubtful whether a selectionist explanation can be applied to changing homicide rates, even those occurring over a thousand years.*

The same argument applies in the context of Rushton's work: increases in offending by blacks over a period of ten to fifteen years cannot possibly be explained by reference to genetic influence.

In the United States as well, the proportional involvement of blacks in crime has risen over the past few decades. One major factor in this rise has been the proliferation of illicit drug usage. Heroin use became pervasive in the 1950s and "crack" cocaine is creating an explosion of violent crime in this decade. As well, the erosion of taboos relating to inter-racial crimes has been associated with increased victimization of whites by blacks (Silberman 1978). A third major development has been the greater accessibility of firearms. These are three potent environmental factors affecting black criminality. One would be hard-pressed to find a genetic explanation for the changing criminal activity pattern of a race over such a short period of time.

(b) Comparisons across Jurisdictions

The variations in black, white, and oriental crime from one society to another also demonstrate the potency of environmental factors in the etiology of crime. Levels of violent crime in the American South are greater for both blacks *and* whites than they are in other parts of the country. As well, there is substantial variation in the homicide rates for blacks in different American states. For example, in Delaware the homicide rate for blacks is 16.7 per 100,000. This is considerably lower than the homicide rate for black residents of other states; in Missouri, for example, the rate is 65 per 100,000 (Carroll and Mercy 1989).

Cross-national, within-race comparisons make the same point. Black Americans have a higher homicide rate than their more racially-pure counterparts in Africa: this fact directly contradicts Rushton's thesis. The author (Bohannan 1960: 123) of a study of African homicide concludes:

> *if it needed stressing, here is overwhelming evidence that it is a cultural and not biological factor which makes for a high homicide rate among American negroes.*

More recent data (International Criminal Police Organization 1988) demonstrate the same variations: the homicide rate per 100,000 inhabitants varies from .01 (Mali) to 29 (Bahamas) and 22.05 (Jamaica). It is noteworthy also that the Caribbean homicide rates are far in excess of even the African countries with the highest rates (e.g., Rwanda, 11 per 100,000; Tanzania, 8 per 100,000). This despite the fact that residents of the Caribbean are more racially mixed than blacks from Africa. According to Rushton's theory, homicide rates should be higher not lower in the more racially pure African states.

Furthermore, orientals do not constitute a monolith of law-abiding citizens. The homicide rates in the Far East also vary considerably, from 39 per 100,000 residents in the Philippines to 1.3 per 100,000 in Hong Kong. In Thailand, the homicide rate exceeds the rate of homicide in Japan by a factor of twelve (International Criminal Police Organization 1988). In all these comparisons, the genetic explanation falls short. The magnitude of these intra-racial differences suggests that the potency of environmental factors to explain crime rates far exceeds that of genetic factors. In statistical terms, these data imply that the percentage of variation in crime rates explained by genetic factors is negligible, if it exists at all.

5. Victimization Patterns

There is another form of over-representation of which Professor Rushton appears unaware: blacks are at much higher risk of becoming the victims of violent crime. In the United States, black males are 20 times more likely than whites to be shot, cut, or stabbed, and black females are 18 times more likely to be raped than white women (Wolfgang and Cohen 1981). Black Americans are also more likely than whites to be victims of burglary, motor vehicle theft, assault, robbery and many other offences (United States Bureau of Justice Statistics 1983). Although blacks constitute only 12% of the general United States population, over 40% of homicide victims are black. See Barnett and Schwartz (1989) for recent data showing black victimization rates to be approximately four times higher than white rates. The same trends are apparent in other countries, such as England. The over-representation of blacks as victims is substantial, yet no-one has posited that such over-representation is due to a genetically-based susceptibility to criminal victimization. While this finding is not inconsistent with an explanation based upon genetic factors, it does underscore the importance of environmental factors such as propinquity and accessibility.

Violent crimes are a result of an interaction between offender and victim. To posit an over-riding genetic basis of crime is to ignore the role of the victim and situational factors (Boyd 1988; Wolfgang 1958). When we examine the dynamics of the violent crime most commonly associated with blacks — armed robbery — we readily see the importance of situational determinants. Actually, recourse to physical violence occurs only in a small minority of robberies. Usually the violence that does occur arises in response to victims who resist the robbers' demands (Gabor et al. 1987). The violence, therefore, is often instrumental and situation-specific.

If blacks are more likely to be both offenders and victims in relation to certain types of crime, then a plausible explanation for their over-representation on both counts is that they tend to live in areas in which violence is a normal consequence of stress, threat, and frustration. This essentially is Wolfgang and Ferracuti's (1982) subculture of violence thesis. Aside from living in environments where violence is normative behaviour, blacks tend disproportionately to live in poverty. Furthermore, they are over-represented among urban dwellers. Economic status and urban residence are linked to a number of crime indices. A fair examination of black and white criminality would therefore necessitate comparison between persons situated similarly in society.

But even the presence of a correlation between race and certain indices of crime, after other plausible environmental factors have been pointed out, does not demonstrate a genetically-based race/crime link. As Charles Silberman (1978) has pointed out, the experience of black Americans has been very different from the experience of any other disadvantaged group. The generations of violence, deprivation, disenfranchisement, and exclusion from educational and vocational opportunities to which they have been subjected has not been shared by any other ethnic or racial group. Moreover, much of this racial discrimination persists, to this day, and in this country, as recent research has documented (Henry and Ginzberg 1985). Discrimination of this kind can engender social patterns and attitudes towards authority that lead to law breaking.

Careful epidemiological research can result in samples of black and white citizens that are "matched" on many important background variables such as social class, income, education, age, family size and composition. Comparisons between such groups is preferable to comparison based upon unmatched samples, but the effects of long-term discrimination, brutality, and oppression over generations cannot be captured by the most rigorous multiple regression analysis. As John Conklin (1989: 140) notes:

> *to argue that blacks and whites of similar backgrounds will have the same crime rate is to argue that centuries of discrimination have had no long-term effects on blacks that are conducive to criminal behaviour.*

Our opposition to Rushton's views should not be interpreted to mean that we deny the existence of any genetic influences upon human behaviour. Rather, we take issue with the attribution of racial differences in criminality to genetic factors. In our view, there is little scientific basis for his rather sweeping assertions about the relative "law-abidingness" of different racial groups. The few statistics he provides are susceptible of a multitude of highly probable alternative explanations derived from an environmental perspective. Given the incendiary nature of the theory and its policy implications, we feel that the burden of proof is upon Professor Rushton to provide more convincing data than the few ambiguous statistics he has to date brought forth. We leave it to others (Lynn 1989; Zuckerman and Brody 1988) to evaluate the scientific credibility of Professor Rushton's genetic explanation of other phenomena such as: intelligence, sexual restraint, personality, political preferences, and the efficacy of the German army in World War II (*The Globe and Mail* 1989). In the area of criminality, his evidence, in our view, falls short of discharging a scientific burden of proof.

NOTE

The authors would like to acknowledge that this manuscript has benefitted from the comments of Michael Petrunik, from the University of Ottawa, the editorial committee of the *Canadian Journal of Criminology*, and two anonymous reviewers.

REFERENCES

Albonetti, Celesta, Robert Hauser, John Hagan, and Ilene Nagel. 1989. "Criminal justice decision making as a stratification process: The role of race and stratification resources in pre-trial release." *Journal of Quantitative Criminology* 5: 57–82.

Barnett, Arnold and Elliot Schwartz. 1989. "Urban homicide: Still the same." *Journal of Quantitative Criminology* 5: 83–100.

Black, D. and Albert Reiss. 1967. *Studies of Crime and Law Enforcement in Major Metropolitan Areas*. Washington, D.C.: Government Printing Office.

Bohannan. Paul. 1960. *African Homicide and Suicide.* Princeton, N.J.: Princeton Univ. Press.

Bonger, Willem. 1969. *Race and Crime.* New Jersey: Patterson Smith. (Originally published 1943).

Boyd, Neil. 1988. *The Last Dance: Murder in Canada.* Toronto: Prentice Hall.

Carroll, Patrick and James Mercy. 1989. "Regional variation in homicide rates: Why is the west violent?" *Violence and Victims* 4: 17–25.

Cloward, Richard A. and Lloyd Ohlin. 1960. *Delinquency and Opportunity: A Theory of Delinquent Gangs.* New York: The Free Press.

Conklin, John. 1989. *Criminology.* (Third edition) New York: Macmillan.

Curie, Elliot. 1985. *Confronting Crime.* New York: Pantheon.

Daly, Martin and Margo Wilson. 1988. *Homicide.* New York: Aldine.

Doob, Anthony N. and Julian V. Roberts. 1982. *Crime: Some Views of the Canadian Public.* Ottawa: Department of Justice.

Fishman, G., Arye Rattner, and Gabriel Weimann. 1987. "The effect of ethnicity on crime attribution." *Criminology* 25: 507–24.

Fiske, Susan T. and Shelley E. Taylor. 1984. *Social Cognition.* Reading, Mass.: Addison-Wesley.

Gabor, Thomas. 1991. "Crime by the public." In Curt Griffiths and Margaret Jackson, eds., *Canadian Criminology: Perspectives on Crime and Criminality.* Toronto: Harcourt Brace Jovanovich.

Gabor, Thomas, Micheline Baril, M. Cusson, D. Elie, Marc LeBlanc, and Andre Nommandeau. 1987. *Armed Robbery: Cops, Robbers, and Victims.* Springfield, Ill.: Charles C. Thomas.

The Globe and Mail. 1989. February 11, 14.

Gordon, Paul. 1988. "Black people and the criminal law: Rhetoric and reality." *International Journal of the Sociology of Law* 16: 295–313.

Gould, Stephen Jay. 1981. *The Mismeasure of Man.* New York: W.W. Norton.

Griffiths, Curt and Simon Verdun-Jones. 1989. *Canadian Criminal Justice.* Toronto: Butterworths.

Hartshome, M. and M.A. May. 1928. *Studies in Deceit.* New York: Macmillan.

Haskell, M.R. and L. Yablonsky. 1983. *Criminology: Crime and Criminality.* Boston: Houghton Mifflin.

Henry, F. and E. Ginzberg. 1985. *Who Gets the Work: A Test of Racial Discrimination in Employment.* Toronto: Urban Alliance on Race Relations and the Social Planning Council.

Herskovits, Melville J. 1930. *The Anthropometry of the American Negro.* New York: Columbia University Press.

Hindelang, Michael. 1982. "Race and Crime." In Leonard D. Savitz and N. Johnston, eds., *Contemporary Criminology.* Toronto: John Wiley.

Hirschi, Travis. 1969. *Causes of Delinquency.* Berkeley: University of California Press.

Hooton, Ernest A. 1939. *Crime and the Man.* Cambridge, Mass.: Harvard University Press.

International Criminal Police Organization. 1988. *International Crime Statistics* 1985–86.

Jefferson, Tony. 1988. "Race, crime and policing: Empirical, theoretical and methodological issues." *International Journal of the Sociology of Law* 16: 521–39.

Landau, Simha. 1981. "Juveniles and the police." *British Journal of Criminology* 21: 27–46.

Landau, Simha and G. Nathan. 1983. "Selecting delinquents for cautioning in the London metropolitan area." *British Journal of Criminology* 28: 128–49.

LaPrairie, Carol. 1989. *The Role of Sentencing in the Over-Representation of Aboriginal People in Correctional Institutions.* Ottawa: Department of Justice.

Lombroso, Caesare. 1968. *Crime. Its Causes and Remedies.* (English edition) Montclair, N.J.: Patterson Smith. (Original publication: *Le Crime, causes et remèdes,* 1899).

Lombroso-Ferrero, Gina. 1972. *Criminal Man According to the Classification of Cesare Lombroso.* Montclair, N.J.: Patterson Smith, 1972 (Originally published 1911).

Lundman, R., R. Sykes and J. Clark. 1978. "Police control of juveniles: A replication." *Journal of Research in Crime and Delinquency* 15: 74–91.

Lynn, Michael. 1989. "Race difference in sexual behaviour: A critique of Rushton and Bogaert's evolutionary hypothesis." *Journal of Research in Personality* 23: 1–6.

Mawson, Anthony. 1989. "Review of Homicide" (Daly and Wilson, 1988). *Contemporary Sociology* March 238–40.

Merton, Robert K. 1968. *Social Theory and Social Structure.* Glencoe: The Free Press.

Nisbett, Richard and Lee Ross. 1980. *Human Inference: Strategies and Shortcomings of Social Judgement.* Englewood Cliffs, N.J.: Prentice Hall.

Pope, Carl E. 1979. "Race and crime re-visited." *Crime and Delinquency* 25: 345–57.

Radzinowicz, Leon and Joan King. 1977. *The Growth of Crime: The International Experience.* London: Penguin.

Roberts, Julian V. and Nicholas R. White. 1986. "Public estimates of recidivism rates: Consequences of a criminal stereotype." *Canadian Journal of Criminology* 28: 229–41.

Rojek, Dean G. 1983. "Social status and delinquency: Do self-reports and official reports match?" In Gordon P. Waldo, ed., *Measurement Issues in Criminal Justice.* Beverly Hills: Sage.

Rushton, J. Philippe. 1987. "Population differences in rule-following behaviour: race, evolution and crime." Paper presented to the 39th Annual Meeting of the American Society of Criminology, Montreal, November 11–14.

———. 1988. "Race differences in behaviour: A review and evolutionary analysis." *Personality and Individual Differences* 9: 1009–24.

———. 1989. "Race differences in sexuality and their correlates: Another look and physiological models." *Journal of Research in Personality* 23: 35–54.

Silberman, Charles. 1978. *Criminal Violence, Criminal Justice*. New York: Vintage.

The Toronto Star. 1989. February 17, 20.

United States Department of Justice. 1983. *Sourcebook of Criminal Justice Statistics*. Washington, D.C.: Bureau of Justice Statistics.

———. 1986. *Criminal Victimization in the United States*. Washington, D.C.: Bureau of Justice Statistics.

———. 1987. *Sourcebook of Criminal Justice Statistics*. Washington, D.C.: Bureau of Justice Statistics.

———. 1989. *Sourcebook of Criminal Justice Statistics*. Washington, D.C.: Bureau of Justice Statistics.

Wallerstein, James S. and Clement J. Wyle. 1947. "Our law-abiding lawbreakers." *Probation* 25: 107–12.

Williams, Jay and Martin Gold. 1972. "From delinquent behaviour to official delinquency." *Social Problems* 20: 209–29.

Wolfgang, Marvin. 1958. *Patterns in Criminal Homicide*. Philadelphia: University of Pennsylvania Press.

Wolfgang, Marvin and Bernard Cohen. 1981. "Crime and race: The victims of crime." In Burt Galaway and Joe Hudson, eds., *Perspectives on Crime Victims*. St. Louis: C.V. Mosby.

———. 1970. *Crime and Race: Conceptions and Misconceptions*. New York: Institute of Human Relations Press.

Wolfgang, Marvin and Franco Ferracuti. 1982. *The Subculture of Violence*. Beverly Hills: Sage.

Zuckerman, Marvin and Nathan Brody. 1989. "Oysters, rabbits and people: A critique of 'race differences in behaviour' by J.P. Rushton." *Personality and Individual Differences* 9: 1025–33.

Chapter 29

CULTURE AND HOMICIDE IN CANADA AND THE USA

RHONDA L. LENTON

One of the most striking and well-known differences between Canada and the United States concerns their crime rates. Americans are roughly four times more likely than Canadians to commit homicide and rape, two and one-half times more likely to commit robbery and one and one-quarter times more likely to commit burglary. While some of these differences may result partly from crossnational variations in legal definitions of crime, methods of counting crime and levels of police surveillance, it is generally agreed that for the most violent crimes — homicide in particular — official crime rates reflect real behavioural differences between the two countries (Hagan, 1984 [1977]: 48–55).

John Hagan refers to the most serious forms of deviance as "consensus crimes." In his judgement members of society broadly agree that the most violent crimes are the most serious crimes, and that their perpetrators deserve the most severe forms of punishment. Violent crime involves avoiding, neutralizing and rejecting deeply and widely held societal norms and values. The rate of violent crime therefore hinges on the ability of a culture to define achievable goals, impose constraints on behaviour, and prevent both the neutralization of community standards and the creation of subcultures that oppose the dominant value system (Hagan, 1984 [1977]: 80–120).

In explaining Canadian–American differences in homicide rates, Hagan follows this cultural approach. Borrowing from the work of S.D. Clark (1976), Seymour Martin Lipset (1986) and others, Hagan argues that two sets of historical forces created Canadian and American value systems that differ in important respects and that account for the lower rate of homicide in Canada (Hagan, 1984 [1977]: 117–18, 147–48, 230–35; Hagan and Leon, 1977). First, in the early years of North American economic development, Canada's frontier was "harder" than that of the United States. That is, Canada was a vast and inhospitable country compared with the U.S., and its natural resources were less accessible. While the development of the American frontier could therefore be left to the initiative of the lone, relatively lawless entrepreneur, the exploitation of the Canadian frontier required the assistance of state-supported armies, police forces, and other social organizations such as the established Roman Catholic and Anglican Churches. The "wild West" shaped American attitudes towards authority, the state, and law and order quite differently from the way the harmonious development of the Canadian frontier influenced Canadians' attitudes: Canadians became more respectful of authority and less inclined to break the law.

According to Hagan, the second main historical force that produced lower Canadian rates of violent crime was the tenacity of Canada's ties to elitist and conservative Britain. Presumably, those ties were reinforced during the American Revolution, when loyalist tories migrated northward, and persisted well into the twentieth century. Canadians' characteristic deference to authority supposedly derived in part from the British connection. In contrast, the American Revolution

---

Source: "Homicide in Canada and the U.S.A.: A Critique of the Hagan Thesis," *Canadian Journal of Sociology* 14, 2 (1989): 163–78. Reprinted by permission of the publisher.

severed the American bond to Britain and institutionalized a deep and abiding anti-authoritarianism in the American psyche. Presumably, that attitude is reflected in the greater propensity of Americans to commit violent crimes.

My purpose in this chapter is not to dispute the accuracy of the violent crime statistics, historical interpretations, or attitudinal differences discussed by Hagan. Other analysts have already raised serious questions about the precision of some of the "facts" he uncritically accepts. For example, there is a considerable body of historical scholarship contesting the old view, endorsed by Hagan, that the Loyalists were tories (Jones, 1985; Upton, 1967). Similarly, an analysis of recent sample survey data indicates that the purported Canadian–American value differences either do not exist or are in the opposite direction from that predicted by Hagan (and Clark and Lipset before him). According to Baer, Grabb, and Johnston (forthcoming 1989), Canadians are *less* respectful of government leaders and institutions than are Americans, and *less* traditional than Americans about the need for crime control.[1]

Whether or not the predicted Canadian–American value differences actually exist, my aim is to demonstrate that variation in homicide rates is better explained by structural factors. I argue that the relationship posited by Hagan between some measured value differences and homicide rates may be largely an artifact of his choice of data. Hagan bases his argument mainly on a comparison of only two cases over a relatively short period of time. By increasing the cross-sectional and longitudinal variation in his independent and dependent variables, however, I cast doubt on the accuracy of Hagan's generalizations.

I also suggest an alternative explanation of Canadian–American differences in homicide rates. I argue that certain features of American and Canadian social structure account for Canadian–American differences in homicide rates better than do alleged cultural differences. Specifically, variations in the racial composition of the two countries and in the level of income inequality stand out as the two most important determinants of crossnational differences in my analysis. In general, I agree with Ian Taylor's view that "[there is a clear need to examine the *structure* of ... society (its demography, political economy and social institutions) and to relate these to ... pathological social interactions like homicide" (Taylor, 1983: 97; emphasis in the original). Apart from criticizing Hagan's thesis, then, my paper adds modest empirical substance to Taylor's assertion.

The persuasiveness of my argument is compromised by the type of data I employ to make my case. It is by now widely recognized that, ideally, the study of homicide etiology should combine data on the characteristics of individual perpetrators and victims with structural data on community and regional characteristics. Such data would help researchers guard against making ecologically fallacious inferences and enable them to explain how individual-level behaviour accounts for aggregate statistical patterns. In practice, however, most analyses of homicide in North America are based on aggregated data for provinces and territories (in Canada), or states and Standard Metropolitan Statistical Areas (in the U.S.). Individual-level data are difficult to obtain from official sources, and when they are available they are usually presented in the form of nation-wide, two- or three-variable contingency tables. Thus, my approach, if deficient, is at least standard. For the most part I use provinces and territories as units of analysis. I also inspect some Statistics Canada contingency tables containing individual-level data for Canada as a whole and report relevant results of the past fifteen years of (almost exclusively American) research on homicide etiology. The result is less a definitive refutation of Hagan's thesis than an attempt to underscore some of its weaknesses and propose an alternative approach. I do, however, claim that the alternative theoretical argument I offer is both plausible and apparently more consistent with available data than is Hagan's thesis.

VARIATION OVER TIME

A key argument in Hagan's thesis is that the ratio of American to Canadian homicide rates has remained about the same or increased over time. A relatively constant or increasing ratio suggests that values which first crystallized 100 to 200 years ago remain obdurate and that cultural differences between the two North American countries exert an enduring influence on criminal behaviour despite vast economic, political, and legal changes. A widely fluctuating or declining ratio of American to Canadian homicide rates, in contrast, would suggest that the values discussed by Hagan have no persistent effect on criminal behaviour.

When Hagan first made his case he compared American and Canadian homicide rates in 1957, 1960, 1967, 1968, and 1970. He concluded that the ratio of American to Canadian homicide rates is increasing over time (Hagan and Leon, 1977: 198–99). He later compared homicide rates for the years 1960–80 and concluded that the ratio has remained constant over time (Hagan, 1984 [1977]: 50).

It is unclear why Hagan selected these particular years for comparison. It does, however, seem that he based his conclusions on a simple visual inspection of the data. Table 29.1 assembles American and Canadian homicide rates from 1954 (the first year for which Canadian data are readily accessible from secondary sources) to 1986 (the last year for which data are currently available). Although the ratio of American to Canadian rates does not fluctuate widely from year to year, it appears to be very slowly *declining*. Rather than substantiating Hagan's thesis, these findings offer some support for Irving Louis Horowitz's contrary claim that homicide data reveal a tendency for the "cultural gap" between Canada and the United States to be closing over time. Horowitz asserts that this gap is narrowing due to the Americanization of Canada that is caused by such structural forces as increasing American economic and political influence (Horowitz, 1973: 341 and *passim*).

VARIATION BY REGION

A second problem with Hagan's analysis is that he considers only two cases — Canada and the United States — and is consequently unable to determine whether the relationship he observes between homicide rates and culture patterns is fortuitous or generalizable. One way of getting around this problem is by comparing units of analysis smaller than countries, such as provinces or states.[2] This seems sensible because there is more variation in homicide rates *within* both Canada and the United States than *between* the two countries. In 1986, the coefficient of variation (the standard deviation over the mean) of homicide rates within Canada was 1.534. Within the U.S. the coefficient of variation was .664, and between Canada and the U.S. it was only .593 (raw data sources: Department of Justice, 1987: 44–50; Statistics Canada, 1987: 61). The range of homicide rates across the Canadian provinces was almost the same in 1986 (27) as the range of homicide rates across the American states (30). The ranges and coefficients of variation show that national comparisons mask wide regional variations within the two countries. This raises the question of whether it makes much sense to assume national homogeneity in values and homicidal behaviour, as does a simple comparison of national mean rates.

In order to test the stability of correlations across time, I calculated zero-order correlations for 1986, 1981, 1976, and 1971.[3] In order to test the robustness of correlations across groups of cases, I used all twelve

Table 29.1 Homicide Rates (per 100,000 Population), Canada and U.S.A., 1954–1986

	Canada	U.S.A.	U.S.A./Canada ratio
1954	1.2	4.8	4.0
1955	1.2	4.5	3.8
1956	1.3	4.6	3.5
1957	1.2	4.5	3.8
1958	1.4	4.5	3.1
1959	1.2	4.5	3.8
1960	.9	5.1	5.7
1961	1.2	4.8	4.0
1962	1.4	4.5	3.3
1963	1.3	4.6	3.5
1964	1.3	4.9	3.8
1965	1.4	5.1	3.6
1966	1.2	5.6	4.7
1967	1.7	6.2	3.7
1968	1.8	6.9	3.8
1969	1.8	7.3	4.1
1970	2.2	7.9	3.6
1971	2.2	8.6	3.9
1972	2.4	9.0	3.8
1973	2.5	9.4	3.8
1974	2.7	9.8	3.6
1975	3.1	9.6	3.1
1976	2.9	8.8	3.0
1977	3.0	8.8	2.9
1978	2.8	9.0	3.2
1979	2.7	9.7	3.6
1980	2.5	10.2	4.1
1981	2.7	9.8	3.7
1982	2.7	9.1	3.4
1983	2.7	8.3	3.0
1984	2.7	7.9	3.0
1985	2.8	7.9	2.8
1986	2.2	8.6	3.9

Sources: Canada, 1954–59: Statistics Canada (1973c: 8); Canada and U.S.A., 1960–80: Hagan (1984 [1977]: 50); Canada, 1981–86: Statistics Canada (1987: 85); U.S.A., 1954–59: Bureau of the Census (1976: 414); U.S.A., 1981–86; Statistics Canada (1987: 83).

cases. Next, the Northwest Territories, which has the highest homicide rate and the second smallest population of the twelve jurisdictions, was removed and the correlations recalculated. Then the Yukon, which generally has the second highest homicide rate and the smallest population of the twelve jurisdictions, was removed and the correlations calculated for a third time. Finally, both the Northwest Territories and the Yukon were removed and the correlations calculated for a fourth time.[4]

In Hagan's view, one correlate of homicide rates is the strength of the "Imperial connection." Presumably, an indicator of British influence is the proportion of British-origin people in each province or territory: it follows from Hagan's argument that the greater the proportion British-origin, the lower the homicide rate. In fact, out of the sixteen correlations between proportion British and the homicide rate, only ten are in the predicted direction and statistically significant at the .05 level.[5] Proportion British is in the predicted direction and statistically significant across time only if the two northern territories are omitted; and proportion British is in the predicted direction and statistically significant across groups of cases only in 1971 and 1981.

Hagan also suggests that Canadian values have been profoundly influenced by the predominance of the Anglican and Roman Catholic Churches, which provided Canada with "a set of hierarchical and traditionally rooted control mechanisms" that reinforced the effects of the hard frontier and the British connection (Hagan and Leon, 1977: 184; cf. Lipset, 1986: 124–28). In contrast, Protestant sectarianism flourished in the U.S., thus reinforcing individualism and lack of respect for authority in that country. Yet of the thirty-two correlations between provincial and territorial homicide rates, on the one hand, and proportion Catholic and proportion Anglican, on the other, none is in the predicted direction and statistically significant. Combining proportion Catholic and proportion Anglican into one index does not alter the conclusion that provincial and territorial homicide rates do not increase with the greater numerical prevalence of Catholics and Anglicans.

VARIATION BY RACE AND ECONOMIC CONDITION

The foregoing analysis generates only weak support for Hagan's thesis. The best that can be said for his argument is that proportion British predicts homicide rates well for the ten provinces. However, once the territories are included in the analysis, proportion British fails to perform very well. And proportion Catholic and proportion Anglican systematically fail to predict homicide rates.

An alternative explanation of the Canadian–American difference in homicide rates can be derived from research on homicide conducted mainly in the U.S. over the past fifteen years. Perhaps the best substantiated finding of both ecological and individual-level analyses of homicide etiology in the U.S. is that poor, young, urban blacks and Hispanics are tremendously overrepresented among homicide offenders (e.g., Williams, 1984). In 1986, for example, blacks accounted for 48.0 percent and Hispanics for 15.7 percent of American murderers, yet they composed, respectively, only 12 percent and 6 percent of the American population (Department of Justice, 1987: 182, 185). Significantly, Canadian homicide statistics for poor Native Canadians are equally startling. In 1986, for instance, Native Canadians accounted for 21 percent of Canadian murderers for whom race could be ascertained, yet Natives represented a mere 2 percent of the population (Statistics Canada, 1987: 95). There is a consistently strong and statistically significant association between homicide rates in the Canadian provinces and territories and the proportion of the population that is of Native origin: fifteen of the sixteen relevant correlations are in the predicted direction and statistically significant.

The racial skewedness of homicide in both Canada and the U.S., and the dissimilar racial compositions of the two countries, have important implications for Hagan's thesis. Consider, for instance, that the 1986 non-black, non-Hispanic American homicide rate was 3.1 (compared with 8.6 for the entire American population). The 1986 non-Native Canadian rate was 1.7 (compared with 2.2 for the entire Canadian population). If one compares American non-blacks and non-Hispanics with Canadian non-Natives, then the 1986 American–Canadian homicide ratio of 3.9 falls to a much less dramatic 1.8.[6] Hagan virtually dismisses the significance of the racial composition of Canada and the U.S. in interpreting the two countries' different homicide rates (Hagan and Leon, 1977: 199; contrast Horowitz, 1973: 341). The fact is, however, that differences in racial composition account for over half the discrepancy that Hagan set out to explain.

Despite the fact that Hagan makes no mention of the higher level of poverty and inequality in the U.S. as compared with Canada, some portion of the remaining discrepancy is likely the result of the different distribution of economic advantages in the two countries (cf. Horowitz, 1973: 341). Consider the following:

1. We know from American research that measures of economic well-being, both at the aggregate and individual level, are associated with homicide rates (Blau and Blau, 1982; Loftin and Hill, 1974; Smith and Parker, 1980; Williams, 1984; Williams and Flewelling, 1988). To varying degrees in different studies, unemployment, poverty, levels of inequality, and so forth, have been reported to promote homicidal behaviour independent of the effects of race. While there has been some inconsistency in findings on the effects of economic

variables, recent research suggests that that is because such effects are indirect and mediated by levels of family disruption (Sampson, 1987).

2. In Canada, too, economic condition appears to be associated with propensity to commit homicide. Thus, from 1961 to 1974, fully 56 percent of murder suspects had a primary education or less (compared with 35 percent of the population in 1971); and only 3 percent of murder suspects had a university education (compared with 10 percent of the population in 1971) (Statistics Canada, 1976: 99). In that same period, 61 percent of homicide suspects were blue-collar workers or self-employed workers in the primary sector (Statistics Canada, 1976: 102) compared with 36 percent of the population in those occupational categories in 1971 (Kalbach and McVey, 1979 [1971]: 290).

3. Crossnational studies including Canada and the U.S. as cases have also found that homicide rates are positively associated with levels of inequality (Krahn, Hartnagel, and Gartrell, 1986; Messner, 1982). In this connection it is of interest that the level of income inequality in Canada is considerably lower than that in the U.S. In the mid-1970s the Gini index of income inequality was .33 in Canada and .41 in the U.S. (Krahn, Hartnagel, and Gartrell, 1986: 295), and the gap between the two countries seems to have widened during the 1980s (cf. Banting, 1987 and Rothschild, 1988).

In my analysis, structural poverty (cf. Loftin and Hill, 1974: 719) is operationalized as an index constructed from two items: the infant mortality rate and the proportion of households reporting no income.[7] Scores on both these items were standardized and added together to create the index. Family disruption (cf. Sampson, 1987: 356) is operationalized as an index constructed from three items: the proportion of lone-parent families, the incidence of marital separation and the incidence of divorce. As with the structural poverty index, scores on these items were standardized and added together to create the index.

As a predictor of homicide, structural poverty performs nearly as well as percent Native, with thirteen of sixteen relevant correlations attaining statistical significance. The correlations between family disruption and homicide are much less robust and stable, with only four of the sixteen relevant correlations attaining statistical significance. I surmise that my family disruption index performs poorly in the Canadian context because it is derived from research on Black Americans

Figure 29.1 A Causal Model of Homicide Etiology in Canada

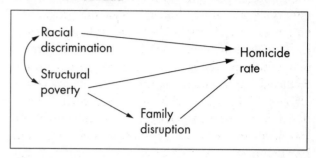

and therefore fails to tap manifestations of family disruption among Native Canadians. Divorce, separation, and single-parent families are relatively common in American urban ghettos, but Native Canadians do not appear to be more prone to these forms of family breakdown than other Canadians. For Native Canadians, family violence and incest seem to be more valid indicators of family breakdown (Shkilnyk, 1985). Unfortunately, however, systematically collected national data on family violence and incest by ethnic group are unavailable.

In the light of these findings it is tempting to model my argument along the lines of Figure 29.1. I propose that structural poverty and racial discrimination are the two principal causes of homicide. Structural poverty exerts its impact both directly and indirectly through its effects on family disruption.

DISCUSSION

If murder is the prototypical crime of passion, it seems evident that passion is much more likely to take such a violent course in particular types of communities. Cross-sectional data from both Canada and the U.S. suggest that when racial discrimination, endemic poverty, and family disruption cause hopelessness and rage, murder rates increase.

This social-structural interpretation is of course at variance with Hagan's argument, which borrows heavily from the "subculture of violence" thesis, until recently the dominant explanation of homicide in the U.S. (Wolfgang and Ferracuti, 1967). Darnell Hawkins, a student of homicide among American blacks and a critic of the subculture of violence thesis, summarizes the thesis by noting that it

tends to identify the value system of a given subculture as the locus of crime causation. Emphasis is also placed upon the role of social learning as the principal process by which aggressive behaviour is acquired. While there is some attention paid to the social, economic and political deprivation within subcultures, such deprivation is itself seldom seen as a direct cause of crime. That is, the impact of deprivation on crime is mediated by social values — in particular the existence or a positive attitude toward the use of violence. (Hawkins, 1986: 112)

In like fashion, Hagan tries to account for American–Canadian differences in homicide rates by examining value differences between the two countries and, in the process, ignoring differences in racial composition and the distribution of economic advantages.

The data assembled here do not unequivocally undermine the cultural thesis and support a structural interpretation of variation in homicide rates across Canadian regions and between Canada and the U.S. This is partly due to problems stemming from the highly aggregated nature of most of the data reviewed here and partly due to measurement problems. Although my inspection of individual-level contingency tables from Canadian government sources does suggest that my argument is not ecologically fallacious, I cannot be absolutely certain that the relationships discovered here hold at lower levels of aggregation or at the individual level because most of my data are highly aggregated. Moreover, partly because I use ecological data, my independent variables are highly correlated, thus preventing the construction of a multivariate model. On these grounds alone there is much room for additional research.

In addition, some of the measures used here — such as proportion British and proportion Native — are not unambiguously structural or cultural (cf. Loftin and Hill, 1974). Thus, it is unclear to what degree the prevalence of members of a given group indicates something about the value system of a particular region or about its social structure. Better measures are clearly needed. Until they are available one is obliged to note that there is apparently considerable variation in homicide rates across Native Canadian groups (compare, for example, Fisher, 1987; French, 1988; and Shkilnyk, 1985). This casts doubt on the notion that there is some culturally uniform cause of homicide among Native Canadians.

All these qualifications notwithstanding, available evidence suggests that the conviction with which Hagan endorses the cultural theory of Canadian–American differences in homicide rates is unwarranted. The evidence supporting a structural theory is somewhat stronger, but considerably more research is needed before one can hope to call closure on the debate.

CONCLUSION

I noted at the beginning of this chapter that homicide is considered by Hagan to be one variant of a broad class of "consensus" crimes, including murder, rape, incest, and kidnapping. According to Hagan, these are the most violent crimes and, as a result, members of society generally agree that they are the most serious crimes; their perpetrators receive the most severe forms of punishment; attitudes towards these crimes are weakly, if at all, related to status group membership; social and economic forces play a relatively small role in designating such acts as deviant; and these crimes are best explained by consensus theories, which focus on how cultures succeed or fail in imposing constraints on deviant behaviour. Hagan argues that, in contrast, crimes that do not match the criteria listed above are better explained by labelling, conflict, and Marxist theories, which emphasize the historical variability of crime and the manner in which dominant groups define and punish criminal behavior.

My critique has questioned the applicability of a consensus theory to one of the most violent types of crime in two countries. But, more broadly, the foregoing analysis calls into question the utility of viewing the most violent crimes as consensus crimes. For in two senses — one concerning social definition, the other etiology — even homicide is a conflict crime. Consider, first, that some types of widespread killing are not socially defined as serious crimes because to do so would harm corporate interests; while homicide is "allowed" to be socially defined as a serious crime because it does not harm corporate interests. Thus, deaths that result from industrial pollution and the failure to implement more stringent worker safety legislation account for many more deaths per year than homicide. Yet these acts are not consensually defined as serious crimes, they are not subject to strict surveillance, they are often not detected and counted by authorities and their perpetrators are typically not punished severely when detected. Corporate influence is surely a major socioeconomic force that prevents such killing from being classified as a crime on a par with homicide. As these examples illustrate, to the degree that there is consensus about what kind of killing is a serious crime, that consensus is not "given" by culture but is manufactured by the distribution of power in society.[8] Crimes like homicide are *mala en sa* (wrong in themselves), but they are also *mala prohibita* (wrong by prohibition).

Homicide is also a conflict crime from an etiological point of view. The distribution of homicide by race, class, sex, age, and level of inequality indicates that most homicide is a manifestation of social conflict, a violent response to racial, class, and sexual antagonism.[9] As Ian Taylor (1983: 84) writes, "antagonistic or competitive social relationships in patriarchal, capitalist societies tend to produce violent solutions to individuals' social, sexual or financial problems." Cultural interpretations of violent crime like Hagan's deflect our attention from the ways in which homicide and other violent crimes are, like all forms of deviance, socially constructed and socially caused.[10] Such interpretations should therefore be treated with appropriate sociological skepticism.

NOTES

I would like to thank Robert Brym, John Fox, Graham Lowe and three anonymous *CJS* reviewers for helpful comments on an earlier version of this paper.

1. More generally, Hagan fails to cite some published evidence that refutes the subculture of violence thesis (e.g., Erlanger, 1974).
2. One could also compare more countries. This strategy is adopted by Tom Truman (1971: 505–508), for example, whose findings, like mine, are inconsistent with Hagan's argument.
3. I correlated 1986 and 1981 homicide data with 1981 data on the ethnic and religious composition and family disruption rates of the provinces and territories and 1980–81 data on structural poverty. Similarly, I correlated 1976 and 1971 homicide data with 1971 data on the ethnic and religious composition and family disruption rates of the provinces and territories and 1970–71 data on structural poverty. This was mainly because of limitations on the availability of published data (e.g., 1986 data on the ethnic and religious composition of the provinces and territories are not yet available from Statistics Canada). In addition, over the course of a decade the provinces and territories are unlikely to change their ranks on a variable like the rate of divorce or the infant mortality rate, so I collected data on these variables for only one year per decade for the sake of parsimony.
4. Although there are some outliers in the provincial-territorial scatterplots, there are none in the province-only scatterplots.
5. The use of tests of significance on population data is now fairly common and is justified by Blalock (1979 [1960]: 241–43) on the grounds that such tests help eliminate "explanations" based on the existence of chance processes.
6. American Native people and Canadian blacks also seem to have higher homicide rates than one would expect on the basis of their representation in the population, but they are relatively small groups and their overrepresentation is not as striking as that of the racial minorities mentioned above. Thus, in 1986 American Native people amounted to very roughly 0.5 percent of the American population and accounted for 0.9 percent of homicide arrests (Department of Justice, 1987: 183). In the period 1961–74, about 1.2 percent of murders in Canada were committed by blacks, very roughly double the proportion of blacks in the population (Statistics Canada, 1976: 86–87).
7. I also constructed a measure of income inequality, but it performed poorly as a predictor of homicide, reaching statistical significance in only five of the sixteen relevant cases. This is probably because large regional differences in the cost of living make income inequality a problematic measure of economic disadvantage in Canada.
8. In fact, where homicide is economically beneficial it may be positively sanctioned. See, for example, Eisenberg's (1981: 300) discussion of infanticide among the !Kung San of the Kalahari and the Netsilik Inuit of northwestern Hudson Bay — peoples who are warm and indulgent toward their children and yet defend the practice of infanticide because of an "unpredictable subsistence base."
9. This by no means implies that the violence is directed principally at superordinate groups. Quite the contrary: most suspect–victim relationships do not in fact cross racial, class, and family lines. For example, from 1961 to 1974, 39.3 percent of suspect–victim relationships in Canada were domestic relationships and another 30.2 percent were social or business relationships (Taylor, 1983: 101).
10. My argument holds even more emphatically for violent crimes other than homicide that Hagan classifies as consensus crimes, such as rape and incest. All aspects of rape and incest reflect power imbalances and social conflict (Toronto Rape Crisis Centre 1985; Lenton, 1989). For example, there is dissensus, especially between men and women, over how rape should be defined, over how serious a crime rape is, and over how severely rapists should be punished; and the likelihood of detection, apprehension, and punishment appears to vary inversely with the ratio of the victim's to the perpetrator's power.

REFERENCES

Baer, Doug, Edward Grabb, and William A. Johnston. 1989. "The values of Canadians and Americans: a critical analysis and reassessment." *Social Forces*. Forthcoming.

Banting, Keith. 1987. "The welfare state and inequality in the 1980s." *Canadian Review of Sociology and Anthropology* 24: 309–38.

Blalock, Hubert M., Jr. 1979. *Social Statistics*. Rev. 2nd ed. New York: McGraw-Hill [1960].

Blau, Judith R. and Peter M. Blau. 1982. "The cost of inequality: metropolitan structured and violent crime." *American Sociological Review* 47: 114–29.

Bureau of the Census. 1976. *The Statistical History of the United States.* Washington, D.C.: U.S. Bureau of the Census.

Clark, S.D. 1976. *Canadian Society in Historical Perspective.* Toronto: McGraw-Hill Ryerson.

Department of Justice. 1983. *Report to the Nation on Crime and Justice.* Washington: U.S. Department of Justice.

———. 1987. *Uniform Crime Reports, 1986.* Washington, D.C.: U.S. Department of Justice, Federal Bureau of Investigation.

Devine, Joel A., Joseph F. Sheley, and M. Dwayne Smith. 1988. "Macroeconomic and social-control policy influences on crime rate changes, 1945–1985." *American Sociological Review* 53: 407–20.

Eisenberg, Leon. 1981. "Cross-cultural and historical perspectives on child abuse and neglect." *Child Abuse and Neglect* 5: 299–308.

Erlanger, Howard S. 1974. "The empirical status of the subculture of violence thesis." *Social Problems* 22: 280–92.

Fisher, A.D. 1987. "Alcoholism and race: the misapplication of both concepts to North American Indians." *Canadian Review of Sociology and Anthropology* 24: 81–98.

French, Orland. 1988. "Where man belongs to the land." *The Globe and Mail* (24 September), D5.

Hagan, John. 1984. *The Disreputable Pleasures: Crime and Deviance in Canada.* 2nd ed. Toronto: McGraw-Hill Ryerson [1977].

Hagan, John and Jeffrey Leon. 1977. "Philosophy and sociology of crime control." *Sociological Inquiry* 47: 181–208.

Hawkins, Darnell F. 1986. "Black and white homicide differentials: alternatives to an inadequate theory." In Darnell F. Hawkins, ed., *Homicide Among Black Americans*, pp. 109–35. New York: University Press of America.

Horowitz, Irving Louis. 1973. "The hemispheric connection: a critique and corrective to the entrepreneurial thesis of development with special emphasis on the Canadian case." *Queen's Quarterly* 80: 327–59.

Jones, Elwood. 1985. "The Loyalists and Canadian history." *Journal of Canadian Studies* 20(3): 149–56.

Kalbach, Warren E. and Wayne W. McVey. 1979. *The Demographic Bases of Canadian Society.* 2nd ed. Toronto: McGraw-Hill Ryerson [1971].

Krahn, Harvey, Timothy F. Hartnagel, and John W. Gartrell. 1986. "Income inequality and homicide rates: cross-national data and criminological theories." *Criminology* 24: 269–95.

Lenton, Rhonda L. 1989. "Parental discipline and child abuse." Unpublished PhD dissertation. Toronto: Department of Sociology, University of Toronto.

Lipset, Seymour Martin. 1986. "Historical traditions and national characteristics: a comparative analysis of Canada and the United States." *Canadian Journal of Sociology* 11: 113–55.

Loftin, Colin and Robert H. Hill. 1974. "Regional subculture and homicide: an examination of the Gastil-Hackney thesis." *American Sociological Review* 39: 714–24.

Messner, Steven F. 1982. "Societal development, social equality, and homicide: a cross-national test of a Durkheimian model." *Social Forces* 61: 225–40.

Rothschild, Emma. 1988. "The real Reagan economy." *New York Review of Books* 35 (11) 30 June: 46–53.

Sampson, Robert J. 1987. "Urban black violence: the effect of male joblessness and family disruption." *American Journal of Sociology* 3: 348–82.

Shkilnyk, Anastasia M. 1985. *A Poison Stronger than Love: The Destruction of an Ojibwa Community.* New Haven: Yale University Press.

Smith, M. Dwayne and Robert Nash Parker. 1980. "Type of homicide and variation in regional rates." *Social Forces* 59: 136–47.

Statistics Canada. 1973a. *1971 Census of Canada: Families: Family by Size and Type.* Ottawa: Statistics Canada.

———. 1973b. *1971 Census of Canada: Population: Ethnic Groups.* Ottawa: Statistics Canada.

———. 1973c. *Murder Statistics, 1971.* Ottawa: Statistics Canada, Judicial Division.

———. 1973d. *Murder Statistics, 1961–1970.* Ottawa: Statistics Canada, Judicial Division.

———. 1974. *Vital Statistics.* Volume III. *Deaths: 1971.* Ottawa: Statistics Canada.

———. 1975. *1971 Census of Canada: Families: One-Parent Families.* Ottawa: Statistics Canada.

———. 1976. *Homicide in Canada: A Statistical Synopsis.* Ottawa: Statistics Canada, Justice Statistics Division.

———. 1978. *Homicide Statistics, 1976.* Ottawa: Statistics Canada, Justice Statistics Division.

———. 1982a. *1981 Census of Canada: Census Families in Private Households: Persons, Children at Home, Structure and Type, Living Arrangements.* Ottawa: Statistics Canada.

———. 1982b. *1981 Census of Canada: Population: Age, Sex and Marital Status: Canada, Provinces, Urban Size Groups, Rural Non-Farm and Rural Farm.* Ottawa: Statistics Canada.

———. 1982c. *Crime and Traffic Enforcement Statistics, 1981.* Ottawa: Statistics Canada, Canadian Centre for Justice Statistics.

———. 1983a. *1981 Census of Canada: Population: Religion.* Ottawa: Statistics Canada.

———. 1983b. *Vital Statistics.* Volume I. *Births and Deaths: 1981.* Ottawa: Statistics Canada.

———. 1984a. *1981 Census of Canada: Ethnic Origin: Canada, Provinces, Urban Size Groups, Rural Non-Farm and Rural Farm.* Ottawa: Statistics Canada.

———. 1984b. *1981 Census of Canada: Private Households: Income: Canada, Provinces, Urban Size Groups, Rural Non-Farm and Rural Farm.* Ottawa: Statistics Canada.

———. 1986. *Homicide in Canada, 1984: A Statistical Perspective.* Ottawa: Statistics Canada, Canadian Centre for Justice Statistics, Law Enforcement Programme.

————. 1987. *Homicide in Canada, 1986.* Ottawa: Statistics Canada, Canadian Centre for Justice Statistics, Law Enforcement Programme.

Taylor, Ian. 1983. "Some reflections on homicide and violence in Canada." In *Crime, Capitalism and Community: Three Essays in Socialist Criminology*, 83–115. Toronto: Butterworths.

Toronto Rape Crisis Centre. 1985. "Rape." In Connie Guberman and Margie Wolfe, eds., *No Safe Place: Violence Against Women and Children*, pp. 61–86. Toronto: Women's Press.

Truman, Tom. 1971. "A critique of Seymour Martin Lipset's article, 'Value differences, absolute or relative: the English-speaking democracies.'" *Canadian Journal of Political Science* 4: 473–96.

Upton, L.F.S., ed. 1967. *The United Empire Loyalists: Men and Myths.* Toronto: Copp Clark.

Williams, Kirk R. 1984. "Economic sources of homicide: reestimating the effects of poverty and inequality." *African Sociological Review* 49: 283–89.

Williams, Kirk R. and Robert L. Flewelling. 1988. "The social production of criminal homicide: a comparative study of disaggregated rates in American cities." *American Sociological Review* 53: 421–31.

Wolfgang, Marvin E. and Franco Ferracuti. 1967. *The Subculture of Violence: Towards an Integrated Theory in Criminology.* London: Tavistock.

PART 6

GLOBAL DEVELOPMENT AND THE ENVIRONMENT

T HE INDUSTRIAL REVOLUTION began in Britain in the 1780s. For the next 200 years nature seemed exploitable without limit, a thing to be subdued and dominated in the name of economic progress and human development. In the last few decades of this century, however, circumstances have forced a growing number of people to recognize that industrial-era attitudes toward nature are not just naïve, but arrogant and foolhardy. For example:

- Since the Industrial Revolution, humans have been using increasing quantities of fossil fuels (coal, oil, gasoline, etc.). When burned, they release carbon dioxide into the atmosphere. The accumulation of CO_2 allows more solar radiation to enter the atmosphere and less solar radiation to escape. The result of this "greenhouse effect" is global warming and, eventually, potentially catastrophic climactic change, including the partial melting of the polar ice caps and the flooding of heavily populated coastal regions.

- CFCs (chlorofluorocarbons) are widely used in industry and by consumers, and they are burning a hole in the atmosphere's ozone layer. Ozone is a form of oxygen that blocks ultraviolet radiation from the sun. Let more ultraviolet radiation reach ground level and, as we are now witnessing, rates of skin cancer and crop damage increase.

- A wide range of toxic gases and liquids enter the environment as a result of industrial production, often with devastating consequences. For example, sulphur dioxide and other gases emitted by coal-burning power plants, pulp and paper mills, and motor-vehicle exhaust help to form an acid in the atmosphere which rains down on the earth, destroying forests and lakes.

- The world's forests help to clean the air since photosynthesis uses up carbon dioxide and produces oxygen. The tropical rain forests contain a large and variegated plant life that is an important source of new drugs. The rain forests also produce moisture that is carried by wind currents to other parts of the globe and falls as rain. Despite the enormously important role the forests play, however, they are being rapidly depleted as a result of strip mining, the construction of huge pulp and paper mills and hydro-electric projects, and the deforestation of land by farmers and cattle grazers.

• A huge fleet of trawlers belonging to the highly industrialized countries has been equipped with sonar to help locate large concentrations of fish. Some of these ships use fine mesh nets to increase their catch. They have been enormously "successful." Fish stocks in some areas of the world, such as off the coast of Newfoundland, have been greatly depleted, devastating fishing communities and endangering one of the world's most important sources of protein.

Two main lessons may be drawn from these examples. First, issues of economic development can no longer be separated from those of the environment. Second, development problems have become **globalized**: increasingly, local developments have worldwide repercussions while worldwide developments shape local events.

Both of these points are well illustrated by Joel Novek and Karen Kampen of the University of Winnipeg in Chapter 30. They highlight the difficulty of reconciling economic development and environmental preservation by analyzing the controversy surrounding the proposed construction of two pulp and paper megaprojects in northern Alberta and Manitoba. They also show how the growth of urban bureaucracies in Japan and the United States negatively affect social, economic, and environmental conditions even in remote areas of Canada.

In general, because less industrialized countries are poor and relatively powerless, the people living there suffer disproportionately from the effects of environmental degradation. Only the rich countries can enjoy the luxury of locating some of their dirtiest industries far from their population centres (including abroad) and cleaning up some of the local mess. Moreover, disparity in environmental quality between rich and poor countries is growing, in part because the so-called population bomb is placing tremendous pressure on the environment in less industrialized countries.

From a demographic point of view, the less industrialized countries are now in the position that Europe and North America were in between 1700 and 1870. Their populations are growing very rapidly because people are living longer and women's birth rates are high and barely falling. The 5.8 billion inhabitants of the planet in 1995 are expected to multiply to 10.2 billion by the year 2100, and during that period the less developed countries are expected to increase their share of world population from 75 percent to 86 percent of the total.

Some very populous but still relatively poor countries are now industrializing rapidly. The Chinese, Indians, Brazilians, Mexicans, Malaysians, and Thais, who constitute nearly half the world's population, want electricity, cars, VCRs, Pepsi, and Guess jeans just as much as Canadians do. They cannot, however, afford expensive pollution control measures. Consider only the fact that motor vehicles are the single biggest source of pollution in the world. Imagine the consequences when the proportion of car owners in the populous industrializing areas of Asia and Latin America increases from 5 percent to even 25 percent of the adult population!

A frequently voiced and increasingly popular solution to the problem of overpopulation in the less industrialized countries is compulsory sterilization and other forms of coercive birth control. Some advocates even claim that economic development aid should be redirected to coercive family planning. In Chapter 31, Harvard University economist Amartya Sen shows how misguided such recommendations are. By carefully analyzing the situation in China, India, and other countries, he demonstrates that forced birth control often results in higher infant mortality and discrimination against female children, while the surest way of bringing down the birth rate in the less industrialized countries is by encouraging economic development and improving the economic status and education of women. Once women enter the non-agricultural paid labour force, they quickly recognize the advantages of having few children and the birth rate plummets.

Economic development is, however, very difficult to achieve, as Paul Kennedy, perhaps the most popular historian in the English-speaking world, shows in Chapter 32. Kennedy demonstrates that the countries that have managed to undergo rapid economic growth in the past 25 years — South Korea, Taiwan, Singapore, and Hong Kong — all emphasize the need for education (in order to create a highly trained work force), personal saving (to make investment capital readily available), centralized economic co-ordination (to help plan and subsidize industrial development), and export-led growth (to stimulate economic expansion). He predicts that while a few more countries in Asia and Latin America may move from "have-not" to "have" status in the 21st century, most countries, especially those in Africa, will remain destitute because they lack one or more of the four main social and political conditions that encourage economic growth.

The difficulty that the less industrialized countries have in paying for pollution prevention and control, clean water, vaccines, soil irrigation, and basic sanitation services is closely related to the problem of international debt. The prices paid on world markets for the raw materials exported by less developed countries dropped by 50 percent between 1974 and 1987. As a result, the less developed countries were forced to borrow enormous sums from banks in the rich industrialized countries. Debt in the less industrialized countries increased by 1,200 percent between 1974 and 1987, and now stands at over US $1.2 trillion. Some people in the rich countries complain that they are giving too much aid to the poor countries of the world, but the plain fact is that the poor countries now receive US $50 billion dollars less per year in the form of aid than they pay to the rich countries in the form of interest and repayments of debt principal.

In Chapter 33, Sandra Postel and Christopher Flavin, associate directors of the Worldwatch Institute, make concrete and sensible suggestions about how debt in the less industrialized countries can be reduced and restructured. They also show how development aid can be redirected in order to maximize the growth potential of the less industrialized countries in an environmentally sound way. They are firm believers in **sustainable growth**; in their view, economic growth and environmental degradation do not have to go hand in hand. They argue that government incentives throughout the world can be used to promote sustainable growth and that substantial "green taxes" should be levied on products that pollute, deplete, or degrade natural systems. Such taxes would simultaneously act as a disincentive to ruin the environment and create a pool of capital for pollution prevention and control.

Whether individuals and governments in the rich industrialized countries will be willing to act along the lines recommended by Postel and Flavin is an open question. My guess is that it will probably take many serious environmental disasters to convince us to do so; public opinion polls show that while many people pay lip service to environmental concerns, most are unwilling to do much about them unless it is convenient and cheap.

One thing is, however, crystal clear. If people continue to think of themselves only as members of a particular nation, class, or race, Postel's and Flavin's recommendations are likely to fall on deaf ears. In that event, many citizens of the privileged countries will believe that it is in their self-interest to cut aid to the less industrialized countries, to use just as many scarce resources as they wish to and can afford, and to object to the imposition of high environmental taxes on, say, fossil fuels. They will be blind to the fact that such a narrow definition of self-interest may devastate all of humanity.

Much now seems to depend on whether we will be able to think and act as members of a single human group whose members share a common interest in survival. If we fail to take such a global view, if we insist instead on fighting to protect our narrow group privileges rather than humanity's general interest, we may not go the way of the dinosaurs, but future generations will in all likelihood suffer an existence that is nastier, more brutish, and shorter than that which we now enjoy.

GLOSSARY

Globalization is the increasing tendency for local social processes to have implications for the entire planet; and the increasing tendency for worldwide social forces to shape local events.

Sustainable growth refers to environmentally sound economic development.

Chapter 30

SUSTAINABLE OR UNSUSTAINABLE DEVELOPMENT IN WESTERN CANADA?

JOEL NOVEK AND KAREN KAMPEN

During the 1980s a growing literature on "sustainable development" has tried to reconcile the contradiction between economic development and environmental preservation. A combination of wise state regulation, the market system working at its best and international cooperation would ward off the threat of "limits to growth" caused by excessive environmental degradation (Brown, 1981; Repetto, 1985). The contradiction between economic development and environmental preservation would disappear as would the distributional conflicts associated with a steady state or no-growth economy (Rees, 1990).

The focus on economic growth as a desirable end explains the positive reception afforded the conclusions of the World Commission on the Environment and Development (WCED, 1987) with respect to sustainable development. In the Commission's view, economic growth in the advanced nations would be sustainable if the mix of economic activities could be shifted from those industries which are heavily resource-intensive to those which are less: "[Economic] growth rates could be environmentally sustainable if industrialized nations can continue the recent shifts in the content of their growth towards less material and energy intensive industries and the improvement of their efficiency in using materials and resources" (WCED, 1987: 51).

This is to be accomplished by shifting the mix of economic activity from manufacturing to information industries which are seen as less resource intensive. The Science Council of Canada has identified information technologies as "important building blocks of a sustainable economy" (Science Council of Canada, 1988: 15). Environmentalist Robert Paehlke suggests that, "Desirable technologies include computers, telecommunications, and the whole array of information industries" (Paehlke, 1989: 108). Such views have been termed "shallow environmentalism" (Alexander, 1990) for their assumption that economic growth and ecology are easily compatible.

We suggest the opposite: the relationship between economic expansion and environmental preservation remains fundamentally contradictory. Schnaiberg (1975; 1980) refers to the "societal-environmental dialectic" in which economic expansion imposes costs on the natural and social environments which can ultimately threaten economic expansion itself. This dialectic is part of the commodification/de-commodification process endemic to industrial capitalist states (Habermas, 1976; Offe, 1984). Environmental preservation requires non-market intervention to counter the commodification of resources and to protect them from market pressures. Such non-market interventions, however, restrict economic growth and illustrate the contradictory commitments of governments to economic expansion and environmental protection (Redclift, 1987).

These themes will be explored through an analysis of the environmental controversy surrounding two proposed pulp and paper megaprojects for the prairie boreal forest. One is the Japanese-owned Alberta-Pacific (ALPAC) mill to be sited on the Athabasca River in northern Alberta and billed as the world's largest pulp mill. When completed, it will have the

Source: Excerpted from "Sustainable or Unsustainable Development? An Analysis of an Environmental Controversy," *Canadian Journal of Sociology* 17, 3 (1992): 249–73. Reprinted by permission of the publisher.

capacity to produce 1500 tonnes per day of bleached hardwood pulp. The other is the proposed expansion and conversion of the former provincially owned Manfor mill located in The Pas in northern Manitoba. In this deal, Repap Enterprises of Montreal would convert the latter mill into a bleached pulp operation and expand production from 400 to 500 tonnes per day. Both are large-scale bleached kraft mills designed to process virgin fibre from the prairie boreal forest into export market pulp.

In our analysis of the controversy surrounding the Repap and ALPAC projects, we take the position that there are three principal reasons why the conflict between economic development and environmental preservation cannot be easily overcome. For one thing, the information society model fails to provide a panacea for non-polluting, non-depleting growth in the industrial world. Instead, the spread of information technology is part of the general commodification process. Information technology promotes the consumption of commodities, including paper, which is a driving force behind the expansion of pulp mills into the boreal forest.

Second, from the point of view of political economy, globalization of world trade has transformed distributional conflicts over environmental externalities, such as pollution, which may be defined as the social costs of economic expansion (Elliot, 1981: 5). In a world economy dominated by trans-national corporations, ownership, extraction, production, and consumption are often geographically and politically separate. Environmental externalities may accrue in jurisdictions far removed from ownership or consumption of a resource such as forest products.

Finally, the state and state institutions are in a contradictory position as promoters of economic development and as environmental regulators. New institutions, notably the environmental review process, have been developed to mediate between these contradictory functions as well as to legitimate ongoing state and private activities. However, public controversy surrounding the environmental review process has challenged efforts of the state to regulate the pulp and paper industry in a technical and depoliticized manner. We will now discuss these issues in greater detail.

THE INFORMATION SOCIETY AS TECHNOCENTRIC IDEAL

One of the major concepts to emerge from the literature on social and technological change over the past decade has been that of the information society (Bell,

1981; Oettinger, 1980; Masuda, 1981). In an information society the production, transformation, and exchange of information displaces the production and exchange of tangible goods as the primary focus of economic activity. It is clear that information related activities have increased in the advanced nations. Between 1960 and 1980 in the United States such activities grew at an average rate of 8.4 percent per annum (Hurwitz, 1987: 89) The mass media, advertising, printing and publishing, data processing, and communications have expanded enormously in the postwar period.

In a path-breaking study for the United States Department of Commerce, Porat (1977) has documented the transition to an information economy. His work provided the empirical basis for subsequent theorizing by Bell, Oettinger, and others. He argued that information-based occupations are now dominant in the American labour force, accounting for about 45 percent of all occupations. This would include information occupations in industrial and service organizations as well as information industries such as telecommunications, broadcasting, advertising, computers, education, and financial services. Similar trends have been noted in Canada, Western Europe, and Japan.

Along with these trends, predictions were made that the "office of the future" would be virtually paperless, i.e., that electronic information management would eliminate heavy paper usage. Bell stated that an information explosion would continue throughout the 1980s and 1990s which could only be handled by an automated system.

> *The really major social change of the next two decades will come in the third major infrastructure, as the merging of technologies of telephone, computer, facsimile, cable television and video discs lead to a vast reorganization in the modes of communication between persons; the transmission of data; the reduction if not the elimination of paper in transactions and exchanges. (Bell, 1981: 533)*

Similar predictions of the trend toward the "paperless office" were made by Giuliano (1982: 149) and Taylor (1981: 10), who foresaw the breakup of traditional paper-based bureaucracies — the theoretical legacy of Harold Innis and Max Weber — and their replacement by new forms of electronic networking.

We argue that such predictions of a paperless information society, similar to predictions of a post-industrial society made a decade earlier, represent the expression of a technocentric ideology (O'Riordan, 1981). Economic

Table 30.1 Proportion of the Labour Force in Information Occupations, Selected Countries, 1951–1982

	1951	1961	1971	1975	1981	1982
Canada	29.4	34.2	39.9			
W. Germany	18.3[a]	23.4	29.3[d]	32.8[e]	33.5	34.8
Japan	17.9[b]	22.2[c]	25.4[d]	29.6		
U.K.	26.7	32.1	35.6		41.0	
U.S.	30.7[a]	34.7[b]	41.1[d]		45.8[f]	

[a]1950; [b]1960; [c]1965; [d]1970; [e]1976; [f]1980.

Source: Organisation for Economic Co-operation and Development. 1986. *Trends in the Information Economy.* Paris: OECD, p. 8. © OECD, 1986. Reproduced by permission of the OECD.

activity is reduced to pure information and pure technology which is abstracted from the physical and social environments in which it is embedded. Unlike industrial society with its characteristic pollution and resource depletion, economic activity in an information society can continue to expand ad infinitum with only minimal demands on the environment. Environmental limits to growth are breached through an intellectual sleight of hand. Prevailing beliefs in the control of nature for human betterment through technological progress are maintained.

Environmental economist Herman Daly (1977: 118) has criticized such views for assuming a non-physical "angelized G.N.P." independent of its material base. Schnaiberg (1980: 171) has noted that in a service-based society, consumption of goods continues to increase and the resources necessary for the production of those goods must come from somewhere. In fact, the spread of information technology is part of a larger process termed the "commodification of time and space" (Giddens, 1981: 9) in which information is transformed into a commodity and used to promote the increased production and consumption of resources. One of the consequences associated with the spread of information technology has been a large increase in the institutionalized consumption of paper.

Despite the reliance on electronic communications, paper remains the preferred communications medium. Information producers, transformers, and consumers all demand a hard copy. There has been a pronounced upward trend in office paper use for the past several decades. According to Paul Strassman, "Office paper usage, per information worker, has been growing steadily since 1946 at a rate about double that of the growth in the G.N.P." (Strassman, 1985: 167). The spectacular growth of fax machines and laser printing in recent years confirms the preference for paper-based means of communications.

Data on Canadian consumption of paper illustrate this trend. While overall consumption has increased in the 1980s, there has been a switch to the forms of paper associated with the newer information technologies. Demand for newsprint has levelled off as newspapers have been affected by inroads made by the electronic media (Hurwitz, 1987: 93). The strongest increase has come in the category of fine papers which includes the bond paper used in office information processing and the coated paper used in glossy magazine publishing. Printing and writing paper (used in a variety of printing methods from magazines to computer printers) has risen to first place in per capita consumption at 61 kg. per capita, ahead of newsprint and containerboard for packaging at 47 and 57 kg. per capita, respectively. Per capita consumption of printing and writing paper increased 105 percent between 1970 and 1988, compared with an average increase of 41 percent for all grades of paper (Canadian Pulp and Paper Association [CPPA], 1989: 25).

The trend toward increased use of paper for the office is worldwide with most of the increase coming in consumption of paper for computers and copiers. Between 1980 and 1987, worldwide shipments of printing and writing paper used in information industries increased by 40 percent while the other mainstays

Figure 30.1 Paper Consumption in Canada, 1970–1988

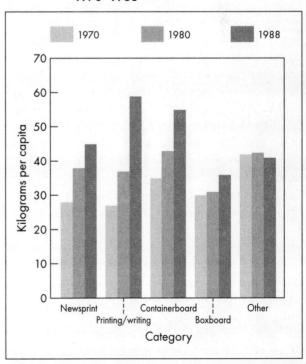

Source: Canadian Pulp and Paper Association, *Reference Tables,* 43rd ed. Montreal, 1989, p. 25.

of the paper industry, newsprint and packaging, increased by 19 percent and 18 percent, respectively (CPPA, 1989: 31–34). Rennel estimated that between 1970 and 1980, world copying volume by xerography increased 800 percent from 38 to 342 billion copies while offset reproduction increased only 50 percent from 302 to 454 billion copies (Rennel, 1984: 188). Bleecker (1987: 15) estimated that American business generates 190 billion pages of documentation every day.

It is beyond the scope of this essay to discuss in detail why the growth of the newer information technologies has not displaced the paper medium. A number of theories have been advanced. Braten offers a variant of the cultural lag hypothesis in asserting that the paper medium serves a need to "touch and feel" information. This need is a heritage of our long dependence on clay- and later paper-based media (Braten, 1984: 15). Similarly, Strassman stresses the importance of "touching" information, especially that provided by visual display units (Strassman, 1985: 172). Zuboff (1988) provides support for this view with her observation that information workers have had difficulty making the transition from paper files to more abstract computerized systems. Bleecker, interestingly, argues that an emphasis on quantitative measures of output in the office environment contributes to an intensified paper flow rather than a creative approach to working with information (Bleecker, 1987: 34).

Most of this paper chase ends up as paper waste. Data from 1988 indicate that paper accounts for 35 percent of Manitoba's solid waste versus less than 5 percent for plastics (Manitoba Recycling Action Committee, 1990: 11). Recycled waste paper accounts for only 10 percent of the fibre used in Canadian paper production, the second lowest figure in the industrial world (McClay, 1990: 4). The corresponding figures for other industrialized nations range from 24 percent in the United States to 69 percent in the Netherlands. Paper accumulation in dump sites represents the detritus of an information society.

The spread of information industries throughout North America, Western Europe and Japan in the 1980s has led to increased demand for wood fibre, the basic ingredient in paper-making. World pulpwood consumption increased by 12 percent or 16 million tonnes between 1980 and 1987 with North America accounting for 46 percent of consumption, Western Europe 24 percent and Japan 8 percent (CPPA, 1989: 29). Softwood forests in the temperate zones of North America and Western Europe, long the mainstay of the world pulp and paper industry, have been depleted or subject to environmental restriction. Just as the oil

industry has stepped up its search for new sources of oil as existing sources run out, so the paper industry has looked for new sources of wood fibre in the rain forests of the southern hemisphere (Kellison and Zobel, 1987) and in the boreal forests of the Canadian north.

The vast boreal forest — huge strands of slow growing spruce, jackpine, tamarack, and aspen stretching across the central and northern tier of the prairie provinces — represents the last great untapped forest resource in the nation. The size of this western forest has been estimated at 4241 million cubic metres or 18 percent of Canada's supply of merchantable timber (Statistics Canada, 1986: 15–20). However, in 1986 this area produced only 8.8 percent of Canada's total primary forest output and 8.9 percent of pulpwood production. Until recently the harsh climate, distance from major markets, and relatively low density of tree growth inhibited resource exploitation (Mathias, 1971). Increasing world demand for paper has made the boreal forest more attractive as a source of pulpwood fibre.

Hence the linkage between the expansion of the information industry worldwide and the announcement of pulp and paper megaprojects in the boreal forest, notably ALPAC and Repap. Furthermore, information industry requirements have included demands for whiter, brighter, and stronger papers to produce glossier magazines or more sharply defined laser printing. The market has shifted toward the stronger bleached and chemical pulps used for printing and writing paper and away from the unbleached and mechanical pulps used for newsprint (Sinclair, 1988: 84–85). The bleached kraft method of chemical pulping which uses sodium sulphate and sodium hydroxide to "cook" the pulp and chlorine to bleach it produces a stronger pulp than alternative methods and has become dominant in the industry.

In 1965 the bleached kraft method accounted for 48 percent of Canadian pulp exports but by 1988 that figure had risen to 74 percent (CPPA, 1989: 10). Thus it is not surprising that both the Repap and the ALPAC projects are bleached kraft mills. The bleached product, however, makes heavy demands on the environment through the generation of greater volumes of chemical waste. One estimate holds the pulp and paper industry responsible for about 50 percent of all waterborne pollution in Canada (Sinclair, 1988: 63). Much concern has been expressed about toxic organochlorines, notably dioxins and furans, products of the bleaching process which must be disposed of in the form of sewered effluent (von Stackelberg, 1989). The environmental risks associated with bleaching and resource harvesting are borne at the production rather than the consumption end.

Harvey Brooks (1986: 336) uses the concept of "technological monocultures" to describe technological systems that have become so powerfully ingrained that alternative modes of production and consumption are precluded. We argue that the development of information technology and its spread throughout the world, along with the concomitant increased demand for paper, is linked to a "technological monoculture" in the pulp and paper industry which feeds the information hunger. The elements of this dominant technological regime include dependence on bleached and chemically processed paper made from virgin fibre; the concentration of production in megamills which must draw on vast forest resources in order to be economically viable; and the growth of industrial forestry in which huge sections of public forestland are turned into privately managed tree farms for the production of pulp.

All of these elements are present in the Repap and ALPAC projects under which the sparsely utilized boreal forest will be subject to the regime of industrial forestry for the benefit of global markets. The Repap facility, for example, will discharge 750 kilograms of highly toxic adsorbable organic halogens per day into the North Saskatchewan River.[1] Estimates for the ALPAC mill are 525 kilograms of adsorbable organic halogens per day into the Athabasca River based on revised and probably somewhat optimistic estimates.[2] The information industry, usually portrayed as environmentally benign, is a potential threat to the vast boreal region.

THE POLITICAL ECONOMY OF PULPMILL DEVELOPMENT: EXTERNALIZING THE EXTERNALITIES?

Information industries are quintessentially urban, associated with the bureaucracies of business, government, advertising, communications, and education. They are characteristic of the built environment (Dunlap and Catton, 1983) of the modern city which appears separate and cut off from the natural world. Yet the streams of paper that drive the information economy come from forests further and further afield and hence "invisible" (Schnaiberg, 1980: 132) to the average urban dweller. The spread of information industries is related to the expansion of the global economy into new regions in search of scarce raw materials — in this case virgin fibre to maintain the constant paper flow.

The geographical separation of consumption from resource harvesting masks the distributional and environmental consequences of a globalized economy.

Political economists have looked on Canadian economic history as a series of episodes devoted to the production and export of particular natural resource products or "staples" into metropolitan markets (Watkins, 1989). A staples economy, however, has presented Canadian society with a number of long-term problems. Chief among them is dependence on the vagaries of supply and demand in the global economy and limited control of our own economic destiny (Clement, 1983). There has also been an evident failure to expand resource processing into the manufacture of finished goods.

The pulp and paper industry mirrors many of the problems outlined above. It is one of Canada's leading industries whose annual output throughout the 1980s has been about 3 percent of GNP. Pulp and paper shipments represent 12 percent of the value of all manufacturing shipments and between 9 percent and 12 percent of total exports (CPPA, 1989: 2). However, in the higher value-added areas of paper-making the Canadian industry is weakest. Canada has about 10 percent of the world's forest stock and accounts for 15 percent of world pulp and 32 percent of newsprint production but only 3 percent of paper and paperboard output (Sinclair, 1988: 15). Not only are the hinterland regions exposed to environmental risk but the job creation potential is limited by the lack of downstream further processing.

In the developments slated for the western boreal forest, semi-processed pulp is to be exported for the benefit of paper-making and information industries in the U.S. and Japan. The Repap conversion in Manitoba will eliminate the present paper-making capacity and transform it into purely a pulpmill to supply an American plant which makes glossy magazine grade paper. The Japanese-owned ALPAC mill will supply markets in Japan and the U.S. with raw market pulp.

Manitoba and Alberta expected that pulpmills would open up a new economic frontier of development in the north. Large-scale pulp exports, however, accentuate the position of both provinces as resource suppliers to a competitive global marketplace. They become highly sensitive to a variety of factors currently affecting the world market for pulp and paper. Northern suppliers face increasing competition from fast growing tropical sources of pulp with eucalyptus being especially important (Gundersby and Rennel, 1990: 121). Furthermore, demand for virgin fibre is expected to level off as consumption of recycled fibre in North

America increases to approach the much higher levels currently the norm in Europe and Japan (1990: 121).

While modern pulpmills are expensive to build they create relatively few permanent jobs in comparison with their capital cost. They rely heavily on mechanization and automation to maintain efficient operations. As a study of the British Columbia forest products industry has well documented, much of this capital equipment originates abroad (Marchak, 1983). Skilled and craft jobs often go to southern immigrants rather than northern and aboriginal residents. The initial Repap expansion and conversion, for example, will not increase permanent employment despite higher output. Employment expansion will only come with the construction of a new supermill sometime in the future. The ALPAC mill will create about 1,000 jobs for an investment of about $1.5 billion or about $1.5 million per job. We can ask whether it is worthwhile to place our northern forests at risk for only modest employment gains.

Conflicts are not only about jobs and the terms of trade. Increasingly the international division of externalities mirrors the international division of labour. Just as poorer nations and regions function as manufacturing platforms, producing labour-intensive goods for consumption in the affluent world, so they are also forced to accept developments which are environmentally risky, supplying resources which affluent nations require but do not wish to produce themselves. Less affluent regions assume environmental costs or externalities in order to gain the benefits of economic development. Environmental externalities are themselves externalized to less economically favoured parts of the world. Are the benefits of such economic developments worth the environmental risks which may threaten alternative forms of economic and social activity?

The march of pulpmill developments into the boreal forest is part of the international division of externalities. The Japanese situation is a good case in point. The Japanese paper industry is the second largest in the world, after the United States, and the fastest growing among industrial nations (Food and Agriculture Organization, 1986: 20–22). During the 1980s per capita paper consumption in Japan grew by 50 percent (British Paper and Board Federation, 1990) reflecting expanding information industries and growing affluence. Japan has achieved this despite severely limited domestic sources of wood fibre which have been subject to strict controls on logging. About 49 percent of Japanese paper is manufactured from recycled fibre (McClay, 1990: 4). Most of the rest originates abroad in the form of imported logs and, increasingly, pulp from Japanese-owned mills operating in North America and Southeast Asia.

Investments in the boreal forest by companies such as Mitsubishi-Honshu — the owners of ALPAC — offer Japanese industry an important new source of fibre so Japanese paper-making capacity can continue to increase. At the same time, Japan need not run the environmental risks associated with clear-cutting and chlorine bleaching. These risks can be exported to other jurisdictions, such as the boreal forest, where environmental controls are less strict and forest resources available at a comparatively low price. Japanese pulp and paper companies have long been active in the rain forests of Southeast Asia where their logging methods have come under criticism (Morrow, 1989: 13; Nectoux and Kuroda, 1989). Globalization of the forest industry allows externalities to be borne in regions far removed from further processing or final consumption.

Provincial governments in Alberta and Manitoba have enthusiastically supported exploitation of the boreal forest as a means of achieving job creation and diversification of the northern economy. In this strategy, termed "administrative recommodification" (Offe, 1984: 124), the state attempts to create conditions under which its citizens and resources can better function as commodities in the global marketplace. The northern economies in both provinces have long been characterized by higher unemployment and lower incomes than the south and a dependence on extractive industries such as nickel mining in Manitoba and petroleum in Alberta.

The rapid commitment of the western boreal forest to large scale pulpmill developments has aroused political controversy. Northern pulpmill development will affect fishing, trapping, tourism, and other resource industries on which the northern economy is dependent. The bleached kraft method of chemical pulping will dump thousands of cubic metres of highly toxic effluent containing organochlorines into northern rivers every day, threatening the productive fisheries and other aspects of the northern eco-system (Bonsor, McCubbin, and Sprague, 1988: 163). In assessing the environmental impact of these projects, two points must be considered. One is the transfer of vast tracts of public forest land from common to private usage and control. The second related point is the significance to the northern economy of traditional activities such as fishing and trapping which are the major economic activities on northern Indian Reserves (Keewatin Community College, undated) and which have depended on common use of the land and water.

The fishery will be used as an example. Information supplied by the Freshwater Fish Marketing Corporation — a federal agency based in Winnipeg — indicates that the Saskatchewan River Basin, into which the Repap mill will drain, supports 100 licenced commercial fishermen each employing one or two assistants. The region has the capability to produce 2.2 million lbs. of walleye, pike, and other quota species worth about $3.5 million annually (Hay, 1989). There is also a large domestic fishery for Natives and a growing sport fishery. Spokesmen for the fishery have raised concerns about the impact of pulpmill effluent on fish health and quality, especially as some of the best areas are located downstream from the plant (Bodnar, 1989; Manitoba Keewatinowi Okimakanak, 1989).

In Alberta the stakes are even higher because the Peace-Athabasca Delta, which will receive effluent from ALPAC as well as three other kraft mills, supports a wide variety of traditional and aboriginal activities in northern Alberta and the Northwest Territories. The federal Department of the Environment (1989) estimated that the four tonnes of total organic chlorine which these mills will deposit daily into the Peace-Athabasca river system will affect the 200 largely Native hunters and trappers who depend on the delta for their livelihood. The delta is also the best fur-bearing region in Alberta with plentiful supplies of muskrat, beaver, mink, and otter. Trapping alone provides several hundred thousand dollars worth of annual income to area residents (Peace Athabasca Trappers Association, 1989).

However, the greatest impact will be on the northern fishery. The Lac La Biche Fisheries Task Force Report (1988) estimated that the commercial fishery generates $0.5 billion annually for the Alberta economy. The town of Fort Chipewyan on Lake Athabasca, for instance, has 42 fishermen whose catch of 80,000 kg. of walleye benefits 400 people, one-third of the community (Morrow and Wagg, 1989: 2). The environmental impact does not stop at the Alberta border. Since the Athabasca River flows into the Northwest Territories, the buildup of organochlorines can affect the fishery on Great Slave Lake which employs 200 and produces 3.7 million lbs. of fish with an annual value of $3.0 million for the northern economy (Government of the Northwest Territories, 1989; Bergunder, 1989).

Analysis of the submissions before the Manitoba Clean Environment Commission, which conducted an environmental review of the Repap proposal in 1989, indicated that the major issue was not development versus no development, but rather the future sustainability of traditional northern activities with competing claims on the resource base (Tobacco, 1989; Henderson, 1989; Bercier, 1989). Is extensive logging and pulping compatible with continued multiple use of the forest, land, and water for fishing, hunting, and trapping? As an expression of this concern, there were demands by local residents for the creation of an official body to ensure some degree of local monitoring of Repap's environmental impact, a demand endorsed by some of the most enthusiastic local proponents of development (Unfried, 1989; Fahlgren, undated).

CONTRADICTIONS OF THE ROLE OF THE STATE

While the Manitoba and Alberta governments have been heavily involved in promoting pulp and paper projects in their respective provinces, their roles have in fact been contradictory as both promoter and referee. O'Connor (1973), Habermas (1976), and Offe (1984) have noted the complex relationship between the state's role as promoter of economic development (accumulation) and as welfare state provider (legitimation). A somewhat similar mechanism drives the state's position on environmental issues. The state requires a degree of environmental preservation in order to support economic growth over the long run and to enhance its public acceptance. This would be a politically acceptable form of sustainable development.

However, the primary commitment of the state is to economic growth and environmental constraints can hamper economic growth. Regulating the negative externalities of economic expansion, such as pollution, runs the risk of slowing down the drive toward economic expansion or "decelerating the treadmill" (Schnaiberg, 1980: 244). This is a risk that most governments would rather not run. On the other hand, the goal of environmental preservation has received considerable public support over the past decade and governments have come under pressure to take a more active role in protecting the environment. Paehlke (1989: 156) has noted that environmental movements, despite ideological support for decentralization and local initiatives, have come to rely on the state as the prime guarantor of compliance with environmental norms. Environmentalism challenges neo-conservatism by demanding that the state take a more active role in society as environmental protector.

Torn between the "deep structure" of its traditional commitment to economic development (Liess, 1990: 106) and growing public support for environmental protection, state policy has searched for a compromise which would involve some political response to the claims of environmentalists while preserving intact the priority of economic growth. Redclift (1987) has termed this compromise "environmental management." This is characterized by interventions of a modest nature designed to facilitate rather than curtail economic development. It is usually concerned with reactive responses to the negative externalities of growth: "Environmental management, imbued with the contradictions that afflict all management science, represents an attempt to mediate the contradictions of industrialised society by minimizing the social costs of conflict" (Redclift, 1987: 136–37).

The environmental assessment and review process has become the chief means through which governments have attempted to resolve their contradictory commitments to economic development and environmental protection, or commodification and de-commodification. The scope of this approach is typically narrow while a facade of technological objectivity is maintained (Rees, 1980; Hoos, 1979; Schnaiberg, 1985). The conflict between the political and the technical inherent in the environmental review process has been observed in the Canadian context by Sadler and Armour: "Because basic differences in interests and values are involved, environment and development issues are not matters of misunderstanding that can be cleared up by additional information" (Sadler and Armour, 1989: 2).

This perspective applies to the environmental assessment and review processes carried out in relation to the Repap and ALPAC projects. Environmental assessment in Canada was established by the federal government in 1973 in the form of the Environmental Assessment and Review Process (EARP) under the Minister of the Environment (Richardson, 1989: 28). In 1984 EARP was strengthened when new guidelines were issued by an Order in Council under the Government Organization Act. EARP was designed to initiate a planning process which would supplement the traditional regulatory approach to environmental pollution (Richardson, 1989: 10). However, since EARP is a set of administrative guidelines rather than a statutory requirement, the provinces have subsequently initiated their own environmental assessment procedures. Manitoba and Alberta based their environmental assessments of Repap and ALPAC, respectively, on provincial responsibility for forestry matters.

In both provinces the environmental assessment process is similar (Manitoba Environment, undated a; Alberta Environment, 1985). A company presents a development proposal, conducts its own review of the anticipated environmental impact, and presents the report to the provincial Ministry of the Environment. Ministry officials review the report, may hold public hearings to identify citizens' concerns, and may address comments or criticisms, based on the report, back to the company. When the provincial government is satisfied that its environmental concerns have been dealt with, it issues a licence to proceed. It should be noted that the review process is largely worked out in consultation between the officials of the provincial government and the companies concerned. The governments of Manitoba and Alberta attempted to depoliticize the review process and present it as an exercise in technological legitimation for development. Neither government was entirely successful in this endeavour.

Both governments sought to ensure that the review process would be narrowly focused on the technical regulation of the externalities of the megaprojects. The main focus in both cases was to be water-borne pollution from the pulping and bleaching process. Broader social and environmental concerns, such as the forest management agreements which gave both companies effective control over huge sections of the boreal forest, were excluded from the initial environmental impact statements and review processes.

The efforts to avoid controversy and turn the environmental review process into a legitimation exercise proved futile. Neither government could escape the contradiction between its traditional commitment to economic development and its newfound and somewhat halfhearted commitment to sustainability. In Manitoba the Phase One hearings were held in August and September, 1989, and, in November, the Clean Environment Commission recommended that Repap could proceed with its planned expansion and conversion (Manitoba Clean Environment Commission, 1989). The provincial cabinet, to no one's surprise, agreed and granted Repap its licence (Manitoba Environment, 1990). However, the public hearing process had aired substantial concerns about the Repap project from northern aboriginal groups worried about the impact on their livelihood and from urban environmental groups.[3] Repap, reacting to the negative publicity generated by the review process and to a downturn in the world pulp market, announced that it would not proceed with its planned expansion and conversion until the review process was complete and all licences had been granted (Stevenson, 1990: 23). The effort to fast track the licensing procedure had failed.

In Alberta, the attempt of the provincial government to turn the review process into a legitimation exercise with little public input ran into substantial opposition. In June, 1989 a petition signed by 300,000 Albertans, one-eighth the provincial population, called for a moratorium on pulp mill developments until after full public hearings (Nikiforuk and Struzik, 1989: 64). Although forestry is a provincial responsibility, the impact of the pulp mill effluent on rivers and fisheries comes under federal jurisdiction. The Athabasca River, which will receive effluent from the ALPAC mill as well as four other mills, flows north into the Mackenzie basin and will affect the Northwest Territories as well as Alberta. The federal responsibility was reinforced by a 1989 court ruling concerning the Rafferty-Alameda dams in Saskatchewan which upheld the EARP guidelines for environmental review of all projects which come under federal jurisdiction (Robertson, 1989: 1).

In July, 1989, a joint federal–provincial assessment panel was announced to conduct a public review of the ALPAC proposal as well as the cumulative impact of other mills on the Peace-Athabasca River system. The provincial government agreed to this joint review panel in return for the right to select four of the seven panel members and to exclude all forestry and logging concerns from the terms of reference (Environmental Impact Assessment Review Board, 1990: 4–5). However, under EARP guidelines, the review process required public hearings. These hearings were held in October, November, and December, 1989, and, similar to the ones held in Manitoba, generated considerable public interest and much opposition to the proposed mill from northern aboriginal groups and urban environmentalists.[4]

One of the strongest critiques of the ALPAC proposal came from the federal Department of the Environment (1989) which raised the issue of the cumulative impact of pulp mill pollution on the Peace-Athabasca Rivers system. This argument appeared convincing and in March, 1990, the federal–provincial review panel issued a report recommending that ALPAC not proceed pending further study of the issue (Environmental Impact Assessment Review Board, 1990).

After considerable debate, the Alberta cabinet reluctantly supported the panel's recommendation. However, the pressures for development were too great to let the matter rest for any length of time. ALPAC (Alberta Pacific Forest Industries, 1990) issued a revised proposal under which its bleaching process would be modified so that the amount of adsorbable organic halogen discharged into the Athabasca River would be reduced from 1.3 to 0.35 kilograms per tonne of pulp. A second Alberta Pacific Scientific

Review Panel (1990) was convened by the Alberta government with a mandate to review the technical feasibility of the revised proposal. No other issues could be considered within the panel's mandate. After two months of deliberation the Scientific Review Panel recommended in favour of the revised ALPAC proposal in a report which was quickly accepted by the Alberta cabinet and made public in December, 1990. ALPAC had finally received its licence to proceed.

The environmental review process reinforced the commitment of both provincial governments to strategies of promoting economic development. Public concern, however, forced both provincial governments to pay more attention than they might otherwise to their alternative commitment to environmental preservation. The environmental review processes, in the end, were lengthier, more public, and more controversial than originally intended. Both projects were delayed; the Repap mill indefinitely, while the ALPAC proposal was substantially modified so as to be less environmentally obtrusive. The demands of economic development may remain paramount but the need for a politically legitimate response to environmental concerns can push the state in contradictory directions.

CONCLUSIONS

Contrary to the views expressed by proponents of the sustainable development perspective, analysis of the Repap and ALPAC controversies indicates that the demands of economic development and environmental preservation remain contradictory. The growth of information industries intensifies the commodification process. The expansion of the global economy leads to the commodification of resources in the world's hinterland regions and their transfer from common to private control. The western Canadian boreal forest is to be mulched into pulp to supply global information industries. The externalities of information-led growth in Japan, the United States, and Southern Canada are themselves externalized to the boreal forest. This process is encouraged by provincial governments anxious to promote administrative re-commodification by selling their resources in global markets.

However, the government role in promoting resource-based development has attracted considerable opposition. Public opposition to pulp and paper megaprojects in Western Canada has reinforced the contradiction between the state's role as development promoter and as protector of northern resources and aboriginal populations from the global market economy. The contradictory commitment to economic development and environmental preservation, to commodification and de-commodification, has been played out through the rapidly evolving environmental review process. This has tested the procedures in place for political legitimation which were designed more for technical assessment than for public debate. As a result of the highly political legitimation process, the incorporation of the boreal forest into the global economy proceeds, but at a slower pace and in a more publicly visible manner than previously intended.

NOTES

This research was based on a detailed examination of submissions before the Manitoba Clean Environment Commission and the Alberta-Pacific Environmental Impact Assessment Review Board. We would like to thank Manitoba Environment, Alberta Environment, and Environment Canada for their invaluable cooperation in making a wide range of documentation available to us. We would also like to thank the Strategic Grants Division of the Social Sciences and Humanities Research Council of Canada for supporting our research. In addition, Dr. Peter Miller of the Department of Philosophy, University of Winnipeg, as well as two anonymous reviewers, deserve to be thanked for their helpful suggestions and encouragement.

1. Based on Repap's estimate of 1.5 kg. AOX per air dried tonne. See Richards (undated).
2. ALPAC revised its estimated AOX emissions downward from an initial 1.5 kg. per air dried tonne to .35 kg. per air dried tonne (Alberta Pacific Scientific Review Panel, 1990; 30–39).
3. There were 75 submissions, many of them critical of the review process as well as the pulp mill.
4. There were 750 submissions to the Review Board, the majority critical of the mill and the way the environmental assessment had been carried out.

REFERENCES

Alexander, Don. 1990. "Left ecology, deep ecology and shallow environmentalism." *Canadian Dimension* 24(1) 16–18.

Bell, Daniel. 1981. "The social framework of the information society." In Tom Forester, ed., *The Microelectronics Revolution*, pp. 500–49. Cambridge, MA: MIT Press.

Bleecker, Samuel. 1987. "Rethinking how we work: The office of the future." *The Futurist* 21(4) 15–21.

Bonsor, Norman, Neal McCubbin, and John Sprague. 1988. *Kraft Mill Effluents in Ontario*. Toronto: Environment Ontario.

Braten, Stein. 1984. "Prologue." In Jan Rennel, *The Future of Paper in a Telematic World*. Helsinki: Jaakko Poyry.

Brooks, Harvey. 1986. "The typology of surprise in technology, institutions and development." In W.E. Clark and R.E. Munn, eds., *Sustainable Development in the Biosphere*, pp. 325–50. Cambridge: Cambridge University Press.

Brown, Lester. 1981. *Building a Sustainable Society*. New York: Norton.

Clement, Wallace. 1983. *Class, Power and Property*. Toronto: Methuen.

Daly, Herman. 1977. *Steady State Economics*. San Francisco: W.H. Freeman and Company.

Dunlap, Riley and William Catton. 1983. "What environmental sociologists have in common." *Sociological Inquiry* 53(2/3): 113–35.

Elliot, John. 1981. *The Sociology of Natural Resources*. Toronto: Butterworths.

Food and Agricultural Organization. 1986. *The Outlook for Pulp and Paper to 1995*. Rome: FAO.

Flood, Gerald. 1989. "Repap denies financial woes factor in delay." *Winnipeg Free Press* (30 November): 10.

Giddens, Anthony. 1981. *A Contemporary Critique of Historical Materialism*. Berkeley: University of California Press.

Giuliano, Vincent. 1982. "The mechanization of office work." *Scientific American* 247(3): 148–64.

Gundersby, Per and Jan Rennel. 1990. "New market pulp capacity." *Pulp and Paper* 64(8): 120–24.

Habermas, Jürgen. 1976. *Legitimation Crisis*. London: Heinemann.

Hoos, Ida. 1979. "Societal aspects of technology assessment." *Technological Forecasting and Social Change* 13: 191–202.

Hurwitz, Roger. 1987. "Patterns of media use in developed and developing countries." In FAO, *World Pulp and Paper Supply and Demand*, pp. 89–98. Rome: FAO.

Kellison, R.C. and B.J. Zobel. 1987. "Technological advances to improve the wood supply for the pulp and paper industry in developing countries." In FAO, *World Pulp and Paper Supply and Demand*, pp. 136–44. Rome: FAO.

Lett, Dan. 1989. "Repap review assailed." *Winnipeg Free Press* (18 December): 1, 4.

Liepa, Ingrid. 1989. "Alberta commits forests to pulp." *Alternatives* 16(3): 8–9.

Liess, William. 1990. *Under Technology's Thumb*. Montreal and Kingston: McGill-Queen's University Press.

Marchak, Patricia. 1983. *Green Gold: The Forest Industry in British Columbia*. Vancouver: UBC Press.

Masuda, Yoneji. 1981. *The Information Society as Post Industrial Society*. Bethesda, MD: World Future Society.

Mathias, Philip. 1971. *Forced Growth*. Toronto: James Lewis and Samuel.

McClay, Brian. 1990. "Paper recycling in Canada: An established practice on the verge of significant growth." Presented to Globe 90 Conference, Vancouver, B.C.

Morrison, Helen. 1989. *Arguments in Favour of Applying the Federal Environmental Assessment and Review Process to the Proposed Alterations to the Manfor Pulp Mill.* Ottawa: Research Branch, Library of Parliament.

Morrow, Jeff. 1989. "Pulp mills endanger aborigine culture." *Windspeaker* 7(19): 13.

Morrow, Jeff and Diana Wagg. 1989. "Northern bands to rally against pulp mills." *Windspeaker* 7(37): 1–2.

Mosco, Vincent. 1989. *The Pay-Per Society.* Toronto: Garamond Press.

Nectoux, Francois and Yoichi Kuroda. 1989. *Timber from the South Seas: An Analysis of Japan's Tropical Timber Trade and Its Environmental Impact.* Washington, D.C.: World Wildlife Fund.

Nikiforuk, Andrew and Ed Struzik. 1989. "The great forest sell-off." *Globe and Mail Report on Business Magazine* (November): 56–68.

————. 1990. "Going to pulp." *Canadian Forum* 68: 8–11.

O'Connor, James. 1973. *The Fiscal Crisis of the State.* New York: St. Martin's Press.

Oettinger, Anthony. 1980. "Information resources: Knowledge and power in the 21st century." *Science* 209: 191–98.

Offe, Claus. 1984. *Contradictions of the Welfare State.* Cambridge, MA: MIT Press.

O'Riordan, Tim. 1981. *Environmentalism.* London: Pion.

Paehlke, Robert. 1989. *Environmentalism and the Future of Progressive Politics.* New Haven: Yale University Press.

Porat, Marc. 1977. *The Information Economy.* Washington, D.C.: U.S. Department of Commerce.

Redclift, Michael. 1987. *Sustainable Development: Exploring the Contradictions.* London and New York: Methuen.

Rees, William. 1980. "Comment on Demirdache and Carpenter." In Ted Schecker and C.A. Hooker, eds., *Proceedings of the Conference on the Human Context for Science and Technology,* pp. 204–8. Ottawa: Supply and Services Canada.

————. 1990. "The ecology of sustainable development." *The Ecologist* 20(1): 18–23.

Rennel, Jan. 1984. *The Future of Paper in a Telematic World.* Helsinki: Jaakko Poyry.

Repetto, Robert, ed. 1985. *The Global Possible.* New Haven: Yale University Press.

Richardson, Nigel. 1989. *Land Use Planning and Sustainable Development in Canada.* Ottawa: Supply and Services Canada.

Robertson, James. 1989. *Environmental Impact Assessment in Canada: Proposals for Change.* Ottawa: Research Branch, Library of Parliament.

Sadler, Barry and Audrey Armour. 1989. "Common ground: On the relationship of environmental assessment and negotiation." In *The Place of Negotiation in Environmental Assessment,* pp. 1–6. Hull: Canadian Environmental Assessment Research Council.

Schnaiberg, Allan. 1975. "Social syntheses of the societal-environmental dialectic: The role of distributional impacts." *Social Science Quarterly* 56(1): 5–20.

————. 1980. *The Environment: From Surplus to Scarcity.* New York: Oxford University Press.

————. 1985. "The retreat from political to technical environmentalism." In Augustine Brannigan and Sheldon Goldenberg, eds., *Social Responses to Technological Change,* pp. 19–36. Westport, Connecticut: Greenwood Press.

Science Council of Canada. 1988. *Environmental Peacekeepers: Science, Technology and Sustainable Development in Canada.* Ottawa: Supply and Services Canada.

Sinclair, William. 1988. *Controlling Pollution from Canadian Pulp and Paper Manufacturers: A Federal Perspective.* Ottawa: Environment Canada.

Stevenson, Mark. 1990. "The high cost of green." *Western Report* 5(8): 22–25.

Strassman, Paul. 1985. *Information Payoff: The Transformation of Work in the Electronic Age.* New York: The Free Press.

Taylor, James. 1981. "The office of the future: Weber and Innis revisited." *In Search* 8(3): 2–13.

von Stackelberg, Peter. 1989. "Whitewash: The dioxin cover-up." *Greenpeace* 14(2): 7–11.

Watkins, Mel. 1989. "The political economy of growth." In Wallace Clement and Glenn Williams, eds., *The New Canadian Political Economy,* pp. 16–35. Montreal: McGill-Queen's University Press.

World Commission on Environment and Development. 1987. *Our Common Future.* New York: Oxford University Press.

Zuboff, Shoshona. 1988. *In the Age of the Smart Machine.* New York: Basic Books.

Documents

Alberta Environment. 1985. *Environmental Impact Assessment Guidelines.* Edmonton: Alberta Environment.

Alberta Pacific Forest Industries Inc. 1989. *Environmental Impact Assessment: Summary Report.*

————. 1990. *Fact Sheet. ALPAC Pulp Mill.*

Alberta Pacific Scientific Review Panel. 1990. *A Review of the Modified Wood Pulping and Bleaching Processes Proposed for Alberta Pacific Forest Industries Inc. Pulp Mill.* Edmonton: Alberta Environment.

British Paper and Board Federation. 1990. "Statistics." Quoted in *The Globe and Mail,* June 16, 1990.

Canadian Pulp and Paper Association. 1989. *Reference Tables.* 43rd ed. Montreal: CPPA.

Keewatin Community College. n.d. *North of 53 Environmental Scan.* The Pas: Keewatin Community College.

Environmental Impact Assessment Review Board. 1990. *The Proposed Alberta-Pacific Pulp Mill: Report of the EIA Review Board.* Edmonton: Alberta Environment.

Expert Review Panel. 1990. *Forest Management in Alberta.* Edmonton: Alberta Energy, Forestry, Lands and Wildlife.

Government of Alberta. 1990. "News Release." Athabasca, Alberta, December 20.

Manitoba Clean Environment Commission. 1989. *Report on Hearings Repap Manitoba Inc.* Winnipeg: Manitoba Environment.

Manitoba Environment. n.d. a. *Guide to the Manitoba Environment Act.* Winnipeg: Manitoba Environment.

———. n.d. b. "Guidelines for the preparation of an environmental impact assessment for the proposed modification and expansion to the Manfor Complex at The Pas."

———. n.d. c. "Guidelines for the preparation of an environmental impact assessment for the proposed Phase I forest management plan for Repap Manitoba Inc."

———. 1990. "Fact sheet." 26 January, Winnipeg: Manitoba Environment.

Manitoba Recycling Action Committee. 1990. *Action Plan: A Waste Minimization Strategy for Manitoba in the 1990s.* Winnipeg: Manitoba Environment.

Northern Alberta Development Council. 1990. *Trends in Northern Alberta 1970–1990: A Statistical Overview.* Peace River, Alberta: NADC.

Organisation for Economic Co-operation and Development. 1986. *Trends in the Information Economy.* Paris: OECD.

Statistics Canada. 1986. *Canadian Forestry Statistics* (25–202). Ottawa: Supply and Services Canada.

Selected submissions to the Manitoba Clean Environment Commission hearing H-11-89/90, Repap Phase I (August–September), 1989

Bercier, Ted, Mayor. 1989. Moose Lake Community Council, *Submission,* 22 August.

Bodnar, J.P. 1989. Commerical Fisherman's Union, *Submission,* 21 August.

Fahlgren, D.I., Director. n.d. The Pas and District Chamber of Commerce, *Submission,* undated.

Hay, Rick, Northern Zone Manager. 1989. Freshwater Fish Marketing Corporation, *Brief,* 21 August.

Henderson, Jerry. 1989. Swampy Tree Tribal Council, *Brief,* 12 July.

Manitoba Keewatinowi Okimakanak. 1989. *Letters,* 4, 17, and 22 August.

MacLaren Plansearch Inc. 1989. *Environmental Impact Assessment for Phase I Modification and Expansion of the Manfor Complex,* May.

Richards, Paul, Vice President and General Manager. n.d. Repap Manitoba, Inc., *Slides,* undated.

Tobacco, Jim, Chief. 1989. Moose Lake Indian Band, *Brief,* 11 August.

Unfried, Bruce, Mayor. 1989. The Pas, *Brief,* 30 August.

Selected submissions to the Alberta-Pacific Environmental Impact Assessment Review Board (October, November, and December), 1989

Aboriginal Resource Development Group. 1989. *Filed Document J-31,* 1 December.

Asch, Michael. 1989. Edmonton Inter-Church Committee on the North, *Filed Document J-24,* 30 November.

Bergunder, Dave, Zone Manager. 1989. Northwest Territories, Freshwater Fish Marketing Corporation, *Filed Document H-6,* 25 November.

Department of the Environment. 1989. *Filed Document G-21,* 18 November.

Fort Providence Dene Band. 1989. *Filed Document H-4,* 23 November.

Government of the Northwest Territories. 1989. *Filed Document F-11,* 16 November.

Janvier Tribal Administration. 1989. *Filed Document B-1,* 1 November.

Lac La Biche Fisheries. 1988. Task Force Report, *Filed Document C-10,* September, 1988.

Métis Association of the Northwest Territories. 1989. *Filed Document F-7,* 16 November.

Peace Athabasca Trappers Association. 1989. *Filed Document E-5,* 10 November.

Chapter 31

POPULATION: DELUSION AND REALITY

Amartya Sen

1.

Few issues today are as divisive as what is called the "world population problem." With the approach this autumn of the International Conference of Population and Development in Cairo, organized by the United Nations, these divisions among experts are receiving enormous attention and generating considerable heat. There is a danger that in the confrontation between apocalyptic pessimism, on the one hand, and a dismissive smugness, on the other, a genuine understanding of the nature of the population problem may be lost.[1]

Visions of impending doom have been increasingly aired in recent years, often presenting the population problem as a "bomb" that has been planted and is about to "go off." These catastrophic images have encouraged a tendency to search for emergency solutions which treat the people involved not as reasonable beings, allies facing a common problem, but as impulsive and uncontrolled sources of great social harm, in need of strong discipline.

Such views have received serious attention in public discussions, not just in sensational headlines in the popular press, but also in seriously argued and widely read books. One of the most influential examples was Paul Ehrlich's *The Population Bomb*, the first three sections of which were headed "Too Many People," "Too Little Food," and "A Dying Planet."[2] A more recent example of a chilling diagnosis of imminent calamity is Garrett Hardin's *Living within Limits*.[3] The arguments on which these pessimistic visions are based deserve serious scrutiny.

If the propensity to foresee impending disaster from overpopulation is strong in some circles, so is the tendency, in others, to dismiss all worries about population size. Just as alarmism builds on the recognition of a real problem and then magnifies it, complacency may also start off from a reasonable belief about the history of population problems and fail to see how they may have changed by now. It is often pointed out, for example, that the world has coped well enough with fast increases in population in the past, even though alarmists had expected otherwise. Malthus anticipated terrible disasters resulting from population growth and a consequent imbalance in "the proportion between the natural increase of population and food."[4] At a time when there were fewer than a billion people, he was quite convinced that "the period when the number of men surpass their means of subsistence has long since arrived." However, since Malthus first published his famous *Essay on Population* in 1798, the world population has grown nearly six times larger, while food output and consumption per person are considerably higher now, and there has been an unprecedented increase both in life expectancies and in general living standards.[5]

The fact that Malthus was mistaken in his diagnosis as well as his prognosis two hundred years ago does not, however, indicate that contemporary fears about population growth must be similarly erroneous. The increase in the world population has vastly accelerated

Source: "Population: Delusion and Reality," *The New York Review of Books* 41, 15 (22 September 1994): 62–71. Copyright © 1994 Nyrev, Inc. Reprinted with permission from *The New York Review of Books*.

over the last century. It took the world population millions of years to reach the first billion, then 123 years to get to the second, 33 years to the third, 14 years to the fourth, 13 years to the fifth billion, with the sixth billion to come, according to one UN projection, in another 11 years.[6] During the last decade, between 1980 and 1990, the number of people on earth grew by about 923 million, an increase nearly the size of the total world population in Malthus's time. Whatever may be the proper response to alarmism about the future, complacency based on past success is no response at all.

Immigration and Population

One current worry concerns the regional distribution of the increase in world population, about 90 percent of which is taking place in the developing countries. The percentage rate of population growth is fastest in Africa — 3.1 percent per year over the last decade. But most of the large increases in population occur in regions other than Africa. The largest absolute increases in numbers are taking place in Asia, which is where most of the world's poorer people live, even though the rate of increase in population has been slowing significantly there. Of the worldwide increase of 923 million people in the 1980s, well over half occurred in Asia — 517 million in fact (including 146 million in China and 166 million in India).

Beyond concerns about the well-being of these poor countries themselves, a more self-regarding worry causes panic in the richer countries of the world and has much to do with the current anxiety in the West about the "world population problem." This is founded on the belief that destitution caused by fast population growth in the third world is responsible for the severe pressure to emigrate to the developed countries of Europe and North America. In this view, people impoverished by overpopulation in the "South" flee to the "North." Some have claimed to find empirical support for this thesis in the fact that pressure to emigrate from the South has accelerated in recent decades, along with a rapid increase in the population there.

There are two distinct questions here: first, how great a threat of intolerable immigration pressure does the North face from the South, and second, is that pressure closely related to population growth in the South, rather than to other social and economic factors?" There are reasons to doubt that population growth is the major force behind migratory pressures, and I shall concentrate here on that question. But I should note in passing that immigration is now severely controlled in

Europe and North America, and insofar as Europe is concerned, most of the current immigrants from the third world are not "primary" immigrants but dependent relatives — mainly spouses and young children — of those who had come and settled earlier. The United States remains relatively more open to fresh immigration, but the requirements of "labor certification" as a necessary part of the immigration procedure tend to guarantee that the new entrants are relatively better educated and more skilled. There are, however, sizable flows of illegal immigrants, especially to the United States and to a lesser extent to southern Europe, though the numbers are hard to estimate.

What causes the current pressures to emigrate? The "job-worthy" people who get through the immigration process are hardly to be seen as impoverished and destitute migrants crated by the sheer pressure of population. Even the illegal immigrants who manage to evade the rigors of border control are typically not starving wretches but those who can make use of work prospects in the North.

The explanation for the increased migratory pressure over the decades owes more to the dynamism of international capitalism than to just the growing size of the population of the third world countries. The immigrants have allies in potential employers, and this applies as much to illegal farm laborers in California as to the legally authorized "guest workers" in automobile factories in Germany. The economic incentive to emigrate to the North from the poorer Southern economies may well depend on differences in real income. But this gap is very large anyway, and even if it is presumed that population growth in the South is increasing the disparity with the North — a thesis I shall presently consider — it seems unlikely that this incentive would significantly change if the Northern income level were, say, twenty times that of the Southern as opposed to twenty-five times.

The growing demand for immigration to the North from the South is related to the "shrinking" of the world (through revolutions in communication and transport), reduction in economic obstacles to labor movements (despite the increase in political barriers), and the growing reach and absorptive power of international capitalism (even as domestic politics in the North has turned more inward-looking and nationalistic). To try to explain the increase in immigration pressure by the growth rate of total population in the third world is to close one's eyes to the deep changes that have occurred — and are occurring — in the world in which we live, and the rapid internationalization of its cultures and economies that accompanies these changes.

Fears of Being Engulfed

A closely related issue concerns what is perceived as a growing "imbalance" in the division of the world population, with a rapidly rising share belonging to the third world. That fear translates into worries of various kinds in the North, especially the sense of being over-run by the South. Many Northerners fear being engulfed by people from Asia and Africa, whose share of the world population increased from 63.7 percent in 1950 to 71.2 percent by 1990, and is expected, according to the estimates of the United Nations, to rise to 78.5 percent by 2050 AD.

It is easy to understand the fears of relatively well-off people at the thought of being surrounded by a fast growing and increasingly impoverished Southern population. As I shall argue, the thesis of growing impoverishment does not stand up to much scrutiny; but it is important to address first the psychologically tense issue of racial balance in the world (even though racial composition as a consideration has only as much importance as we choose to give it). Here it is worth recollecting that the third world is right now going through the same kind of demographic shift — a rapid expansion of population for a temporary but long stretch — that Europe and North America experienced during their industrial revolution. In 1650 the share of Asia and Africa in the world population is estimated to have been 78.4 percent, and it stayed around there even in 1750.[7] With the industrial revolution, the share of Asia and Africa diminished because of the rapid rise of population in Europe and North America; for example, during the nineteenth century while the inhabitants of Asia and Africa grew by about 4 percent per decade or less, the population of "the area of European settlement" grew by around 10 percent every decade.

Even now the combined share of Asia and Africa (71.2 percent) is considerably *below* what its share was in 1650 or 1750. If the United Nations' prediction that this share will rise to 78.5 percent by 2050 comes true, then the Asians and the Africans would return to being proportionately almost exactly as numerous as they were before the European industrial revolution. There is, of course, nothing sacrosanct about the distributions of population in the past; but the sense of a growing "imbalance" in the world, based only on recent trends, ignores history and implicitly presumes that the expansion of Europeans earlier on was natural, whereas the same process happening now to other populations unnaturally disturbs the "balance."

Collaboration versus Override

Other worries involving the relation of population growth to food supplies, income levels, and the environment reflect more serious matters.[8] Before I take up those questions, a brief comment on the distinction between two rival approaches to dealing with the population problem may be useful. One involves voluntary choice and a collaborative solution, and the other over-rides voluntarism through legal or economic coercion.

Alarmist views of impending crises tend to produce a willingness to consider forceful measures for coercing people to have fewer children in the third world. Imposing birth control on unwilling people is no longer rejected as readily as it was until quite recently, and some activists have pointed to the ambiguities that exist in determining what is or is not "coercion."[9] Those who are willing to consider — or at least not fully reject — programs that would use some measure of force to reduce population growth often point to the success of China's "one child policy" in cutting down the national birth rate. Force can also take an indirect form, as when economic opportunities are changed so radically by government regulations that people are left with very little choice except to behave in ways the government would approve. In China's case, the government may refuse to offer housing to families with too many children — thus penalizing the children as well as the dissenting adults.

In India the policy of compulsory birth control that was initiated during the "emergency period" declared by Mrs. Gandhi in the 1970s was decisively rejected by the voters in the general election in which it — along with civil rights — was a major issue. Even so, some public health clinics in the northern states (such as Uttar Pradesh) insist, in practice, on sterilization before providing normal medial attention to women and men beyond a certain age. The pressures to move in that direction seem to be strong, and they are reinforced by the rhetoric of "the population bomb."

I shall call this general approach the "override" view, since the family's personal decisions are overridden by some agency outside the family — typically by the government of the country in question (whether or not it has been pressed to do so by "outside" agencies, such as international organizations and pressure groups). In fact, overriding is not limited to an explicit use of legal coercion or economic compulsion, since people's own choices can also be effectively overridden by simply not offering them the opportunities for jobs or welfare that they can expect to get from a responsible government. Override can take many different forms and can be of varying intensity (with the Chinese "one child policy" being something of an extreme case of a more general approach).

A central issue here is the increasingly vocal demand by some activists concerned with the population growth that the highest "priority" should be given in third world countries to family planning over other public commitments. This demand goes much beyond supporting family planning as a part of development. In fact, proposals for shifting international aid away from development in general to family planning in particular have lately been increasingly frequent. Such policies fit into the general approach of "override" as well, since they try to rely on manipulating people's choices through offering them only some opportunities (the means of family planning) while denying others, no matter what they would have themselves preferred. Insofar as they would have the effect of reducing health care and educational services, such shifts in public commitments will not only add to the misery of human lives, they may also have, I shall argue, exactly the opposite effect on family planning than the one intended, since education and health care have a significant part in the *voluntary* reduction of the birth rate.

The "override" approach contrasts with another, the "collaborative" approach, that relies not on legal or economic restrictions but on rational decisions of women and men, based on expanded choices and enhanced security, and encouraged by open dialogue and extensive public discussions. The difference between the two approaches does not lie in government's activism in the first case as opposed to passivity in the second. Even if solutions are sought through the decisions and actions of people themselves, the chance to take reasoned decisions with more knowledge and a greater sense of personal security can be increased by public policies, for example, through expanding educational facilities, health care, and economic well-being, along with providing better access to family planning. The central political and ethical issue concerning the "override" approach does not lie in its insistence on the need for public policy but in the ways it significantly reduces the choices open to parents.

The Malthus–Condorcet Debate

Thomas Robert Malthus forcefully argued for a version of the "override" view. In fact, it was precisely this preference that distinguished Malthus from Condorcet, the eighteenth-century French mathematician and

social scientist from whom Malthus had actually derived the analysis of how population could outgrow the means of living. The debate between Condorcet and Malthus in some ways marks the origin of the distinction between the "collaborative" and the "override" approaches, which still compete for attention.[10]

In his *Essay on Population*, published in 1798, Malthus quoted — extensively and with approval — Condorcet's discussion, in 1795, of the possibility of overpopulation. However, true to the Enlightenment tradition, Condorcet was confident that this problem would be solved by reasoned human action: through increases in productivity, through better conservation and prevention of waste, and through education (especially female education) which would contribute to reducing the birth rate.[11] Voluntary family planning would be encouraged, in Condorcet's analysis, by increased understanding that if people "have a duty toward those who are not yet born, that duty is not to give them existence but to give them happiness." They would see the value of limiting family size "rather than foolishly ... encumber the world with useless and wretched beings."[12]

Even though Malthus borrowed from Condorcet his diagnosis of the possibility of overpopulation, he refused to accept Condorcet's solution. Indeed, Malthus's essay on population was partly a criticism of Condorcet's enlightenment reasoning, and even the full title of Malthus's famous essay specifically mentioned Condorcet. Malthus argued that

> there is no reason whatever to suppose that anything beside the difficulty of procuring in adequate plenty the necessaries of life should either indispose *this greater number of persons to marry early, or* disable *them from rearing in health the largest families.*[13]

Malthus thus opposed public relief of poverty: he saw the "poor laws" in particular as contributing greatly to population growth.[14]

Malthus was not sure that any public policy would work, and whether "overriding" would in fact be possible: "The perpetual tendency in the race of man to increase beyond the means of subsistence is one of the great general laws of animated nature which we can have no reason to expect will change."[15] But insofar as any solution would be possible, it could not come from voluntary decisions of the people involved, or acting from a position of strength and economic security. It must come from overriding their preferences through the compulsions of economic necessity, since their poverty was the only thing that could "indispose the greater number of persons to marry early, or disable them from rearing in health the largest families."

Development and Increased Choice

The distinction between the "collaborative" approach and the "override" approach thus tends to correspond closely to the contrast between, on the one hand, treating economic and social development as the way to solve the population problem and, on the other, expecting little from development and using, instead, legal and economic pressures to reduce birth rates. Among recent writers, those such as Gerard Piel[16] who have persuasively emphasized our ability to solve problems through reasoned decisions and actions have tended — like Condorcet — to find the solution of the population problem in economic and social development. They advocate a broadly collaborative approach, in which governments and citizens would together produce economic and social conditions favoring slower population growth. In contrast, those who have been thoroughly skeptical of reasoned human action to limit population growth have tended to go in the direction of "override" in one form or another, rather than concentrate on development and voluntarism.

Has development, in fact, done much to reduce population growth? There can be little doubt that economic and social development, in general, has been associated with major reductions in birth rates and the emergence of smaller families as the norm. This is a pattern that was, of course, clearly observed in Europe and North America as they underwent industrialization, but that experience has been repeated in many other parts of the world.

In particular, conditions of economic security and affluence, wider availability of contraceptive methods, expansion of education (particularly female education), and lower mortality rates have had — and are currently having — quite substantial effects in reducing birth rates in different parts of the world.[17] The rate of world population growth is certainly declining, and even over the last two decades its percentage growth rate has fallen from 2.2 percent per year between 1970 and 1980 to 1.7 percent between 1980 and 1992. This rate is expected to go steadily down until the size of the world's population becomes nearly stationary.[18]

There are important regional differences in demographic behavior; for example, the population growth rate in India peaked at 2.2 percent a year (in the 1970s) and has since started to diminish, whereas most Latin American countries peaked at much higher rates before coming down sharply, while many countries in Africa currently have growth rates between 3 and 4 percent, with an average for sub-Saharan Africa of 3.1 percent. Similarly, the different factors have varied in their respective influence from region to region. But there can be little dispute that economic and social development tends to reduce fertility rates. The regions of the third world that lag most in achieving economic and social development, such as many countries in Africa, are, in general, also the ones that have failed to reduce birth rates significantly. Malthus's fear that economic and social development could only encourage people to have more children has certainly proved to be radically wrong, and so have all the painful policy implications drawn from it.

This raises the following question: in view of the clear connection between development and lower fertility, why isn't the dispute over how to deal with population growth fully resolved already? Why don't we reinterpret the population problem simply as a problem of underdevelopment and seek a solution by encouraging economic and social development (even if we reject the oversimple slogan "development is the most reliable contraceptive")?

In the long run, this may indeed be exactly the right approach. The problem is more complex, however, because a "contraceptive" that is "reliable" in the long run may not act fast enough to meet the present threat. Even though development may dependably work to stabilize population if it is given enough time, there may not be, it is argued, time enough to give. The death rate often falls very fast with more widely available health care, better sanitation, and improved nutrition, while the birth rate may fall rather slowly. Much growth of population may meanwhile occur.

This is exactly the point at which apocalyptic prophecies add force to the "override" view. One claim, then, that needs examination is that the world is facing an imminent crisis, one so urgent that development is just too slow a process to deal with it. We must try right now, the argument goes, to cut down population growth by drastic and forceful means if necessary. The second claim that also needs scrutiny is the actual feasibility of adequately reducing population growth through these drastic means, without fostering social and economic development.

2.

Population and Income

It is sometimes argued that signs of an imminent crisis can be found in the growing impoverishment of the South, with falling income per capita accompanying high population growth. In general, there is little evidence for this. As a matter of fact, the average population of "low-income" countries (as defined by the World Bank) has been not only enjoying a rising gross national product (GNP) per head, but a growth rate of GNP per capita (3.9 percent per year for 1980–1992) that is much faster than those for the "high-income" countries (2.4 percent) and for the "middle-income" ones (0 percent).[19]

The growth of per capita GNP of the population of low-income countries would have been even higher had it not been for the negative growth rates of many countries in sub-Saharan Africa, one region in which a number of countries have been experiencing economic decline. But the main culprit causing this state of affairs is the terrible failure of economic production in sub-Saharan Africa (connected particularly with political disruption, including wars and military rule), rather than population growth, which is only a subsidiary factor. Sub-Saharan Africa does have high population growth, but its economic stagnation has contributed much more to the fall in its per-capita income.

With its average population growth rate of 3.1 percent per year, had sub-Saharan Africa suddenly matched China's low population growth of 1.4 percent (the lowest among the low-income countries), it would have gained roughly 1.7 percent in per-capita GNP growth. The real income per person would still have fallen, even with that minimal population growth, for many countries in the region. The growth of GNP per capita is *minus* 1.9 percent for Ethiopia, *minus* 1.8 percent for Togo, *minus* 3.6 percent for Mozambique, *minus* 4.3 percent for Niger, *minus* 4.7 percent for Ivory Coast, not to mention Somalia, Sudan, and Angola, where the political disruption has been so serious that no reliable GNP estimates even exist. A lower population growth rate could have reduced the magnitude of the fall in per capita GNP, but the main roots of Africa's economic decline lie elsewhere. The complex political factors underlying the troubles of Africa include, among other things, the subversion of democracy and the rise of combative military rulers, often encouraged by the cold war (with Africa providing "client states" — from Somalia and Ethiopia to Angola and Zaire — for the superpowers, particular from the 1960s onward). The explanation of sub-Saharan Africa's problems has to be sought in these political troubles, which affect economic stability, agricultural and industrial incentives, public health arrangements, and social services — even family planning and population policy.[20]

There is indeed a very powerful case for reducing the rate of growth of population in Africa, but this problem cannot be dissociated from the rest of the continent's woes. Sub-Saharan Africa lags behind other developing regions in economic security, in health care, in life expectancy, in basic education, and in political and economic stability. It should be no great surprise that it lags behind in family planning as well. To dissociate the task of population control from the politics and economics of Africa would be a great mistake and would seriously mislead public policy.

Population and Food

Malthus's exact thesis cannot, however, be disputed by quoting statistics of income per capita, for he was concerned specifically with food supply per capita, and he had concentrated on "the proportion between the natural increase of population and food." Many modern commentators, including Paul Ehrlich and Garrett Hardin, have said much about this, too. When Ehrlich says, in his *Population Bomb*, "too little food," he does not mean "too little income," but specifically a growth shortage of food.

Is population beginning to outrun food production? Even though such an impression is often given in public discussions, there is, in fact, no serious evidence that this is happening. While there are some year-to-year fluctuations in the growth of food output (typically inducing, whenever things slacken a bit, some excited remarks by those who anticipate an impending doom), the worldwide trend of food output per person has been firmly upward. Not only over the two centuries since Malthus's time, but also during recent decades, the rise in food output has been significantly and consistently outpacing the expansion of world population.[21]

But the total food supply in the world as a whole is not the only issue. What about the regional distribution of food? If it were to turn out that the rising ratio of food to population is mainly caused by increased production in richer countries (for example, if it appeared that US wheat output was feeding the third world, in which much of the population expansion is taking place), then the neo-Malthusian fears about "too many people" and "too little food" may have some plausibility. Is that what is happening?

In fact, with one substantial exception, exactly the opposite is true. The largest increases in the production of food — not just in the aggregate but also per person — are actually taking place in the third world, particularly in the region that is having the largest absolute increases in the world population, that is, in Asia. The many millions of people who are added to the populations of India and China may be constantly cited by the terrorized — and terrorizing — advocates of the apocalyptic view, but it is precisely in these countries that the most rapid rates of growth in food output per capita are to be observed. For example, between the three-year averages of 1979–1981 and 1991–1993, food production per head in the world moved up by 3 percent, while it went up by only 2 percent in Europe and went down by nearly 5 percent in North America. In contrast, per capita food production jumped up by 22 percent in Asia generally, including 23 percent in India and 39 percent in China.[22] (See Table 31.1).

During the same period, however, food production per capita went down by 6 percent in Africa, and even the absolute size of food output fell in some countries (such as Malawi and Somalia). Of course, many countries in the world — from Syria, Italy, and Sweden to Botswana in Africa — have had declining food production per head without experiencing hunger or starvation since their economies have prospered and grown; when the means are available, food can be easily bought in the international market if it is necessary to do so. For many countries in sub-Saharan Africa the problem arises from the fact that the decline in food production is an integral part of the story of overall economic decline, which I have discussed earlier.

Difficulties of food production in sub-Saharan Africa, like other problems of the national economy, are not only linked to wars, dictatorships, and political chaos. In addition, there is some evidence that climatic shifts have had unfavorable effects on parts of that continent. While some of the climatic problems may be caused partly by increases in human settlement and environmental neglect, that neglect is not unrelated to the political and economic chaos that

has characterized sub-Saharan Africa during the last few decades. The food problem of Africa must be seen as one part of a wider political and economic problem of the region.[23]

The Price of Food

To return to "the balance between food and population," the rising food production per capita in the world as a whole, and in the third world in general, contradicts some of the pessimism that characterized the gloomy predictions of the past. Prophecies of imminent disaster during the last few decades have not proved any more accurate than Malthus's prognostication nearly two hundred years ago. As for new prophecies of doom, they cannot, of course, be contradicted until the future arrives. There was no way of refuting the theses of W. Paddock and P. Paddock's popular book *Famine — 1975!*, published in 1968, which predicted terrible cataclysm for the world as a whole by 1975 (writing off India, in particular, as a basket case), until 1975 actually arrived. The new prophets have learned not to attach specific dates to the crises they foresee, and past failures do not seem to have reduced the popular appetite for this creative genre.

However, after noting the rather dismal forecasting record of doomsayers, we must also accept the general methodological point that present trends in output do not necessarily tell us much about the prospects of further expansion in the future. It could, for example, be argued that maintaining growth in food production may require proportionately increasing investments of capital, drawing them away from other kinds of production. This would tend to make food progressively more expensive if there are "diminishing returns" in shifting resources from other fields into food production. And, ultimately, further expansion of food production may become so expensive that it would be hard to maintain the trend of increasing food production without reducing other outputs drastically.

But is food production really getting more and more expensive? There is, in fact, no evidence for that conclusion either. In fact, quite the contrary. Not only is food generally much cheaper to buy today, in constant dollars, than it was in Malthus's time, but it also has become cheaper during recent decades. As a matter of fact, there have been increasing complaints among food exporters, especially in the third world, that food prices have fallen in relation to other commodities. For example, in 1992 a United Nations report recorded a 38 percent fall in the relative prices of "basic foods" over the last decade.[24] This is entirely in line with the

Table 31.1 Indices of Food Production per Capita

	1979–1981 Base Period	1991–1993
World	100	103
Europe	100	102
North America	100	95
Africa	100	94
Asia	100	122
including		
India	100	123
China	100	139

Source: FAO Quarterly Bulletin of Statistics, Food and Agriculture Organization of the United States.

trend, during the last three decades, toward declining relative prices of particular food items, in relation to the prices of manufactured goods. The World Bank's adjusted estimates of the prices of particular food crops, between 1953–1955 and 1983–1985, show similarly steep declines for such staples as rice (42 percent), wheat (57 percent), sorghum (39 percent), and maize (37 percent).[25]

Not only is food getting less expensive, but we also have to bear in mind that the current increase in food production (substantial and well ahead of population growth, as it is) is itself being kept in check by the difficulties in selling food profitably, as the relative prices of food have fallen. Those neo-Malthusians who concede that food production is now growing faster than population often point out that it is growing "only a little faster than population," and they are inclined to interpret this as evidence that we are reaching the limits of what we can produce to keep pace with population growth.

But that is surely the wrong conclusion to draw in view of the falling relative prices of food, and the current difficulties in selling food, since it ignores the effects of economic incentives that govern production. When we take into account the persistent cheapening of food prices, we have good grounds to suggest that food output is being held back by a lack of effective demand in the market. The imaginary crisis in food production, contradicted as it is by the upward trends of total and regional food output per head, is thus further debunked by an analysis of the economic incentives to produce more food.

Deprived Lives and Slums

I have examined the alleged "food problem" associated with population growth in some detail because it has received so much attention both in the traditional Malthusian literature and in the recent writings of neo-Malthusians. In concentrating on his claim that growing populations would not have enough food, Malthus differed from Condorcet's broader presentation of the population question. Condorcet's own emphasis was on the possibility of "a continual diminution of happiness" as a result of population growth, a diminution that could occur in many different ways — not just through the deprivation of food, but through a decline in living conditions generally. That more extensive worry can remain even when Malthus's analysis of the food supply is rejected.

Indeed, average income and food production per head can go on increasing even as the wretchedly deprived living conditions of particular sections of the population get worse, as they have in many parts of the third world. The living conditions of backward regions and deprived classes can decline even when a country's economic growth is very rapid on the average. Brazil during the 1960s and 1970s provided an extreme example of this. The sense that there are just "too many people" around often arises from seeing the desperate lives of people in the large and rapidly growing urban slums — *bidonvilles* — in poor countries, sobering reminders that we should not take too much comfort from aggregate statistics of economic progress.

But in an essay addressed mainly to the population problem, what we have to ask is not whether things are just fine in the third world (they obviously are not), but whether population growth is the root cause of the deprivations that people suffer. The question is whether the particular instances of deep poverty we observe derive mainly from population growth rather than from other factors that lead to unshared prosperity and persistent and possibly growing inequality. The tendency to see in population growth an explanation for every calamity that afflicts poor people is now fairly well established in some circles, and the message that gets transmitted constantly is the opposite of the old picture postcard: "Wish you weren't here."

To see in population growth the main reason for the growth of overcrowded and very poor slums in large cities, for example, is not empirically convincing. It does not help to explain why the slums of Calcutta and Bombay have grown worse at a faster rate than those of Karachi and Islamabad (India's population growth rate is 2.1 percent per year, Pakistan's 3.1), or why Jakarta has deteriorated faster than Ankara or Istanbul (Indonesian population growth is 1.8 percent, Turkey's 2.3), or why the slums of Mexico City have become worse more rapidly than those of San José (Mexico's population growth rate is 2.0, Costa Rica's 2.8), or why Harlem can seem more and more deprived when compared with the poorer districts of Singapore (US population growth rate is 1.0, Singapore's is 1.8). Many causal factors affect the degree of deprivation in particular parts of a country — rural as well as urban — and to try to see them all as resulting from overpopulation is the negation of social analysis.

This is not to deny that population growth may well have an effect on deprivation, but only to insist that any investigation of the effects of population growth must be part of the analysis of economic and political processes, including the effects of other variables. It is the isolationist view of population growth that should be rejected.

Threats to the Environment

In his concern about "a continual diminution of happiness" from population growth, Condorcet was a pioneer in considering the possibility that natural raw materials might be used up, thereby making living conditions worse. In his characteristically rationalist solution, which relied partly on voluntary and reasoned measures to reduce the birth rate, Condorcet also envisaged the development of less improvident technology: "The manufacture of articles will be achieved with less wastage in raw materials and will make better use of them."[26]

The effects of a growing population on the environment could be a good deal more serious than the food problems that have received so much attention in the literature inspired by Malthus. If the environment is damaged by population pressures, this obviously affects the kind of life we lead, and the possibilities of a "diminution in happiness" can be quite considerable. In dealing with this problem, we have to distinguish once again between the long and the short run. The short-run picture tends to be dominated by the fact that the per-capita consumption of food, fuel, and other goods by people in third world countries is often relatively low; consequently the impact of population growth in these countries is not, in relative terms, so damaging to the global environment. But the problems of the local environment can, of course, be serious in many developing economies. They vary from the "neighborhood pollution" created by unregulated industries to the pressure of denser populations on rural resources such as fields and woods.[27] (The Indian authorities had to close down several factories in and around Agra, since the façade of the Taj Mahal was turning pale as a result of chemical pollution from local factories.) But it remains true that one additional American typically has a larger negative impact on the ozone layer, global warmth, and other elements of the earth's environment than dozens of Indians and Zimbabweans put together. Those who argue for the immediate need for forceful population control in the third world to preserve the global environment must first recognize this elementary fact.

This does not imply, as is sometimes suggested, than as far as the global environment is concerned, population growth in the third world is nothing to worry about. The long-run impact on the global environment of population growth in the developing countries can be expected to be large. As the Indians and Zimbabweans develop economically, they too will consume a great deal more, and they will pose, in the future, a threat to the earth's environment similar to that of people in the rich countries today. The long-run threat of population to the environment is a real one.

3.

Women's Deprivation and Power

Since reducing the birth rate can be slow, this and other long-run problems should be addressed right now. Solutions will no doubt have to be found in the two directions to which, as it happens, Condorcet pointed: (1) developing new technology and new behavior patterns that would waste little and pollute less, and (2) fostering social and economic changes that would gradually bring down the growth rate of population.

On reducing birth rates, Condorcet's own solution not only included enhancing economic opportunity and security, but also stressed the importance of education, particularly female education. A better-educated population could have a more informed discussion of the kind of life we have reason to value; in particular it would reject the drudgery of a life of continuous child bearing and rearing that is routinely forced on many third world women. That drudgery, in some ways, is the most immediately adverse consequence of high fertility rates.

Central to reducing birth rates, then, is a close connection between women's well-being and their power to make their own decisions and bring about changes in the fertility pattern. Women in many third world countries are deprived by high birth frequency of the freedom to do other things in life, not to mention the medical dangers of repeated pregnancy and high maternal mortality, which are both characteristic of many developing countries. It is thus not surprising that reductions in birth rates have been typically associated with improvement of women's status and their ability to make their voices heard — often the result of expanded opportunities for schooling and political activity.[28]

There is nothing particularly exotic about declines in the birth rate occurring through a process of voluntary rational assessment, of which Condorcet spoke. It is what people do when they have some basic education, know about family planning methods and have access to them, do not readily accept a life of persistent drudgery, and are not deeply anxious about their economic security. It is also what they do when they are not forced by high infant and child mortality rates to be so worried that no child will survive to support them in their old age that they try to have many children. In country after country the birth rate has come down with more female education, the reduction of mortality rates, the expansion of economic means and security, and greater public discussion of ways of living.

Development versus Coercion

There is little doubt that this process of social and economic change will over time cut down the birth rate. Indeed the growth rate of world population is already firmly declining — it came down from 2.2 percent in the 1970s to 1.7 percent between 1980 and 1992. Had imminent cataclysm been threatening, we might have had good reason to reject such gradual progress and consider more drastic means of population control, as some have advocated. But that apocalyptic view is empirically baseless. There is no imminent emergency that calls for a breathless response. What is called for is systematic support for people's own decisions to reduce family size through expanding education and health care, and through economic and social development.

It is often asked where the money needed for expanding education, health care, etc., would be found. Education, health services, and many other means of improving the quality of life are typically highly labor-intensive and are thus relatively inexpensive in poor countries (because of low wages).[29] While poor countries have less money to spend, they also need less money to provide these services. For this reason many poor countries have indeed been able to expand educational and health services widely without waiting to become prosperous through the process of economic growth. Sri Lanka, Costa Rica, Indonesia, and Thailand are good examples, and there are many others. While the impact of these social services on the quality and length of life have been much studied, they are also major means of reducing the birth rate.

By contrast with such open and voluntary developments, coercive methods, such as the "one child policy" in some regions, have been tried in China, particularly since the reforms of 1979. Many commentators have pointed out that by 1992 the Chinese birth rate has fallen to 19 per 1,000, compared with 29 per 1,000 in India, and 37 per 1,000 for the average of poor countries other than China and India. China's total fertility rate (reflecting the number of children born per woman) is now at "the replacement level" of 2.0, compared with India's 3.6 and the weighted average of 4.9 for low-income countries other than China and India.[30] Hasn't China shown the way to "solve" the population problem in other developing countries as well?

4.

China's Population Policies

The difficulties with this "solution" are of several kinds. First, if freedom is valued at all, the lack of freedom associated with this approach must be seen to be a social loss in itself. The importance of reproductive freedom has been persuasively emphasized by women's groups throughout the world.[31]

The loss of freedom is often dismissed on the grounds that because of cultural differences, authoritarian policies that would not be tolerated in the West are acceptable to Asians. While we often hear references to "despotic" Oriental traditions, such arguments are not more convincing than a claim that compulsion in the West is justified by the traditions of the Spanish Inquisition or of the Nazi concentration camps. Frequent references are also made to the emphasis on discipline in the "Confucian tradition"; but that is not the only tradition in the "East," nor is it easy to assess the implications of that tradition for modern Asia (even if we were able to show that discipline is more important for Confucius than it is for, say, Plato or Saint Augustine).

Only a democratic expression of opinion could reveal whether citizens would find a compulsory system acceptable. While such a test has not occurred in China, one did in fact take place in India during "the emergency period" in the 1970s, when Indira Gandhi's government imposed compulsory birth control and suspended various legal freedoms. In the general elections that followed, the politicians favoring the policy of coercion were overwhelmingly defeated. Furthermore, family planning experts in India have observed how the briefly applied programs of compulsory sterilization tended to discredit voluntary birth control programs generally, since people became deeply suspicious of the entire movement to control fertility.

Second, apart from the fundamental issue of whether people are willing to accept compulsory birth control, its specific consequences must also be considered. Insofar as coercion is effective, it works by making people do things they would not freely do. The social consequences of such compulsion, including the ways in which an unwilling population tends to react when it is coerced, can be appalling. For example, the demands of a "one child family" can lead to the neglect — or worse — of a second child, thereby increasing the infant mortality rate. Moreover, in a country with a strong preference for male children — a preference shared by China and many other countries in Asia and North Africa — a policy of allowing only one child per family can easily lead to the fatal neglect of a female child. There is much evidence that this is fairly widespread in China, with very adverse effects on infant mortality rates. There are reports that female children have been severely neglected as well as suggestions that female infanticide occurs with considerable frequency. Such consequences are hard to tolerate morally, and perhaps politically also, in the long run.

Third, what is also not clear is exactly how much additional reduction in the birth rate has been achieved through these coercive methods. Many of China's longstanding social and economic programs have been valuable in reducing fertility, including those that have expanded education for women as well as men, made health care more generally available, provided more job opportunities for women, and stimulated rapid economic growth. These factors would themselves have reduced the birth rates, and it is not clear how much "extra lowering" of fertility rates has been achieved in China through compulsion.

For example, we can determine whether many of the countries that match (or outmatch) China in life expectancy, female literacy rates, and female participation in the labor force actually have a higher fertility rate than China. Of all the countries in the world for which data are given in the *World Development Report 1994*, there are only three such countries: Jamaica (2.7), Thailand (2.2), and Sweden (2.1) — and the fertility rates of two of these are close to China's (2.0). Thus the additional contribution of coercion to reducing fertility in China is by no means clear, since compulsion was superimposed on a society that was already reducing its birth rate and in which education and jobs outside the home were available to large numbers of women. In some regions of China the compulsory program needed little enforcement, whereas in other — more backward — regions, it had to be applied with much severity, with terrible consequences in infant mortality and discrimination against female children. While China may get too much credit for its authoritarian measures, it gets far too little credit for the other, more collaborative and participatory, policies it has followed, which have themselves helped to cut down the birth rate.

China and India

A useful contrast can be drawn between China and India, the two most populous countries in the world. If we look only at the national averages, it is easy to see that China with its low fertility rate of 2.0 has achieved much more than India has with its average

fertility rate of 3.6. To what extent this contrast can be attributed to the effectiveness of the coercive policies used in China is not clear, since we would expect the fertility rate to be much lower in China in view of its higher percentage of female literacy (almost twice as high), higher life expectancy (almost ten years more), larger female involvement (by three quarters) in the labor force, and so on. But India is a country of great diversity, whose different states have very unequal achievements in literacy, health care, and economic and social development. Most states in India are far behind the Chinese provinces in educational achievement (with the exception of Tibet, which has the lowest literacy rate of any Chinese or Indian state), and the same applies to other factors that affect fertility. However, the state of Kerala in southern India provides an interesting comparison with China, since it too has high levels of basic education, health care, and so on. Kerala is a state within a country, but with its 29 million people, it is larger than most countries in the world (including Canada). Kerala's birth rate of 18 per 1,000 is actually lower than China's 19 per 1,000, and its fertility rate is 1.8 for 1991, compared with China's 2.0 for 1992. These low rates have been achieved without any state coercion.[32]

The roots of Kerala's success are to be found in the kinds of social progress Condorcet hoped for, including, among others, a high female literacy rate (86 percent, which is substantially higher than China's 68 percent). The rural literacy rate is in fact higher in Kerala — for women as well as men — than in every single province in China. Male and female life expectancies at birth in China are respectively 67 and 71 years; the provisional 1991 figures for men and women in Kerala are 71 and 74 years. Women have been active in Kerala's economic and political life for a long time. A high proportion do skilled and semi-skilled work and a large number have taken part in educational movements.[33] It is perhaps of symbolic importance that the first public pronouncement of the need for widespread elementary education in any part of India was made in 1817 by Rani Gouri Parvathi Bai, the young queen of the princely state of Travancore, which makes up a substantial part of modern Kerala. For a long time public discussions in Kerala have centered on women's rights and the undesirability of couples marrying when very young.

This political process has been voluntary and collaborative, rather than coercive, and the adverse reactions that have been observed in China, such as infant mortality, have not occurred in Kerala. Kerala's low fertility rate has been achieved along with an infant mortality rate of 16.5 per 1,000 live births (17 for boys and 16 for girls), compared with China's 31 (28 for boys and 33 for girls). And as a result of greater gender equality in Kerala, women have not suffered from higher mortality rates than men in Kerala, as they have in China. Even the ratio of females to males in the total population in Kerala (above 1.03) is quite close to that of the current ratios in Europe and America (reflecting the usual pattern of lower female mortality whenever women and men receive similar care). By contrast, the average female to male ratio in China is 0.94 and in India as a whole 0.93.[34] Anyone drawn to the Chinese experience of compulsory birth control must take note of these facts.

The temptation to use the "override" approach arises at least partly from impatience with the allegedly slow process of fertility reduction through collaborative, rather than coercive, attempts. Yet Kerala's birth rate has fallen from 44 per 1,000 in the 1950s to 18 by 1991 — not a sluggish decline. Nor is Kerala unique in this respect. Other societies, such as those of Sri Lanka, South Korea, and Thailand, which have relied on expanding education and reducing mortality rates — instead of on coercion — have also achieved sharp declines in fertility and birth rates.

It is also interesting to compare the time required for reducing fertility in China with that in the two states in India, Kerala and Tamil Nadu, which have done most to encourage voluntary and collaborative reduction in birth rates (even though Tamil Nadu is well behind Kerala in each respect).[35] Table 31.2 shows the fertility rates both in 1979, when the one-child policy and related programs were introduced in China, and in 1991. Despite China's one-child policy and other coercive measures, its fertility rate seems to have fallen much less sharply than those of Kerala and Tamil Nadu. The "override" view is very hard to defend on

Table 31.2 Fertility Rates in China, Kerala, and Tamil Nadu

	1979	1991
China	2.8	2.0
Kerala	3.0	1.8
Tamil Nadu	3.5	2.2

Sources: For China, Xizhe Peng, *Demographic Transition in China* (Oxford University Press, 1991), Li Chengrui, *A Study of China's Population* (Beijing: Foreign Language Press, 1992), and *World Development Report 1994*. For India, *Sample Registration System 1979–80* (New Delhi: Ministry of Home Affairs, 1982) and *Sample Registration System: Fertility and Mortality Indicators 1991* (New Delhi: Ministry of Home Affairs, 1993).

the basis of the Chinese experience, the only systematic and sustained attempt to impose such a policy that has so far been made.

Family Planning

Even those who do not advocate legal or economic coercion sometimes suggest a variant of the "override" approach — the view, which has been getting increasing support, that the highest priority should be given simply to family planning, even if this means diverting resources from education and health care as well as other activities associated with development. We often hear claims that enormous declines in birth rates have been accomplished through making family planning services available, without waiting for improvements in education and health care.

The experience of Bangladesh is sometimes cited as an example of such success. Indeed, even though the female literacy rate in Bangladesh is only around 22 percent and life expectancy at birth no higher than 55 years, fertility rates have been substantially reduced there through the greater availability of family planning services, including counseling.[36] We have to examine carefully what lessons can, in fact, be drawn from this evidence.

First, it is certainly significant that Bangladesh has been able to cut its fertility rate from 7.0 to 4.5 during the short period between 1975 and 1990, an achievement that discredits the view that people will not voluntarily embrace family planning in the poorest countries. But we have to ask further whether family planning efforts may themselves be sufficient to make fertility come down to really low levels, without providing for female education and the other features of a fuller collaborative approach. The fertility rate of 4.5 in Bangladesh is still quite high — considerably higher than even India's average rate of 3.6. To begin stabilizing the population, the fertility rates would have to come down closer to the "replacement level" of 2.0, as has happened in Kerala and Tamil Nadu, and in many other places outside the Indian subcontinent. Female education and the other social developments connected with lowering the birth rate would still be much needed.

Contrasts between the records of Indian states offer some substantial lessons here. While Kerala, and to a smaller extent Tamil Nadu, have surged ahead in achieving radically reduced fertility rates, other states in India in the so-called "northern heartland" (such as Uttar Pradesh, Bihar, Madhya Pradesh, and Rajasthan), have very low levels of education, especially female education, and of general health care (often combined with pressure on the poor to accept birth control measures, including sterilization, as a qualifying condition for medical attention and other public services). These states all have high fertility rates — between 4.4 and 5.1. The regional contrasts within India strongly argue for the collaborative approach, including active and educated participation of women.

The threat of an impending population crisis tempts many international observers to suggest that priority be given to family planning arrangements in the third world countries over other commitments such as education and health care, a redirection of public efforts that is often recommended by policy-makers and at international conferences. Not only will this shift have negative effects on people's well-being and reduce their freedoms, it can also be self-defeating if the goal is to stabilize population.

The appeal of such slogans as "family planning first" rests partly on misconceptions about what is needed to reduce fertility rates, but also on mistaken beliefs about the excessive costs of social development, including education and health care. As has been discussed, both these activities are highly labor-intensive, and thus relatively inexpensive even in very poor economies. In fact, Kerala, India's star performer in expanding education and reducing both death rates and birth rates, is among the poorer Indian states. Its domestically produced income is quite low — lower indeed in per capita terms than even the Indian average — even if this is somewhat deceptive, for the greatest expansion of Kerala's earnings derives from citizens who work outside the state. Kerala's ability to finance adequately both educational expansion and health coverage depends on both activities being labor-intensive; they can be made available even in a low-income economy when there is the political will to use them. Despite its economic backwardness, an issue which Kerala will undoubtedly have to address before long (perhaps by reducing bureaucratic controls over agriculture and industry, which have stagnated), its level of social development has been remarkable, and that has turned out to be crucial in reducing fertility rates. Kerala's fertility rate of 1.8 not only compares well with China's 2.0, but also with the US's and Sweden's 2.1, Canada's 1.9, and Britain's and France's 1.8.

The population problem is serious, certainly, but neither because of "the proportion between the natural increase in population and food" nor because of some impending apocalypse. There are reasons for worry about the long-term effects of population growth on the environment; and there are strong reasons for concern about the adverse effects of high birth rates on the quality of life, especially of women. With greater opportunities for education (especially female education), reduction of mortality rates (especially of children), improvement in economic security (especially in old age), and greater participation of women in employment and in political action, fast reductions in birth rates can be expected to result through the decisions and actions of those whose lives depend on them.

This is happening right now in many parts of the world, and the result has been a considerable slowing down of world population growth. The best way of dealing with the population problem is to help to spread these processes elsewhere. In contrast, the emergency mentality based on false beliefs in imminent cataclysms leads to breathless responses that are deeply counterproductive, preventing the development of rational and sustainable family planning. Coercive polices of forced birth control involve terrible social sacrifices, and there is little evidence that they are more effective in reducing birth rates than serious programs of collaborative action.

NOTES

1. This chapter draws on a lecture by Amartya Sen arranged by the "Eminent Citizens Committee for Cairo '94" at the United Nations in New York on April 18, 1994, and also on research supported by the National Science Foundation.

2. Paul Ehrlich, *The Population Bomb* (Ballantine, 1968). More recently Paul Ehrlich and Anne H. Ehrlich have written *The Population Explosion* (Simon and Schuster, 1990).

3. Garrett Hardin, *Living within Limits* (Oxford University Press, 1993).

4. Thomas Robert Malthus, *Essay on the Principle of Population As It Affects the Future Improvement of Society with Remarks on the Speculation of Mr. Godwin, M. Condorcet, and Other Writers* (London: J. Johnson, 1798), chapter 8; in the Penguin classics edition, *An Essay on the Principle of Population* (1982), p. 123.

5. See Simon Kuznets, *Modern Economic Growth* (Yale University Press, 1966).

6. Note by the Secretary-General of the United Nations to the Preparatory Committee for the International Conference on Population and Development, Third Session, A/Conf.171/PC/5, February 18, 1994, p. 30.

7. Philip Morris Hauser's estimates are presented in the National Academy of Sciences publication *Rapid Population Growth: Consequences and Policy Implications*, Vol. 1 (Johns Hopkins University Press, 1971). See also Simon Kuznets, *Modern Economic Growth*, chapter 2.

8. For an important collection of papers on these and related issues, see Sir Francis Graham-Smith, F.R.S., ed., *Population — The Complex Reality: A Report of the Population Summit of the World's Scientific Academies*, issued by the Royal Society and published in the US by North American Press, Golden, Colorado. See also D. Gale Johnson and Ronald D. Lee, eds., *Population Growth and Economic Development, Issues and Evidence* (University of Wisconsin Press, 1987).

9. Garrett Hardin, *Living within Limits*, 274.

10. Paul Kennedy, who has discussed important problems in the distinctly "social" aspects of population growth, has pointed out that this debate "has, in one form or another, been with us since then," and "it is even more pertinent today than when Malthus composed his Essay," in *Preparing for the Twenty-First Century* (Random House, 1993), pp. 5–6.

11. On the importance of "enlightenment" traditions in Condorcet's thinking, see Emma Rothschild, "Condorcet and the Conflict of Values," forthcoming in *The Historical Journal*.

12. Marie Jean Antoine Nicholas de Caritat Marquis de Condorcet's *Esquisse d'un Tableau Historique des Progrès de l'Esprit Humain*, Xe Epoque (1795). English translation by June Barraclough, *Sketch for a Historical Picture of the Progress of the Human Mind*, with an introduction by Stuart Hampshire (Weidenfeld and Nicolson, 1955), pp. 187–92.

13. T.R. Malthus, *A Summary View of the Principle of Population* (London: John Murray, 1830); in the Penguin classics edition (1982), p. 243; italics added.

14. On practical policies, including criticism of poverty relief and charitable hospitals, advocated for Britain by Malthus and his followers, see William St. Clair, *The Godwins and the Shelleys: A Biography of a Family* (Norton, 1989).

15. Malthus, *Essay on the Principle of Population*, chapter 17; in the Penguin classics edition, *An Essay of the Principle of Population*, pp. 198–99. Malthus showed some signs of weakening in this belief as he grew older.

16. Gerard Piel, *Only One World: Our Own to Make and to Keep* (Freeman, 1992).

17. For discussions of these empirical connections, see R.A. Easterlin, editor, *Population and Economic Chance in Developing Countries* (University of Chicago Press, 1980); T.P. Schultz, *Economics of Population* (Addison-Wesley, 1981); J.C. Caldwell, *Theory of Fertility Decline* (Academic Press, 1982); E. King and M.A. Hill, eds., *Women's Education in Developing Countries* (Johns Hopkins University Press, 1992); Nancy Birdsall, "Economic Approaches to Population Growth," in *The Handbook of Development Economics*, H.B. Chenery and T.N. Srinivasan, eds. (Amsterdam: North Holland, 1988); Robert Cassen et al., *Population and Development: Old Debates, New Conclusions* (New Brunswick: Overseas Development Council/Transaction Publisher, 1994).

18. World Bank, *World Development Report 1994* (Oxford University Press, 1994), Table 25, pp. 210–11.

19. World Bank, *World Development Report 1994*, Table 2.

20. These issues are discussed in Amartya Sen and Jean Drèze, *Hunger and Public Action* (Oxford University Press, 1989), and the three volumes edited by them, *The Political Economy of Hunger* (Oxford University Press, 1990), and also in Amartya Sen, "Economic Regress: Concepts and Features," in *Proceedings of the World Bank Annual Conference on Development Economics 1993* (World Bank, 1994).

21. This is confirmed by, among other statistics, the food production figures regularly presented by the United Nations Food and Agricultural Organization (see the *FAO Quarterly Bulletin of Statistics, and also the FAO Monthly Bulletins*).

22. For a more detailed picture and references to data sources, see Amartya Sen, "Population and Reasoned Agency: Food, Fertility and Economic Development," in *Population, Economic Development, and the Environment*, Kerstin Lindahl-Kiessling and Hans Landberg, eds. (Oxford University Press, 1994); see also the other contributions in this volume. The data presented here have been slightly updated from later publications of the FAO.

23. On this see Amartya Sen, *Poverty and Famines* (Oxford University Press, 1981).

24. See UNCTAD VIII, Analytical Report by the UNCTAD Secretariat to the Conference (United Nations, 1992), Table V-S, p. 235. The period covered is between 1979–1981 and 1988–1990. These figures and related ones are discussed in greater detail in Amartya Sen, "Population and Reasoned Agency."

25. World Bank, *Price Prospects for Major Primary Commodities*, Vol. II (World Bank, March 1993), Annex Tables 6, 12, and 18.

26. Condorcet, *Esquisse d'un Tableau Historique des Progrès de l'Esprit Humain*; in the 1968 reprint, p. 187.

27. The importance of "local" environmental issues is stressed and particularly explored by Partha Dasgupta in *An Inquiry into Well-Being and Destitution* (Oxford University Press, 1993).

28. In a forthcoming monograph by Jean Drèze and Amartya Sen tentatively called "Indian: Economic Development and Social Opportunities," they discuss the importance of women's political agency in rectifying some of the more serious lapses in Indian economic and social performance — not just pertaining to the deprivation of women themselves.

29. See Jean Drèze and Amartya Sen, *Hunger and Public Action* (Oxford University Press, 1989), which also investigates the remarkable success of some poor countries in providing widespread educational and health services.

30. World Bank, *World Development Report 1994, p. 212; and Sample Registration System: Fertility and Mortality*

Indicators 1991 (New Delhi: Ministry of Home Affairs, 1993).

31. See the discussions, and the literature cited, in Gita Sen, Adrienne German, and Lincoln Chen, eds., *Population Policies Reconsidered: Health, Empowerment, and Rights* (Harvard Center for Population and Development Studies/International Women's Health Coalition, 1994).

32. On the actual processes involved, see T.N. Krishnan, "Demographic Transition in Kerala: Facts and Factors," in *Economic and Political Weekly*, Vol. 11 (1976), and P.N. Mari Bhat and S.I. Rajan, "Demographic Transition in Kerala Revisited," in *Economic and Political Weekly*, Vol. 25 (1990).

33. See, for example, Robin Jeffrey, "Culture and Governments: How Women Made Kerala Literate," in *Pacific Affairs*, Vol. 60 (1987).

34. On this see Amartya Sen, "More Than 100 Million Women Are Missing," *New York Review of Books*, December 20, 1990; Ansley J. Coale, "Excess Female Mortality and the Balance of the Sexes: An Estimate of the Number of 'Missing Females,'" *Population and Development Review*, No. 17 (1991); Amartya Sen, "Missing Women," *British Medical Journal*, No. 304 (March 1992); Stephan Klasen, "Missing Women Reconsidered," *World Development*, forthcoming.

35. Tamil Nadu has benefited from an active and efficient voluntary program of family planning, but these efforts have been helped by favorable social conditions as well, such as a high literacy rate (the second highest among the sixteen major states), a high rate of female participation in work outside the home (the third highest), a relatively low infant mortality rate (the third lowest), and a traditionally higher age of marriage. See also T.V. Antony, "The Family Planning Programme — Lessons from Tamil Nadu's Experience," *Indian Journal of Social Science*, Vol. 5 (1992).

36. World Bank and Population Reference Bureau, *Success in a Challenging Environment: Fertility Decline in Bangladesh* (World Bank, 1993).

Chapter 32

WINNERS AND LOSERS IN THE 21ST CENTURY

PAUL KENNEDY

1.

Everyone with an interest in international affairs must be aware that broad, global forces for change are bearing down upon humankind in both rich and poor societies alike. New technologies are challenging traditional assumptions about the way we make, trade, and even grow things. Automated workplaces in Japan intimate the end of the "factory system" that first arose in Britain's Industrial Revolution and spread around the world. Genetically engineered crops, cultivated in biotech laboratories, threaten to replace naturally grown sugar, vanilla, coconut oil, and other staple farm produce, and perhaps undermine field-based agriculture as we know it. An electronically driven, twenty-four-hour-a-day financial trading system has created a global market in, say, yen futures over which nobody really has control. The globalization of industry and services permits multinationals to switch production from one country to another (where it is usually cheaper), benefitting the latter and hurting the former.

In addition to facing these technology-driven forces for change, human society is grappling with the effects of fast-growing demographic imbalances throughout the world. Whereas birth-rates in richer societies plunge well below the rates that would replace their populations, poorer countries are experiencing a population explosion that may double or even treble their numbers over the next few decades. As these fast-swelling populations press upon the surrounding forests, grazing lands, and water supplies, they inflict dreadful damage upon local environments and may also be contributing to that process of global warming first created by the industrialization of the North a century and a half ago. With overpopulation and resource depletion undermining the social order, and with a global telecommunications revolution bringing television programs like *Dallas* and *Brideshead Revisited* to viewers everywhere from Central America to the Balkans, a vast illegal migration is under way as millions of families from the developing world strive to enter Europe and North America.

Although very different in form, these various trends from global warming to twenty-four-hour-a-day trading are *transnational* in character, crossing borders all over our planet, affecting local communities and distant societies at the same time, and reminding us that the earth, for all its divisions, is a single unit. Every country is challenged by these global forces for change, to a greater or lesser extent, and most are beginning to sense the need to prepare themselves for the coming twenty-first century. Whether *any* society is at present "well prepared" for the future is an open question;[1] but what is clear is that the regions of the globe most affected by the twin impacts of technology and demography lie in the developing world. Whether they succeed in harnessing the new technologies in an environmentally prudent fashion, and at the same time go through a demographic transition, will probably affect the prospects of global peace in the next century more than any other factor. What, then, are their chances?

Source: "Preparing for the 21st Century: Winners and Losers," *The New York Review of Books* 40, 4 (11 February 1993): 32–44. Copyright © 1993 Nyrev, Inc. Reprinted with permission from *The New York Review of Books*.

Before that question can be answered, the sharp contrasts among the developing countries in the world's different regions need to be noted here.[2] Perhaps nothing better illustrates those differences than the fact that, in the 1960s, South Korea had a per capita GNP exactly the same as Ghana's (US $230), whereas today it is ten to twelve times more prosperous.[3] Both possessed a predominantly agrarian economy and had endured a half-century or more of colonial rule. Upon independence, each faced innumerable handicaps in their effort to "catch up" with the West, and although Korea possessed a greater historical and cultural coherence, its chances may have seemed less promising, since it had few natural resources (apart from tungsten) and suffered heavily during the 1950–1953 fighting.

Decades later, however, West African states remain among the most poverty-stricken countries in the world — the per capita gross national products of Niger, Sierra Leone, and Chad today, for example, are less than $500[4] — while Korea is entering the ranks of the high-income economies. Already the world's thirteenth largest trading nation, Korea is planning to become one of the richest countries of all in the twenty-first century,[5] whereas the nations of West Africa face a future, at least in the near term, of chronic poverty, malnutrition, poor health, and underdevelopment. Finally, while Korea's rising prosperity is attended by a decrease in population growth, most African countries still face a demographic explosion that erodes any gains in national output.

This divergence is not new, for there have always been richer and poorer societies; the prosperity gap in the seventeenth century — between, say, Amsterdam and the west coast of Ireland, or between such bustling Indian ports as Surat and Calcutta[6] and the inhabitants of New Guinean hill villages — must have been marked, although it probably did not equal the gulf between rich and poor nations today. The difference is that the twentieth-century global communications revolution has made such disparities widely known. This can breed resentments by poorer peoples against prosperous societies, but it can also provide a desire to emulate (as Korea emulated Japan). The key issue here is: What does it take to turn a "have not" into a "have" nation? Does it simply require imitating economic techniques, or does it involve such intangibles as culture, social structure, and attitudes toward foreign practices?

This discrepancy in performance between East Asia and sub-Saharan Africa clearly makes the term "third world" misleading. However useful the expression might have been in the 1950s, when poor, non-aligned, and recently decolonized states were attempting to remain independent of the two superpower blocs,[7] the rise of super-rich oil-producing countries a decade later already made the term questionable. Now that prosperous East Asian societies — Korea, Taiwan, and Singapore — possess higher per capita GNPs than Russia, Eastern Europe, and even West European states like Portugal, the word seems less suitable than ever. With Taiwanese or Korean corporations establishing assembly plants in the Philippines, or creating distribution networks within the European Community, we need to recognize the differences that exist among non-Western economies. Some scholars now categorize *five* separate types of "developing" countries in assessing the varied potential of societies in Asia, Africa, and Latin America.[8]

Relative national growth in the 1980s confirms these differences. Whereas East Asian economies grew on average at an impressive annual rate of 7.4 percent, those in Africa and Latin America gained only 1.8 and 1.7 percent respectively[9] — and since their populations grew faster, the net result was that they slipped backward, absolutely and relatively. Differences of economic structure also grew in this decade, with African and other primary commodity-producing countries eager for higher raw-material prices, whereas the

Figure 32.1 Shares of World Trade in Manufactures

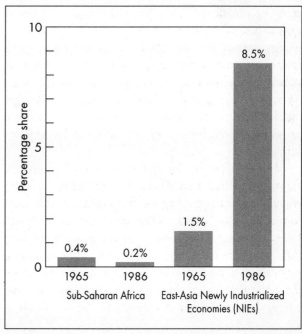

Source: S. Fardoust and A. Dhareshwan, *Long-Term Outlook for the World Economy: Issues and Projections for the 1990s,* World Bank Policy and Research Report, No. 12 (February 1990), p. 9, Table 3.

export-oriented manufacturing nations of East Asia sought to keep commodity prices low. The most dramatic difference occurred in the shares of world trade in manufactures, a key indicator of economic competitiveness. Thus, while some scholars still refer to a dual world economy[10] of rich and poor countries, what is emerging is increasing differentiation. Why is this so?

The developing countries most successfully catching up with the West are the trading states of the Pacific and East Asia. Except for Communist regimes there, the Pacific rim countries (including the western provinces of Canada and the United States, and in part Australia) have enjoyed a lengthy boom in manufacturing, trade, and investment; but the center of that boom is on the *Asian* side of the Pacific, chiefly fuelled by Japan's own spectacular growth and the stimulus given to neighboring economies and trans-Pacific trade. According to one source:

> In 1962 the Western Pacific (notably East Asia) accounted for around 9 percent of world GNP, North America for 30 percent, and Western Europe for 31 percent. Twenty years later, the Western Pacific share had climbed to more than 15 percent, while North America's had fallen to 28 percent and Europe's to 27 percent. By the year 2000 it is likely that the Western Pacific will account for around one-quarter of world GNP, with the whole Pacific region increasing its share from just over 43 percent to around half of world GNP.[11]

East Asia's present boom is not, of course, uniform, and scholars distinguish between the different stages of economic and technological development in this vast region. Roughly speaking, the divisions would be as follows:

(a) Japan, now the world's largest or second largest financial center and, increasingly, the most innovative high-tech nation in the nonmilitary field;

(b) the four East Asian "tigers" or "dragons," the Newly Industrialized Economies (NIEs) of Singapore, Hong Kong, Taiwan, and South Korea, of which the latter two possess bigger populations and territories than the two port-city states, but all of which have enjoyed export-led growth in recent decades;

(c) the larger Southeast Asian states of Thailand, Malaysia, and Indonesia which, stimulated by foreign (chiefly Japanese) investment, are becoming involved in manufacturing, assembly, and export — it is doubtful whether the Philippines should be included in this group;

(d) finally, the stunted and impoverished Communist societies of Vietnam, Cambodia, and North Korea, as well as isolationist Myanmar pursuing its "Burmese Way to Socialism."

Because of this staggered level of development, economists in East Asia invoke the image of the "flying geese," with Japan the lead bird, followed by the East Asian NIEs, the larger Southeast Asian states, and so on. What Japan produced in one decade — relatively low-priced toys, kitchenware, electrical goods — will be imitated by the next wave of "geese" in the decade following, and by the third wave in the decade after that. However accurate the metaphor individually, the overall picture is clear; these birds are flying, purposefully and onward, to an attractive destination.

Of those states, it is the East Asian NIEs that have provided the clearest example of successful transformation. Although distant observers may regard them as similar, there are notable differences in size, population,[12] history, and political system. Even the economic structures are distinct; for example, Korea, which began its expansion at least a decade later than Taiwan (and democratized itself even more slowly), is heavily dependent upon a few enormous industrial conglomerates, or *chaebol*, of whom the top four alone (Samsung, Hyundai, Lucky-Goldstar, and Daewoo) have sales equal to half Korea's GNP. By contrast, Taiwan possesses many small companies, specializing in one or two kinds of products. While Taiwanese are concerned that their firms may lose out to foreign giants, Koreans worry that the *chaebol* will find it increasingly difficult to compete in large-scale industries like petrochemicals and semiconductors and shipbuilding at the same time.[13]

Despite such structural differences, these societies each contain certain basic characteristics, which, *taken together*, help to explain their decade-upon-decade growth. The first, and perhaps the most important, is the emphasis upon education. This derives from Confucian traditions of competitive examinations and respect for learning, reinforced daily by the mother of the family who complements what is taught at school.

To Western eyes, this process — like Japan's — appears to concentrate on rote learning and the acquisition of technical skills, and emphasizes consensus instead of encouraging individual talent and the habit of questioning authority. Even if some East Asian educators would nowadays admit that criticism, most believe that their own educational mores create social harmony and a well-trained work force. Moreover, the uniformity of the system does not exclude intense individual competitiveness; in Taiwan (where, incidentally, twelve members of the fourteen-member cabinet of 1989 had acquired Ph.D.s abroad), only the top one third of each year's 110,000 students taking the national university entrance examinations are selected, to emphasize the importance of college education.[14]

Perhaps nothing better illustrates this stress upon learning than the fact that Korea (43 million population) has around 1.4 million students in higher education, compared with 145,000 in Iran (54 million), 15,000 in Ethiopia (46 million), and 159,000 in Vietnam (64 million); or the further fact that already by 1980 "as many engineering students were graduating from Korean institutions as in the United Kingdom, West Germany and Sweden combined."[15]

The second common characteristic of these countries is their high level of national savings. By employing fiscal measures, taxes, and import controls to encourage personal savings, large amounts of low-interest capital were made available for investment in manufacture and commerce. During the first few decades of growth, personal consumption was constrained and living standards controlled — by restrictions upon moving capital abroad, or importing foreign luxury goods — in order to funnel resources into industrial growth. While average prosperity rose, most of the fruits of economic success were plowed back into further expansion. Only when economic "take-off" was well under way has the system begun to alter; increased consumption, foreign purchases, capital investment in new homes, all allow internal demand to play a larger role in the country's growth. In such circumstances, one would expect to see overall savings ratios decline. Even in the late 1980s, however, the East Asians NIEs still had high national savings rates.

Table 32.1 Comparative Savings Ratios, 1987

Taiwan	38.8%
Malaysia	37.8%
Korea	37.0%
Japan	32.3%
Indonesia	29.1%
US	12.7%

Source: Lest this 1987 figure appear too distant, note that Korea's sixth Five-Year Plan calls for a national savings rate of 33.5 percent in the early 1990s: see *Trends in Developing Economies*, p. 300. This table is taken from T. Fukuchi and M. Kagami, editors, *Perspectives on the Pacific Basin Economy: A Comparison of Asia and Latin America* (Tokyo: Asian Club Foundation, Institute of Developing Economics, 1990), p. 31, Table 10.

The third feature has been a strong political system within which economic growth is fostered. While entrepreneurship and private property are encouraged, the "tigers" never followed a laissez-faire model. Industries targeted for growth were given a variety of supports — export subsidies, training grants, tariff protection from foreign competitors. As noted above, the fiscal system was arranged to produce high savings ratios. Taxes assisted the business sector, as did energy policy. Trade unions operated under restrictions. Democracy was constrained by the governor of Hong Kong, *dirigiste* administrations in Singapore, and the military regimes in Taiwan and Korea. Only lately have free elections and party politics been permitted. Defenders of this system argued that it was necessary to restrain libertarian impulses while concentrating on economic growth, and that democratic reforms are a "reward" for the people's patience. The point is that domestic politics were unlike those in the West yet did not hurt commercial expansion.

The fourth feature was the commitment to exports, in contrast to the policies of India, which emphasize locally produced substitutes for imports, and the consumer-driven policies of the United States. This was traditional for a small, bustling trading state like Hong Kong, but it involved substantial restructuring in Taiwan and Korea, where managers and workers had to be trained to produce what foreign customers wanted. In all cases, the value of the currency was kept low, to increase exports and decrease imports. Moreover, the newly industrialized economies of East Asia took advantage of favorable global circumstances: labor costs were much lower than in North America and Europe, and they benefitted from an open international trading order, created and protected by the United States, while shielding their own industries from foreign competition.

Eventually, this led to large trade surpluses and threats of retaliation from European and American governments, reminding us of the NIEs' heavy dependence upon the current international economic system. The important thing, however, is that they targeted export-led growth in manufactures, whereas other developing nations continued to rely upon commodity exports and made little effort to cater to foreign consumers' tastes.[16] Given this emphasis on trade, it is not surprising to learn that Asia now contains seven of the world's twelve largest ports.

Finally, the East Asian NIEs possess a local model, namely Japan, which Yemen, Guatemala, and Burkina Faso simply do not have. For four decades East Asian peoples have observed the dramatic success of a non-

Western neighbor, based upon its educational and technical skills, high savings ratios, long-term, state-guided targeting of industries and markets, and determination to compete on world markets, though this admiration of Japan is nowadays mixed with a certain alarm at becoming members of a yen block dominated by Tokyo. While the Japanese domestic market is extremely important for the East Asian NIEs, and they benefit from Japanese investments, assembly plants, engineers, and expertise, they have little enthusiasm for a new Greater East Asia co-prosperity sphere.[17]

The benefits of economic success are seen not merely in East Asia's steadily rising standards of living. Its children are on average four or five inches taller than they were in the 1940s, and grow up in some of the world's healthiest countries:

> *A Taiwanese child born in 1988 could expect to live 74 years, only a year less than an American or a West German, and 15 years longer than a Taiwanese born in 1952; a South Korean born in 1988 could expect 70 years on earth, up from 58 in 1965. In 1988 the Taiwanese took in 50 percent more calories each day than they had done 35 years earlier. They had 200 times as many televisions, telephones and cars per household; in Korea the rise in the possession of these goods was even higher.[18]*

In addition, the East Asian NIEs enjoy some of today's highest literacy rates, once again confirming that they are altogether closer to "first" world nations than poor, developing countries.

Will this progress last into the twenty-first century? Politically, Hong Kong's future is completely uncertain, and many companies are relocating their headquarters elsewhere; Taiwan remains a diplomatic pariah-state because of Beijing's traditional claims; and South Korea still worries about the unpredictable, militarized regime in the north. The future of China — and of Siberia — is uncertain, and causes concern. The 1980s rise in Asian stock-market prices (driven by vast increases in the money supply) was excessive and speculative, and destined to tumble. Protectionist tendencies in the developed world threaten the trading states even more than external pressures to abandon price supports for local farmers. A rise in the value of the Korean and Taiwanese currencies has cut export earnings and reduced their overall rate of growth. Some Japanese competitors have moved production to neighboring low-cost countries such as Thailand or southern China. Sharp rises in oil prices increase the import bills. High wage awards (in Korea they increased by an average 14 percent in 1988, and by 17 percent in 1989) affect labor costs and competitiveness. The social peace, precarious in these recent democracies, is damaged by bouts of student and industrial unrest.[19]

On the other hand, these may simply be growing pains. Savings ratios are still extremely high. Large numbers of new engineers and technicians pour out of college each year. The workers' enhanced purchasing power has created a booming domestic market, and governments are investing more in housing, infrastructure, and public facilities. The labor force will not grow as swiftly as before because of the demographic slowdown, but it will be better educated and spend more.[20] A surge in overseas investments is assisting the long-term balance of payments. As the populous markets of Indonesia, Thailand, and Malaysia grow at double-digit rates, there is plenty of work for the trading states. A hardening of the currency can be met by greater commitment to quality exports, high rates of

Table 32.2 Comparative Living Standards

	Life Expectancy at Birth (years), 1987	Adult Literacy Rate (%), 1985	GNP per capita, 1988 US$
Niger	45	14	300
Togo	54	41	310
India	59	43	340
Singapore	73	86	9,070
South Korea	70	95	5,000
Spain	77	95	7,740
New Zealand	75	99	10,000

Source: For the first two columns, "Development Brief," *The Economist*, May 26, 1990, p. 81. © 1990 The Economist Newspaper Group, Inc. Reprinted with permission. Further reproduction prohibited; the GNP per capita comes from *World Development Report* (Oxford University Press, 1990), pp. 178–79.

industrial investment, and a move into newer, high-technology manufacture — in imitation of the 1980s re-tooling of Japanese industry when its currency hardened swiftly. Nowhere else in the world would growth rates of "only" 5 or 6 percent be considered worrying, or a harbinger of decline. Barring a war in East Asia, or a widespread global slump, the signs are that the four "tigers" are better structured than most to grow in wealth and health.

2.

For confirmation of that remark, one need only consider the present difficult condition of Latin America, which lost ground in the 1980s just as East Asia was gaining it. Here again, distinctions have to be made between various countries within the continent, with its more than 400 million people in an area almost 7 million square miles stretching from the Rio Grande to Antarctica, and with a range of political cultures and socioeconomic structures. Argentina, which around 1900 had a standard of living suggesting that it was a "developed" economy, is very different from Honduras and Guyana. Similarly, population change in Latin America occurs in three distinct forms: such nations as Bolivia, the Dominican Republic, and Haiti have high fertility rates and lower life expectancies; a middle group — Brazil, Colombia, Mexico, Venezuela, Costa Rica, and Panama — is beginning to experience declines in fertility and longer life expectancy; and the temperate-zone countries of Argentina, Chile, and Uruguay have the demographic characteristics of developed countries.[21]

Despite this diversity, there are reasons for considering Latin America's prospects as a whole: the economic challenges confronting the region are similar, as are its domestic politics — in particular, the fragility of its recently emerged democracies; and each is affected by its relationship with the developed world, especially the United States.

Several decades ago, Latin America's future appeared encouraging. Sharing in the post-1950 global boom, benefitting from demand for its coffee, timber, beef, oil, and minerals, and enjoying foreign investments in its agriculture, industry, and infrastructure, the region was moving upward. In the thirty years after 1945, its production of steel multiplied twenty times, and its output of electric energy, metals, and machinery grew more than tenfold.[22] Real gross domestic product (GDP) per person rose at an annual average of 2.8 percent during the 1960s and spurted to an annual average increase of 3.4 percent in the 1970s. Unfortu-

nately, the growth then reversed itself, and between 1980 and 1988 Latin America's real GDP per person steadily fell by an annual average of 0.9 percent.[23] In some states, such as Peru and Argentina, real income dropped by as much as one quarter during the 1980s. With very few exceptions (Chile, Colombia, the Dominican Republic, Barbados, the Bahamas), most Latin American countries now have per capita GDPs lower than they were a decade earlier, or even two decades earlier (see Table 32.3).

The reasons for this reversal offer a striking contrast to the East Asian NIEs. Instead of encouraging industrialists to target foreign markets and stimulate the economy through export-led growth, many Latin American governments pursued a policy of import substitution, creating their own steel, cement, paper, automobiles, and electronic-goods industries, which were given protective tariffs, government subsidies, and tax-breaks to insulate them from international competition. As a result, their products became less attractive abroad.[24] Moreover, while it was relatively easy to create a basic iron and steel industry, it proved harder to establish high-tech industries like computers, aerospace, machine-tools, and pharmaceuticals — most of these states therefore still depend on imported manufactured goods, whereas exports chiefly consist of raw materials like oil, coffee, and soybeans.[25]

Secondly, economic growth was accompanied by lax financial policies and an increasing reliance upon foreign borrowings. Governments poured money not only into infrastructure and schools but also into state-owned enterprises, large bureaucracies, and oversized armed forces, paying for them by printing money and raising loans from Western (chiefly US) banks and international agencies. The result was that public spending's share of GDP soared, price inflation accelerated, and was further increased by index-linked rises in salaries and wages. Inflation became so large that it was difficult to comprehend, let alone to combat. According to the 1990 *World Resources* report, "in 1989, for example, annual inflation in Nicaragua was more than 3,400 percent; in Argentina inflation reached 3,700 percent, in Brazil almost 1,500 percent, and in Peru nearly 3,000 percent. Ecuador, with only 60 percent inflation, did comparatively well."[26] In such circumstances the currency becomes worthless, as does the idea of seeking to raise national savings rates for long-term capital investment.

Another result is that some Latin American countries find themselves among the most indebted in the world, as Table 32.4 shows. Total Latin American indebtedness now equals about $1,000 for every man,

Table 32.3 Per Capita GDP of Latin American Countries (1988 US Dollars)

Country	1960	1970	1980	1988
Chile	1,845	2,236	2,448	2,518
Argentina	2,384	3,075	3,359	2,862
Uruguay	2,352	2,478	3,221	2,989
Brazil	1,013	1,372	2,481	2,449
Paraguay	779	931	1,612	1,557
Bolivia	634	818	983	724
Peru	1,233	1,554	1,716	1,503
Ecuador	771	904	1,581	1,477
Colombia	927	1,157	1,595	1,739
Venezuela	3,879	4,941	5,225	4,544
Guyana	1,008	1,111	1,215	995
Suriname	887	2,337	3,722	3,420
Mexico	1,425	2,022	2,872	2,588
Guatemala	1,100	1,420	1,866	1,502
Honduras	619	782	954	851
El Salvador	832	1,032	1,125	995
Nicaragua	1,055	1,495	1,147	819
Costa Rica	1,435	1,825	2,394	2,235
Panama	1,264	2,017	2,622	2,229
Dominican Republic	823	987	1,497	1,509
Haiti	331	292	386	319
Jamaica	1,610	2,364	1,880	1,843
Trinidad & Tobago	3,848	4,927	8,116	5,510
Barbados	2,000	3,530	3,994	4,233
Bahamas	8,448	10,737	10,631	11,317

Source: Taken from G.W. Landau et al., *Latin America at a Crossroads* (The Trilateral Commission, 1990), p. 5, which reports the source as being *Economic and Social Progress in Latin America: 1989 Report* (Washington, DC: Inter-American Development Bank, 1989), Table B1, p. 463.

woman, and child. But instead of being directed into productive investment, that money has been wasted domestically or disappeared as "capital flight" to private accounts in US and European banks. This has left most countries incapable of repaying even the interest on their loans. Defaults on loans (or suspension of interest payments) then produced a drying up of capital from indignant Western banks and a net capital *outflow* from Latin America just when it needed capital to aid economic growth.[27] Starved of foreign funds and with currencies made worthless by hyperinflation, many countries are in a far worse position than could

Table 32.4 Growth of Latin American Indebtedness (Selected Countries)

Country	Total External Debt (billion US $)			Long-Term Public Debt as a Percentage of GNP		
	1977	1982	1987	1977	1982	1987
Argentina	8.1	32.4	53.9	10	31	62
Brazil	28.3	68.7	109.4	13	20	29
Chile	4.9	8.5	18.7	28	23	89
Guyana	0.4	0.9	1.2	100	158	353
Honduras	0.6	1.6	3.1	29	53	71
Jamaica	1.1	2.7	4.3	31	69	139
Mexico	26.6	78.0	93.7	25	32	59
Venezuela	9.8	27.0	29.0	10	16	52

Source: World Resources 1990–91, p. 246. Copyright © by the World Resources Institute. Reprinted by permission of Oxford University Press, Inc.

have been imagined twenty-five years ago.[28] For a while, it was even feared that the region's financial problems might undermine parts of the international banking system. It now appears that the chief damage will be in the continent itself, where 180 million people (40 percent) are living in poverty — a rise of 50 million alone in the 1980s.

Given such profligacy, and the conservative, "anti-big government" incumbents in the White House during the 1980s, it was predictable that Latin America would come under pressure — from the World Bank, the IMF, private bankers, Washington itself — to slash public spending, control inflation, and repay debts. Such demands were easier said than done in the existing circumstances. Islands of democracy (e.g., Costa Rica) did exist, but many states were ruled by right-wing military dictatorships or social revolutionaries; internal guerrilla wars, military *coups d'état,* labor unrest were common. Even as democracy began to reassert itself in the 1980s, the new leaders found themselves in a near-impossible situation: inheritors of the high external debts contracted by the outgoing regimes, legatees in many cases of inflationary index-linked wage systems, targets of landowner resentment and/or of guerrilla attacks, frustrated by elaborate and often corrupt bureaucracies, and deficient in trained personnel. While grappling with these weaknesses, they discovered that the Western world, which applauded the return to democracy, was unsympathetic to fresh lending, increasingly inclined to protectionism, and demanding unilateral measures (e.g., in the Amazon rain forests) to stop global warming.

Two other weaknesses have also slowed any hoped-for recovery. One is the unimpressive accomplishments of the educational systems. This is not due to an absence of schools and universities, as in parts of Africa. Many Latin American countries have extensive public education, dozens of universities, and high adult literacy rates; Brazil, for example, has sixty-eight universities, Argentina forty-one.[29] The real problem is neglect and under-investment. One citizen bemoaned the collapse in Argentina as follows:

Education, which kept illiteracy at bay for more than a century, lies in ruins. The universities are unheated and many public schools lack panes for their window frames. Last summer [1990] an elementary school teacher with ten years' experience earned less than $110 a month. An associate professor at the Universidad de Buenos Aires, teaching ten hours a week, was paid $37 a month. A doctor's salary at a municipal hospital
was $120 a month.... At times, teachers took turns teaching, or cut their class hours, because they and their students could not afford transportation.[30]

Presumably, if resources were available, those decaying educational and health-care structures could be resuscitated, helping national recovery; but where the capital can be raised in present circumstances is difficult to see. Moreover, in the strife-torn countries of Central America there is little education to begin with; in Guatemala, the latest census estimated that 63 percent of those ten years of age and older were illiterate, while in Honduras the illiteracy rate was 40 percent.[31] Unfortunately, it is in the educationally most deprived Latin American countries that resources are being eroded by swift population increases.

Despite these disadvantages, recent reports on Latin America have suggested that the "lost decade" of the 1980s will be followed by a period of recovery. The coming of democratic regimes, the compromises emerging from protracted debt-recycling talks, the stiff economic reforms (cutting public spending, abandoning indexation) to reduce inflation rates, the replacement of "state protectionism with import liberalization and privatization,"[32] the conversion of budget deficits into surpluses — all this has caused the Inter-American Development Bank to argue that "a decisive and genuine takeoff" is at hand, provided the new policies are sustained.[33] Growth has resumed in Argentina, Mexico, and Venezuela. Even investment bankers are reported to be returning to the continent.

Whether these changes are going to be enough remains uncertain, especially since the newly elected governments face widespread resentment at the proposed reforms. As one commentator put it, "Much of Latin America is entering the 1990s in a race between economic deterioration and political progress."[34] Whereas Spain, Portugal, and Greece moved to democracy while enjoying reasonable prosperity, Latin America (like Eastern Europe) has to make that change as its economies flounder — which places immense responsibilities upon the political leadership.

Although it can be argued that the region's future is in its own hands, it will also be heavily influenced by the United States. In many ways, the US–Latin America leadership is similar to that between Japan and the East Asian NIEs, which are heavily dependent upon Japan as their major market and source of capital.[35] Yet there is more to this relationship than Latin America's economic dependence upon the United States, whose banking system has also suffered because of Latin

American indebtedness. United States exports, which are fifty times larger to this region than to Eastern Europe, were badly hurt by Latin America's economic difficulties, and they would benefit greatly from a resumption of growth. The United States' own environment may now be threatened by the diminution of the Amazon and Central American rain forests. Its awful drug problem, driven by domestic demand, is fuelled by Latin American supplies — more than 80 percent of the cocaine and 90 percent of the marijuana entering the United States are produced or move through this region.

Finally, the population of the United States is being altered by migration from Mexico, the Caribbean, and Central America; if there should be a widespread socioeconomic collapse south of the Rio Grande, the "spillover" effects will be felt across the United States. Instead of being marginalized by the end of the cold war, Latin America may present Washington with formidable and growing challenges — social, environmental, financial, and ultimately political.[36] Thus, while the region's own politicians and citizens have to bear the major responsibility for recovery, richer nations — especially the United States — may find it in their own best interest to lend a hand.

3.

If these remarks disappoint readers in Brazil or Peru, they may care to glance, in grim consolation, at the world of Islam. It is one thing to face population pressures, shortage of resources, educational/technological deficiencies, and regional conflicts, which would challenge the wisest governments. But it is another when regimes themselves stand in angry resentment of global forces for change instead of (as in East Asia) selectively responding to such trends. Far from preparing for the twenty-first century, much of the Arab and Muslim world appears to have difficulty in coming to terms with the nineteenth century, with its composite legacy of secularization, democracy, laissez-faire economics, industrial and commercial linkages among different nations, social change, and intellectual questioning. If one needed an example of the importance of cultural attitudes in explaining a society's response to change, contemporary Islam provides it.

Before analyzing the distinctive role of Islamic culture, one should first note the danger of generalizing about a region that contains such variety. After all, it is not even clear what *name* should be used to describe this part of the earth. To term it the "Middle East"[37] is, apart from its Atlantic-centered bias, to leave out such

North African states as Libya, Tunisia, Algeria, and Morocco. To term it the "Arab World"[38] is to exclude Iran (and, of course, Israel), the Kurds, and the non-Muslim tribes of southern Sudan and Mauritania. Even the nomenclature Islam, or the Muslim world, disguises the fact that millions of Catholics, Copts, and Jews live in these lands, and that Islamic societies extend from West Africa to Indonesia.[39]

In addition, the uneven location of oil in the Middle East has created a division between super-rich and dreadfully poor societies that has no equivalent in Central America or sub-Saharan Africa.[40] Countries like Kuwait (2 million), the United Arab Emirates (1.3 million), and Saudi Arabia (11.5 million) enjoy some of the world's highest incomes, but exist alongside populous neighbors one third as rich (Jordan, Iran, Iraq) or even one tenth as rich (Egypt, Yemen). The gap is accentuated by different political systems: conservative, antidemocratic, traditionalist in the Gulf sheikdoms; demagogic, populist, militarized in countries such as Libya, Syria, Iraq, and Iran.

The 1990 Iraqi attack upon Kuwait, and the different responses of the Saudi elites on the one hand and the street masses in Amman or Rabat on the other, illustrated this divide between "haves" and "have-nots" in the Muslim world. The presence of millions of Egyptian, Yemeni, Jordanian, and Palestinian *Gastarbeiter* in the oil-rich states simply increased the mutual resentments, while the Saudi and Emirate habit of giving extensive aid to Iraq during its war against Iran, or to Egypt to assist its economic needs, reinforces the impression of wealthy but precarious regimes seeking to achieve security by bribing their larger, jealous neighbors.[41] Is it any wonder that the unemployed, badly housed urban masses, despairing of their own secular advancement, are attracted to religious leaders or "strongmen" appealing to Islamic pride, a sense of identity, and resistance to foreign powers and their local lackeys?

More than in any other developing region, then, the future of the Middle East and North Africa is affected by issues of war and conflict. The region probably contains more soldiers, aircraft, missiles, and other weapons than anywhere else in the world, with billions of dollars of armaments having been supplied by Western, Soviet, and Chinese producers during the past few decades. In view of the range and destructiveness of these weapons, another Arab–Israeli war would be a nightmare, yet many Muslim states still regard Israel with acute hostility. Even if the Arab–Israeli antagonism did not exist, the region is full of other rivalries, between Syria and Iraq, Libya and Egypt, Iran and Iraq, and so on. Vicious one-man dictatorships glare threateningly at arch-conservative, antidemocratic, feudal sheikdoms. Fundamentalist regimes exist from Iran to the Sudan. Terrorist groups in exile threaten to eliminate their foes. Unrest among the masses puts a question mark over the future of Egypt, Algeria, Morocco, Jordan.[42] The recent fate of Lebanon, instead of serving as a warning against sectarian fanaticism, is more often viewed as a lesson in power politics, that the strong will devour the weak.

To the Western observer brought up in Enlightenment traditions — or, for that matter, to economic rationalists preaching the virtues of the borderless world — the answer to the Muslim nations' problems would appear to be a vast program of *education*, not simply in the technical, skills-acquiring sense but also to advance parliamentary discourse, pluralism, and a secular civic culture. Is that not the reason, after all, for the political stability and economic success of Scandinavia or Japan today?

If that argument is correct, then such an observer would find few of those features in contemporary Islam. In countries where fundamentalism is strong, there is (obviously) little prospect of education or advancement for the female half of the population.[43] Where engineers and technicians exist, their expertise has all too often been mobilized for war purposes, as in Iraq. Tragically, Egypt possesses a large and bustling university system but a totally inadequate number of jobs for graduates and skilled workers, so that millions of both are underemployed. In Yemen, to take an extreme example, the state of education is dismal. By contrast, the oil-rich states have poured huge resources into schools, technical institutes, and universities, but these alone are insufficient to create an "enterprise culture" that would produce export-led manufacturing along East Asian lines. Ironically, possession of vast oil reserves could be a disadvantage, since it reduces the incentive to rely upon the skills and quality of the people, as occurs in countries (Japan, Switzerland) with few natural resources. Such discouraging circumstances may also explain why many educated and entrepreneurial Arabs, who passionately wanted their societies to borrow from the West, have emigrated.

It is difficult to know whether the reason for the Muslim world's troubled condition is cultural or historical. Western critics pointing to the region's religious intolerance, technological backwardness, and feudal cast of mind often forget that, centuries before the Reformation, Islam led the world in mathematics, cartography, medicine, and many other aspects of science and industry; and contained libraries, universities, and

observatories, when Japan and America possessed none and Europe only a few. These assets were later sacrificed to a revival of traditionalist thought and the sectarian split between Shi'ite and Sunni Muslims, but Islam's retreat into itself — its being "out of step with History," as one author termed it[44] — was probably also a response to the rise of a successful, expansionist Europe.

Sailing along the Arab littoral, assisting in the demise of the Mughal Empire, penetrating strategic points with railways, canals, and ports, steadily moving into North Africa, the Nile Valley, the Persian Gulf, the Levant, and then Arabia itself, dividing the Middle East along unnatural boundaries as part of a post-First World War diplomatic bargain, developing American power to buttress and then replace European influences, inserting an Israeli state in the midst of Arab peoples, instigating coups against local popular leaders, and usually indicating that this part of the globe was important only for its oil — the Western nations may have contributed more to turning the Muslim world into what it is today than outside commentators are willing to recognize.[45] Clearly, the nations of Islam suffer many self-inflicted problems. But if much of their angry, confrontational attitudes toward the international order today are due to a long-held fear of being swallowed up by the West, little in the way of change can be expected until that fear is dissipated.

4.

The condition of sub-Saharan Africa — "the third world's third world," as it has been described — is even more desperate.[46] When one considers recent developments such as perestroika in the former Soviet Union, the coming integration of Europe, and the economic miracle of Japan and the East Asian NIEs, remarked a former president of Nigeria, General Olusegun Obasanjo, and "contrasting all this with what is taking place in Africa, it is difficult to believe that we inhabit the same historical time."[47] Recent reports upon the continent's plight are extraordinarily gloomy, describing Africa as "a human and environmental disaster area," as "moribund," "marginalized," and "peripheral to the rest of the world," and having so many intractable problems that some foreign development experts are abandoning it to work elsewhere. In the view of the World Bank, virtually everywhere else in the world is likely to experience a decline in poverty by the year 2000 *except* Africa, where things will only get worse.[48] "Sub-Saharan Africa," concludes one economist, "suffers from a combination of economic, social, political, institutional and environmental handicaps which have so far largely defied development efforts by the African countries and their donors."[49] How, an empathetic study asks, can Africa survive?[50]

The unanimity of views is remarkable, given the enormous variety among the forty-five states that comprise sub-Saharan Africa.[51] Nine of them have fewer than one million people each, whereas Nigeria contains about 110 million. Some lie in the desert, some in tropical rain forests. Many are rich in mineral deposits, others have only scrubland. While a number (Botswana, Cameroon, Congo, Gabon, Kenya) have seen significant increases in living standards since independence, they are the exception — suggesting that the obstacles to growth on East Asian lines are so deep-rooted and resistant to the "development strategies" of foreign experts and/or their own leaders that it may require profound changes in attitude to achieve recovery.

This was not the mood thirty years ago, when the peoples of Africa were gaining their independence. True, there was economic backwardness, but this was assumed to have been caused by decades of foreign rule, leading to dependency upon a single metropolitan market, monoculture, lack of access to capital, and so on. Now that Africans had control of their destinies, they could build industries, develop cities, airports, and infrastructure, and attract foreign investment and aid from either Western powers or the USSR and its partners. The boom in world trade during the 1950s and 1960s, and demand for commodities, strengthened this optimism. Although some regions were in need, Africa as a whole was self-sufficient in food and, in fact, a net food exporter. Externally, African states were of increasing importance at the United Nations and other world bodies.

What went wrong? The unhappy answer is "lots of things." The first, and perhaps most serious, was that over the following three decades the population mushroomed as imported medical techniques and a reduction in malaria-bearing mosquitoes drastically curtailed infant mortality. Africa's population was already increasing at an average annual rate of 2.6 percent in the 1960s, jumped to 2.9 percent during the 1970s, and increased to over 3 percent by the late 1980s, implying a doubling in size every twenty-two years; this was, therefore, the highest rate for any region in the world.[52]

In certain countries, the increases were staggering. Between 1960 and 1990, Kenya's population quadrupled, from 6.3 million to 25.1 million, and Côte d'Ivoire's jumped from 3.8 million to 12.6 million. Altogether Africa's population — including the North African states — leapt from 281 to 647 million in three decades.[53] Moreover, while the majority of Africans inhabit rural settlements, the continent has been becoming urban at a dizzying speed. Vast shanty-cities have already emerged on the edges of national capitals (such as Accra in Ghana, Monrovia in Liberia, and Lilongwe in Malawi). By 2025, urban dwellers are predicted to make up 55 percent of Africa's total population.

The worst news is that the increase is unlikely to diminish in the near future. Although most African countries spend less than 1 percent of GNP on health care and consequently have the highest infant mortality rates in the world — in Mali, for example, there are 169 infant deaths for every 1,000 live births — those rates are substantially less than they were a quarter century ago and will tumble further in the future, which is why demographers forecast that Africa's population in 2025 will be nearly three times that of today.[54]

There remains one random and tragic factor which may significantly affect all these (late 1980s) population projections — the AIDS epidemic, which is especially prevalent in Africa. Each new general study has raised the global total of people who are already HIV positive. For example, in June 1991, the World Health Organization abandoned its earlier estimate that 25–30 million people throughout the world would be infected by the year 2000, and suggested instead that the total could be closer to 40 million, and even that may be a gross underestimate.[55] Without question, Africa is the continent most deeply affected by AIDS, with entire families suffering from the disease. Tests of pregnant women in certain African families reveal that 25–30 percent are now HIV positive.[56] Obviously, this epidemic would alter the earlier projections of a doubling or trebling of Africa's total population over the next few decades — and in the worst possible way: family sizes would still be much larger than in most other regions of the globe, but tens of millions of Africans would be dying of AIDS, further crushing the world's most disadvantaged continent.

The basic reason why the present demographic boom will not otherwise be halted swiftly is traditional African belief-systems concerning fecundity, children, ancestors, and the role of women. Acutely aware of the invisible but pervasive presence of their ancestors, determined to expand their lineage, regarding childlessness or small families as the work of evil spirits, most Africans seek to have as many children as possible; a woman's virtue and usefulness are measured by the number of offspring she can bear. "Desired family size," according to polls of African women, ranges from five to nine children. The social attitudes that lead women in North America, Europe, and Japan to delay childbearing — education, career ambitions, desire for independence — scarcely exist in African societies; where such emerge, they are swiftly suppressed by familial pressures.[57]

This population growth has not been accompanied by equal or larger increases in Africa's productivity, which would of course transform the picture. During the 1960s, farm output was rising by around 3 percent each year, keeping pace with the population, but since 1970 agricultural production has grown at only half that rate. Part of this decline was caused by the drought, hitting countries south of the Sahara. Furthermore, existing agricultural resources have been badly eroded by overgrazing — caused by the sharp rise in the number of cattle and goats — as well as by deforestation in order to provide fuel and shelter for the growing population. When rain falls, the water runs off the denuded fields, taking the topsoil with it.

None of this was helped by changes in agricultural production, with farmers encouraged to grow tea, coffee, cocoa, palm oil, and rubber for export rather than food for domestic consumption. After benefitting from high commodity prices in the early stages, producers suffered a number of blows. Heavy taxation on cash crops, plus mandatory governmental marketing, reduced the incentives to increase output; competition grew from Asian and Latin American producers; many African currencies were overvalued, which hurt exports; and in the mid-1970s, world commodity prices tumbled. Yet the cost of imported manufactures and foodstuffs remained high, and sub-Saharan Africa was badly hurt by the quadrupling of oil prices.[58]

These blows increased Africa's indebtedness in ways that were qualitatively new. Early, postcolonial borrowings were driven by the desire for modernization, as money was poured into cement works, steel plants, airports, harbors, national airlines, electrification schemes, and telephone networks. Much of it, encouraged from afar by international bodies like the World Bank, suffered from bureaucratic interference, a lack of skilled personnel, unrealistic planning, and inadequate basic facilities, and now lies half-finished or (where completed) suffers from lack of upkeep. But borrowing to pay for imported oil, or to feed half the nation's population, means that indebtedness rises without any possible return on the borrowed funds. In consequence, Africa's total debt expanded from $14 billion in 1973 to $125 billion in 1987, when its capacity to repay was dropping fast; by the mid-1980s, payments on loans consumed about half of Africa's

export earnings, a proportion even greater than for Latin American debtor nations. Following repeated debt reschedulings, Western bankers — never enthusiastic to begin with — virtually abandoned private loans to Africa.[59]

As a result, Africa's economy is in a far worse condition now than at independence, apart from a few countries like Botswana and Mauritius. Perhaps the most startling illustration of its plight is the fact that "excluding South Africa, the nations of sub-Saharan Africa with their 450 million people have a total GDP less than that of Belgium's 11 million people"; in fact, the entire continent generates roughly 1 percent of the world GDP.[60] Africa's share of world markets has shriveled just as East Asia's share has risen fast. Plans for modernization lie unrealized. Manufacturing still represents only 11 percent of Africa's economic activity — scarcely up from the 9 percent share in 1965; and only 12 percent of the continent's exports is composed of manufactures (compared with Korea's 90 percent). There is a marked increase in the signs of decay: crumbling infrastructure, power failures, broken-down communications, abandoned projects, and everywhere the pressure of providing for increasing populations. Already Africa needs to import 15 million tons of maize a year to achieve minimal levels of food consumption, but with population increasing faster than agricultural output, that total could multiply over the next decade — implying an even greater diversion of funds from investment and infrastructure.[61]

Two further characteristics worsen Africa's condition. The first is the prevalence of wars, *coups d'état*, and political instability. This is partly the legacy of the European "carve-up" of Africa, when colonial boundaries were drawn without regard for the differing tribes and ethnic groups,[62] or even of earlier conquests by successful tribes of neighboring lands and peoples; Ethiopia, for example, is said to contain 76 ethnic groups and 286 languages.[63] While it is generally accepted that those boundaries cannot be unscrambled, most of them are clearly artificial. In extreme cases like Somalia, the "state" has ceased to exist. And in most other African countries, governments do not attract the loyalty of citizens (except perhaps kinsmen of the group in power), and ethnic tensions have produced innumerable civil wars — from Biafra's attempt to secede from Nigeria, to the conflict between Arab north and African south in the Sudan, to Eritrean struggles to escape from Ethiopia, to the Tutsi–Hutu struggle in Burundi, to clashes and suppressions and guerrilla campaigns from Uganda to the Western Sahara, from Angola to Mozambique.[64]

These antagonisms have often been worsened by struggles over ideology and government authority. The rulers of many new African states rapidly switched either to a personal dictatorship, or single-party rule. They also embraced a Soviet or Maoist political economy, instituting price controls, production targets, forced industrialization, the takeover of private enterprises, and other features of "scientific socialism" that — unknown to them — were destroying the Soviet economy. Agriculture was neglected, while bureaucracy flourished. The result was the disappearance of agricultural surpluses, inattention to manufacturing for the world market, and the expansion of party and government bureaucracies, exacerbating the region's problems.

The second weakness was the wholly inadequate investment in human resources and in developing a culture of entrepreneurship, scientific inquiry, and technical prowess. According to one survey, Africa has been spending less than $1 each year on research and development per head of population, whereas the United States was spending $200 per head. Consequently, Africa's scientific population has always trailed the rest of the world.

In many African countries — Malawi, Zambia, Lesotho — government spending on education has fallen, so that, after some decades of advance, a smaller share of children are now in school. While there is a hunger for learning, it cannot be satisfied beyond the secondary level except for a small minority. Angola, for example, had 2.4 million pupils in primary schools in 1982–1983, but only 153,000 in secondary schools and a mere 4,700 in higher education.[65] By contrast, Sweden, with a slightly smaller total population, had 570,000 in secondary education and 179,000 in higher education.[66]

Despite these relative weaknesses, some observers claim to have detected signs of a turnaround. With the

Table 32.5 Numbers of Scientists and Engineers per Million of Population

Japan	3,548
US	2,685
Europe	1,632
Latin America	209
Arab States	202
Asia (minus Japan)	99
Africa	53

Source: T.R. Odhiambo, "Human resources development: problems and prospects in developing countries," *Impact of Science on Society*, No. 155 (1989), p. 214.

exception of intransigent African socialists,[67] many leaders are now attempting to institute reforms. In return for "structural adjustments," that is, measures to encourage free enterprise, certain African societies have secured additional loans from Western nations and the World Bank. The latter organization has identified past errors (many of them urged on African governments and funded by itself), and encouraged economic reforms. Mozambique, Ghana, and Zambia have all claimed recent successes in reversing negative growth, albeit at considerable social cost.

Democratic principles are also returning to the continent: the dismantling of apartheid in South Africa, the cease-fire in Angola, the independence of Namibia, the success of Botswana's record of democracy and prosperity, the cries for reforms in Gabon, Kenya, and Zaire, the rising awareness among African intellectuals of the transformations in East Asia, may all help — so the argument goes — to change attitudes, which is the prerequisite for recovery.[68] Moreover, there are local examples of economic self-improvement, cooperative ventures to halt erosion and improve yields, and village-based schemes of improvement.[69] This is, after all, a continent of enormous agricultural and mineral resources, provided they can be sensibly exploited.

Despite such signs of promise, conditions are likely to stay poor. Population increases countered only by the growing toll of AIDS victims, the diminution of grazing lands and food supplies, the burdens of indebtedness, the decay of infrastructures and reduced spending on health care and education, the residual strength of animist religions and traditional belief-systems, the powerful hold of corrupt bureaucracies and ethnic loyalties ... all those tilt against the relatively few African political leaders, educators, scientists, and economists who perceive the need for changes.

What does this mean for Africa's future? As the Somalian disaster unfolds, some observers suggest that parts of the continent may be taken over and administered from the outside, rather like the post-1919 League of Nations mandates. By contrast, other experts argue that disengagement by developed countries might have the positive effect of compelling Africans to begin a *self-driven* recovery, as well as ending the misuse of aid monies.[70] Still others feel that Africa cannot live without the West, although its leaders and people will have to abandon existing habits, and development aid must be more intelligently applied.[71] Whichever view is correct, the coming decade will be critical for Africa. Even a partial recovery would give grounds for hope; on the other hand, a second decade of decline, together with a further surge in population, would result in catastrophe.

5.

From the above, it is clear that the developing countries' response to the broad forces for global change is going to be uneven. The signs are that the gap between success and failure will widen; one group enjoys interacting beneficial trends, while others suffer from linked weaknesses and deficiencies.[72]

This is most clearly the case with respect to demography. As noted earlier, the commitment of the East Asian trading states to education, manufacturing, and export-led growth produced a steady rise in living standards, and allowed those societies to make the demographic transition to smaller family sizes. This was in marked contrast to sub-Saharan Africa where, because of different cultural attitudes and social structures, improved health care and rising incomes led, *not* to a drop in population growth, but to the opposite. Just before independence in 1960, for example, the average Kenyan woman had 6.2 children, whereas by 1980 she had 8.2[73] — and that in a period when Africa's economic prospects were fading.

In Africa's case the "global trend" which drives all others is, clearly, the demographic explosion. It spills into every domain — overgrazing, local conflicts over water and wood supplies, extensive unplanned urbanization, strains upon the educational and social structures, reliance upon imported food supplies (at the cost of increasing indebtedness), ethnic tensions, domestic unrest, border wars. Only belatedly are some African governments working to persuade families to limit their size as people become aware that access to family planning, plus improved educational opportunities for women, produce significant declines in birth rates. Against such promising indications stand the many cultural, gender-related, and economic forces described above that encourage large families. This resistance to change is aided by Africa's general lack of resources. Raising Somalia's female literacy rate (6 percent) to South Korea's (88 percent) to produce a demographic transition sounds fine until one considers how so ambitious a reform could be implemented and paid for. Unfortunately, as noted above, the projections suggest that, as Africa's population almost trebles over the next few decades, the only development curtailing it could be the rapid growth of AIDS.[74]

In many parts of Latin America, the demographic explosion will also affect the capacity to handle globally driven forces for change. While wide differences in total fertility rates exist between the moderate-climate countries and those in the tropics, the overall picture is that Latin America's population, which was roughly equal to that of United States and Canada in 1960, is increasing so swiftly that it will be, more than double the latter in 2025.[75] Even if birth-rates are now declining in the larger countries, there will still be enormous increases: Mexico's population will leap to 150 million by 2025 and Brazil's to 245 million.[76] This implies a very high incidence of child poverty and malnutrition, further strain upon already inadequate health-care and educational services, the crowding of millions of human beings into a dozen or more "megacities," pollution, the degradation of grazing land, forests, and other natural resources. In Mexico, for example, 44 million people are without sewers and 21 million without potable water, which means that when disease (e.g., cholera) strikes, it spreads swiftly.[77] These are not strong foundations upon which to improve the region's relative standing in an increasingly competitive international economic order.

In this regard, many Muslim states are in a similar or worse position; in no Arab country is the population increasing by less than 2 percent a year,[78] and in most the rate is considerably higher. The region's total population of more than 200 million will double in less than twenty-five years and city populations are growing twice as fast as national averages. This puts enormous pressures upon scarce food, water, and land resources, and produces unbalanced populations. Already, in most Arab countries at least four out of every ten people are under the age of fifteen — the classic recipe for subsequent social unrest and political revolution. One in five Egyptian workers is jobless, as is one in four Algerian workers.[79] In what is widely regarded as the most turbulent part of the world, therefore, demography is contributing to the prospects of future unrest year by year. Even the Israeli–Palestine quarrel has become an issue of demography, with the influx of Soviet Jews seen as countering the greater fertility of the Palestinians.

There is, moreover, little likelihood that population growth will fall in the near future. Since infant mortality rates in many Muslim countries are still high, further improvements in prenatal care will produce rises in the numbers surviving, as is happening in the Gulf States and Saudi Arabia.

As elsewhere, politics intrudes; many regimes are deliberately encouraging women to have large families, arguing that this adds to the country's military strength. "Bear a child," posters in Iraq proclaim, "and

Table 32.6 Comparative Infant Mortality Rates
(Infant Deaths per 1,000 live Births)

	1965–1970	1985–1990
Algeria	150	74
Egypt	170	85
Sudan	156	108
Yemen Arab Republic	186	116
Saudi Arabia	140	71
Kuwait	55	19
Iraq	111	69
Japan	16	5
US	22	10
Sweden	13	6

Source: World Resources 1990–91, p. 258–259. Copyright © by the World Resources Institute. Reprinted by permission of Oxford University Press, Inc.

you pierce an arrow in the enemy's eye."[80] Countries such as Iraq and Libya offer many incentives for larger families, as do the Gulf States and Saudi Arabia, anxious to fill their oil-rich lands with native-born rather than foreign workers. Only in Egypt are propaganda campaigns launched to curb family size, but even if that is successful — despite resistance from the Muslim Brotherhood — present numbers are disturbing. With a current population of over 55 million Egyptians, six out of ten of whom are under twenty, and with an additional one million being born every eight months, the country is in danger of bursting at the seams during the next few decades.

6.

For much the same reasons, we ought to expect a differentiated success rate among developing countries in handling environmental challenges, with the newly industrializing East Asian economies way ahead of the others. This is not to ignore significant local schemes to improve the ecology that are springing up in Africa and the interesting proposals for "sustainable development" elsewhere in the developing world,[81] or to forget that industrialization has caused environmental damage in East Asia, from choked roads to diminished forests. Yet the fact is that nations with lots of resources (capital, scientists, engineers, technology, a per capita GNP of over US $4,000) are better able to deal with environmental threats than those without money, tools, or personnel. By contrast, it is the poorer societies (Egypt, Bangladesh, Ethiopia) that, lacking financial and personnel resources, find it difficult to respond to cyclones, floods, drought, and other natural dis-

asters — with their devastated populations augmenting the millions of refugees and migrants. Should global warming produce sea-level rises and heightened storm surges, teeming island populations from the Caribbean to the Pacific are in danger of being washed away.[82]

Finally, it is the population explosion in Latin America and South Asia and Africa that is the major cause for the overgrazing, soil erosion, salinization, and clearing of the tropical rain forests, which, while contributing to global warming, also hurts the local populations and exacerbates regional struggles for power. Elsewhere in the Middle East, for example, supplies of water are the greatest concern, especially in view of growing demographic pressures. The average Jordanian now uses only one third the amount of domestic water consumed in Israel and has little hope of increasing the supply, yet Jordan's population, which is now roughly equal to Israel's, is expected to double during the next twenty years.[83]

With all governments in the region striving to boost agricultural output and highly sensitive to famine and unrest among their peasant farmers, the search for secure water influences domestic politics, international relations, and spending priorities. Egypt worries that either the Sudan or Ethiopia might dam the Nile in order to increase irrigation. Syria and Iraq have taken alarm at Turkey's new Ataturk dam, which can interrupt the flow of the Euphrates. Jordan, Syria, and Israel quarrel over water rights in the Litani, Yarmuk, and Jordan river valleys, as do Arabs and Jews over well supplies in the occupied West Bank. Saudi Arabia's ambition to grow wheat is draining its aquifers, and the same will occur with Libya's gigantic scheme to tap water from under the Sahara.[84] As more and more people struggle for the same — or diminishing — amounts of water, grand ideas about preparing for the twenty-first century look increasingly irrelevant; surviving *this* century becomes the order of the day.

What are the implications for these societies of the new technologies being developed by Western scientists? The revolution in biotech farming, for example, is of great relevance to developing countries, even if the consequences will be mixed. Improved strains of plants and more sophisticated pesticides and fertilizers could, potentially, enhance yields in the developing world, reduce pressures upon marginal lands, restore agricultural self-sufficiency, improve the balance of payments, and raise standards of living. Since much biotech does not involve expensive enterprise, we could witness farmers' groups experimenting with new seeds, improved breeding techniques, cultivation of gene tissue, regional gene-banks, and other developments.

Yet it is also possible that giant pharmaceutical and agro-chemical firms in the "first" world may monopolize much of the knowledge — and the profits — that this transformation implies. Surpluses in global foodstuffs caused by the biotech revolution could be used to counter malnutrition. They could also undermine commodity prices and hurt societies in which most inhabitants were employed in agriculture. Removing food production from the farm to the laboratory — which is what is implied by recent breakthroughs in biotech agriculture — would undercut agrarian societies, which is why some biotech experts in the development field call for serious planning in "agricultural conversion," that is, conversion into other economic activities.[85]

While the uses of biotechnology are relatively diverse, that is not the case with robotics and automated manufacture. The requirements for an indigenous robotics industry — capital, an advanced electronics sector, design engineers, a dearth of skilled labor — suggest that countries like Taiwan and Korea may follow Japan's example out of concern that Japan's automation will make their own products uncompetitive. On the other hand, automated factories assembling goods more swiftly, regularly, and economically than human beings pose a challenge to *middle-income* economies (Malaysia, Mexico), whose comparative advantage would be undercut. As for countries without a manufacturing base, it is difficult to see how the robotics revolution would have any meaning — except to further devalue the resource which they possess in abundance, masses of impoverished and undereducated human beings.

Finally, the global financial and communications revolution, and the emergence of multinational corporations, threatens to increase the gap between richer and poorer countries, even in the developing world. The industrial conglomerates of Korea are now positioning themselves to become multinational, and the East Asian NIEs in general are able to exploit the world economy (as can be seen in their trade balances, stockmarkets, electronics industries, strategic marketing alliances, and so on). Furthermore, if the increasingly borderless world rewards entrepreneurs, designers, brokers, patent-owners, lawyers, and dealers in high value-added services, then East Asia's commitment to education, science, and technology can only increase its lead over other developing economies.

By contrast, the relative lack of capital, high-technology, scientists, skilled workers, and export industries in the poorer countries makes it difficult for them

to take part in the communications and financial revolution, although several countries (Brazil, India) clearly hope to do so. Some grimmer forecasts suggest the poorer parts of the developing world may become more marginalized, partly because of the reduced economic importance of labor, raw materials, and foodstuffs, partly because the advanced economies may concentrate upon greater knowledge-based commerce among themselves.

7.

Is there any way of turning these trends around? Obviously, a society strongly influenced by fundamentalist mullahs with a dislike of "modernization" is unlikely to join the international economy; and it does not *have* to enter the borderless world if its people believe that it would be healthier, spiritually if not economically, to remain outside. Nor ought we to expect that countries dominated by selfish, authoritarian elites bent upon enhancing their military power — developing world countries spent almost $150 billion on weapons and armies in 1988 alone — will rush to imitate Japan and Singapore.

But what about those societies that wish to improve themselves yet find that they are hampered by circumstances? There are, after all, many developing countries, the vast majority of which depend upon exporting food and raw materials. With dozens of poor countries seeking desperately to sell their cane sugar or bananas or timber or coffee in the global market, prices fall and they are made more desperate.[86] Moreover, although much international aid goes to the developing world, in fact far more money flows out of impoverished countries of Africa, Asia, and Latin America and *into* the richer economies of Europe, North America, and Japan — to the tune of at least $43 billion each year.[87] This outward flow of interest repayments, repatriated profits, capital flight, royalties, fees for patents and information services, makes it difficult for poorer countries to get to their feet; and even if they were able to increase their industrial output, the result might be a large rise in "the costs of technological dependence."[88] Like their increasing reliance upon Northern suppliers for food and medical aid, this has created another dependency relationship for poorer nations.

In sum, as we move into the next century the developed economies appear to have all the trump cards in their hands — capital, technology, control of communications, surplus foodstuffs, powerful multinational companies[89] — and, if anything, their advantages are growing because technology is eroding the value of labor and materials, the chief assets of developing countries. Although nominally independent since decolonization, these countries are probably more dependent upon Europe and the United States than they were a century ago.

Ironically, three or four decades of efforts by developing countries to gain control of their own destinies — nationalizing Western companies, setting up commodity-exporting cartels, subsidizing indigenous manufacturing to achieve import substitution, campaigning for a new world order based upon redistribution of the existing imbalances of wealth — have all failed. The "market," backed by governments of the developed economies, has proved too strong, and the struggle against it has weakened developing economies still further — except those (like Korea and Taiwan) which decided to join.

While the gap between rich and poor in today's world is disturbing, those who have argued that this gap is unjust have all too often supported heavy-handed state interventionism and a retreat from open competition, which preserved indigenous production in the short term but rendered it less efficient against those stimulated by market forces. "Scientific socialism for Africa" may still appeal to some intellectuals,[90] but by encouraging societies to look inward it made them less well equipped to move to newer technologies in order to make goods of greater sophistication and value. And a new "world communications order," as proposed a few years ago by UNESCO to balance the West's dominance, sounds superficially attractive but would in all likelihood become the pawn of bureaucratic and ideological interests rather than function as an objective source of news reporting.

On the other hand, the advocates of free market forces often ignore the vast political difficulties which governments in developing countries would encounter in abolishing price controls, selling off national industries, and reducing food subsidies. They also forget that the spectacular commercial expansion of Japan and the East Asian NIEs was carried out by strong states which eschewed laissez-faire. Instead of copying either socialist or free market systems, therefore, the developing countries might imitate East Asia's "mixed strategies" which combine official controls and private enterprise.[91]

Although the idea of a mixed strategy is intriguing, how can West or Central African countries imitate East Asia without a "strong state" apparatus, and while having a weak tradition of cooperation between government and firms, far lower educational achievements, and a different set of cultural attitudes toward family size or international economics? With the global scene less welcoming to industrializing newcomers, how likely are they to achieve the same degree of success as the East Asian NIEs did, when they "took off" a quarter-century ago?[92] Even if, by an economic miracle, the world's poorest fifty nations *did* adopt the Korean style of export-led growth in manufactures, would they not create the same crisis of overproduction as exists in the commodity markets today?

How many developing nations will be able to follow East Asia's growth is impossible to tell. The latest *World Development Report* optimistically forecast significant progress across the globe, provided that poorer nations adopted "market friendly" policies and richer nations eschewed protectionism.[93] Were Taiwan and Korea to be followed by the larger states of Southeast Asia such as Malaysia and Thailand, then by South Asia and a number of Latin American countries, that would blur the North–South divide and make international economic alignments altogether more variegated. Moreover, sustained manufacturing success among developing countries *outside* East Asia might stimulate imitation elsewhere.

At the moment, however, the usual cluster of factors influencing relative economic performance — cultural attitudes, education, political stability, capacity to carry out long-term plans — suggests that while a small but growing number of countries is moving from a "have-not" to a "have" status, many more remain behind. The story of winners and losers in history will continue, therefore, only this time modern communications will remind us all of the growing disparity among the world's nations and regions.

NOTES

1. Discussed further in Paul Kennedy, *Preparing for the Twenty-First Century* (Random House, 1993).
2. For reasons of size and organization, China and India (containing around 37 percent of the world's population) are not treated here: for coverage, see chapter 9, "India and China," of *Preparing for the Twenty-First Century*.
3. *World Tables 1991* (Washington, DC: World Bank, 1991), pp. 268–69, 352–53.
4. *World Tables 1991*, pp. 268–69, 352–53.
5. See the World Bank publication *Trends in Developing Economies*, 1990, pp. 299–303, for Korea.
6. For descriptions, see F. Braudel, *Civilization and Capitalism: Vol. 3, The Perspective of the World* (Harper and Row, 1986), pp. 506–11.
7. See P. Lyon, "Emergence of the Third World," in H. Bull and A. Watson, eds., *The Expansion of International Society* (Oxford University Press, 1983), p. 229

ff.; G. Barraclough, *An Introduction to Contemporary History* (Penguin, 1967), chapter 6, "The Revolt Against the West."

8. J. Ravenhill, "The North–South Balance of Power," *International Affairs*, Vol. 66, No. 4 (1990), pp. 745–46. See also J. Cruickshank, "The Rise and Fall of the Third World: A Concept Whose Time Has Passed," *World Review*, February 1991, pp. 28–29. Ravenhill's divisions are high-income oil-exporting countries; industrializing economies with strong states and relatively low levels of indebtedness (Taiwan, etc.); industrializing economies with the state apparatus under challenge and/or with debt problems (Argentina, Poland); potential newly industrializing countries (Malaysia, Thailand); primary commodity producers (in sub-Saharan Africa, Central America).

9. Ravenhill, "The North–South Balance of Power," p. 732.

10. W.L.M. Adriaansen and J.G. Waardensburg, eds., *A Dual World Economy* (Groningen: Wolters-Noordhoff, 1989).

11. P. Drysdale, "The Pacific Basin and Its Economic Vitality," in J.W. Morley, ed., *The Pacific Basin: New Challenges for the United States* (Academy of Political Science with the East Asian Institute and the Center on Japanese Economy and Business, 1986), p. 11.

12. While Korea has a population of around 43 million and Taiwan about 20 million, Hong Kong possesses 5.7 million and Singapore only 2.7 million.

13. See especially, "Taiwan and Korea: Two Paths to Prosperity," *The Economist*, July 14, 1990, pp. 19–21; also "South Korea" (survey), *The Economist*, August 18, 1990. There is a useful comparative survey in L.A. Veit, "Time of the New Asian Tigers," *Challenge*, July–August 1987, pp. 49–55.

14. N.D. Kristof, "In Taiwan, Only the Strong Get US Degrees," *The New York Times*, March 26, 1989, p. 11.

15. Figures taken, respectively, from J. Paxton, ed., *The Statesman's Yearbook 1990–1991* (St. Martin's Press, 1990); and from R.N. Gwynne, *New Horizons? Third World Industrialization in an International Framework* (New York/London: Wiley, 1990), p. 199.

16. Table 1 of Fukuchi and Kagami shows the different rates of growth, and of export's share of total GDP, of the Asian Pacific nations compared with those of Latin America. See also H. Hughes, "Catching Up: The Asian Newly Industrializing Economies in the 1990s," *Asian Development Review*, Vol. 7, No. 2 (1989), p. 132 (and Table 32.3).

17. "The Yen Block" (survey), *The Economist*, July 15, 1989; "Japan Builds a New Power Base," *Business Week*, March 20, 1989, pp. 18–25.

18. "Taiwan and Korea: Two Paths to Prosperity," *The Economist*, p. 19; "South Korea: A New Society," *The Economist*, April 15, 1989, pp. 23–25.

19. "When a Miracle Stalls," *The Economist*, October 6, 1990, pp. 33–34 (on Taiwan); *Trends in Developing Economies*, 1990, pp. 299–300 (Korea); R.A. Scalapino, "Asia and the United States: The Challenges Ahead," *Foreign Affairs*, Vol. 69, No. 1 (1989–1990), especially pp. 107–12; "Hong Kong, In China's Sweaty Palm," *The Economist*, November 5, 1988, pp. 19–22.

20. See the detailed forecasts in "Asia 2010: The Power of People," *Far Eastern Economist Review*, May 17, 1990, pp. 27–58. On industrial retooling, see pp. 8–9 of "South Korea" (survey), *The Economist*, August 18, 1990, pp. 8–9.

21. Sadik, editor, *Population: The UNFPA Experience* (New York University Press, 1984), chapter 4, "Latin America and the Caribbean," pp. 51–52.

22. A.F. Lowenthal, "Rediscovering Latin America," *Foreign Affairs*, Vol. 69, No. 4 (Fall 1990), p. 34.

23. Figure from "Latin America's Hope," *The Economist*, December 9 1989, p.14.

24. As mentioned earlier, Japan and its East Asian emulators also sought to protect fledgling domestic industries, but that was in order to create a strong base from which to mount an export offensive — *not* to establish an economic bastion within which their industries would be content to remain.

25. For details, see the various national entries in *The Statesman's Year-Book 1990–91; and The Economist World Atlas and Almanac* (Prentice Hall 1989), pp. 131–157. R.N. Gwynne's *New Horizons?* has useful comments on Latin America's "inward-oriented industrialization" (chapter 11), which he then contrasts with East Asia's "outward orientation" (chapter 12).

26. World Resources Institute, *World Resources 1990–91* (Oxford University Press, 1990), p. 39.

27. In 1989, the net transfer of capital leaving Latin America was around $25 billion.

28. For the above, see *World Resources 1990–91*, pp. 33–48; "Latin America at a Crossroads," B.J. McCormick, *The World Economy: Patterns of Growth and Change* (Oxford University Press, 1988), chapter 13; "Latin American debt: The banks' great escape," *The Economist*, February 11, 1989, pp. 73–74.

29. For educational details, see *The Statesman's Year-Book 1990–91*, pp. 95, 236; for literacy rates, see especially those of Uruguay, Costa Rica, Argentina, and Venezuela in the table "Development Brief," *The Economist*, May 26, 1990, p.81.

30. T.E. Martinez, "Argentina: Living with Hyperinflation," *The Atlantic Monthly*, December 1990, p. 36.

31. *The Statesman's Year-Book 1990–91*, pp. 584, 605.

32. T. Kamm, "Latin America Edges Toward Free Trade," *The Wall Street Journal*, November 30, 1990, p. A10.

33. C. Farnsworth, "Latin American Economies Given Brighter Assessments," *The New York Times*, October 30, 1990; "Latin America's New Start," *The Economist*, June 9, 1990, p. 11; N.C. Nash, "A Breath of Fresh Economic Air Brings Change to Latin America," *The New York Times*, November 13, 1991, pp. A1, D5.

34. "Latin America's Hope," *The Economist*, December 9, 1989, p. 15; Nash, "A Breath of Fresh Economic Air Brings Change to Latin America."

35. J. Brooke, "Debt and Democracy," *The New York Times*, December 5, 1990, p. A16; P. Truell, "As the U.S. Slumps, Latin America Suffers," *The Wall Street Journal*, November 19, 1990, p. 1.

36. For these arguments, see especially Lowenthal's fine summary, "Rediscovering Latin America," in *Foreign Affairs*; also G.A. Fauriol, "The Shadow of Latin American Affairs," *Foreign Affairs*, Vol. 69, No. 1 (1989–1990), pp. 116–34; and M.D. Hayes, "The U.S. and Latin America: A Lost Decade?" *Foreign Affairs*, Vol. 68, No. 1 (1988–1989), pp. 180–98.

37. This is the subdivision preferred by *The Economist World Atlas and Almanac*, pp. 256–71, which discusses the North African states (except Egypt) in a later section, under "Africa."

38. "The Arab World" (survey), *The Economist*, May 12, 1990.

39. See "Religions" in the *Hammond Comparative World Atlas* (Hammond, Inc., 1993 edition), p. 21.

40. The few oil-producing countries in Africa, such as Gabon and Nigeria, still have relatively low per capita GNPs compared with the Arab Gulf states.

41. G. Brooks and T. Horwitz, "Shaken Sheiks," *The Wall Street Journal*, December 28, 1990, pp. A1, A4.

42. "The Arab World," *The Economist*, p. 12.

43. In 1985, adult female literacy in the Yemen Arab Republic was a mere 3 percent, in Saudi Arabia 12 percent, in Iran 39 percent. On the other hand, many women from the middle and upper-middle classes in Muslim countries are educated, which suggests that poverty, as much as culture, plays a role.

44. M.A. Heller, "The Middle East: Out of Step with History," *Foreign Affairs*, Vol. 69, No. 1 (1989–1990), pp. 153–71.

45. See also the remarks by S.F. Wells and M.A. Bruzonsky, eds., *Security in the Middle East: Regional Change and Great Power Strategies* (Westview Press, 1986), pp. 1–3.

46. D.E. Duncan, "Africa: The Long Good-bye," *The Atlantic Monthly*, July 1990, p. 20.

47. J.A. Marcum, "Africa: A Continent Adrift," *Foreign Affairs*, Vol. 68, No. 1 (1988–1989), p.177. See also the penetrating article by K.R. Richburg, "Why Is Black Africa Overwhelmed While East Asia Overcomes?" *The International Herald Tribune*, July 14, 1992, pp. 1, 6.

48. C.H. Farnsworth, "Report by World Bank Sees Poverty Lessening by 2000 Except in Africa," *The New York Times*, July 16, 1990, p. A3; Marcum, "Africa: A Continent Adrift"; Duncan, "Africa: The Long Good-bye"; and "The bleak continent," *The Economist*, December 9, 1989, pp. 80–81.

49. B. Fischer, "Developing Countries in the Process of Economic Globalisation," *Intereconomics* (March/April 1990), p. 55.

50. J.S. Whitaker, *How Can Africa Survive?* (Council on Foreign Relations Press, 1988).

51. As will be clear from the text, this discussion excludes the Republic of South Africa.

52. T.J. Goliber, "Africa's Expanding Population: Old Problems, New Policies," *Population Bulletin*, Vol. 44, No. 3 (November 1989), pp. 4–49, an outstandingly good article.

53. *World Resources 1990–91*, p. 254.

54. *World Resources 1990–91*, p. 254 (overall population growth to 2025), and p. 258 (infant mortality). L.K. Altman, "W.H.O. Says 40 Million Will Be Infected with AIDS by 2000," *The New York Times*, June 18, 1991, p. C3 (for percentage of GNP devoted to health care).

55. L.K. Altman, "W.H.O. Says 40 Million Will Be Infected with AIDS Virus by 2000"; and for further figures, see Kennedy, *Preparing for the Twenty-First Century*, chapter 3.

56. K.H. Hunt, "Scenes from a Nightmare," *The New York Times Magazine*, August 12, 1990, pp. 26, 50–51.

57. See Whitaker, *How Can Africa Survive?*, especially chapter 4, "The Blessings of Children," for a fuller analysis; and J.C. Caldwell and P. Caldwell, "High Fertility in Sub-Saharan Africa," *Scientific American*, May 1990, pp. 118–25.

58. "The bleak continent," *The Economist*; Whitaker, *How Can Africa Survive?*, chapters 1 and 2; Goliber, "Africa's Expanding Population," pp. 12–13.

59. Whitaker, *How Can Africa Survive?*; Duncan, "Africa: The Long Good-bye."

60. "Fruits of Containment" (op-ed), *The Wall Street Journal*, December 18, 1990, p. A14, for the Africa–Belgium comparison; H. McRae, "Visions of tomorrow's world," *The Independent* (London), November 26, 1991, for Africa's share of world GDP.

61. "Aid to Africa," *The Economist*, December 8, 1990, p. 48.

62. In this regard, East Asian nations like Taiwan and Korea, possessing coherent indigenous populations, are once again more favorably situated.

63. *The Economist World Atlas and Almanac* (Prentice Hall, 1989), p. 293.

64. Apart from the country by country comments in *The Economist World Atlas and Almanac*, see also K. Ingham, *Politics in Modern Africa: The Uneven Tribal Dimension* (Routledge, 1990); "Africa's Internal Wars of the 1980s — Contours and Prospects," United States Institute of Peace, *In Brief*, No. 18 (May 1990).

65. *The Statesman's Yearbook 1989*, p. 84; Goliber, "Africa's Expanding Population," p. 15.

66. *The Statesman's Yearbook 1989*, pp. 1,159–60 (certain smaller groups of students are excluded from these totals).

67. P. Lewis, "Nyere and Tanzania: No Regrets at Socialism," *The New York Times*, October 24, 1990.

68. "Wind of change, but a different one," *The Economist*, July 14, 1990, p. 44. See also the encouraging noises made — on a country by country basis — in the World Bank's own *Trends in Developing Economies*, 1990, as well as in its 1989 publication *Sub-Saharan Africa: From Crisis to Sustainable Growth* (summarized in "The bleak continent," *The Economist*, pp. 80–81).

69. See especially P. Pradervand *Listening to Africa: Developing Africa from the Grassroots* (Greenwood, 1989); B. Schneider, *The Barefoot Revolution* (London: I.T. Publications, 1988); K. McAfee, "Why the Third World Goes Hungry," *Commonweal*, June 15, 1990, pp. 384–85.

70. See Edward Sheehan's article "In the Heart of Somalia," *The New York Review*, January 14, 1993. See also Duncan, "Africa: The Long Good-bye," p. 24; G. Hancock, *Lords of Poverty: The Power, Prestige, and Corruption of the International Aid* (Atlantic Monthly Press, 1989); G.B.N. Ayittey, "No More Aid for Africa," *The Wall Street Journal*, October 18, 1991 (op-ed), p. A14.

71. Whitaker, *How Can Africa Survive?*, p. 231.

72. See, for example, the conclusions in B. Fischer, "Developing Countries in the Process of Economic Globalisation," pp. 55–63.

73. Caldwell and Caldwell, "High Fertility in Sub-Saharan Africa," *Scientific American*, p. 88.

74. AIDS in Africa," *The Economist*, November 24, 1989, p. 1B; E. Eckholm and J. Tierney, "AIDS in Africa: A Killer Rages On," *The New York Times*, September 16, 1990, pp. 1, 4; C.M. Becker, "The Demo-Economic Impact of the AIDS Pandemic in Sub-Saharan Africa," *World Development*, Vol. 18, No. 12 (1990), pp. l,599–1,619.

75. *World Resources 1990–91*, p. 254. The US–Canada total in 1960 was 217 million to Latin America's 210 million; by 2025 it is estimated to be 332 million to 762 million.

76. *World Resources 1990–91*, p. 254.

77. Apart from chapters 2 and 4 above, see again *World Resources 1990–91*, pp. 33–48; T. Wicker, "Bush Ventures South," *The New York Times*, December 9, 1990, p. E17; T. Golden, "Mexico Fights Cholera But Hates to Say Its Name," *The New York Times*, September 14, 1991, p. 2.

78. "The Arab World," *The Economist*, p.4.

79. "The Arab World," p. 6; Y.F. Ibrahim, "In Algeria, Hope for Democracy But Not Economy," *The New York Times*, July 26, 1991, pp. A1, A6.

80. As quoted in "The Arab World," p. 5.

81. See again Pradervand, *Listening to Africa*. Also important is D. Pearce et al., *Sustainable Development: Economics and Environment in the Third World* (Gower, 1990).

82. F. Gable, "Changing Climate and Caribbean Coastlines," *Oceanus*, Vol. 30, No. 4 (Winter 1987–1988), pp. 53–56; G. Gable and D.G. Aubrey, "Changing Climate and the Pacific," *Oceanus*, Vol. 32, No. 4 (Winter 1989–1990), pp. 71–73.

83. "The Arab World," p. 12.

84. *World Resources 1990–91*, pp. 176–77; *State of the World 1990*, pp. 48–49.

85. C. Juma, *The Gene Hunters: Biotechnology and the Scramble for Seeds* (Princeton University Press, 1989).

86. D. Pirages, *Global Technopolitics: The International Politics of Technology and Resources* (Brooks-Cole, 1989), p. 152.

87. McAfee, "Why the Third World Goes Hungry," p. 380.

88. See P.K. Ghosh, ed., *Technology Policy and Development: A Third World Perspective* (Greenwood, 1984), p. 109.

89. C.J. Dixon et al., eds., *Multinational Corporations and the Third World* (Croom Helm, 1986).

90. For a good example, see B. Onimode, *A Political Economy of the African Crisis* (Humanities Press International, 1988), especially p. 310 ff.

91. M. Clash, "Development Policy, Technology Assessment and the New Technologies," *Futures*, November 1990, p. 916.

92. L. Cuyvers and D. Van den Bulcke, "Some Reflections on the 'Outward-oriented' Development Strategy of the Far Eastern Newly Industrialising Countries," especially pp. 196–97, in Adriaansen and Waardenburg, *A Dual World Economy*.

93. *World Development Report 1991: The Challenge of Development*, a World Bank report (Oxford University Press, 1991). See also the World Bank's *Global Economic Prospects and the Developing Countries* (1991).

Chapter 33

RESHAPING THE GLOBAL ECONOMY

SANDRA POSTEL AND CHRISTOPHER FLAVIN

The vast scale and rapid growth of the $20-trillion global economy are hailed as great achievements of our time. But as the pace of environmental deterioration quickens, the consequences of failing to bridge the gap between the workings of economic systems and natural ones are becoming all too clear.[1]

Rising material consumption multiplied by unprecedented growth in human numbers has translated into mounting stress on local, regional, and global life-support systems. Atmospheric stability is among the major casualties. Powered by fossil fuels, the fivefold expansion of the world economy since 1950 caused the concentration of carbon dioxide (CO_2) to climb by 40 parts per million, whereas it took the previous two centuries to rise by 30 parts per million. Scientists now believe this rapid and continuing assault on the atmosphere will make the world warmer in the next few decades than it has been for thousands of years.[2]

Nearly 1 billion people will be added to the planet during the nineties, each of them striving for a materially satisfying life. Much of the increase will occur in parts of the developing world sliding toward ecological bankruptcy, including a good deal of Africa and parts of Latin America and the Indian subcontinent. The prospects are daunting, given that in 1989 some 1.2 billion people — 23 percent of humanity — lived in the grim state called absolute poverty, where their most basic needs for food, clothing, and shelter were not being met. Per capita incomes in more than 40 poor countries declined during the eighties.[3]

Despite what leading economic indicators may imply, no economy can be called successful if its prosperity comes at the expense of future generations and if the ranks of the poor continue to grow. With mounting evidence that environmental deterioration and economic decline feed on each other, the fate of the poor and the fate of the planet have become tightly entwined.

Redirecting the global economy toward environmental sustainability requires fundamental reforms at both the international and national levels. In an age when deforestation in one country reduces the entire earth's biological richness, when chemicals released on one continent can lead to skin cancer on another, and when CO_2 emissions anywhere hasten climate change everywhere, economic policymaking is no longer exclusively a national concern.

Two of the primary forces shaping prospects in developing countries today are their heavy debt burdens and the tens of billions of dollars of development assistance they receive. By 1989, the Third World's external debt stood at $1.2 trillion, 44 percent of its collective gross national product (GNP). In some countries, the figure was far higher — 140 percent in Egypt and Zaire, and a staggering 400 percent in Mozambique. Developing nations paid $77 billion in interest on their debts that year, and repaid $85 billion worth of principal. Since 1983, the traditional flow of capital from North to South has been reversed: the poor countries pay more to the rich than they receive in return, a net hemorrhage that now stands at more than $50 billion a year.[4]

Source: "Reshaping the Global Economy," in Lester R. Brown et al., eds., *State of the World 1991* (Washington, DC: Worldwatch Institute, 1991), pp. 170–88. Copyright © 1991 by Worldwatch Institute. Reprinted with the permission of W.W. Norton & Company, Inc.

Lack of capital has made it nearly impossible for developing countries to invest adequately in forest protection, soil conservation, irrigation improvements, more energy-efficient technologies, or pollution control devices. Even worse, growing debts have compelled them to sell off natural resources, often their only source of foreign currency. Like a consumer forced to hock the family heirlooms to pay credit card bills, developing countries are plundering forests, decimating fisheries, and depleting water supplies — regardless of the long-term consequences. Unfortunately, no global pawnbroker is holding on to this inheritance until the world can afford to buy it back. Greatly lessening the debt burden is thus a prerequisite for an environmentally sustainable world economy.

Very little of the aid money disbursed to developing countries by governments and international lending institutions supports ecologically sound development. The World Bank, the largest single funder, lacks a coherent vision of a sustainable economy, and thus its lending priorities often run counter to the goal of creating one. Bilateral aid agencies, with a few important exceptions, do little better. Moreover, the scale of total lending falls far short of that needed to help the Third World escape from the overlapping traps of poverty, overpopulation, and ecological decline.

At the heart of the dilemma at the national level is the failure of economies to incorporate environmental costs into private decisions, which results in society at large bearing them, often in unanticipated ways. Automobile drivers do not pay the full costs of local air pollution or long-term climate change when they fill their gas tanks, nor do farmers pick up the whole tab for the health and ecological risks of using pesticides. This blinkered view of societal expenses has burdened many nations with huge environmental cleanup bills. In the United States, for instance, cleaning up thousands of abandoned hazardous waste sites is expected to cost $500 billion. And the Soviet Union's total bill from the Chernobyl nuclear accident is now expected to reach $358 billion, 14 percent of the country's GNP in 1988.[5]

Many industrial nations now spend 1–2 percent of their total economic output on pollution control, and these figures will increase in the years ahead. Such large sums spent on capturing pollutants at the end of the pipe, while necessary, are to some extent a measure of the economy's failure to foster practices that curb pollution at its source. Governments mandate catalytic converters for cars, but neglect energy-efficient transport systems that would lessen automobile dependence. They require expensive methods of treating hazardous waste, while doing little to encourage industries to reduce their generation of waste.[6]

Of the many tools governments can use to reorient economic behavior, environmental taxes are among the most promising. Designed to make prices better reflect true costs, they would help ensure that those causing environmental harm pay the price, rather than society as a whole. In addition, eliminating government incentives that unwittingly foster resource destruction and establishing ones that encourage environmentally sound practices is essential to moving national economies quickly onto a stable path.

Many of these changes will only come about if policymakers replace growth with sustainability as their central goal. As long as GNP expands through massive releases of greenhouse gases into the atmosphere, rampant deforestation, and health-threatening air pollution, it no longer makes sense to equate this common measure with progress. With sustainability as the yardstick, what counts is not whether the economy grows but whether needs and wants are met without destroying the resource base. Examined in this light, it becomes clear that sustainability can only be achieved by slowing and then stopping population growth and by reducing the material consumption of the world's fortunate.

Not only do global environmental threats now constrain economic activity, they raise the wrenching question of whether the world our children inherit will provide for their needs as well as it does our own. Never before have economic policymakers had to be so concerned about future generations. A wholly new set of goals have been added to the traditional ones of creating jobs, spurring growth, and allocating resources efficiently.

AID FOR SUSTAINABLE DEVELOPMENT

After a decade of economic and environmental decline, many developing countries are at a dangerous crossroads. Unless poor nations are able to invest sufficient resources in such things as conserving soil, improving energy efficiency, and providing family planning to the impoverished majority, their life-support systems will be irreparably damaged. And as environmental problems become global in scale, the world as a whole has a growing stake in the ability to marshal an ecologically sound development effort in the Third World.

Bilateral nonmilitary aid provided by rich nations to poor ones in 1989 reached a net total of $41 billion. Loans from the World Bank and the regional development banks totaled $28 billion in 1989, most of it borrowed on commercial markets. For 50 nations, annual net receipts exceed 10 percent of their individual GNPs.[7]

U.S. aid has actually declined in real terms, to $7.7 billion in 1989, while Japan has emerged as the world's largest donor, contributing nearly $9 billion that year. (See Table 33.1.) Measured as a share of GNP, the differences among aid levels are notable — from less than 0.2 percent in the United States to more than 1 percent in Norway.[8]

The Organisation for Economic Co-operation and Development (OECD) has set a goal of boosting annual aid levels to 0.7 percent of each member's GNP, which would double current assistance to over $80 billion a year. Unfortunately, in many donor countries aid levels are actually declining. Moreover, the shift of aid toward such sustainable development priorities as reforestation, family planning, or energy efficiency is proceeding slowly if at all. Just 7 percent of bilateral aid funds go to population and health, for example.[9]

As much as two thirds of some countries' aid is tied to the domestic purchase of goods and services, essentially a form of export promotion. Furthermore, the Soviet Union and the United States give most of their assistance to just a handful of nations deemed strategically important. Soviet aid is now dwindling rapidly, and Washington provides 39 percent of its nonmilitary aid to Israel, Egypt, and El Salvador, which together have only 1.2 percent of the world's population. Fortunately, other donor nations in Europe and elsewhere tend to spread their development assistance more widely.[10]

Aid programs are therefore badly in need of an overhaul. Norway, in many ways the world leader in development assistance, might serve as a model. Not only does this small nation provide more aid as a share of its GNP than any other country, it is increasingly focused on sustainable development, as mandated by Parliament in 1987. Agriculture and fisheries receive 19 percent of Norwegian development assistance, and education gets 8 percent. In addition, a special environment fund disbursed more than $10 million to developing countries in 1990. The leading recipients of Norwegian aid are the neediest countries — including, for example, Tanzania, Bangladesh, and India. If the world as a whole had the priorities reflected in Norway's aid budget, Third World environmental reforms would be much further along.[11]

The World Bank and the three regional development banks are well situated to help the Third World develop sustainably. Their influence is even greater than the $28 billion they lent in 1989 suggests, since their prejudices are reflected in the lending patterns of commercial banks and in the investment priorities of many poor nations. A clearly articulated sustainable development strategy by the World Bank would provide badly needed intellectual leadership for the world.[12]

At the moment, the World Bank continues its traditional bread and butter lending for large capital-intensive projects such as road building, dam construction, and irrigation projects, making it an accomplice to the pollution of rivers, the burning of rain forests, and the strip-mining of vast areas, often in countries that cannot even monitor the damage. In several cases, Bank-supported projects are now the object of vehement opposition by local people — usually the rural poor, who are most affected.[13]

Serious efforts to reform the Bank began slowly in the early eighties under pressure from environmental groups worldwide. In a 1987 speech, Bank president Barber Conable acknowledged the institution's problems and pledged new initiatives. This was followed by the creation of a central Environment Department as well as four regional environment divisions. Yet today, the professional environmental staff numbers just 54, assisted by 23 consultants — out of a total World Bank professional staff of more than 4,000.[14]

Among the accomplishments touted by World Bank officials are 11 "freestanding" environmental loans in 1990. Some are indeed laudable, such as $237 million given for sewerage, drainage, and water supply improvements in several Indonesian cities. Included,

Table 33.1 Development Assistance from Selected Industrial Nations, 1989

Country	Development Aid	Share of GNP
	(billion dollars)	(percent)
Norway	0.92	1.04
Netherlands	2.09	0.94
France	7.45	0.78
Canada	2.32	0.44
Italy	3.61	0.42
Germany	4.95	0.41
Australia	1.02	0.38
Japan	8.95	0.32
United Kingdom	2.59	0.31
United States	7.66	0.15

Source: Organisation for Economic Co-operation and Development, *Development Co-operation: Efforts and Policies of the Members of the Development Assistance Committee. 1994 Report.* (Paris: OECD, 1995). © OECD, 1995. Reproduced by permission of the OECD.

however, is a "sustainable forestry" project in Côte d'Ivoire that is likely to result in accelerated logging and deforestation. Even more suspect is the Bank's claim that half its loans now include "environmental components." This classification is often little more than a new label on old projects.[15]

Barber Conable has found it easy to get inspiring reports written, but harder to motivate the people who continue to churn out loans for dams and roads. Bank staffers are rewarded for the quantity of loans they process, not their quality. The Bank is also plagued by a culture of secrecy and arrogance that makes it resistant both to its own internal reformers and to pressures exerted from the outside by governments and nongovernmental organizations (NGOs). Staff who push for faster and more fundamental reforms have sometimes been reassigned to less influential posts.[16]

Although new priorities, such as improved energy efficiency, are recommended in World Bank policy papers, they are still badly underfunded. Energy supply projects such as coal plants and hydro dams are the largest area of Bank lending, receiving 16–18 percent of the loans in recent years. Energy efficiency loans, however, still represent less than 3 percent of the Bank's lending to energy and industry.[17]

An environmental assessment process has also been set up to review the potential impact of proposed projects. But its effectiveness is undermined by the fact that the borrowing countries, eager to obtain loans, are responsible for the assessment; often they have neither the staff nor the skills to do the job. As a result, destructive projects are still going forward with only minor restrictions.[18]

Part of the problem is that within this huge bureaucracy, the new Environment Department is weak — appended to the Policy, Research, and External Affairs complex, with no direct involvement in lending operations. The department will need to be strengthened and the environmental review process more carefully controlled by in-house staff if the list of environmental disasters supported by the World Bank is to be shortened.[19]

It is time for a second generation of fundamental reforms at the World Bank — ones that address the institutional resistance to change and set genuinely new priorities. Even a strengthened Environment Department is not enough. Without a coherent vision of ecologically sound development, the Bank will continue to stumble from one environmental confrontation to another.

Restructuring lending programs will involve tackling some thorny issues. The World Bank's current portfolio of large, capital-intensive project loans requires less staff time to design and oversee than a program of smaller loans would. This allows the institution to finance its lending using the small margin between its own borrowing costs and the rate it charges developing countries — which is lower than comparable commercial lending rates. To support smaller, more labor-intensive projects such as community woodlots, integrated pest management for small farmers, rural cookstove industries, or urban bicycle factories, new financing mechanisms are needed.

One possibility is to shift the balance between project and policy lending. This latter category now accounts for 20–30 percent of the Bank's loan portfolio and is used to meet government funding needs, including structural adjustment lending that has been used recently to reduce subsidies and otherwise streamline Third World governments. Policy loans involve lower overhead costs than project loans do; if their share were increased, the project loans could be made at lower interest rates, making it possible to support smaller, more labor-intensive development efforts. At the same time, however, it is essential that policy loans be reoriented to encourage environmentally sound development, in effect using structural adjustment lending to foster environmental as well as economic reforms. Levying pollution taxes, for example, or cutting pesticide subsidies would improve the fiscal health of Third World governments and reduce their environmental problems.[20]

On the project lending side, an environmentally responsible development bank might, at least in the initial years, be one that provided more loans but less money. The Bank needs to emphasize the nature and effect of its loans rather than the dollars disbursed. It could support such projects as raising irrigation efficiency, building factories that turn out efficient light bulbs, and training workers in everything from planting trees to installing solar collectors. Directing even a small portion of loans to facilities such as Bangladesh's Grameen Bank, which makes "micro loans" to the rural poor, could spur myriad grassroots projects.[21]

For sustainable development to become the priority, it is essential that the development banks do more to involve local people in decision making. This would require easing the oppressive secrecy that now prevents both the affected public and even the Bank's directors from learning essential details of proposed projects. Ideally, the World Bank would become a force for openness and provide avenues for public participation. Many groups in the Third World are ready and willing to get involved in this process.[22]

Beyond the reform of aid and lending, debt reduction is essential to sustainable economic progress in many developing countries. Although the first step out of the morass is for the poor nations to continue their fundamental economic reforms, richer countries have their own responsibility to help reduce Third World debts, many of them accrued with their encouragement. Unfortunately, efforts to date have only nibbled at the problem. Neither the Baker plan of the mid-eighties nor the Brady plan that followed has appreciably reduced the debt burden, though they did give the commercial banks enough breathing room to reduce their risk of default.[23]

Turning the debt crisis around will require more than rescheduling payments or issuing new loans. The international financial institutions and commercial banks that hold most of the outstanding notes will almost certainly need to write down many debts and entirely forgive others. The governments of Canada, Germany, the United Kingdom, and the United States have between them already forgiven over $5 billion worth of public loans to sub-Saharan African countries. This is the right approach, but commercial loans will also need to be written off.[24]

A number of imaginative proposals to reduce Third World debt have been floated, but so far the leadership needed to implement them has been lacking. By definition, any successful debt-reduction strategy is one that brings Third World debt down to a level that allows environmentally sound development to be restored. Achieving this may require debt reduction on the order of 60 percent, a cut from $1.2 trillion to $500 billion. As several economists have suggested, it is logical to build incentives for environmental protection into a debt-reduction strategy.[25]

On a more limited scale, U.S. biologist Thomas Lovejoy has introduced an environmental financing concept known as "debt-for-nature swaps." Under his proposal, a conservation organization buys a portion of a debtor's obligation from a commercial bank on the open market, usually at just 15–30 percent of its face value. The developing country's central bank then issues bonds in local currency, at something less than the value of the original debt, which are used by an indigenous environmental group for conservation purposes.[26]

By August 1990, 15 such debt-for-nature swaps had been arranged in eight countries, including Bolivia, Madagascar, and Poland. One of the largest and most far-reaching is the Dutch government's purchase of $33 million worth of Costa Rica's debt in exchange for $10 million of local investments in refor-

estation, watershed management, and soil conservation. The face value of all debt eliminated in this way so far amounts to less than $100 million, or one ten-thousandth of the total. This is clearly not a solution to the debt problem, but it is an important source of funds for environmental NGOs and for a broader array of sustainable development programs. If other governments or even private banks were to follow the Dutch approach, the far larger sums involved could meaningfully reduce debt as well as help more countries onto a sustainable development path.[27]

Another financing idea whose time may have come is that of establishing one or more international environmental funds to provide resources to address global concerns such as climate change and ozone depletion that individual nations do not have sufficient incentive to tackle on their own. The bulk of the money raised would go to poor nations that are short of capital for needed investments.

The notion of an international environmental fund was proposed by former Indian prime minister Rajiv Gandhi in 1989, and has been endorsed by the French government and the Executive Director of the United Nations Environment Programme (UNEP), Mostafa Tolba. Such a fund could either be paid for through government donations, such as those used to replenish the World Bank and U.N. agencies, or by levying a new environmental tax, possibly on carbon emitted by burning fossil fuels. The creation of a new financing mechanism of this kind will be high on the agenda for the U.N. Conference on Environment and Development in Brazil in 1992.[28]

In September 1989, the international community agreed to set up an environmental fund — to be managed by the World Bank in cooperation with the U.N. Development Programme and UNEP and to be in place by early 1991. Although the Bank's reputation for efficiency led governments to place the fund there, some environmental NGOs have opposed this, given the Bank's poor environmental record.[29]

The new fund is to be dedicated to four key priorities: protecting the ozone layer, limiting greenhouse gas emissions, preserving biodiversity, and protecting international water resources. Initial financing of the ozone portion was set at $240 million at a June 1990 conference on revising the Montreal Protocol held in London. Additional government commitments are still being discussed — reportedly aiming at a total fund of more than $1 billion for the first three years. The U.S. government opposed establishing such a fund, but finally agreed in November 1990 to provide financing if certain conditions were met.[30]

So far, the world community is making only halting progress in mobilizing the financial resources to stop the process of global environmental decline. The central issues are how to reduce the debt burden, how to increase and rechannel development aid, and how to overcome the institutional biases and inertia of the World Bank and other multilateral lenders. Unless nations address the twin problems of growing Third World poverty and increasing international inequity, global economic and environmental decline are certain to accelerate.

REDIRECTING GOVERNMENT INCENTIVES

At the national level, governments employ a wide variety of tools to shape economic and social activity. Unfortunately, and rather surprisingly, many deliberate government policies are stacked squarely against sustainability. Road building, biased utility regulation, subsidized irrigation services, and below-cost timber sales are but a sampling of the numerous public programs that result in environmental damage. Often just where taxes are justified to reduce a harmful activity, a public subsidy instead promotes it. Collectively, governments spend tens of billions of dollars a year supporting environmentally unsound economic practices.

Government subsidies for pesticides, which take such forms as tax exemptions and below-cost sales by government-controlled distributors, provide one example of these perverse incentives. In examining policies among nine developing countries — three each in Asia, Africa, and Latin America — Robert Repetto of the World Resources Institute in Washington, D.C., found pesticide subsidies in the early eighties ranging from 19 percent of the unsubsidized retail cost (in China) to 89 percent (in Senegal). The median subsidy was Colombia's 44 percent. In Egypt, subsidies equal to 83 percent of full retail costs drained the treasury of more than $200 million per year. The Egyptian government spent more per capita on pesticide subsidies in 1982 than it currently spends on health.[31]

By keeping pesticide costs low, governments aim to help farmers reduce pest damage and thereby increase crop yields. But it also encourages them to use pesticides excessively, increasing the myriad risks associated with toxic farm chemicals. And subsidies undermine the development and use of integrated pest management (IPM), a package of measures designed to control pests in a safer, more ecologically sound way. To name but a few successes, IPM has proved effective with soybeans in Brazil, with cotton in China,

Nicaragua, and Texas, with cassava in equatorial Africa, and with rice in Indonesia — often reducing pesticide use by more than half. Heavy subsidies for chemicals prevent these promising methods from taking hold.[32]

Similarly, forests have suffered in rich and poor countries alike from government efforts to "develop" their economies and promote growth. Many governments are in effect subsidizing wholesale forest destruction, a practice that costs public treasuries vast sums each year. Laden with debt and looking for quick revenues, many tropical-country governments — often aided by international donors — have instituted tax credits and other fiscal incentives to encourage the conversion of forests to pasture, cash crops, and other land uses that may earn short-term profits but rarely prove sustainable on poor tropical soils. Harvesting contracts excessively favorable to loggers have fueled "timber booms" that not only deplete and degrade forests but give colonizing farmers access to lands with soils that often will not sustain agriculture.[33]

Brazil, Indonesia, and the Philippines are among the countries losing from $500 million to more than $1 billion annually through such economic policies. Much of the deforestation of the Brazilian Legal Amazon, totaling by 1989 some 40 million hectares (an area larger than Japan), can be linked to government road building, resettlement schemes, and various fiscal and land tenure policies. One particularly powerful incentive was hefty income tax credits — up to 50 percent in some cases — if the resulting savings were invested in the Amazon region. A good deal of this money went into clearing land to plant pasture for livestock ranches, many of which now yield only a small fraction of planned production; some no longer produce anything at all.[34]

Recent deforestation trends in Brazil suggest how rapidly change can occur once subsidies are removed. Former president José Sarney suspended most tax credits that encouraged forest clearing in 1988 and the new administration of Fernando Collor de Mello has curtailed them further. Satellite data show that deforestation in the Amazon peaked in 1987 at 8 million hectares, dropping to 4.8 million in 1988 and to 3 million in 1989. An unusually rainy dry season, when most of the burning takes place, coupled with stepped-up enforcement against illegal burning, helped stem the loss in 1989. But the elimination of financial incentives appears to have played a major role.[35]

In addition to the immediate environmental benefits, reducing such subsidies often lessens a source of social inequity and frees up funds for programs that benefit the poor. Those in place today often enrich the politically powerful and relatively well-off, who can successfully lobby for economic favors. Pesticide and irrigation subsidies, for instance, do nothing for the cash-poor, dryland farmer who has no access to these inputs. Likewise, subsidies for cattle ranching and logging bypass those on the lower economic rungs.[36]

Eliminating environmentally destructive incentives helps ensure that people and industries pay the full costs of their activities. Reshaping economies rapidly enough to avoid the breakdown of critical environmental systems requires a distinctly different set of incentives, however — ones that reward ecologically sound practices, and thus makes them attractive. Such incentives would not remain in place indefinitely, but would jump-start the economy, moving it quickly onto a sustainable track.

There is almost no limit to the innovative ways of marshaling private investment to work for the good of the environment. It demands, however, a systematic look at how current rules, regulations, and incentives shape behavior, and how they can be changed to foster sound decisions.

In the United States, for example, the Conservation Reserve Program gives farmers an economic reason to conserve soil. By agreeing to plant their most erodible land in trees or grass for 10 years, farmers receive about $120 per hectare in annual rental payments. As of 1990, almost 14 million hectares had entered the five-year-old program, and excessive soil erosion nationwide had been cut by nearly a third, from 1.6 billion tons to 1.1 billion.[37]

Reforming the way utilities are regulated could unleash the vast money-saving potential of energy efficiency while slowing global warming, reducing acid rain, and curbing urban air pollution. Under most current regulations, utility profits rise in tandem with electricity sales. Even though utilities could save energy — for example, through consumer service programs that install efficient lighting, low-flow showerheads, and insulation in homes and offices — at far less cost than supplying more, they have little incentive to do so.[38]

In the United States, new programs in California, New York, Oregon, and five New England states are "decoupling" profits from power sales, and giving utilities a direct financial incentive to invest in efficiency. In California, a proposal by the three largest electric utilities, approved in August 1990 by the Public Utilities Commission, ties earnings to energy savings. If conservation targets are met, one utility will be allowed electricity rates that yield an annual return of 14.6 percent on its conservation investments, substantially higher than the 10.7 percent the company would get

from investing those funds in a new power plant. The other two will receive in profits 15–17 percent of the value of the energy savings they undertake for customers. Together, the efficiency programs will cost an estimated $500 million over the next two years, but are expected to save more than twice that in reduced power bills.[39]

Per capita energy use in developing countries is far lower than in industrial ones; in many cases, increased supplies are essential to raising living standards. But efficiency improvements have an enormous untapped potential here as well. Energy analyst Howard Geller has found, for instance, that over the next two decades Brazil could cut its growth in electricity use in half, from 5.2 percent per year to 2.6 percent, by promoting efficient technologies. Indeed, by using economic incentives to encourage conservation and efficiency investments — instead of subsidizing energy use — developing countries could avoid more than $1.4 trillion in energy supply costs over the next 20 years, saving scarce capital and improving the environment at the same time.[40]

Creative incentives could also give a much-needed boost to family planning efforts in the Third World, which unfortunately have been neglected during the eighties. Setting up education savings accounts for the children of couples who limit their family size, allowing higher income tax deductions for couples with no more than two children, and providing free family planning services are but a few of the incentives possible.[41]

Well-designed incentive programs are cost-effective, since expenditures to reduce fertility levels avoid larger social service costs later on. In Mexico, for example, every peso spent on family planning by the urban social security system between 1972 and 1984 saved nine pesos that would have been spent on maternal and infant health care. By providing nearly 800,000 women with contraceptives, the program averted 3.6 million unwanted births and resulted in a net savings of some 318 billion pesos ($2 billion).[42]

Relatively little attention has been given to the environmental effects of trade policies, but they are undoubtedly as serious as they are difficult to untangle. Trade rules and agreements are a major determinant of how natural resources are used, what pressures are placed on the environment, and who benefits from the huge money flows — now $3 trillion annually — that cross borders with the exchange of goods.[43]

From the standpoint of economic efficiency alone, trade distortions — including import quotas, tariffs, export subsidies, and domestic price supports — are undesirable, since they restrict competition in the global marketplace. It was a pre-world-war trading system plagued by such measures that spurred the creation of the General Agreement on Tariffs and Trade (GATT), which began operating in 1948 and now covers nearly 90 percent of world merchandise trade. Seven rounds of negotiations to amend the GATT have left many restrictions in place, particularly in politically sensitive areas such as agriculture. In recent years, the rich nations' trade barriers and domestic farm price supports for commodities such as sugar have cost the Third World an estimated $30 billion annually in lost agricultural income, and industrial-country consumers some $245 billion in higher prices and taxes.[44]

Freer trade, however, would not necessarily help the poorest people in the Third World, nor be a net benefit to the environment. Much depends, for instance, on who gains from the added export revenue — peasant farmers or wealthy landowners. Much depends, too, on whether opening world markets would cause scarce land and water to be diverted from subsistence to export crops, at the expense of the poor and of food self-sufficiency.[45]

Moreover, freer trade could draw countries to the least common denominator in environmental protection and undermine conservation efforts. A U.S. proposal to "harmonize" international food safety standards under the GATT could force countries that have strict limits on pesticide residues in food to lower them to the established international standard. Removing a country's prerogative to set restrictions could eliminate important conservation tools, such as the import ban placed on ivory to help protect the African elephant, or the bans on raw log exports instituted by Indonesia, the Philippines, and Thailand to help preserve their forests.[46]

When the Danish government decided that all beer and soft drinks, whether produced domestically or imported, should be sold in refillable bottles, it was taken to the European Community's Court of Justice on the grounds that the requirement restricted free trade. Setting what may be a key precedent, the Court upheld Denmark's right to refuse imports of canned beverages on environmental grounds. That the Danish initiative even was challenged, however, underscores the need to ensure that trade rules explicitly permit countries to set high standards and to freely pursue their environmental goals. Unfortunately, as of November 1990, with the Uruguay Round slated to end in December, the GATT negotiators had not seriously considered the environmental implications of their proposals.[47]

In establishing a comprehensive incentive structure to promote sustainability, governments might now consider one overarching guideline: no net environmental damage. This would preclude projects that destroy forests, add carbon to the atmosphere, or pave over croplands unless additional investments were made to compensate for the damage done. Enforcing such a policy would be politically difficult, to say the least, yet one or two modest steps in this direction have been suggested.

The Netherlands has launched a project to plant 125,000 hectares of trees in five Latin American countries over the next 25 years to offset the estimated carbon emissions from a Dutch coal-fired power plant to be completed during the nineties. Ideally, of course, the coal plant would not be built in the first place, and the Dutch would instead meet new energy demands through improved efficiency and renewable sources. But since trees absorb carbon from the atmosphere through photosynthesis, planting more of them can counteract emissions from fossil fuels and help lessen the risk of greenhouse warming.[48]

Making such compensating investments mandatory, for both public and private investors, would ensure that those who profit from "development" plow some of their expected proceeds back into safeguarding the natural systems they place in jeopardy. It is no more radical a notion than that of requiring investors to pay back their creditors. In this case, the creditor is the global ecosystem.

GREEN TAXES

Perhaps the single most powerful instrument for redirecting national economies toward environmental sustainability is taxation. Taxing products and activities that pollute, deplete, or otherwise degrade natural systems is a way of ensuring that environmental costs are taken into account in private decisions — whether to commute by car or bicycle, for example, or to generate electricity from coal or sunlight. Each individual producer or consumer decides how to adjust to the higher costs: a tax on air emissions would lead some factories to add pollution controls, some to change their production processes, and others to redesign products so as to generate less waste. By raising a large proportion of revenue from such "green taxes" and reducing income taxes or others to compensate, governments can help move economies swiftly onto a sustainable track.

Taxes are appealing because they offer an efficient way of correcting for the market's failure to value environmental services. If the atmosphere is a free repository for waste products, industries will pollute heavily, and society at large will bear the costs in terms of health care, lost agricultural output, and climate change. Similarly, if farmers pay nothing for using nearby waterways to carry off pesticide residues, they will use more of these chemicals than society would want, and rural people will pay the price in contaminated drinking water.[49]

So far, most governments trying to correct such market failures have turned to regulatory standards, dictating what measures must be taken to meet environmental goals. This approach has measurably improved the environment in many cases, and is especially important where there is little room for error, such as in disposing of high-level radioactive waste or safeguarding an endangered species. But it has often turned out to be a costly and cumbersome way of bringing about widespread change. Taxes can help meet broad environmental goals efficiently, since they adjust prices and then let the market do the rest.[50]

Many countries have already established green taxes. A survey of OECD members turned up more than 50 environmental charges, including levies on air and water pollution, waste, and noise, as well as various product charges, such as fees on fertilizers and batteries. In most cases, however, these fees have been set too low to motivate major changes in behavior, and have been used instead to raise a modest amount of revenue for an environmental program or other specific purpose. Norway's surcharge on fertilizers and pesticides, for instance, raises funds for programs in sustainable agriculture — certainly a worthy cause — but is too low to reduce greatly the amount of chemicals farmers use in the short term.[51]

There are, however, some notable exceptions. In the United Kingdom, a higher tax on leaded gasoline increased the market share of unleaded gas from 4 percent in April 1989 to 30 percent in March 1990. And in late 1989, the U.S. Congress passed a tax on the sale of ozone-depleting chlorofluorocarbons (CFCs) in order to hasten their phaseout, which the nation has agreed to do by the end of the decade, and to capture the expected windfall profits as the chemicals' prices rise. The most widely used CFCs are initially being taxed at $3.02 per kilogram ($1.37 per pound), roughly twice the current price; the tax will rise to $6.83 per kilogram by 1995 and to $10.80 per kilogram by 1999. During the first five years, this is expected to generate $4.3 billion in revenues.[52]

A comprehensive set of environmental taxes, designed as part of a broader restructuring of fiscal policy, could do much more to steer the economy toward sustainability. Most governments raise the bulk of their revenues by taxing income, profits, and the value added to goods and services. This has the perverse effect of discouraging work, savings, and investment — things that are generally good for an economy. If governments substituted taxes on pollution, waste, and resource depletion for a large portion of current levies, both the environment and the economy could benefit.

Completely shifting the tax base would not be desirable, since income taxes can be designed to ensure that the wealthy pay a proportionately higher share; green taxes, on balance, would not serve this equity goal. Indeed, to offset any regressive effect, income tax rates would need to be lowered for poorer people, who would suffer, for example, from higher heating fuel prices. Government payments could compensate the very poor, who may not pay any income taxes at all now but who might experience higher living costs under an environmental tax code. Moreover, since green-tax revenues would diminish as production and consumption patterns shift away from the taxed activity, they would not be as constant a source of revenue as income taxes are. For all these reasons, some blend of taxes seems best.

A tax on carbon emissions from fossil fuels, urgently needed to slow the pace of global warming, is the one likely to raise the most revenue. Levied on the carbon content of coal, oil, and natural gas, an effective charge must be high enough to reduce emissions of carbon dioxide, now the official goal of more than a dozen industrial nations. Carbon taxes went into effect in Finland and the Netherlands in early 1990; Sweden is expected to begin collecting carbon taxes in January 1991. Unfortunately, none of these levies seems high enough to spur major changes in energy use.[53]

In late September 1990, the 12 environment ministers from the European Community (EC) gathered in Rome to discuss the possibility of community-wide green taxes. Though they failed to reach agreement, the meeting placed environmental taxes squarely on Europe's political agenda. The European Commission itself supports a common EC tax on carbon emissions, as do Belgium, Denmark, France, and Germany. The less wealthy EC members fear, however, that a harmonized tax would be too high, jeopardizing their growth, while the Netherlands worries that it might be too low. Even if community-wide taxes are not set, however, it seems likely that many countries will introduce them individually over the next few years.[54]

In the United States, several energy taxes have been proposed, including higher levies on gasoline, new fees on imported oil, and taxes on the carbon content of fossil fuels. Among these, the carbon tax — levied on coal at the mine, on oil at the wellfield or dock, and on natural gas at the wellhead — would most efficiently and effectively reduce CO_2 emissions. An August 1990 study by the U.S. Congressional Budget Office (CBO) examined the effect of phasing in a carbon tax over the next decade, beginning with $11 per ton of carbon in 1991 and rising to $110 per ton in 2000 (in 1988 dollars). When fully implemented, the tax would generate an estimated $120 billion in annual revenues, equal to 30 percent of federal receipts from individual income taxes in 1988.[55]

The CBO estimates that the fee of $110 per ton of carbon would raise oil and natural gas prices by about half over the levels currently projected for 2000, and the expected price of coal — the most carbon-rich of the fossil fuels — by 256 percent. This would encourage industries and consumers to invest in efficiency measures, and to switch to noncarbon energy sources.[56]

The model used by CBO that best reflects business and consumer responses to changed energy prices shows that carbon emissions would be 37 percent lower than now projected in the year 2000, while the nation's energy efficiency would improve by 23 percent. (See Table 33.2.) The nation would also meet the much discussed international target of cutting CO_2 emissions 20 percent from the 1988 level by the year 2005. The model projects a drop of $45 billion in the GNP in 2000, a modest 0.6 percent, which could likely be avoided by pairing the carbon tax with reductions in income or other taxes.[57]

A comprehensive environmental tax code would alter economic activity in many other areas. It could penalize the use of virgin materials, the generation of toxic waste, emissions of acid rain-forming pollutants, and the overpumping of groundwater. A team of researchers at the Umwelt und Prognose Institut (Environmental Assessment Institute) in Heidelberg proposed a varied set of taxes for the former West Germany that would have collectively raised more than 210 billion deutsche marks ($136 billion). The researchers analyzed more than 30 possible "eco-taxes," and determined tax levels that would markedly shift consumption patterns for each item. In some cases, a doubling or tripling of prices was needed to cut consumption substantially. For example, halving pesticide use would require a tax on the order of 200 percent of current pesticide prices.[58]

No study as comprehensive has been done yet for the United States. But a list of just eight possible green taxes suggests they have substantial revenue-raising potential while working to protect the environment. (See Table 33.3.) Determining the appropriate tax levels — ones that reduce harm to human health and the environment without damaging the economy — is complicated; the ones shown here are simply for illustration. Moreover, data on all the activities that would be taxed are not up to date. The estimate for groundwater depletion, for example, is for 1980; pesticide sales are for 1988. It is impossible to say what level of activity would exist when the taxes were fully in force.[59]

Because some taxes have multiple effects (a carbon tax, for example, would reduce emissions of sulfur dioxide by lowering fossil fuel consumption), and because levels of the taxed activity will decline even before the tax is completely in place, revenues shown

---

Table 33.2 United States: Estimated Effects of a $110–Per-Ton Carbon Tax in the Year 2000[1]

Options	Energy Consumption	Energy Intensity	Carbon Emissions	Real GNP[2]
	(quadrillion Btus)	(1,000 Btus per 1988 dollar of GNP)	(billion tons)	(billion 1988 dollars)
Year 2000 without Tax	90	13	1.6	7,137
Year 2000 with Tax	69	10	1.0	7,092
		(percent)		
Change	−23	−23	−37	−0.6

[1]Assumes tax is phased in, starting at $11 per ton in 1991. Since these carbon figures are all metric, they differ from those in the source, which also gives emissions of carbon dioxide rather than carbon.
[2]Does not assume any offsetting reductions in income taxes.

Source: U.S. Congressional Budget Office, *Carbon Charges as a Response to Global Warming: The Effects of Taxing Fossil Fuels* (Washington, D.C.: U.S. Government Printing Office, 1990).

Table 33.3 United States: Potential Green Taxes

Tax Description	Quantity of Taxed Activity	Assumed Charge[1]	Resulting Annual Revenue[2]
			(billion dollars)
Carbon content of fossil fuels	1.3 billion tons	$100 per ton	130.0
Hazardous wastes generated	266 million tons	$100 per ton	26.6
Paper and paperboard produced from virgin pulp	61.5 million tons	$64 per ton	3.9
Pesticide sales	$7.38 billion	half of total sales	3.7
Sulfur dioxide emissions[3]	21 million tons	$150 per ton	3.2
Nitrogen oxides emissions[3]	20 million tons	$100 per ton	2.0
Chlorofluorocarbon sales[4]	225 million kilograms	$5.83 per kilogram	1.3
Groundwater depletion	20.4 million acre-feet	$50 per acre-foot	1.0

[1]Charges shown here are for illustration only, and are based simply on what seems reasonable given existing costs and prices. In some cases several taxes would exist in a given category to reflect differing degrees of harm; the hazardous waste tax shown, for instance, would be the average charge.

[2]Since revenue would diminish as the tax shifted production and consumption patterns, and since some taxes have multiple effects, the revenue column cannot be added to get a total revenue estimate.

[3]The Clean Air Act passed in October 1990 requires utility sulfur dioxide emissions to drop by 9 million tons and nitrogen oxide emissions by 1.8 million tons by the end of the decade.

[4]This tax already exists. Revenues shown here are expected for 1994.

Source: Worldwatch Institute. See endnote 59 for sources on the quantity of taxed activity.

in Table 33.3 cannot be totaled. But it seems likely that more than $100 billion could be raised just from the eight listed here.

Phasing in each tax over, say, 5 or 10 years would ease the economic effects and allow for a gradual adjustment. Countries wishing to keep the total tax burden the same so as to avoid slowing their economies could reduce income and other taxes in proportion to the added revenues. Others might choose to use some of the green-tax revenues for unmet fiscal needs — in the United States, for instance, to reduce the federal budget deficit. Virtually anywhere environmental taxes are applied, other taxes would need to be adjusted to ensure a progressive overall tax structure.

Beyond their role in reshaping national economies, green taxes can raise funds for global initiatives that require transfers from rich countries to poorer ones, transfers that would begin to pay back the ecological debt industrial countries have incurred by causing most of the damage to the global environment thus far. An extra tax of $10 per ton of carbon emitted in industrial countries (excluding Eastern Europe and the Soviet Union) would initially generate $25 billion per year for a global fund.[60]

Fiscal policy is a highly sensitive political issue. Opinion polls show that a good share of the public thinks more should be spent on protecting the environment, but most people harbor strong aversions to higher taxes. By shifting the tax base away from income and toward environmentally damaging activities, governments can reflect new priorities without increasing the total tax burden.[61]

FROM GROWTH TO SUSTAINABLE PROGRESS

Even if development aid is rechanneled, government incentives are restructured, and green taxes are instituted — all to encourage environmentally sound economic activity — there remains the vexing problem of scale. Listening to most economists and politicians, unlimited expansion of the economy seems not only possible but desirable. Political leaders tout growth as the answer to unemployment, poverty, ailing industries, fiscal crises, and myriad other societal ills. To question the wisdom of growth seems almost blasphemous, so ingrained is it in popular thinking about how the world works.

Yet to agree that creating an environmentally sustainable economy is necessary is to acknowledge that limits on some forms of growth are inevitable — in particular the consumption of physical resources. Textbook models often portray the economy as a self-contained system, with money flowing between consumers and businesses in a closed loop. In reality, however, the economy is not isolated. It operates within the boundaries of a global ecosystem with finite capacities to produce fresh water, form new topsoil, and absorb pollution. As a subset of the biosphere, the economy cannot outgrow its physical limits and still remain intact.[62]

With an annual output of $20 trillion, the global economy now produces in 17 days what it took an entire year to generate in 1900. Already, economic activity has breached numerous local, regional, and global thresholds, resulting in the spread of deserts, acidification of lakes and forests, and the buildup of greenhouse gases. If growth proceeds along the lines of recent decades, it is only a matter of time before global systems collapse under the pressure.[63]

One useful measure of the economy's size relative to the earth's life-supporting capacity is the share of the planet's photosynthetic product now devoted to human activity. "Net primary production" is the amount of solar energy fixed by green plants through photosynthesis minus the energy used by those plants themselves. It is, in essence, the planet's total food resource, the biochemical energy that supports all forms of animal life, from earthworms to humans.

Biologist Peter Vitousek at Stanford University and his colleagues estimate that 40 percent of the earth's annual net primary production on land now goes directly to meet human needs or is indirectly used or destroyed by human activity — leaving 60 percent for the millions of other land-based species with which humans share the planet. While it took all of human history to reach this point, the share could double to 80 percent by 2030 if current rates of population growth and consumption continue; rising per capita consumption could shorten the doubling time considerably. Along the way, with people usurping an ever larger share of the earth's life-sustaining energy, natural systems will unravel faster. Exactly when vital thresholds will be crossed irreversibly is impossible to say. But as Vitousek and his colleagues state, those "who believe that limits to growth are so distant as to be of no consequence for today's decision makers appear unaware of these biological realities."[64]

For humanity to avoid the wholesale breakdown of natural systems requires not just a slowing in the expansion of our numbers but a shift from the pursuit of growth to that of sustainable progress — human betterment that does not come at the expense of future generations. The first and easiest phase in the transition is to increase greatly the efficiency with which water, energy, and materials are used, which will allow people's needs to be satisfied with fewer resources and less environmental harm. This shift is already under way, but is proceeding at a glacial pace compared with what is needed.

One example of the necessary approach is in California. Pioneering energy policies there have fostered utility investments in efficiency, causing electricity use per person to decline 0.3 percent between 1978 and 1988, compared with an 11-percent increase in the rest of the United States. Californians suffered no drop in living standards as a result; indeed, their overall welfare improved since their electricity bills were reduced and their cooking, lighting, and other electrical needs were met with less sacrifice of air quality.[65]

Producing goods and services as efficiently as possible and with the most environmentally benign technologies available will move societies a long way toward sustainability, but it will not allow them to achieve it. Continuing growth in material consumption — the number of cars and air conditioners, the amount of paper used, and the like — will eventually overwhelm gains from efficiency, causing total resource use (and all the corresponding environmental damage) to rise. A halving of pollution emissions from individual cars, for example, will not result in much improvement in air quality if the total distance driven doubles, as it has in the United States since 1965.[66]

This aspect of the transition from growth to sustainability is thus far more difficult, as it goes to the heart of people's consumption patterns. In poorer countries, simply meeting the basic needs of growing human numbers will require that consumption of water, energy, and forest products increases, even if these resources are used with the utmost efficiency. But the wealthier industrial countries — especially the dozen that have stabilized their population size, including Austria, Germany, Italy, Norway, Sweden, and Switzerland — are in the best position to begin satisfying their needs with no net degradation of the natural resource base. These countries could be the first to benefit from realizing that some growth costs more than it is worth, and that an economy's optimum size is not its maximum size.[67]

GNP becomes an obsolete measure of progress in a society striving to meet people's needs as efficiently as possible and with the least damage to the environment. What counts is not growth in output, but the quality of services rendered. Bicycles and light rail, for instance, are less resource-intensive forms of transportation than automobiles are, and contribute less to GNP. But a shift to mass transit and cycling for most passenger trips would enhance urban life by eliminating traffic jams, reducing smog, and making cities safer for pedestrians. GNP would go down, but overall well-being would increase — underscoring the need for new indicators of progress.[68]

Likewise, investing in water-efficient appliances and irrigation systems instead of building more dams and diversion canals would meet water needs with less harm to the environment. Since massive water projects consume more resources than efficiency investments do, GNP would tend to decline. But quality of life would improve. It becomes clear that striving to boost GNP is often inappropriate and counterproductive. As ecologist and philosopher Garrett Hardin puts it, "For a statesman to try to maximize the GNP is about as sensible as for a composer of music to try to maximize the number of notes in a symphony."[69]

Abandoning growth as an overriding goal does not mean forsaking the poor. Rising incomes and material consumption are essential to improving well-being in much of the Third World. But contrary to what political leaders imply, global economic growth as currently pursued is not the solution to poverty. Despite the fivefold rise in world economic output since 1950, 1.2 billion people — more than ever — live in absolute poverty today. More growth of the sort engineered in recent decades will not save the poor; only a new set of priorities can.[70]

Formidable barriers stand in the way of shifting from growth to real progress as the central goal of economic policy. The vision that growth conjures up of an expanding pie of riches is a powerful and convenient political tool because it allows the tough issues of income inequality and skewed wealth distribution to be avoided. People assume that as long as there is growth, there is hope that the lives of the poor can be bettered without sacrifices from the rich. The reality, however, is that achieving an environmentally sustainable global economy is not possible without the fortunate limiting their consumption in order to leave room for the poor to increase theirs.

With the ending of the cold war and the fading of ideological barriers, an opportunity has opened to build a new world upon the foundations of peace. A sustainable economy represents nothing less than a higher social order — one as concerned with future generations as with our own, and more focused on the health of the planet and the poor than on material acquisitions and military might. While it is a fundamentally new endeavor, with many uncertainties, it is far less risky than continuing with business as usual.

The basic elements involved in getting there are no mystery; all the needed technologies, tools, and instruments of change exist. The real hurdle is deciding to commit ourselves to a new path. That commitment needs to come from each of us individually. And from all of us together.

NOTES

1. Throughout this chapter, the $20-trillion dollar world economy is a Worldwatch Institute estimate based on 1988 gross world product from Central Intelligence Agency (CIA), *Handbook of Economic Statistics, 1989* (Washington, D.C.: 1989), with Soviet and Eastern Europe gross national products extrapolated from Paul Marer, *Dollar GNP's of the USSR and Eastern Europe* (Baltimore: Johns Hopkins University Press, 1985), with adjustments to 1990 based on growth rates from International Monetary Fund (IMF), *World Economic Outlook* (Washington, D.C.: October 1990), and CIA, *Handbook of Economic Statistics*, and with the composite deflator from Office of Management and Budget, *Historical Tables, Budget of the United States Government, Fiscal Year 1990* (Washington, D.C.: U.S. Government Printing Office, 1989).

2. Fivefold global expansion from Angus Maddison, *The World Economy in the 20th Century* (Paris: Organisation of Economic Co-operation and Development (OECD), 1989), and from IMF, *World Economic Outlook*; carbon emissions from "Mauna Loa, 30 Years of Continuous CO_2 Measurements," *CDIAC Communications*, Carbon Dioxide Information Analysis Center, Oak Ridge National Laboratory, Oak Ridge, Tenn., Summer 1988; Charles D. Keeling, "Measurements of the Concentration of Atmospheric Carbon Dioxide at Mauna Loa Observatory, Hawaii, 1958–1986," Final Report for the Carbon Dioxide Information and Analysis Center, Martin-Marietta Energy Systems Inc., Oak Ridge, Tenn., April 1987; Neftel et al., "Evidence from Polar Ice Cores for the Increase in Atmospheric CO_2 in the Last Two Centuries," *Nature*, May 2, 1985; Intergovernmental Panel on Climate Change, "Policymakers' Summary of the Scientific Assessment of Climate Change," Report from Working Group I, June 1990.

3. Population estimates from Population Reference Bureau (PRB), *1989* and *1990 World Population Data Sheet* (Washington, D.C. 1989 and 1990); poverty figures from Alan B. Durning, *Poverty and the Environment: Reversing the Downward Spiral*, Worldwatch Paper 92 (Washington, D.C.: Worldwatch Institute, November 1989).

4. World Bank, *World Debt Tables 1989–1990: External Debt of Developing Countries, Vols. I and II* (Washington, D.C.: 1989).

5. Office of Technology Assessment, *Assessing Contractor Use in Superfund* (Washington, D.C.: 1989); WISE (World Information Service on Energy), "State of the

Soviet Nuclear Industry," Paris, May 18, 1990; Soviet GNP from CIA, *Handbook of Economic Statistics, 1989*.

6. OECD, *OECD in Figures* (Paris: 1990); Kit D. Farber and Gary L. Rutledge, "Pollution Abatement and Control Expenditures, 1984–87," *Survey of Current Business*, U.S. Department of Commerce, June 1989.

7. OECD, *Development Co-operation: Efforts and Policies of the Members of the Development Assistance Committee* (Paris: in press); OECD, *Development Co-operation in the 1990s: Efforts and Policies of the Members of the Development Assistance Committee* (Paris: 1989).

8. OECD, *Development Co-operation in the 1990s*; OECD, *Development Co-operation* (in press).

9. OECD, *Development Co-operation* (in press).

10. OECD, *Development Co-operation in the 1990s*; Agency for International Development, *Agency for International Development Fiscal Year 1991 Summary Tables* (Washington, D.C.: 1990); PRB, *1990 World Population Data Sheet*.

11. OECD, *Development Co-operation* (in press); Sigismund Niebel, Reporting System Division, OECD, Paris, private communication, November 18, 1990.

12. OECD, *Development Co-operation* (in press); World Bank, *The World Bank Annual Report 1990* (Washington, D.C.: 1990).

13. World Bank, *The World Bank Annual Report 1990*; Bruce Rich, Environmental Defense Fund, "The Environmental Performance of the Public International Financial Institutions and Other Related Issues," Testimony before the Committee on Appropriations, U.S. Senate, Washington, D.C., July 25, 1990; Stephan Schwartzman, *Bankrolling Disasters: International Development Banks and the Global Environment* (Washington, D.C.: Sierra Club, 1986).

14. Barber B. Conable, President, World Bank, "The World Bank and International Finance Corporation," presented to the World Resources Institute, Washington, D.C., May 5, 1987; World Bank, *The World Bank and the Environment: First Annual Report Fiscal 1990* (Washington, D.C.: 1990); Personnel Office, World Bank, Washington D.C., private communication, November 1, 1990.

15. World Bank, *The World Bank and the Environment*; Bruce Rich, "The Emperor's New Clothes: The World Bank and Environmental Reform," *World Policy Journal*, Spring 1990.

16. Michael Irwin, "Why I've Had It with the World Bank," *Wall Street Journal*, March 30, 1990; World Bank staff, private communications, October 1990.

17. Howard Geller, "End-Use Electricity Conservation: Options for Developing Countries," Energy Department Paper No. 32, World Bank, Washington, D.C., 1986; World Bank, *The World Bank Annual Report 1990*; Rich, "The Environmental Performance of the Public International Financial Institutions and Other Related Issues."

18. Environmental assessment process detailed in World Bank, *The World Bank and the Environment*; Rich, "The Environmental Performance of the Public International Financial Institutions and Other Related Issues."

19. Location of the Environment Department in World Bank, *The World Bank and the Environment*.

20. World Bank staff, private communications.

21. Mahabub Hossain, *Credit for Alleviation of Rural Poverty: The Grameen Bank in Bangladesh*, Research Report 65 (Washington, D.C.: International Food Policy Research Institute, 1988).

22. NGO Working Group on the World Bank, "Position Paper of the NGO Working Group on the World Bank," Geneva, December 1989; Irwin, "Why I've Had It with the World Bank."

23. Overseas Development Council, "The Brady Plan: An Interim Assessment," Washington, D.C., 1990; *Securing Our Global Future: Canada's Stake in the Unfinished Business of Third World Debt*, Minutes of Proceedings and Evidence of the Standing Committee on External Affairs and International Affairs, Canadian House of Commons, June 7, 1990.

24. World Bank, *World Debt Talks*; Canadian House of Commons, *Securing Our Global Future*; Jane Perlez, "U.S. Forgives Loans to 12 African Countries," *New York Times*, January 10, 1990.

25. Robert Repetto and Frederik van Bolhuis, *Natural Endowments: Financing Resource Conservation for Development* (Washington, D.C.: World Resources Institute, 1989); David Bigman, "A Plan to End LDC Debt and Save the Environment Too," *Challenge*, July/August 1990.

26. Thomas E. Lovejoy, "Aid Debtor Nations' Ecology," *New York Times*, October 4, 1984; Diana Page, "Debt-for-Nature Swaps: Experience Gained, Lessons Learned," *International Environmental Affairs*, January 1990.

27. The Nature Conservancy, "Officially Sanctioned Debt-for-Nature Swaps to Date," Washington, D.C., August 1990; Roque Sevilla Larrea and Alvaro Umaña, "Por qué Canjear Deuda por Naturaleza?" World Wildlife Fund, World Resources Institute, and Nature Conservancy, Washington, D.C., 1989.

28. Address by Rajiv Gandhi, Prime Minister of India, at the Ninth Conference of Heads of State or Government of Non-Aligned Countries, Belgrade, Yugoslavia, September 5, 1989; France's endorsement was delivered at the World Bank's annual meeting, "French Proposal on the Environment," Press Communique from the Development Committee Meeting, September 25, 1989, Washington, D.C.; "Tolba Advocates World Environment Fund," *Our Planet*, Vol. 1, No. 2/3, 1989; funding mechanism as a centerpiece of the Brazil Conference from Mostafa Tolba quoted in Linda Starke, *Signs of Hope: Working Towards Our Common Future* (Oxford: Oxford University Press, 1990).

29. World Bank, *The World Bank and the Environment*; World Bank, "Funding for the Global Environment," Discussion Paper, Washington, D.C., February 1990; Steven Mufson, "World Bank Wants Fund to Protect Environment," *Washington Post*, May 3, 1990; Letter to Barber Conable, president, World Bank, from David A. Wirth et al., National Resources Defense Council (NRDC), on behalf of NRDC and six other national environmental groups, Washington, D.C., March 9, 1990.

30. World Bank, *The World Bank and the Environment*; "Parties to Montreal Protocol Agree to Phase Out CFCs, Help Developing Nations," *International Environment Reporter*, July 11, 1990; Philip Shabecoff, "U.S. Backs World Bank Environment Unit," *New York Times*, November 30, 1990.

31. Robert Repetto, *Paying the Price: Pesticide Subsidies in Developing Countries* (Washington, D.C.: World Resources Institute, 1985); Egyptian gross domestic product from World Bank, *World Development Report 1990* (New York: Oxford University Press, 1990); Egyptian health spending based on various Egyptian ministry reports provided by the World Bank.

32. Sandra Postel, *Defusing the Toxics Threat: Controlling Pesticides and Industrial Waste*, Worldwatch Paper 79 (Washington, D.C.: Worldwatch Institute, September 1987).

33. See Robert Repetto, *The Forest for the Trees? Government Policies and the Misuse of Forest Resources* (Washington, D.C.: World Resources Institute, 1988); Robert Repetto, "Deforestation in the Tropics," *Scientific American*, April 1990.

34. Estimate of $500 million to $1 billion from Repetto and van Bolhuis, *Natural Endowments*; Philip M. Fearnside et al., *Deforestation Rate in Brazilian Amazonia* (São Paulo, Brazil: Instituto de Pesquisas Espaciais and Instituto National de Pesquisas da Amazônia, 1990).

35. "Brazil: Latest Deforestation Figures," *Nature*, June 28, 1990; Vera Machado, Head of the Environment Sector, Embassy of Brazil, Washington, D.C., private communication, October 30, 1990.

36. Repetto, *Paying the Price*; Robert Repetto, *Skimming the Water: Rent-Seeking and the Performance of Public Irrigation Systems* (Washington, D.C.: World Resources Institute, 1986); Repetto, *The Forest for the Trees?*

37. U.S. Department of Agriculture (USDA), Economic Research Service, *Agricultural Resources: Cropland, Water and Conservation: Situation and Outlook Report*, Washington, D.C., September 1990.

38. David Moskovitz, *Profits & Progress Through Least-Cost Planning* (Washington, D.C.: National Association of Regulatory Utility Commissioners, 1989).

39. California Public Utilities Commission (CPUC), "CPUC, Major Utilities Promote Energy Efficiency and Conservation Programs," press release, San Francisco, Calif., August 29, 1990; Elizabeth Kolbert, "Utility's Rates Tied to Saving of Electricity," *New York Times*, September 1, 1990; "NEES to 'Mine' Customers' kWh," *Electrical World*, October 1989; Oregon Public Utility Commission, "PUC Lauds PP&L's Conservation Program as an Oregon 'First,'" press release, Salem, Oreg., July 19, 1990; Armond Cohen, Conservation Law Foundation, Boston, Mass., private communication, October 29, 1990.

40. Howard S. Geller, "Electricity Conservation in Brazil: Status Report and Analysis," American Council for an Energy-Efficient Economy, Washington, D.C., August 1990; David A. Wirth, "Climate Chaos," *Foreign Policy*, Spring 1989.

41. Judith Jacobsen, *Promoting Population Stabilization: Incentives for Small Families*, Worldwatch Paper 54 (Washington, D.C.: Worldwatch Institute, June 1983).

42. D.L. Nortman et al., "A Cost Benefit Analysis of Family Planning Program of Mexican Social Security Administration," paper presented at the general conference of the International Union for the Scientific Study of Population, Florence, Italy, June 5–12, 1985, cited in Jodi L. Jacobson, *Planning the Global Family*, Worldwatch Paper 80 (Washington, D.C.: Worldwatch Institute, December 1987).

43. IMF, *International Financial Statistics* (Washington, D.C.: various years).

44. Information and Media Relations Division, "General Agreement on Tariffs and Trade (GATT): What It Is, What It Does," (Geneva: General Agreement on Tariffs and Trade, 1990); Third World lost income estimate from Paul Shaw, "Rapid Population Growth and Environmental Degradation: Ultimate versus Proximate Factors," *Environmental Conservation*, Autumn 1989; Steven Shrybman, "International Trade and the Environment: An Environmental Assessment of Present GATT Negotiations," *Alternatives*, Vol. 17, no. 2, 1990; Jeffrey J. Schott, "Uruguay Round: What Can Be Achieved," in Jeffrey J. Schott, ed., *Completing the Uruguay Round* (Washington, D.C.: Institute for International Economics, 1990); Dale E. Hathaway, "Agriculture," ibid.

45. Ann Davison, "Developing Country Concerns," in *IOCU (International Organization of Consumers Unions) Newsletter*, No. 5, 1990; Herman E. Daly and John B. Cobb, *For the Common Good: Redirecting the Economy Toward Community, the Environment, and a Sustainable Future* (Boston: Beacon Press, 1989).

46. Stewart Hudson, "Trade, Environment, and the Negotiations on the General Agreement on Trade and Tariffs (GATT)," National Wildlife Federation, Washington, D.C., September 24, 1990.

47. Ebba Dohlman, "The Trade Effects of Environmental Regulation," *The OECD Observer*, February/March 1990; Court decision from Evy Jordan, Embassy of Denmark, Washington, D.C., private communication,

October 29, 1990; Shrybman, "International Trade and the Environment."

48. Dutch Electricity Generating Board, "Dutch Plan for Reforestation in Latin America," press release, Arnhem, The Netherlands. March 30, 1990; Irene Carsouw, Dutch Electricity Generating Board, private communication, October 29, 1990.

49. David Pearce et al., *Blueprint for a Green Economy* (London: Earthscan Ltd., 1989).

50. Allen V. Kneese, *The United States in the 1980s* (Stanford: The Hoover Institution, 1980); Pearce et al., *Blueprint for a Green Economy*.

51. OECD, *Economic Instruments for Environmental Protection* (Paris: 1989).

52. U.K. example from European Community Commission, "Report of the Working Group of Experts from the Member States on the Use of Economic and Fiscal Instruments in EC Environmental Policy," Brussels, May 1990; CFC figures from U.S. House of Representatives, "Omnibus Budget Reconciliation Act of 1989, Conference Report to Accompany H.R. 3299," Washington, D.C., November 21, 1989; Joint Committee on Taxation, "Estimated Revenue Effects of Conference Agreement on Revenue Provisions of H.R. 3299," Washington, D.C., November 21, 1989; Michael Weisskopf, "A Clever Solution for Pollution: Taxes," *Washington Post*, December 12, 1989.

53. Carbon dioxide emissions goals from "Ministerial Declaration of the Second World Climate Conference," Geneva, November 7, 1990, from "Germany and the Greenhouse: A Closer Look," *Global Environmental Change Report*, August 17, 1990, from "East Germany: Country Will Comply with CFC Ordinance of West Germany, Seeks Smaller CO_2 Cut," *International Environment Reporter*, July 1990, from "Japan to Stabilize Greenhouse Gas Emissions by 2000," *Global Environmental Change Report*, July 20, 1990, from "Switzerland to Announce Stabilization Goal at Second World Climate Conference," *Global Environmental Change Report*, July 20, 1990, from "The Netherlands Sets CO_2 Emissions Tax for 1990," *Global Environmental Change Report*, December 22, 1989, from "Country Profiles: Denmark," *European Energy Report*, May 1990, from The Ministry of Environment and Energy, *Action for a Common Future: Swedish National Report for Bergen Conference*, May 1990 (Stockholm 1989), from U.K. Department of the Environment, *This Common Inheritance: Britain's Environmental Strategy* (London: 1990), from Gunnrr Mathisen, Secretariat for Climate Affairs, Ministry of the Environment, Oslo, Norway, private communication, January 30, 1990, from "Austria to Reduce CO_2 Emissions 20% by 2005," *Global Environmental Change Report*, September 14, 1990, from Emmanuele D'Achon, First Secretary, Embassy of France, Washington, D.C., private communication,

October 10, 1990, and from Ron Scherer, "Australia to Press for Worldwide Gas-Emissions Limits," *Christian Science Monitor*, October 18, 1990; carbon taxes from Geraldine C. Kay, "Global Climate Change Timeline," *Global Environmental Change Report*, July 28, 1990, from "Nation Adopts Carbon Dioxide Tax; Measure to be Higher on Coal than Gas," *International Environment Report*, March 1990, and from Anders Boeryd, Fuel Market Division, National Energy Administration, Sweden, private communication, August 10, 1990.

54. Debora MacKenzie, "... as Europe's Ministers Fail to Agree on Framework for Green Taxes," *New Scientist*, September 29, 1990.

55. Kennedy Maize, "Budget Summit Looking at Carbon Tax," *Energy Daily*, June 1, 1990; U.S. Congressional Budget Office (CBO), *Carbon Charges as a Response to Global Warming: The Effects of Taxing Fossil Fuels* (Washington, D.C.: August 1990); income tax receipts from U.S. Bureau of the Census, *Statistical Abstract of the United States: 1990* (Washington, D.C.: U.S. Government Printing Office, 1990).

56. CBO, *Carbon Charges as a Response to Global Warming*.

57. Ibid.; CBO estimates are based on pre-Iraqi invasion oil price projections.

58. Dieter Teufel et al., "Kosteuern als marktwirtschaftliches Instrument im Umweltschutz: Vorschläge für eine ökologische Steuerreform," Umwelt und Prognose Institut, Heidelberg, April 1988.

59. Estimated tax revenues based on Gregg Marland et al., *Estimates of CO_2 Emissions from Fossil Fuel Burning and Cement Manufacturing, Based on the United Nations Energy Statistics and the U.S. Bureau of Mines Cement Manufacturing Data* (Oak Ridge, Tenn.: Oak Ridge National Laboratory, 1989), and on British Petroleum (BP), *BP Statistical Review of World Energy* (London: 1990); hazardous waste estimates are 1985 figures from World Resources Institute, *World Resources 1990–1991* (New York: Oxford University Press, 1990); virgin pulp estimate based on 1987 figures in Alice H. Ulrich, *U.S. Timber Production, Trade, Consumption. and Price Statistics 1950–87* (Washington, D.C.: USDA, December 1989); pesticide sales are 1988 figures in U.S. Environmental Protection Agency (EPA), *Pesticides Industry Sales and Usage* (Washington, D.C.: 1990); sulfur dioxide and nitrogen oxide emission estimates are for 1988 in EPA, *National Air Quality Emissions and Trends Report*, 1988 (Research Triangle Park, N.C.: 1990); CFC tax and revenue estimates for 1994 from U.S. House of Representatives, "Omnibus Budget Reconciliation Act of 1989," and from Joint Committee on Taxation, "Estimated Revenue Effects"; groundwater depletion estimates are for 1980 in U.S. Geological Survey, *National Water Summary 1983 — Hydrologic Events and Issues* (Washington, D.C.: U.S. Government Printing Office, 1983).

60. Estimate for climate fund revenues based on Marland et al., *Estimates of CO$_2$ Emissions*, and on BP, *BP Statistical Review*.

61. Louis Harris & Associates et al., *The Rising Tide: Public Opinion, Policy & Politics* (Washington, D.C.: Americans for the Environment, 1989).

62. See Herman Daly, "Towards an Environmental Macroeconomics," presented at "The Ecological Economics of Sustainability: Making Local and Short-Term Goals Consistent with Global and Long-Term Goals," the International Society for Ecological Economics, Washington, D.C., May 1990; see also Paul R. Ehrlich, "The Limits to Substitution: Meta-Resource Depletion and a New Economic-Ecological Paradigm," *Ecological Economics*, No. 1, 1989.

63. 1900 global world output from Lester R. Brown and Sandra Postel, "Thresholds of Change," in Lester Brown et al., *State of the World 1987* (Washington, D.C.: W.W. Norton & Company, 1987).

64. Peter M. Vitousek et al., "Human Appropriation of the Products of Photosynthesis," *BioScience*, June 1986; PRB, *1990 World Population Data Sheet*.

65. U.S. Department of Energy (DOE), Energy Information Agency (EIA), *State Energy Data Report, Consumption Estimates, 1960–1988* (Washington, D.C.: 1990); DOE, EIA, *Annual Energy Review 1989* (Washington, D.C.: 1990); Bureau of the Census, *Statistical Abstract of the United States: 1990*.

66. Total vehicle kilometers for 1965–70 from U.S. Department of Commerce, *Historical Statistics of the United States, Colonial Times to 1970, Bicentennial Edition* (Washington, D.C., 1975); 1970–88 from DOE, EIA, *Annual Energy Review 1989*.

67. PRB, *1990 World Population Data Sheet*.

68. See Hazel Henderson, "Moving Beyond Economism: New Indicators for Culturally Specific, Sustainable Development," in The Caracas Report on Alternative Development Indicators, *Redefining Wealth and Progress: New Ways to Measure Economic, Social and Environmental Change* (New York: The Bootstrap Press, 1989); Daly and Cobb, *For the Common Good*.

69. Garrett Hardin, "Paramount Positions in Ecological Economics," presented at "The Ecological Economics of Sustainability."

70. Durning, *Poverty and the Environment*.

Appendix

LIST OF GLOSSARY TERMS

1. THE FIELD OF SOCIOLOGY

2. FOUNDATIONS OF SOCIETY

abstraction
co-operation
culture
production
role
social interaction
socialization
social structure

2A. Socialization and Social Interaction

gender
impression management
secondary socialization

2B. Culture

division of labour
postmodern culture
rites of passage

2C. Social Structure

business cycle
formal organization
network
personal community
power
protest ideology
social movement
traditional community

3. SOCIAL INEQUALITY

3A. Class and Gender Inequality

postindustrial society
poverty rate

3B. Ethnic and Racial Inequality

discrimination
ethnic group
prejudice
race

4. SOCIAL INSTITUTIONS

institution
macrostructure
megastructure
microstructure

4A. Families

neoconservatism
non-family household
non-nuclear family
non-traditional nuclear family
nuclear family
patriarchy
traditional nuclear family

4B. Politics

concentration of ownership
enterprise

4C. The Economy and Work

bureaucracy
late-industrializing countries
quality of working life

5. CRIME AND DEVIANCE

deviance
victimization survey

6. GLOBAL DEVELOPMENT AND THE ENVIRONMENT

globalization
sustainable growth

INDEX

READER REPLY CARD

We are interested in your reaction to *Society in Question: Sociological Readings for the 21st Century*, by Robert J. Brym. You can help us to improve this book in future editions by completing this questionnaire.

1. What was your reason for using this book?

    ❑ university course   ❑ continuing education course
    ❑ college course   ❑ personal interest
    ❑ professional development   ❑ other_____

    _____

2. If you are a student, please identify your school and the course in which you used this book.

3. Which chapters or parts of this book did you use? Which did you omit?

4. What did you like best about this book?

5. What did you like least about this book?

6. Please identify any topics you think should be added to future editions.

7. Please add any comments or suggestions.

8. May we contact you for further information?

Name: _____

Address: _____

           _____

Phone: _____

(fold here and tape shut)

0116870399-M8Z4X6-BR01

Heather McWhinney
Publisher, College Division
HARCOURT BRACE & COMPANY, CANADA
55 HORNER AVENUE
TORONTO, ONTARIO
M8Z 9Z9